URBAN MAN AND SOCIETY

ALBERT N. COUSINS and
HANS NAGPAUL

URBAN MAN
AND
SOCIETY

A Reader in Urban Sociology

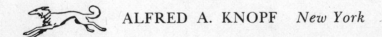 ALFRED A. KNOPF   *New York*

THIS IS A BORZOI BOOK

PUBLISHED BY ALFRED A. KNOPF, INC.

First printing

Copyright © 1970 by Alfred A. Knopf, Inc.
All rights reserved under International and Pan-American Copyright Conventions.
Published in the United States by Alfred A. Knopf, Inc., New York, and
simultaneously in Canada by Random House of Canada Limited, Toronto.
Distributed by Random House, Inc., New York.

Library of Congress Catalog Card Number: 75–102390

Manufactured in the United States of America

FOR

Julia
Daniel
Ashish
Arun

*who will inhabit
the city of the future*

Preface

LIKE THE MODERN CITY ITSELF, urban sociology is a vast sprawl. And like the city, it is less a distinct entity than a nebulous universe. In the densely populated, heterogeneous, mobile, and formally coordinated type of society that has now evolved to such a high degree, the definition of what is urban and what is not, and what is sociological rather than, say, economic or political becomes ever more difficult. The urban sociologist evidences this uncertainty toward his subject matter in the variety of perspectives that he employs, and also in his participation along with other disciplines in what has come loosely to be called urban studies.

The independence of sociology is of course far less important than the total intellectual enterprise, if only because the practical benefits that knowledge can produce have taken on singular significance in the light of today's urban crisis. Accordingly, the readings that make up this volume are the work of a number of specialties besides sociology, including those of the historian, political scientist, geographer, anthropologist, and city planner. Sociology, however, predominates, particularly in regard to theoretical approaches to the urban community, the character of urban life, and the social structure of the city.

Within the framework of sociology, then, our overriding aim has been to provide the reader with a balanced survey of man's urban experience. Therefore, we have selected "classical" writings, empirical studies, and official reports that convey a coherent picture of the urban community and urban society and of the people who inhabit them.

Starting with a lengthy section tracing the history of the city, this volume deals in turn with the basic conceptions of the urban phenomenon, the social psychology of man in the city, the city as a social system, urban ills, attempts at the social reconstruction of the city, and finally the newer paths which urban sociology if not urbanology is taking. Although the focus is the contemporary American metropolis, attention is also given to some cross-cultural insights. The substantial introductions and head-notes together with the bibliographical appendix may make it feasible for instructors to use this book as a text rather than merely supplementary reading.

We are indebted to Barbara G. Frisch and Alice M. Tassoff for invaluable assistance in producing this volume and to the staff of the Cleveland State University library for their cooperation. Professors Charles H. Page and John Edwards made many useful suggestions regarding the selection of readings as well as their presentation. We are grateful to them for doing this. We wish also to thank the authors and publishers who generously granted us permission to make use of the material that appears here. Theodore Caris, Arthur Strimling, Leonore C. Hauck, and Judith Rosenberg of the Random House and Alfred A. Knopf College Department have earned our gratitude for their patience, encouragement, and resourcefulness. To our professional friends and colleagues who in different ways helped us with ideas and interpretations we owe a good deal although none of the errors and shortcomings of this book are attributable to them.

Mr. Dooley once remarked that "Everything that's worth having goes to the city; the country takes what's left." We would like to think that these readings on the city do indeed partake of the very best.

Albert N. Cousins

Hans Nagpaul

Contents

URBAN MAN AND SOCIETY

CHAPTER ONE

EMERGENCE AND GROWTH OF CITIES

If the history of the human species stretches back over a period of 500,000 years, its habitation of cities amounts to merely one percent of that time. And even at that, since 4,000 B.C. when the earliest cities appeared, only a very small part of the world's population has actually been urban. Despite unprecedented concentrations of people during the past two centuries only 20 percent of the world's population is urban even today. Nonetheless, few scholars would disagree with Kingsley Davis' judgment that urbanized society is "a new and fundamental step in man's social evolution." [1] We are compelled to recognize that the city represents a distinct and permanent alteration of human thought and behavior and of social institutions as well.

The origin of the city is traceable to a combination of change agents—environmental, technological, and social. In the Fertile Crescent of the Tigris-Euphrates river valleys beyond the Mediterranean littoral, neolithic man encountered conditions that made the dense agglomeration of a diverse population possible. Independently in at least three other geographic settings, one of them in the Western Hemisphere, analogous circumstances also produced the urban revolution. Where preurban Paleolithic society had maintained population densities of from one-half to one person per square mile, the domestication of animals and sedentary cultivation, assisted by shaped tools, made possible densities of thirty people per square mile. It was these changes that lay behind the settlement of such cities as Erech, Kish, Ubaid, and Lagash in southern Iraq. Once underway, the growth of urban society continued. Fifteen hundred years would elapse as urbanization took hold, but eventually the early city of Uruk would embrace 1,100 acres and house 50,000 persons.

Cities and civilization have from the first had a mutually reinforcing cycle of change and growth. Basic to both cities and civilization is complex social organization in which people who are unrelated by kinship, who do not necessarily share the same religious faith, and who are not under the compulsion of force, cooperate for their mutual benefit. To be sure, civilizations, like cities, show an underlying and sustaining political and ethical unity among their members. Yet their lietmotif is the association of large numbers of people in the pursuit of a great variety of ends. This outlook animated the emergence of the first distinctly recognizable cities in the Near East, northern India, and pre-Columbian Latin America. This spirit, furthermore, is the revolutionary element in the urban social order that essentially sets it apart from the preurban folk society. It is also the reason why technological progress alone will not suffice to explain the origin of cities in the world, and why civilization is coeval with—not anterior to—the urban revolution.

Until the beginning of the Industrial Revolution the growth of urban communities was generally slow and discontinuous. In many areas cities were uncommon before 1750, and at times whole regions that had had prosperous cities relapsed into a local rural condition. During the past two hundred years, however, the history of urbanization has been very clearly defined. Not only have many new cities appeared, but cities have expanded greatly, and the proportion of people living in them in relation to the total population has risen sharply. For this reason two broad periods of urbanization are recognized. Within each of these periods numerous cities were established and, in different ways, were influenced by the communities that had produced them.

The Preindustrial Era began even before the Bronze Age of 3,000 B.C., and certainly it preceded the Age of Iron by about two thousand years. Suffice it to say that the accumulation of technology was an indispensable cause, if not a sufficient one, for the first cities to arise. Similarly, as Charles Horton Cooley recognized, other contributory factors were present, such as transport breaks, which determined the location of cities, as well as sheer technological advances in ship design and construction.[2] At the water's edge were Knossos, Massilia, Byzantium, Ostia, and Piraeus, and athwart the rivers, rudiments of modern Frankfurt, Cologne, Stettin, and Vienna.

In the Preindustrial Era cities with populations of 5,000 to 10,000 were common. Cities of 100,000 were rare, although Rome, under Caesar Augustus, had a population of one million. Fifth century Athens in the pre-Christian world had 150,000 people, and the capital of Byzantium, Constantinople, reached the half-million mark in 1,000 A.D. Baghdad, Edo (Tokyo), Osaka, the fortress of Carcassonne in France, and the African city of Sofara (Mali) were other notable preindustrial population giants.

Preindustrial cities were primarily a result of military, dynastic, and religious causes. Economic interests were certainly present but did not have the saliency that they achieved following the introduction, in the eighteenth century, of power-driven machinery. The interworkings of these preindustrial factors are to be observed, for instance, in the ceremonial and ritualistic use of the networks of roads that served Rome, Cuzco, and Damascus. The intermingling is equally apparent in the city-state (the polis) of Classical Greece centering on Eretria, Samos, Aegina, Sparta, Corinth, Miletus, and Chalcis. It is also inherent in two other types of urban settlements —the "bourgs," defensive camps situated on islands or hills, or located within a strategic valley, and the "episcopal cities" of Tours, Amiens, Treves, and Laon, where the church nobility wrested control from the feudal monarchs and were therefore guaranteed sufficient security to fashion a theocratic hierarchy.

Some of the architecture that the military, dynastic, and religious forces produced still stands today: moated, walled, and towering fortresses that protected or terrorized the countryside; and, churches, chapels, and cathedrals that provided for the spiritual salvation of the surrounding countryside. They are a reminder of the conditions that existed when the first cities arose. With the achievement of agricultural production above subsistence level, and with the crystallization of cooperative methods of flood control and irrigation, the need arose for specialists who could supply goods and services for the rural peasantry. The exchange process, however, required a working consensus, a basis for trust and predictability of response. Undoubtedly, the warrior, craftsman, and concubine of the prehistoric city profited from the priestly ability that was applied to appropriate and allocate the grain, field-peas, livestock or meat, fowl, sesame, melons and other fruits, cotton, fish, and lumber that the New Stone Age expertise was producing.

Although the general process of urbanization was common wherever the first cities were to be found, it differed in detail from one region to another. For instance, Mesopotamian cities reached a greater size than did Egyptian cities, probably owing to the ease with which Egypt achieved military security and political integration. As Eric Lampard has pointed out, the regular inundations of the Nile no doubt simplified the problems of water management, and the severe mountains and deserts that screened the fertile river valley provided safety from invasion. A secure household economy that kept the population scattered on large landed estates arose in

Egypt. Industry was very limited, and as a result the growth of
Egyptian cities was checked. Once set in motion, indigenous cultural forces thereafter shaped the urban revolution in particular localities. Thus, there might be much geometric land use at Harappa
and little in the Sumerian cities. The result is that we can observe
no single pattern of early city establishment and administration,
but only somewhat different manifestations of an evolutionary tendency.

   The decline of urbanism that followed the fall of the Roman Empire was widespread. Even though Byzantium continued relatively
intact in the East and the walled marketplaces of the Ukraine and
the Russian Steppes on the Varangian route to the north came
into existence, western Europe of the Dark Ages returned to rural
simplicity. Rome had shrunk to only 50,500 inhabitants in the sixth
century. Similarly, Marseilles and the other port cities of the Mediterranean succumbed to the inability of feudal Europe to maintain
commerce on the Mediterranean in the face of Moslem opposition.
Only later, beginning perhaps with trade in salt and fish with the
Byzantines in the eleventh century, was there an urban revival; it
centered on northern Italy. Venice, which is at the head of naviga-
tion on the Adriatic, rose by 1330 to a population of 200,000. Pisa,
Genoa, and Florence grew in size too, as Italian commerce, including shipbuilding, textiles, metal working, and banking, developed.
The Hanseatic League along the Baltic and the Flemish towns of
the northwest also progressed. Commercial to be sure, these Renaissance cities were still preindustrial. In them flourished the traditional values of dynastic politics, religious ritual, and hierarchical
status relations. The essential noneconomic character of the preindustrial urban community is revealed, as Gideon Sjoberg reminds
us, in the fact that "the city's center [was] the hub of governmental
and religious activity more than of commercial ventures." [3]

   Nonetheless, ecclesiastical and political interests stimulated economic activities in Europe and thus caused further maturation of
the urban process. Nowhere, perhaps, is this more apparent than in
the effects on the cities of the Iberian peninsula of Portuguese and
Spanish explorations of the South Atlantic and the Indian Ocean.
Under the Moors in the twelfth century, Lisbon had been a town of
15,000. By the fifteenth century, however, when Vasco da Gama was
sailing to Calcutta, its population had grown to 50,000. And when
in the next century Lisbon had become Europe's emporium for the
Oriental trade, it had swelled to fully 200,000, a third of this number Negroes from Africa. In like manner Seville, which through the
Casa de Contratacion controlled all of Spain's overseas commerce,
had a population of 400,000 in the sixteenth century.

   However impressive preindustrial urbanization may at times have been, in scale, at least, it has since been dwarfed. Manchester, the first industrial city of modern times, was a market town of 25,000 in 1780. Only 40 years later, when 72 textile mills had been built, it had a population of 100,000. By 1850 even that number had quadrupled. Most of England and Wales felt the sweeping changes in the distribution of population brought about by machine technology and the factory system. The multiplication of cities where the new industrial facilities were being located was as rapid as the migration of people from the farms. Only 10 percent of the population of the United Kingdom lived in cities of 100,000 or more in 1800. That figure rose to 30 percent by 1890. In fact, by 1890, two-thirds of the nation's people were living in communities of at least 10,000. Urbanization had become an alternative to English rural society, not an addition to it.

More decisively than ever before, economic considerations were determining the location, establishment, and viability of the new industrial cities. Breaks in the terrain, the pull of raw materials, the availability of transport, and the lure of markets all figured in the modern industrial urbanism. However, other factors, particularly political decisions, were also influential. Amsterdam, for example, prospered as a virtually free city because of its successful struggle with the House of Orange that culminated in 1672. Asiatic despotism more than anything else proved to be responsible for the creation on the swampy estuary of the Neva of St. Petersburg as the northern capital and monument to the Romanoffs. Everywhere in the Americas, Asia, and South Africa, colonial cities were rising out of the wilderness. And in Europe too, aggressive statesmen were at work altering the demographic constitution of their countries; among them, for example, was Frederick the Great, whose protectionist policy in eighteenth-century Germany was turning Berlin into the heart of the northern principalities.

The sheer economic determinism that one is tempted to read into the urbanizing effects of the Industrial Revolution is an over-simplification of modern history. A group of social variables at least contributed to, if they did not wholly determine, the rapid urbanization of Europe and the United States. Among these were an enterprising middle class, the legitimation of social mobility, the social organization of scientific activity, and a high degree of literacy. Without such facilitating conditions the efficient exploitation of natural resources together with the successful application of the new technology would not have been possible. New York is an obvious illustration. Although New York had a magnificent harbor, the use of the harbor was long inhibited by English colonial regulations. National independence, however, meant the establishment of a vast common market, and New York became the major

East Coast distribution center for goods and immigrants alike. On the eve of the American Revolution, New York had scarcely 25,000 people. A hundred years later its population exceeded a million.

Industrialization laid the foundation for the modern city and for the urbanization of society. Once the big city came into existence and served to organize the economic potentialities of the surrounding region, however, secondary economic growth soon transformed it into the metropolis. Industries arose in response to the newer needs that the large population of the city were experiencing. The demand for household appliances, modish dress, personal adornment, recreation, and edification grew. The metropolis was also stimulated by the necessity for more comprehensive administrative control of this exceedingly complex economy. The twentieth century metropolis was thus the seat of educational, esthetic, medical, communication, financial, and governmental institutions that served a region and even an entire nation.

Nor is the urbanization process at an end. Studies, such as those conducted by the International Population and Urban Research Center at Berkeley, have revealed that more than 50 cities in the world now have populations over 1,000,000, fourteen of them in the United States alone.[4] And by the year 2,000, urban residence will have engulfed upwards of four-fifths of the entire world's population. This will affect the nonindustrialized underdeveloped countries most significantly. Although they have some large cities—indeed, with their mammoth populations they may have the majority of the large cities of the world—they enjoy a low level of overall urbanization. For example, India in 1961 was only 20 percent urban, and Thailand 12 percent. Cities are growing in such countries, although surprisingly without appreciably reducing the rural proportion of the population. This fact indicates that city growth is not enhancing the economic opportunities of the general population, a condition in striking contrast to the experience of Western Europe and the United States during the era of industrialization.

Urbanization is not without its problems today even among the advanced nations of the world. The meritocracy and affluence of the great population centers reflect enormous technological advances in production, transportation, and communication. Tides of in-migration from the relatively depressed and deprived hinterland attest to urban prosperity no less than does the large-scale out-migration of population to the wealthy suburban fringe. Yet there are also obvious and alarming signs of decline and discord. Disaffection is present at both ends of the socioeconomic spectrum, among the most underprivileged, who are experiencing hopeless misery, and among the most affluent, who are vexed by their ever-inflated wants. A lack of consensus handicaps urban administration in coping with environmental dangers to health and problems of congestion and decay inimical to comfort and safety.

The buildup of cities goes on in the less well-developed lands. Brasília, Brazzaville, Nairobi, and New Delhi are only a few, though arresting, cases among many. Often lacking an adequate economic base, these new urban centers suffer from technological backwardness, status-conscious reactionary élites, and deeply ingrained localism. Their development has proven to be painful even in the face of the most determined administration. Many people, it must be acknowledged, legitimately struggle to preserve a way of life traditional to them; even today this happens in some of the most urbanized nations. France is an example. In large measure it remains rural, with a proclivity to small business and handicrafts. Nevertheless, the continued diffusion of the industrial-urban social order is probably irresistible. Not only are its material benefits obvious to all, but the different major ideological systems support both technology and the city, however much they may otherwise disagree.

The material that makes up this first section is a composite history of the city. Childe reviews the very beginnings of urban settlement in the world. Then Turner and Pirenne analyze urbanism from the time of the Roman Empire to the end of the first millennium of the Christian era. Following these two articles, Sjoberg and Adna Weber deal with the preindustrial and industrial cities and their many salient contrasts. Finally, the concluding document traces the emergence of the metropolitan center, the megalopolis, and the urbanization of society in general during the first three decades of the twentieth century.

1. THE URBAN REVOLUTION

V. Gordon Childe

The prehistory of the city is to be found in the archaeological recon-struction of human settlements that arose in the post-Pleistocene Neo-lithic Age. The urban revolution that occurred at that time witnessed an unprecedented concentration of people and the initiation of a new stage of economic development. The revolution presupposed a level of social organization capable of securing the cooperation of specialists who ex-changed their crafts and also provided military, religious, and recrea-tional services in return for the available surplus of food produced by the surrounding hinterland. A significant factor that made possible the emer-gence of cities was the presence of fertile river valleys. These river valleys, present in Egypt, Mesopotamia, and the Indus basin (and in somewhat different form in Central and South America), yielded the necessary sur-plus of food. But more importantly they facilitated the establishment of social cooperation, principally for the task of irrigation, on a sizable scale. It was this that laid the socio-cultural foundation for cities—and civiliza-tion.

The emergence of the earliest cities was by no means a sudden depar-ture from the past. Any number of generations died away before the ten characteristics by which Gordon Childe defines urban formation had fully come into existence: namely—a large and dense population; a divi-sion of labor; an effective (transported) surplus of foodstuffs; public buildings; hierarchy; literacy; mathematics; the pictorial and plastic arts; commerce; and political organization. Though tenuous at first and de-

From *The Town Planning Review* (April, 1950). Reprinted by permission of *The Town Planning Review*.

spite subsequent regional declines, once it had materialized man's urban capacity was never relinquished. Cuzco and Ur might succumb, but they would only be succeeded by Athens, Carthage, and Rome.

ABOUT 5,000 YEARS AGO irrigation cultivation (combined with stockbreeding and fishing) in the valleys of the Nile, the Tigris-Euphrates and the Indus had begun to yield a social surplus, large enough to support a number of resident specialists who were themselves released from food-production. Water-transport, supplemented in Mesopotamia and the Indus valley by wheeled vehicles and even in Egypt by pack animals, made it easy to gather food stuffs at a few centres. At the same time, dependence on river water for the irrigation of the crops restricted the cultivable areas while the necessity of canalizing the waters and protecting habitations against annual floods encouraged the aggregation of population. Thus arose the first cities—units of settlement ten times as great as any known neolithic village. It can be argued that all cities in the old world are offshoots of those of Egypt, Mesopotamia and the Indus basin. So the latter need not be taken into account if a minimum definition of civilization is to be inferred from a comparison of its independent manifestations.

But some three millennia later cities arose in Central America, and it is impossible to prove that the Mayas owed anything directly to the urban civilizations of the Old World. Their achievements must therefore be taken into account in our comparison, and their inclusion seriously complicates the task of defining the essential preconditions of the Urban Revolution. In the Old World the rural economy which yielded the surplus was based on the cultivation of cereals combined with stock-breeding. But this economy had been made more efficient as a result of the adoption of irrigation (allowing cultivation without prolonged fallow periods) and of important inventions and discoveries—metallurgy, the plough, the sailing boat and the wheel. None of these devices was known to the Mayas; they bred no animals for milk or meat; though they cultivated the cereal maize, they used the same sort of slash-and-burn method as neolithic farmers in prehistoric Europe or in the Pacific Islands today. Hence the minimum definition of a city, the greatest factor common to the Old World and the New will be substantially reduced and impoverished by the inclusion of the Maya. Nevertheless ten rather abstract criteria, all deducible from archaeological data, serve to distinguish even the earliest cities from any older or contemporary village.

(1) In point of size the first cities must have been more extensive and more densely populated than any previous settlements, although considerably smaller than many villages today. It is indeed only in Mesopotamia and India that the first urban populations can be estimated with any confidence or precision. There excavation has been sufficiently extensive

and intensive to reveal both the total area and density of building in sample quarters and in both respects has disclosed significant agreement with the less industrialized Oriental cities today. The population of Sumerian cities, thus calculated, ranged between 7,000 and 20,000; Harappa and Mohenjo-daro in the Indus valley must have approximated to the higher figure. We can only infer that Egyptian and Maya cities were of comparable magnitude from the scale of public works, presumably executed by urban populations.

(2) In composition and function the urban population already differed from that of any village. Very likely indeed most citizens were still also peasants, harvesting the lands and waters adjacent to the city. But all cities must have accommodated in addition classes who did not themselves procure their own food by agriculture, stock-breeding, fishing or collecting—full-time specialist craftsmen, transport workers, merchants, officials and priests. All these were of course supported by the surplus produced by the peasants living in the city and in dependent villages, but they did not secure their share directly by exchanging their products or services for grains or fish with individual peasants.

(3) Each primary producer paid over the tiny surplus he could wring from the soil with his still very limited technical equipment as tithe or tax to an imaginary deity or a divine king who thus concentrated the surplus. Without this concentration, owing to the low productivity of the rural economy, no effective capital would have been available.

(4) Truly monumental public buildings not only distinguish each known city from any village but also symbolize the concentration of the social surplus. Every Sumerian city was from the first dominated by one or more stately temples, centrally situated on a brick platform raised above the surrounding dwellings and usually connected with an artificial mountain, the staged tower or ziggurat. But attached to the temples were workshops and magazines, and an important appurtenance of each principal temple was a great granary. Harappa, in the Indus basin, was dominated by an artificial citadel, girt with a massive rampart of kiln-baked bricks, containing presumably a palace and immediately overlooking an enormous granary and the barracks of artisans. No early temples nor palaces have been excavated in Egypt, but the whole Nile valley was dominated by the gigantic tombs of the divine pharaohs while royal granaries are attested from the literary record. Finally the Maya cities are known almost exclusively from the temples and pyramids of sculptured stone round which they grew up.

Hence in Sumer the social surplus was first effectively concentrated in the hands of a god and stored in his granary. That was probably true in Central America while in Egypt the pharaoh (king) was himself a god. But of course the imaginary deities were served by quite real priests who, besides celebrating elaborate and often sanguinary rites in their honour, administered their divine masters' earthly estates. In Sumer indeed the god very soon, if not even before the revolution, shared his wealth and power with a mortal viceregent (the 'City-King') who acted as civil ruler and leader in war. The divine pharaoh was naturally assisted by a whole hierarchy of officials.

(5) All those not engaged in food-production were of course supported in the first instance by the surplus accumulated in temple or royal granaries and were thus dependent on temple or court. But naturally priests, civil and military leaders and officials absorbed a major share of the concentrated surplus and thus formed a 'ruling class.' Unlike a palaeolithic magician or a neolithic chief, they were, as an Egyptian scribe actually put it, 'exempt from all manual tasks. On the other hand, the lower classes were not only guaranteed peace and security, but were relieved from intellectual tasks which many find more irksome than any physical labour. Besides reassuring the masses that the sun was going to rise the next day and the river would flood again next year (people who have not five thousand years of recorded experience of natural uniformities behind them are really worried about such matters!), the ruling classes did confer substantial benefits upon their subjects in the way of planning and organization.

(6) They were in fact compelled to invent systems of recording and exact, but practically useful, sciences. The mere administration of the vast revenues of a Sumerian temple or an Egyptian pharaoh by a perpetual corporation of priests or officials obliged its members to devise conventional methods of recording that should be intelligible to all their colleagues and successors, that is, to invent systems of writing and numeral notation. Writing is thus a significant, as well as a convenient, mark of civilization. But while writing is a trait common to Egypt, Mesopotamia, the Indus valley and Central America, the characters themselves were different in each region and so were the normal writing materials—papyrus in Egypt, clay in Mesopotamia. The engraved seals or stelae that provide the sole extant evidence for early Indus and Maya writing no more represent the normal vehicles for the scripts than do the comparable documents from Egypt and Sumer.

(7) The invention of writing—or shall we say the inventions of scripts —enabled the leisured clerks to proceed to the elaboration of exact and predictive sciences—arithmetic, geometry and astronomy. Obviously beneficial and explicitly attested by the Egyptian and Maya documents was the correct determination of the tropic year and the creation of a calendar. For it enabled the rulers to regulate successfully the cycle of agricultural operations. But once more the Egyptian, Maya and Babylonian calendars were as different as any systems based on a single natural unit could be. Calendrical and mathematical sciences are common features of the earliest civilizations and they too are corollaries of the archaeologists' criterion, writing.

(8) Other specialists, supported by the concentrated social surplus,

gave a new direction to artistic expression. Savages even in palaeolithic times had tried, sometimes with astonishing success, to depict animals and even men as they saw them—concretely and naturalistically. Neolithic peasants never did that; they hardly ever tried to represent natural objects, but preferred to symbolize them by abstract geometrical patterns which at most may suggest by a few traits a fantastical man or beast or plant. But Egyptian, Sumerian, Indus and Maya artist-craftsmen—full-time sculptors, painters, or seal-engravers—began once more to carve, model, or draw likenesses of persons or things, but no longer with the naïve naturalism of the hunter, but according to conceptualized and sophisticated styles which differ in each of the four urban centres.

(9) A further part of the concentrated social surplus was used to pay for the importation of raw materials, needed for industry or cult and not available locally. Regular 'foreign' trade over quite long distances was a feature of all early civilizations and, though common enough among barbarians later, is not certainly attested in the Old World before 3,000 B.C. nor in the New before the Maya 'empire.' Thereafter regular trade extended from Egypt at least as far as Byblos on the Syrian coast while Mesopotamia was related by commerce with the Indus valley. While the objects of international trade were at first mainly 'luxuries,' they already included industrial materials, in the Old World notably metal the place of which in the New was perhaps taken by obsidian. To this extent the first cities were dependent for vital materials on long distance trade as no neolithic village ever was.

(10) So in the city, specialist craftsmen were both provided with raw materials needed for the employment of their skill and also guaranteed security in a State organization based now on residence rather than kinship. Itinerancy was no longer obligatory. The city was a community to which a craftsman could belong politically as well as economically.

Yet in return for security they became dependent on temple or court and were relegated to the lower classes. The peasant masses gained even less material advantages; in Egypt for instance metal did not replace the old stone and wood tools for agricultural work. Yet, however imperfectly, even the earliest urban communities must have been held together by a sort of solidarity missing from any neolithic village. Peasants, craftsmen, priests and rulers form a community, not only by reason of identity of language and belief, but also because each performs mutually complementary functions, needed for the well-being (as redefined under civilization) of the whole. In fact the earliest cities illustrate a first approximation to an organic solidarity based upon a functional complementarity and interdependence between all its members such as subsist between the constituent cells of an organism. Of course this was only a very distant approximation. However necessary the concentration of the surplus really were with the existing forces of production, there seemed a glaring conflict on economic interests between the tiny ruling class, who annexed the bulk of the social surplus, and the vast majority who were left with a bare subsistence and effectively excluded from the spiritual benefits of civilization. So solidarity had still to be maintained by the ideological devices appropriate to the mechanical solidarity of barbarism as expressed in the preeminence of the temple or the sepulchral shrine, and now supplemented by the force of the new State organization. There could be no room for sceptics or sectaries in the oldest cities.

These ten traits exhaust the factors common to the oldest cities that archaeology, at best helped out with fragmentary and often ambiguous written sources, can detect. No specific elements of town planning for example can be proved characteristic of all such cities; for on the one hand the Egyptian and Maya cities have not yet been excavated; on the other neolithic villages were often walled, an elaborate system of sewers drained the Orcadian hamlet of Skara Brae; two-storeyed houses were built in pre-Columbian pueblos, and so on.

The common factors are quite abstract. Concretely, Egyptian, Sumerian, Indus and Maya civilizations were as different as the plans of their temples, the signs of their scripts and their artistic conventions. In view of this divergence and because there is so far no evidence for a temporal priority of one Old World centre (for instance, Egypt) over the rest nor yet for contact between Central America and any other urban centre, the four revolutions just considered may be regarded as mutually independent. On the contrary, all later civilizations in the Old World may in a sense be regarded as lineal descendants of those of Egypt, Mesopotamia or the Indus.

But this was not a case of like producing like. The maritime civilizations of Bronze Age Crete or classical Greece for example, to say nothing of our own, differ more from their reputed ancestors than these did among themselves. But the urban revolutions that gave them birth did not start from scratch. They could and probably did draw upon the capital accumulated in the three allegedly primary centres. That is most obvious in the case of cultural capital. Even today we use the Egyptians' calendar and the Sumerians' divisions of the day and the hour. Our European ancestors did not have to invent for themselves these divisions of time nor repeat the observations on which they are based; they took over and very slightly improved systems elaborated 5,000 years ago! But the same is in a sense true of material capital as well. The Egyptians, the Sumerians and the Indus people had accumulated vast reserves of surplus food. At the same time they had to import from abroad necessary raw materials like metals and building timber as well as 'luxuries.' Communities controlling these natural resources could in exchange claim a slice of the urban surplus. They could use it as capital to support full-time specialists —craftsmen or rulers—until the latters' achievement in technique and organization had so enriched barbarian economies that they too could produce a substantial surplus in their turn.

2. THE GRECO-ROMAN URBAN CULTURE

Ralph Turner

*Greco-Roman culture was urban. Indeed, the Roman order re-
mained intact only as long as its cities did. With the transposition of
Hellenism to a West still at the tribal level, urban life came to encircle
the Mediterranean. Although noteworthy feats of engineering—principally roads and aqueducts—linked the Roman cities into a farflung network, it was the evolution of an economic and administrative system that
fundamentally made this network possible. An elaborate civil law sustained the corporate municipality of the Romans, and a system of rights
and obligations expressed in terms of citizenship, ownership, exchange,
and contract insured the reality of property. It was this economic and administrative system that stimulated economic activity for 1,500 years over
an area that embraced the Baltic Sea, equatorial Africa, and even southern China.*

BY WIDENING THE AREA of social interaction the Roman conquest of the
Mediterranean Basin and western Europe carried further the cultural
tendencies of the Hellenistic age, particularly as they moved toward the
creation of a cosmopolitan culture. Rome built a political regime suited
to this culture, but the culture itself belonged to many peoples, among
whom, of course, the Greeks were the most important. But local cultures
did not disappear. Greco-Roman culture was peculiarly the possession of
the thousand or more cities and towns which were the centers of Roman
administration, and its social bearers were mainly the members of the

From *The Great Cultural Traditions: The Foundations of Civilization* (Volume II,
The Classical Empires) by Ralph Turner (1941). Reprinted by permission.

aristocratic wealth-holding classes who resided there. In the second century, when Roman rule was at its height, there were three clearly marked culture areas within the empire: (1) the Greco-oriental, or Hellenized, East, (2) the Latin West—Italy, Africa, and Spain, and (3) the Gallic West—Gaul and Britain. And beneath the stratum of literate culture in both the East and the West persisted the ancient local cultures—mainly peasant-village in character—of the conquered peoples. In the fourth century, under the reorganized Roman Empire, the forces of cosmopolitanism reached their climax and found expression, as will be described subsequently, in the Christian reorientation of the Western cultural tradition. The Roman Empire was little more than the instrument that guided these forces to fruition.[1]

THE URBAN QUALITY OF GRECO-ROMAN CULTURE

The literary, intellectual, and artistic elements of Greco-Roman culture, as well as its political and economic organization, were identified with cities. "It would scarcely be an exaggeration to say that the history of Greco-Roman civilization is the history of cities." [2] Indeed, the great work of the Roman Empire, based as it was on the interests of urban groups, consisted of a stabilization and extension of urban life throughout the Mediterranean Basin. In the eastern Mediterranean area the work was mainly the matter of putting an end to the revolutionary movements that had threatened the Greek and Hellenistic cities. In Italy it was the organization of urban patterns among an ancient peasant population. In the western area it involved the founding of new cities among the peoples still at the tribal level of social organization. And Greco-Roman culture endured only so long as these cities retained their historic social structures; it disappeared when changes weakened the urban ruling classes, which were the carriers of its literary, intellectual, and artistic elements.

The great structures whose ruins give historic grandeur to a modern Rome that staggers with the memory of the past they represent suggest the fundamental patterns which, identified by buildings repeating their purpose if not their splendor in other cities, both large and small, in every part of the empire, were the characteristic elements of Greco-Roman culture. The Forum was the center of public life. About it were shops, markets, halls of justice—basilicas—and offices of the bureaucrats who really governed, and near by were the palaces of those who held power—the emperor and his associates. The Pantheon was originally the temple of local gods. Other temples, dedicated to the Divine Julius, Apollo, the Great Mother, and Fortuna, testified not only to the sources of imperial strength—genius, courage, fecundity, and luck—but also to the social amalgamation which had produced Greco-Roman culture. About the Portico of Octavia were grouped museums and libraries where

artists, poets, and philosophers found the works of their illustrious predecessors. The first triumphal arches celebrated the victories of Roman
commanders, but in time they were used for other commemorative and
even decorative purposes. Among the many that graced imperial Rome
those remaining are credited to the emperors Titus, Septimius Severus,
and Constantine. Constantine's is decorated with sculptures from Tra-
jan's arch. The Colosseum, the Amphitheatre, and the great baths recall
the amusements which played such a part in the life of the populace. The
walls, the aqueducts, the sewers, and the roads testify to the political and
economic organization that supported urban life.[3]

Altogether these structures constitute an architectural rendering of the
institutions, outlook, and values of Greco-Roman culture. They are even
now beautiful and were in their day no doubt a fitting setting for a life of
power, ease, and luxury. Indeed, they are the monuments of a culture
which made an art of consumption but considered unworthy any effort to
understand production. In this connection it is pertinent to emphasize
that the tradition of rural life founded by the representatives of Greco-
Roman culture was that of the gentleman landlord, not that of the working peasant. Its essential element was an amplification of the life of ease
and luxury of the urban aristocrat with the pleasant aspects of life in the
country. "If you read—read every ancient writer you like—you will find
that life, really civilized life, was a city life." [4]

. . .

ROMAN LAW

The single intellectual development which the Romans initiated and significantly contributed to was the formation of a body of law which became as time went on an instrument to realize a justice based not on custom but on reason. The necessity of ruling the divers peoples of the
conquered lands was the chief incentive to the substitution of principles
for customs, and acquaintance with the laws of other peoples, as well as
with Greek philosophy, guided the substitution. In the end, however, the
systematization of the law was almost as much the work of non-Romans
as it was of Romans. In fact when Roman law is viewed as a cultural
growth and not as a creation of the Roman state, it appears as a product
of the mingling of peoples and the assimilation of local cultures that influenced every other aspect of cultural change in Roman times.[5]

. . .

Although Roman public, religious, and criminal law had lasting influence, only civil law, as elaborated by the jurisconsults, became a funda-

mental element in the Western cultural tradition; as Gaius said, it dealt with *persons, things,* and *actions.*

The Roman law of personality drew a distinction between a *man* and a *person,* with the result that a man might actually be several persons. For example, the Roman might be a magistrate, a head of a family, a soldier, a partner in a business, and an agent, and in each capacity special rights and obligations constituted him a person. Furthermore, individuals organized for a common purpose and having a common treasury were regarded as a person; this is the legal conception which survives today in the corporation. Such corporate persons, known to Romans as *universitates,* were common in municipal, religious, industrial, and commercial affairs. Because slaves had no rights, they were not regarded as persons. Foreigners became persons when granted rights under Roman law. Besides the rights to bear arms and to vote in the assemblies, the chief rights of the citizen were to head a family and to possess a patrimony, i.e., to own part of the soil of Italy. The loss of citizenship deprived a man of these rights. . . .

. . .

The Roman law of things, which was grounded in custom, recognized several classes of property, such as sacred property, i.e., the lands, temples, and utensils which belonged to the gods: common property, i.e., the air, the sea, and running water; public property, i.e., walls, gates, streets, aqueducts, and roads; and private property, i.e., things that could be owned by individuals. All things were divided into two classes, corporeal and incorporeal. Chief among corporeal things were lands, buildings, livestock, slaves, implements, and furnishings. Among incorporeal things were the rural and urban servitudes. The rural servitudes were the right to an eight-foot roadway for heavy traffic, the right to a footpath or a bridle road, the right to drive cattle to water across another's land, the right to take water in an artificial channel across another's land, and the right to draw water from another's well. The urban servitudes were the right to seat timbers in a neighbor's wall, the right to discharge rain water in gutters, and the right to allow water from a roof to drip on another's land. The urban dweller was required to build his wall strong enough to bear the weight of his neighbor's construction. The law defined three modes of private ownership: (1) the full right of use and abuse, (2) the right of usufruct, i.e., the right to use but not to change, and (3) the right to use for a limited time under the compulsion of necessity. . . .

. . . By developing a special form of ownership for things sold under the jus gentium, the praetors replaced the formal process of transfer of the jus civile with a flexibility which, while protecting the rights of both the seller and the purchaser, permitted transactions of all kinds to be made easily. . . .

With the development of flexibility in the law of transfer of property, came the elaboration of legal means of possessing and using it. Chief among these means were the leasehold and the loan secured by mortgage. Leases for a period, in perpetuity, and at will developed. Originally a leaseholder had no rights against an owner except those stipulated in a contract, and he could not assign the leased property to a third party. In time, however, he obtained the right of assignment. The loan secured by mortgage was a special form of credit transaction. The mortgage was dead property given by a debtor to a creditor as security for a loan. The debtor retained possession as a tenant at will, but ownership was transferred to the creditor by formal conveyance. The right of the debtor to recover ownership when the loan was repaid was provided for in a collateral agreement. If the creditor sold the property to a third party, which he had a right to do, the debtor could bring an action to protect his rights. If the debtor failed to repay the loan, his rights were completely extinguished by the sale of the property under the order of the court. Interest was the compensation due a creditor when a debtor failed to repay a loan. . . .

The making of profit on lent money, known as usury, developed from this practice of allowing a creditor to collect compensation when a debtor defaulted. As the traditional agrarian economy gave way before the development of commerce, opportunities for lending money at a profit multiplied, and moneylending became a lucrative business. It was first subjected to legal regulation in the Twelve Tables. The rate of interest was fixed at 12 per cent, and those who collected more were punished twice as severely as thieves. From the fourth century B.C. to the end of the republic there is ample evidence to support the view that the struggle of debtors and moneylenders was a significant factor in politics. In 347 B.C. the legal rate of interest was fixed at 5, and five years later the right to collect interest was abolished. Since this law applied only to citizens, it was evaded by making loans in the names of aliens. Apparently the praetors winked at the practice for a long time, for it was not suppressed until the opening of the second century B.C. As Roman power grew, the profits of moneylending increased because in the provinces the moneylenders could charge as much as the traffic would bear. In some cases they collected about 50 per cent per year. In the time of the Gracchi open hostility between creditors and debtors appeared, and in the Social War violence broke out between them. Sulla eased the situation by fixing the interest rate at 1 per cent per month. In the middle of the first century B.C. this rate, which amounted to 12 per cent, was extended to the provinces. . . . More important, however, than these limitations was the law of bankruptcy, which revolutionized the ancient law of debt by allowing a debtor to cede his estate to his creditors and begin anew with liability for obligations proceeding from the earlier periods only if they could be paid without financially ruining him. This reform, it should be noted, was designed more to protect the creditor against fraud than to ease the debtor's burden. All modern systems of bankruptcy stem from this legislation. In the course of these developments the ancient right of the creditor to enslave the debtor disappeared and a system of exemptions which withdrew certain chattels from seizure took its place. . . . Under the empire moneylending as a business declined, and the greatest evils of usury ceased. But the lower classes remained the prey of petty creditors. Imprisonment of the debtor and holding the debtor for ransom were common, as was the old custom of seizing the corpse of a defaulting debtor as a means of enforcing payment from his heirs. The general tendency of imperial legislation was to lessen the rights of the creditor over the debtor.

. . .

The most distinctive element of the civil law was the law of contract. Like other elements of the civil law it was originally formal, but in time, largely as the result of the diversification of economic activity, it developed a high degree of flexibility. A contract was a legal form that made enforceable the promises of individuals, particularly those entered into by bargaining. A contractual relation was regarded as involving three distinct acts: (1) the offer, (2) the acceptance, and (3) the delivery or the performance. Offer and acceptance together constituted the agreement that was enforceable; delivery or performance was the act which the parties to the agreement could be legally compelled to perform. . . . The Roman law of contract standardized transactions involving property rights and the performance of labor by making the intentions of individuals in their private relations legally binding.

The Characteristics of the Roman Legal System

The development of Roman law was continuous from the ancient tribes to the oriental monarchy—a period of about fifteen hundred years. Although the Twelve Tables and many legislative enactments contributed to this development, the enduring force was an unwritten legal tradition, originally preserved by priests but ultimately perpetuated and elaborated by lawyers. The process of legal growth was twofold: (1) modification of the tradition to meet changing circumstances and (2) perpetuation of the fundamental rule of the law through new circumstances. The concrete forms of this twofold process were (1) the judicial precedent and (2) the legal principle. Although each gave stability to the law, each also contributed to its flexibility, for as new circumstances appeared, the application of a principle involved the creation of new precedent. Thus the Roman legal system became systematic and abstract and, under the influence of Greek philosophy, rational, i.e., the law was conceived as grounded in a fundamental order of justice which was worked out in practice by reason. In essence, therefore, the law grew by interpretation and comment. The role of the judge and the legal scholar was not only to render justice in specific cases but also to refine constantly the practical justice that stemmed from universal justice. Notable, in this connection, were the procedures which gave parties to litigation full opportunity to develop the issue according to their divergent interests, for by such procedure justice was rendered without arbitrary action. There was truth in the jurisconsult's assertion that the law is "the art of the good and the fair."

The distinctive achievement of Roman legal development was the most complete elaboration of the right of private property found in any legal system before modern times. By liberating individual intention from governmental control, this part of the civil law contributed to the free disposal of property and led to competition rather than regimentation in economic relations. . . .

. . .

3. THE NINTH CENTURY

Henri Pirenne

Pirenne's thesis is that the decline of cities in the Frankish Empire re-sulted from Islamic control of the Mediterranean. Once the foundation of Rome's urban centers, the Frankish Empire's commerce dwindled in the ninth century as the southern world was sealed off to the Carolingi-ans. The closed domestic market therefore witnessed the replacement of an economy of exchange by an economy of consumption, and the cities of Augustus grew silent and lifeless. At the same time, however, Russia was a scene of flourishing trade carried on from fortified enclosures, such as Smolensk, Novgorod, and Kiev. Russian commerce flowed to the Bagdad Caliphate lying to the east and the Empire of Byzantium to the south. The latter's influence on Russian life was to become incalculable, much of it channeled through Czarograd—the city of the Emperors.

. . . IN THE DAYS OF THE MEROVINGIANS, Gaul was still a maritime country and trade and traffic flourished because of that fact. The Empire of Char-lemagne, on the contrary, was essentially an inland one. No longer was there any communication with the exterior; it was a closed State, a State without foreign markets, living in a condition of almost complete isolation.

To be sure, the transition from one era to the other was not clear-cut. The trade of Marseilles did not suddenly cease but, from the middle of the seventh century, waned gradually as the Moslems advanced in the

An abridgement of "The Ninth Century," in Henri Pirenne, *Medieval Cities, Their Origins and the Revival of Trade* (Princeton University Press, 1969). Copyright 1925, 1952 by Princeton University Press. Reprinted by permission of the publisher.

Mediterranean. Syria, conquered by them in 633–638, no longer kept it thriving with her ships and her merchandise. Shortly afterwards, Egypt passed in her turn under the yoke of Islam (638–640), and papyrus no longer came to Gaul. A characteristic consequence is that, after 677, the royal chancellery stopped using papyrus. The importation of spices kept up for a while, for the monks of Corbie, in 716, believed it useful to have ratified for the last time their privileges of the *tonlieu* of Fos. A half century later, solitude reigned in the port of Marseilles. Her fostermother, the sea, was shut off from her and the economic life of the inland regions which had been nourished through her intermediary was definitely extinguished. By the ninth century Provence, once the richest country of Gaul, had become the poorest.

More and more, the Moslems consolidated their domination over the sea. In the course of the ninth century they seized the Balearic Isles, Corsica, Sardinia, Sicily. On the coasts of Africa they founded new ports: Tunis (698–703); later on, Mehdia to the south of this city; then Cairo, in 973. Palermo, where stood a great arsenal, became their principal base in the Tyrrhenian Sea. Their fleets sailed it in complete mastery; commercial flotillas transported the products of the West to Cairo, whence they were redispatched to Bagdad, or pirate fleets devastated the coasts of Provence and Italy and put towns to the torch after they had been pillaged and their inhabitants captured to be sold as slaves. . . .

The efforts of Charlemagne and his successors to protect the coasts from Saracen raiders were as impotent as their attempts to oppose the invasions of the Norsemen in the north and west. The hardihood and seamanship of the Danes and Norwegians made it easy for them to plunder the coasts of the Carolingian Empire during the whole of the eleventh century. They conducted their raids not only from the North Sea, the Channel, and the Gulf of Gascony, but at times even from the Mediterranean. Every river which emptied into these seas was, at one time or another, ascended by their skilfully constructed barks, splendid specimens whereof, brought to light by recent excavations, are now preserved at Oslo. Periodically the valleys of the Rhine, the Meuse, the Scheldt, the Seine, the Loire, the Garonne and the Rhône were the scene of systematic and persistent pillaging. The devastation was so complete that, in many cases indeed, the population itself disappeared. And nothing is a better illustration of the essentially inland character of the Frankish Empire than its inability to organize the defense of its coasts, against either Saracens or Norsemen. For that defense, to be effective, should have been a naval defense, and the Empire had no fleets, or hastily improvised ones at best.

Such conditions were incompatible with the existence of a commerce of first-rate importance. The historical literature of the ninth century contains, it is true, certain references to merchants (*mercatores, negociatores*), but no illusion should be cherished as to their importance. Compared to the number of texts which have been preserved from that era, these references are extremely rare. The capitularies, those regulations touching upon every phase of social life, are remarkably meagre in so far as applies to commerce. From this it may be assumed that the latter played a rôle of only secondary, negligible importance. It was only in the north of Gaul that, during the first half of the ninth century, trade showed any signs of activity.

. . .

It is, then, most likely that the commerce of Carolingian times was very much reduced. Except in the neighborhood of Quentovic and Duurstede, it consisted only in the transport of indispensable commodities, such as wine and salt, in the prohibited traffic of a few slaves, and in the barter, through the intermediary of the Jews, of a small number of products from the East.

Of a regular and normal commercial activity, of steady trading carried on by a class of professional merchants, in short, of all that constitutes the very essence of an economy of exchange worthy of the name, no traces are to be found after the closing off of the Mediterranean by the Islamic invasion. The great number of markets (*mercatus*), which were to be found in the ninth century, in no way contradicts this assertion. They were, as a matter of fact, only small local marketplaces, instituted for the weekly provisioning of the populace by means of the retail sale of foodstuffs from the country. As a proof of the commercial activity of the Carolingian era, it would be equally beside the point to speak of the existence of the street occupied by merchants (*vicus mercatorum*) at Aix-la-Chapelle near the palace of Charlemagne, or of similar streets near certain great abbeys such as, for example, that of St. Riquier. The merchants with whom we have to do here were not, in fact, professional merchants but servitors charged with the duty of supplying the Court or the monks. They were, so to speak, employees of the seignorial household staff and were in no respect merchants.

. . .

We are so accustomed to consider the reign of Charlemagne as an era of revival that we are unconsciously led to imagine an identical progress in all fields. Unfortunately, what is true of literary culture, of the religious State, of customs, institutions and statecraft is not true of communications and commerce. Every great thing that Charlemagne accomplished was accomplished either by his military strength or by his alliance with the Church. For that matter, neither the Church nor arms could overcome the circumstances in virtue of which the Frankish Empire found itself deprived of foreign markets. It was forced, in fact, to accommodate itself to a situation which was inevitably prescribed. History is obliged to recognize that, however brilliant it seems in other respects, the cycle of Charlemagne, considered from an economic viewpoint, is a cycle of regression.

.   .   .

The economic base of the State, as of society, was from this time on the landed proprietor. Just as the Carolingian Empire was an inland State without foreign markets, so also was it an essentially agricultural State. The traces of commerce which were still to be found there were negligible. There was no other property than landed property, and no other work than rural work. As has already been stated above, this predominance of agriculture was no new fact. It existed in a very distinct form in the Roman era and it continued with increasing strength in the Merovingian era. As early as the close of antiquity, all the west of Europe was covered with great demesnes belonging to an aristocracy the members of which bore the title of senators (*senatores*). More and more, property was disappearing in a transformation into hereditary tenures, while the old free farmers were themselves undergoing a transformation into "cultivators" (*coloni*) bound to the soil, from father to son. The Germanic invasions did not noticeably alter this state of things. We have definitely given up the idea of picturing the Germanic tribes in the light of a democracy of peasants, all on an equal footing. Social distinctions were very great among them even when they first invaded the Empire. They comprised a minority of the wealthy and a majority of the poor. The number of slaves and half-free (*liti*) was considerable.

The arrival of the invaders in the Roman provinces brought with it, then, no overthrow of the existing order. The newcomers preserved, in adapting themselves thereto, the status quo. Many of the invaders received from the king or acquired by force or by marriage, or otherwise, great demesnes which made them the equals of the "senators." The landed aristocracy, far from disappearing, was on the contrary invigorated by new elements.

.   .   .

As long as urban life and commerce flourished, the great demesnes had a market for the disposal of their produce. There is no room for doubt that during all the Merovingian era it was through them that the city groups were provisioned and that the merchants were supplied. But it could not help be otherwise when trade disappeared and therewith the merchant class and the municipal population. The great estates suffered the same fate as the Frankish Empire. Like it, they lost their markets. The possibility of selling abroad existed no longer because of the lack of buyers, and it became useless to continue to produce more than the indispensable minimum for the subsistence of the men, proprietors or tenants, living on the estate.

For an economy of exchange was substituted an economy of consumption. Each demesne, in place of continuing to deal with the outside, constituted from this time on a little world of its own. It lived by itself and for itself, in the traditional immobility of a patriarchal form of government. The ninth century is the golden age of what we have called the closed domestic economy and which we might call, with more exactitude, the economy of no markets.[1]

This economy, in which production had no other aim than the sustenance of the demesnial group and which in consequence was absolutely foreign to the idea of profit, can not be considered as a natural and spontaneous phenomenon. It was, on the contrary, merely the result of an evolution which forced it to take this characteristic form. The great proprietors did not give up selling the products of their lands of their own free will; they stopped because they could not do otherwise. Certainly if commerce had continued to supply them regularly with the means of disposing of these products abroad, they would not have neglected to profit thereby. They did not sell because they could not sell, and they could not sell because markets were wanting. The closed demesnial organization, which made its appearance at the beginning of the ninth century, was a phenomenon due to compulsion. That is merely to say that it was an abnormal phenomenon.

This can be most effectively shown by comparing the picture which Carolingian Europe presents with that of Southern Russia at the same era.

We know that bands of sea-faring Norsemen, that is to say of Scandinavians originally from Sweden, established their domination over the Slavs of the watershed of the Dnieper during the course of the ninth century. These conquerors, whom the conquered designated by the name of Russians, naturally had to congregate in groups in order to insure their safety in the midst of the populations they had subjected.

For this purpose they built fortified enclosures, called *gorods* in the Slavic tongue, where they settled with their princes and the images of their gods. The most ancient Russian cities owe their origin to these entrenched camps. There were such camps at Smolensk, Suzdal and Novgorod; the most important and the most civilized was at Kiev, the prince of which ranked above all the other princes. The subsistence of the invaders was assured by tributes levied on the native population.

It was therefore possible for the Russians to live off the land, without seeking abroad to supplement the resources which the country gave them in abundance. They would have done so, without doubt, and been content to use the prestations of their subjects if they had found it impossible, like their contemporaries in Western Europe, to communicate with the exterior. But the position which they occupied must have early led them to practise an economy of exchange.

Southern Russia was placed, as a matter of fact, between two regions of a superior civilization. To the east, beyond the Caspian Sea, extended the Caliphate of Bagdad; to the south, the Black Sea bathed the coasts of the Byzantine Empire and pointed the way towards Constantinople. The barbarians felt at once the effect of these two strong centers of attraction. To be sure, they were in the highest degree energetic, enterprising and adventurous, but their native qualities only served to turn circumstances to the best account. Arab merchants, Jews, and Byzantines were already frequenting the Slavic regions when they took possession, and showed them the route to follow. They themselves did not hesitate to plunge along it under the spur of the love of gain, quite as natural to primitive man as to civilized.

The country they occupied placed at their disposal products particularly well suited for trade with rich empires accustomed to the refinements of life. Its immense forests furnished them with a quantity of honey, precious in those days when sugar was still unknown, and furs, sumptuousness in which was a requisite, even in southern climes, of luxurious dress and equipment.

. . .

In the region of Kiev they followed to the south the course of the Dnieper, to the east the Volga, and to the north the direction marked by the Western Dvina or the lakes which abut the Gulf of Bothnia. Information from Jewish or Arab travellers and from Byzantine writers fortunately supplements the data from archaeological records. It will suffice here to give a brief résumé of what Constantine Porphyrogenetus reports in the ninth century. He shows the Russians assembling their boats at Kiev each year after the ice melts. Their flotilla slowly descends the Dnieper, whose numerous cataracts present obstacles that have to be avoided by dragging the barks along the banks. The sea once reached, they sail before the wind along the coasts towards Constantinople, the supreme goal of their long and perilous voyage. There the Russian merchants had a special quarter and made commercial treaties, the oldest of which dates back to the ninth century, regulating their relations with the population. Many of them, seduced by its attractions, settled down there and took service in the Imperial Guard, as had done, before that time, the Germans in the legions of Rome.

The City of the Emperors (Czarograd) had for the Russians a fascination the influence of which has lasted across the centuries. It was from her that they received Christianity (957–1015); it was from her that they borrowed their art, their writing, the use of money and a good part of their administrative organization. Nothing more is needed to demon-

strate the rôle played by Byzantine commerce in their social life. It occupied so essential a place therein that without it their civilization would
remain inexplicable. To be sure, the forms in which it is found are very
primitive, but the important thing is not the forms of this traffic; it is the
effect it had.

Among the Russians of the late Middle Ages it actually determined the
constitution of society. By striking contrast with what has been shown to
be the case with their contemporaries of Carolingian Europe, not only
the importance but the very idea of real estate was unknown to them.
Their notion of wealth comprised only personal property, of which slaves
were the most valuable. They were not interested in land except in so far
as, by their control of it, they were able to appropriate its products. And
if this conception was that of a class of warrior-conquerors, there is but
little doubt that it was held for so long because these warriors were, at
the same time, merchants. We might, incidentally, add that the concentration of the Russians in the *gorods,* motivated in the beginning by military necessity, is itself found to fit in admirably with commercial needs.
An organization created by barbarians for the purpose of keeping conquered populations under the yoke was well adapted to the sort of life
which theirs became after they gave heed to the economic attraction of
Byzantium and Bagdad. Their example shows that a society does not necessarily have to pass through an agrarian stage before giving itself over to
commerce. Here commerce appears as an original phenomenon. And if
this is so, it is because the Russians instead of finding themselves isolated
from the outside world like Western Europe were on the contrary pushed
or, to use a better word, *drawn* into contact with it from the
beginning. . . .

4. THE PREINDUSTRIAL CITY

Gideon Sjoberg

Although the urban community is meaningful in terms of population density and an exchange process, distinct differences may be observed between preindustrial and industrial cities. Ecological, economic, and social contrasts are apparent in the cities of medieval Europe as well as those of present-day Africa and Asia on the one hand, and the industrialized communities of the Western world, on the other. Industrialization requires an economic structure in which recruitment of personnel is based upon universalistic instead of particularistic criteria. Industrialization is also consistent with a class system embodying achievement values rather than an estate system of ascriptive standards. Similarly, the true industrial city is one which possesses a system of mass education and communication that is essentially secular in character. Besides illuminating these variables, the present article traces the persistence of preindustrial elements in the cities of many regions of the world and suggests that their recognition will help in the development of more sophisticated comparative community studies. Theoretical and methodological, Sjoberg's paper is also an apt picture of that phase of urban history which preceded the contemporary era.

IN THE PAST FEW DECADES social scientists have been conducting field studies in a number of relatively non-Westernized cities. Their recently acquired knowledge of North Africa and various parts of Asia, combined

Excerpts from "The Preindustrial City" (*American Journal of Sociology,* March 1955).
Reprinted by permission of the author and the University of Chicago Press. Copyright 1955 by the University of Chicago.

with what was already learned, clearly indicates that these cities are not like typical cities of the United States and other highly industrialized areas but are much more like those of medieval Europe. Such communities are termed herein "preindustrial," for they have arisen without stimulus from that form of production which we associate with the European industrial revolution.

Recently Foster, in a most informative article, took cognizance of the preindustrial city.[1] His primary emphasis was upon the peasantry (which he calls "folk"); but he recognized this to be part of a broader social structure which includes the preindustrial city. He noted certain similarities between the peasantry and the city's lower class. Likewise the present author sought to analyze the total society of which the peasantry and the preindustrial city are integral parts.[2] For want of a better term this was called "feudal." Like Redfield's folk (or "primitive") society, the feudal order is highly stable and sacred; in contrast, however, it has a complex social organization. It is characterized by highly developed state and educational and/or religious institutions and by a rigid class structure.

Thus far no one has analyzed the preindustrial city per se, especially as it differs from the industrial-urban community, although Weber, Tonnies, and a few others perceived differences between the two. Yet such a survey is needed for the understanding of urban development in so-called underdeveloped countries and, for that matter, in parts of Europe. Such is the goal of this paper. The typological analysis should also serve as a guide to future research.

ECOLOGICAL ORGANIZATION

Preindustrial cities depend for their existence upon food and raw materials obtained from without; for this reason they are marketing centers. And they serve as centers for handicraft manufacturing. In addition, they fulfill important political, religious, and educational functions. Some cities have become specialized; for example, Benares in India and Karbala in Iraq are best known as religious communities, and Peiping in China as a locus for political and educational activities.

The proportion of urbanites relative to the peasant population is small, in some societies about 10 per cent, even though a few preindustrial cities have attained populations of 100,000 or more. Growth has been by slow accretion. These characteristics are due to the nonindustrial nature of the total social order. The amount of surplus food available to support an urban population has been limited by the unmechanized agriculture, transportation facilities utilizing primarily human or animal power, and inefficient methods of food preservation and storage.

The internal arrangement of the preindustrial city, in the nature of the case, is closely related to the city's economic and social structure.[3] Most streets are mere passageways for people and for animals used in transport. Buildings are low and crowded together. The congested conditions, combined with limited scientific knowledge, have fostered serious sanitation problems.

More significant is the rigid social segregation which typically has led to the formation of "quarters" or "wards." In some cities (e.g., Fez, Morocco, and Aleppo, Syria) these were sealed off from each other by walls, whose gates were locked at night. The quarters reflect the sharp local social divisions. Thus ethnic groups live in special sections. And the occupational groupings, some being at the same time ethnic in character, typically reside apart from one another. Often a special street or sector of the city is occupied almost exclusively by members of a particular trade; cities in such divergent cultures as medieval Europe and modern Afghanistan contain streets with names like "street of the goldsmiths." Lower-class and especially "outcaste" groups live on the city's periphery, at a distance from the primary centers of activity. Social segregation, the limited transportation facilities, the modicum of residential mobility, and the cramped living quarters have encouraged the development of well-defined neighborhoods which are almost primary groups.

Despite rigid segregation the evidence suggests no real specialization of land use such as is functionally necessary in industrial-urban communities. In medieval Europe and in other areas city dwellings often serve as workshops, and religious structures are used as schools or marketing centers.[4] Finally, the "business district" does not hold the position of dominance that it enjoys in the industrial-urban community. Thus, in the Middle East the principal mosque, or in medieval Europe the cathedral, is usually the focal point of community life. The center of Peiping is the Forbidden City.

ECONOMIC ORGANIZATION

The economy of the preindustrial city diverges sharply from that of the modern industrial center. The prime difference is the absence in the former of industrialism which may be defined as that system of production in which *inanimate* sources of power are used to multiply human effort. Preindustrial cities depend for the production of goods and services upon *animate* (human or animal) sources of energy—applied either directly or indirectly through such mechanical devices as hammers, pulleys, and wheels. The industrial-urban community, on the other hand, employs inanimate generators of power such as electricity and steam which greatly enhance the productive capacity of urbanites. This basically new form of energy production, one which requires for its development and survival a special kind of institutional complex, effects striking changes in the ecological, economic, and social organization of cities in which it has become dominant.

Other facets of the economy of the preindustrial city are associated with its particular system of production. There is little fragmentation or specialization of work. The handicraftsman participates in nearly every phase of the manufacture of an article, often carrying out the work in his own home or in a small shop near by and, within the limits of certain guild and community regulations, maintaining direct control over conditions of work and methods of production.

In industrial cities, on the other hand, the complex division of labor requires a specialized managerial group, often extra-community in character, whose primary function is to direct and control others. And for the supervision and co-ordination of the activities of workers, a "factory system" has been developed, something typically lacking in preindustrial cities. (Occasionally centralized production is found in preindustrial cities—e.g., where the state organized slaves for large-scale construction projects.) Most commercial activities, also, are conducted in preindustrial cities by individuals without a highly formalized organization; for example, the craftsman has frequently been responsible for the marketing of his own products. With a few exceptions, the preindustrial community cannot support a large group of middlemen.

The various occupations are organized into what have been termed "guilds."[5] These strive to encompass all, except the elite, who are gainfully employed in some economic activity. Guilds have existed for merchants and handicraft workers (e.g., goldsmiths and weavers) as well as for servants, entertainers, and even beggars and thieves. Typically the guilds operate only within the local community, and there are no large-scale economic organizations such as those in industrial cities which link their members to their fellows in other communities.

Guild membership and apprenticeship are prerequisites to the practice of almost any occupation, a circumstance obviously leading to monopolization. To a degree these organizations regulate the work of their members and the price of their products and services. And the guilds recruit workers into specific occupations, typically selecting them according to such particularistic criteria as kinship rather than universalistic standards.

The guilds are integrated with still other elements of the city's social structure. They perform certain religious functions; for example, in medieval European, Chinese, and Middle Eastern cities each guild had its "patron saint" and held periodic festivals in his honor. And, by assisting members in time of trouble, the guilds serve as social security agencies.

The economic structure of the preindustrial city functions with little rationality judged by industrial-urban standards. This is shown in the general nonstandardization of manufacturing methods as well as in the products and is even more evident in marketing. In preindustrial cities throughout the world a fixed price is rare; buyer and seller settle their bargain by haggling. (Of course, there are limits above which customers will not buy and below which merchants will not sell.) Often business is conducted in a leisurely manner, money not being the only desired end.

Furthermore, the sorting of goods according to size, weight, and quality is not common. Typical is the adulteration and spoilage of produce. And weights and measures are not standardized: variations exist not only between one city and the next but also within communities, for often different guilds employ their own systems. Within a single city there may be different kinds of currency, which, with the poorly developed accounting and credit systems, signalized a modicum of rationality in the whole of economic action in preindustrial cities.[6]

SOCIAL ORGANIZATION

The economic system of the preindustrial city, based as it has been upon animate sources of power, articulates with a characteristic class structure and family, religious, educational, and governmental systems.

Of the class structure, the most striking component is a literate elite controlling and depending for its existence upon the mass of the populace, even in the traditional cities of India with their caste system. The elite is composed of individuals holding positions in the governmental, religious, and/or educational institutions of the larger society, although at times groups such as large absentee landlords have belonged to it. At the opposite pole are the masses, comprising such groups as handicraft workers whose goods and services are produced primarily for the elite's benefit.[7] Between the elite and the lower class is a rather sharp schism, but in both groups there are gradations in rank. The members of the elite belong to the "correct" families and enjoy power, property, and certain highly valued personal attributes. Their position, moreover, is legitimized by sacred writings.

Social mobility in this city is minimal; the only real threat to the elite comes from the outside—not from the city's lower classes. And a middle class—so typical of industrial-urban communities, where it can be considered the "dominant" class—is not known in the preindustrial city. The system of production in the larger society provides goods, including food, and services in sufficient amounts to support only a small group of leisured individuals; under these conditions an urban middle class, a semi-leisured group, cannot arise. Nor are a middle class and extensive social mobility essential to the maintenance of the economic system.

Significant is the role of the marginal or "outcaste" groups (e.g., the Eta of Japan), which are not an integral part of the dominant social system. Typically they rank lower than the urban lower class, performing tasks considered especially degrading, such as burying the dead. Slaves, beggars, and the like are outcastes in most preindustrial cities. Even such groups as professional entertainers and itinerant merchants are often viewed as outcastes, for their rovings expose them to "foreign" ideas from which the dominant social group seeks to isolate itself. Actually many outcaste groups, including some of those mentioned above, are ethnic groups, a fact which further intensifies their isolation. (A few, like the Jews in the predominantly Muslim cities of North Africa, have their own small literate religious elite which, however, enjoys no significant political power in the city as a whole.)

An assumption of many urban sociologists is that a small, unstable kinship group, notably the conjugal unit, is a necessary correlate of city life. But this premise does not hold for preindustrial cities.[8] At times sociologists and anthropologists, when generalizing about various traditional societies, have imputed to peasants typically urban kinship patterns. Actually, in these societies the ideal forms of kinship and family life are most closely approximated by members of the urban literate elite, who are best able to fulfill the exacting requirements of the sacred writings. Kinship and the ability to perpetuate one's lineage are accorded marked prestige in preindustrial cities. Children, especially sons, are highly valued, and polygamy or concubinage or adoption help to assure the attainment of large families. The pre-eminence of kinship is apparent even in those preindustrial cities where divorce is permitted. Thus, among the urban Muslims or urban Chinese divorce is not an index of disorganization; here, conjugal ties are loose and distinctly subordinate to the bonds of kinship, and each member of a dissolved conjugal unit typically is absorbed by his kin group. Marriage, a prerequisite to adult status in the preindustrial city, is entered upon at an early age and is arranged between families rather than romantically, by individuals.

The kinship and familial organization displays some rigid patterns of sex and age differentiation whose universality in preindustrial cities has generally been overlooked. A woman, especially of the upper class, ideally performs few significant functions outside the home. She is clearly subordinate to males, especially her father or husband. Recent evidence indicates that this is true even for such a city as Lhasa, Tibet, where women supposedly have had high status.[9] The isolation of women from public life has in some cases been extreme. In nineteenth-century Seoul, Korea, "respectable" women appeared on the streets only during certain hours of the night when men were supposed to stay at home.[10] Those women in preindustrial cities who evade some of the stricter requirements are members of certain marginal groups (e.g., entertainers) or of the lower class. The role of the urban lower-class woman typically resembles that of the peasant rather than the urban upper-class woman. Industrialization, by creating demands and opportunities for their employment outside the home, is causing significant changes in the status of women as well as in the whole of the kinship system in urban areas.

A formalized system of age grading is an effective mechanism of social control in preindustrial cities. Among siblings the eldest son is privileged. And children and youth are subordinate to parents and other adults. This, combined with early marriage, inhibits the development of a "youth culture." On the other hand, older persons hold considerable power and prestige, a fact contributing to the slow pace of change.

As noted above, kinship is functionally integrated with social class. It also reinforces and is reinforced by the economic organization: the occupations, through the guilds, select their members primarily on the basis of kinship, and much of the work is carried on in the home or immediate vicinity. Such conditions are not functional to the requirements of a highly industrialized society.

The kinship system in the preindustrial city also articulates with a special kind of religious system, whose formal organization reaches fullest development among members of the literate elite.[11] The city is the seat of the key religious functionaries whose actions set standards for the rest of society. The urban lower class, like the peasantry, does not possess the education or the means to maintain all the exacting norms prescribed by the sacred writings. Yet the religious system influences the city's entire social structure. (Typically, within the preindustrial city one religion is dominant; however, certain minority groups adhere to their own beliefs.) Unlike the situation in industrial cities, religious activity is not separate from other social action but permeates family, economic, governmental, and other activities. Daily life is pervaded with religious significance. Especially important are periodic public festivals and ceremonies like Ramadan in Muslim cities. Even distinctly ethnic outcaste groups can through their own religious festivals maintain solidarity.

Magic, too, is interwoven with economic, familial, and other social activities. Divination is commonly employed for determining the "correct" action on critical occasions; for example, in traditional Japanese and Chinese cities, the selection of marriage partners. And nonscientific procedures are widely employed to treat illness among all elements of the population of the preindustrial city.

Formal education typically is restricted to the male elite, its purpose being to train individuals for positions in the governmental, educational, or religious hierarchies. The economy of preindustrial cities does not require mass literacy, nor, in fact, does the system of production provide the leisure so necessary for the acquisition of formal education. Considerable time is needed merely to learn the written language, which often is quite different from that spoken. The teacher occupies a position of honor, primarily because of the prestige of all learning and especially of knowledge of the sacred literature, and learning is traditional and characteristically based upon sacred writings.[12] Students are expected to memorize rather than evaluate and initiate, even in institutions of higher learning.

Since preindustrial cities have no agencies of mass communication, they are relatively isolated from one another. Moreover, the masses within a city are isolated from the elite. The former must rely upon verbal communication, which is formalized in special groups such as story-tellers or their counterparts. Through verse and song these transmit upper-class tradition to nonliterate individuals.

The formal government of the preindustrial city is the province of the elite and is closely integrated with the educational and religious systems. It performs two principal functions: exacting tribute from the city's masses to support the activities of the elite and maintaining law and order through a "police force" (at times a branch of the army) and a court system. The police force exists primarily for the control of "outsiders," and the courts support custom and the rule of the sacred literature, a code of enacted legislation typically being absent.

In actual practice little reliance is placed upon formal machinery for regulating social life.[13] Much more significant are the informal controls exerted by the kinship, guild, and religious systems, and here, of course, personal standing is decisive. Status distinctions are visibly correlated with personal attributes, chiefly speech, dress, and personal mannerisms which proclaim ethnic group, occupation, age, sex, and social class. In nineteenth-century Seoul, not only did the upper-class mode of dress differ considerably from that of the masses, but speech varied according to social class, the verb forms and pronouns depending upon whether the speaker ranked higher or lower or was the equal of the person being addressed.[14] Obviously, then, escape from one's role is difficult, even in the street crowds. The individual is ever conscious of his specific rights and duties. All these things conserve the social order in the preindustrial city despite its heterogeneity.

CONCLUSIONS

Throughout this paper there is the assumption that certain structural elements are universal for all urban centers. This study's hypothesis is that their form in the preindustrial city is fundamentally distinct from that in the industrial-urban community. A considerable body of data not only from medieval Europe, which is somewhat atypical,[15] but from a variety of cultures supports this point of view. Emphasis has been upon the static features of preindustrial city life. But even those preindustrial cities which have undergone considerable change approach the ideal type. For one thing, social change is of such a nature that it is not usually perceived by the general populace.

Most cities of the preindustrial type have been located in Europe or Asia. Even though Athens and Rome and the large commercial centers of Europe prior to the industrial revolution displayed certain unique features, they fit the preindustrial type quite well.[16] And many traditional Latin-American cities are quite like it, although deviations exist, for, excluding pre-Columbian cities, these were affected to some degree by the industrial revolution soon after their establishment.

It is postulated that industrialization is a key variable accounting for the distinctions between preindustrial and industrial cities. The type of social structure required to develop and maintain a form of production utilizing inanimate sources of power is quite unlike that in the preindustrial city.[17] At the very least, extensive industrialization requires a rational, centralized, extra-community economic organization in which recruitment is based more upon universalism than on particularism, a class system which stresses achievement rather than ascription, a small and flexible kinship system, a system of mass education which emphasizes universalistic rather than particularistic criteria, and mass communication. Modification in any of these elements affects the others and induces changes in other systems such as those of religion and social control as well. Industrialization, moreover, not only requires a special kind of social structure within the urban community but provides the means necessary for its establishment.

Anthropologists and sociologists will in the future devote increased attention to the study of cities throughout the world. They must therefore recognize that the particular kind of social structure found in cities in the United States is not typical of all societies. Miner's recent study of Timbuctoo,[18] which contains much excellent data, points to the need for recognition of the preindustrial city. His emphasis upon the folk-urban continuum diverted him from an equally significant problem: How does Timbuctoo differ from modern industrial cities in its ecological, economic, and social structure? Society there seems even more sacred and organized than Miner admits.[19] For example, he used divorce as an index of disorganization, but in Muslim society divorce within certain rules is justified by the sacred literature. The studies of Hsu and Fried would have considerably more significance had the authors perceived the generality of their findings. And, once the general structure of the preindustrial city is understood, the specific cultural deviations become more meaningful.

Beals notes the importance of the city as a center of acculturation.[20] But an understanding of this process is impossible without some knowledge of the preindustrial city's social structure. Although industrialization is clearly advancing throughout most of the world, the social structure of preindustrial civilizations is conservative, often resisting the introduction of numerous industrial forms. Certainly many cities of Europe (e.g., in France or Spain) are not so fully industrialized as some presume; a number of preindustrial patterns remain. The persistence of preindustrial elements is also evident in cities of North Africa and many parts of Asia; for example, in India and Japan,[21] even though great social change is currently taking place. And the Latin-American city of Merida, which Redfield studied, had many preindustrial traits.[22] A conscious awareness of the ecological, economic, and social structure of the preindustrial city should do much to further the development of comparative urban community studies.

5. THE GROWTH OF INDUSTRIAL CENTERS IN THE NINETEENTH CENTURY

Adna Ferrin Weber

Adna Weber saw the evolution of industry as having passed through four specific stages: (1) the household system, (2) the era of handicrafts, (3) the cottage system, and (4) the centralized industry of the factory system. It was the last stage that ushered in the big city of modern times. Written late in the nineteenth century, Weber's analysis depicts the emergence of large-scale production within a populous market—all made possible, of course, by the technological advances and consequent economies of the trunk-line railroad. Weber describes the process of industrial concentration, the decline of the small town, the plight of unskilled and unorganized labor, and even the early phases of the drift of factories to the urban fringe that characterized the metropolitan scene a hundred years ago.

THE FACTORY SYSTEM has come to stay. But how does it affect the distribution of population? First, by destroying family industry prosecuted in the farm houses, it diminishes the number of agriculturists; . . . secondly, by destroying industries in the handicraft stage (village shoemaking, milling, etc.) , it removes population from the villages. The entire effect on the distribution of population is therefore centralizing. But it remains a question whether it favors the growth of large cities, as commerce does, or of small cities and towns. It is a question of the advantageous location of the large factory. If local facilities for transportation preponderate among the natural advantages, then the factory will go to the great city;

Excerpts from *The Growth of Cities in the Nineteenth Century, A Study in Statistics* by Adna Ferrin Weber (1899) .

while, if local facilities for production determine the site, the factory is likely to go to the small city.

. . .

In manufacturing, the raw material that comes from the soil is but a single factor in production; other factors are capital, labor, rent, taxes, market for the sale, and facilities for the shipment, of the manufactured products. Now the effect of improved transportation is to cheapen the raw materials, and as a consequence diminish their relative importance as a factor of production. The very fact therefore that railways have so cheapened transportation as to permit the shipment of bulky and heavy commodities (i.e., raw materials) has diminished the importance of local *natural* advantages and increased the importance of the non-natural or artificial advantages for production. The crude manufactures (e.g., lumber mills, tanneries) are still located near the source of supply of raw materials, but not the finer manufactures, and the question arises, is their location determined by other conditions of production, or by the conditions of consumption, i.e., facilities for marketing, and cheap shipment to consumers? If nearness to consumers is the most important advantage in a manufacturing site, then it might be expected that the great commercial centers would also be the manufacturing centers, for they not only contain a rich and numerous body of consumers, but apparently afford superior facilities for distributing goods to the remaining consuming population. The tendency in manufacturing would then be toward centralization, and the great cities would grow at an enormous rate. Such, indeed, has been the actual tendency. In former times, the manufacturer located his plant chiefly with regard to two advantages, water power and nearness to raw materials. Steam applied to stationary engines has made him independent of water power; applied to engines of locomotion it has made him all but independent of the source of his raw materials. Cheap transportation may put the great city on a level with the small town adjacent to the raw materials, i.e., one tendency of modern improvements is to make the commercial center also a manufacturing center.

The centralizing influence of railways is particularly strong in countries where competition has had full sway; the competitive points, enjoying lower rates than rival towns on a single line, absorb all the growth of a region. This fact has been a matter of every-day observation in many parts of the United States, and it is confirmed by all railway authorities. It is asserted that "the entire net increase of the population from 1870 to 1890 in Illinois, Wisconsin, Iowa and Minnesota, except in the new sections, was in cities and towns possessing competitive rates, while those having non-competitive rates decreased in population"; and in Iowa it is the general belief that the absence of large cities is due to the earlier policy of the railways in giving Chicago discriminating rates.

If in the United States excessive competition among the railways has concentrated population in a few competitive points, the absence of competition in France has produced a similar effect. The French government supervised the construction of railways very closely and never permitted the waste involved in building more than one line between the same two points; each road therefore had a monopoly in its own district, and as it could earn a higher rate of profit on through business than on the local traffic, it neglected the latter. Local branches remained unbuilt until subsidies were forthcoming from the central government and local authorities (1865). Ten years later an attempt was made to divert the local roads from their true purpose, and by building connecting links bring them into competition with the old roads for the through traffic; general insolvency of the local roads resulted, which was followed by a new monopoly. The state's guarantee of dividends (1883) undoubtedly prevents the French railways from building many new lines to develop new business; but in America this has been overdone, and it is probable that the smaller places are better served in France than they are in the United States—at least in the West.

In Germany, too, there was a tendency for manufacturers to settle in the cities upon the opening up of railway communication. A careful statistical study of the effect of railways upon the growth of places of different size was made several years ago by Dr. Schwabe, of the Berlin Statistical Bureau. He calculated the rates of growth of 125 cities for a certain period (ranging from six to twenty-one years) before and after the formation of railway connections. The result was as follows: (A) Of 80 cities having less than 10,000 inhabitants each, the increase in population was greater in 23 and less in 57 after the opening of the railway. (B) Of 37 cities with populations 10,000–50,000, 18 showed an increased rate of growth, 19 a decreased rate. (C) Of 8 cities of more than 50,000 inhabitants, all but one (Cologne) grew more rapidly after the introduction of railways than before. It thus appears that the railways stopped the increase of population in the smaller cities, except those of an industrial character, and hastened the growth of the large cities. The railways concentrate transportation in a few channels, and the termini get the benefit. . . .

The statistics of manufactures furnished by the United States government are not altogether trustworthy, but they at least show that in the period 1860–90 the movement was a centralizing one, toward the larger cities. In 1860 the annual production of manufactures per capita was $60 for the United States as a whole, $193.50 for ten cities having a population of 50,000 or more, $424 for ten cities under 50,000, and $44 for the rural districts. Thus the per capita production was at that time largest in the smaller cities. In 1890, however, the per capita product of manufactures was $455 in the 28 great cities, $355 in the 137 cities of 20,000–100,000 population, and $58 for the remainder of the country.

The superiority of the smaller cities in 1860 had in 1890 given way to that of the great cities.

But it is probably safe to affirm that the centralization of manufacturing industry has reached its limit. A reaction toward decentralization began when manufacturers located their mills in the suburbs of large cities in order to escape the high city rents and still avail themselves of the city's superior shipping facilities. Suburban enterprises have in the last decade become increasingly familiar phenomena, not only in the United States, but also in England and Germany, and have brought hope to social philanthropists disheartened with the poverty and misery of congested cities. The statistics of manufactures do not portray the tendency, because it is comparatively recent; but the Twelfth Census, . . . will show how rapidly manufacturing industries are leaving the larger cities. To give one example: the writer was informed by William A. Perrine, of the Ironmoulders' Conference Board of New York, that of some 65 iron foundries in New York City fourteen years ago, only fifteen now remain. Some have gone out of existence; but most of the remaining establishments have removed to Brooklyn, or suburban towns on the Hudson or in New Jersey.

In recent years the decentralizing movement has taken a still more favorable turn, largely as a result of continued improvements in transportation methods and a more enlightened policy on the part of railway managers, who have learned that the factor of distance is of minor importance in the expense account as compared with the additions to the revenue that result from a judicious encouragement of industries in small cities along their lines. Today, practically every shipping point in New England enjoys precisely the same freight rates to points south and west of New York city as does the metropolis itself. This is in effect the zone tariff system, which has been fully developed in Hungary; it gives one and the same rate to all points within each zone. . . .

The effect of a single, uniform railway rate, if it is ever realized (and we have seen that it is, to a certain extent, already a reality for New England manufacturers), would be to eliminate the factor of transportation facilities from the advantages or disadvantages of particular localities for production. The great city would then distribute its products no more cheaply than the small city.

Of the remaining facilities for production, there is no preponderance on the side of the great commercial centers. The important functions of buying and selling, and the securing of capital and credit, which formerly determined the location of many enterprises in the commercial centers, can now all be accomplished by means of a city office; there is not the slightest need of bringing the factory itself to the city. On the other hand, the small town has the great advantage of much lower rents and taxes, which in most cases will be decisive, especially if the town offers freedom from taxation and sufficient land for a building site as an inducement, a policy that has been the making of many a small city in Michigan, New Jersey and other commonwealths. As regards the supply of labor, the relative advantages of city and country differ according to the kind of occupations. As a rule, the wages of skilled workmen are higher in the city than in the village, largely because of the greater efficiency of labor organizations. Even where wages rule the same, many employers have abandoned the great city to escape other exactions of the labor unions. The typographers have one of the strongest of trade unions, and their aggressiveness has already caused the removal to suburbs or small cities of the printing houses of several New York and Boston publishers. It is difficult to say how far this movement will extend; it is opposed now with all the strength of the trade unions in the city, and on the other hand, improved means of communication may in the course of time permit the formation of labor organizations in the country that will be as strong and efficient as those in the city, where large numbers who can meet together on short notice render a powerful association easier of formation. When that time arrives, the small town loses one of its attractions for the manufacturer.

With regard to unskilled labor, the case is somewhat different. The great city contains a large population that is uneducated, unskilled and poverty-stricken. Incapable of organization, it sells its energies to the bidder at starvation wages. Its standard of living is that of the "submerged tenth" of London, or the slum population of New York and Chicago. Although rent and the necessaries of life are higher in the great city than in the rural districts, the middleman who runs the "sweat-shop" finds cheap city labor more submissive and profitable. In England such industries as glovemaking, hand-made lace, etc., are pursued successfully in the rural districts, where female labor is to be secured cheaply. The disadvantage of such labor, however, is its irregularity, which has prevented its employment in this country.

On the whole, the great city seems now to be at a disadvantage in manufacturing, except in the case of cheap and unskilled labor, such as that engaged in the clothing trade.

The existence of other manufacturing enterprises in the metropolis may probably be set down to one of the following causes: (1) Certain old establishments started on the outskirts of the city in an earlier period, and now loath to remove, when the city's growth has enclosed them. (2) Certain industries requiring either traditionally skilled labor, which is not yet to be found outside the original seat, or a high development of technique and art. (3) Many industries whose product is chiefly for local consumption. The number of these is large, since the cities contain so large a proportion of scientific and mechanical contrivances of the age. New York and Chicago together probably possess a larger number of the modern web-perfecting printing presses than all the rest of the United States. Putting together all the paraphernalia of a great commercial city, vehicles of all kinds, vaults and safes, elevated railway apparatus, etc., one will see the necessity of the existence in the great city of a large number of mechanical industries. To these must be added the enterprises that cater to the wants of the rich consumers of a commercial city—furniture, table-ware, carriages, etc. Some of the articles might, indeed, be made outside the city, but there is considerable advantage in "being on the ground." (4) Certain industries whose raw materials come equally by land and water routes. In this case the point of intersection—a commercial center—will be the most economical place of assemblage. An instance in point is the iron and steel industry of Chicago.

. . .

With all the advantages for manufacturing industry possessed by the village or small city, it may look as if the country were destined to be covered with industrial villages built up around one or two immense factories. But there are many forces to oppose the tendency. In the first place, one large modern factory alone gives employment to hundreds of operatives and tends to attract other industries, for it is a well understood fact that place-specialization is extended not to a single trade but to a group of allied trades. Hence, when the benefits of specialization cause a manufacturer to confine himself to a single process in any industry, say weaving in the textile trade, it is natural for other firms carrying on the processes of carding, dyeing, etc., to locate their establishments in the vicinity. Auxiliary trades and repair shops also attach themselves to the group. Further, there are by-products to be utilized; thus it happened that the erection of a large tannery in a western New York village was shortly followed by that of a glue-factory. Finally, in a factory town where the labor of one sex is exclusively employed, other industries will frequently spring up to utilize the labor of the opposite sex. Thus one of the earliest factories in the city of New Britain, Conn., was devoted to the manufacture of carpenters' rules and levels, and employed male labor alone; it was not long before a cotton factory, in which the cheap and abundant labor of women and children could be used to advantage, was planted in the town. A similar tendency has caused the location of textile factories in mining, metal and machine towns in England.

These are some of the reasons why an industrial village soon becomes a large town. But the process does not stop there. New factories are apt to seek the neighborhood of old establishments in the same industry on account of the "initial difficulties" (familiar in the "infant industry" tariff argument) which attend the upbuilding of an industry in an entirely new atmosphere. The advantages of inherited skill and traditions favorable to the genesis of improvements, created by friction among the followers of the same skilled trade in one place, have been well described by Professor Marshall: "The mysteries of the trade become no mysteries; but are as it were in the air, and children learn of them unconsciously. Good work is rightly appreciated, inventions and improvements in machinery, in processes, and the general organization of the business have their merits promptly discussed; if one man starts a new idea, it is taken up by others and combined with suggestions of their own; and thus it becomes the source of new ideas. And presently subsidiary trades grow up in the neighborhood, supplying it with implements and materials, organizing its traffic and in many ways conducing to the economy of its materials."

6. THE PROCESS OF URBANIZATION: UNDERLYING FORCES AND EMERGING TRENDS

The Urbanism Committee of the National Resources Committee

This official document narrates the history of cities during the first third of the twentieth century. Electricity, the automobile, and the airplane were responsible for turning the big city, which at the beginning of the twentieth century had been the product of steam, into the gigantic metropolitan region of the 1930's. Other technological advances, such as aluminum refining, household appliances, diesel engines, synthetics and plastics, and linotype printing, which gave industry fresh power to satisfy an ever rising standard of living and thereby further enlarge the metropolitan community, contributed to the process of urban growth. In fact, two other urbanization trends went on at the same time. The first was the emergence of an urban nation characterized by a network of metropolitan aggregates linked together by highways, airlines, and telephone communication. The second was the centrifugal tendency of cities to disperse into suburban rings surrounding inner cities stricken more and more by severe social problems. Thus, tendencies toward both large-scale interdependence and centrifugal localism gave impetus to the "rurbanization" ideal in cities which originally arose when a fruitful countryside had produced an agricultural surplus.

THE GROWTH OF CITIES since about the beginning of the 19th century in Western Europe and in the United States in particular is attributable . . . to the scientific discoveries and mechanical inventions which facilitated the development of power-driven machinery. Of these revolutioniz-

Excerpts from *Our Cities, Their Role in the National Economy* (1937), United States Government Printing Office.

ing innovations none was probably more fundamental than the application of steam as a source of power for industry and transportation to supplement and replace the previously available sources of power, especially water. Prior to the steam era, few cities exceeded 100,000 and it is doubtful whether any city, even such renowned centers as Rome, Peking, or Nanking, ever exceeded 1 million in population. Not until the great economic and social changes that we identify as the Industrial Revolution had been set in motion did the modern great city become possible.

.   .   .

In recent years, and while steam was molding the pattern of urbanization, a new force has come upon the scene. Whereas steam has had a concentrative effect, electricity and the internal-combustion engine, which became available after the pattern of American cities had already become fixed, have tended to have precisely the opposite effect. The dispersive influence of electricity is due to the fact that it can be transmitted economically even now over distances up to about 300 miles and that it can be used as power with almost equal efficiency in large or small units. It also has decided advantages over steam for rapid local transportation. It has at least the potentiality of exercising a centrifugal influence upon cities as contrasted with the centripetal force exerted by steam. Up to the present, however, electricity, through its use as power for the fast electric elevator and for urban and suburban transit, has mainly accentuated concentration as in the skyscraper and in the overdeveloped, congested, central business district.

In addition to its use as power, electricity, as distinguished from steam, has a quality which has to be reckoned with as a reconstructive element in urban life, the urban structure and our entire social order, namely its use in communication. This use in the form of the telegraph, the telephone, and the radio has only recently been felt and appreciated. It gives promise of having at least as great an influence in reshaping our cities and our civilization during the twentieth century as steam did during the nineteenth.

If to the influences of electricity we add the flexibility, the speed and the individualization of transportation effected by the internal-combustion engine as embodied in the automobile and the airplane, we may say that these new technological devices are likely to alter the structure of the urban community and national life profoundly whether or not we consciously use them as instruments to improve our mode of living.

.   .   .

The outstanding factor in the urbanization of the United States is the speed with which it has progressed. In addition, the urbanization of the

United States has continued apace even after the major western industrial countries have already reached an approximately stable rural-urban equilibrium. This may be attributed to our enormous reserves of unexploited resources which stimulated domestic population growth and attracted immigrants from the economically hard-pressed countries of Europe.

Within a single generation, 1900 to 1930, the urban population of the United States grew from 30 million to nearly 69 million, or by about 130 percent. During the most recent of these census decades (1920–1930), urban population growth had slowed down to 26 percent, and in the period from 1930 to 1935 it was still further reduced to an estimated 3 percent. While this indicates a considerable retardation in the pace of urban growth, it is still significant because it exceeds the rate of growth of the population as a whole and contrasts with the relative stabilization of rural America.

The large cities of the country as a whole have grown more rapidly than the small cities, indicating that the national urban pattern is becoming fixed. Most of the larger cities which have lost population in recent decades are located in New England. The cities along the Atlantic seaboard, which in general had their most rapid growth at an earlier period of national development, grew in the decade 1920–1930 by about 25 percent, those in the Great Lakes region by 36 percent, those in the South by about 53 percent, and those of the West coast by 65 percent. The settlement of the western frontier and the accompanying agricultural expansion, the attraction of the climate in Florida, California, and the Southwest, both because of specialized agriculture and the growing class of people who can afford to live or retire where they please, the phenomenal expansion of the oil industry, the development of heavy industry in the Great Lakes region, symbolized by the rise of the Detroit region in connection with the automobile industry, and Gary in the Chicago district in connection with steel—these account for the recent shifts of urban development into newer regions or into areas offering greater economic opportunity and other special advantages.

In view of the relatively limited quantity of agricultural products which the national and world market can absorb, and of the relatively unlimited human capacity to consume the products of industry, and in the light of the perceivable reflux from the frontier, as well as the probable increase in the mechanization of agriculture, it is to be expected that regions of intensive manufacturing and commercial activity will attract an increasing share of the population, particularly of the urban portion. Consequently, the conditions of living, which are characteristic of the largest cities and which have affected an ever-increasing proportion of the population, may be expected to become even more widely diffused throughout the Nation.

. . .

There is a significant trend in urbanization which in recent decades has become quite marked. It is revealed by the extraordinarily rapid growth of small satellite towns and rural communities within the orbit of metropolitan centers as compared with the central cities themselves. This is in a sense an expression of the coming into more general use of the automobile, electric service, the telephone, and the extension of urban utilities into the surrounding territory. As a result, a new type of urban community has come upon the scene—the metropolitan region.

The metropolis subsists not merely upon its own hinterland but it has become the most vital link in world affairs so that the lines of communication and transportation that link the great metropolitan centers with one another may be thought of as the Main Streets of the world. Since the trend toward a greater concentration of the Nation's population and industry into great metropolitan centers is almost wholly the unplanned product of interacting forces of which we are as yet scarcely conscious, we may infer that these metropolitan aggregations perform essential functions in the national and world economy and owe their genesis and growth to the vital role they play in modern civilization.

Nearly one-half of the population of the United States at the time of the last census lived within a radius of from 20 to 50 miles of cities of over 100,000 inhabitants. These metropolitan areas have absorbed a steadily increasing proportion of the Nation's total population growth, ranging from 46.4 percent of the total national population increment in the decade 1890–1900 to 74 percent in the decade 1920–1930.

The growth of the 96 metropolitan districts recognized by the United States Census in 1930 will serve to illustrate the nature of this regional development of the urban community in the United States. Since 1900 the rate of population increase has been greater in the satellite areas surrounding those large cities than that within their limits. While the central cities in the decade 1920–1930 increased 22.3 percent, those portions of the metropolitan districts lying outside the central cities increased at about twice this rate, or nearly six times as much as the nonmetropolitan part of the United States. The central cities contain a declining proportion of the total population of the metropolitan districts, indicating that metropolitan growth is in even larger degree than formerly a suburban trend. But what might at first glance appear to be a decentralization of population, therefore, is revealed upon closer inspection to be merely a redistribution of the urban population within metropolitan regions or a dispersion from the central city into the adjacent suburban periphery. It is not a general devolution of cities or a flight from the city. What is actually happening is, rather, that the urbanite is steadily being transformed into the suburbanite. While the movement of the last 100 years toward the centralization of population apparently continues, actually satellite cities and satellite rural areas are increasing so rapidly as to evidence a powerful dispersive force within urban regions. This dispersion has not yet become a definite centrifugal movement, but might well develop into one.

Far from being on the decline, the city thus gives evidence mainly of a new phase of its growth by emptying at the center and spilling over its own corporate boundaries. The basis of this centrifugal tendency is to be sought in the urge on the part of those who have the means to escape the congestion, the disadvantageous family life, the undesirable and expensive housing and living conditions, and the high taxation which urban life so frequently involves. The hegira from the city is motivated by the ease of commutation and communication giving ready access to urban technical and cultural facilities combined with the lower taxes and land values, the better housing, more desirable family and community life, and more healthful conditions of existence prevailing in the suburbs. The intraregional dispersion of industry follows in the main from the same factors. Sometimes it precedes and stimulates and at other times it follows and accentuates the centrifugal movement of population.

The redistribution of the urban population into the peripheries of metropolitan regions involves the close and constant dependence of the suburban communities upon the economic and technical functions and cultural opportunities which the metropolis provides. The model suburb, whether it is industrial or residential, however superior, aloof, and detached it may believe itself to be, has its basis of existence and draws much of its sustenance from the noisy, grimy city of which economically and culturally it is an integral part, but from which it has managed to remain independent politically.

It has been said that the suburbanite shuttles back and forth from a place where he would rather live to a place where he would rather not work. In his daily or periodical pendular movement, of which the clock and the time schedule are symbolic, the suburban commuter exhibits the peculiar segmentalization between working and living so characteristic of modern urban society. The bedrooms of American cities are increasingly to be found in the dormitory colonies of the suburbs. The suburbanite, who in his daily routine oscillates between his vocation involving the humdrum, high-speed, technical work of business, industry, and the professions in the heart of the metropolis, and his avocation, which may range from amateur gardening and similar pastoral activities to suburban politics, is not an exception to the urban type of personality but is merely a variety of it. The motives leading to this type of existence are to be sought in the urge to escape the obnoxious aspects of urban life without at the same time losing access to its economic and cultural advantages. In the process, the form and the functions of the city are being revolutionized.

. . .

As the city grew and as new technological factors were introduced, it became increasingly difficult and costly to readapt the fundamental urban street and building pattern to changed needs. As a consequence, there has emerged a public attitude of placid resignation which too generally accepts what is as inevitable and irremediable. Even when disasters such as fires or earthquakes reduced the major part of the city to ruins, as in Chicago and San Francisco, respectively, the rebuilding on the same site has usually been guided by little more than intensified speculative fervor.

While during the colonial period there was evidence of building restrictions and some indication of an interest in community design, the subsequent irresistible expansion and the undaunted spirit of private enterprise swept most of these away. Laws designed to curb the greed and heedlessness of the individual owner and speculator in the interests of order, health, safety, and public welfare were allowed to lapse and were resuscitated only when it was too late to repair most of the damage that had been done through generations of neglect.

As cities have grown big, they have also, in general, grown more sordid and uninhabitable. Building regulations and their enforcement came into use only after the evils of the tenements in the large cities had become glaringly manifest and had been exposed through arduous campaigns of urban social reform. It was not actually until the "muckrakers" through journalism, the social survey, and social research had awakened the public conscience in regard to some of the most disreputable phases of urban living, that legislation designed to mitigate the disastrous consequences of civic apathy and neglect was enacted and some effort made to enforce it. The tremendous growth of cities during the last half of the nineteenth century, the wreckage left behind by periodic depressions, and the appalling congestion in the urban slums helped to call attention to the social and individual cost of land gambling and to the absence of social control of housing and of the physical development of the community.

Today over 1,500 municipalities have building codes and the number of municipal zoning ordinances in force, which have increased phenomenally since 1916, has grown to over 1,300. Legislation authorizing city planning commissions now exists in 42 States, and county planning, which is essential to effective metropolitan planning, is authorized in 26 States.

The nonexistence or nonenforcement of rational land policies, combined with an overemphasis on individualistic enterprise and speculation, in the face of unparalleled opportunities for private gain because of enormous growth and expansion, are the underlying factors in some of the most acute problems of urban life. Such problems include congestion of traffic, the herding of the low-income groups into dark, poorly ventilated dwellings, the contagion of blight near the heart of the city, the uneconomical, unsafe, and disorderly distribution of structures, a deficiency of public open spaces combined with a surplus of unused private space, undue concentration of land values, inequitable apportionment of local tax burdens, and inadequate public services. In varying degrees these are to be found in practically every city.

. . .

Even though, through the development of modern systems of communication and the close interdependence between country and city, the rural and the urban world tend to be more alike, the differences and conflicts between them still persist. The city holds such fascination for country inhabitants that it often leads them to migration. The city dweller, on the other hand, having failed to find a satisfactory life in the city, often generates a nostalgic longing for more "natural" ways of living and seeks a refuge in the country. Because the city has become indispensable to civilized existence, but at the same time subjects man to so many frustrations of his deepest longings, the notion of an ideal mode of life lying somewhere between these two extremes has been a force ever since cities have been in existence. In modern times this ideal expresses itself in a movement known as "rurbanization." It embodies the effort to find a balance between agriculture and industry, between the open natural landscape and the congestion of the city. Model suburbs, garden cities, and suburban homesteads represent variations of this ideal, and the promoters of large scale decentralization of industry have also found argument for their program in the attempt to combine the advantages of urban and rural life in the same community.

If conscious social effort may be assumed to play a significant role in shaping the conditions under which man lives, the present crisis and opportunity in our national life calls for a prompt examination of the alternative modes of life that we might follow. If rural life or living in communities of small size is either wholly or in certain respects more desirable than living in small or large cities, the evidence to that effect should have a bearing upon the formulation of our national policy, insofar as that policy will further or hinder the rural or urban trend. It may well be that the future of our civilization will in large measure depend not upon man's ability to escape from the city but upon his ability to master and use the forces that move and control it. It is doubtful whether without the city we can hope to enjoy the plane of living that contemporary civilization makes possible. The central problem of national life in regard to cities is a problem of creating those conditions that are required to make cities livable for human beings in a machine age.

CHAPTER TWO

THE URBAN GENUS

Long before scholars were concerned about scientifically identifying their subjects they freely declared themselves on the relative value of urban and rural life, most often with a pronounced antiurban bias. The writer of Genesis, it will be recalled, condemned Sodom and Gomorrah. Old Persian, Hindu, Japanese, and Chinese philosophy largely regarded agriculture as the most noble of all the occupations. It is true that Xenophon, Aristotle, and Plato praised the farmer, yet in their estimation he still fell far below the full urban citizen. Even in so urbanized a society as Rome, both for military and moral virtues, Virgil, Horace, Seneca, and Tacitus all extolled the agriculturist.

Medieval and early-modern thought on the opposing claims of rural and urban existence is mixed. The Egyptian historian Ibu-Khaldun saw the city as the center of cultural innovation, but he also feared its tendency to moral degeneration. Regardless of the predominance of rural life at the time, Thomas Aquinas visualized the city as the fitting and proper setting for the expression of human nature. On the other hand, Sir Thomas More in his *Utopia* saw the countryside as the beneficient way to achieve Christian brotherhood. Machiavelli, of course, depicted urban life as particularly disorganized and demoralized, much more so than that of the simple village and farm. Later social philosophers, including Montesquieu, Hume, and Adam Smith, held balanced views. Strong antipathy to the city, however, received fresh impetus at the hands of Jean Jacques Rousseau in his *Discourse about Science and the Arts* and in the *Social Contract,* so much so that his American counter-

parts, Jefferson and Jackson, continue to have enormous sentimental if not practical support even today.

Much of our contemporary rural and not a little of our urban sociology also embodies the traditional antiurban bias. In fact, in
large measure it is a plea for the retention of earlier rural modes of
behavior. A great deal of thought has also been devoted, however,
to simply identifying the phenomena that previous writers approached with a naïveté that often led to confusing results. Practical
as well as academic motives impel this interest. For example, census results are divided into rural and urban sections in many countries. These efforts have had varying emphases: density of settlement, political boundaries, and size of the population. None,
however, has had complete success in describing farm, nonfarm,
town, city, and metropolis. Fundamental to this scientific study is
the basic assumption that rural, on the one hand, and urban, on the
other, represent ontological realities that have significantly different
sociocultural implications, and therefore, that this conceptualization is a prerequisite for theoretical progress in sociology.

A set of dichotomous classifications that attempt to clarify the
matter occupies a very prominent place in contemporary sociological thought. These include Tonnies' *Gemeinschaft* and *Gesellschaft*
communities; Maine's status and contract; Spencer's military and
industrial societies; Durkheim's two types of solidarity—mechanical
and organic; and Weber's traditional and rational forms of action.[1]
Although broader and not entirely equivalent, in one way or another all relate to the distinction drawn by layman, historian, and
philosopher between rural and urban society. And these formulations may indeed raise as many questions as they answer. Their
contribution to theoretical sociology is obvious nevertheless, for
they address themselves to the intrinsic differences between manifestations of society that earlier writers merely condemned or
extolled.

A *typology* is the basis for theory building because it permits the
statement of testable propositions in terms of the classes that have
been defined by the person making the typology. For example, both
Louis Wirth and Georg Simmel drew deductive theories from a few
basic assumptions about urban society. Wirth began with an ecological model and took a dense, large population as given. From that
he postulated that heterogeneity would arise, and that this heterogeneity would in turn produce segmental contacts, anonymity, and
a high rate of mobility.[2] Simmel, on the other hand, used social not
ecological premises. He deduced that given multiple interactions, a
pervasive psychology of rationality and calculation would ensue.[3]
Such inferences as Wirth and Simmel made are susceptible to fac-

tual validation. And with this proof, more refined theory then emerges as conditions are specified, subtypes defined, and rates of change calculated.

Theory is a system of propositions that weave together a multitude of factual relationships expressed in terms of abstract concepts. Three such concepts are important to urban theory—although there is at present no complete agreement on their use. (1) *Urbanization* may be defined as the movement of people from sparsely populated areas to densely populated areas and a change from agricultural to industrial occupations, with a resulting increase in the population at these points, as well as an increase in the number of these points of dense population. (2) *Urbanism,* on the other hand, represents a mode of life evidencing impersonality, receptivity to change, and similar related cosmopolitan traits. (3) The *city* is a major urban community differentiated from the smaller urban community, the town, and at the other end of the scale, the metropolis, although no precise line of demarcation other than an arbitrary one is commonly recognized. It is obvious that these concepts all presuppose the urban genus as their basic reference.

The urban order that is denoted in the several outstanding sets of polarities subsumes a combination of objective referents. One of these is a *physical structure* with a population base, a territorial complex, a technology, and a dependent economy. The second is a *social system,* and the third, a *personality-attitude structure*. In somewhat more detailed form, the urban genus comprises individual self-expression, special interest groups, esthetic-scientific institutions, a complex administrative system, occupational diversity, specialized services, recreational pluralism, socioeconomic heterogeneity, varied styles of life, ethnic and religious variation, and the prevalence of special problems in housing, social control, and transport, among others. By comparison, the prime characteristics assigned to the rural community are a contiguous territorial location together with a rudimentary, extractive technology; a self-sufficient economy; a social system in which intimacy, kinship, and traditional sanctions are prominent features; and a homogeneous common culture.

As much as half a century ago Max Weber was writing, "A rural society, separate from the urban social community, does not exist at the present time in a great part of the modern civilized world."[4] Nor, he might have added, was the completely nonisolated, heterogeneous, rational, and secular community in existence either. Their abstract counterparts are, however, readily available to the imagination, and in that manner they inform the ideal-type conceptions of rural and urban.

In fact, it was the rapid buildup of urban communities and the

equally swift disappearance of rural life in Europe and here in the
United States during the nineteenth century that contributed materially to the dichotomous classifications of the typologists. Accordingly, the urban theory of this period placed greatest stress on the
comparison of urban and unurban societies, each conceived of in
the most general and sweeping terms. Later the ecological interest
of the Chicago school became dominant. This was not a complete
change, however, for the evolutionary hypothesis that the ideal-type
theorizing had implied was simply imposed on a narrower field,
that of the single urban microcosm. One change was very apparent
in this shift: the careful scrutiny of minute facts. Urban sociology
became far more concrete than it had been. Although they did see
the internal complexity of any given city, the older theorists had
thought about cities as a whole. Park, Burgess, Wirth, and Thomas
were simply fascinated by the urban kaleidoscope.[5] In this of course
they erred, as may be seen in the temporocentrism of their studies,
for they lacked the very broad historical perspective of their more
theoretical predecessors.

The earlier sociology that we are discussing saw the city as transforming what had hitherto in history always been a predominantly
rural society. With urbanization at an advanced stage, as it is today,
interest has shifted and now centers on the quality of the urban life
that has been brought about and on the problems confronting municipal administration and national coordination. The transition
corresponds without any doubt to the new metropolitan social order
that has evolved. It also is attributable to the failure of the early
theory, a failure inherent perhaps in the primitive character of the
dichotomous typology.

One aspect of the critique that has developed regarding typological urban theory has been supplied by Gideon Sjoberg. He argues
that, far from being a unitary concept, rural society must be definitely subdivided if it is to have true research value. Though both
share rural properties, Sjoberg says, feudal society has a separate
identity from folk society, and this delineation is a necessary second
approximation if we are to achieve greater research success than the
mere idea of rurality has been able to supply us with. Whether it be
European, Japanese, Spanish, or perhaps even Aztec, a feudal society has an élite that resists industrialization. A feudal society is
also overpopulated, with the result that labor is cheap and so serves
as a further barrier to the adoption of machine technology. If feudal and folk societies are indiscriminately lumped together important differences are obscured.[6]

The original rural-urban typology had had the value of directing
attention to social change. If, as Hofsommer has observed, the qualities of what is essentially rural were drawn from observations of the

South Rhodesian Kraal, the Andaman islanders, and such "plain people" as the Amish, Mennonites, and Dunkers, this was done in an evolutionary context. The writers who followed the pioneers of sociology have built on this premise. For instance, one scheme organizes a lineal progression of advancement, in turn, from the original traditional system to a stage of rural underdevelopment; then to the period of nationalization; afterward industrialization; and finally urbanization. It will be noted that social, cultural, and technological systems are interwoven in this evolutionary process, so it is possible not only to reach mathematical precision from what was at first a qualitative concept, but also to fashion an analytical tool for pragmatic policy purposes.

Four variables are enough to encompass these disparate, though functionally interdependent, urban elements in quantitative terms. The urban status of a nation can be stated as the percentage of the population in cities of 100,000 or more. Its industrial status can be defined as the proportion of the labor force engaged in nonagricultural occupations. The degree to which a middle class has evolved is supplied by the per capita income as a measure of professional development. And, finally, assuming that literacy is indispensable to the comprehension of nationalism, the prevalence of a nationalist ideology is measurable by the proportion of the adult population that is literate. One result of applying such an index is that the ordinal position of the nations of the world can be determined with some precision, certainly an advance over the original qualitative model. Another possible result is the recognition of latent political instability. It may be argued, for example, that the lack of a large enough middle class, a sufficient industrial base, and a spirit of nationalism in large metropolitan cities, as in Argentina and Chile, are indications of continuing political tensions.

Besides making a methodological attack on urban typology, sociologists have also been critical of its theoretical premises. The effect has been a reexamination of some of the basic assumptions of the several schools of social thought. It will be recalled that Wirth viewed the competitiveness of urban residents as the indisputable absence of moral consensus.[7] Parsons, on the other hand, regards this very condition as representing the institutionalization of universalism as the dominant achievement pattern.[8] Behind the debate is the question of whether competition is a subsocial process whose normative control is an illusory rationalization for a predatory power system or whether competition is truly transcended into value-oriented behavior at the level of symbolic interaction. In other words, can the biotic struggle for existence be extinguished by incorporating it into a cultural system superior in controlling force to the original impulse? The contention between the positivist and the functionalist has not been resolved by any means. Urban theory has merely sharpened it.

The rural-urban continuum is fundamentally a sociological approach. That is, it postulates a distinctive pair of antithetical social, cultural, and economic systems. Although these may be derived from demographic and ecological variables, they are *sui generis,* things of their own particular kind. Consequently the roots of the rural-urban typology are in contrasting conceptions of community and personality structure. Admittedly, empirical sociologists have experienced great difficulty in making such qualitative entities operational. One result has been a tendency toward the elucidation of simple correlations involving size, economic function, occupational distribution, and social-area analysis. These have the defect, first, of treating variables in isolation and, second, of seldom rising above the level of mere description. Robert Angell has been one sociologist who has struck out upon the task of measuring the moral integration of communities, and with appreciable success.[9] Other writers have followed the original systems analysis of Park and Burgess, that a city is "a constellation of institutions." However, because of the incommensurate nature of a government, a school system, a system of environmental health processes, and the like, cities have been hampered by having to deal with presences that are logically related but without the necessary methodology cannot be empirically systematized.

Postulates of the rural-urban typology have come under careful scrutiny and negative findings have cast doubt on the original formulations. Rural personalities are, thus, supposedly more integrated and since they enjoy more primary interaction they experience a higher level of expressive gratification. Better methods of analysis than those available earlier fail, however, to show that there are sharp psychological differences between rural and urban personalities. To be sure metropolitan dominance of the hinterland may have erased traditional disparities. Yet, on one hand, the homogeneous character of the urban environment has been discredited and, on the other, heterogeneity and the acceptance of rapid social change need not be psychically disturbing. Even studies of nonindustrialized countries that have much traditional rural life still intact fail to reveal the simple, homogeneous social structure and the sacred, kin-dominated, mechanical solidary-character structure that supposedly corresponded to rural life.

If rural and urban are thought of as polar entities on the same continuum, the massive presence of mixed, intermediate phenomena commonly referred to as the urban fringe needs clear definition that the typology does not supply. Often this question is answered by simply treating it as a residual category remaining after the urban, rural-farm, and unincorporated-village categories have been accounted for. Sometimes the fringe is regarded as that part of the Standard Metropolitan Area that lies outside the urbanized territory. However, the distinctly mixed land-use characteristics and the mixed occupational distribution throw into relief the unsatisfactory nature of crude dichotomous types.

Enough has probably been said to cast serious doubt on both the validity and the utility of the rural-urban typology. In the first of the subsequent three readings, McKinney and Loomis show that the several major typologies are not equivalent by any means. Although they are commonly used to illuminate rural and urban communities, as Dewey shows later, the many separate traits that these typologies specify do not enjoy a consensus. Reiss, for one, has questioned these concepts.[10] So have others, among them Lewis and Miner.[11] On close examination it turns out that urban residence has not entirely eclipsed the primary relationship nor does the rural community wholly lack formal interaction. Even the fundamental demographic conditions of density and numbers, Stewart has observed, are not exclusively urban.[12]

In *The Folk Culture of Yucatan,* Redfield attempted to determine the factual soundness of the rural-urban dichotomy by postulating an evolutionary process, from the homogeneous-isolated community to the heterogeneous-cosmopolitan social system, with three conditions attendant on the transition—namely, cultural disorganization, secularization, and a growing tendency toward individual self-expression. Making a restudy, Oscar Lewis was unable to corroborate Redfield's affirmative findings.[13] Homogeneity and the supposedly communal nature of rural life turned out on inspection to be conspicuous by their absence. Lewis concluded that the folk-urban, or rural-urban, dichotomy is an over-simplification of social reality.

More careful conceptualization would, therefore, appear to be in order, requiring the identification of salient intervening variables. Following Lewis' lead, perhaps it might be assumed that urban society provides the individual with a greater range of alternative modes of conduct, and that this is the definitive trait of urbanism. Such a quantitative approach would be useful for differentiating degrees of urbanization within the segments of a single urban population and for taking account of the cultural characteristics shared by city and country alike in any given region.

Despite the impressive critique of typological theory that has materialized, however, the rural-urban continuum unquestionably reflects a vital cleavage in human experience. Sorokin and Zimmerman ably express this below. That the typological categories convey an evolutionary dynamism, that they comprehend a unity of cultural, social, and psychological characteristics, and that as constructs they penetrate to the level of motivation—these values are generally recognized. It is in regard to concrete application and research utility that their chief weaknesses are cited. It may be that as their methods are refined, sociologists will not only conclusively test the implications of typological theory but will discover that properly qualified the theory possesses a substantial measure of validity as well. Prior to that time, it remains the most illuminating understanding that we have of the contrasting modes of society, one of which is now so extensive as to make it largely coincident with human society while the other is passing out of existence perhaps forever.

7. THE TYPOLOGICAL TRADITION

John C. McKinney and Charles P. Loomis

The components of urbanism—whether as attributes of a social system, a cultural order, or a mode of personality—may be forcibly brought to light by means of typological construction. Many sociologists have, in fact, formulated various dualities that reveal the nature of the urban phenomenon. McKinney and Loomis recognize the disparities which these typologies possess although they stress the degree to which they overlap and even duplicate one another. The Gesellschaft concept of Tönnies is, of course, basic to any grasp of urban life, as is perhaps Durkheim's idea of the organically solidary society. Cooley's delineation of the primary group has entailed the derivation of the secondary type of interaction that is synonymous with the city. These and other abstractions pertaining to urban relationships are reviewed in this article, among them the work of Redfield, Becker, Sorokin, Weber, and Parsons. In each case, what is essentially and typically urban is juxtaposed with its antithesis—the rural mode of human existence.

ONE OF THE persistent aspects of sociological enterprise is the very old tradition of typing social entities antithetically. . . . Such familiar conceptualizations as Maine's status society and contract society; Spencer's militant and industrial forms; Ratzenhofer's conquest state and culture state; Wundt's natural and cultural polarity; Tönnies' *Gemeinschaft* and *Gesellschaft* forms; Durkheim's mechanical and organic solidarity; Cooley's primary and secondary (implicit) groups; MacIver's communal and asso-

Excerpts from *Contemporary Sociology* edited by Joseph S. Roucek (1958). Reprinted by permission of Philosophical Library, Publishers.

ciational relations; Zimmerman's localistic and cosmopolitan communities; Odum's folk-state pair; Redfield's folk-urban continuum; Sorokin's familistic vs. contractual relations; Becker's sacred and secular societies; as well as such non-personalized but common dichotomies as primitive-civilized; literate–non-literate; and, rural vs. urban are examples of this tradition.

Obviously these varied polarizations are not interchangeable and do not abstract the "same things" out of the social world, but they do have something in common. Not only do they frequently represent similar "content," but perhaps more important, they in common exemplify the view that it is necessary to distinguish fundamentally different types of social organization in order to establish a range within which transitional or intermediate forms can be comprehended. . . .

TÖNNIES: GEMEINSCHAFT *AND* GESELLSCHAFT

. . .

A *Gemeinschaft*-like entity may be distinguished by virtue of its possession of the following attributes: unity, a division of labor based upon mutual aid and helpfulness; an equilibrium of individual wills in mutual interdependence; authority based upon age, wisdom and benevolent force; common habitat; common action directed toward common goals understood as given; kinship; friendship; reciprocal and binding sentiment; diffuse or blanket obligations, common language, custom, and belief; mutual possession and enjoyment; sacred tradition; and the spirit of brotherhood. In sum, *Gemeinschaft* is a relationship of concord based upon bonds of: (a) blood (kinship), (b) place (neighborhood), or (c) mind (friendship).

In contrast a *Gesellschaft* may be distinguished in terms of the following characteristics: separation rather than unification, individualism; action in terms of self-interest; conventions or positive and specific definitions and regulations; delimited spheres of contact; money and credit relationships, dominance by merchants, capitalists, and a power elite; obligations limited and the feelings and strivings of others disregarded on the level of sentiment; and lack of mutual familiar relations. In sum, the *Gesellschaft*-like entity based upon rational will consists in contractual and functionally specific relationships consciously established for the attainment of planned objectives. The *Gesellschaft* is articulated through (a) convention, (b) legislation, and (c) public opinion, and exists in city, national, and cosmopolitan life.

Tönnies utilized the concepts of *Gemeinschaft* and *Gesellschaft* first of all as "normal types," or what Weber later called "ideal types" in the

analysis of social structure. In addition, however, he utilized them to analyze the data of history and discovered them to be trans-historical sociological categories. Tönnies found the main evolutionary path of history to
be the transition from *Gemeinschaft* to *Gesellschaft* and in so doing indicated that they may coexist and be intertwined in various empirical structures in different degrees at different times. . . .

DURKHEIM: MECHANICAL AND ORGANIC SOLIDARITY

Describing not merely the range of human existence, but what to him appeared as an irreversible historical trend, Durkheim in his study of the division of labor polarized society into two types.[1] The first type is the *mechanically solidary society* wherein beliefs and conduct are alike. People
are homogeneous mentally and morally, hence communities are uniform
and nonatomized. It is in this type of society that a totality of beliefs and
sentiments common to all men exists, and which Durkheim called the
conscience collective. This conscience is characterized by the attributes of
exteriority and *constraint*. Exteriority refers to the fact that the conscience as totality is never a product of the members of society at any one
point in time; constraint has reference to the significant point that the
membership of a mechanically solidary society cannot morally refute its
collective conscience. Offense against the collective conscience is moral offense and is punishable by repressive law.

Durkheim's second polar type, defining the direction of historical development, is the *organically solidary society* wherein society is held together by the interdependence of its parts. The division of labor is a result of the struggle for existence, and the specialization of labor
stimulated individualism and differentiation. People in the society are
heterogeneous; their mental and moral similarities have disappeared.
Volume, and material and moral density of people are the necessary conditions for the division as they make it possible for more individuals to
make sufficient contact to be able to act and react upon one another. This
in turn makes possible the contact and interconnection of formerly separate collectivities and breaks down the insulation between them, with resultant diversification. The primary consequence of his whole process is
the weakening of the *conscience collective*. Crime ceases to be an offense
against common moral sentiments and becomes an offense against personal "rights." Spontaneous relations between individuals are replaced by
contractual associations. Offensive acts then lose their sacrilegious character and "repressive" law is replaced by "restitutive" law.

. . . .

COOLEY: THE PRIMARY GROUP

Cooley, an American contemporary of Durkheim's, maintained that neither the individual nor the group has primacy in social action. Contrary to Durkheim, who gave the group primacy over its individual members, and contrary to Spencer who asserted that the individual is basic and the group only the sum total of its members, Cooley perceived the importance of interactive process, of mutual influence betwen group and individual. For him the most important groups in the formation of individual human nature and the development of norms and ends are what he called *primary groups*.[2]

> Type examples of the primary group are the family, or household group, the old-fashioned neighborhood, and the spontaneous play-group of children. In such groups all children everywhere participate, and the intimate association there realized works upon them everywhere in much the same way. It tends to develop sympathetic insight into the moods and states of mind of other people and this in turn underlies the development of both the flexible type of behavior and the common attitudes and sentiments which we have mentioned. . . .
> The chief characteristics of a primary group are:
> 1) Face-to-face association.
> 2) The unspecialized character of that association.
> 3) Relative permanence.
> 4) The small number of persons involved.
> 5) The relative intimacy among the participants.
> Such groups are primary in several senses, but chiefly in that they are fundamental in forming the social nature and ideals of the individual. The result of intimate association, psychologically, is a certain fusion of individualities in a common whole, so that one's very self, for many purposes at least, is the common life and purpose of the group. Perhaps the simplest way of describing this wholeness is by saying that it is a "we"; it involves the sort of sympathy and mutual identification for which "we" is the natural expression. One lives in the feeling of the whole and finds the chief aims of his will in that feeling.[3]

Cooley's combination of organic theory and psychological orientation which led him to the invention of the concept, "looking-glass" self, and to say that "self and society are twin born," [4] resulted in the conceptualization of the primary group, apparently independently of the other theorists we discuss. He did not use the term "secondary group," permitting the implicit type under which groups with characteristics opposite to the primary groups to go unnamed. . . .

REDFIELD: THE FOLK-URBAN CONTINUUM

The folk-urban typology of Redfield has been the best known and most controversial typological formulation in cultural anthropology for the past twenty-five years. It has often been criticized, particularly by idiographically-minded field workers, but it nevertheless has been the stimulant for a great amount of research.[5]

Redfield has formulated an ideal-type version of folk society by linking together a set of attributes. In the absence of explicit delineation the "urban" type is simply composed of the opposite attributes, and hence becomes the polar antithesis.

To Redfield, the folk society is a small collectivity containing no more people within it than can know each other well. It is an isolated, non-literate, homogeneous grouping with a strong sense of solidarity. Technology is simple, and aside from the division of function between the sexes there is little other division of labor, hence the group is economically independent of other groups. The ways in which problems are met by the society are conventionalized by long intercommunication within the group, and these ways have become interrelated with one another to constitute a coherent and self-consistent system: a culture. Behavior is spontaneous, traditional, personal, and there is no motivation toward reflection, criticism, or experimentation. Kinship, its relations and institutions, is central to all experience, and the family is the unit of action. The value of traditional acts and objects is not to be questioned; hence they are sacred. The sacredness of objects is apparent in the ways in which objects are hedged in with restraints and taboos that keep them from being commonplace. All activities, even those of economic production, are ends in themselves. The more remote ends of living are taken as given; hence the folk society exists not so much on the basis of exchange of useful functions as in common understandings as to what is to be done.

Redfield contends that understanding of society in general and of our own modern urbanized society in particular can be gained through consideration of the societies least like our own—folk societies. His scheme defines an ideal type, the *folk society,* which is the polar opposite of urban society. The type is a construct and no known society precisely corresponds to it. It is "created only because through it we may hope to understand reality. Its function is to suggest aspects of real societies which deserve study, and especially to suggest hypotheses as to what, under certain defined conditions, may be generally true about society."[6]

. . .

BECKER: SACRED AND SECULAR SOCIETIES

The sacred-secular antithesis has been utilized by many people, but it finds its most elaborate construction in the work of Howard Becker.[7] . . .

The *sacred society* is isolated vicinally, socially, and mentally. This isolation leads to fixation of habit and neophobia, relations of avoidance, and traditional in-group–out-group attitudes. The concrete is emphasized at the expense of abstraction; social contacts are primary and tradition and ritual play a large part in the life of the individual. There is the dominance of sacredness even in the economic sphere which works toward the maintenance of self-sufficiency, and against any development of the pecuniary attitude. The division of labor is simple. Kinship ties are strong and are manifest in "great family" relationships. All forms of activity are under sacred sanctions, and hence violent social control is at a minimum. The forces of gossip and tradition are powerful tools of control. Non-rational behavior is predominant, with an important element of supernaturalism present. Rationalism, particularly in the form of science, is largely absent. The value system is impermeable.

The *secular society* lies at the opposite pole of the continuum and is vicinally, socially, and mentally accessible. Habit fixation is rendered difficult by the accessibility of the social structure. There is an absence of social barriers. Social circulation is unimpeded. Ends are evaluated in terms of "happiness," and means according to the norm of efficiency. Tradition and ritual are minimal. Rationality is dominant, and science is pervasive and powerful. The kinship group is manifest in the conjugal family form. Innovation is frequent; change is sought after and idealized as progress. Informal sanctions are weak and formal law prevails. Offense against the law invokes little social disapproval. Legal contracts are the rule. Individuation is prominent in society and the value system is permeable.

. . .

SOROKIN: FAMILISTIC AND CONTRACTUAL RELATIONS

As Sorokin states in the foreword to the English edition of *Gemeinschaft and Gesellschaft,* these types are reiterated up to and presumably in his own thinking. Sorokin's *familistic* and *contractual* relationships correspond respectively to *Gemeinschaft and Gesellschaft* and have been used as pairs to accompany these concepts, i.e., *familistic Gemeinschaft* and *contractual Gesellschaft.*[8] . . . For Sorokin *familistic* relationships are permeated by mutual love, sacrifice and devotion. They are most frequently found among members of a devoted family and among real friends. Familistic relations represent a fusion of the ego into "we." Both joys and sorrows are shared in common and those involved need one another. Norms of such relations require that the participation be all-embracing, all-forgiving, all-bestowing and unlimited.

The *contractual* relationship is limited and specified, covering only one narrow sector of the lives of the parties involved. Typical contractual relationships are those of employer and employee, buyer and seller, plumber and householder. The rights and duties of each party are specified by contract. The unity of such groups is rooted in the sober calculation of advantage. It is self-centered and utilitarian. Typically one member of the relationship tries to get as much from the other as possible with the smallest possible contribution. They may remain strangers to each other, one party little interested in the well-being, activities and philosophy of the other. There is no fusion to produce a homogeneous "we." Such relations are usually of limited duration, voluntary and stand in contrast to those which are compulsory. Relationships may develop from familistic to contractual or vice versa.[9]

WEBER: TYPES OF ACTION ORIENTATION

Although not following properly in the tradition of dichotomously typing society, the types of action constructed by Weber are directly relevant to the Tönnies formulation, the Parsons formulation which is to follow, and the present context in general. All the relationships discussed here, indeed all relations, are based upon a continuity of social action.[10] Weber starts by typing the action context. . . .

. . . in terms of rational orientation to a system of discrete individual ends (*zweckrational*), that is, through expectations as to the behavior of some objects in the external situation and of other human individuals, making use of these expectations as 'condition' or 'means' for the successful attainment of the actor's own rationally chosen ends; (2) in terms of rational orientation to an absolute value (*wertrational*); involving a conscious belief in the absolute value of some ethical, aesthetic, religious, or other form of behavior, entirely for its own sake and independently of any prospects of external success; (3) in terms of affectual orientation (*affektuell*), especially emotional, determined by the specific affects and states of feeling of the actor; (4) as traditionally oriented (*traditionell*) through the habituation of long practice.[11]

It may be seen that *zweckrational* is essentially expedient rationality and denotes a system of action involving an actor's motives, conditions, means, and ends wherein the actor weighs the possible alternative ends and means available to him in terms of his purposes and selects the course of action most expedient to him. A system of discrete ends exist for the actor, and an orientation toward them involves such considerations as "efficiency," "counting the cost," "undesirable consequences," "amount of return," and "figuring the results" which condition the otherwise unrestrained adaptation of means to the achievement of ends. . . .

Wertrational orientation is differentiated from expedient rationality by Weber through the inclusion of an "absolute value" which eliminates the possibility of the actor's selection from alternative ends, and ultimately, therefore, bars the possible selection of certain means. This is a sanctioned form of rationality wherein the actual adaptation of means toward the achievement of the absolute, or ultimate end (value), may comply with the criteria of expedience but cannot in itself be *zweckrational* in view of the lack of a discrete system of ends and the possibility of weighing them in terms of available means and prevailing conditions. The sole important consideration of the actor is the realization of the value.

Affectual action is actually treated by Weber as a form of non-rationality (possibly even irrationality) wherein means and ends become fused, and therefore insusceptible of delineation in behavior. This form of action is dominated by emotional states of feeling of the actor and involves an impulsive or uncontrolled reaction to some exceptional stimulus. It occurs as a release from tension, and therefore the later phases of an affectual act may become increasingly "rational."

Traditional action is also treated by Weber as a deviation from rational orientation in that the means involved become ends in themselves or hold the same rank as ends. This type of action is an almost automatic reaction to habitual stimuli which guide behavior in repeatedly followed and prevailing courses. Typically this means a conformity with the accepted and prevalent ways of behavior, with little evaluation or consideration of their expedience.

. . . It is easy to see . . . how Weber reached his conclusion that the main trend of history was that of increased rationalization. This compares directly with Tönnies' conclusions regarding the trend toward *Gesellschaft,* and also with the related conclusions of Sorokin, Becker, Durkheim, and Redfield.

PARSONS: THE PATTERN VARIABLES
OF ACTION ORIENTATION

. . . Parsons ends his classic discussion of *Gemeinschaft* and *Gesellschaft* with the following comment:

> . . . this discussion of *Gemeinschaft* and *Gesellschaft* should not be taken to mean that these concepts are unreservedly acceptable as the basis for a general classification of social relationships or, indeed, that it is possible to start from any dichotomy of only two types. The basic types cannot be reduced to two, or even to the three that Weber used. To attempt to develop such a scheme of classification would be definitely outside the scope of the present study. Such an attempt would, however, have to make critical examination of the schemes of Tönnies, Weber and some others one of its main tasks. However, the aspects of Tönnies' classification with which this discussion has been concerned do involve distinctions of basic importance for any such scheme and would hence have to be built into the wider scheme, which would probably involve considerable alteration in their form of statement.[12]

At base the attitude of Parsons indicated a recognition of the fact that general "sponge" types had inherent limitations with respect to the handling of many specific problems. Weber manifested some recognition of this; Becker has been acutely aware of it; . . . Parsons, in line with his propensity for systematic theory, chose the approach of deriving the components of action orientation directly from the structure of social action.

In starting his analysis with an actor in a situation Parsons contends that any actor must make five separate choices before the action will have a determinate meaning for him. Meaning does not automatically emerge in a situation, but rather, is based upon the actor's selections from the five sets of alternatives posed for him in any situation. These dichotomies are termed the pattern variables of action orientation, and the problems of choice between them are termed the dilemmas of action.

Affectivity vs *affective* neutrality is the gratification-discipline dilemma and involves the problem of accepting an opportunity for gratification without regard for its consequences. It is a matter really of whether evaluation will take place or not in a given situation.

Particularism vs *universalism* is the dilemma of choice between types of value standards, and involves evaluating an object of action in terms of its relations to the actor and his specific object relationship situation, or in terms of its relations to a generalized frame of reference. This dilemma is one concerning primacy of cathectic or cognitive standards.

Ascription vs *achievement* is the dilemma of choice between "modalities" of the social object, and involves the actor's seeing the social object as a composite of ascribed qualities, or conversely, as a composite of performances. This dilemma concerns the conception of objects as "attribute" or "action" complexes.

Diffuseness vs *specificity* is the dilemma of the definition of the scope of interest in the object, and involves the concession to a social object of an undefined set of rights to be delimited only by conflicting demands, as over and against the concession to a social object of a clearly specified and limited set of rights. This dilemma concerns the scope of significance of the object in action.

Collective orientation vs *self orientation* is the collective interest vs private interest dilemma and involves the problem of considering an act with respect to its significance for a collectivity or a moral code, or with respect to its personal significance. This dilemma concerns the primacy of moral standards in a procedure of evaluation.[13]

Parsons contends that these pattern-variables are the single most important thread of continuity in the action frame of reference and that they enter in at four different levels. On the concrete level of empirical action they exist as five discrete choices an actor must explicitly make before he can act. They enter on the collectivity level as role definitions wherein actions of role-incumbents tend to be specified in terms of one side or another of a dilemma. The variables also enter on the cultural level as aspects of value standards. In that value-standards are rules governing action and insofar as an actor is committed to a standard he will habitually choose the horn of the dilemma specified by adherence to that standard. As a consequence the variables also enter at the personality level.

In view of their history, derivation, and content, it seems justifiable to conclude that the pattern-variables represent a further and more elaborate specification of the aspects of society dealt with by *Gemeinschaft* and *Gesellschaft*.[14]. . .

8. RURAL AND URBAN WORLDS

Pitirim Sorokin and Carle C. Zimmerman

The combination of factors comprising the urban realm and setting it apart from what is essentially rural is not a loose assortment of separate elements but, rather, a tightly knit system of interdependent characteristics. In its original form Sorokin and Zimmerman's presentation of their eight-fold schema manifests a broad range of empirical data from American and European sources. It carefully derives the demographic and sociocultural differentia of urban communities from their presumed occupational and environmental foundations, and does so with much factual support. The part of their work that appears here contains the authors' methodological principles and general conclusions, and although it can only suggest the original, it does, nonetheless, succinctly represent the polar types of the rural and urban worlds in the skeleton form which they constructed.

"THE CITY AND THE COUNTRY!" It seems nothing can be simpler than a definition of the urban and the rural aggregates. And yet, when a serious attempt is made to define them it meets many obstacles. Neither the size of a community, nor the density of population, nor official qualification of some communities, as "the city" or "town," and others, as "village or open country," nor any of these usual criteria are sufficient by themselves to give a sound and scientifically acceptable definition of the city and the country, or of the rural and urban social world.[1] If for statistical and other practical purposes, it is necessary to take either size or density as a criterion of rural or urban societies, neither statistician nor others may think that such a single criterion really expresses and describes all the essential characteristics of both social worlds and that their differences consist only in the size or density of official qualification. This means that an adequate definition of these complex phenomena must indicate not one trait of difference but *several* traits which are specific for each of these societies and in which they differ from each other. Rural and urban societies and their differences are undescribable in terms of *one* characteristic, and require a definition which combines several typical traits. . . .

Such a "compound definition," through its indication of several specific traits, although it appears to be more adequate than the "single trait definition," may also have its minuses or bad points. It may be merely eclectic in its complexity and be only a purely "mechanical" unification in one formula of several traits which are not bound together by real causal or functional relations. Any such purely mechanical "piling together" of various unrelated traits in the "attic" of a compound definition is rather fruitless scientifically. Such a "compound definition" is only really scientific when it puts together several traits causally connected in reality. For these reasons a "compound" definition of the city and the rural community must not be "eclectic" but a logical unification of traits functionally correlated with one another.

One who intends to give such a definition must be ready to meet another difficulty. In reality the transition from a purely rural community to an urban one, whatever may be the definition, is not abrupt but gradual; from an open farm through a small settlement of agriculturists, a hamlet with a slight admixture of a few non-farming people, a village, a small town, to larger and larger towns and cities. Each step is associated with a proportionately decreasing agricultural population and an increasing of the proportion of the people engaged in other than agricultural pursuits. There is no absolute boundary line which would show a clearly cut cleavage between the rural and the urban community. Correspondingly, many differential characteristics of the rural and urban community would consist not so much in the presence of certain traits in rural, and their absence in urban communities, as much as in a quantitative increase or decrease of these characteristics or in their positive or negative correlation with "rurality" and "urbanity." . . . we must not be embarrassed by such mere "quantitative" differences. They have great cognitive value and are unavoidable if one does not wish to disfigure the reality and overlook many important traits.

Side by side with this necessity for demarcation by relative-quantitative-differential traits, in the case of a gradual seriation of the phenomena studied, science uses, almost invariably, another device of study, namely, *the typological method* in the sense already clearly outlined by Max Weber.[2] When scholars construct a type of an animal or a plant species, a type of race, a type of mind such as "introvert" or "extrovert," a type of society such as "Feudal, Capitalist, or Socialist," a type of economy such as "natural, money, or credit," a type of personality such as "conservative or radical" and so on, they all use, consciously or unconsciously, in a poor or a perfect form, the typological method. Through the classification of a complex and an uninterrupted series of phenomena into a few types or classes, they overcome the complexity of the concrete reality and give its important traits in the form of a few classes or types of phenomena. The same may be done in our definition of the rural and urban community. Side by side with the indication of the qualitative differences between them, and the increasing or decreasing, positive or negative, correlations of given traits with urbanity or rurality, we need to recur to the use of the typological method. In other words, we need to construct a type of urban and rural community. When such a procedure is carefully done, and the elements of each type are properly selected and backed by factual data, such a method proves itself highly productive and enriches our knowledge.

After these methodological remarks let us now turn to a description of the differential characteristics of the urban and rural community whose totality gives the type of each of these social aggregates. In accordance with the above characteristics of sociology we must study only such differences as are . . .

. . .

. . . relatively constant, and causally connected qualitative and quantitative characteristics of the urban and rural worlds.

These fundamental characteristics . . . are all causally connected, or interrelated. As soon as one takes the agricultural occupation and the people engaged in it, he finds the other differences enumerated. The first "variable," so to speak, carries the others with it. In their totality, they compose the typical and constant "cradle" or "framework" within which rural and urban phenomena carry on. . . . [See Table 1.—Editors' note.]

TABLE 1

	Rural World	Urban World
Occupation.	Totality of cultivators and their families. In the community are usually few representatives of several non-agricultural pursuits. They, however, do not compose the proper object of rural sociology.	Totality of people engaged principally in manufacturing, mechanical pursuits, trade, commerce, professions, governing, and other non-agricultural occupations.

TABLE 1 (*Continued*)

	Rural World	Urban World
Environment.	Predominance of nature over anthropo-social environment. Direct relationship to nature.	Greater isolation from nature. Predominance of man-made environment over natural. Poorer air. Stone and iron.
Size of community.	Open farms or small communities, "agriculturalism" and size of community are negatively correlated.	As a rule in the same country and at the same period, the size of urban community is much larger than the rural community. In other words, urbanity and size of community are positively correlated.
Density of population.	In the same country and at the same period the density is lower than in urban community. Generally density and rurality are negatively correlated.	Greater than in rural communities. Urbanity and density are positively correlated.
Heterogeneity and homogeneity of the population.	Compared with urban populations the populations of rural communities are more homogeneous in racial and psycho-social traits. (Negative correlation with heterogeneity.)	More heterogeneous than rural communities (in the same country and at the same time). Urbanity and heterogeneity are positively correlated.
Social differentiation and stratification.	Rural differentiation and stratification less than urban.	Differentiation and stratification show positive correlation with urbanity.
Mobility.	Territorial, occupational, and other forms of social mobility of the population are comparatively less intensive. Normally the migration current carries more individuals from the country to the city.	More intensive. Urbanity and mobility are positively correlated. Only in the periods of social catastroph is the migration from the city to the country greater than from the country to the city.
System of interaction.	Less numerous contacts per man. Narrower area of the interaction system of its members and the whole aggregate. More promi-	More numerous contacts. Wider area of interaction system per man and per aggregate. Predominance of secondary contacts.

TABLE 1 (*Continued*)

Rural World	Urban World
nent part is occupied by primary contacts. Predominance of personal and relatively durable relations. Comparative simplicity and sincerity of relations. "Man is interacted as a human person."	Predominance of impersonal casual and short-lived relations. Greater complexity, manifoldedness, superficiality, and standardized formality of relations. Man is interacted as a "number" and "address."

9. THE RURAL-URBAN CONTINUUM

Richard Dewey

Although commonly accepted by social scientists and laymen alike, the idea of the rural-urban dichotomy enjoys altogether too little consensus as far as its objective referents are concerned. Size, density, and heterogeneity or homogeneity of population are generally understood to be basic. Disagreement or confusion arises, however, over the cultural characteristics that writers ascribe to the two different modes of social organization that accompany the demographic variables.

Cities are said to exhibit predatory relations. Similarly, the nuclear family is held to be typical of the urban community, as are also the attitudes and conditions of secularism, tolerance, commercialization, literacy, creativity, and utilitarianism. To be sure, authorities differ in the emphasis that they place on these various dimensions. Nevertheless, the more general and more important question is whether these dimensions are in any case the necessary concomitants of the urban environment or whether they are inherent in the culture of the surrounding, and larger, social system.

This insight draws attention to the probable temporocentrism of the rural-urban typology. Though it is suggestive of possibly valid differentiations between institutions, modes of thought, and of systematic interaction, the rural-urban schema, at least as it has been formulated,

Excerpts from *American Journal of Sociology* (1960). Reprinted by permission of the author and The University of Chicago Press. Copyright 1960 © by The University of Chicago.

corresponds perhaps to a particular stage in European-American social history, namely, the late nineteenth and early twentieth century, and not general sociological principles.

EVIDENCE ABOUNDS to show that many of the things which are uncritically taken as part and parcel of urbanism do not depend upon cities for their existence. History reveals that creativity in the form of invention and discovery is not limited to cities, that literacy is not tied to urbanization, and that sacred ties are stronger in some cities than in many small towns and farming areas. Cultural variety in language and religion may be greater in some rural areas than in certain large cities. Complex technology is common in certain farming regions and scarce in some urban communities. In brief, "it is too frequently assumed that the correlation between a variable and urbanness represents a causal connection between the two." [1]

However, it is not logical to hold that the rural-urban continuum has no universal or general referents, merely because of the mistaken assignment to urbanism of a welter of cultural items which can be, and are, independent of city environments. In the first place, it is probably futile to argue for the abandonment of the terms "rural" and "urban" as indicators of size and density of population. There is little, if any, evidence that the established usage of these words is in process of change: their abandonment would require the invention of a new pair of terms to denote the large, densely associated communities, distinguished from the small and sparsely settled groups of the world.

In Figure 1, instead of paralleling the cultural continua, the rural-urban continuum is perceived as intersecting them. This orientation sharply distinguishes things rural and urban per se from sociocultural relations based upon knowledge, beliefs, and feelings. Although there is no novelty in basing the conception of the rural-urban continuum upon numbers and density, most, if not all, definitions of urbanism include cultural components. The inclusion of both population and cultural bases in the term "urbanism" renders it useless except for labeling time-bound phenomena. Assuredly, people and culture cannot be separated, but the influences upon human attitudes and actions of the two can, and logically must, be distinguished. Man appears to be no exception to the general rule that significant variation in numbers and density of objects brings about equally significant changes in the nature of the objects' relationships. In Wirth's article there are, mingled with items which are clearly cultural, characteristics which plausibly at least, are to be discovered in accentuated form at the urban extreme and in minimal degree or not at all at the rural end of the continuum. Evidence seems to support Wirth's observations that variations in size and density of population induce concomitant variations in five qualities:

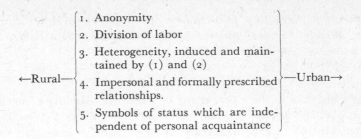

The logic of custom and of the English language supports the retention of "rural" and "urban" to designate the extremes of the continuum defined by the five items.

If this reorientation (Fig. 1) is valid, then it is a misrepresentation of facts to speak of the export or spread of urban culture to rural areas. Some have agreed among themselves that acculturation is reducing, and will in time obliterate, the differences between rural and urban commun-

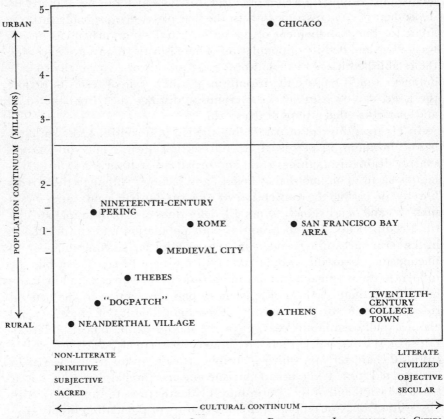

FIGURE 1. RELATIONSHIP BETWEEN CULTURAL AND POPULATION INFLUENCES ON CITIES

ities, thus eliminating the usefulness of the concepts. This hardly appears realistic. Culture can, and obviously does, move bilaterally between open country and city, but this does not mean that ruralism and urbanism are exportable commodities. There is no such thing as urban culture or rural culture but only various culture contents somewhere on the rural-urban continuum. The movement of zoot suits, jazz, and antibiotics from city to country is no more a spread of urbanism than is the transfer or diffusion of blue jeans, square dancing, and tomatoes to the cities a movement of ruralism to urban centers. As Figure 1 shows, there can be, and most assuredly are, small rural communities which are secular, civilized, dynamic, and highly literate as well as large, sacred, essentially primitive, illiterate, and relatively static urban communities.

That each of the five items listed above as definitive of the rural-urban continuum can be culturally influenced in quite remarkable degree is not deniable, but this in no way reduces their validity as delineators of ruralism or urbanism. Designs in housing, techniques of communication, and segregation can, and indeed do, increase anonymity, but anonymity is inevitable for the vast majority of a city's population and impossible at the rural extreme, save for the hermit. That industrialization has multiplied occupational specialties is obvious, but it should be quite equally obvious that, whereas a small rural community can present an undifferentiated occupational pattern, a city of a million most certainly cannot. Great complexity in the division of labor can exist in an industrial culture's city, but a certain minimum must exist in increasing degree as the size and density of the community increases. That there is a minimum of heterogeneity in large cities, regardless of the culture (George Orwell and *1984* to the contrary notwithstanding), is clearly perceivable. The very clear, and seemingly contradictory, fact that American cities are more homogeneous today in the folkways involving food, clothing, language, national allegiance, and the like does not in any way negate the argument that minimal heterogeneity is inescapable in large cities and that it will increase as the city increases in size. The reduction of cultural heterogeneity in American cities is a product of neither urbanism nor ruralism. Likewise, the increase in their occupational heterogeneity is basically cultural.

The situation is similar with respect to the items of instituted rules and symbols of status. Culture can enlarge upon them, but it cannot eliminate them from the city. When people interact socially, they must, except on rare occasions, know the status of their associates, and the pervasive anonymity of the large city demands some means of identifying the functionaries essential to daily living there. The waitress, the clerk, the policeman, the priest, and others must be identified. Even the less uniform symbols of "good standing" are important in the city. A salesman whose clothes were soiled and ill pressed and whose face and hair were unkempt would stand little chance of gaining an audience with a prospective customer in the city. This is not to say, of course, that the less functional items of "conspicuous consumption" are part and parcel of life in a large city; rather, they are products of a special kind of culture, plus urban settings, and not urban features as such. Life in a large metropolis without some formally and explicitly instituted rules (which, to be sure, may in time become customary) is unthinkable and certainly does not exist. Good intentions and informality will not suffice to induce even the minimal order requisite for life in a metropolis, regardless of time or place.

It may occur to one that, if this be all that there is to the rural-urban continuum, it is of minor importance for sociology. He would be quite correct. The importance rests in the recognition that the five elements are inevitable accompaniments of urbanization and must be taken into consideration in understanding it. Some city planners, unaware of this, have been enticed into ill-advised attempts to eliminate some of these intrinsic qualities. The controversy over the principle of the neighborhood as a unit is a case in point.[2] Conversely, planners at times seem to have taken as inevitable certain features which are mere cultural correlates of urbanization at a particular time and place.

The failure of sociologists to reach consensus concerning the rural-urban continuum is attributable in part to the reductionism which has been popular in American sociology in recent decades and which has led to various attempts to discover, through analysis, some easily manipulable part of the larger society. Thus, some students of the city, misperceiving the city as sufficiently detached from society and culture to warrant study as a separate object, have unintentionally inflated the rural-urban concepts with extraneous cultural elements, reducing the concepts' real, if minor, significance for research. If they had not been enticed into taking their eyes off their principal datum, society in the large, the rural-urban continuum might not have been overemphasized. No evidence suggests that these concepts can acquire more than incidental importance in the understanding of the complexities of human relations in cities or hamlets. There is evidence of a growing recognition of this fact in the emphasis upon cultural settings as distinguished from urbanism by such writers as Axelrod, Beers, Greer and Kube, Haer, Sjoberg.[3]

However, to argue, as has been done here, for reduced importance of the rural-urban continuum is not to seek its elimination from sociology. The influences of rural and urban environments upon social organization and individual behavior will remain important facts, to be considered with the more important cultural facts, form and content, which are the sociologist's stock in trade.

CHAPTER THREE

APPROACHES TO
URBAN SOCIOLOGY

A city is obviously a complex system. It consists of a territory, a population, a mode of life, and a form of social organization. Not only these but also their subsystems and even their various interrelations are each a basis for study and understanding. Historians may seek a comprehensive account of the formation and course of development of particular cities chiefly as centers of intellectual, political, and cultural leadership. To economists, the city is a system of exchange that is both independent and a part of a larger order. Legal scholars, social administrators, geographers, anthropologists, psychologists, and others have other special interests regarding the city.

Although their focus of attention is the city as a community, sociologists recognize the fact that urban communities are inseparable from constituent and related elements, such as physical mechanisms, aggregations of personalities, social structures, and systems of control. This has produced an intellectual state of affairs in which four distinct approaches exist in urban sociology. Each of these—the ecological, the demographic, the sociocultural, and the juridical— provides valuable insight into urban phenomena. Each is also correlative with one another.

For example, studying the city as a population means in the first instance to describe the composition, the totality, and the changes in its population, and to attribute these characteristics to three variables, fertility, mortality, and migration. The latter, however, are far from being first causes. In fact, they are readily capable of interpretation in the light of environmental and cultural conditions. And these in turn yield to still further influences, say, in the social structure where political controls shape the economy independently of either the physical setting or the system of institutionalized values. Finally, it may be observed that demographic factors reenter the picture and further impinge on the political constitution of the community, changing it still further in the course of time.

The population balance is the product of three distinct but interdependent elements: the amount of land available, knowledge concerning the use of land, and the level of living to which a community is attuned. Population is of course patently dependent on subsistence. Yet the means of subsistence are probably equally dependent on the state of the technical arts and on the system of allocation that prevails. Neither of these two is itself entirely free of the influence of the social structure, which allots rights and responsibilities, legitimizing some at the expense of others, notably so in the crystallization of social classes. Thus the population of a community depends on the social order, while the makeup of the social order is itself contingent on the aggregate size, density, and internal composition of the population in the first place. Witness the formal relations that come into being in a large population as it carries on social life, and then the attitude of secularization that is fostered, and finally the restraining effect that this subsequently has on fertility.

For these reasons what we have in urban sociology are different modes of discourse, and not entirely separate and independent manifestations of urban man and society. Ecological, demographic, sociocultural, and juridical dimensions of urban life do exist although they are interrelated, circular, and mutually reinforcing. Each is capable of yielding coherent descriptions and significant generalizations. Nonetheless, no wholly satisfactory way has yet been devised to establish the primacy of any one of these conceptual models. They remain salient dimensions of a complex structure and process, each of which gives us valuable though incomplete knowledge of urban reality.

Human ecology is not a discipline but a point of view. Its frame of reference is the spatial position occupied by a given social activity, for it looks at people from the perspective of their relations with their habitat. Ecology takes cognizance of the physical, territorial, and technological aspects of human life in contrast with the ideological, interactional, and purposive parts of the social order. Consequently, ecological questions concern the reasons why given spatial distributions exist and how these patterns relate to the physical environment. Not only urban sociologists but economists and historians too are concerned with the influences that a site has on the activities in which people are engaged. In sociology, however, ecological study has perhaps been the most prominent basis for urban research.

Robert E. Park and Ernest W. Burgess first introduced the term *human ecology* into American sociology when in 1921 they began a systematic effort to apply the principles of plant and animal adaptation to the study of human communities.[1] Paying attention to the spatial distribution of human activities, however, has had a much longer history. Studies of crime were conducted in this fashion in England as long ago as the 1830's. Park's rationale for human ecology was borrowed from the so-called classical position, that is, that the basic process underlying human behavior is competition for scarce resources. Furthermore, the various forms of struggle that this implies can all be summed up in the constant contention that goes on for the control of space. This is not to say that within the overall competitive system symbiotic, or advantageous, relationships do not exist. In fact, it is characteristic of human beings that they compete as members of groups—families, social classes, castes, fraternal orders, occupational ranks, communities, and nations— rather than as unaided individuals. However, even within these bodies, sub-groups carry on rivalry and competition, and individuals interpersonal strife.

Although Park's original hypothesis was derived from the biotic struggle for existence that characterizes the lower animals, Burgess transposed human ecology into economic terms that allow for the operation of purposive group life. The human counterpart of symbiosis is the division of labor. This is far more complex than what is observed among nonhuman species. It is, moreover, subject to cultural influences, which give rise to secondary needs, such as esthetic interests and group symbols. Nevertheless, sustenance needs persist and dictate our unrelenting ecological determinism. In other words, the balance of nature is never absent from the web of life.

Burgess' concentric-zone hypothesis of the city clearly represents the working out of a competitive economic system, with dominance centralized in the downtown business district. At the University of Chicago he led a large number of scholars in the ecological study of the city, with the result that numerous social facts were discovered to have distinct spatial configurations. Among these were divorce, desertion, social status, emotional illness, crime and delinquency, family types, and age groups. Reckless, Faris and Dunham, Cressey, Thrasher, Anderson, Zorbaugh, Mowrer, and Wirth all contributed specific ecological studies.[2]

As a consequence of his intensive research into a small part of just one of Burgess' zones, Zorbaugh suggested that it would be appropriate to view a city as composed of many natural areas that are produced by unplanned growth. Later writers have added other units to the ecological study of the urban community, such as Hoyt's sectors, Harris and Ullman's nuclei, and Shevky and Bell's social areas.[3] And a number of processes have been described as operating within them, like the concentration of people, the centralization of services, decentralization, segregation, assimilation, invasion and succession, and migration.

Another development in social ecology was the shift of interest from the individual city to the environs, with the purpose of analyzing the zones and corridors that the wider metropolitan area reveals. Among the pioneers in this transition were Charles Merriam, Calvin F. Schmid, Roderick D. McKenzie, Graham R. Taylor, Nathan L. Whetten, the National Resources Committee, and Walter Firey.[4] Don Bogue, for example, followed McKenzie's lead in depicting the modern United States as a nation in which a number of metropolises are dominant, each in its own region. Smaller cities are subdominants, while rural nonfarm communities are influents, and rural farm communities are subinfluents. Dickinson varied the terminology and the units of classification by conceiving of groupings of metropolitan regions into belts not unlike stellar galaxies, each of which has a national economic role as a manufacturing center, livestock producer, or granary.[5] Thus urban ecologists are concerned about dominance and regional networks, the relations between communities, production economics, residential structure, inter-community conflict, and service dependencies, among others.

As Stuart Dodd has observed, the ecological approach lends support to sociology as a positivist discipline.[6] When one considers populations en masse in terms of migration and mobility rates, he is soon impressed with the apparent absence of volition from behavior. However, the vast ecological literature, which Albert J. Reiss has reviewed, takes note of "the symbiotic and commensalistic aspects of communities," with the result that environmental determinism is qualified by consideration of sociocultural, symbiotic phenomena.[7] Certainly ecological studies of cities around the world do support central-place and break-in-transportation hypotheses to a considerable degree. But they do not show a clear pattern despite the fact that in capitalist industrial cities economic values have definite locational significance. Consequently, as Theodorson observes, ecological writers fall into four categories according to the stress they place on the sufficiency of environment as against the importance of cultural values in regard to urban location and structure. These are the classicists, neo-orthodox analysts, social-area analysts, and socioculturists.[8]

By 1945 there was intense criticism of the classical ecological approach. Maurice Davie contended that concentric zones were not apparent in New Haven. Milla Alihan took up the distinction between the biotic and cultural levels of human society. Hollingshead, Gettys, Hatt, Gehlke, Biehl, and Duncan and Davis all entered the controversy, stressing the importance of cultural values and questioning both the crude biologizing and correlation techniques that had been used in the early research. There is no doubt that the classical position was seriously undermined.[9]

Radhakamal Mukerjee in India [10] and Theodore Caplow in France [11] have shown that cultural values keep land values from being all important in determining urban patterns. In India cities are often divided into caste quarters, each with its own sacred grove and shrine. In France historic parks and squares evidence similarly strong influence. Spatial determination thus becomes a clear oversimplification. Even Chicago, where the orthodox ecologists most systematically applied their principles, was shown, as in Homer Hoyt's *One Hundred Years of Land Values in Chicago*, to have been strikingly subject to historical accident. Chicago is no better situated than Rockford, Beloit, and Kankakee. Political activity and aggressive business practices no doubt contributed to Chicago's emergence as the major metropolitan center of the Middle West. Nor was Chicago alone in sustaining cultural influence. The effect of law over land settlement in the history of the United States is striking. While it is true that geographic considerations rapidly modified the village form of settlement imported from Europe, it was federal law that perpetuated the particular and rigid rectilinear system of land holdings west of the Alleghenies following the Northwest Ordinance (1787).

Few will disagree with the conclusion that the sociocultural order is significant in urban patterning and further that it is not wholly reducible to the bioeconomic rationale of the ecological perspective. The ecological setting may indeed be the limiting framework within which community organization develops. It does not, however, demonstrably explain the specific form that it takes. Neo-orthodox ecologists, such as Quinn and Hawley,[12] reject the primacy of culture, although they do not believe that society is essentially biotic. Hawley places greatest stress on the division of labor, Quinn on the subsocial utilization of resources, including space. On the other hand, sociocultural ecologists concede major importance to cultural values in accounting for the spatial distribution of human activities. Firey in Boston, Jonassen in New York, Meyers in New Haven, and Seeman among Utah's Mormons have each attempted to demonstrate the primacy of symbolic considerations.[13]

Social-area analysis (one application of which appears in Chapter Five of this book) has been described by Theodore R. Anderson and Lee L. Bean as possibly providing "a clear conceptual base upon which to build a theory relating space to social behavior." [14] This method, developed by Efrem Shevky, Marilyn Williams, and Wendell Bell, selects three variables as crucial to modern industrial urban society—social rank or economic status; urbanization in the sense of low fertility, a high proportion of females in the labor force, and a large percentage of the population in multiple dwellings; and, finally, segregation, or the proportion of foreign-born and nonwhite population. Crescive communities, then, are those clusters of census tracts that are similar with respect to these variables. Forms of social participation such as primary interaction and anomie, can thus be ascertained and correlated with these demographic indexes of the social structure viewed as a measurable ecological phenomenon.

Interwoven with economic forces the population factor has been responsible for much urban history. Kingsley Davis has been one who has ably demonstrated the significance of demographic analysis in urban study. By differentiating the proportion of a population living in cities from mere city growth, he has thrown into relief the essential difference between the earlier period of urbanization and the current evolution going on in the underdeveloped areas of the world. Cities used to grow as a result of migration from the countryside. This alleviated widespread agrarian distress. In fact, a benign S-curve of urbanization emerged, with the affluent suburban movement characteristic of the mature state of urbanization. But now, because of the natural increase of population in the underdeveloped countries, the urbanization process is faltering, despite obvious growth in the numbers of urban inhabitants. This threatens to freeze any number of preindustrial lands in unrelieved backwardness.

Beginning in the eighteenth century, it was the harnessing of inanimate energy that greatly stimulated population growth and also the centering of population in cities. Economic progress was intimately associated with urbanization and has continued to be. The factory system required people to be concentrated together, and subsequently the control of communicable disease became imperative if the crowded cities were going to continue. Epidemics were eventually curbed and the resulting reduction in mortality further crowded the industrial centers. As a matter of fact, where in the middle of the nineteenth century the cities of Manchester, London, and Liverpool had had a shorter expectation of life than rural England by some 25 percent, by 1950 the entire differential had been erased.

The demographic basis of urban life has been explored if not fully circumscribed. Density of population accounts for formal interaction, instrumental relationships, and a variety of other structural effects. The urban birth rate is typically lower than that of the rural population. Owing to the urbanization of the countryside in the sense of the diffusion of individualistic and hedonistic urban values, however, the difference is diminishing though it has not been entirely eliminated. Thus if population has been shown to be socially consequential for the city, it itself has also been clearly established as a consequence of the city. Not only in regard to fertility but also to migration is this indicated. The elasticity of demand, or in other words the multiplication of secondary needs that leads to increased production in the urban economy, results in rising wages and a correspondingly greater power of attraction that cities have for the relatively deprived rural hinterland. In the United States, for instance, by the mid-1960s only seven percent of the nation's labor force made their living from farming.

The demographic approach has yet another contribution to make to urban sociology because it convincingly shows the swiftness and depth of the currents of urbanization, suburbanization, metropolitanization, and reurbanization. The International Population and Urban Research Center at Berkeley has authoritatively documented the rising tide of urbanization in modern times. One index, that of people living in cities of 100,000 or more, shows that the rate of concentration accelerated from 1850 to 1960 and that if the degree of increase in the decade 1950–1960 is maintained over the next quarter of a century, more than half of the world's population will be living in cities of 100,000 or larger in 1990. One-third of the world's population was already so urbanized in 1960.

An urban community is not simply a large, dense population but an organized aggregation. Central to the sociological conception of the urban community is the recognition that any organized group possesses a consensus, or pattern of cohesion in usages and mores. Such sentimental cohesion may indeed outweigh all considerations of objective utility. As Walter Firey has shown, space, which is the essence of ecology, may itself be symbolized and made use of, regardless of economic values. Albert Reiss has observed that scholars who view the local community as a social system are interested in showing it to be a microcosmic representation of the larger system simply rooted in a definite, particular territorial locale. As such, the community has a system of stratification, of political control, kinship, and the like. The lacuna is the failure to show in what manner the given community is unique, in other words how its stratification system and other institutions deviate from those of the greater society. What is needed may be an interaction-space, or social-group, approach to uncover the essential differences.

The city is a marketplace. It may also be a military camp or the seat of a church and hence perform integrative functions for the surrounding countryside. However, a social system that effectively allocates rights and duties and, consequently, coordinates the behavior of a sizable and functionally heterogeneous population is a prerequisite for the provision of such services. As Max Weber insists, the city is first and foremost a political community. This is the essence of the juridical approach to the city.

Once in being as a cultural entity, a city may generate sweeping changes in the patterns of life of a society by giving birth to new ideologies and effective social movements. As Spengler declares below, after folk societies evolve into urban concentrations further urbanization ensues in which diverse sociocultural trends are unleashed, with fateful consequences for all. In its totality, of course, this process has ecological, demographic, and juridical facets as well.

10. THE NATURE OF CITIES

Edward Ullman and Chauncey Harris

*Both of these geographers, Harris and Ullman, grasp two basic aspects of the nature of cities—their economic relationships to physical environments and their internal morphology. They picture urban communities as being either service centers, transportation hubs, or concentration points for specialized services. In addition, they review the literature on land-use patterns, with the result that cities are seen as arrangements consisting of concentric zones, sectors, and multiple nuclei. This paper is a model of the concise and orderly presentation of concepts that are fundamental to the study of urban concentrations. Moreover, in the paper's specification of the various modes by which land is utilized within a city, it represents a distinct advance over the earlier efforts of such social ecologists as Roderick D. McKenzie. McKenzie identified the cyclical process by which the population of cities grow and distribute themselves. In his contribution to Park and Burgess' *The City, published in 1925, McKenzie called attention to the demographic "invasions" and "displacements" that give rise to destructive socio-cultural "natural areas" in the urban community.*

As ONE APPROACHES A CITY and notices its tall buildings rising above the surrounding land and as one continues into the city and observes the crowds of people hurrying to and fro past stores, theaters, banks, and other establishments, one naturally is struck by the contrast with the rural countryside. What supports this phenomenon? What do the people of the city do for a living?

Excerpts from *The Annals of the American Academy of Political and Social Science*, November 1945. Reprinted by permission of the authors and the publisher.

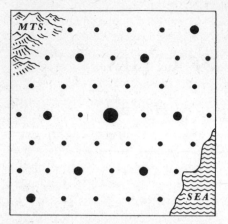

FIGURE 1. THEORETICAL DISTRIBUTION OF
CENTRAL PLACES

In a homogeneous land, settlements are
evenly spaced; largest city in center surrounded by 6 medium-size centers which
in turn are surrounded by 6 small centers.
Tributary areas are hexagons, the closest
geometrical shapes to circles which completely fill area with no unserved spaces.

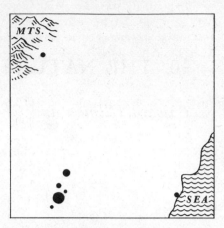

FIGURE 3. SPECIALIZED-FUNCTION
SETTLEMENTS

Large city is manufacturing and mining
center surrounded by a cluster of smaller
settlements located on a mineral deposit.
Small centers on ocean and at edge of
mountains are resorts.

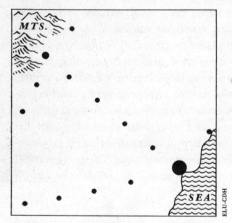

FIGURE 2. TRANSPORT CENTERS, ALIGNED
ALONG RAILROADS OR AT COAST

Large center is port; next largest is railroad junction and engine-changing point
where mountain and plain meet. Small
centers perform break of bulk principally
between rail and roads.

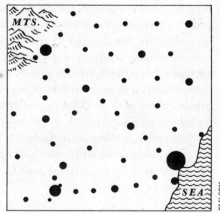

FIGURE 4. THEORETICAL COMPOSITE
GROUPING

Port becomes the metropolis and, although
off center, serves as central place for whole
area. Manufacturing-mining and junction
centers are next largest. Railroad alignment of many towns evident. Railroad
route in upper left of Fig. 2 has been diverted to pass through manufacturing and
mining cluster. Distribution of settlements
in upper right follows central-place arrangement.

The support of a city depends on the services it performs not for itself but for a tributary area. Many activities serve merely the population of the city itself. Barbers, dry cleaners, shoe repairers, grocerymen, bakers, and movie operators serve others who are engaged in the principal activity of the city, which may be mining, manufacturing, trade, or some other activity.

The service by which the city earns its livelihood depends on the nature of the economy and of the hinterland. Cities are small or rare in areas either of primitive, self-sufficient economy or of meager resources. As Adam Smith stated, the land must produce a surplus in order to support cities. This does not mean that all cities must be surrounded by productive land, since strategic location with reference to cheap ocean highways may enable a city to support itself on the specialized surplus of distant lands. Nor does it mean that cities are parasites living off the land. Modern mechanization, transport, and a complex interdependent economy enable much of the economic activity of mankind to be centered in cities. Many of the people engaged even in food production are actually in cities in the manufacture of agricultural machinery.

The support of cities as suppliers of urban services for the earth can be summarized in three categories, each of which presents a factor of urban causation: [1]

1. Cities as central places performing comprehensive services for a surrounding area. Such cities tend to be evenly spaced throughout productive territory (Figure 1). For the moment this may be considered the "norm" subject to variation primarily in response to the ensuing factors.

2. Transport cities performing break-of-bulk and allied services along transport routes, supported by areas which may be remote in distance but close in connection because of the city's strategic location on transport channels. Such cities tend to be arranged in linear patterns along rail lines or at coasts (Figure 2).

3. Specialized-function cities performing one service such as mining, manufacturing, or recreation for large areas, including the general tributary areas of hosts of other cities. Since the principal localizing factor is often a particular resource such as coal, water power, or a beach, such cities may occur singly or in clusters (Figure 3).

Most cities represent a combination of the three factors, the relative importance of each varying from city to city (Figure 4).

. . .

Application of the three types of urban support

Although examples can be cited illustrating each of the three types of urban support, most American cities partake in varying proportions of all three types. New York City, for example, as the greatest American port is a break-of-bulk point; as the principal center of wholesaling and retailing it is a central-place type; and as the major American center of manufacturing it is a specialized type. The actual distribution and functional classification of cities in the United States, more complex than the simple sum of the three types (Figure 4), has been mapped and described elsewhere in different terms.[2]

The three basic types therefore should not be considered as a rigid framework excluding all accidental establishment, although even fortuitous development of a city becomes part of the general urban-supporting environment. Nor should the urban setting be regarded as static; cities are constantly changing, and exhibit characteristic lag in adjusting to new conditions.

Ample opportunity exists for use of initiative in strengthening the supporting base of the future city, particularly if account is taken of the basic factors of urban support. Thus a city should examine: (1) its surrounding area to take advantage of changes such as newly discovered resources or crops, (2) its transport in order to adjust properly to new or changed facilities, and (3) its industries in order to benefit from technological advances.

INTERNAL STRUCTURE OF CITIES

Any effective plans for the improvement or rearrangement of the future city must take account of the present pattern of land use within the city, of the factors which have produced this pattern, and of the facilities required by activities localized within particular districts.

Although the internal pattern of each city is unique in its particular combination of details, most American cities have business, industrial, and residential districts. The forces underlying the pattern of land use can be appreciated if attention is focused on three generalizations of arrangement—by concentric zones, sectors, and multiple nuclei.

Concentric zones

According to the concentric-zone theory, the pattern of growth of the city can best be understood in terms of five concentric zones [3] (Figure 5).

1. *The central business district*   This is the focus of commercial, social, and civic life, and of transportation. In it is the downtown retail district with its department stores, smart shops, office buildings, clubs, banks, hotels, theaters, museums, and organization headquarters. Encircling the downtown retail district is the wholesale business district.

2. *The zone in transition*   Encircling the downtown area is a zone of residential deterioration. Business and light manufacturing encroach

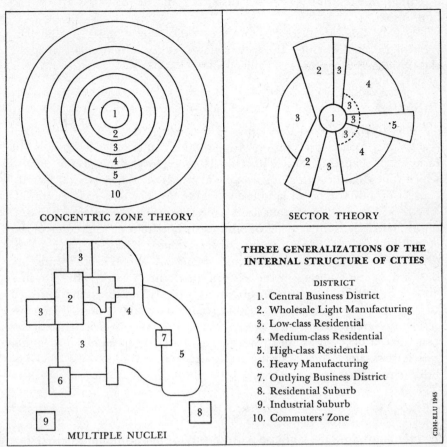

CONCENTRIC ZONE THEORY

SECTOR THEORY

THREE GENERALIZATIONS OF THE INTERNAL STRUCTURE OF CITIES

DISTRICT

1. Central Business District
2. Wholesale Light Manufacturing
3. Low-class Residential
4. Medium-class Residential
5. High-class Residential
6. Heavy Manufacturing
7. Outlying Business District
8. Residential Suburb
9. Industrial Suburb
10. Commuters' Zone

MULTIPLE NUCLEI

CDH-ELU 1945

FIGURE 5. GENERALIZATIONS OF INTERNAL STRUCTURE OF CITIES

The concentric-zone theory is a generalization for all cities. The arrangement of the sectors in the sector theory varies from city to city. The diagram for multiple nuclei represents one possible pattern among innumerable variations.

on residential areas characterized particularly by rooming houses. In this zone are the principal slums, with their submerged regions of poverty, degradation, and disease, and their underworlds of vice. In many American cities it has been inhabited largely by colonies of recent immigrants.

3. *The zone of independent workingmen's homes*   This is inhabited by industrial workers who have escaped from the zone in transition but who desire to live within easy access of their work. In many American cities second-generation immigrants are important segments of the population in this area.

4. *The zone of better residences*   This is made up of single-family dwellings, of exclusive "restricted districts," and of high-class apartment buildings.

5. *The commuters' zone*   Often beyond the city limits in suburban areas or in satellite cities, this is a zone of spotty development of high-class residences along lines of rapid travel.

Sectors

The theory of axial development, according to which growth takes place along main transportation routes or along lines of least resistance to form a star-shaped city, is refined by Homer Hoyt in his sector theory, which states that growth along a particular axis of transportation usually consists of similar types of land use [4] (Figure 5). The entire city is considered as a circle and the various areas as sectors radiating out from the center of that circle; similar types of land use originate near the center of the circle and migrate outward toward the periphery. Thus a high-rent residential area in the eastern quadrant of the city would tend to migrate outward, keeping always in the eastern quadrant. A low-quality housing area, if located in the southern quadrant, would tend to extend outward to the very margin of the city in that sector. The migration of high-class residential areas outward along established lines of travel is particularly pronounced on high ground toward open country, to homes of community leaders, along lines of fastest transportation, and to existing nuclei of buildings or trading centers.

Multiple nuclei

In many cities the land-use pattern is built not around a single center but around several discrete nuclei (Figure 5). In some cities these nuclei have existed from the very origins of the city; in others they have developed as the growth of the city stimulated migration and specialization. An example of the first type is Metropolitan London, in which "The City" and Westminster originated as separate points separated by open country, one as the center of finance and commerce, the other as the center of political life. An example of the second type is Chicago, in which heavy industry, at first localized along the Chicago River in the heart of the city, migrated to the Calumet District, where it acted as a nucleus for extensive new urban development.

The initial nucleus of the city may be the retail district in a central-place city, the port or rail facilities in a break-of-bulk city, or the factory, mine, or beach in a specialized-function city.

The rise of separate nuclei and differentiated districts reflects a combination of the following four factors:

1. Certain activities require specialized facilities. The retail district, for

example, is attached to the point of greatest intracity accessibility, the port district to suitable water front, manufacturing districts to large blocks of land and water or rail connection, and so on.

2. Certain like activities group together because they profit from cohesion.[5] . . . Retail districts benefit from grouping which increases the concentration of potential customers and makes possible comparison shopping. Financial and office-building districts depend upon facility of communication among offices within the district. The Merchandise Mart of Chicago is an example of wholesale clustering.

3. Certain unlike activities are detrimental to each other. The antagonism between factory development and high-class residential development is well known. The heavy concentrations of pedestrians, automobiles, and streetcars in the retail district are antagonistic both to the railroad facilities and the street loading required in the wholesale district and to the rail facilities and space needed by large industrial districts, and vice versa.

4. Certain activities are unable to afford the high rents of the most desirable sites. This factor works in conjunction with the foregoing. Examples are bulk wholesaling and storage activities requiring much room, or low-class housing unable to afford the luxury of high land with a view.

The number of nuclei which result from historical development and the operation of localization forces varies greatly from city to city. The larger the city, the more numerous and specialized are the nuclei. The following districts, however, have developed around nuclei in most large American cities.

The central business district   This district is at the focus of intracity transportation facilities by sidewalk, private car, bus, streetcar, subway, and elevated. Because of asymmetrical growth of most large cities, it is generally not now in the area center of the city but actually near one edge, as in the case of lake-front, riverside, or even inland cities; examples are Chicago, St. Louis, and Salt Lake City. Because established internal transportation lines converge on it, however, it is the point of most convenient access from all parts of the city, and the point of highest land values. The retail district, at the point of maximum accessibility, is attached to the sidewalk; only pedestrian or mass-transportation movement can concentrate the large numbers of customers necessary to support department stores, variety stores, and clothing shops, which are characteristic of the district. In small cities financial institutions and office buildings are intermingled with retail shops, but in large cities the financial district is separate, near but not at the point of greatest intracity facility. Its point of attachment is the elevator, which permits three-dimensional access among offices, whose most important locational factor is accessibility to other offices rather than to the city as a whole. Government buildings also are commonly near but not in the center of the retail district. In most cities a separate "automobile row" has arisen on the edge of the central business district, in cheaper rent areas along one or more major high-ways; its attachment is to the highway itself.

The wholesale and light-manufacturing district   This district is conveniently within the city but near the focus of extra city transportation facilities. Wholesale houses, while deriving some support from the city itself, serve principally a tributary region reached by railroad and motor truck. They are, therefore, concentrated along railroad lines, usually adjacent to (but not surrounding) the central business district. Many types of light manufacturing which do not require specialized buildings are attracted by the facilities of this district or similar districts: good rail and road transportation, available loft buildings, and proximity to the markets and labor of the city itself.

The heavy industrial district   This is near the present or former outer edge of the city. Heavy industries require large tracts of space, often beyond any available in sections already subdivided into blocks and streets. They also require good transportation, either rail or water. With the development of belt lines and switching yards, sites on the edge of the city may have better transportation service than those near the center. In Chicago about a hundred industries are in a belt three miles long, adjacent to the clearing freight yards on the southwestern edge of the city. Furthermore, the noise of boiler works, the odors of stockyards, the waste disposal problems of smelters and iron and steel mills, the fire hazards of petroleum refineries, and the space and transportation needs which interrupt streets and accessibility—all these favor the growth of heavy industry away from the main center of the large city. The Calumet District of Chicago, the New Jersey marshes near New York City, the Lea marshes near London, and the St. Denis district of Paris are examples of such districts. The stockyards of Chicago, in spite of their odors and size, have been engulfed by urban growth and are now far from the edge of the city. They form a nucleus of heavy industry within the city but not near the center, which has blighted the adjacent residential area, the "back-of-the-yards" district.

The residential district   In general, high-class districts are likely to be on well-drained, high land and away from nuisances such as noise, odors, smoke, and railroad lines. Low-class districts are likely to arise near factories and railroad districts, wherever located in the city. Because of the obsolescence of structures, the older inner margins of residential districts are fertile fields for invasion by groups unable to pay high rents. Residential neighborhoods have some measure of cohesiveness. Extreme cases are the ethnically segregated groups, which cluster together although including members in many economic groups; Harlem is an example.

Minor nuclei   These include cultural centers, parks, outlying business districts, and small industrial centers. A university may form a nucleus for a quasi-independent community; examples are the University of

Chicago, the University of California, and Harvard University. Parks and recreation areas occupying former wasteland too rugged or wet for housing may form nuclei for high-class residential areas; examples are Rock Creek Park in Washington and Hyde Park in London. Outlying business districts may in time become major centers. Many small institutions and individual light manufacturing plants, such as bakeries, dispersed throughout the city may never become nuclei of differentiated districts.

Suburb and Satellite   Suburbs, either residential or industrial, are characteristic of most of the larger American cities.[6] The rise of the automobile and the improvement of certain suburban commuter rail lines in a few of the largest cities have stimulated suburbanization. Satellites differ from suburbs in that they are separated from the central city by many miles and in general have little daily commuting to or from the central city, although economic activities of the satellite are closely geared to those of the central city. Thus Gary may be considered a suburb but Elgin and Joliet are satellites of Chicago.

Appraisal of land-use patterns

Most cities exhibit not only a combination of the three types of urban support, but also aspects of the three generalizations of the land-use pattern. An understanding of both is useful in appraising the future prospects of the whole city and the arrangement of its parts.

As a general picture subject to modification because of topography, transportation, and previous land use, the concentric-zone aspect has merit. It is not a rigid pattern, inasmuch as growth or arrangement often reflects expansion within sectors or development around separate nuclei.

The sector aspect has been applied particularly to the outward movement of residential districts. Both the concentric-zone theory and the sector theory emphasize the general tendency of central residential areas to decline in value as new construction takes place on the outer edges; the sector theory is, however, more discriminating in its analysis of that movement.

Both the concentric zone, as a general pattern, and the sector aspect, as applied primarily to residential patterns, assume (although not explicitly) that there is but a single urban core around which land use is arranged symmetrically in either concentric or radial patterns. In broad theoretical terms such an assumption may be valid, inasmuch as the handicap of distance alone would favor as much concentration as possible in a small central core. Because of the actual physical impossibility of such concentration and the existence of separating factors, however, separate nuclei arise. The specific separating factors are not only high rent in the core, which can be afforded by few activities, but also the natural attachment of certain activities to extraurban transport, space, or other facilities, and the advantages of the separation of unlike activities and the concentration of like functions.

The constantly changing pattern of land use poses many problems. Near the core, land is kept vacant or retained in antisocial slum structures in anticipation of expansion of higher-rent activities. The hidden costs of slums to the city in poor environment for future citizens and excessive police, fire, and sanitary protection underlie the argument for a subsidy to remove the blight. The transition zone is not everywhere a zone of deterioration with slums, however, as witness the rise of high-class apartment development near the urban core in the Gold Coast of Chicago or Park Avenue in New York City. On the fringe of the city, overambitious subdividing results in unused land to be crossed by urban services such as sewers and transportation. Separate political status of many suburbs results in a lack of civic responsibility for the problems and expenses of the city in which the suburbanites work.

11. THE PROCESS OF URBANIZATION

Hope Tisdale

In the far-reaching essay that follows, Hope Tisdale calls attention to the demographic underpinnings of the city. Neither its power and influence over the surrounding hinterland nor its cosmopolitan culture can satisfactorily identify the city, because each of these, in fact, presupposes that urbanization has already taken place. Only the preexisting urban community can control its geographic environment and only the already established city can demonstrate the possession of urban psychosocial characteristics.

Accordingly, population concentration alone is the essential condition of urbanism and urbanization. The development of a dense aggregation of people is necessary if any of the other properties of the city is to be observed. Yet population growth is obviously dependent on technological proficiency. As a result, Tisdale acknowledges that the advancement of technology is an indispensable basis for the concentration of population without which the urban condition is a literal impossibility.

The long-range, almost global point of view of this selection ably demonstrates why the demographic perspective is part of the basic orientation of urban sociology.

URBANIZATION IS A PROCESS of population concentration. It proceeds in two ways: the multiplication of points of concentration and the increase in size of individual concentrations. It may occasionally or in some areas

From *Social Forces*, March 1942. Reprinted by permission of the University of North Carolina Press.

stop or actually recede, but the tendency is inherent in society for it to proceed until it is inhibited by adverse conditions. Whether or not a saturation point, an "urban maturity," followed by stabilization or subsidence of the process, can or will be reached is not known. There is some evidence that points toward such a development, but the contingent and derivative nature of urbanization makes this a difficult question to answer.

The restriction of the definition of urbanization to terms of population concentration may at first seem too limited, but an investigation of the possibilities of broader or different definition will show that this is the only one which does not lead to ambiguity and other forms of intellectual distress. Its concreteness and simplicity further recommend it; it gives us something definite to lay hold of. Logically and etymologically, it is unassailable. The societal point of view demands it, since it comprehends the totality of the process both in time and in space. It eliminates or throws into different categories other processes which, though associated with urbanization, may have opposing effects upon it. The concomitants of urbanization are not to be ignored; they are simply to be distinguished from it.

Consistent with the definition of urbanization, cities may be defined as points of concentration. There is no need at this juncture to fix lower limits to the size and density which qualify a concentration as a city. There is no clear-cut level of concentration at which a city suddenly springs into being. It is convenient from time to time arbitrarily to name certain levels beyond which concentrations are designated as cities. This is necessary in analyzing data and identifying characteristics of various size groups, but it does not alter the validity of the original concept.

In defending the strictness and simplicity of the definitions offered here, it is in order to examine some other definitions and explain why they have been rejected. There are two classes of definition which are deemed unacceptable. The first regards urbanization as a process of radiation whereby ideas and practices spread out from the urban center into surrounding areas. This is an objectionable definition because it makes the city the cause of urbanization rather than the result or the product of urbanization. It does not explain the appearance and growth of cities. It posits the pre-existence of cities. It says, "In the beginning, there were cities." Not that cities do not radiate powerful influences. Indeed they do. But calling this radiation urbanization introduces the element of ambiguity mentioned earlier in this discussion. If the process by which people congregate in cities (and surely it cannot be said that this is not urbanization) and the process by which influences go out from the city are both called urbanization, we have a hybrid definition, a definition on two levels, in two senses. It will be necessary always to specify the sense in which it is being used. To use it in both senses at once is to be abstruse. The two types of phenomena are related. They act upon each other. But unless we dissect them apart, we cannot understand the nature of their association.

The second class of definition is more objectionable than the first, and more peculiar. It defines urbanization as the increase in intensity of problems or traits or characteristics that are essentially urban. Again, we have the confusion of cause and effect, the pre-supposition of cities before urbanization, which gives the definition only a strictly contemporary application. The chief objection to it, however, lies in the necessity of admitting its corollary, that as problems are solved, as traits disappear, as characteristics change, deurbanization sets in. This cannot be true unless we are able to discover some problems, traits and characteristics which are so essentially urban that they never diminish or disappear as cities increase, only as they decrease. The one trait which can be demonstrated to have a complete and consistent positive association with urban growth is population concentration. If this is the only trait, it should itself be the definition.

In our time, we observe many urban traits. We must refuse to call their intensification urbanization until we are sure that the growth of cities cannot proceed without their intensification, and also that the traits cannot intensify without a concomitant urban increase.

There is a third class of definition which is partially acceptable. It is the implied definition. Perhaps the best way to understand what is meant by a word is to study how it is used rather than to accept a formal definition. This does not belittle the importance of scientific definition, which is the chief object of the present discussion, but rather emphasizes the importance of making the definition consistent with the use of a word. Some writers do not attempt to define urbanization; they merely use the term with a meaning made obvious by its context. Occasionally, it is defined one way and used another. This is a serious blunder.

In most cases, the implied meaning of urbanization is the one we have chosen, the concentration of population. This is the only meaning it should be given. No wonder at the miracles of modern technology, no bewilderment with the complexity of modern urban life, no impotence before the stubbornness of modern social problems should be allowed to obscure this fact. Any definition of urbanization which calls for a transcendence of cities is a definition of something else, because urbanization must culminate in the city if it is to be the process which makes the city.

Just as long as cities grow in size or multiply in number, urbanization is taking place. It can stop, recede or go on at any point in time or space. There can be urbanization at one time and not at another. There can be urbanization in one area and not in another. There can be rapid urbanization and slow urbanization; there can be deurbanization. There can be urbanization before there are cities and after there have been cities. Furthermore, there can be absence of urbanization even though there are many cities. As soon as population concentration stops, urbanization stops. How far urbanization can go, we are unable to say, because we do not know what limits of concentration society may be able to tolerate.

Urbanization is a process of becoming. It implies a movement, not necessarily direct or steady or continuous, from a state of non-urbanism toward a state of complete urbanism, or rather from a state of less concentration toward a state of more concentration. It is put in motion by events or conditions which make concentration both possible and desirable. These events are not to be confused with the process itself. The discovery and utilization of electricity, for example, constitute a series of events which have served to stimulate urbanization, but they are not to be identified with urbanization because urbanization is not their sole effect; they also de-urbanize.

For much the same reasons that the definition of urbanization must be restricted, that of cities must also be restricted. Cities have been defined as ways of life, states of mind, collections of traits, types of occupation and the like. Such definitions are bound to get us in trouble sooner or later because none of the attributes named are constants of the city and all of them spill over into other areas. Traits change, occupations change, political organization changes, the economic system changes. The only trait that is constant is that the city is different from what is not the city. The nature of this difference varies. If we say that the city is a collection of traits, we cut ourselves loose from the only solid base on which we can set up definite criteria and find ourselves neck-deep in a sea of difficulties connected with the isolation of urban traits. It means that whatever we find more of in the city is an urban trait. But what is the city? Why, it is a collection of urban traits. How do we identify these traits? By their high intensity in the city. But what is the city? A collection of traits. And so forth. The only way to break this deadlock is to go back to population concentration. The criterion must be in terms of population. Then we can study traits, relationships, and characteristics to our heart's content.

Of course there are many things about these concentrations which are different. Of course there are ways of behaving, physical aspects, kinds of organization, types of activity which develop in and by virtue of the city. Some are different because they are in the city; some are in the city because they are different. Some are in society, if not in the city, because the city is in society. We call them civilization. Civilization is a pattern, or a group of patterns, in the matrix of social change which is concomitant of urbanization but which transcends the city. It is the culture of an urban or citified society. It is not one kind of thing, like urbanization, but many kinds of things, and it has to be studied in parts. There are civilizations, but only one urbanization. With the exercise of a little imagination, we can pick out from the matrix of social change the basic pattern of urbanization and relate it to other patterns.

In a sense, everything that affects population movement affects urbanization one way or the other. Most events of any significance are complex enough to have a bifurcated effect upon it. Because of the intricate interdependence and the almost infinite ramifications of consequences of everything that does happen in a society, we are brought to the conclusion that it is the total effect of social change in all of a society upon population distribution that determines the course of urbanization. This is one reason why it is so important to lay hold of something definite like population and work backward, forward, and outward from it.

Social change is a name we can give to all the processes by which social organization continually adapts to new conditions, new problems, and new ideas. If we can place a finger upon the mainspring of human action, we shall have it also upon the source of social change. What is the dynamic force which launches man on countless enterprises, scatters him over the earth, and makes society forever different though always the same? It is man's urge to live on, his tireless quest of fulfilled desire. Survival? Yes, but survival on a dozen planes; survival on earth, survival in heaven, survival in his children, survival in the minds of other men, survival in his own conscience, survival in every way that he was born demanding or has learned to value. We need no more than this to account for the immense diversity of human behavior and the persistence of social change.

We posit that social change has existed as long as social life has existed. This may well be as long as man has existed in any significant numbers. Human beings show a disposition to live together. Whether this "consciousness of kind," as Giddings called it, is an inherited urge or an accident of association or a result of necessity does not matter a great deal. The biological peculiarities of human birth and infancy would be enough to establish habits of togetherness, regardless of whether the chromosomes carry genes for such behavior or not. If human beings had not stuck together to some extent, there probably would be none of them now. The fact that they stuck together as much as they did is one reason for there being so many of them now.

This being together in scattered and wandering groups, this original differential density, might be called urbanization of a sort. Certainly, it carried the germ of urbanization. But urbanization is togetherness of a progressive nature, that is, an increasing concentration. Insofar as these groups were increasing in size, as some of them must have done, urbanization was taking place, even though there were as yet no cities in any acceptable sense of the word, not even any villages.

Somewhere along the line, groups began to take up more or less permanent abode. We infer this from the observation that man now pretty generally lives in permanent dwellings. We can guess at the way it happened. A localized means of sustenance was necessary to a permanent abode. Agriculture was the answer. Agriculture developed, not through the operation of some external force inexorably set upon such a course, but because somebody thought of it, or several or many somebodies. Maybe it was thought of because people did not want to wander any more and were casting about for ways and means of settling down. Possibly, someone just stumbled on the idea and then people stopped wandering because they did not like to leave the crops. Perhaps groups were getting too big to wander conveniently and they did not want to separate because they were safer and happier together. All of these things may have happened. However the idea was born, agriculture filled some sort of felt need or it would never have been adopted. Historically, agriculture did not always appear in conjunction with permanent habitation, but except where it did, urbanization would have been stalemated at a relatively low level.

With habitation fixed and agriculture developing, urbanization was moving along. Now that they no longer wandered, groups could grow larger without becoming unwieldy. Concentration tolerance was increased. Death rates may well have decreased at this time. Probably other groups, still wandering, came upon the settled groups, liked the idea, and themselves settled there or elsewhere, if they were not killed off by a militant village population. Thus we see that agriculture, which is now the chief occupation of non-urban dwellers, was one of the earliest steps in the long process of urbanization that could one day make a New York. No doubt, hunting, fishing, and the domestication of animals also played their part in urbanization, but they could not have tied the people to the land so effectively as agriculture did.

But agriculture was to play a further role in the process. The next step that had to be made in order for urbanization to proceed was the releasing of some of the population from the necessity of working on the land. It had to be possible for a part of the population to produce enough to feed all the population. Just how this came about is a matter of conjecture. It probably came about in many ways. But some method or methods of food production and preservation, some technological devices, which allowed one person to produce as much as had been produced before by more than one person, must have been discovered. And from that time to this, it has been improvement in agricultural methods and the increase in per capita agricultural productivity that have created a surplus of population which could leave the land and follow other pursuits. Reduce agriculture to the subsistence level today and our cities will be gone tomorrow.

This freeing of part of the population from the land in no direct way forced the appearance of cities. It merely furnished the personnel which made cities a possibility. In order for cities to appear, there had to be both motivation and means for their development. These were provided by a combination of predisposing conditions. Among them were the survival complex already described, the patent advantages of mutual aid and cooperative enterprise, the safety of concentration, geography, and the general improbability that man would think up only those projects which he could carry out single-handed or in small groups. Consequently, productive activity which required people's living in compact groups began to grow and the groups with it, in the same unplanned expediential manner as characterized agricultural development. When conditions prompted, urbanization proceeded and cities eventually emerged and grew. Not everywhere or all at once, but gradually as need and ideas arose. Each stage of urbanization was pregnant with the possibility of further urbanization, though it did not always and everywhere come to fruition.

Probably there has never been such perfect coordination between people and technics that the expansion of nonagricultural activity and attendant urbanization neatly took up the slack produced by agricultural improvements. Perhaps there never will be. The difficulties of planned social change are enormous. It has been the tendency, however. One point that should be clear by now is that cities are not creatures of spontaneous generation with a life of their own, but gradual accumulations in the grand concourse of a society, made possible by population surpluses, replenished and nurtured by the society as a whole, and as long as they last, an integral part of that society.

At the beginning of this discussion, it was stated that urbanization is inherent in society. This raises the question of inevitability. There are two ways to look at inevitability. One is to regard it as the inescapable approach of the predestined march of fate. The other is to see it as the simple outgrowth of what has gone before. If we accept the latter, we may say that urbanization was inevitable, inevitable in the limited sense that it was quite natural, inevitable in the way that a man will put on his coat when the wind blows cold.

When you compress the whole of human history into a few pages, as we have just done, history looks much simpler than it was, even though we are dealing with but a single aspect of it. The process of urbanization looks much smoother from where we sit than it was. Actually, for hundreds of thousands of years it had its ups and downs, its advances and retreats. There were interferences like the ice age and other cataclysms of nature, pillage and conquest by predatory peoples, epidemics and scourges, droughts and crop failures, and thousands of things that we know nothing about. Occasionally, there were concatenations of circumstances such that a certain amount of isolation and a certain amount of intergroup contact conspired to produce a local urbanism of impressive proportions. There were Egypt and Greece and Rome, the Mayan urbanization in America, the Chinese urbanization in Asia, and a number of others. Some of them were swallowed up in waves of social change; some of them were only heavily drained.

In our time, urbanization has been so rapid that we can see it happening, but there were other times when it moved so slowly that the trend would have been imperceptible. Now, it occurs on an almost world-wide scale. In the past, it was sporadic and localized. In this country, we have a laboratory in which we can trace the process rather closely from a very early stage, at least so far as this one area and this civilization are concerned.

Two conditions appear to be necessary for urbanization. One is people and the other is technology. Population increase and surplus feed the process; technology and urbanization work along together. A population does not necessarily reach a certain density before it begins to urbanize. Technology does not have to wait on population. The whole thing is a spiral arrangement whereby technology produces population surplus and encourages population increase, population surplus and increase encourage further technology, and the upshot is urbanization.

As to population increase, the tendency to multiply up to the limit of the food supply is probably just as characteristic of human beings as of any order of organic life. But Malthusian law could operate freely only under conditions of status quo. Man often circumvents it by exercising his ingenuity to increase the population tolerance of the area he inhabits. Not that this idea is uppermost in his mind. His immediate objective is to achieve life, satisfaction, and security for himself and those in whom he is interested. He naturally seeks the easiest and most effective way to do this. He never consciously takes the hard way. The result is technology. Population increase is bound to give some impulse to this kind of enterprise, but it is not the sole incentive. Technology can develop to some extent without it. It so happens that the net effect of technology has been to permit the increase of both total and concentrated populations, but its specific application is usually in terms of immediate and individual wants and problems, and it often acts to decrease populations. At this very moment, an application of technology is doing a competent job of decreasing populations, both total and concentrated.

Urbanization is so closely bound up with technology that we can say without qualification that technology is the sine qua non of urbanization. The reverse is not true. Technology is not the exclusive property of the city; it operates in every province and pocket of society. It was technology that released potential urban dwellers from the land. Although urbanization could not proceed without it, technology may prove to be the means of deurbanizing our own civilization. This has happened before. If technology has been the means for population concentration, it has also been the means of population spread, through exploration, trade, and commerce. Commerce, by the way, is a technological complex with unusually bifid urbanizational potentialities. It appears absolutely essential to a high degree of urbanization, but it involves at the same time a dispersal of population which goes beyond anything that unconcentrated society ever dreamed of. It is by the grace of technological achievement that Europeans people the Americas, that Britishers live in India, and that Africans are at home in the Southeast.

Technology is our name for the ways that man has discovered and invented of doing things which he wanted to do but could not do with any already known methods. This includes both the doing of things which had never been done before and the doing of old things by quicker and more effective methods. In these matters, man does not act as a group; society does not function as a unit. The total effect of the execution of a technological idea is not anticipated and provided for. Consequently, many difficulties and contradictions arise. Each technological innovation solves certain problems but creates others. Many of these problems have to do with population distribution.

The close interrelation between urbanization and technology is perhaps one reason why the definition of urbanization has not been clearer. The double-edged effect of technology upon society whereby it both disperses and compacts, both facilitates and frustrates, both preserves life and destroys it, has given rise to every conceivable emotional state and all manner of confusion. The identification of cities with technology has confounded the issue by directing the intensity of every passion from love to loathing upon them both.

But cities are both good and bad, no matter what moral criterion we choose to apply. It is not justifiable even to say they are more one than the other. By the same token, technology is not one instrument in the hands of a clumsy society, but many instruments in the hands of many groups and individuals, which they are using rather cleverly on the whole, looking at it from their viewpoints. It remains to be seen whether our society will acquire a consciousness of common interest and become organized in such a way that the groups who now find themselves technologically disadvantaged will be allowed to participate more fully in what are considered to be the benefits of technology.

To recapitulate, urbanization is a process of population concentration. It comes about through the utilization of technological devices, the result if not the object of which is to increase the population tolerance of the areas in which they operate. Population increase is an incentive to technological advance and urbanization, but it is not the sole incentive. Both can develop somewhat independently of it, given the indefinite expansibility and diversity of man's desires and his capacity for exercising ingenuity in achieving them. The products of the concentrative process, cities, give to society a cultural character which we call civilization. Different people and different technologies produce different civilizations, but urbanization is one and the same throughout though it varies in rate and scope from time to time and from place to place.

The problem of the urban sociologist is to measure and study the process and its products and attempt to determine as specifically as possible the relationships which obtain between it and other elements in the general flow of social change.

12. THE CITY AS A CULTURE FORM

Oswald Spengler

The city, declares Spengler, is possessed of a unique culture. Urbanism is free intellect. It is participatory democracy. It is commercial values. It is scientific objectivity. And finally it is also sterility, futility, and doom. The city originates in a market place but eventually comes to feel itself differentiated from the countryside surrounding it. In time, the city's cultural influence spreads over these environs and corrupts the pristine, timeless, virile mode of life with its own artificial, monetary, and political values. At last, as the folk culture is fully extinguished, factionalism mounts, the birth rate declines, and urban man loses his desire even to survive.

Spengler's apocalyptic view of the city as culture conforms, of course, to his organic analogy in which sociocultural forms are seen to obey an irresistible logic from birth to death. The high drama that Spengler thus imparts to history may draw attention away from his depiction of the city as being a particular type of culture, to be sure, but one which may be very durable and which may also be most productive in terms of the invention, diffusion, and preservation of constructive features of society. Spengler's view of the city was colored by events in Germany, such as religious wars and economic competition from the New World which had undermined and even depopulated Germany's earlier urban centers and which had elevated rural mysticism to the stature of a ruling principle in German politics and philosophy.

An interesting, and contrasting, interpretation of urban cultural influence has been made by the anthropologists Robert Redfield and Milton

Excerpts from *The Decline of the West*, Vol. 2 (1928), translated by Charles Francis Atkinson. Reprinted by permission of Alfred A. Knopf.

B. Singer. A city arises from the antecedent folk culture. Intellectuals elaborate a "Great Tradition" (such as the Mayan, Hellenic, and the like) out of indigenous materials, and this is morally creative because it integrates the whole system of social institutions. Then, however, given an advanced stage of urbanization, alien cultures may impinge on peoples from cities beyond their own cultural orbit, with disturbing effects resulting. Though Redfield and Singer recognize the rationalistic and alienating capacities of urbanism, it is intercultural contact, they observe, not simply diffusion from the city that is primarily disorganizing.

IT IS A CONCLUSIVE FACT—yet one hitherto never appreciated—that all great Cultures are town-Cultures. Higher man of the Second Age is a town-tied animal. Here is the real criterion of "world-history" that differentiates it with utter sharpness from man's history—*world-history is the history of civic man*. Peoples, states, politics, religion, all arts, and all sciences rest upon *one* prime phenomenon of human being, the town. As all thinkers of all Cultures themselves live in the town (even though they may reside bodily in the country), they are perfectly unaware of what a bizarre thing a town is. To feel this we have to put ourselves unreservedly in the place of the wonder-struck primitive who for the first time sees this mass of stone and wood set in the landscape, with its stone-enclosed streets and its stone-paved squares—a domicile, truly, of strange form and strangely teeming with men!

But the real miracle is the birth of the *soul* of a town. A mass-soul of a wholly new kind—whose last foundations will remain hidden from us forever—suddenly buds off from the general spirituality of its Culture. As soon as it is awake, it forms for itself a visible body. Out of the rustic group of farms and cottages, each of which has its own history, arises a *totality*. And the whole lives, breathes, grows, and acquires a face and an inner form and history. Thenceforward, in addition to the individual house, the temple, the cathedral, and the palace, the town-figure itself becomes a unit objectively expressing the form-language and style-history that accompanies the Culture throughout its life-course.

It goes without saying that what distinguishes a town from a village is not size, but the presence of a soul. Not only in primitive conditions, such as those of central Africa, but in Late conditions too—China, India, and industrialized Europe and America—we find very large settlements that are nevertheless not to be called cities. They are centres of landscape; they do not inwardly form worlds in themselves. They have no soul. Every primitive population lives wholly as peasant and son of the soil— the being "City" does not exist for it. That which in externals develops from the village is not the city, but the market, a mere meeting-point of rural life-interests. Here there can be no question of a separate existence. The inhabitant of a market may be a craftsman or a tradesman, but he lives and thinks as a peasant. We have to go back and sense accurately what it means when out of a primitive Egyptian or Chinese or Germanic village—a little spot in a wide land—a city comes into being. It is quite possibly not differentiated in any outward feature, but spiritually it is *a place from which the countryside is henceforth regarded, felt, and experienced as "environs,"* as something different and subordinate. From now on there are two lives, that of the inside and that of the outside, and the peasant understands this just as clearly as the townsman. The village smith and the smith in the city, the village headman and the burgomaster, live in two different worlds. The man of the land and the man of the city are different essences. First of all they feel the difference, then they are dominated by it, and at last they cease to understand each other at all. To-day a Brandenburg peasant is closer to a Sicilian peasant than he is to a Berliner. From the moment of this specific attunement, the City comes into being, and it is this attunement which underlies, as something that goes without saying, the entire waking-consciousness of every Culture.

Every springtime of a Culture is *ipso facto* the springtime of a new city-type and civism. The men of the pre-Culture are filled with a deep uneasiness in the presence of these types, with which they cannot get into any inward relation. On the Rhine and the Danube the Germans frequently, as at Strassburg, settled down at the gates of Roman cities that remained uninhabited. In Crete the conquerors built, on the ruins of the burnt-out cities like Gournia and Cnossus—villages. The Orders of the Western pre-Culture, the Benedictines, and particularly the Cluniacs and Premonstratensians, settled like the knights on free land; it was the Franciscans and Dominicans who began to build in the Early Gothic city. There the new soul had just awakened. But even there a tender melancholy still adheres to the architecture, as to Franciscan art as a whole—an almost mystical fear of the individual in presence of the new and bright and conscious, which as yet was only dully accepted by the generality. Man hardly yet dared to cease to be peasant; the first to live with the ripe and considered alertness of genuine megalopolitans are the Jesuits. It is a sign that the countryside is still unconditionally supreme, and does not yet recognize the city, when the ruler shifts his court every spring from palace to palace. In the Egyptian Old Kingdom the thickly-populated centre of the administration was at the "White Wall" (Memphis), but the residences of the Pharaohs changed incessantly as in Sumerian Babylon and the Carolingian Empire. The Early Chinese rulers of the Chóu dynasty had their court as a rule at Lo-Yang (the present Ho-nan-fu) from about 1160, but it was not until 770—corresponding to our sixteenth century—that the locality was promoted to be the permanent royal residence.

Never has the feeling of earth-boundness, of the plantwise-cosmic, expressed itself so powerfully as it did in the architecture of the petty early towns, which consisted of hardly more than a few streets about a market-place or a castle or a place of worship. Here, if anywhere, it is manifest that every grand style is itself plantlike. The Doric column, the Egyptian pyramid, the Gothic cathedral, *grow out of* the ground, earnest, big with destiny, Being without waking-consciousness. The Ionic column, the buildings of the Middle Kingdom and those of the Baroque, calmly aware and conscious of themselves, free and sure, *stand on* the ground. There, separated from the power of the land—cut off from it, even, by the pavement underfoot—Being becomes more and more languid, sensation and reason more and more powerful. Man becomes intellect, "free" like the nomads, whom he comes to resemble, but narrower and colder than they. "Intellect," *"Geist,"* *"esprit,"* is the specific urban form of the understanding waking-consciousness. All art, all religion and science, become slowly intellectualized, alien to the land, incomprehensible to the peasant of the soil. With the Civilization sets in the climacteric. The immemorially old roots of Being are dried up in the stone-masses of its cities. And the free intellect—fateful word!—appears like a flame, mounts splendid into the air, and pitiably dies.

. . .

The new Soul of the City speaks a new language, which soon comes to be tantamount to the language of the Culture itself. The open land with its village-mankind is wounded; it no longer understands that language, it is nonplussed and dumb. All genuine style-history is played out in the cities. It is exclusively the city's destiny and the life-experience of urban men that speaks to the eye in the logic of visible forms. The very earliest Gothic was still a growth of the soil and laid hold of the farmhouse with its inhabitants and its contents. But the Renaissance style flourished only in the Renaissance *city,* the Baroque only in the Baroque *city*—not to mention the wholly megalopolitan Corinthian column or Rococo. There was perhaps some quiet infiltration from these into the landscape; but the land itself was no longer capable of the smallest creative effort—only of dumb aversion. The peasant and his dwelling remained in all essentials Gothic, and Gothic it is to this day. The Hellenic *countryside* preserved the geometric style, the Egyptian village the cast of the Old Kingdom.

It is, above all, the expression of the city's "visage" that has a history. The play of this facial expression, indeed, is almost the spiritual history of the Culture itself. First we have the little proto-cities of the Gothic and other Early Cultures, which almost efface themselves in the landscape, which are still genuine peasant-houses crowded under the shadow of a stronghold or a sanctuary, and without inward change become town-houses merely in the sense that they have neighbour-houses instead of fields and meadows around them. The peoples of the Early Culture grad-

ually became town-peoples, and accordingly there are not only specifically Chinese, Indian, Apollinian, and Faustian town-forms, but, moreover, Armenian and Syrian, Ionian and Etruscan, German and French
and English town-physiognomies. There is a city of Phidias, a city of
Rembrandt, a city of Luther. These designations, and the mere names of
Granada, Venice, and Nürnberg conjure up at once quite definite images,
for all that the Culture produces in religion, art, and knowledge has been
produced in such cities. While it was still the spirit of knights' castles and
rural monasteries that evoked the Crusades, the Reformation is urban
and belongs to narrow streets and steep-gabled houses. The great Epic,
which speaks and sings of the blood, belongs to *Pfalz* and *Burg,* but the
Drama, in which *awakened* life tests itself, is city-poetry, and the great
Novel, the survey of all things human by the *emancipated* intellect, presupposes the world-city. Apart from really genuine folk-song, the only
lyrism is of the city. Apart from the "eternal" peasant-art, there is
only urban painting and architecture, with a swift and soon-ended
history.

And these stone visages that have incorporated in their light-world the
humanness of the citizen himself and, like him, are all eye and intellect—
how distinct the language of form that they talk, how different from the
rustic drawl of the landscape! The silhouette of the great city, its roofs
and chimneys, the towers and domes on the horizon! What a language is
imparted to us through *one* look at Nürnberg or Florence, Damascus or
Moscow, Peking or Benares. What do we know of the Classical cities,
seeing that we do not know the lines that they presented under the Southern noon, under clouds in the morning, in the starry night? The courses
of the streets, straight or crooked, broad or narrow; the houses, low or tall,
bright or dark, that in all Western cities turn their façades, *their faces,*
and in all Eastern cities turn their backs, blank wall and railing, towards
the street; the spirit of squares and corners, impasses and prospects, fountains and monuments, churches or temples or mosques, amphitheatres
and railway stations, bazaars and town-halls! The suburbs, too, of neat
garden-villas or of jumbled blocks of flats, rubbish-heaps and allotments;
the fashionable quarter and the slum area, the Subura of Classical Rome
and the Faubourg Saint-Germain of Paris, ancient Baiæ and modern
Nice, the little town-picture like Bruges and Rothenburg and the sea of
houses like Babylon, Tenochtitlan, Rome, and London! All this has history and *is* history. One major political event—and the visage of the town
falls into different folds. Napoleon gave to Bourbon Paris, Bismarck gave
to worthy little Berlin, a new mien. But the Country stands by, uninflu-
enced, suspicious and irritated.

In the earliest time the *landscape-figure alone* dominates man's eyes. It
gives form to his soul and vibrates in tune therewith. Feelings and wood-
land rustlings beat together; the meadows and the copses adapt themselves to its shape, to its course, even to its dress. The village, with its

quiet hillocky roofs, its evening smoke, its wells, its hedges, and its beasts, lies completely fused and embedded in the landscape. The country town *confirms* the country, is an intensification of the picture of the country. It is the Late city that first defies the land, contradicts Nature in the lines of its silhouette, *denies* all Nature. It wants to be something different from and higher than Nature. These high-pitched gables, these Baroque cupolas, spires, and pinnacles, neither are, nor desire to be, related with anything in Nature. And then begins the gigantic megalopolis, the *city-as-world*, which suffers nothing beside itself and sets about *annihilating* the country picture. The town that once upon a time humbly accommodated itself to that picture now insists that it shall be the same as itself. *Extra muros,* chaussées and woods and pastures become a park, mountains become tourists' view-points; and *intra muros* arises an imitation Nature, fountains in lieu of springs, flower-beds, formal pools, and clipped hedges in lieu of meadows and ponds and bushes. In a village the thatched roof is still hill-like and the street is of the same nature as the baulk of earth between fields. But here the picture is of deep, long gorges between high, stony houses, the like of which no nature-being has ever conceived. Costumes, even faces, are adjusted to a background of stone. By day there is a street traffic of strange colours and tones, and by night a new light that outshines the moon. And the yokel stands helpless on the pavement, understanding nothing and understood by nobody, tolerated as a useful type in farce and provider of this world's daily bread.

It follows, however—and this is the most essential point of any—that we cannot comprehend political and economic history at all unless we realize that the city, with its gradual detachment from and final bankrupting of the country, is the determinative form to which the course and sense of higher history generally conforms. *World history is city history.*

An obvious case in point is, of course, the Classical world, in which the Euclidean feeling of existence connected the city-idea with its need of minimizing extension and thus, with ever-increasing emphasis, identified the State with the stone body of the individual Polis. But, quite apart from this instance, we find in every Culture (and very soon) the type of the *capital city*. This, as its name pointedly indicates, is that city whose spirit, with its methods, aims, and decisions of policy and economics, dominates the land. The land with its people is for this controlling spirit a tool and an object. The land does not understand what is going on, and is not even asked. In all countries of all Late Cultures, the great parties, the revolutions, the Caesarisms, the democracies, the parliaments, are the form in which the spirit of the capital tells the country what it is expected to desire and, if called upon, to die for. The Classical forum, the Western press, are, essentially, intellectual engines of the ruling City. Any country-dweller who really understands the meaning of politics in such periods, and feels himself on their level, moves into the City, not perhaps in the body, but certainly in the spirit. The sentiment and public opinion of the peasant's country-side—so far as it can be said to exist—is prescribed and guided by the print and speech of the city. Egypt is Thebes, the *orbis terrarum* is Rome, Islam is Baghdad, France is Paris. The history of every springtime phase is played out in the many small centres of many separate districts. The Egyptian nomes, the Greek peoples of Homer, the Gothic counties and free cities, were the makers of history of old. But gradually Policy gathers itself up into a very few capitals, and everything else retains but a shadow of political existence. Even in the Classical world, the atomizing tendency towards city-states did not hold out against the major movement. As early as the Peloponnesian War it was only Athens and Sparta that were really handling policy, the remaining cities of the Aegean being merely elements within the hegemony of the one or the other; of policies of *their own* there is no longer any question. Finally it is the Forum of the City of Rome alone that is the scene of Classical history. Caesar might campaign in Gaul, his slayers in Macedonia, Antony in Egypt, but, whatever happened in these fields, *it was from their relation to Rome that events acquired meaning.*

. . .

All effectual history begins with the primary classes, nobility and priesthood, forming themselves and elevating themselves above the peasantry as such. The opposition of greater and lesser nobility, between king and vassal, between worldly and spiritual power, is the basic form of all primitive politics, Homeric, Chinese, or Gothic, until with the coming of the City, the burgher, the *Tiers État,* history changes its style. But it is exclusively in these classes as such, in their class-consciousness, that the whole meaning of history inheres. *The peasant is historyless.* The village stands outside world-history, and all evolution from the "Trojan" to the Mithridatic War, from the Saxon emperors to the World War of 1914, passes by these little points on the landscape, occasionally destroying them and wasting their blood, but never in the least touching their inwardness.

The peasant is the eternal man, independent of every Culture that ensconces itself in the cities. He precedes it, he outlives it, a dumb creature propagating himself from generation to generation, limited to soil-bound callings and aptitudes, a mystical soul, a dry, shrewd understanding that sticks to practical matters, the origin and the ever-flowing source of the blood that makes world-history in the cities.

Whatever the Culture up there in the city conceives in the way of state-forms, economic customs, articles of faith, implements, knowledge, art, he receives mistrustfully and hesitatingly; though in the end he may accept these things, never is he altered in kind thereby. Thus the West-European peasant outwardly took in all the dogmas of the Councils from the great Lateran to that of Trent, just as he took in the products of mechanical engineering and those of the French Revolution—but he remains what he was, what he already was in Charlemagne's day. The present-day piety of the peasant is older than Christianity; his gods are more ancient than those of any higher religion. Remove from him the pressure of the great cities and he will revert to the state of nature without feeling that he is losing anything. His real ethic, his real metaphysic, which no scholar of the city has yet thought it worth while to discover, lie outside all religious and spiritual history, have in fact no history at all.

The city is intellect. The Megalopolis is "free" intellect. It is in resistance to the "feudal" powers of blood and tradition that the burgherdom or bourgeoisie, the intellectual class, begins to be conscious of its own separate existence. It upsets thrones and limits old rights in the name of reason and above all in the name of "the People," which henceforward means exclusively the people of the city. Democracy is the political form in which the townsman's outlook upon the world is demanded of the peasantry also. The urban intellect reforms the great religion of the springtime and sets up by the side of the old religion of noble and priest, the new religion of the *Tiers État, liberal science*. The city assumes the lead and control of economic history in replacing the primitive values of the land, which are for ever inseparable from the life and thought of the rustic, by the *absolute idea of money* as distinct from goods. The immemorial country word for exchange of goods is "barter"; even when one of the things exchanged is precious metal, the underlying idea of the process is not yet *monetary*—i.e., it does not involve the abstraction of value from things and its fixation in metallic or fictitious quantities intended to *measure* things qua "commodities." Caravan expeditions and Viking voyages in the springtime are made between land-settlements and imply barter or booty, whereas in the Late period they are made between cities and mean "money." This is the distinction between the Normans before and the Hansa and Venetians after the Crusades, and between the seafarers of Mycenaean times and those of the later colonization period in Greece. The City means not only intellect, but also money.

Presently there arrived an epoch when the development of the city had reached such a point of power that it had no longer to defend itself against country and chivalry, but on the contrary had become a despotism against which the land and its basic orders of society were fighting a hopeless defensive battle—in the spiritual domain against nationalism, in the political against democracy, in the economic against money. At this period the number of cities that really counted as historically dominant had already become very small. And with this there arose the profound distinction—which was above all a spiritual distinction—between the great city and the little city or town. The latter, very significantly called the country-town, was a part of the no longer co-efficient countryside. It was not that the difference between townsman and rustic had become lessened in such towns, but that this difference had become negligible as compared with the new difference between them and the great city. The sly-shrewdness of the country and the intelligence of the megalopolis are two forms of waking-consciousness between which reciprocal understanding is scarcely possible. Here again it is evident that what counts is not the number of inhabitants, but the spirit. It is evident, moreover, that in all great cities nooks remained in which relics of an almost rural mankind lived in their byeways much as if they were on the land, and the people on the two sides of the street were almost in the relation of two villages. In fact, a pyramid of mounting civism, of decreasing number and increasing field of view, leads up from such quasi-rural elements, in ever-narrowing layers, to the small number of genuine megalopolitans at the top, who are at home wherever their spiritual postulates are satisfied.

With this the notion of money attains to full abstractness. It no longer merely *serves* for the understanding of economic intercourse, but *subjects* the exchange of goods to *its own* evolution. It values things, no longer as between each other, but *with reference to itself*. Its relation to the soil and to the man of the soil has so completely vanished, that in the economic thought of the leading cities—the "money-markets"—it is ignored. Money has now become a power, and, moreover, a power that is wholly intellectual and merely figured in the metal it uses, a power the reality of which resides in the waking-consciousness of the upper stratum of an economically active population, a power that makes those concerned with it just as dependent upon itself as the peasant was dependent upon the soil. There is monetary thought, just as there is mathematical or juristic.

But the earth is actual and natural, and money is abstract and artificial, a mere "category"—like "virtue" in the imagination of the Age of Enlightenment. And therefore every primary, pre-civic economy is dependent upon and held in bondage by the cosmic powers, the soil, the climate, the type of man, whereas money, as the pure form of economic intercourse within the waking-consciousness, is no more limited in potential scope by actuality than are the quantities of the mathematical and the logical world. Just as no view of facts hinders us from constructing as many non-Euclidean geometries as we please, so in the developed megalopolitan economics there is no longer any inherent objection to increasing "money" or to thinking, so to say, in other money-dimensions. This has nothing to do with the availability of gold or with any values in actuality at all. There is no standard and no sort of goods in which the value of the talent in the Persian Wars can be compared with its value in the Egyptian booty of Pompey. Money has become, for man as an economic animal, a form of the activity of waking-consciousness, having no longer any roots in Being. This is the basis of its monstrous power over every beginning Civilization, which is always an unconditional *dictatorship of money*, though taking different forms in different Cultures. But this is the reason, too, for the want of solidity, which eventually leads to its losing its power and its meaning, so that at the last, as in Diocletian's time, it disappears from the thought of the closing Civilization, and the primary values of the soil return anew to take its place.

Finally, there arises the monstrous symbol and vessel of the completely emancipated intellect, the world-city, the centre in which the course of a world-history ends by winding itself up. A handful of gigantic places in each Civilization disfranchises and disvalues the entire motherland of its own Culture under the contemptuous name of "the provinces." The "provinces" are now everything whatsoever—land, town, *and* city—except these two or three points. There are no longer noblesse and bourgeoisie, freemen and slaves, Hellenes and Barbarians, believers and unbelievers, *but only cosmopolitans and provincials.* All other contrasts pale before this one, which dominates all events, all habits of life, all views of the world.

The earliest of all world-cities were Babylon and the Thebes of the New Empire—the Minoan world of Crete, for all its splendour, belonged to the Egyptian "provinces." In the Classical the first example is Alexandria, which reduced old Greece at one stroke to the provincial level, and which even Rome, even the resettled Carthage, even Byzantium, could not suppress. In India the giant cities of Ujjaina, Kanauj, and above all Pataliputra were renowned even in China and Java, and everyone knows the fairy-tale reputation of Baghdad and Granada in the West. In the Mexican world, it seems, Uxmal (founded in 950) was the first world-city of the Maya realms, which, however, with the rise of the Toltec world-cities Tezcuco and Tenochtitlan sank to the level of the provinces.

It should not be forgotten that the word "province" first appears as a constitutional designation given by the Romans to Sicily; the subjugation of Sicily, in fact, is the first example of a once pre-eminent Culture-landscape sinking so far as to be purely and simply an object. Syracuse, the first real great-city of the Classical world, had flourished when Rome was still an unimportant country town, but thenceforward, *vis-à-vis* Rome, it becomes a provincial city. In just the same way Habsburg Madrid and Papal Rome, leading cities in the Europe of the seventeenth century, were from the outset of the eighteenth depressed to the provincial level by the world-cities of Paris and London. And the rise of New York to the position of world-city during the Civil War of 1861–5 may perhaps prove to have been the most pregnant event of the nineteenth century.

. . .

The stone Colossus "Cosmopolis" stands at the end of the life's course of every great Culture. The Culture-man whom the land has spiritually formed is seized and possessed by its own creation, the City, and is made into its creature, its executive organ, and finally its victim. This stony mass is the *absolute* city. Its image, as it appears with all its grandiose beauty in the light-world of the human eye, contains the whole noble death-symbolism of the definitive thing-become. The spirit-pervaded stone of Gothic buildings, after a millennium of style-evolution, has become the soulless material of this daemonic stone-desert.

13. THE POLITICO-ADMINISTRATIVE CONCEPT OF THE CITY

Max Weber

Weber directs critical attention to the juridical systems of the city. Both markets and military garrisons presuppose first, the actual presence of the city, and second, that the city will be protected. Hence, the political structure of the urban area is a basic element in understanding cities and the exchange relationships carried on within them. The city as a community requires the existence of a corporate unit. This mode of autonomous administration, or self-determination, of the urban group, Weber concludes, arose indigenously only in the Occident. All the eastern end of the ancient Mediterranean and along the Euphrates appeared the civic development that later was to exist so extensively in classical Greece and Rome.

BESIDE POSSESSING an accumulation of abodes the city also has an economic association with its own landed property and a budget of receipts and expenditure. Such an economic association may also appear in the village no matter how great the quantitative differences. Moreover, it was not peculiar to the city alone, at least in the past, that it was both an economic and a regulatory association. Trespass restrictions, pasture regulations, the prohibition of the export of wood and straw, and similar regulations are known to the village, constituting an economic policy of the association as such.

The cities of the past were differentiated only by the kinds of regula-

Excerpts from *The City* by Max Weber reprinted with permission of The Macmillan Company. Translated and edited by Don Martindale and Gertrud Neuwirth. © by The Free Press, a Corporation, 1958.

tions which appeared. Only the objects of political economic regulation on behalf of the association and the range of characteristic measures embraced by them were peculiar. It goes without saying that measures of the "urban economic policy" took substantial account of the fact that under the transportation conditions of the time the majority of all inland cities were dependent upon the agricultural resources of the immediate hinterland. As shown by the grain policies of Athens and Rome this was true for maritime cities. In a majority, not all, of urban trades areas, opportunity was provided for the natural "play of the market." The urban market supplied the normal, not the sole, place for the exchange of products, especially food.

.   .   .

On the basis of customer relations and specialized small establishments operating without capital, the local urban market with its exchange between agricultural and non-agricultural producers and resident merchants, represents a kind of economic counterpart to barter as against systematically divided performances in terms of work and taxes of a specialized dependent economy in connection with the *oikos,* having its basis in the accumulation and integration of work in the manner, without exchange occurring inside. Following out the parallel: the *regulation* (*urban economic policy*) of the exchange and production conditions in the city represent the counterpart to the *organization* (traditional and feudal-contractual) of activities united in the economy of the *oikos.*

The very fact that in drawing these distinctions we are led to use the concepts of an "urban economic area" and "urban area," and "urban authority," already indicates that the concept of the "city" can and must be examined in terms of a series of concepts other than the purely economic categories so far employed.

The additional concepts required for analysis of the city are political. This already appears in the fact that the urban economic policy itself may be the work of a prince to whom political dominion of the city with its inhabitants belongs. In this case when there is an urban economic policy it is determined *for* the inhabitants of the city not *by* them. However even when this is the case the city must still be considered to be a partially autonomous association, a "community" with special political and administrative arrangements.

The economic concept . . . must be entirely separated from the political-administrative concept of the city. Only in the latter sense may a special *area* belong to the city. A locale can be held to be a city in a political-administrative sense though it would not qualify as a city economically. In the Middle Ages there were areas legally defined as "cities" in which the inhabitants derived ninety percent or more of their livelihood from agriculture, representing a far larger fraction of their income than that of the inhabitants of many localities legally defined as "villages."

Naturally, the transition from such semi-rural cities to consumers', producers' or commercial cities is quite fluid. In those settlements which differ administratively from the village and are thus dealt with as cities only one thing, namely, the kind of regulations of land-owning, is customarily different from rural land-owning forms. Economically such cities are differentiated by a special kind of rent situation presented in urban real estate which consists in house ownership to which land ownership is accessory. The position of urban real estate is connected administratively with special taxation principles. It is bound even more closely to a further element decisive for the political-administrative concept of the city and standing entirely outside the purely economic analysis, namely, the fortress.

FORTRESS AND GARRISON

It is very significant that the city in the past, in Antiquity and the Middle Ages, outside as well as within Europe, was also a special fortress or garrison. At present this property of the city has been entirely lost, but it was not universal even in the past. In Japan, for example, it was not the rule. Administratively one may, with Rathgen,[1] doubt the existence of cities at all. In contrast to Japan, in China every city was surrounded with a gigantic ring of walls. However, it is also true that many economically rural localities which were not cities in the administrative sense, possessed walls at all times. In China such places were not the seat of state authorities.

In many Mediterranean areas such as Sicily, a man living outside the urban walls as a rural worker and country resident is almost unknown. This is a product of century-long insecurity. By contrast in old Hellas the Spartan polis sparkled by the absence of walls, yet the property of being a "garrison-town" was met. Sparta despised walls for the very reason that it was a permanent open military camp.

. . .

The city was neither the sole nor oldest fortress. In disputed frontier territory and during chronic states of war, every village fortified itself. Under the constant danger of attack in the area of the Elbe and Oder Rivers Slavic settlements were fortified; the national form of the rural village seems early to have been standardized in the form of the "hedge-enclosed" circular area with a single entrance which could be locked and through which at night cattle were driven to the central protection of the village area. Similarly, walled hill retreats were diffused throughout the world from Israelite East Jordan to Germanic territories. Unarmed persons and cattle took refuge within in times of danger. The so-called "cities" of Henry I in the German East were merely systematically established fortresses of this sort.

In England during the Anglo-Saxon period a "burgh" (borough) belonged to each shire whose name it took. Guard and garrison duty as the oldest specifically "civic" obligations were attached to certain persons or pieces of land. When in normal times such fortresses were occupied, guards or vassals were maintained as a permanent garrison and paid in salaries or in land. There were fluid transitions from the permanently garrisoned fortress to the Anglo-Saxon burgh, the "garrison-city," in the sense of Maitland's theory, with a "burgess" as inhabitants. The burgess received its name from its political position which like the legal nature of its civic land and house property was determined by the duty of maintaining and guarding the fortress.

However, historically neither the palisaded village nor the emergency fortification are the primary fore-runners of the city fortress, which was, rather, the manorial castle. The manorial castle was a fortress occupied by the lord and warriors subordinated to him as officials or as a personal following, together with their families and servants.

Military castle construction is very old, doubtlessly older than the chariot and military use of the horse. Like the war chariot the importance of the castle was determined by the development of knightly and royal warfare. In old China of the classic songs, in India of the Vedas, in Egypt and Mesopotamia, in Canaan, in Israel at the time of the Song of Deborah, in Greece during the period of the Homeric epics, and among the Etruscans, Celts, and Irish, the building of castles and the castle-principality were diffused universally. . . .

In the period of Christianization, castle construction was pressed in Russia. It appears also during the dynasty of Thutmose in Syria at the time of the Israelite confederation (Abimelech). Old Chinese literature also provides irrefutable evidence of its original occurrence. The Hellenic and Asia Minor sea-castle was as universally diffused as piracy. There must have been an interim period of especially deep pacification to allow the Cretan unfortified palaces to arise in the place of the castle. In this area later castles like the Decelia,[2] so important in the Peloponnesian Wars, were originally fortresses of noble families.

The medieval development of a politically independent gentry opened with the *castelli* in Italy. In Northern Europe the independence of the vassals was also bound up with enormous castle construction as established by Below.[3] Even in modern times individual deputyship in Germany has been dependent upon possession by the family of a castle, even if only the meager ruins of one. Disposal of a castle originally signified military dominion over the country. The only question was: In whose hands? It could be in the hands of the individual lords, or confederations of knights, or of a ruler who could depend on the trustworthiness of his vassals, ministers, or officers.

THE CITY AS THE FUSION OF FORTRESS AND MARKET

In the first stage of its development into a special political form the fortified city was incorporated in or dependent upon a castle, the fortress of a
king, noblemen, or association of knights. Such nobles either resided in
the fortress themselves or maintained a garrison of mercenaries, vassals,
or servants therein. In Anglo-Saxon England the right to possess a "haw,"
a fortified house in a "burgh," was bestowed as a privilege on certain land
owners of the surrounding countryside. In Antiquity and Medieval Italy
the cityhouse of the nobleman was held in addition to his rural castle.
The inhabitants or residents adjoining the castle, sometimes all, sometimes special strata, were bound as citizens (burgess) to the performance
of certain military duties such as building and repair of the walls, guard
duty, defense service and, at times, other military services such as communication and supply for the urban military noble. In this instance the
burger is a member of his estate because, and insofar as, he participates in
the military association of the city.

.   .   .

The relation between the garrison of the political fortress and the civil
economic population is complicated but always decisively important for
the composition of the city. Wherever a castle existed artisans came or
were settled for the satisfaction of manorial wants and the needs of the
warriors. The consumption power of a prince's military household and
the protection it guaranteed attracted the merchants. Moreover the lord
was interested in attracting these classes since he was in position to procure money revenues through them either by taxing commerce or trade
or participating in it through capital advances. At times the lord engaged
in commerce on his own, even monopolizing it. In maritime castles as
ship owner or ruler of the port the lord was in a position to procure a
share in piratical or peacefully won sea-borne profits. His followers and
vassals resident in the place were also in position to profit whether he vol-
untarily gave them permission or, being dependent on their good will,
was forced to do so.

.   .   .

. . . in early Antiquity and in the Middle Ages the urban commercial
capitalists, the financiers of commerce, the specific notable persons of the
city, have to be separated in principle from the domiciled holders of commercial "establishments," the merchants proper. To be sure, the strata

often blended into each other. However, with this we already anticipate later explanations.

In the hinterland, shipping points, terminals, crossings of rivers and caravan routes (for example, Babylon) could become locations of similar developments. At times competition arose between the priest of the temple, and priestly lord of the city, for temple districts of famous gods offered sacred protection to inter-ethnic elements. Such areas could provide locations for politically unprotected commerce. Thus a city-like settlement, economically supplied by temple revenues, could attach itself to the temple district in a matter similar to the princely city with its tributes to the prince.

Individual cases varied depending on the extent to which the prince's interest in monetary revenues predominated in the granting of privileges for merchandising and manufacturing independent of the lordly household and taxed by the lord. On the other hand, the lord could be interested in satisfying his own needs, hence in acting in ways strengthening his own powers and monopolizing trade in his own hands. When attracting foreigners by offering special privileges the lord also had to take into consideration the interests and "established" ability (which was also important for himself) of those already resident, who were dependent on his political protection or manorial supplies.

To this variety of possible development must be added the effects of the political-militaristic structure of the dominating group within which the founding of the city or its development occurred. We must consider the main antitheses in city development arising therefrom.

ASSOCIATIONAL AND STATUS PECULIARITIES OF THE OCCIDENTAL CITY

Neither the "city," in the economic sense, nor the garrison, the inhabitants of which are accoutred with special political-administrative structures, necessarily constitute a "community." An urban "community," in the full meaning of the word, appears as a general phenomenon only in the Occident. Exceptions occasionally were to be found in the Near East (in Syria, Phoenicia, and Mesopotamia) but only occasionally and in rudiments. To constitute a full urban community a settlement must display a relative predominance of trade-commercial relations with the settlement as a whole displaying the following features: 1. a fortification, 2. a market; 3. a court of its own and at least partially autonomous law; 4. a related form of association; and 5. at least partial autonomy and autocephaly, thus also an administration by authorities in the election of whom the burghers participated.

In the past, rights such as those which define the urban community were normally privileges of the estates. The peculiar political properties of the urban community appeared only with the presence of a special stratum, a distinct new estate. Measured by this rule the "cities" of the Occidental Middle Ages only qualify in part as true cities; even the cities of the eighteenth century were genuine urban communities only in minor degree. Finally measured by this rule, with possible isolated exceptions, the cities of Asia were not urban communities at all even though they all had markets and were fortresses.

All large seats of trade and commerce in China and most of the small ones were fortified. This was true also for Egyptian, Near Eastern, and Indian centers of commerce and trade. Not infrequently the large centers of trade and commerce of those countries were also separate jurisdictional districts. In China, Egypt, the Near East, and India the large commercial centers have also been seats of large political associations—a phenomenon not characteristic of Medieval Occidental cities, especially those of the North. Thus, many, but not all of the essential elements of the true urban community were at hand. However, the possession by the urbanites of a special substantive or trial law or of courts autonomously nominated by them were unknown to Asiatic cities. Only to the extent that guilds or castes (in India) were located in cities did they develop courts and a special law. Urban location of these associations was legally incidental. Autonomous administration was unknown or only vestigial.

If anything, even more important than the relative absence of autonomous administration, the appearance in the city of an association of urbanites in contradiction to the countryman was also found only in rudiments. The Chinese urban dweller legally belonged to his family and native village in which the temple of his ancestors stood and to which he conscientiously maintained affiliation. This is similar to the Russian village-comrade, earning his livelihood in the city but legally remaining a peasant. The Indian urban dweller remained a member of the caste. As a rule urban dwellers were also members of local professional associations, such as crafts and guilds of specific urban location. Finally they belonged to administrative districts such as the city wards and street districts into which the city was divided by the magisterial police.

. . .

In Near Eastern Egyptian antiquity the cities were fortresses and official administrative centers with royal market privileges. However, in the period of the dominion of the great kingdom they lacked autonomy, community organizations, and a privileged citizen estate. In Egypt during the Middle Empire office feudalism existed; in the New Empire a bureaucratic administration of clerks appeared. "Civic privileges" were bestowed on feudal or prebendal office holders in localities comparable to the privileges of bishops in old Germany. However, civic rights were not bestowed on an autonomous citizenry and even the beginnings of a "city patriciate" have not been found.

In contrast to the complete absence of a citizenry in ancient Egypt were the phenomena in Mesopotamia, Syria and especially Phoenicia, where at an early period typical city-kingdoms emerged at intersection points of sea and caravan traffic. Such civic kingdoms were of intensified sacred-secular character. They were also typified by the rising power of patrician families in the "city-house" (bitu in the Tel-el-Amarna tablets) in the period of charioteering.[4] In the Canaanite city an association of chariot-fighting knights possessing urban residences appeared. This knighthood kept the peasant farmers in a state of debt servitude and clientship as in the case of the early Hellenic polis. It was obviously similar in Mesopotamia where the "patrician," as a land-owning full burgher economically qualified for war service, is separated from the peasant. Immunities and privileges of this stratum were chartered by the king. However, with the mounting military power of the government this also disappeared. Politically autonomous cities and a burgher stratum of Occidental type are as little to be found in Mesopotamia as is a special urban law alongside royal law.

Only in Phoenicia did the landed patriciate engaging in commerce with its capital manage to maintain its dominion over the city state. However, the coins of the time *am Sôr* and *am Karthadast* in Tyre and Carthage hardly indicate the presence of a ruling "demos" and if such was ever the case it was only at a later time. Thus a true citizenry only partly developed. In Israel, Juda became a city-state but the elders (*sekenium*) who in the early period governed the administration as chieftains of patrician sibs were thrust into the background by the royal administration. The *gibborim* (knights) became royal attendants and soldiers. In contrast to the countryside, the royal *sarim* (officials) ruled in the large cities. Only after the exile did the community (*kahal*) or fellowship (*cheber*) appear as an institution on a confessional basis under the rule of priestly families.[15]

Nevertheless, all these phenomena indicate that here on the coasts of the Mediterranean Sea and on the Euphrates appeared the first real analogies of a civic development equivalent to that of Rome at the time of the reception of the Gens Claudia. The city is ruled by a patriciate resident in the city with powers resting on monetary wealth primarily won in commerce and secondarily invested in landed property, debt slaves and war slaves. The military power of the urban patriciate was a product of its training for knightly warfare, a training often spent in feuds against one another. The patricians were interlocally diffused and united with the king or *schofeten* or *sekenim* as *primus inter pares*. Such a patriciate like the Roman nobility with consuls was threatened by the tyranny of the charismatic war king relying upon recruited bodyguards (Abimelech, Jepthah, David). Prior to the Hellenic period this stage of urban development was nowhere permanently surpassed.

CHAPTER FOUR

URBAN MAN

Simmel, Wirth, Marx, Gans, Whyte, and Riesman—the authors of the selections that make up this chapter—all write about one or another aspect of urban man as a personality. Each in turn examines the characteristic intellectual processes of the urbanite, his typical attitudes and values, particularly the estrangement that is thought to be one of his most fundamental attributes, and also the ways in which the modern, changing city is affecting him psychologically. The psychology of urban life is both the cause and effect of the city as an ecological, demographic, and institutional system, and though serious issues are raised in the literature concerning the social psychology of the city, a fairly unified body of thought does exist on the subject.

Urban personality has been likened to the "psychic space" of the city in contrast with its physical space, and the ecology of this space has been mapped by numerous theorists and empirical investigators. Their basic insight has been the principle of the economy of effort. More than anything else this has been thought to characterize urban man, for urban society is largely the organization of individuals pursuing their own personal self-interests, and as such the city conditions its participants to manifest functionally valuable and expeditious forms of behavior.

Four cardinal directions of sociopsychological development have thus been observed, or at least postulated, in the city. Urbanites segmentalize their social contacts, and though their relationships may at times become very intense, at any given moment they remain narrowly focused on single tasks or needs. Much role switching is there-

fore required in order to exist effectively. Secondly, this mode of behavior means that the city person stereotypes others, thereby
quickly orienting himself to situations. Such crude classifications
may distort reality but they are essential if multiple associations are
to be carried on. In the third place, city life calls for one to heed
standardized symbols and to respond promptly to the codes of behavior that are in force. And, finally, urbanism dictates that the individual cultivate an emotionally shallow mode of response, or a
sense of indifferent detachment in order to conserve his psychic energy by avoiding strong emotional ties that would prevent prompt
reorientation whenever that became necessary.

Urban personality is, therefore, situation-centered. That is, instead of possessing persistent attitudes, the urbanite learns to behave in terms of specific settings and relationships. James Quinn observes that the urban psychological type embodies a calculating
attitude, that he is sensitive to appearances, that he is conscious of
time, and that he has confidence in the efficacy of deliberate, rational social controls.[1] Rose Hum Lee echoes this delineation, at-
tributing it to "the social interaction, competition, accommodation,
and selective segregation" that prevails in the urban milieu.[2] One
may readily cite empirical field studies by, for example, Wirth, Anderson, Zorbaugh, and Samuel Strong in support of this conclusion.[3]

Economic pressures are a major source of social control in the
city. They are related to the cultural values placed on pecuniary
success and style of life but they do indicate the basic rationality of
urban life, a point emphasized in the writings of Max Weber. Law
is another primary component of control, although despite apparent specificity, as in housing codes, business regulations, educational
administration, and domestic statutes, minute specifications are the
product of localized social routines structured to maximize convenience, the economy of behavior, and the efficient definition of situations.

These considerations suggest that the urban mass is typically engaged in nonconsensual relations. In contrast to folk society, which
relies on traditions and customary ceremonials to invoke, express,
and reinforce cultural unity and individual identity, the urban social order enjoys whatever concensus it has chiefly, it seems, as the
result of negotiation, contract, and other equally formal means.
True, as Louis Wirth has pointed out, other methods, such as force,
identification with great heroes, and the invocation of tradition, are
not entirely absent from urban society. However, the maintenance
of solidarity in the urban environment seems to fall most squarely
on the mass media, and this turns out to be an unending process of
continuous adjustment. Television, radio, newspapers, and movies

appear in large measure to have replaced the school and the church as the primary sources of information, influence, and control. Even here though, following Lazarsfeld's research, we are reminded that ideational diffusion finally rests on individual "influentials" and interpersonal relations rather than on the direct impact of the media.[4] In this respect then, the general conception of urban personality that has been theorized needs further clarification.

In fact, close scrutiny of the urban social system and urban personalities has cast some serious doubt on the soundness of the typological characterization of urban personality. C. A. McMahan's review of a number of urban-personality studies concludes that no distinct type actually exists and that the literature itself is unclean.[5] This unitary concept has indeed been refined to the point where three ideal-type urban personalities have been hypothesized. One personality type cultivates detachment in order to preserve his integrity, but in so doing suffers from feelings of resignation, insignificance, and powerlessness. The second relinquishes every desire for self-expression and compulsively adheres to the prevailing patterns. The third, in an unsophisticated way, accepts the urban social system as a moral order but also retains a conviction of some deeper meaning and of an ultimate system of values apart from and greater than its economic calculus, careerism, and expediency. Each of these types denotes the instability that is inherent in the theoretically postulated urban type and the existence of other elements in the urbanite's makeup.

Status symbols take on greater importance in the city, where anonymity amidst a large, dense, and heterogeneous population is so prevalent among persons who must interact for functional reasons alone if nothing else. Such symbols—speech patterns, dress, accouterments, and manners—not only signify rank but as Erving Goffman has demonstrated, also express different value-orientations and styles of life.[6] Personality, in the sense of projecting oneself in a favorable light, is valued by the urbanite. As Goethe has said, character is built in solitude, style in public. This tendency is understandable when one realizes that the city dweller is seldom in a position to weigh complex questions carefully. He has to rely on appearances, on brief utterances made in a welter of competing claims that are both genuine and spurious. It is often true, however, that underneath the surface coolness and sang-froid attitude of the urbanite there exists a neurotic-like agitation over one's tense, estranged participation in a segmented, role-playing society, a great deal of insecurity, and correspondingly a hungry search for adherence to truly moral and dependable persons.

For all of its gratifications, such as a relatively high level of living, short hours and good conditions of work, cultural opportunities, and psychological stimulation, city life also creates tensions—the tension of subservience to the machine, to the press of the population, to gross inequalities in power and the amenities of life. Role conflict is perhaps endemic in urban society: between the ideal of freedom and the actuality of dependence on being employed; between the code of Christian charity, or magnanimity, and economic individualism; between democratic participation and inter-group discrimination. It was Karl Marx who first advanced the idea of alienation as arising from the new factory system of the Industrial Revolution and as being reinforced by the mode of life in the new cities that were growing up. The worker, he observed, was now separated from the ownership of his tools and also from the management of the work process. As a result, he had been rendered powerless, since he had become merely an instrument toward others' ends. With the loss of his autonomy, the industrial, urban worker had also lost his morale. True, this persuasive theory ignores the diversity of the social systems that make up industrial society and, like informal organization and countervailing power, help to allocate control and, correspondingly, restore morale. It does, however, make a vital point.

The reality of alienation cannot be simply dismissed. It crops up when the city dweller experiences himself as a stranger, as an insignificant cipher in a vast calculus. Neighboring is attenuated. Local groups find themselves merely cells in larger organizations with whom they have become affiliated in an attempt to express themselves at the city, state, and national levels. Dissociation also results from the lack of property ownership as well as from mobility and the spurious public opinion articulated by the leaders of complex organizations striving to advance their own interests and policies.

Anxiety, or dull displeasure, may indeed be the normal urban condition. Riesman has certainly sensitized modern scholarship to the "vague disquietude of lonely individuals" in the urban social structure.[7] And endemic culture conflict might also be assumed to be the result of the divergent standards of the many subcultures that coexist in a city. Numerous role-switches habituate one to fluid priorities and criteria instead of stable standards. These are also conducive to schizophrenic-like disorientation. For example, the need for affiliation may result in group membership, but owing to the lack of intimate experience the urbanite may address himself to stereotypes, that is, the kind of people he imagines himself to be dealing with in trying to cope with his problems. Thus the labor leader is viewed as a reformer instead of a bureaucratic administrator, and the citizens' group president as an effective diplomat instead of a deprived, compensating personality. In fact, status differences themselves give rise to differences in perception and evaluation. For example, high status persons tend to believe that their social inferiors are more pecuniarily motivated than they themselves are. The result is mutual misunderstanding and uncertainty of expectation.

It is scarcely any wonder then that scholars have repeatedly hurled imprecations at urban man. In *Democratic Vistas,* Walt Whitman contrasted "the splendor, picturesqueness, and oceanic amplitude and rush" of the great cities, with their populations consisting of "petty grotesques, malformations, phantoms, playing meaningless antics," pervaded by "flippancy and vulgarity, low cunning, infidelity . . . an abnormal libidinousness . . . with a range of manners, or rather lack of manners (considering the advantages enjoy'd) , probably the meanest to be seen in the world." Whitman is not alone in his attitude. Indeed, a large volume of criticism, often presented as objective analysis, has long been directed against urban man as a personality. Two newer lines of thought have, moreover, recently begun to be pursued in relation to this—one condemning the suburban variant of the basic urban personality and the other criticizing the dehumanized personality of man in mass society. Both of these, of course, constitute critiques on the basic conception of urban man.

The sociology of suburbia is typically deprecatory, with life in the suburbs described as dull, hypocritical, crass, and slothful. Strictures against the suburban mentality, however, shade into the condemnation of mass society so that the two subjects are not uncommonly assimilated to each other. Thus, Daniel Bell has disclosed that as a term mass society is used to refer to lack of differentiation, incompetence, mechanization, bureaucratic organization, and also alienation and aimlessness.[8] With the massive movement of population to the suburbs, suburbia has come to be considered the incipient urbanism of the future. It has also been thought the model of mass society, at least its contemporary form. In the minds of perhaps the majority of writers mass society denotes the standardization of taste, of attitude, of style of life, and of behavior. These attributes are supposed to result from mass fabrication, for one thing, so that limited-choice processed foods, like tasteless bread, tend to erase ethnic differences. National firms undercut local businesses and suppliers. Standardization is clearly economical though critics deplore the vulgarization of culture that commercial enterprise has helped cultivate or produce.

Of late, however, a counter trend has been emerging in the sociological literature. Leonard Reissman and Thomas Ktsanes have questioned the suburban critique with the observation that similar architecture and position in the life cycle may have been mistaken for sociopsychological homogeneity, though they are only outward or transitory similarities.[9] They say that suburban value conflicts have been ignored, as between the Protestant ethic and hedonism. In passing it may be noted that unanticipated reversals are taking place, like the Democratic resurgence and ethnic reidentification of suburbanites.

Defenders of suburban and mass culture reject the reactionary élitism of the critics who they say are defending an essentially "literary" culture. Instead they view the leisure culture as classless and are more sympathetic toward it. Paradoxically, the qualities of mass society that critical observers have felt were adverse to democracy are coming to be viewed as supportive of democratic institutions. Among these are a national instead of local orientation; a nationwide consensus in place of a pluralism of values (the former stemming, it may be conjectured, from horizontal professional groupings); tolerance and blandness rather than philosophic intensity; and the ready acceptance of change and innovation.

Some writers conclude that the suburbs represent a new subculture that is a significant departure from the mode of life and corresponding personality type of traditional theory. It is not always recognized, however, that suburbs vary, and vary a good deal, too. There are, among other variations, the marginal fringe, the planned community, the exurb, and the industrial satellite. These have been documented by Walter Firey, A. C. Spectorsky, Herbert Gans, and Evelyn M. Kitagawa and Donald J. Bogue.[10] Socio-psychological correlates have been drawn from various suburban populations, such as proclivities to child-centering and mutual aid. In his selection, David Riesman ascribes non-vocationalism, low-key hedonism, moral blandness, and general aimlessness to the suburban mind.

Riesman's study of character change in history, which associates other-directedness with modern Western urban society, sees commercial contacts as being more and more carried out in a spirit of friendliness quite in contrast with the predatory nature attributed to urban man by the typologists. No hard distinction is any longer being made between business and play, for instance. The tasteful use of leisure is now a requirement. The expected cultural consequences of crass exploitation are thus being put in doubt. Yet the dire implications of early theory are not entirely inconsistent with Riesman's formulations. Other-directed political involvement, to take one case, is a mixture of participation and passivity where the individual knows what he likes but not what he wants, and sincerity counts for more than competence. Another is the multiplication of veto groups, which gives us again the picture of urban society that Wirth drew of it a long time ago, that is, a mosaic of discrete self-interest associations and publics.

Svend Riemer is among those who have cogently raised the question of just how valid the concept of urban personality is.[11] He has, in fact, proposed "tertiary group" as expressive of urban behavior, in other words, an emotional attachment such as we find in the primary group but one that is oriented to the institutions and processes of the community—shopping centers, bond issues, the local school system, and the rest—rather than to specific personalities. This conception skirts the rational, egotistic, instrumental relationships of secondary organization. And there is much evidence to support this new idea. Economic ties are certainly present in the city, but pure economic man is a myth. In fact, social relationships are inseparable from economic behavior. For example, only people who are indifferent to economic loss fail to carry on the quasi-personal social contacts that are expected in the neighborhood, service club, church, labor union, business association, and political community. Exclusively economic action is self-defeating. Indeed, participation in voluntary and informal group life correlates very strongly with social status, education, and wealth, the very factors that epitomize urbanism.

Walter Firey has observed that although the city is a remarkably functional system, there are many nonutilitarian elements in it. So, too, the personality of urban man. It may at bottom be economically motivated and rationally oriented. But it also gives signs of sentimental and purely social attachments as well. Not only are these latter configurations in need of more precise understanding, they appear to be in the process of rapid change.

14. THE METROPOLIS AND MENTAL LIFE

Georg Simmel

Simmel's analysis of urban consciousness is handicapped by two things—an outmoded sensory psychology and the romantic German philosophy of the nineteenth century, which condemned the city as spiritually pernicious. Nevertheless, his trenchant insights into the sociopsychological consequences of the urban milieu have had lasting scientific value. One need only call attention to Veblen, Wirth, and Riesman.

Whatever the time or place, the city exerts a variety of conditioning forces upon the people that live within its social and cultural framework. Intensive stimulation creates a sophisticated, blasé personality. The city's money economy gives rise to a trucking and bartering posture in which the mental habits of precise calculation are at a premium, and cool reserve becomes essential to competitive success. Indeed, dissociative, defensive hostility is required to give one protection from predatory exploitation at the hands of one's fellow city residents.

However, in spite of these pejorative findings, Simmel recognizes that the urban marketplace occasions a greater and greater division of labor and, accordingly, individual specialization to the point where each person is capable of providing a virtually unique, hence saleable, service. Yet such freedom of expression is spurious, for it does not embody "true" human character. No matter how diverse men become in the city, the social distance they maintain and the competitive stance they exhibit toward their neighbors rob them of real independence, which is the manifestation of the "general human being" in every individual.

Excerpts from *The Sociology of Georg Simmel*, edited and translated by Kurt Wolff, reprinted with permission of The Macmillan Company. © 1955 by The Free Press, a Corporation.

THE PSYCHOLOGICAL BASIS of the metropolitan type of individuality consists in the *intensification of nervous stimulation* which results from the swift and uninterrupted change of outer and inner stimuli. . . . With each crossing of the street, with the tempo and multiplicity of economic, occupational and social life, the city sets up a deep contrast with small town and rural life with reference to the sensory foundations of psychic life. The metropolis exacts from man as a discriminating creature a different amount of consciousness than does rural life. Here the rhythm of life and sensory mental imagery flows more slowly, more habitually, and more evenly. Precisely in this connection the sophisticated character of metropolitan psychic life becomes understandable—as over against small town life which rests more upon deeply felt and emotional relationships. . . .

The metropolis has always been the seat of the money economy. Here the multiplicity and concentration of economic exchange gives an importance to the means of exchange which the scantiness of rural commerce would not have allowed. Money economy and the dominance of the intellect are intrinsically connected. They share a matter-of-fact attitude in dealing with men and with things; and, in this attitude, a formal justice is often coupled with an inconsiderate hardness. The intellectually sophisticated person is indifferent to all genuine individuality, because relationships and reactions result from it which cannot be exhausted with logical operations. In the same manner, the individuality of phenomena is not commensurate with the pecuniary principle. Money is concerned only with what is common to all: it asks for the exchange value, it reduces all quality and individuality to the question: How much? All intimate emotional relations between persons are founded in their individuality, whereas in rational relations man is reckoned with like a number, like an element which is in itself indifferent. Only the objective measurable achievement is of interest. Thus metropolitan man reckons with his merchants and customers, his domestic servants and often even with persons with whom he is obliged to have social intercourse. These features of intellectuality contrast with the nature of the small circle in which the inevitable knowledge of individuality as inevitably produces a warmer tone of behavior, a behavior which is beyond a mere objective balancing of service and return. In the sphere of the economic psychology of the small group it is of importance that under primitive conditions production serves the customer who orders the good, so that the producer and the consumer are acquainted. The modern metropolis, however, is supplied almost entirely by production for the market, that is, for entirely unknown purchasers who never personally enter the producer's actual field of vision. Through this anonymity the interests of each party acquire an unmerciful matter-of-factness; and the intellectually calculating economic egoism of both parties need not fear any deflection because of the imponderables of personal relationships. The money economy dominates the metropolis; it has displaced the last survivals of domestic production and the direct barter of goods; it minimizes, from day to day, the amount of work ordered by customers. The matter-of-fact attitude is obviously so intimately interrelated with the money economy, which is dominant in the metropolis, that nobody can say whether the intellectualistic mentality first promoted the money economy or whether the latter determined the former. The metropolitan way of life is certainly the most fertile soil for this reciprocity, a point which I shall document merely by citing the dictum of the most eminent English constitutional historian: throughout the whole course of English history, London has never acted as England's heart but often as England's intellect and always as her moneybag!

In certain seemingly insignificant traits, which lie upon the surface of life, the same psychic currents characteristically unite. Modern mind has become more and more calculating. The calculative exactness of practical life which the money economy has brought about corresponds to the ideal of natural science: to transform the world into an arithmetic problem, to fix every part of the world by mathematical formulas. Only [the] money economy has filled the days of so many people with weighing, calculating, with numerical determinations, with a reduction of qualitative values to quantitative ones. Through the calculative nature of money a new precision, a certainty in the definition of identities and differences, an unambiguousness in agreements and arrangements has been brought about in the relations of life-elements—just as externally this precision has been effected by the universal diffusion of pocket watches. However, the conditions of metropolitan life are at once cause and effect of this trait. The relationships and affairs of the typical metropolitan usually are so varied and complex that without the strictest punctuality in promises and services the whole structure would break down into an inextricable chaos. Above all, this necessity is brought about by the aggregation of so many people with such differentiated interests, who must integrate their relations and activities into a highly complex organism. If all clocks and watches in Berlin would suddenly go wrong in different ways, even if only by one hour, all economic life and communication of the city would be disrupted for a long time. In addition an apparently mere external factor: long distances, would make all waiting and broken appointments result in an ill-afforded waste of time. Thus, the technique of metropolitan life is unimaginable without the most punctual integration of all activities and mutual relations into a stable and impersonal time schedule. Here again the general conclusions of this entire task of reflection become obvious; namely, that from each point on the surface of existence—however closely attached to the surface alone—one may drop a sounding into the depth of the psyche so that all the most banal externalities of life finally are connected with the ultimate decisions concerning the meaning and style of life. Punctuality, calculability, exactness are forced upon life by the complexity and extension of metropolitan existence and are not only most intimately connected with its money economy and intellectual-istic character. These traits must also color the contents of life and favor the exclusion of those irrational, instinctive, sovereign traits and impulses which aim at determining the mode of life from within, instead of receiving the general and precisely schematized form of life from without. Even though sovereign types of personality, characterized by irrational impulses, are by no means impossible in the city, they are, nevertheless, opposed to typical city life. The passionate hatred of men like Ruskin and Nietzsche for the metropolis is understandable in these terms. Their natures discovered the value of life alone in the unschematized existence which cannot be defined with precision for all alike. From the same source of this hatred of the metropolis surged their hatred of [the] money economy and of the intellectualism of modern existence.

The same factors which have thus coalesced into the exactness and minute precision of the form of life have coalesced into a structure of the highest impersonality; on the other hand, they have promoted a highly personal subjectivity. There is perhaps no psychic phenomenon which has been so unconditionally reserved to the metropolis as has the blasé attitude. The blasé attitude results first from the rapidly changing and closely compressed contrasting stimulations of the nerves. . . . In the same way, through the rapidity and contradictoriness of their changes, more harmless impressions force such violent responses, tearing the nerves so brutally hither and thither that their last reserves of strength are spent; and if one remains in the same milieu they have no time to gather new strength. An incapacity thus emerges to react to new sensations with the appropriate energy. This constitutes that blasé attitude which, in fact, every metropolitan child shows when compared with children of quieter and less changeable milieus.

This physiological source of the metropolitan blasé attitude is joined by another source which flows from the money economy. The essence of the blasé attitude consists in the blunting of discrimination. . . . For money expresses all qualitative differences of things in terms of "how much?" Money, with all its colorlessness and indifference, becomes the common denominator of all values; irreparably it hollows out the core of things, their individuality, their specific value, and their incomparability. All things float with equal specific gravity in the constantly moving stream of money. All things lie on the same level and differ from one another only in the size of the area which they cover. . . . The large cities, the main seats of the money exchange, bring the purchasability of things to the fore much more impressively than do smaller localities. That is why cities are also the genuine locale of the blasé attitude. In the blasé attitude the concentration of men and things stimulate the nervous system of the individual to its highest achievement so that it attains its peak. Through the mere quantitative intensification of the same conditioning

factors this achievement is transformed into its opposite and appears in
the peculiar adjustment of the blasé attitude. . . .

. . . This mental attitude of metropolitans toward one another we
may designate, from a formal point of view, as reserve. If so many inner
reactions were responses to the continuous external contacts with innumerable people as are those in the small town, where one knows almost
everybody one meets and where one has a positive relation to almost
everyone, one would be completely atomized internally and come to an
unimaginable psychic state. Partly this psychological fact, partly the right
to distrust which men have in the face of the touch-and-go elements of
metropolitan life, necessitates our reserve. As a result of this reserve we
frequently do not even know by sight those who have been our neighbors
for years. And it is this reserve which in the eyes of the small-town people
makes us appear to be cold and heartless. Indeed, if I do not deceive myself, the inner aspect of this outer reserve is not only indifference but,
more often than we are aware, it is a slight aversion, a mutual strangeness
and repulsion, which will break into hatred and fight at the moment of a
closer contact, however caused. . . . A latent antipathy and the prepara-
tory stage of practical antagonism effect the distances and aversions without which this mode of life could not at all be led. The extent and the
mixture of this style of life, the rhythm of its emergence and disappearance, the forms in which it is satisfied—all these, with the unifying motives in the narrower sense, form the inseparable whole of the metropolitan style of life. What appears in the metropolitan style of life directly as
dissociation is in reality only one of its elemental forms of socialization.

This reserve with its overtone of hidden aversion appears in turn as the
form or the cloak of a more general mental phenomenon of the metropolis: it grants to the individual a kind and an amount of personal freedom
which has no analogy whatsoever under other conditions. The metropolis
goes back to one of the large developmental tendencies of social life as
such, to one of the few tendencies for which an approximately universal
formula can be discovered. The earliest phase of social formations found
in historical as well as in contemporary social structures is this: a relatively small circle firmly closed against neighboring, strange, or in some
way antagonistic circles. However, this circle is closely coherent and allows its individual members only a narrow field for the development of
unique qualities and free, self-responsible movements. Political and kinship groups, parties and religious associations begin in this way. . . . The
small-town life in Antiquity and in the Middle Ages set barriers against
movement and relations of the individual toward the outside, and it set
up barriers against individual independence and differentiation within
the individual self. These barriers were such that under them modern
man could not have breathed. Even today a metropolitan man who is
placed in a small town feels a restriction similar, at least, in kind. The
smaller the circle which forms our milieu is, and the more restricted those

relations to others are which dissolve the boundaries of the individual, the more anxiously the circle guards the achievements, the conduct of life, and the outlook of the individual, and the more readily a quantitative and qualitative specialization would break up the framework of the whole little circle.

The ancient *polis* in this respect seems to have had the very character of a small town. The constant threat to its existence at the hands of enemies from near and afar effected strict coherence in political and military respects, a supervision of the citizen, a jealousy of the whole against the individual whose particular life was suppressed to such a degree that he could compensate only by acting as a despot in his own household. The tremendous agitation and excitement, the unique colorfulness of Athenian life, can perhaps be understood in terms of the fact that a people of incomparably individualized personalities struggled against the constant inner and outer pressure of a de-individualizing small town. . . . Just as in the feudal age, the "free" man was the one who stood under the law of the land, that is, under the law of the largest social orbit, and the unfree man was the one who derived his right merely from the narrow circle of a feudal association and was excluded from the larger social orbit—so today metropolitan man is "free" in a spiritualized and refined sense, in contrast to the pettiness and prejudices which hem in the small-town man. For the reciprocal reserve and indifference and the intellectual life conditions of large circles are never felt more strongly by the individual in their impact upon his independence than in the thickest crowd of the big city. This is because the bodily proximity and narrowness of space makes the mental distance only the more visible. It is obviously only the obverse of this freedom if, under certain circumstances, one nowhere feels as lonely and lost as in the metropolitan crowd. For here as elsewhere it is by no means necessary that the freedom of man be reflected in his emotional life as comfort.

It is not only the immediate size of the area and the number of persons which, because of the universal historical correlation between the enlargement of the circle and the personal inner and outer freedom, has made the metropolis the locale of freedom. It is rather in transcending this visible expanse that any given city becomes the seat of cosmopolitanism. The horizon of the city expands in a manner comparable to the way in which wealth develops; a certain amount of property increases in a quasi-automatical way in ever more rapid progression. As soon as a certain limit has been passed, the economic, personal, and intellectual relations of the citizenry, the sphere of intellectual predominance of the city over its hinterland, grow as in geometrical progression. Every gain in dynamic extension becomes a step, not for an equal, but for a new and larger extension. From every thread spinning out of the city, ever new threads grow as if by themselves, just as within the city the unearned increment of ground rent, through the mere increase in communication, brings the owner automatically increasing profits. At this point, the quantitative aspect of life is transformed directly into qualitative traits of character. . . . a city consists of its total effects which extend beyond its immediate confines. Only this range is the city's actual extent in which its existence is expressed. This fact makes it obvious that individual freedom, the logical and historical complement of such extension, is not to be understood only in the negative sense of mere freedom of mobility and elimination of prejudices and petty philistinism. The essential point is that the particularity and incomparability, which ultimately every human being possesses, be somehow expressed in the working-out of a way of life. . . .

Cities are, first of all, seats of the highest economic division of labor. They produce thereby such extreme phenomena as in Paris the remunerative occupation of the *quatorzième*. They are persons who identify themselves by signs on their residences and who are ready at the dinner hour in correct attire, so that they can be quickly called upon if a dinner party should consist of thirteen persons. In the measure of its expansion, the city offers more and more the decisive conditions of the division of labor. It offers a circle which through its size can absorb a highly diverse variety of services. At the same time, the concentration of individuals and their struggle for customers compel the individual to specialize in a function from which he cannot be readily displaced by another. It is decisive that city life has transformed the struggle with nature for livelihood into an inter-human struggle for gain, which here is not granted by nature but by other men. For specialization does not flow only from the competition for gain but also from the underlying fact that the seller must always seek to call forth new and differentiated needs of the lured customer. In order to find a source of income which is not yet exhausted, and to find a function which cannot readily be displaced, it is necessary to specialize in one's services. This process promotes differentiation, refinement, and the enrichment of the public's needs, which obviously must lead to growing personal differences within this public.

All this forms the transition to the individualization of mental and psychic traits which the city occasions in proportion to its size. There is a whole series of obvious causes underlying this process. First, one must meet the difficulty of asserting his own personality within the dimensions of metropolitan life. Where the quantitative increase in importance and the expense of energy reach their limits, one seizes upon qualitative differentiation in order somehow to attract the attention of the social circle by playing upon its sensitivity for differences. Finally, man is tempted to adopt the most tendentious peculiarities, that is, the specifically metropolitan extravagances of mannerism, caprice, and preciousness. Now, the meaning of these extravagances does not at all lie in the contents of such behavior, but rather in its form of "being different," of standing out in a striking manner and thereby attracting attention. For many character types, ultimately the only means of saving for themselves some modicum of self-esteem and the sense of filling a position is indirect, through the awareness of others. In the same sense a seemingly insignificant factor is operating, the cumulative effects of which are, however, still noticeable. I refer to the brevity and scarcity of the inter-human contacts granted to the metropolitan man, as compared with social intercourse in the small town. The temptation to appear "to the point," to appear concentrated and strikingly characteristic, lies much closer to the individual in brief metropolitan contacts than in an atmosphere in which frequent and prolonged association assured the personality of an unambiguous image of himself in the eyes of the other.

The most profound reason, however, why the metropolis conduces to the urge for the most individual personal existence—no matter whether justified and successful—appears to me to be the following: the development of modern culture is characterized by the preponderance of what one may call the "objective spirit" over the "subjective spirit." This is to say, in language as well as in law, in the technique of production as well as in art, in science as well as in the objects of the domestic environment, there is embodied a sum of spirit. The individual in his intellectual development follows the growth of this spirit very imperfectly and at an ever increasing distance. If, for instance, we view the immense culture which for the last hundred years has been embodied in things and in knowledge, in institutions and in comforts, and if we compare all this with the cultural progress of the individual during the same period—at least in high status groups—a frightful disproportion in growth between the two becomes evident. Indeed, at some points we notice a retrogression in the culture of the individual with reference to spirituality, delicacy, and idealism. This discrepancy results essentially from the growing division of labor. For the division of labor demands from the individual an ever more onesided accomplishment, and the greatest advance in a onesided pursuit only too frequently means dearth to the personality of the individual. In any case, he can cope less and less with the overgrowth of objective culture. The individual is reduced to a negligible quantity, perhaps less in his consciousness than in his practice and in the totality of his obscure emotional states that are derived from this practice. The individual has become a mere cog in an enormous organization of things and powers which tear from his hands all progress, spirituality, and value in order to transform them from their subjective form into the form of a purely objective life. It needs merely to be pointed out that the metropolis is the genuine arena of this culture which outgrows all personal life. Here in buildings and educational institutions, in the wonders and comforts of space-conquering technology, in the formations of community life, and in the visible institutions of the state, is offered such an overwhelming fullness of crystallized and impersonalized spirit that the personality, so to speak, cannot maintain itself under its impact. On the one hand, life is made infinitely easy for the personality in that stimulations, interests, uses of time and consciousness are offered to it from all sides. They carry the person as if in a stream, and one needs hardly to swim for oneself. On the other hand, however, life is composed more and more of these impersonal contents and offerings which tend to displace the genuine personal colorations and incomparabilities. This results in the individual's summoning the utmost in uniqueness and particularization, in order to preserve his most personal core. He has to exaggerate this personal element in order to remain audible even to himself. The atrophy of individual culture through the hypertrophy of objective culture is one reason for the bitter hatred which the preachers of the most extreme individualism, above all Nietzsche, harbor against the metropolis. But it is, indeed, also a reason why these preachers are so passionately loved in the metropolis and why they appear to the metropolitan man as the prophets and saviors of his most unsatisfied yearnings.

If one asks for the historical position of these two forms of individualism which are nourished by the quantitative relation of the metropolis, namely, individual independence and the elaboration of individuality itself, then the metropolis assumes an entirely new rank order in the world history of the spirit.

15. URBANISM AS A WAY OF LIFE

Louis Wirth

Wirth's paper on the social psychology of the urbanite has become a standard in American sociological literature. Defining the city as "a relatively large, dense and permanent settlement of socially heterogeneous individuals," Wirth proceeds to derive the attitudes and modes of behavior characteristic of the urban resident from the basic demographic variables of the urban community. City life, he finds, exhibits secondary relationships that are impersonal, segmental, superficial, transitory, and often predatory in nature. As a result of such social participation, urban man becomes anonymous, isolated, secular, relativistic, rational, and sophisticated in his cognitive and emotional orientations. These states of mind underlie a way of life in which the individual is reduced to virtual insignificance in a large and complex mass. Only when the individual joins with others of similar interests into organized associations does he attain his ends, and then, indeed; frequently at an advanced level of development.

EVER SINCE ARISTOTLE's *Politics,* it has been recognized that increasing the number of inhabitants in a settlement beyond a certain limit will affect the relationships between them and the character of the city. Large numbers involve, as has been pointed out, a greater range of individual variation. Furthermore, the greater the number of individuals participating in a process of interaction, the greater is the *potential* differentiation be-

Excerpts from the *American Journal of Sociology,* July 1938. Reprinted by permission of the University of Chicago Press.

tween them. The personal traits, the occupations, the cultural life, and the ideas of the members of an urban community may, therefore, be expected to range between more widely separated poles than those of rural inhabitants.

That such variations should give rise to the spatial segregation of individuals according to color, ethnic heritage, economic and social status, tastes and preferences, may readily be inferred. The bonds of kinship, of neighborliness, and the sentiments arising out of living together for generations under a common folk tradition are likely to be absent or, at best, relatively weak in an aggregate the members of which have such diverse origins and backgrounds. Under such circumstances competition and formal control mechanisms furnish the substitutes for the bonds of solidarity that are relied upon to hold a folk society together.

Increase in the number of inhabitants of a community beyond a few hundred is bound to limit the possibility of each member of the community knowing all the others personally. Max Weber, in recognizing the social significance of this fact, pointed out that from a sociological point of view large numbers of inhabitants and density of settlement mean that the personal mutual acquaintanceship between the inhabitants which ordinarily inheres in a neighborhood is lacking. The increase in numbers thus involves a changed character of the social relationships. As Simmel points out:

> [If] the unceasing external contact of numbers of persons in the city should be met by the same number of inner reactions as in the small town, in which one knows almost every person he meets and to each of whom he has a positive relationship, one would be completely atomized internally and would fall into an unthinkable mental condition.

The multiplication of persons in a state of interaction under conditions which make their contact as full personalities impossible produces that segmentalization of human relationships which has sometimes been seized upon by students of the mental life of the cities as an explanation for the "schizoid" character of urban personality. This is not to say that the urban inhabitants have fewer acquaintances than rural inhabitants, for the reverse may actually be true; it means rather that in relation to the number of people whom they see and with whom they rub elbows in the course of daily life, they know a smaller proportion, and of these they have less intensive knowledge.

Characteristically, urbanites meet one another in highly segmental roles. They are, to be sure, dependent upon more people for the satisfactions of their life-needs than are rural people and thus are associated with a greater number of organized groups, but they are less dependent upon particular persons, and their dependence upon others is confined to a highly fractionalized aspect of the other's round of activity. This is essentially what is meant by saying that the city is characterized by secondary rather than primary contacts. The contacts of the city may indeed be face to face, but they are nevertheless impersonal, superficial, transitory, and segmental. The reserve, the indifference, and the blasé outlook which urbanites manifest in their relationships may thus be regarded as devices for immunizing themselves against the personal claims and expectations of others.

The superficiality, the anonymity, and the transitory character of urban-social relations make intelligible, also, the sophistication and the rationality generally ascribed to city-dwellers. Our acquaintances tend to stand in a relationship of utility to us in the sense that the role which each one plays in our life is overwhelmingly regarded as a means for the achievement of our own ends. Whereas, therefore, the individual gains, on the one hand, a certain degree of emancipation or freedom from the personal and emotional controls of intimate groups, he loses, on the other hand, the spontaneous self-expression, the morale, and the sense of participation that comes with living in an integrated society. This constitutes essentially the state of _anomie_ or the social void to which Durkheim alludes in attempting to account for the various forms of social disorganization in technological society.

The segmental character and utilitarian accent of interpersonal relations in the city find their institutional expression in the proliferation of specialized tasks which we see in their most developed form in the professions. The operations of the pecuniary nexus leads to predatory relationships, which tend to obstruct the efficient functioning of the social order unless checked by professional codes and occupational etiquette. The premium put upon utility and efficiency suggests the adaptability of the corporate device for the organization of enterprises in which individuals can engage only in groups. The advantage that the corporation has over the individual entrepreneur and the partnership in the urban-industrial world derives not only from the possibility it affords of centralizing the resources of thousands of individuals or from the legal privilege of limited liability and perpetual succession, but from the fact that the corporation has no soul.

The specialization of individuals, particularly in their occupations, can proceed only, as Adam Smith pointed out, upon the basis of an enlarged market, which in turn accentuates the division of labor. This enlarged market is only in part supplied by the city's hinterland; in large measure it is found among the large numbers that the city itself contains. The dominance of the city over the surrounding hinterland becomes explicable in terms of the division of labor which urban life occasions and promotes. The extreme degree of interdependence and the unstable equilibrium of urban life are closely associated with the division of labor and the specialization of occupations. This interdependence and instability is increased by the tendency of each city to specialize in those functions in which it has the greatest advantage.

In a community composed of a larger number of individuals than can know one another intimately and can be assembled in one spot, it becomes necessary to communicate through indirect mediums and to articulate individual interests by a process of delegation. Typically in the city, interests are made effective through representation. The individual counts for little, but the voice of the representative is heard with a deference roughly proportional to the numbers for whom he speaks.

. . .

DENSITY

As in the case of numbers, so in the case of concentration in limited space, certain consequences of relevance in sociological analysis of the city emerge. Of these only a few can be indicated.

As Darwin pointed out for flora and fauna and as Durkheim noted in the case of human societies, an increase in numbers when area is held constant (i.e., an increase in density) tends to produce differentiation and specialization, since only in this way can the area support increased numbers. Density thus reinforces the effect of numbers in diversifying men and their activities and in increasing the complexity of the social structure.

On the subjective side, as Simmel has suggested, the close physical contact of numerous individuals necessarily produces a shift in the mediums through which we orient ourselves to the urban milieu, especially to our fellow-men. Typically, our physical contacts are close but our social contacts are distant. The urban world puts a premium on visual recognition. We see the uniform which denotes the role of the functionaries and are oblivious to the personal eccentricities that are hidden behind the uniform. We tend to acquire and develop a sensitivity to a world of artifacts and become progressively farther removed from the world of nature.

We are exposed to glaring contrasts between splendor and squalor, between riches and poverty, intelligence and ignorance, order and chaos. The competition for space is great, so that each area generally tends to be put to the use which yields the greatest economic return. Place of work tends to become dissociated from place of residence, for the proximity of industrial and commercial establishments makes an area both economically and socially undesirable for residential purposes.

Density, land values, rentals, accessibility, healthfulness, prestige, aesthetic consideration, absence of nuisances such as noise, smoke, and dirt determine the desirability of various areas of the city as places of settlement for different sections of the population. Place and nature of work, income, racial and ethnic characteristics, social status, custom, habit, taste, preference, and prejudice are among the significant factors in accordance with which the urban population is selected and distributed into more or less distinct settlements. Diverse population elements inhabiting a compact settlement thus tend to become segregated from one another in the degree in which their requirements and modes of life are incompatible with one another and in the measure in which they are antagonistic to one another. Similarly, persons of homogeneous status and needs unwittingly drift into, consciously select, or are forced by circumstances into, the same area. The different parts of the city thus acquire specialized functions. The city consequently tends to resemble a mosaic of social worlds in which the transition from one to the other is abrupt. The juxtaposition of divergent personalities and modes of life tends to produce a relativistic perspective and a sense of toleration of differences which may be regarded as prerequisites for rationality and which lead toward the secularization of life.

The close living together and working together of individuals who have no sentimental and emotional ties foster a spirit of competition, aggrandizement, and mutual exploitation. To counteract irresponsibility and potential disorder, formal controls tend to be resorted to. Without rigid adherence to predictable routines a large compact society would scarcely be able to maintain itself. The clock and the traffic signal are symbolic of the basis of our social order in the urban world. Frequent close physical contact, coupled with great social distance, accentuates the reserve of unattached individuals toward one another and, unless compensated for by other opportunities for response, gives rise to loneliness. The necessary frequent movement of great numbers of individuals in a congested habitat gives occasion to friction and irritation. Nervous tensions which derive from such personal frustrations are accentuated by the rapid tempo and the complicated technology under which life in dense areas must be lived.

HETEROGENEITY

The social interaction among such a variety of personality types in the urban milieu tends to break down the rigidity of caste lines and to complicate the class structure, and thus induces a more ramified and differentiated framework of social stratification than is found in more integrated societies. The heightened mobility of the individual, which brings him within the range of stimulation by a great number of diverse individuals and subjects him to fluctuating status in the differentiated social groups that compose the social structure of the city, tends toward the acceptance of instability and insecurity in the world at large as a norm. This fact helps to account, too, for the sophistication and cosmopolitanism of the urbanite. No single group has the undivided allegiance of the individual. The groups with which he is affiliated do not lend themselves readily to a simple hierarchical arrangement. By virtue of his different interests arising out of different aspects of social life, the individual acquires member-ship in widely divergent groups, each of which functions only with refer-ence to a single segment of his personality. Nor do these groups easily permit of a concentric arrangement so that the narrower ones fall within the circumference of the more inclusive ones, as is more likely to be the case in the rural community or in primitive societies. Rather the groups with which the person typically is affiliated are tangential to each other or intersect in highly variable fashion.

Partly as a result of the physical footlooseness of the population and partly as a result of their social mobility, the turnover in group member-ship generally is rapid. Place of residence, place and character of employ-ment, income and interests fluctuate, and the task of holding organiza-tions together and maintaining and promoting intimate and lasting acquaintanceship between the members is difficult. This applies strik-ingly to the local areas within the city into which persons become segre-gated more by virtue of differences in race, language, income, and social status, than through choice or positive attraction to people like them-selves. Overwhelmingly the city-dweller is not a home-owner, and since a transitory habitat does not generate binding traditions and sentiments, only rarely is he truly a neighbor. There is little opportunity for the indi-vidual to obtain a conception of the city as a whole or to survey his place in the total scheme. Consequently he finds it difficult to determine what is to his own "best interests" and to decide between the issues and leaders presented to him by the agencies of mass suggestion. Individuals who are thus detached from the organized bodies which integrate society comprise the fluid masses that make collective behavior in the urban community so unpredictable and hence so problematical.

Although the city, through the recruitment of variant types to perform its diverse tasks and the accentuation of their uniqueness through compe-tition and the premium upon eccentricity, novelty, efficient performance, and inventiveness, produces a highly differentiated population, it also ex-ercises a leveling influence. Wherever large numbers of differently consti-tuted individuals congregate, the process of depersonalization also enters. This leveling tendency inheres in part in the economic basis of the city. The development of large cities, at least in the modern age, was largely dependent upon the concentrative force of steam. The rise of the factory made possible mass production for an impersonal market. The fullest ex-ploitation of the possibilities of the division of labor and mass produc-tion, however, is possible only with standardization of processes and prod-ucts. A money economy goes hand in hand with such a system of production. Progressively as cities have developed upon a background of this system of production, the pecuniary nexus which implies the pur-chasability of services and things has displaced personal relations as the basis of association. Individuality under these circumstances must be re-placed by categories. When large numbers have to make common use of facilities and institutions, an arrangement must be made to adjust the facilities and institutions to the needs of the average person rather than to those of particular individuals. The services of the public utilities, of the recreational, educational, and cultural institutions must be adjusted to mass requirements. Similarly, the cultural institutions, such as the schools, the movies, the radio, and the newspapers, by virtue of their mass clientele, must necessarily operate as leveling influences. The political process as it appears in urban life could not be understood without taking account of the mass appeals made through modern propaganda techniques. If the individual would participate at all in the social, political, and economic life of the city, he must subordinate some of his individuality to the demands of the larger community and in that measure immerse himself in mass movements.

16. THE MACHINE, THE WORKER AND ALIENATION

Karl Marx

Both Marx and Engels were appalled by the hideousness of the prole-tarian districts of England's cities in the mid-nineteenth century. Never-theless, they regarded urban society as being at the forefront of prog-ress. In their interpretation of modern history, the underlying unity of economic interests between worker and intellectual would eventually sweep aside both the exploitative employer and the reactionary, parasitic land holder; the result would be the emergence of a national, secular so-cial order in which all people would spontaneously cooperate for their mutual and common welfare. For this reason, Marx felt no inherent dis-taste for urban life, but saw it rather as the harbinger of a more highly developed society.

It was the perversion of human nature by the machine in the hands of its predatory owners that aroused Marx's concern. The factory system which had created the industrial cities was blighting humanity by sub-jecting the worker to regimentation. Marx saw the result as a state of dis-affection, isolation, and estrangement. The unreasonable discipline im-posed on the helpless machine-tender by unconscionable managers, themselves caught in the grip of the false values of "commodity fetish-ism," could only produce people demoralized by their sense of worthless-ness and helplessness. Although he did not clearly foresee that an im-proved technology demands greater responsibility from the labor force, Marx definitely added the dimension of alienation to urban, industrial sociology.

In this selection from Marx's writings, the quotation on the incessant

Excerpts from *Capital* by Karl Marx. Edited by Frederick Engels and translated by Samuel Moore and Edward Aveling. Published by Random House, Inc.

toil of the factory laborer is from Engels, and that on the low estate of
labor is from the 1854 Manchester Committee of the Master Spinners'
and Manufacturers' Defence Fund. Frederick Engels, The Condition of
the Working-Class in England in 1844 *(London: George Allen and*
Unwin, 1892, translated by Florence Kelley Wischnewetzky) is the fac-
tual basis of his conclusion that Marx cited.

AT THE COMMENCEMENT of this chapter we considered that which we may
call the body of the factory, i.e., machinery organised into a system. We
there saw how machinery, by annexing the labour of women and children, augments the number of human beings who form the material for
capitalistic exploitation, how it confiscates the whole of the workman's
disposable time, by immoderate extension of the hours of labour, and
how finally its progress, which allows of enormous increase of production
in shorter and shorter periods, serves as a means of systematically getting
more work done in a shorter time, or in exploiting labour-power more in-
tensely. We now turn to the factory as a whole, and that in its most perfect form.

Dr. Ure, the Pindar of the automatic factory, describes it, on the one
hand as "Combined co-operation of many orders of workpeople, adult
and young, in tending with assiduous skill, a system of productive machines, continuously impelled by a central power" (the prime mover) ;
on the other hand, as "a vast automaton, composed of various mechanical
and intellectual organs, acting in uninterrupted concert for the production of a common object, all of them being subordinate to a self-regulated
moving force." These two descriptions are far from being identical. In
one, the collective labourer, or social body of labour, appears as the dominant subject and the mechanical automaton as the object; in the other,
the automaton itself is the subject, and the workmen are merely conscious
organs, co-ordinate with the unconscious organs of the automaton, and
together with them, subordinated to the central moving-power. The first
description is applicable to every possible employment of machinery on a
large scale, the second is characteristic of its use by capital, and therefore
of the modern factory system. Ure prefers therefore, to describe the central machine, from which the motion comes, not only as an automaton,
but as an autocrat. "In these spacious halls the benignant power of steam
summons around him his myriads of willing menials."

Along with the tool, the skill of the workman in handling it passes over
to the machine. The capabilities of the tool are emancipated from the restraints that are inseparable from human labour-power. Thereby the
technical foundation on which is based the division of labour in Manufacture, is swept away. Hence, in the place of the hierarchy of specialised
workmen that characterises manufacture, there steps, in the automatic
factory, a tendency to equalise and reduce to one and the same level every

kind of work that has to be done by the minders of the machines; in the place of the artificially produced differentiations of the detail workmen, step the natural differences of age and sex.

So far as division of labour re-appears in the factory, it is primarily a distribution of the workmen among the specialised machines; and of masses of workmen, not however organised into groups, among the various departments of the factory, in each of which they work at a number of similar machines placed together; their co-operation, therefore, is only simple. The organised group, peculiar to manufacture, is replaced by the connexion between the head workman and his few assistants. The essential division is, into workmen who are actually employed on the machines (among whom are included a few who look after the engine), and into mere attendants (almost exclusively children) of these workmen. Among the attendants are reckoned more or less all "Feeders" who supply the machines with the material to be worked. In addition to these two principal classes, there is a numerically unimportant class of persons, whose occupation it is to look after the whole of the machinery and repair it from time to time; such as engineers, mechanics, joiners, etc. This is a superior class of workmen, some of them scientifically educated, others brought up to a trade; it is distinct from the factory operative class, and merely aggregated to it. This division of labour is purely technical.

To work at a machine, the workman should be taught from childhood, in order that he may learn to adapt his own movements to the uniform and unceasing motion of automaton. When the machinery, as a whole, forms a system of manifold machines, working simultaneously and in concert, the co-operation based upon it, requires the distribution of various groups of workmen among the different kinds of machines. But the employment of machinery does away with the necessity of crystallizing this distribution after the manner of Manufacture, by the constant annexation of a particular man to a particular function. Since the motion of the whole system does not proceed from the workman, but from the machinery, a change of persons can take place at any time without an interruption of the work. The most striking proof of this is afforded by the relays system, put into operation by the manufacturers during their revolt from 1848–1850. Lastly, the quickness with which machine work is learnt by young people, does away with the necessity of bringing up for exclusive employment by machinery, a special class of operatives. With regard to the work of the mere attendants, it can, to some extent, be replaced in the mill by machines, and owing to its extreme simplicity, it allows of a rapid and constant change of the individuals burdened with this drudgery.

Although, then, technically speaking, the old system of division of labour is thrown overboard by machinery, it hands on in the factory, as a traditional habit handed down from Manufacture, and is afterwards systematically re-moulded and established in a more hideous form by capital, as a means of exploiting labour-power. The life-long speciality of handling one and the same tool, now becomes the life-long speciality of serving one and the same machine. Machinery is put to a wrong use, with the object of transforming the workman, from his very childhood, into a part of a detail-machine. In this way, not only are the expenses of his reproduction considerably lessened, but at the same time his helpless dependence upon the factory as a whole, and therefore upon the capitalist, is rendered complete. Here as everywhere else, we must distinguish between the increased productiveness due to the development of the social process of production, and that due to the capitalist exploitation of that process. In handicrafts and manufacture, the workman makes use of a tool, in the factory, the machine makes use of him. There the movements of the instrument of labour proceed from him, here it is the movements of the machine that he must follow. In manufacture the workmen are parts of a living mechanism. In the factory we have a lifeless mechanism independent of the workman, who becomes its mere living appendage. "The miserable routine of endless drudgery and toil in which the same mechanical process is gone through over and over again, is like the labour of Sisyphus. The burden of labour, like the rock, keeps ever falling back on the wornout labourer." At the same time that factory work exhausts the nervous system to the uttermost, it does away with the many-sided play of the muscles, and confiscates every atom of freedom, both in bodily and intellectual activity. The lightening of the labour, even, becomes a sort of torture, since the machine does not free the labourer from work, but deprives the work of all interest. Every kind of capitalist production in so far as it is not only a labour-process, but also a process of creating surplus-value, has this in common, that it is not the workman that employs the instruments of labour, but the instruments of labour that employ the workman. But it is only in the factory system that this inversion for the first time acquires technical and palpable reality. By means of its conversion into an automaton, the instrument of labour confronts the labourer, during the labour-process, in the shape of capital, of dead labour, that dominates, and pumps dry, living labour-power. The separation of the intellectual powers of production from the manual labour, and the conversion of those powers into the might of capital over labour, is, as we have already shown, finally completed by modern industry erected on the foundation of machinery. The special skill of each individual insignificant factory operative vanishes as an infinitesimal quantity before the science, the gigantic physical forces, and the mass of labour that are embodied in the factory mechanism and, together with that mechanism, constitute the power of the "master." This "master," therefore, in whose brain the machinery and his monopoly of it are inseparably united, whenever he falls out with his "hands," contemptuously tells them: "The factory operatives should keep in wholesome remembrance the fact that theirs is really a low species of skilled labour; and that there is none which is more easily acquired, or of its quality more amply remunerated, or which by a short training of the least expert can be more quickly, as well as abundantly, acquired. . . . The master's machinery really plays a far more important part in the business of production than the labour and the skill of the operative, which six months' education can teach, and a common labourer can learn." The technical subordination of the workman to the uniform motion of the instruments of labour, and the peculiar composition of the body of workpeople, consisting as it does of individuals of both sexes and of all ages, give rise to a barrack discipline, which is elaborated into a complete system in the factory, and which fully develops the before mentioned labour of overlooking, thereby dividing the workpeople into operatives and overlookers, into private soldiers and sergeants of an industrial army. "The main difficulty (in the automatic factory) . . . lay . . . above all in training human beings to renounce their desultory habits of work, and to identify themselves with the unvarying regularity of the complex automaton. To devise and administer a successful code of factory discipline, suited to the necessities of factory diligence, was the Herculean enterprise, the noble achievement of Arkwright! Even at the present day, when the system is perfectly organised and its labour lightened to the utmost, it is found nearly impossible to convert persons past the age of puberty, into useful factory hands." The factory code in which capital formulates, like a private legislator, and at his own good will, his autocracy over his workpeople, unaccompanied by that division of responsibility, in other matters so much approved of by the bourgeoisie, and unaccompanied by the still more approved representative system, this code is but the capitalism caricature of that social regulation of the labour-process which becomes requisite in co-operation on a great scale, and in the employment in common, of instruments of labour and especially of machinery. The place of the slave driver's lash is taken by the overlooker's book of penalties. All punishments naturally resolve themselves into fines and deductions from wages, and the law-giving talent of the factory Lycurgus so arranges matters, that a violation of his laws is, if possible, more profitable to him than the keeping of them.

17. URBANISM AND SUBURBANISM

Herbert J. Gans

Wirth had earlier contrasted city life with folk community life. His data were drawn principally from European villagers transplanted to Chicago's mass society by the great wave of late nineteenth-century immigration. Later attention directed to the new suburbs showed, however, marked sociocultural differentiation that failed to bear out the uniform anonymity and isolation Wirth attributed to the urban pattern. True, the inner city does approximate that configuration described by Wirth, but even here, owing to the variety of city types, the atomistic secondary character is only a partially warranted generalization. In the suburbs, by comparison, a quasi-primary way of life is clearly prevalent, and it little resembles the picture drawn by Wirth. Herbert Gans discusses this contrast and also examines a number of popular myths concerning the individual and society in suburbia. Gans, however, is inclined to believe that differences in modes of life between the central city and its surrounding ring of suburbs are likely to have a closer relationship with the social-class system and the life-cycle variations of their respective populations than with urban residence per se.

WIRTH'S DIAGNOSIS of the city as *Gesellschaft* must be questioned on three counts. First, the conclusions derived from a study of the inner city cannot be generalized to the entire urban area. Second, there is as yet not enough evidence to prove—nor, admittedly, to deny—that number, dens-

Excerpts from *Human Behavior and Social Processes*, edited by Arnold M. Rose (1962). Reprinted by permission of the Houghton Mifflin Company.

ity, and heterogeneity result in the social consequences which Wirth proposed. Finally, even if the causal relationship could be verified, it can be shown that a significant proportion of the city's inhabitants were, and are, isolated from these consequences by social structures and cultural patterns which they either brought to the city, or developed by living in it. Wirth conceived the urban population as consisting of heterogeneous individuals, torn from past social systems, unable to develop new ones, and therefore prey to social anarchy in the city. While it is true that a not insignificant proportion of the inner city population was, and still is, made up of unattached individuals, Wirth's formulation ignores the fact that this population consists mainly of relatively homogeneous groups, with social and cultural moorings that shield it fairly effectively from the suggested consequences of number, density, and heterogeneity. This applies even more to the residents of the outer city, who constitute a majority of the total city population.

The social and cultural moorings of the inner city population are best described by a brief analysis of the five types of inner city residents. These are:

1. the "cosmopolites";
2. the unmarried or childless;
3. the "ethnic villagers";
4. the "deprived"; and
5. the "trapped" and downward mobile.

The "cosmopolites" include students, artists, writers, musicians, and entertainers, as well as other intellectuals and professionals. They live in the city in order to be near the special "cultural" facilities that can only be located near the center of the city. Many cosmopolites are unmarried or childless. Others rear children in the city, especially if they have the income to afford the aid of servants and governesses. The less affluent ones may move to the suburbs to raise their children, continuing to live as cosmopolites under considerable handicaps, especially in the lower-middle-class suburbs. Many of the very rich and powerful are also cosmopolites, although they are likely to have at least two residences, one of which is suburban or exurban.

The unmarried or childless must be divided into two subtypes, depending on the permanence or transience of their status. The temporarily unmarried or childless live in the inner city for only a limited time. Young adults may team up to rent an apartment away from their parents and close to job or entertainment opportunities. When they marry, they may move first to an apartment in a transient neighborhood, but if they can afford to do so, they leave for the outer city or the suburbs with the arrival of the first or second child. The permanently unmarried may stay in the inner city for the remainder of their lives, their housing depending on their income.

The "ethnic villagers" are ethnic groups which are found in such inner city neighborhoods as New York's Lower East Side, living in some ways as they did when they were peasants in European or Puerto Rican villages. Although they reside in the city, they isolate themselves from significant contact with most city facilities, aside from workplaces. Their way of life differs sharply from Wirth's urbanism in its emphasis on kinship and the primary group, the lack of anonymity and secondary-group contacts, the weakness of formal organizations, and the suspicion of anything and anyone outside their neighborhood.

The first two types live in the inner city by choice; the third is there partly because of necessity, partly because of tradition. The final two types are in the inner city because they have no other choice. One is the "deprived" population: the very poor; the emotionally disturbed or otherwise handicapped; broken families; and, most important, the nonwhite population. These urban dwellers must take the dilapidated housing and blighted neighborhoods to which the housing market relegates them, although among them are some for whom the slum is a hiding place, or a temporary stop-over to save money for a house in the outer city or the suburbs.

The "trapped" are the people who stay behind when a neighborhood is invaded by non-residential land uses or lower-status immigrants, because they cannot afford to move, or are otherwise bound to their present location. The "downward mobiles" are a related type; they may have started life in a higher class position, but have been forced down in the socio-economic hierarchy and in the quality of their accommodations. Many of them are old people, living out their existence on small pensions.

These five types all live in dense and heterogeneous surroundings, yet they have such diverse ways of life that it is hard to see how density and heterogeneity could exert a common influence. Moreover, all but the last two types are isolated or detached from their neighborhood and thus from the social consequences which Wirth described.

When people who live together have social ties based on criteria other than mere common occupancy, they can set up social barriers regardless of the physical closeness or the heterogeneity of their neighbors. The ethnic villagers are the best illustration. While a number of ethnic groups are usually found living together in the same neighborhood, they are able to *isolate* themselves from each other through a variety of social devices. Wirth himself recognized this when he wrote that "two groups can occupy a given area without losing their separate identity because each side is permitted to live its own inner life and each somehow fears or idealizes the other.". . .

The cosmopolites, the unmarried, and the childless are *detached* from neighborhood life. The cosmopolites possess a distinct subculture which causes them to be disinterested in all but the most superficial contacts with their neighbors, somewhat like the ethnic villagers. The unmarried and childless are detached from neighborhood because of their life-cycle stage, which frees them from routine family responsibilities that entail some relationship to the local area. In their choice of residence, the two types are therefore not concerned about their neighbors, or the availability and quality of local community facilities. Even the well-to-do can choose expensive apartments in or near poor neighborhoods, because if they have children, these are sent to special schools and summer camps which effectively isolate them from neighbors. In addition, both types, but especially the childless and unmarried, are transient. Therefore, they tend to live in areas marked by high population turnover, where their own mobility and that of their neighbors creates a universal detachment from the neighborhood.

The deprived and the trapped do seem to be affected by some of the consequences of number, density, and heterogeneity. The deprived population suffers considerably from overcrowding, but this is a consequence of low income, racial discrimination, and other handicaps, and cannot be considered an inevitable result of the ecological make-up of the city. Because the deprived have no residential choice, they are also forced to live amid neighbors not of their own choosing, with ways of life different and even contradictory to their own. If familial defenses against the neighborhood climate are weak, as is the case among broken families and downward mobile people, parents may lose their children to the culture of "the street." The trapped are the unhappy people who remain behind when their more advantaged neighbors move on; they must endure the heterogeneity which results from neighborhood change.

Wirth's description of the urban way of life fits best the transient areas of the inner city. Such areas are typically heterogeneous in population, partly because they are inhabited by transient types who do not require homogeneous neighbors or by deprived people who have no choice, or may themselves be quite mobile. Under conditions of transience and heterogeneity, people interact only in terms of the segmental roles necessary for obtaining local services. Their social relationships thus display anonymity, impersonality, and superficiality.

The social features of Wirth's concept of urbanism seem therefore to be a result of residential instability, rather than of number, density, or heterogeneity. In fact, heterogeneity is itself an effect of residential instability, resulting when the influx of transients causes landlords and realtors to stop acting as gatekeepers—that is, wardens of neighborhood homogeneity. Residential instability is found in all types of settlements, and, presumably, its social consequences are everywhere similar. These consequences cannot therefore be identified with the ways of life of the city.

THE OUTER CITY AND THE SUBURBS

The second effect which Wirth ascribed to number, density, and heterogeneity was the segregation of homogeneous people into distinct neighborhoods, on the basis of "place and nature of work, income, racial and ethnic characteristics, social status, custom, habit, taste, preference and prejudice." This description fits the residential districts of the *outer city*. Although these districts contain the majority of the city's inhabitants, Wirth went into little detail about them. He made it clear, however, that the socio-psychological aspects of urbanism were prevalent there as well.

Because existing neighborhood studies deal primarily with the exotic sections of the inner city, very little is known about the more typical residential neighborhoods of the outer city. However, it is evident that the way of life in these areas bears little resemblance to Wirth's urbanism. Both the studies which question Wirth's formulation and my own observations suggest that the common element in the ways of life of these neighborhoods is best described as *quasi-primary*. I use this term to characterize relationships between neighbors. Whatever the intensity or frequency of these relationships, the interaction is more intimate than a secondary contact, but more guarded than a primary one.

There are actually few secondary relationships, because of the isolation of residential neighborhoods from economic institutions and workplaces. Even shopkeeepers, store managers, and other local functionaries who live in the area are treated as acquaintances or friends, unless they are of a vastly different social status or are forced by their corporate employers to treat their customers as economic units. Voluntary associations attract only a minority of the population. Moreover, much of the organizational activity is of a sociable nature, and it is often difficult to accomplish the association's "business" because of the members' preference for sociability. Thus, it would appear that interactions in organizations, or between neighbors generally, do not fit the secondary-relationship model of urban life. As anyone who has lived in these neighborhoods knows, there is little anonymity, impersonality or privacy. In fact, American cities have sometimes been described as collections of small towns. There is some truth to this description, especially if the city is compared to the actual small town, rather than to the romantic construct of anti-urban critics.

Postwar suburbia represents the most contemporary version of the quasi-primary way of life. Owing to increases in real income and the encouragement of home ownership provided by the FHA, families in the lower-middle class and upper working class can now live in modern single-family homes in low-density subdivisions, an opportunity previously available only to the upper and upper-middle classes.

The popular literature describes the new suburbs as communities in which conformity, homogeneity, and other-direction are unusually rampant. The implication is that the move from city to suburb initiates a new way of life which causes considerable behavior and personality change in previous urbanites. A preliminary analysis of data which I am now collecting in Levittown, New Jersey, suggests, however, that the move from the city to this predominantly lower-middle-class suburb does not result in any major behavioral changes for most people. Moreover, the changes which do occur reflect the move from the social isolation of a transient city or suburban apartment building to the quasi-primary life of a neighborhood of single-family homes. Also, many of the people whose life has changed reported that the changes were intended. They existed as aspirations before the move, or as reasons for it. In other words, the suburb itself creates few changes in ways of life. . . .

A COMPARISON OF CITY AND SUBURB

If urban and suburban areas are similar in that the way of life in both is quasi-primary, and if urban residents who move out to the suburbs do not undergo any significant changes in behavior, it would be fair to argue that the differences in ways of life between the two types of settlements have been overestimated. Yet the fact remains that a variety of physical and demographic differences exist between the city and the suburb. However, upon closer examination, many of these differences turn out to be either spurious or of little significance for the way of life of the inhabitants.

The differences between the residential areas of cities and suburbs which have been cited most frequently are:

1. Suburbs are more likely to be dormitories.
2. They are further away from the work and play facilities of the central business districts.
3. They are newer and more modern than city residential areas and are designed for the automobile rather than for pedestrian and mass-transit forms of movement.
4. They are built up with single-family rather than multi-family structures and are therefore less dense.
5. Their populations are more homogeneous.
6. Their populations differ demographically: they are younger; more of them are married; they have higher incomes; and they hold proportionately more white collar jobs.

Most urban neighborhoods are as much dormitories as the suburbs. Only in a few older inner city areas are factories and offices still located in the middle of residential blocks, and even here many of the employees do not live in the neighborhood.

The fact that the suburbs are farther from the central business district is often true only in terms of distance, not travel time. Moreover, most people make relatively little use of downtown facilities, other than workplaces. The downtown stores seem to hold their greatest attraction for the upper-middle class; the same is probably true of typically urban entertainment facilities. Teen-agers and young adults may take their dates to first-run movie theaters, but the museums, concert halls, and lecture rooms attract mainly upper-middle-class ticketbuyers, many of them suburban.

The suburban reliance on the train and the automobile has given rise to an imaginative folklore about the consequences of commuting on alcohol consumption, sex life, and parental duties. Many of these conclusions are, however, drawn from selected high-income suburbs and exurbs, and reflect jobs tensions in such hectic occupations as advertising and show business more than the effects of residence. It is true that the upper-middle-class housewife must become a chauffeur in order to expose her children to the proper educational facilities, but such differences as walking to the corner drug store and driving to its suburban equivalent seem to me of little emotional, social, or cultural import. In addition, the continuing shrinkage in the number of mass-transit users suggests that even in the city many younger people are now living a wholly auto-based way of life.

The fact that suburbs are smaller is primarily a function of political boundaries drawn long before the communities were suburban. This affects the kinds of political issues which develop and provides somewhat greater opportunity for citizen participation. Even so, in the suburbs as in the city, the minority who participate are the professional politicians, the economically concerned businessmen, lawyers and salesmen, and the ideologically motivated middle- and upper-middle-class people with better than average education.

The social consequences of differences in density and house type also seem overrated. Single-family houses on quiet streets facilitate the supervision of children; this is one reason why middle-class women who want to keep an eye on their children move to the suburbs. House type also has some effects on relationships between neighbors, insofar as there are more opportunities for visual contact between adjacent homeowners than between people on different floors of an apartment house. However, if occupants' characteristics are also held constant, the differences in actual social contact are less marked. Homogeneity of residents turns out to be more important as a determinant of sociability than proximity. If the population is heterogeneous, there is little social contact between neighbors, either on apartment-house floors or in single-family-house blocks; if people are homogeneous, there is likely to be considerable social contact in both house types. One need only contrast the apartment house located in a transient, heterogeneous neighborhood and exactly the same structure in a neighborhood occupied by a single ethnic group. The former is a lively, anonymous building; the latter, a bustling micro-society. I have observed similar patterns in suburban areas: on blocks where people are homogeneous, they socialize; where they are heterogeneous, they do little more than exchange polite greetings.

Suburbs are usually described as being more homogeneous in house

type than the city, but if they are compared to the outer city, the differences are small. Most inhabitants of the outer city, other than well-to-do
homeowners, live on blocks of uniform structures as well—for example,
the endless streets of rowhouses in Philadelphia and Baltimore or of two-
story duplexes and six-flat apartment houses in Chicago. They differ from
the new suburbs only in that they were erected through more primitive
methods of mass production. Suburbs are of course more predominantly
areas of owner-occupied single homes, though in the outer districts of
most American cities homeownership is also extremely high.

Demographically, suburbs as a whole are clearly more homogeneous
than cities as a whole, though probably not more so than outer cities.
However, people do not live in cities or suburbs as a whole, but in specific neighborhoods. An analysis of ways of life would require a determination of the degree of population homogeneity within the boundaries of
areas defined as neighborhoods by residents' social contracts. Such an
analysis would no doubt indicate that many neighborhoods in the city as
well as the suburbs are homogeneous. Neighborhood homogeneity is actually a result of factors having little or nothing to do with the house
type, density, or location of the area relative to the city limits. Brand new
neighborhoods are more homogeneous than older ones, because they have
not yet experienced resident turnover, which frequently results in population heterogeneity. Neighborhoods of low- and medium-priced housing
are usually less homogeneous than those with expensive dwellings because they attract families who have reached the peak of occupational
and residential mobility, as well as young families who are just starting
their climb and will eventually move to neighborhoods of higher status.
The latter, being accessible only to high-income people, are therefore
more homogeneous with respect to other resident characteristics as well.
Moreover, such areas have the economic and political power to slow
down or prevent invasion. Finally, neighborhoods located in the path of
ethnic or religious group movement are likely to be extremely homogeneous.

The demographic differences between cities and suburbs cannot be
questioned, especially since the suburbs have attracted a large number of
middle-class child-rearing families. The differences are, however, much
reduced if suburbs are compared only to the outer city. In addition, a detailed comparison of suburban and outer city residential areas would
show that neighborhoods with the same kinds of people can be found in
the city as well as the suburbs. Once again, the age of the area and the
cost of housing are more important determinants of demographic characteristics than the location of the area with respect to the city limits.

18. THE DECLINE OF THE PROTESTANT ETHIC

William H. Whyte, Jr.

Urbanism may be at a high level in either a free or a planned econ-omy. However, large-scale organization cannot exist in the absence of big cities, and to speak about large-scale organization is to assume urbanism. William Whyte's "organization man" does not refer expressly to urban society. Nonetheless, the metropolitan milieu is unmistakably the back-drop for the transition that has taken place from the ethic of individual-ism and self-reliance to that of consensus, group adherence, and uniform-ity. The interdependence of the members of the big organization set in the midst of an integrated community, and even an urban nation, makes it imperative that entrepreneurial tendencies be curbed and that admin-istrative coordination be cultivated instead. Whyte reminds us that despite the continued mythology of the Protestant Ethic, pragmatic group-mindedness has replaced the Protestant Ethic, the social doctrine that pre-vailed during the earlier stages of industrial development. Society, manifested in the giant corporation and megalopolis alike, is now the object of perfectibility, not the individual.

LET US GO BACK A MOMENT to the turn of the century. If we pick up the Protestant Ethic as it was then expressed we will find it apparently in full flower. We will also find, however, an ethic that already had been strained by reality. The country had changed. The ethic had not.

Here, in the words of banker Henry Clews as he gave some fatherly ad-vice to Yale students in 1908, is the Protestant Ethic in purest form:

Survival of Fittest: You may start in business, or the professions, with your feet on the bottom rung of the ladder; it rests with you to acquire the strength to climb to the top. You can do so if you have the will and the force to back you. There is always plenty of room at the top. . . . Success comes to the man who tries to compel success to yield to him. Cassius spoke well to Brutus when he said, "The Fault is not in our stars, dear Brutus, that we are underlings, but in our natures."

Thrift: Form the habit as soon as you become a money-earner, or money-maker, of saving a part of your salary, or profits. Put away one dollar out of every ten you earn. The time will come in your lives when, if you have a little money, you can control circumstances; otherwise circumstances will control you. . . .

Note the use of such active words as *climb, force, compel, control.* As stringently as ever before, the Protestant Ethic still counseled struggle against one's environment—the kind of practical, here and now struggle that paid off in material rewards. And spiritually too. The hard-boiled part of the Protestant Ethic was incomplete, of course, without the companion assurance that such success was moral as well as practical. To continue with Mr. Clews:

Under this free system of government, whereby individuals are free to get a living or to pursue wealth as each chooses, the usual result is competition. Obviously, then, competition really means industrial freedom. Thus, anyone may choose his own trade or profession, or, if he does not like it, he may change. He is free to work hard or not; he may make his own bargains and set his price upon his labor or his products. He is free to acquire property to any extent, or to part with it. By dint of greater effort or superior skill, or by intelligence, if he can make better wages, he is free to live better, just as his neighbor is free to follow his example and to learn to excel him in turn. If anyone has a genius for making and managing money, he is free to exercise his genius, just as another is free to handle his tools. . . . If an individual enjoys his money, gained by energy and successful effort, his neighbors are urged to work the harder, that they and their children may have the same enjoyment.

It was an exuberantly optimistic ethic. If everyone could believe that seeking his self-interest automatically improves the lot of all, then the application of hard work should eventually produce a heaven on earth. Some, like the garrulous Mr. Clews, felt it already had.

America is the true field for the human race. It is the hope and the asylum for the oppressed and downtrodden of every clime. It is the inspiring example of America—peerless among the nations of the earth, the brightest star in the political firmament—that is leavening the hard lump of aristocracy and promoting a democratic spirit throughout the world. It is indeed the gem of the ocean to which the world may well offer homage. Here merit is the sole test. Birth is nothing. The fittest survive. Merit is the supreme and only qualification essential to success. Intelligence rules worlds and systems of worlds. It is the dread monarch of illimitable space, and in human society, especially in America, it shines as a diadem on the foreheads of those who stand in the foremost ranks of human enterprise. Here only a natural order of nobility is recognized, and its motto, without coat of arms or boast of heraldry, is "Intelligence and integrity." [1]

Without this ethic capitalism would have been impossible. Whether the Protestant Ethic preceded capitalism, as Max Weber argued, or whether it grew up as a consequence, in either event it provided a degree of unity between the way people wanted to behave and the way they thought they *ought* to behave, and without this ideology, society would have been hostile to the entrepreneur. Without the comfort of the Protestant Ethic, he couldn't have gotten away with his acquisitions—not merely because other people wouldn't have allowed him, but because his own conscience would not have. But now he was fortified by the assurance that he was pursuing his obligation to God, and before long, what for centuries had been looked on as the meanest greed, a rising middle class would interpret as the earthly manifestation of God's will.

But the very industrial revolution which this highly serviceable ethic begot in time began to confound it. The inconsistencies were a long while in making themselves apparent. The nineteenth-century inheritors of the ethic were creating an increasingly collective society but steadfastly they denied the implications of it. In current retrospect the turn of the century seems a golden age of individualism, yet by the 1880's the corporation had already shown the eventual bureaucratic direction it was going to take. As institutions grew in size and became more stratified, they made all too apparent inconsistencies which formerly could be ignored. One of the key assumptions of the Protestant Ethic had been that success was due neither to luck nor to the environment but only to one's natural qualities—if men grew rich it was because they deserved to. But the big organization became a standing taunt to this dream of individual success. Quite obviously to anyone who worked in a big organization, those who survived best were not necessarily the fittest but, in more cases than not, those who by birth and personal connections had the breaks.

As organizations continued to expand, the Protestant Ethic became more and more divergent from the reality The Organization was itself creating. The managers steadfastly denied the change, but they, as much as those they led, were affected by it.

Today, some still deny the inconsistency or blame it on creeping socialism; for the younger generation of managers however, the inconsistencies have become importuning.

Thrift, for example. How can the organization man be thrifty? Other people are thrifty *for* him. He stills buys most of his own life insurance, but for the bulk of his rainy-day saving, he gives his proxy to the financial and personnel department of his organization. In his professional capacity also thrift is becoming a little un-American. The same man who will quote from Benjamin Franklin on thrift for the house organ would be horrified if consumers took these maxims to heart and started putting more money into savings and less into installment purchases. No longer can he afford the luxury of damning the profligacy of the public; not in public, at any rate. He not only has to persuade people to buy more but persuade them out of any guilt feelings they might have for following his advice. Few talents are more commercially sought today than the knack of describing departures from the Protestant Ethic as reaffirmations of it.[2]

In an advertisement that should go down in social history, the J. Walter Thompson agency has hit the problem of absolution head-on. It quotes Benjamin Franklin on the benefits of spending. "Is not the hope of being one day able to purchase and enjoy luxuries a great spur to labor and industry? . . . May not luxury therefore produce more than it consumes, if, without such a spur, people would be, as they are naturally enough inclined to be, lazy and indolent?" This thought, the ad says, in a meaningful aside, "appears to be a mature afterthought, qualifying his earlier and more familiar writings on the importance of thrift."

"Hard work?" What price capitalism, the question is now so frequently asked, unless we turn our productivity into more leisure, more of the good life? To the organization man this makes abundant sense, and he is as sensitive to the bogy of overwork and ulcers as his forebears were to the bogy of slothfulness. But he is split. He believes in leisure, but so does he believe in the Puritan insistence on hard, self-denying work—and there are, alas, only twenty-four hours a day. How, then, to be "broad gauge"? The "broad-gauge" model we hear so much about these days is the man who keeps his work separate from leisure and the rest of his life. Any organization man who managed to accomplish this feat wouldn't get very far. He still works hard, in short, but now he has to feel somewhat guilty about it.

Self-reliance? The corporation estates have been expanding so dynamically of late that until about now the management man could suppress the thought that he was a bureaucrat—bureaucrats, as every businessman knew, were those people down in Washington who preferred safety to adventure. Just when the recognition began to dawn, no one can say, but since the war the younger generation of management haven't been talking of self-reliance and adventure with quite the straight face of their elders.

That upward path toward the rainbow of achievement leads smack through the conference room. No matter what name the process is called —permissive management, multiple management, the art of administration—the committee way simply can't be equated with the "rugged" individualism that is supposed to be the business of business. Not for lack of ambition do the younger men dream so moderately; what they lack is the illusion that they will carry on in the great entrepreneurial spirit. Although they cannot bring themselves to use the word bureaucrat, the approved term—the "administrator"—is not signally different in its implications. The man of the future, as junior executives see him, is not the individualist but the man who works through others for others.

Let me pause for a moment to emphasize a necessary distinction. Within business there are still many who cling resolutely to the Protestant Ethic, and some with as much rapacity as drove any nineteenth-century buccaneer. But only rarely are they of The Organization. Save for a small, and spectacular, group of financial operators, most who adhere to the old creed are small businessmen, and to group them as part of the "business community," while convenient, implies a degree of ideological kinship with big business that does not exist.

Out of inertia, the small business is praised as the acorn from which a great oak may grow, the shadow of one man that may lengthen into a large enterprise. Examine businesses with fifty or less employees, however, and it becomes apparent the sentimentality obscures some profound differences. You will find some entrepreneurs in the classic sense—men who develop new products, new appetites, or new systems of distribution— and some of these enterprises may mature into self-perpetuating institutions. But very few.

The great majority of small business firms cannot be placed on any continuum with the corporation. For one thing, they are rarely engaged in primary industry; for the most part they are the laundries, the insurance agencies, the restaurants, the drugstores, the bottling plants, the lumber yards, the automobile dealers. They are vital, to be sure, but essentially they service an economy; they do not create new money within their area and they are dependent ultimately on the business and agriculture that does.

In this dependency they react more as antagonists than allies with the corporation. The corporation, it has become clear, is expansionist—a force for change that is forever a threat to the economics of the small businessman. By instinct he inclines to the monopolistic and the restrictive. When the druggists got the "Fair Trade" laws passed it was not only the manufacturers (and customers) they were rebelling against but the whole mass economy movement of the twentieth century.

The tail wagged the dog in this case and it still often does. That it can, in the face of the growing power of the corporation, illustrates again the dominance mythology can have over reality. Economically, many a small businessman is a counterrevolutionist and the revolution he is fighting is that of the corporation as much as the New or Fair Deal. But the corporation man still clings to the idea that the two are firm allies, and on some particulars, such as fair trade, he often makes policy on this basis when in fact it is against the corporation's interests to do so.

But the revolution is not to be stopped by sentiment. Many anachronisms do remain; in personal income, for example, the corporation man who runs a branch plant on which a whole town depends is lucky to make half the income of the local car dealer or the man with the Coca-Cola franchise. The economy has a way of attending to these discrepancies, however, and the local businessman can smell the future as well as anyone else. The bland young man The Organization sent to town to manage the plant is almost damnably inoffensive; he didn't rent the old place on the hill but a smaller house, he drives an Olds instead of a Caddy, and when he comes to the Thursday luncheons he listens more than he talks. But he's the future just the same.

I have been talking of the impact of organization on the Protestant Ethic; just as important, however, was the intellectual assault. In the great revolt against traditionalism that began around the turn of the century, William James, John Dewey, Charles Beard, Thorstein Veblen, the muckrakers and a host of reformers brought the anachronisms of the Protestant Ethic under relentless fire, and in so doing helped lay the groundwork for the Social Ethic. It would be a long time before organization men would grasp the relevance of these new ideas, and to this day many of the most thoroughgoing pragmatists in business would recoil at being grouped with the intellectuals. (And vice versa.) But the two movements were intimately related. To what degree the intellectuals were a cause of change, or a manifestation, no one can say for certain, but more presciently than those in organization they grasped the antithesis between the old concept of the rational, unbeholden individual and the world one had to live in. They were not rebels against society; what they fought was the denial of society's power, and they provided an intellectual framework that would complement, rather than inhibit, the further growth of big organization.

It is not in the province of this book to go into a diagnosis of the ideas of Dewey and James and the other pragmatists. But there is one point of history I think very much needs making at this time. Many people still look on the decline of the Protestant Ethic as our fall from grace, a detour from Americanism for which we can blame pragmatism, ethical relativism, Freudianism and other such developments. These movements have contributed much to the Social Ethic, and many of their presuppositions are as shaky as those they replaced. To criticize them on this score is in order; to criticize them as having subverted the American temper, however, is highly misleading.

Critics of pragmatism, and followers too, should remember the context of the times in which the pragmatists made their case. The pragmatists' emphasis on social utility may be redundant for today's needs, but when they made their case it was not a time when psychology or adjustment or social living were popular topics but at a time when the weight of conservative opinion denied that there was anything much that needed adjusting. Quite clearly, revolt was in order. The growth of the organization society did demand a recognition that man was not entirely a product of his free will; the country did need an educational plant more responsive to the need of the people. It did need a new breeze, and if there had been no James or no Dewey, some form of pragmatism would probably have been invented anyway. Nonphilosophical Americans sensed that changes were in order too; what the philosophers of pragmatism did was to give them guidance and tell them in intellectually responsible terms that they were right in feeling that way.

Pragmatism's emphasis on the social and the practical, furthermore, was thoroughly in the American tradition. From the beginning, Americans had always been impatient with doctrines and systems; like the Puritans, many came here because of a doctrine, but what they came to was a new environment that required some powerful adapting to, and whenever the doctrine got in the way of practicality, the doctrine lost out. Few people have had such a genius for bending ideals to the demands of the times, and the construction of fundamental theory, theological or scientific, has never excited Americans overmuch. Long before James, *Does it work?* was a respectable question to ask. If impatience at abstract thought was a defect, it was the defect of a virtue, and the virtue, call it what you will, has always been very close to pragmatism as Dewey and James defined it. By defining it they gave it coherence and power at a time when it needed assertion, but the inclination to the practical antedated the philosophy; it was not the product of it.

Reform was everywhere in the air. By the time of the first World War the Protestant Ethic had taken a shellacking from which it would not recover; rugged individualism and hard work had done wonders for the people to whom God in his infinite wisdom, as one put it, had given control of society. But it hadn't done so well for everyone else and now they, as well as the intellectuals, were all too aware of the fact.

The ground, in short, was ready, and though the conservative opinion that drew the fire of the rebels seemed entrenched, the basic temper of the country was so inclined in the other direction that emphasis on the social became the dominant current of U.S. thought. In a great outburst of curiosity, people became fascinated with the discovering of all the environmental pressures on the individual that previous philosophies had denied. As with Freud's discoveries, the findings of such inquiries were deeply disillusioning at first, but with characteristic exuberance Americans found a rainbow. Man might not be perfectible after all, but there was another dream and now at last it seemed practical: the perfectibility of *society.*

19. THE SUBURBAN DISLOCATION

David Riesman

If the suburb is the product of affluence, so too is its new way of life. David Riesman describes the values that comprise the suburban culture of mid-twentieth-century America. These are, first, a defection from Puritanism, with the result that industrial work has become simply a necessary (and boring) means to suburban living and not an end in itself. Unlike his austere cultural predecessors, the modern suburbanite is clearly consumer-minded and devoted to leisure and complacent privatism. True, he does pursue a low-keyed type of local civic enterprise and demonstrates a broad range of communal decencies. Nevertheless, suburbia is an arena of affluent euphoria, even vacuous aimlessness that contrasts sharply with the traditional constraints of the small town. Domesticity, propinquitous relations, and philoprogenitiveness—expressed in terms of the housewife-chauffeur, TV viewing, the backyard barbecue, child-centering, amiable neighboring, and a type of gardening aptly described as outdoor housekeeping—combine to create a new style of living, on a low cultural plateau to be sure, but nonetheless indigenous to the new outer fringe of the megalopolis.

WE EXPECT MORE OF LIFE than did our parents and grandparents—more, even, than freedom from want and the standard package of consumer durables. Our very abundance has increased the scope of our expectations about what life could be like and therefore has made our situation potentially revolutionary.

Excerpts from *The Annals of the American Academy of Political and Social Science,* November 1957. Reprinted by permission of the author and the publisher.

Having said this, I must immediately qualify it by pointing out that, for millions of suburbanites, their post-World War II experience has been prosperous and open far beyond their depression-born expectations. For them, the suburbs have been one vast supermarket, abundantly and conveniently stocked with approved yet often variegated choices. The children are less of a worry there than on city streets; the neighbors often more friendly than those city folk who "keep themselves to themselves"; life in general is more relaxed. The confidence such people often have that things will continue to go well for them is revealed in the story told one journalist in a Southern California suburb where employment depends on nearby defense plants. When he asked people what would happen to them in case of a depression or cancellation of defense contracts, they answered: "Why then the government will stockpile cars." Life on credit has worked out well for many such home owners, allowing them to have their children young and in circumstances far better than those in which they themselves grew up. Whatever the outsider might say about the risks blithely taken, with no allowance made for personal or social setbacks, or about the anemic quality of the relaxed life or its complacency, he would have to admit that such first-generation suburbanites have found the taste of abundance pleasant and, for the younger ones with wages rising faster than prices, not notably problematic.

REVOLT AGAINST INDUSTRIALISM

This subjective attitude does not, however, alter the fact that, among such suburban dwellers and in general in our society, we are witnessing a tremendous but tacit revolt against industrialism. It is a very different sort of revolt from either that of the machine smashers of the early nineteenth century or that of the various anti-industrial sects—socialist, anarchist, agrarian, etc.—of an earlier day. Large manufacturing industry is increasingly moving to the luxury side of the "dual economy," and backbreaking toil and harsh physical conditions are vanishing (except in industrialized farming and the service trades) with the coming of electricity, full employment, unions, and personnel men. But the luxury, which is often used to make the work more gregarious and less of an effort, is seldom used to make it less monotonous.[1] Naturally, men treat their work as delinquents treat school though schools are less likely than plants to pioneer the partial truancy of the four-day week, escaping and sabotaging when they can. Managers and foremen try in vain to restore the "old school spirit" to their employees and, failing, seek through automation and quality control to make up for the deliquescence of the "instinct of workmanship" once so painfully built into the labor force. Observers of factory life have repeatedly pointed out that status within the plant is no longer gained by hard work and craftsmanship, but rather by one's con-

sumer skills outside. Men dream, not of rising in the factory, but of starting a small business such as a motel, gas station, or TV repair shop in the
shabby and open-shop underside of our dual economy.[2] For youngsters
from subsistence farms, for hillbillies, and Southern Negroes, a Detroit or
Gary factory is still glamorous or at least a liberation from drastic poverty
and insecurity; but for second- and third-generation factory workers, it no
longer holds much meaning other than as a (hopefully temporary)
source of funds and fringe benefits.

To be sure, there is a new industrialism of electronics, plastics, avia-
tion, and so on, which retains a certain appeal that the older industries
have so largely lost. However, the new firms, increasingly located in suburbs or where people want to live: California, and the Southwest and
Florida, speed the movement out of heavy industry and merge factory
and suburban life in a blend Patrick Geddes would probably disown. But
we see in these industries precisely the form that the revolt against industrialism has taken today, namely to partially incorporate the "enemy" so
that industrialism is not compartmentalized but rather, in muted form,
spreads into all parts of the culture. This is, of course, what happens in so
many social struggles: One defeats the enemy by becoming more like
him.

LIFE AND WORK VALUES

Let me pursue this further by looking at what is happening to the older
form of industrial and commercial metropolis. When, a few years ago, I
studied interviews done with several hundred college seniors at twenty
representative universities, asking them what they would like or expect to
be doing in fifteen years, I was struck by the fact that the great majority
planned to live in the suburbs. They expected to be married, and in describing their prospective spouses they hoped for what we might call sta-
tion-wagon types: educated, companionable, civic-minded, and profoundly domestic. There were few who recognized some incompatibility
between focus on suburban life and focus on big-city ambitions (for instance, a senior who wanted to go into advertising, yet not live in or near
New York). They were—with some exceptions especially among the
Southerners—willing to sacrifice the heights of achievement, though not
the plateaus of the luxury economy, in favor of their goals of suburban
domesticity and peace. Those who hailed originally from the suburbs suffered from no disenchantment and wanted to return to them—often to
the same one—while both city-bred and small-town boys also preferred
the suburbs. I assume that some of the latter in an earlier day would have
wanted to leave Main Street behind and make their mark in the big city,
whatever lingering agrarian fears and suspicions of it they still harbored.[3]
The city today, for many, spells crime, dirt, and race tensions, more than

it does culture and opportunity. While some people still escape from the small town to the city even more people are escaping from the city to the suburbs.

. . . A recent fragmentary survey presents evidence that managers are less satisfied with their work even than unskilled workers, and it is conceivable that the middle-class occupations in general will soon be regarded as sources of funds and of periodic contacts and activity, much as the working-class occupations are now largely regarded.[4] If work loses its centrality, then the place where it is done also comes to matter less, and the access to variety in work that the central city provides may also come to matter less. Indeed, so much is this the case already that advertising for engineers in *Scientific American* and in trade journals looks more and more like the vacation advertising in *Holiday*. Minneapolis-Honeywell offers seasons and skiing as a counter-lure to the aircraft and electronic suburbs of the Far West. In this regimen, white-collar and blue-collar move towards one another, as each group now emphasizes the consumption aspects of life.

SUBURBAN WAY OF LIFE

This life, as just indicated, is increasingly focused on the suburbs which, since World War II, have grown so in quantity as to change their quality. For, although upper-class and upper-middle-class people have lived in the suburbs of our great cities since the 1880's or earlier, the cities before World War II still retained their hegemony: They engrossed commercial, industrial, and cultural power. The city represented the division and specialization not only of labor but of attitude and opinion: By discovering like-minded people in the city, one developed a new style, a new little magazine, a new architecture. The city, that is, provided a "critical mass" which made possible new combinations—criminal and fantastic ones as well as stimulating and productive ones. Today, however, with the continual loss to the suburbs of the elite and the enterprising, the cities remain big enough for juveniles to form delinquent subcultures, but barely differentiated enough to support cultural and educational activities at a level appropriate to our abundant economy. The elite, moreover, tend to associate with like-income neighbors rather than with like-minded civic leaders, thus dispersing their potential for leadership beyond township boundaries. Ironically, these people sometimes choose to live in communities which might be almost too manageable if millions of others did not simultaneously make the same choice.[5]

Indeed, the suburbs are no longer simply bedroom communities but increasingly absorb the energies of the men as well as the women and children. The men, that is, are not simply being good providers while still attached to the values of the industrial system: They are seekers after the

good life in the suburbs on their own account. Early marriage and the
rise in the birth rate are so many rivulets of individual, only barely self-
conscious protest against the values inherited from industrialism and the
low-birth-rate middle-class metropolis—so many decisions to prefer companionship in the present to some distant goal, and so many mortgages of
the future in the benevolent shadow of the luxury economy and its esca-
lator of slow inflation, promotion, and protection. Whereas men once
identified themselves with commerce and industry—with its power, its abstractions, its achievements—and forced women to remain identified with
domesticity—save for those women who broke through the barrier and
became man-imitating career girls—now, as many observers have pointed
out, a growing homogenization of roles is occurring. Women take jobs to
support the suburban menage periodically while men take part in its
work (do-it-yourself), its civic activities (Parent-Teachers Association,
and so on), and its spirit. Rather than delegating religion to their wom-
enfolk, men go to church in increasing numbers, occasionally as in an earlier day to be respectable or to climb socially, and occasionally out of a
genuine religious call, but more typically because the church, like the
high school and the country club, has become a center for the family as a
social and civic unit.

DECENTRALIZATION OF LEISURE

All this brings with it an increasing decentralization of leisure. Just as the
suburban churches tend, within the boundaries of the "three faiths," to
an amiable syncretism, ignoring doctrinal or liturgical differences, so too
the other leisure activities of the suburbs tend to reduce the specialized
differentiations possible in a metropolis. What I mean here can be illustrated with reference to music. A metropolis has enough music lovers to
organize highly differentiated groups: Mozart lovers may split off from
Bach lovers and would never encounter lovers of Wagner, while in the
suburbs the music lovers—if they are to support communal activities at
all—must in some measure homogenize their tastes and hence create a
local market for "classical music." Indeed, they will be exposed to a good
deal of community pressure to support the musical activities of their
friends in return for having their own enterprises supported. The same
holds, *pari passu,* for the other arts—just as it does for the differentiation of specialty stores, churches, and museums found in a large city. By
the same token, the suburban activist can feel that his own contribution
matters, as he would likely feel in the big city only when he is very rich,
very active, or very influential. People brought up in the suburbs may not
realize what they are missing, and they may relate their emotional ties entirely to their locality, not going downtown to shop or to visit friends or
to go to the theatre.[6]

Suburbs differ, of course, in what they make available, and so, . . .
do central cities; thus, Morris Janowitz showed that many people who, to
the visitor's eye, live in Chicago actually live in a small neighborhood
that might as well be a suburb. Moreover, central cities are increasingly
influenced by suburban styles of life: People trained to a suburban attachment to their cars drive downtown even when good and commodious
public transportation is available, and they wear the casual dress of the
suburbs when they do.

The suburban dweller believes, in fact, that he has the best of both
worlds. In the interviews with college seniors I referred to earlier, in
which such stress was placed on suburban domesticity, many students also
emphasized their wish not to lose the cultural amenities they had enjoyed
in college.[7] Some of these amenities will certainly be distributed in the
suburb though frequently in diluted doses: Piped in through television
and radio and high-fidelity sets; the suburb may even support a theatre
group and, in a few cases, amateur chamber music; the local high school
will provide entertainment of a sort, as well as facilities for adult education.

However, as the radii lengthen on which people move away from the
city—as they must with the crowding of the suburbs leading to the jump
to the exurbs—people either learn as in California to drive great
distances for dinner or confine themselves to their immediate environs:
The central city as a meeting place disappears—a process which has gone
further in Los Angeles and Chicago than in Boston or New York. The
neighbors make up little circles based—as William H. Whyte, Jr., showed
for Park Forest—largely on propinquity.

LOSS OF HUMAN DIFFERENTIATION

The decentralization of leisure in the suburbs goes further than this,
however, as the home itself, rather than the neighborhood, becomes the
chief gathering place for the family—either in the "family room" with its
games, its TV, its informality, or outdoors around the barbecue. And
while there are values in this of family closeness and "togetherness," there
is also a loss of differentiation as the parents play pals to their children
and the latter, while gaining a superficial precocity, lose the possibility of
wider contacts. At worst, there is a tendency for family talk and activity
to seek the lowest common denominator in terms of age and interest.

Some of these matters are illustrated by an interview with a housewife
who had recently bought a house in one of the wealthier suburbs north of
Chicago. Her husband had been transferred to Chicago from a southern
city and had been encouraged by his company to buy a large house for entertaining customers. Customers, however, seldom came since the husband was on the road much of the time. The wife and three children

hardly ever went downtown—they had no Chicago contacts anyway—and after making sporadic efforts to make the rounds of theater and musical activities in the suburbs and to make friends there, they found themselves more and more often staying home, eating outdoors in good weather and looking at TV in bed. Observing that "there is not much formal entertaining back and forth," the wife feared she was almost losing her conversational skills; yet she felt that her family had been pulled closer together by the shared activities, in which the husband joined on weekends, around the home. After listening to her list and discuss the friends made at church and golf, it became evident that her immediate environment just missed providing her with people close enough to her in taste and interest for intimate ties to develop.

. . . there seems to me to be a tendency, though not a pronounced one, in the suburbs to lose the human differentiations which have made great cities in the past the centers of rapid intellectual and cultural advance. The suburb is like a fraternity house at a small college—or the "close propinquity" to which Tocqueville referred—in which like-mindedness reverberates upon itself as the potentially various selves within each of us do not get evoked or recognized. For people who move to the suburb to live when adult, of course, matters are different than among those who never knew another milieu. And, to be sure, creative human contact need not be face to face but can often be vicarious, through print or other mediated channels. Certainly, highly differentiated human beings have grown up in locales which gave them minimal support. Moreover, though the nonneighborly seldom seek the "suburbs," [8] a few doubtless manage to survive there. Ease of movement, in any case, permits periodic access to others, although as these others themselves scatter to the suburbs, this process becomes more difficult.

ROLE OF THE AUTOMOBILE IN SUBURBIA

Indeed, at least until each of us has his own helicopter or rocket, this pattern of life requires us to spend a great deal of time in automobiles, overcoming decentralization—but driving is itself a terribly "decentralized" activity, allowing at best for car-pool sociability, and at worst mitigated by the quiz-bits, frequent commercials, and flatulent music of AM radio. As compared with the older suburbanites who commuted by train and read the paper, did homework, or even read a book, the present and increasing tendency to travel to work by car seems aggressively vacuous and solipsistic.[9] Whereas in preindustrial cultures and in the lower classes in industrial society, people sometimes just hang on a corner or sit vacantly, it is striking that in a society which offers many alternatives, people will consent to drive vacantly but not refreshingly—woe betide the careless or unspry pedestrian or bicyclist who gets in the way of industrial workers pouring out of the factory parking lots or white-collar workers coming home on a throughway. The human waste here is most important, but the waste of resources and land, the roadside *dreck*,[10] the highways which eat space as railroad yards even in St. Louis or Chicago never did, are not negligible even in a huge rich country.

Where the husband goes off with the car to work—and often, in the vicious circle created by the car, there is no other way for him to travel—the wife is frequently either privatized at home or to escape isolation must take a job which will support her own car. Whereas the rental courts of developments like Park Forest provide companionship for the stranded wives—companionship which, given the age and sex homogeneity, is sometimes oppressive—other suburbs are so built and so psychologically "unsociometric" as to limit neighboring and leave many women to the company of Mary Margaret McBride and Arthur Godfrey. Indeed, in a few instances of interviewing in the morning in new suburbs south of Chicago, I have been struck by the eagerness of the housewives to talk to somebody (and not only to a man!) who is not a salesman—once they can be weaned away from the TV which amuses them as a kind of vicarious baby sitter. It is not only the visiting intellectual who finds the lives of these women empty, their associations fragmentary. My colleagues, Donald Horton and R. Richard Wohl, speak of the "parasocial intimacy" they attain with the celebrities of the TV variety shows.[11] The women themselves, if at all sensitive or well educated, complain of having their contacts limited to their young children and to a few other housewives in the same boat. And, as a result of efforts to understand the extraordinary philoprogenitiveness of the suburban middle classes (a theme recurred to below), I have come to entertain the suspicion that, once started on having children, these women continue in some part out of a fear of the emptiness of life without children and of the problems they would face of relating themselves to their menfolk without the static, the noise, the pleasures, the "problems" that the presence of children provides.

The children themselves, in fact before they get access to a car, are captives of their suburb, save for those families where the housewives surrender continuity in their own lives to chauffeur their children to lessons, doctors, and other services which could be reached via public transport in the city. In the suburban public schools, the young are captives, too, dependent on whatever art and science and general liveliness their particular school happens to have—again contrast the metropolis, with its choice of high schools, as most notably in New York.[12]

. . .

SUBURBIA'S POSITIVE AND NEGATIVE ASPECTS

Our Center for the Study of Leisure has been conducting studies of limited scope in several Chicago suburbs in an effort, *inter alia,* to see what

happens to people who leave the city for the suburbs in terms of new
commitments and new demands. We have also done a very inconclusive
study of how people in the city spend their week ends. We have the impression that the suburbanite, tied to his house as the doctor is to his
practice, may actually be less likely to take off for a week end in the country than the urban dweller whose janitor can look after his apartment
and even the cat. Indeed, it is the city people, freed by industrialism from
long hours of grinding work, who (along, of course, with an ample supply of untied suburbanites) make up a large proportion of the outboard
population of our lakes and rivers and of the thirty-five million fishermen
—more than twice the number of those urban sportsmen, the bowlers. Although air-conditioning makes even the most humid and dirty city potentially habitable, people can't wait to leave town on week ends and during
the summer, even though in many parts of the country it means spewing
the city into the countryside and fighting with like-minded crowds for
space on roads, lakes, and at motels.[13]

As I have indicated, I believe that snobbery and imitation of the rich
play a declining part in this exodus to the suburbs and that the quiet revolt against the city and industrialism plays an increasing part. I would
argue that there is often less "front" in the new suburbs than in equivalent sections of a metropolis, and less pressure for a lace-curtain life con-
cealing back-stage scrimping and meanness than there once was. People
do not usually learn the idea of a garden suburb either from British models or Mumford or Clarence Stein. The idea, in its uncomplicated forms,
is an omnipresent dream, carrying overtones of the Bible, peasant life
and folk imagery. The urban wish for contact with nature has been crystallized for many Americans around the habits of the British gentry and
their middle-class imitators. But, more modest than the aspidistra-lovers
of the London suburbs, we prefer not to give fancy names to our own
"villas" but to let this dumb show be done for us by the realtors. In the
Chicago area, for instance, a great many suburbs have either "Park" or
"Forest" in their names, and two of them have both! Furthermore, social
mobility means that many, perhaps most urban dwellers will have suburban relatives or friends. The mass production of suburbs, especially in
the postwar years, has made them accessible to almost everyone. Only in
the rural and impoverished parts of the South and Great Plains farming
regions are we likely to find many people who do not know anybody who
lives in a suburb and have never had occasion to visit one. Beyond that,
the vicarious socialization of Americans into the experiences of consumption they are about to have is the continuous task of the mass media.
Many of these, and at a variety of income levels, are devoted to expound-
ing the suburban way of life directly in ads and features; other media are
indirect vehicles for suburban styles in the homes pictured in stories, the
sport shirts worn, and the idols of consumption portrayed.[14] The whole
American ethos, which once revolved about the dialectic of pure country
versus wicked but exciting city, seems to me now aerated by the suburban

outlook. This produces an homogenization of both city and country, but without full integration.

While on the whole the lower-middle and middle-income suburbs sponsor the relaxed life, there is one area where they impose an imperative which many city dwellers have not met, namely that of having some sort of garden—less as a cultural amenity than as a minimum contribution to civic decency: A kind of compulsory outdoor housekeeping. Indeed, in the study of gardening in two Chicago suburbs conducted by our Center for the Study of Leisure [15] we gained the impression that garden clubs were not extremely active in either one (though we have found very active and prestigeful clubs on the North Shore) ; garden clubs are much more characteristic of older communities, where they represent a familiar activity of some of the earliest families, rather than of the new suburbs, where gardening must compete with many other hobbies and activities, both outdoor and indoor. We found in Fairlawn, a new developer's suburb, for example, that to many housewives the garden was simply one more chore. It represented neither a contrast with the asphalt jungle of the city, nor a pleasure in growing things, nor a rage for order. It was rather a tax imposed by neighborhood consciousness—the neighbors often being interpreted as more concerned and censorious than they, for the most part, were. Thus we find that many people who have moved newly to the suburbs to escape the city come without awareness of the constraints they will find—or mistakenly interpret—in the suburb. Like the appointment in Samarra, they meet pressures they had thought to leave behind, though altered in form and impact.

One of these pressures, already adverted to, is the metropolis itself; its traffic, its ethnic minorities, and its tax rates tend to catch up with them. The waves of succession within the city proper do not halt at its boundaries, and many old and established suburbs are finding themselves cut in two by freeways and by the new kinds of people they bring. In this situation, some of the old kinds of people are among those tempted to become exurbanites, putting the ever-approaching city another few miles away and hoping to solve the dilemma of distance versus intimacy by a superhighway.

However, in this quandary the emphasis on superhighways—and on supercars which require them—takes on much of the lunatic quality of an arms race. As highways get bigger and better, they invite more cars, destroy what undeveloped and unschematized country (or central city) remains, and require still more highways in an unending spiral.[16]

SUBURBAN STYLES OF LIFE AND THOUGHT

People have been drilled by industrialism in the values of efficiency—narrowly defined in terms of speed, performance, and a kind of streamlined look (what Jacques Barzun has referred to as "America's Romance

with Practicality"). Thus even when they flee from the cities and the
style of life industrialism has brought about, they cannot change the style
of thought which sees the solution to ribbon developments in stretching
them still further until our East and West coasts threaten to become continuous roadside slums.

What is true of the planning, or lack of it, of our road-centered
culture as a whole is also true of domestic architecture. Efficiency here
is less stark—and consequently often less attractive—since it must compete with traditional definitions of a suburban free-standing home. But,
as many architects have pointed out, the interiors are highly modern
in the sense of mechanization. Indeed, one reason why husbands have
been willing to become domesticated is that they have been promoted from dishwashers to operators of dishwashers. Similarly, they use
power mowers to give crew cuts to handkerchief-sized lawns and pierce
their wives' and neighbors' ears with the screams of high fidelity music.
The open plan of the very newest ranch-style homes puts the TV set on a
swivel in the center. Here it can be seen from all parts of the house so
that urban news, fashions, gossip, and jokes can circulate in the home
throughout the daily cycle of the members of the family. But all these improvements are bought at the expense of space for the individual whose
bedroom in the suburban development is often smaller than in city tenements. This is especially true, as Albert Roland of *Household* magazine
has pointed out to me, of the newest suburban homes. These have both a
family room and a living room. The latter, like the old parlor, is used only
for state occasions; the family room is big enough for games, the TV, an
inside barbecue, and general clutter.

Nor does the lawn or backyard provide a bounteous free space in most
of the new developments. In comparison with the size and cost of the
house, plots are small (much as they have traditionally been in midwestern cities where people wanted to avoid the row house but not to be too
far from their next-door neighbors). Moreover, the fact that there is both
a front and a backyard—the latter being, in many developments, the
"family room" and the former the "parlor"—means that what space there
is becomes divided. And just as the homes have no interstitial spaces, no
nooks and crannies, so the lots have no texture taken individually or together.[17] I keep asking myself what the lots will look like when the explo-
sion of our population doubles the numbers in the suburban hegira without, in all probability, increasing proportionately the services that our
new expectations crave. Will houses and lots get smaller when people can
no longer spread further afield? People have been moving to the suburbs
in many cases in pursuit of an inchoate dream of spaciousness. They have
looked for a release from urban tensions, from crowded and ugly schools,
from indoors. And ordinarily this release has more than compensated for
losses in urban qualities which are difficult to sense or describe—qualities
of possibility, often, rather than of actual use.[18] What will occur when the

urban qualities have been dissipated, while suburban ones elude all but the rich?

Such questions assume, as I have here been doing, that Americans have ceased being socially inventive outside the corporate or military spheres. They assume that we will not discover the governmental or voluntary channels either to give many people alternative satisfactions to large families or to create forms of life and livelihood appropriate to another age of population expansion—this time with no frontiers left. Certainly, there is now a kind of private inventiveness in the suburbs among people who, having lost "the track of generations" and traditional standards of judgment and taste, are somehow managing, with ambivalent aid from the media, to create new forms and styles. The leaders of Park Forest and several other new communities, surrounded by others as green as they, often managed to develop some communal decencies and controls; in that sense, the townmeeting spirit is far from moribund. It is easy to see the negative and ironical features of the suburbs—harder to see emergent crystallizations.[19]

But one trouble is that the suburbs, like the families within them, can scarcely control their own immediate environs, let alone the larger metropolitan and national orbits that impinge on them and decide their eventual atmosphere. And here is where the suburbanites' immense liking for Ike is portentous. It expresses the wish of so many of the college seniors mentioned above that civics and the Community Chest replace politics; it expresses the hope, built into the very structure of credit and the additive-extrapolative style of thought, that nothing serious will occur, that everything will go on as before. And it expresses this hope, of course, at the very moment when private decisions—irresponsibly influenced—to buy or not to buy, to propagate or not to propagate store up our destinies (quite apart from the similar activities of the rest of our small planet). In interviews done in Chicago suburbs by Louis Harris before the 1956 elections, he asked potential voters how they felt about a part-time, golf-playing president. Many were indignant, saying they would play golf too if they had such problems—though when asked to name serious problems facing the country, they could often get no further than high taxes. Plainly, Ike's complacencies mirrored and supported their own (Eisenhower, of course, like most anyone in Washington, is far less complacent than these constituencies), and their defenses against untoward apprehension were too great to allow thought for the morrow.

THE AIMLESS QUALITY OF SUBURBAN LIFE

In the days of Lincoln Steffens and later, people emphasized the "shame of the cities," and in the 1920's major novelists emphasized the constraints of small-town and occasionally of small-suburban life. Today, the

comparable worry, in the books dealing with the suburbs, is conformity
—*Point of No Return,* with its concern for place and competition, strikes
a somewhat older note; writers point to the uniformity of the ranch style,
the ever-present television antennae, the lamp, if not the crack, in the picture window—which usually provides a view of the nearly treeless street,
the cars, and someone else's picture window. Actually, uniformity and
conformity are quite different matters as Georg Simmel has observed in
his essay on "Fashion." [20] The former may dictate to men only in inessen-
tials, whereas the latter involves some psychological mechanism. And the
conformity of the new suburbs is, in some important ways, far less strin-
gent than that of the old; if it is not quite the case that "anything goes,"
lots of things do go which once would, if known, have brought ostracism.
If one does not seek to force the new suburbanite back across the ethnic
tracks he has just crossed, he is quite tolerant, even bland. If he is political at all—rather than parochially civic-minded, tending to a "garden"
which includes the local schools and waterworks—he is apt to be an Eisenhower Republican, seldom informed, rarely angry, and only spasmodi-
cally partisan.

No, what is missing in suburbia, even where the quality of life has not
overtly deteriorated, is not the result of claustrophobic conformity to
others' sanctions. Rather, there would seem to be an aimlessness, a pervasive low-keyed unpleasure. This cannot be described in terms of traditional sorrows but is one on which many observers of the American scene
and the American visage have commented, notably Erich Fromm in *The
Sane Society* and the Goodmans in *Communitas.* For millions of people,
work no longer provides a central focus for life; and the breadwinner is
no longer the chief protagonist in the family saga—just as Saturday night
no longer provides a central focus for festivity. In fact, the decentralization of leisure in the suburbs is not only spatial but temporal, as evenings
from Thursday through Sunday are oriented to play rather than work
and are not individually accented or collectively celebrated.[21]

CHAPTER FIVE

URBAN SOCIAL STRUCTURE

The city is a functioning social system. Through the city's institutions effective conduct of its population is maintained. Think of certain requirements of social organization in general—motivation, communication, coordination, and adaptation—the city no less than any other social system must provide the responses that are necessary for dealing with them. The sum total of these adaptive measures may be seen as functional processes through which the city copes with its internal and external needs. These processes therefore make up its social structure.

Many sociologists describe and analyze social structure in terms of institutional subsystems, notably kinship, stratification, political organization, the economic distributive system, education, and religion, inasmuch as these subsystems are seen to contribute to the overall social maintenance problem. The writings in this chapter have been chosen to give adequate coverage to institutional complexes, as well as some attention to their interconnections. The articles also convey a sense of the historical process by which urbanization modifies the preexisting folk institutions.

Consequently, Banfield and Wilson discuss the antagonistic economic and ethnic alignments that the modern American city harbors and how these are expressed politically. In like manner, the work of Glazer and Moynihan is directed to the seemingly paradoxical, pluralistic sociocultural forms that accompany political and economic cooperation in the American metropolis at its current stage of development.

Bell and Boat's survey of San Francisco contributes a picture of the persistence of interpersonal relations and the survival of kinship networks even in the largest urban centers. An apt supplement to their article is the abridgment of the study by the Andersons on the modernization process by which isolated communities in Scandinavia grow into sizable cities and witness the decline of familial and religious organization. At the same time, new formal structures arise to take their place. Scott Greer's discussion of the patterns locking the suburb into the functional system of the metropolis broadens the scope of our analysis. Finally, with Bogue's recognition of the dominance and power of attraction that the major city exercises over its surrounding area, the delineation of the urban community as a structured entity is completed.

These selections are perhaps most meaningful when viewed against a broad understanding of urban structure, and that is an objective toward which Max Weber's threefold conception of stratification is a useful point of departure. Weber acknowledges three dimensions of social classes—economic, honorific, and political— with each of these seen as capable of developing somewhat independently of the others. In modern Western history (that is, the period in which urbanization has been a truly major force), industrialization has created occupational opportunity and great wealth. These in turn have been reflected in the growth of a new, powerful urban industrial and commercial élite, a sizable educated middle class of professionals and businessmen, and a large industrial-labor class. Leisure time and conspicuous consumption have been greatly augmented. In addition, republican forms of government have expanded their functions in order to intervene in the economy and effect rational coordination. As a result a large bureaucratic apparatus has been created that, incidentally, has further status implications.

In predominantly agricultural societies, land ownership rather than industry or commerce is the important factor governing stratification. In ancient Greece and Rome, for example, the population was divided into patricians, plebians, and slaves. Similarly, medieval Europe was made up of a feudal aristocracy, vassals, and serfs. There too, however, the control of land was the decisive factor. In modern, primarily rural countries, Cooley and Angell divide the agricultural classes into farm owners, tenants, and laborers; and by comparison, the nonagricultural classes into those of the professionals, businessmen, and workers.[1] Others contend that "businessmen" is too sweeping a category, for it does not distinguish between large-scale executives and the proprietors of small businesses, two somewhat disparate occupations and statuses.

Although there are such uncertainties within rural societies, and also pronounced differences between rural societies themselves, the fact remains, nonetheless, that as a whole rural societies are systematically different in their stratification orders from nations that are essentially urban. Thus, R. L. Beals has outlined a three-class system for Latin America in which parallel strata exist for the rural and urban populations.[2] The rural population includes landholders, storekeepers, small farmers, handicraft workers, and farm laborers. And the urban population is divided into industrialists at the top and then below them, professionals, artisans, and factory laborers.

An urban society means market relations that are very different from those in a rural system. In the urban community there is a much greater range of social space. This is generally attributable to the expansive economy that affords individuals great latitude to develop their capacities and competitive powers. Not only is occupational differentiation effected but also enormous disparities in regard both to wealth and invidiously significant styles of life. The latter of course arise also as a consequence of educational opportunity and cultural expression per se.

Focusing on market relations, the Lynds made a pioneering contribution to urban stratification studies in their 1925 survey of Middletown. There, in Muncie, Indiana, they found that the "outstanding cleavage" was the division of the population into the business and working classes. This basic fact, they observed, had a pervasive influence, having effects on one's family, voluntary associations, possessions, dress, and, "so on indefinitely throughout the daily comings and going of a Middletown man, woman, or child." [3]

Although some scholars insist on the primacy of market position in regard to social-class membership in contemporary Western urban society, major opinion, however, leans toward the recognition of multiple class structures. These indicate that a plurality of stratification bases, including wealth, power, associational participation, and mode-of-life symbolism, crystallize perhaps, as Lenski asserts, in some determinate manner, although this is far from being wholly clear.[4] Thus sociologists are not in agreement on the number of social classes that should be identified in the contemporary American city. Frances E. Merrill and H. W. Eldredge, for instance, uphold the traditional three-class system; Richard Centers, a four-category classification; Hollingshead finds a system of five classes; Warner, a six-class hierarchy; and Harold Kaufman, even an eleven-class typology.[5] Sociologists differ understandably, because they place different weights on occupation, wealth, education, lineage, and life-style in their appraisals of the evaluated participation that is evidenced in social-class placement and membership.

Urban stratification is, moreover, distinctively one in which certain patterns of an amorphous or fluid character are discernible.

Alvin Boskoff has written very persuasively on this subject.[6] Differential association and spatial segregation result in widespread ignorance of the system of graded positions; nevertheless, one is acutely conscious of his own situation. It is thus a condition, first, in which any given individual is unable to evaluate very many statuses; second, in which the material evidence of status is most readily appreciated; and third, in which multiple standards are observed. Therefore, there is much status inconsistency. Insofar as a consensus *does* exist, it focuses on the value of mobility, with the result that although there is much competition for status symbols, it is for the symbols per se; more so perhaps than for their objective counterparts, that is, their corresponding occupational roles. These conditions all contribute to the remarkable "shapelessness" of urban stratification systems.

As a rule, owing to its commitment to rational and secular values, urban society provides a relatively unusual opportunity for mobility. Preindustrial cities must of course be differentiated from those of the industrial era, for in the latter, mobility has become something of a moral imperative, or ethic. For this reason urbanization and its concomitant, industrialization, have undermined, if not obliterated, caste distinctions. Cities and their factory systems require people to live and work together with little ceremonial or traditional behavior. Common carriers militate against separatism. Functional standards of evaluation work against the received canons of deference which depend significantly on nonrational religious faith. In the United States, for example, despite rigid avoidance patterns, endogamous marriage, and the denial of civil rights to nonwhites, the universalistic system of constitutional government, which was the work of the generation that put our society on the road to its becoming an urban social order, has been the greatest single deterrent to the continuation of full caste relations.

Fifty years ago the Negro American was primarily a peasant. His urbanization became a substantial reality only during the two World Wars and the Korean conflict. By 1960, when 69.8 percent of the American population was urban, the Negro rate had reached a surprising 72.4 percent. Even more striking was the fact that the majority of Negroes were located in the core cities, while an appreciable part of the white population was suburban. There is some evidence now that because of a sharp decrease in migration from the South (it amounted to a movement of fully 5,500,000 nonwhites between 1950 and 1966) together with internal movement in the metropolitan area, an actual decline in the numbers of Negroes living in the central cities of our metropolitan centers has taken place. Be this as it may, the recent surge of nonwhites into the core cities of our largest metropolitan concentrations has been aptly described by Paul F. Coe as "one of the outstanding sociological phenomena of our time." This has indeed resulted in a sharp residential polarization of the races together with a number of serious consequences, touching on housing, education, crime, employment, and government.

To a large extent, of course, the plight of the Negro urbanite today duplicates the misery of the earlier rural migrants to the industrial centers of Europe and the United States. It was William Blake who saw on the faces of the desperate lower-class Londoners of the late eighteenth century "marks of weakness, marks of woe," as did Jacob Riis in New York more than a century later. Immigrant groups react to urbanization with personal and collective disorganization. They also, however, put forth purposeful sociocultural, economic, and political organization when confronted with adversity.

The newer nonwhite migrants represent a social-class conflict and also a racial one, and although urban contact produces competition, and hence the further exacerbation of strained ethnic and racial relationships, there are certain valuable ameliorative possibilities in the city today. One is the higher level of education. Another is the advanced productive capacity of industry and technology. And a third is the greater power of government to initiate and coordinate action. Nonetheless, dissensus in America at the beginning of the final third of the twentieth century is very pronounced. The cleavage is reflected in segregation and discrimination, and in antagonistic voluntary association and political organization. Thus black nationalism may represent a fatalistic solution to the race question that is based on the conviction that whites will never accord the Negro equality. The strain on the urban social fabric that such divisive tendencies represent is very great and indeed challenges even its considerable integrative capacities.

Power studies of some note on the degree and character of urban systems of coordination have been made recently by Floyd Hunter, Nelson W. Polsby, Robert A. Dahl, William H. Form and William V. D'Antonio, and Delbert C. Miller.[7] These inquiries presuppose a background of bureaucratic concentration that permits the swift exercise of power over a large population. Indeed, the growth of an apparatus capable of maintaining a very high level of control has taken place in recent years. As an indication in point, Reinhart Bendix has reported that in 1899 there were eight administrative employees for every 100 production workers in the United States, and in 1961, 36.

Bureaucratic organization incorporates specialization of function with hierarchical coordination. Consequently, both a high level of performance and effective control tend to be achieved. In combination these capacities produce great efficiency. Bureaucratic organization is most extensive in the urban setting. It is encountered in manufacturing, business, transportation, government, labor unions, education, social welfare, and even religion.

To be sure, bureaucratic organization exists within an institutional framework of shared values, such as constitutional government and generally accepted standards of justice. And community-wide action does require the development of sufficient consensus to commit funds and combine the efforts of several or even many bureaucratic systems. However, the bureaucratic organization that characterizes urban industrial societies implies oligarchical control by virtue of the access that the managerial elite has to financial and communication resources. It is this unity that gives rise to the hypothesis that power in the urban community tends to be monolithic. Increasingly, however, membership participation has been observed. This would limit the actions of those in authority when the latter are in direct conflict with the values and interests of the rank and file. And yet, control is probably less responsive to such internal pressures than it is to the countervailing power of other bureaucratic structures. But these suggest the possibility of even greater dissensus. A very good illustration is the collective bargaining process by which industrial disputes are increasingly being settled and also paradoxically exacerbated, as in the case of public-service employees in the city.

Such considerations suggest why community-power studies have serious weaknesses. Specifically, there is little agreement on whether "power" is in fact predictably distributed or is merely assumed to be so. Second, issues that supposedly involve the exercise of power are often unspecified. Third, obtaining consent for a given policy is often mistaken for the exercise of control. Fourth, the criterion of decision making is frequently absent. And, finally, outcomes are not uncommonly simply attributed to previously expressed intentions or merely "leaders" recognized earlier.

The several institutional subsystems of the city do comprise a more or less integrated whole. Take, for example, the kinship system and the economy. The nuclear family is conducive to emancipation and an achieving personality. The neolocal pattern of separate households permits considerable geographic and social movement. Similarly, the city's educational and religious structures tend to feed constructively into the maintenance of the political, economic, and domestic institutional complexes. The school takes on a utilitarian role to train technicians. The denominational church permits the separation of affluents from nonaffluents, and a severe or emotional liturgy, as the case may be, that caters to the refinement or expressive gratification sought by the particular status group responding to its unique structural press.

The urban economy has its principal features: a limited market orientation; a corporate, bureaucratic organization; governmental intervention and coordination; a highly advanced and ever more sophisticated technology; well-educated professional and managerial personnel; a disciplined labor force that cultivates the arts of consumption; a system of mass production; and an interest in maintaining an advancing standard of living that amounts to a social ethic.

A modern city's political institutions, even making allowance for major differences in ideology as between East and West, embraces a bureaucratic organization; a system of popular, mass political organization even if only as a means of engineering consent; communication via the media rather than an interpersonal system with, however, intermediate "influentials" filtering messages through primary relationships as a vital factor in the process; a network of voluntary interest groups—labor, commerce, religious, ethnic, and the like; and the fusion of formal and informal organizations by means of interlocking cliques and factions. Finally, all of the foregoing function under an umbrella of cultural values, principally those of universalism, secularism, and rational coordination.

The older theory of urban society postulated the city as a scene of impersonal, segmental contacts with formal arrangements for taking care of needs. Voluntary associations were seen as a means of concentrating power and gaining leverage in the face of competing interests. Indeed, urbanization does weaken the traditional influence of family and church. And voluntary associations do arise, especially where literacy and wealth are present, to render specialized services, as in civic affairs, economic interests, health, and so forth. Voluntary associations are generally very numerous although not uniformly so. A city with a population of moderate size has a facilitating effect on voluntary group establishment and membership while the very large metropolitan center tends to exhibit greater reliance on central, official, formal organization and less on informal, local group formation. Periods of rapid change or transition do, however, stimulate voluntary activity and association both of the formal and informal variety even in the very large urban community.

Voluntary associations play a number of roles in the city. They offer an opportunity for interest groups to exercise influence and power, in the form of private welfare services, for instance, independently of government policy and procedure. Moreover, voluntary associations educate their members, say, by developing social skills. They can, as Harold Wilensky has recognized, provide alternative channels of mobility. Negro churches have long helped compensate for the blocked mobility confronting the caste-burdened colored man. For the larger population now voluntary associations give the career-impeded a substitute warrant of social achievement.

The voluntary group may also serve as a cohesive force by stimulating morale and close interdependence, and if it is a large association, such as a political party, by cutting down on exclusive, conflicting loyalties. Common membership in a fraternal order or lodge will have the same outcome, and a very valuable one, too, when by intersecting social-class boundaries it cuts down on class consciousness and antagonism. Voluntary associations can also institute social change, as by lobbying for the enactment of a statute or the inauguration of an administrative reform. Similarly, too, voluntary associations may play a stabilizing role by helping to preserve the status quo. The self-regulating professions are a good illustration insofar as they place restrictions on the licensing of practitioners.

Despite the profusion of voluntary associations in our own cities at the present time, large numbers of people are still left out of their reach. Mirra Komarovsky has cast doubt on the supposition that nonmembership necessarily implies isolation, deprivation, and alienation. There may be satisfying informal relations within the context of formal association. There may be a lively sense of identification with an institutional organization. There may exist a close tie with relatives. Nevertheless, she has concluded that "sections of our population are cut off from channels of power, information, growth, and a sense of participation in purposive social action." In short, the urban social structure may have serious lacunae and shortcomings that limit its effectiveness as a functioning system.

20. CLEAVAGES IN URBAN SOCIETY

Edward C. Banfield and James Q. Wilson

Defining cleavage as a lasting division within a community, political scientists Banfield and Wilson posit four such separations as both fundamental and widespread in urban America. They use demographic and historical data, as well as controlled studies, in supporting their assessment of the common, recurring competition and conflict that exists in the metropolitan social order. The deft way in which Banfield and Wilson handle their material is perhaps nowhere more in evidence than in the several alignments they identify in city politics as a whole. The upper and lower socioeconomic classes are seen to be pitted against the middle class. The rural hinterland is joined by suburbia in contesting the central city over issues of taxation and public services. And, similarly, Protestant universalism combats Catholic particularism in the city's political and civic organization.

This selection is a source of clear insight into the intricate makeup of the metropolitan community. Its presentation of the ethnic and racial factor in urban politics is, however, admittedly brief. Thus the Negro's central place in urban discord is only suggested. It is surely not developed.

WITHIN THE CITIES and metropolitan areas the most important cleavages are those between (1) haves and have-nots, (2) suburbanites and the cen-

Excerpts reprinted from *City Politics* by Edward C. Banfield and James Q. Wilson, by permission of the publishers, Cambridge, Mass.: Harvard University Press, Copyright, 1963 by the President and Fellows of Harvard College and the Massachusetts Institute of Technology.

tral city, (3) ethnic and racial groups and (4) political parties. These tend to cut across each other and, in general, to become one fundamental cleavage separating two opposed conceptions of the public interest.

HAVES AND HAVE-NOTS

Disparity in kinds and distribution of property, James Madison said is the most fundamental cause of parties and factions in all ages and places. In the city, it is useful to think in terms of three income groups—low,

TABLE 1

CITIES OVER 500,000 POPULATION RANKED BY THE PERCENTAGE OF
FAMILIES WITH INCOMES OF $10,000 A YEAR OR MORE, 1960

Rank	City	Percent	Rank	City	Percent
1	Los Angeles	25.1	12	Cincinnati	15.8
2	Seattle	22.9	13	Baltimore	15.0
3	San Francisco	22.6	14	Pittsburgh	14.3
4	Washington	21.7	15	Philadelphia	14.2
5	Chicago	21.3	16	Boston	13.6
6	San Diego	20.9	17	Buffalo	13.1
7	Dallas	18.9	18	Cleveland	13.0
8	New York	18.5	19	New Orleans	12.9
9	Detroit	17.8	20	St. Louis	10.8
10	Houston	17.5	21	San Antonio	9.6
11	Milwaukee	16.7			

SOURCE: 1960 Census.

middle, and high. Surprising as it may seem to Marxists, the conflict is generally between an alliance of the low-income and high-income groups on the one side and the middle-income groups on the other. The reason is not hard to find. The poorest people in the city favor a high level of expenditure for welfare, housing, and sometimes schools, and rarely oppose expenditure for any purpose whatever. They favor expenditures even for services that they are not likely to use—municipal opera, for example—because they pay no local taxes, or hardly any. Upper-income people also favor a high level of expenditures. They want good public services for the same reason that they want good private ones—they can afford them. But they also want good, or at any rate adequate, services for others, and they willingly support—although no doubt at levels lower than the poor would like—welfare services which they themselves will never use. Table 1 shows how our largest cities vary with respect to this upper-income group; the percentage of families with $10,000 or more income ranges from about 25 to 10 percent.

The middle-income group generally wants a low level of public expenditures. It consists of people who are worrying about the mortgage on their bungalow and about keeping up the payments on the new car. Such people are not especially charitable, no doubt partly because they feel they cannot afford to be, but partly, also, perhaps, because they feel that if others are less well off than they it is mainly because the others have not put forth as much effort as they. Many of these people want to spend their money in status-giving ways, and obviously a new car is more status-giving than a new school or a better equipped police force.

The United Auto Workers had tried for years without success to take control of Detroit's nonpartisan government. Detroit is largely a one-industry and one-union town, and the UAW has been extraordinarily successful in state politics, as evidenced by the fact that G. Mennen Williams, the workingman's friend, was elected governor five times. Nevertheless the mayor of Detroit for four terms was Albert E. Cobo, a conservative businessman who opposed public housing and favored economy and efficiency. Why did the working people who voted for Williams for governor vote for Cobo for mayor? The answer may be that Detroit is a predominantly lower-middle-class homeowning town. In partisan state and national elections, a UAW member votes as a "liberal" because the costs of measures he supports will not be assessed against his bungalow. In nonpartisan city elections, however, he votes as a property owner and taxpayer, and in all probability (if he is white) as one who fears that a progressive city government might make it easier for Negroes to move into his neighborhood.

SUBURBANITES AND THE CENTRAL CITY

The spectacular recent growth of the suburbs and the not unrelated deterioration of the central city have tended to deepen a long-standing line of cleavage between the city and its suburbs. Today many central cities find that their principal antagonist in their legislature is not the rural hinterland but an alliance of the hinterland and the suburbs.[1]

The suburbs are not all of one kind, of course; they are industrial as well as residential, lower-income as well as upper. Not very far from upper-class suburbs where garbage is collected in paper bags and put in fly-proof trucks and where high school teachers are paid as much as many Ivy League college professors, there may be communities (often unincorporated) in which most people cannot afford or else do not want even such basic amenities as sidewalks, police protection, and community sewage disposal. The upper-income suburbanite fears that by annexation or the creation of a metropolitan-area government he may be brought within the jurisdiction of the central city's government and receive a lower level of government service in consequence. The low-income suburbanite also fears being brought within the jurisdiction of the city, but for an opposite reason: it would insist upon providing him with—and taxing him for—services that he would rather do without.

This is not the only basis for the cleavage between city and suburb. Central-city residents often think that the city is being exploited by suburbanites, who use its facilities without paying taxes to it. Because the suburbanite comes to the city to work and shop, the city must spend more than it otherwise would for certain public services—traffic control and police protection, for example—but none of this extra expense, the city resident points out, can be charged against the suburbanite. To this, the suburbanite may reply that by coming to the city to work and shop he creates enough taxable values to make the city a net gainer. He may even assert that it is the suburbanite who is the victim of injustice since suburbs provide expensive public facilities, particularly schools, even though most of the tax base created by suburbanite spending is in the city.[2] When central cities try to annex suburbs or impose taxes upon the earnings of suburbanites who work in the cities, there is always a howl of protest and usually the effort fails.

ETHNIC AND RACIAL GROUPS

Ethnic and racial differences have been, and still are, basic to much of the conflict in the city. Here it will be convenient to speak of three such lines of cleavage: that between native Protestant and all others, that among the various nationality groups of foreign stock, and that between the Negro and all others.

Although the largest waves of immigration ended long ago, some cities, such as New York and Boston, still have, as Table 2 indicates, a sizable number of foreign stock. Other cities, such as Dallas, have scarcely been touched by immigration at all.

TABLE 2

CITIES OVER 500,000 POPULATION RANKED BY THE PERCENTAGE OF
PERSONS FOREIGN-BORN OR WITH AT LEAST ONE FOREIGN-BORN PARENT, 1960

Rank	City	Percent	Rank	City	Percent
1	New York	48.6	12	Philadelphia	29.1
2	Boston	45.5	13	San Antonio	24.0
3	San Francisco	43.5	14	San Diego	21.5
4	Chicago	35.9	15	Baltimore	14.8
5	Buffalo	35.4	16	St. Louis	14.1
6	Los Angeles	32.6	17	Washington	12.6
7	Detroit	32.2	18	Cincinnati	12.0
8	Seattle	31.4	19	Houston	9.7
9	Cleveland	30.9	20	New Orleans	8.6
10	Pittsburgh	30.3	21	Dallas	6.9
11	Milwaukee	30.0			

SOURCE: 1960 Census. The term "foreign-born" does not, of course, include Puerto Ricans.

Until the latter part of the last century, native Protestant industrialists and businessmen ran most cities. Then, in the Northern cities, when the tide of immigration swelled, the newly arrived ethnic groups began to challenge the natives for political control. For a time there was a sharp conflict, but in most cities the natives soon retired from the scene, or, more precisely, they transferred their activity from one sector of the scene to another.

. . .

In a good many cities, where several new ethnic groups competed for control, the old native Protestant elite might conceivably have retained its control by serving—as the Irish so often have—as a neutral force on which all elements of the ethnic struggle could agree. But the elite was incapacitated for this role by its distaste for the political culture of the new immigrant, a distaste that it did not try to conceal. As Peter and Alice Rossi have shown in an unpublished paper on "Bay City," Massachusetts, local politics, which was a source of prestige for the local industrialists until the immigrants became numerous, was "dirty business" afterwards. Accordingly, the old elite turned from elective office and took up instead the control of a relatively new set of institutions, the community service organizations. The local hospital, Red Cross chapter, Community Chest, and Family Welfare Society became the arenas in which the "old families," who of course now asserted that there was no prestige in public office, carried on their public activities.[3]

. . .

The Rossis, who are sociologists, in their report on "Bay City" interpret the change in the character of the old elite's public service as a redirection of its drive for status and recognition. Unwilling to play the status game in the same set with the immigrant, the old elite (according to the Rossis) set up its own game and in effect said that henceforth that was to be *the* game.

We prefer a different explanation. The native middle-class Protestant inherited from his Anglo-Saxon ancestors a political ethos very different from that which the new immigrants brought with them. The ethos of the native could not mix with that of the immigrant, and therefore the natives, who were in the minority, retired to a sphere in which they could conduct public affairs in the manner their culture prescribed.

Richard Hofstadter described the difference of ethos very well in *The Age of Reform:*

> Out of the clash between the needs of the immigrants and the sentiments of the natives there emerged two thoroughly different systems of political ethics. . . . One, founded upon the indigenous Yankee-Protestant

political traditions, and upon middle class life, assumed and demanded the
constant, disinterested activity of the citizen in public affairs, argued that
political life ought to be run, to a greater degree than it was, in accordance
with general principles and abstract laws apart from and superior to
personal needs, and expressed a common feeling that government should
be in good part an effort to moralize the lives of individuals while
economic life should be intimately related to the stimulation and development of individual character. The other system, founded upon the European background of the immigrants, upon their unfamiliarity with independent political action, their familiarity with hierarchy and authority,
and upon the urgent needs that so often grew out of their migration, took
for granted that the political life of the individual would arise out of
family needs, interpreted political and civic relations chiefly in terms of
personal obligations, and placed strong personal loyalties above allegiance
to abstract codes of law or morals.[4]

The Anglo-Saxon Protestant middle-class style of politics, with its emphasis upon the obligation of the individual to participate in public affairs and to seek the good of the community "as a whole" (which implies,
among other things, the necessity of honesty, impartiality, and efficiency)
was fundamentally incompatible with the immigrants' style of politics,
which took no account of the community.

The native elite withdrew to the community service organizations because these constituted the only sphere in which their political style could
prevail. The boards of these organizations were self-perpetuating; they
could not be "crashed" by "outsiders." Because of the nature of their political ethos, Protestants and Jews have been in the vanguard of every
fight for municipal reform. In Worcester, Massachusetts, for example, according to Robert Binstock:

> Yankees are the cultural, business, and social leaders—in short, "the first
> families of Worcester." They are not numerous enough to control the
> governmental apparatus of the city, yet by forming an alliance with the
> Scandinavians, they manage to place two representatives on the City
> Council. The influence of the Yankee within the city government is
> limited, but participation in a strong and active citizens association, the
> CEA, enables this group to enlarge its role in the political process.
> The Jews, more often than not, are political allies of the Yankees and
> Scandinavians. . . .[5]

Conflict as between one immigrant ethnic group and another has
tended to be over "recognition"—the prestige that accrues to a nationality group when one of its members is elected to public office. Since in the
nature of the case there cannot be enough recognition to go around (if
all were equally recognized, none would be recognized at all), the question of which groups are to get it must inevitably lead to conflict. The a-
vidity of the "newer" ethnic groups to see their kind in office has been, and
still is, of great importance, both as a motive force in the political system
and because of certain incidental effects.

When one recalls the contempt with which "micks," "wops," and "po-lacks" were once—and to some extent still are—treated by some other Americans, no further explanation of the appeal of ethnic "recognition" is needed. But an additional reason is that ethnic politics, like sports, en-tertainment, and crime, provided a route of social mobility to people who were to a large extent excluded from power in business and industry. Mayor Daley of Chicago was born behind the stockyards. John E. Powers, the president of the Massachusetts Senate, began life as a clam digger.

One would expect that as the "newer" ethnic groups became assimi-lated to the middle class, they would become assimilated to the Anglo-Saxon Protestant political ethos as well, and that their interest in ethnic politics would decline accordingly. This seems to be happening, but at different rates among different groups. Jews, particularly those in the re-form tradition, seem to acquire the Protestant political ethos very readily.[6] It is interesting that the Jews have not sought ethnic "recognition" in city politics to the extent that other groups have. It may be that they have never doubted their worth as a group, and therefore have not felt any need for public reassurance. More likely, however, their political ethos is such that a politics of ethnic appeal strikes them, as it does the Anglo-Saxon Protestant, as uninteresting and even immoral.

Other ethnic groups also seem to be taking on the middle-class political ethos, but to be doing it more slowly. Third-generation Poles, for exam-ple, usually show a decided preference for Polish candidates, and third-generation Italians usually prefer Italian candidates. Middle-class Irish Catholics who seem entirely to have shed the mentality that caused the immigrant to vote on the basis of personal loyalty to a ward politician are nevertheless rarely found in the ranks of the civic reformers; these are al-most all Protestants and Jews.

Where the taste for ethnic recognition persists, it is for a special kind of recognition, however. The candidate must not be *too* Polish, *too* Italian, or *too* Irish in the old style. . . .

.   .   .

Apparently, nowadays, the nationality-minded voter prefers candidates who represent the ethnic group but at the same time display the attri-butes of the generally admired Anglo-Saxon model. The perfect candi-date, then, is of Jewish, Polish, Italian, or Irish extraction and has the speech, dress, manner, and the public virtues—honesty, impartiality, and devotion to the public interest—of the upper-class Anglo-Saxon.

The cleavage between white and Negro is pervasive in city politics. Until World War II, few Northern cities had many Negroes. As we have already seen, the Negro population of most Northern cities now is grow-ing at a very rapid rate, partly from natural increase and partly from mi-gration from the rural South. The new arrivals go into the Negro slum,

which almost everywhere is the oldest part of the central city, where housing has been swept by successive waves of low-status and low-income migrants. For many years restrictive covenants, written into deeds and prohibiting sale of property to Negroes, made it difficult or impossible for
Negroes to buy in districts that were not already Negro; their districts
therefore became more and more crowded. But after 1948, when the Supreme Court declared such covenants to be unenforceable in the courts,
the Negro community began to spread more rapidly.[7]

In many Northern cities, the question of where Negroes are to live lies
behind almost every proposal for civic action. Will locating a major highway here prevent them from "invading" that white neighborhood? And
where will those Negroes who are displaced by an urban renewal project
resettle? If a school or a hospital is placed here or there, will it bring Negroes to the neighborhood? And if it does, will the neighborhood eventually "tip" and become all Negro?

Many whites have fled to the suburbs to get away from the Negroes.
One reason why many suburbanites want to remain politically separate
from the central city is that they think this will make it easier for them to
resist "invasion" by Negroes.

In all this, upper-class Negroes exhibit much the same attitude as do
whites. Everything that we have said of the reaction of whites to Negroes
can also be said of the reaction of upper-class Negroes to lower-class
ones.

POLITICAL PARTIES

The central cities are almost all heavily Democratic; the suburbs tend to
be heavily Republican, although there are many exceptions, and their
Republicanism is nowhere near as solid or stable as the Democracy of the
central cities.

The Democratic ascendancy is so great in most central cities that cleavage along party lines within the cities is not of great practical importance.
Party cleavage is important, however, in matters that involve both the
central city and the area which lies outside of it. Table 3 shows how the
biggest cities voted in the Presidential election of 1960.

About 60 percent of all cities (but fewer large ones) are nonpartisan,
which means that candidates are not chosen in party primaries and are
not identified by party on the ballot. In some places, there are purely
local parties—the "blues" and the "yellows," so to speak—and in other
places local politics is carried on without anything that could properly be
called a party (it is "unorganized"). Some cities are nominally nonpartisan and actually partisan (Chicago is an example) and others are nominally partisan and actually nonpartisan in the sense of having no connection with the *national* parties (La Guardia, for example, was a nominal

Republican who ran on a Fusion ticket, and so was in this sense nonpartisan).

The most interesting thing about party, with respect to the present analysis, is that it is an *artificially-created* cleavage which cuts across all other cleavages and often supersedes them in importance: party "regularity" requires that the voter ignore all cleavages except the party one. The party cleavage *has* to cut across others because in the nature of things there are no general organizing principles under which all cleavages can be subsumed. The nearest thing to general organizing principles, per-

TABLE 3

CITIES OVER 500,000 POPULATION * RANKED BY THE DEMOCRATIC
PERCENTAGE OF THEIR 1960 PRESIDENTIAL VOTE

Rank	City	Percent	Rank	City	Percent
1	Boston	74.7	9	Baltimore	63.9
2	Detroit	71.0	10	Chicago	63.6
3	Cleveland	70.9	11	New York	62.8
4	Philadelphia	68.1	12	Milwaukee	61.8
5	Pittsburgh	67.0	13	San Francisco	58.0
6	St. Louis	66.6	14	Cincinnati	50.4
7	New Orleans	64.9	15	Seattle	48.8
8	Buffalo	64.9			

* No data available on Dallas, Houston, Los Angeles, San Antonio, or San Diego. Residents of Washington, D.C., could not vote.

SOURCE: Richard M. Scammon, *American Votes 4* (Pittsburgh: University of Pittsburgh Press, 1962).

haps, are "conservatism" and "liberalism." But the cleavages in the city do not fall logically into this or any other pattern; each side of each cleavage stands by itself and ought, in logic, to have its own party. The attachment to party, then, *must* cut across issues. If people were divided into fat men and lean (or Guelfs and Ghibellines, as in medieval Florence) and party feeling then whipped up, the result would be not unlike the American political party. Indeed, in Salt Lake City the party division is said to have been formed in a way as arbitrary as this. The Mormon hierarchy, obliged to liquidate its church political party when it was admitted to the Union, is said to have told people on one side of the street to vote Republican and those on the other side to vote Democratic. Their descendants, some people insist, still vote the same way.

M. I. Ostrogorski wrote on the development of American parties:

> The problems preoccupying public opinion being numerous and varied, it was necessary, instead of grouping the men in accordance with the issues, to adapt the issues to fixed groups of men. With this object confusion of the questions of the day was erected into a system; they were huddled together into "omnibus" programmes; they were put one on top of another; they were shuffled like a pack of cards, some being played at one time and some at another; at a pinch those which caused irreconcilable divergencies were made away with.[8]

This suggests something about the social function of cleavage in general. If cleavages run across each other (so to speak), they may serve to moderate conflict and to prevent "irreconcilable divergencies," because those who are enemies with respect to cleavage *a* are those allies with respect to cleavage *b* and indifferent (and therefore in a position to mediate) with respect to cleavage *c*. The "artificial" cleavage represented by party is especially functional in this respect because it cuts across *all* other cleavages. What Ostrogorski regarded as defects may therefore be great virtues.

Although logically all of these cleavages—between the haves and have-nots, the suburbanites and the central city, the natives and the immigrants, and the major political parties—are separate and often cross-cutting, there is a tendency for them to coalesce into two opposed patterns. These patterns reflect two conceptions of the public interest that are widely held. The first, which derives from the middle-class ethos, favors what the municipal reform movement has always defined as "good government"—namely efficiency, impartiality, honesty, planning, strong executives, no favoritism, model legal codes, and strict enforcement of laws against gambling and vice. The other conception of the public interest (one never explicitly formulated as such, but one all the same) derives from the "immigrant ethos." This is the conception of those people who identify with the ward or neighborhood rather than the city "as a whole," who look to politicians for "help" and "favors," who regard gambling and vice as, at worst, necessary evils, and who are far less interested in the efficiency, impartiality, and honesty of local government than in its readiness to confer material benefits of one sort or another upon them. In the largest, most heterogeneous of our cities, these two mentalities stand forth as distinctly as did those which, in another context, caused Disraeli to write of "The Two Nations."

21. BEYOND THE MELTING POT

Nathan Glazer and Daniel P. Moynihan

Glazer and Moynihan revert to 1908 and Israel Zangwill's melodrama, The Melting Pot, *to strike the keynote of ethnic and racial amalgamation long anticipated on the American continent. "German and Frenchman, Irishman and Englishman, Jews and Russians—into the Crucible with you all! God is making the American." Yet this expected fusion of peoples into a single American nationality has not occurred, least of all in the densely populated quarters of the heterogeneous urban milieu. There the continuity of cultural, religious, and racial differences is obviously, and oftentimes painfully, apparent despite unprecedently successful functional cooperation between groups of people of different persuasions.*

New York City is examined here although what is found would be characteristic of any number of America's other metropolitan centers. Jews, Catholics, Negroes, Puerto Ricans, and Anglo-Saxon Protestants constitute distinct interest groups, if not discrete sub-cultures, in our urban society. Preexisting cultural forces guided these interest groups in different directions; they maintained their distinctiveness even in the race of urban anonymity, but recent historical events elicited perhaps a still greater particularistic response from them. The Nazi holocaust, judicial decisions regarding church-state relations, and the great influx of dark-skinned migrants brought about by two world wars and large-scale economic change are specific influences that have perpetuated urban pluralism.

IT IS STRIKING that in 1963, almost forty years after mass immigration from
Europe to this country ended, the ethnic pattern is still so strong in New
York City. It is true we can point to specific causes that have served to
maintain the pattern. But we know that it was not created by the great
new migrations of Southern Negroes and Puerto Ricans into the city; nor
by the "new" immigration, which added the great communities of East
European Jews and Italians to the city; it was not even created by the
great migration of Irish and Germans in the 1840's. Even in the 1830's,
while the migration from Europe was still mild, and still consisted for the
most part of English-speaking groups, one still finds in the politics of New
York State, and of the city, the strong impress of group differentiation. . . .

There were ways of making distinctions among Welshmen and Eng-
lishmen, Yorkers and New Englanders, long before people speaking
strange tongues and practicing strange religions came upon the scene.
The group-forming characteristics of American social life—more concretely, the general expectation among those of new and old groups that
group membership is significant and formative for opinion and behavior
—are as old as the city. The tendency is fixed deep in American life generally; the specific pattern of ethnic differentiation, however, in every
generation is created by specific events.

We can distinguish four major events or processes that have structured
this pattern in New York during the past generation and whose effects
will remain to maintain this pattern for some time to come—to be replaced by others we can scarcely now discern. These four formative
events are the following:

First, the shaping of the Jewish community under the impact of the
Nazi persecution of the Jews in Europe and the establishment of the state
of Israel; second, the parallel, if less marked, shaping of a Catholic community by the reemergence of the Catholic school controversy; third, the
migration of Southern Negroes to New York following World War I and
continuing through the fifties; fourth, the influx of Puerto Ricans during
the fifteen years following World War II.

THE JEWS

Developments within the Jewish community have had the most immediate significance. A fourth of the city is Jewish; very much more than a
fourth of its wealth, energy, talent, and style is derived from the Jews.
Over the past thirty years this community has undergone profound emotional experiences, centered almost entirely on the fact of Jewishness, has
been measurably strengthened by immigration, and has become involved
in vast Zionist enterprises, the rationale of which is exclusively Jewish.
There are two aspects of these developments as they affect melting tendencies, one negative, the other positive.

The negative aspect has prevented a change that might otherwise have occurred. Prior to the 1930's Jews contributed significantly to the ethnic pattern of New York politics by virtue of their radicalism. This kept them apart from the Catholic establishment in the Democratic party and the Protestant regime within the Republican party but did give them a distinct role of their own. At the time of *The Melting Pot* there were, to be sure, a great many Democratic and Republican Jewish merchants and businessmen. Most East Side Jews probably voted the Tammany ticket. But indigenous Jewish politics, the politics of the *Jewish Daily Forward,* of the Workmen's Circle, and the needle-trades unions were predominantly socialist. The Russian Revolution, in which Russian Jews played a prominent role, had a strong attraction for a small but important number of their kinsmen in New York. It would appear, for example, that during the 1930's most Communist party members in New York City were Jewish.[1] It must be stressed that the vast majority of New York Jews had nothing whatever to do with Communism. Some of the strongest centers of anti-Communist activity were and are to be found within the New York Jewish community. Nonetheless there was an ethnic cast to this form of political radicalism in New York, as there had been to the earlier Socialist movement.

Both Socialism and Communism are now considerably diminished and both have lost almost entirely any ethnic base. But just at the moment when the last distinctly Jewish political activity might have disappeared, a transcendent Jewish political interest was created by the ghastly persecutions of the Nazis, the vast dislocations of World War II, and the establishment of the State of Israel. These were matters that no Jew or Christian could ignore. They were equally matters about which little could be done except through politics. . . .

In a positive sense, events of the Nazi era and its aftermath have produced an intense group consciousness among New York Jews that binds together persons of widely disparate situations and beliefs. A pronounced religious revival has occurred. Among those without formal religious ties there is a heightened sense of the defensive importance of organized Jewish activity. Among intellectuals, the feeling of Jewishness is never far from the surface.

Now, as in the past, the Jewish community in New York is the one most actively committed to the principles of racial integration and group tolerance. But open housing is something different from the melting pot. There is no reason to think that any considerable portion of the Jewish community of New York ever subscribed to Israel Zangwill's vision of a nonreligious, intermarried, homogeneous population, but it surely does not do so today. To the contrary, much of the visible activity of the community is aimed in directions that will intensify Jewish identity: Jewish elementary and secondary schools, Jewish colleges and universities, Jewish periodicals, Jewish investments in Israel, and the like. In the meantime, Jewish politicians make more (or at least not less) of the "Jewish" vote.

. . . Religion plays in many ways the smallest part of the story of American Jews. In New York City in particular the religious definition of the group explains least. Here the formal religious groups are weakest, the degree of affiliation to synagogues and temples smallest. In a city with 2,000,000 Jews, Jews need make no excuses to explain Jewishness and Jewish interests. On the one hand, there is the social and economic structure of the community; on the other, ideologies and emotions molded by the specific history or recent decades. Together they have shaped a community that itself shapes New York and will for generations to come.[2]

THE CATHOLICS

Outwardly, events since World War I have brought Catholics, notably the Irish Catholics, ever closer to the centers of power and doctrine in American life. But following a pattern common in human affairs, the process of closing the gap has heightened resentment, among some at all events, that a gap should exist. Here, as in much else concerning this general subject, it is hardly possible to isolate New York events from those of the nation generally, but because New York tends to be the center of Catholic thinking and publishing, the distinction is not crucial. The great division between the Catholic Church and the leftist and liberal groups in the city during the period from the Spanish Civil War to the era of McCarthy has been narrowed, with most elements of city politics converging on center positions. However issues of church-state relations have become considerably more difficult, and the issue of government aid to Catholic schools has become acute.

Controversy over church-state relations is nothing new to the American Catholic Church. What is new, however, and what is increasingly avowed, is the extent to which the current controversy derives from Catholic-Jewish disagreements rather than from traditional Catholic-Protestant differences. Relations between the two latter groups have steadily improved: to the point that after three centuries of separation Catholics in the 1960's began increasingly to talk of the prospects of reestablishing Christian unity. In general (there are, of course, many individual exceptions) the dominant view within Protestant and Catholic circles is that the United States is and ought to be a Christian commonwealth, to the point at very least of proclaiming "In God We Trust" on the currency and celebrating Christmas in the public schools. However, as this *rapprochement* has proceeded, within the Jewish community a contrary view has arisen which asserts that the separation of church and state ought to be even more complete than it has been, and that the "Post-Protestant era" means

Post-Christian as well, insofar as government relations with religion are concerned.

The most dramatic episode of this development was the decision of the United States Supreme Court on June 25, 1962, that the recitation of an official prayer in the New York school system was unconstitutional. . . . The response to the decision could hardly have been more diametrical. Cardinal Spellman declared, "I am shocked and frightened. . . ." The New York Board of Rabbis, on the other hand, hailed the decision: "The recitation of prayers in the public schools, which is tantamount to the teaching of prayer, is not in conformity with the spirit of the American concept of the separation of church and state. All the religious groups in this country will best advance their respective faiths by adherence to this principle." The American Jewish Committee, the American Jewish Congress, and the Anti-Defamation League of B'nai B'rith strongly supported the Court. Only among the Orthodox was there mild disagreement with the Supreme Court decision.

. . .

Significantly, Protestant reaction to the decision was mixed. The Brooklyn *Tablet* took the cue, stating that the crucial question raised by the decision was "What are the Protestants going to do about it? For, although this is a national problem, it is particularly a Protestant problem, given the large Protestant enrollment in the public schools. Catholics have been fighting long—and sometimes alone—against the Church-State extremists. May we count on Protestants to supply more leadership in this case? If so, we pledge our support to join efforts against the common enemy: secularism." [3]

The subject of aid to Catholic schools is only one aspect of the more general issue of church-state relations, and here again the ethnic composition of New York City tends to produce the same alignment of opposing groups. There are elements within the Jewish community, again the Orthodox, that favor public assistance for religious schools, but the dominant view is opposed. In 1961 the New York Republican party at the state level made a tentative move toward the Catholic position by proposing a Constitutional amendment that would have permitted state construction loans to private institutions of higher learning, sectarian as well as secular. Opposition from Jewish (as well as some Protestant) groups was pronounced, and the measure was beaten at the polls.

The situation developing in this area could soberly be termed dangerous. An element of interfaith competition has entered the controversy. As the costs of education mount, it becomes increasingly difficult to maintain the quality of the education provided by private schools deprived of public assistance. It is not uncommon to hear it stated in Catholic circles that the results of national scholarship competitions already point to the weakness of Catholic education in fields such as the physical sciences. The specter is raised that a parochial education will involve sacrifice for the students as well as for their parents.

. . .

Whether the course of the controversy will lead Catholics further into separatist views . . . is not clear. But it is abundantly evident that so long as Catholics maintain a separate education system and the rest of the community refuses to help support it by tax funds or tax relief, a basic divisive issue will exist. This will be an ethnic issue in measure that the Catholic community continues to include the bulk of the Irish, Italian, and Polish population in the city, at least the bulk of those affiliated with organizations taking a position on the issue. If, as may very well happen, the Catholics abandon elementary and even secondary education to concentrate on their colleges and universities, the larger issue of church-state relations will no doubt subside.

But it is not the single issue of school aid, no matter how important and long-lived it is, that alone shapes the polarization between the Jewish and the emerging Catholic community. There have been other issues in the past—for example, the struggle over the legitimacy of city hospitals giving advice on birth control, which put Jews and liberal Protestants on one side and Catholics on the other. There are the recurrent disputes over government censorship of books and movies and magazines that have become freer and freer in their handling of sex and sexual perversion. This again ranges Jewish and Protestant supporters of the widest possible freedom of speech against Catholics who are more anxious about the impact of such material on young people and family life. One can see emerging such issues as the rigid state laws on divorce and abortion.[4]

Many of these issues involve Catholic *religious* doctrine. But there exists here a situation that is broader than a conflict over doctrines and the degree to which government should recognize them. What is involved is the emergence of two subcultures, two value systems, shaped and defined certainly in part by religious practice and experience and organization but by now supported by the existence of two communities. If the bishops and the rabbis were to disappear tomorrow, the subcultures and subcommunities would remain. One is secular in its attitudes, liberal in its outlook on sexual life and divorce, positive about science and social science. The other is religious in its outlook, resists the growing liberalization in sexual mores and its reflection in cultural and family life, feels strongly the tension between moral values and modern science and technology. . . .

Thus a Jewish ethos and a Catholic ethos emerge: they are more strongly affected by a specific religious doctrine in the Catholic case than in the Jewish, but neither is purely the expression of the spirit of a religion. Each is the result of the interplay of religion, ethnic group, American setting, and specific issues. The important fact is that the differences in values and attitudes between the two groups do not, in general, become smaller with time. On the contrary: there is probably a wider gap between Jews and Catholics in New York today than in the days of Al Smith.[5]

NEGROES AND PUERTO RICANS

A close examination of Catholic-Jewish relations will reveal some of the tendency of ethnic relations in New York to be a form of class relations as well. However, the tendency is unmistakably clear with regard to the Negroes and Puerto Ricans. Some 22 per cent of the population of the city is now Negro or Puerto Rican, and the proportion will increase. (Thirty-six per cent of the births in 1961 were Negro or Puerto Rican.) To a degree that cannot fail to startle anyone who encounters the reality for the first time, the overwhelming portion of both groups constitutes a submerged, exploited, and very possibly permanent proletariat.

New York is properly regarded as the wealthiest city in the nation. Its more affluent suburbs enjoy some of the highest standards of living on earth. . . . But amidst such plenty, unbelievable squalor persists: the line of demarcation is a color line in the case of Negroes, a less definite but equally real ethnic line in the case of Puerto Ricans.

The relationship between the rise of the Negro-Puerto Rican labor supply and the decline of industrial wages is unmistakable. In 1950 there were 246,000 Puerto Ricans in the city. By 1960 this number had increased by two and one-half times to 613,000, or 8 per cent. In 1950 the average hourly earnings of manufacturing production workers in New York City ranked tenth in the nation. By 1960 they ranked thirtieth. In the same period comparable wages in Birmingham, Alabama, rose from thirty-third to tenth. In 1959 median family income for Puerto Ricans was $3,811 as against $6,091 for all the city's families (and $8,052 for suburbs of Westchester). In 1962 average weekly earnings of manufacturing production workers were 19 per cent higher in Birmingham than in New York City, 15 per cent higher in New Orleans, and almost 10 per cent higher in the nation as a whole.

These economic conditions vastly reinforce the ethnic distinctions that serve to separate the Negro community and the Puerto Rican community from the rest of the city. The Negro separation is strengthened by the fact that the colored community is on the whole Protestant, and much of its leadership comes from Protestant clergy. Thus the Negroes provide the missing element of the Protestant-Catholic-Jew triad.

Housing segregation, otherwise an intolerable offense to the persons affected, serves nonetheless to ensure the Negroes a share of seats on the

City Council and in the State Legislature and Congress. This power, as well as their voting power generally, has brought Negro political leaders to positions of considerable prominence. . . . Puerto Ricans have only begun to make their influence felt, but they are clearly on the way to doing so.

Their fate gives them an interest in the same issues: the housing of the poor in a city of perpetual housing shortage; the raising of the wages of the poorly paid service semiskilled occupations in which most of them work; the development of new approaches to raising motivation and capacity by means of education and training in the depressed areas of the city. They live adjacent to each other in vast neighborhoods. And they cooperate on many specific issues—for example, in fighting urban renewal programs that would displace them. But there are deeply felt differences between them. The more Americanized group is also more deeply marked by color. The furtive hope of the new group that it may move ahead as other immigrants have without the barrier of color, and the powerful links of language and culture that mark off the Puerto Ricans, suggest that, despite the fact that the two groups increasingly comprise the proletariat of the city, their history will be distinct.

Thus the cast of major characters for the next decades is complete: the Jews; the Catholics, subdivided at least into Irish and Italian components; the Negroes; the Puerto Ricans; and, of course, the white Anglo-Saxon Protestants. . . .

22. URBAN NEIGHBORHOODS AND INFORMAL SOCIAL RELATIONS [1]

Wendell Bell and Marion D. Boat

Testing the assumption that urban society is uniformly impersonal, anonymous, isolated, segmental, and formal, this empirical study that Bell and Boat conducted in San Francisco draws on the methodology of social-area analysis developed by Shevky and Bell. It seeks to determine the degree to which friendships and personal relations are present in the urban structure. The results of this study throw doubt on the correctness of the idea of big-city life advanced by such earlier sociologists as Simmel and Wirth.

Bell and Boat's examination of interview data on interpersonal contacts in the city reveals that the completely isolated man is a rarity, although isolation from specific informal groups, such as neighbors, co-workers, and relatives, is not uncommon. However, interaction with kin turns out to be a very significant source of satisfaction even though it is true that the calculation of material benefit is not wholly absent even from such contacts. Class differences are also apparent as an influential variable. Nonetheless, primary relations are an integral part of the metropolitan social system.

STUDENTS OF URBAN SOCIAL ORGANIZATION have concerned themselves with several lines of investigation. The study of the city as compared to rural places or non-literate societies and the study of one section of the city as compared to others have been prominent among them. The two interests

Excerpts reprinted from the *American Journal of Sociology*, January 1957 by permission of Professor Wendell Bell and the University of Chicago Press. Copyright 1957 by the University of Chicago.

can be found in Wirth's classic article, "Urbanism as a Way of Life," in which, comparing the city and the country, he says: "Distinctive features of the urban mode of life have often been described sociologically as consisting of the substitution of secondary for primary contacts, the weakening of bonds of kinship, and the declining social significance of the family, the disappearance of the neighborhood, and the undermining of the traditional basis of social solidarity." On the other hand, he emphasizes the differences between urban neighborhoods when he says: "Persons of homogeneous status and needs unwittingly drift into, consciously select, or are forced by circumstances into, the same area. . . . The city consequently tends to resemble a mosaic of social worlds in which the transition from one to the other is abrupt." [2]

Recent writers have both questioned the extent to which the city in general contains impersonal, anonymous, and secondary social relations and suggested that the differences between sections of the city should be considered in making generalizations about urban social relationships in general.[3] Are anonymity, social isolation, impersonal relations, the decline in the importance of the kin group, the disappearance of local community life, and other alleged attributes of life in the city as contrasted with life in the country equally present in every section of the city? Are they characteristic of certain parts of the city and not of others? If the latter is the case, then generalizations contrasting urban with rural social relations need to be elaborated to include a *systematic* analysis of particular urban conditions under which impersonal social relations arise most and those other conditions under which they arise least.

It is the purpose of this paper to contribute to the determination of such conditions by relating informal relations of urban residents to social types of neighborhoods. Specifically, male residents of four different types of neighborhoods are compared with respect to amount of socializing with neighbors, relatives, co-workers, and friends; the nature of informal contacts; the source of friendships; and the amount of personal relations in formal associations.[4]

From an examination of the social area distribution of the census tracts in San Francisco as of 1950, four tracts were selected in which intensive interviewing was carried out. Each tract represents a different social type of neighborhood: Mission, a low-rent rooming-house neighborhood, is characterized by relatively low economic status and a relatively low score on the index of family status. Outer Mission, a neighborhood of low-rent detached houses, is of low economic status and high family status. Pacific Heights, with its high-rent apartment houses, is high in economic status and low in family status; and St. Francis Wood, with its high-rent detached houses, ranks high on both criteria. Each contains relatively few members of subordinate racial and nationality groups.[5]

A probability sample of males over the age of twenty-one was drawn from each census tract, and a total of 701 interviews was completed, mostly during the spring of 1953. The total number of interviews is about equally divided between the four neighborhoods, and the total response rate exceeds 85 per cent.[6]

Table 1 reports the frequency of total informal group participation for each of the four neighborhoods.[7] The majority of men in each of the neighborhoods get together with some informal group at least once a week. In Mission 62.2 per cent, in Pacific Heights 63.4 per cent, in Outer Mission 71.8 per cent, and in St. Francis Wood 73.8 per cent of the men so report. Although the neighborhoods differ in economic and family characteristics, most of the men have fairly frequent informal social contacts.

TABLE 1

PERCENTAGE DISTRIBUTION OF ADULT MALES, BY FREQUENCY OF PARTICIPATION IN ALL INFORMAL GROUPS

Frequency of Informal Group Participation	Low Family, Low Economic Status (Mission)	Low Family, High Economic Status (Pacific Heights)	High Family, Low Economic Status (Outer Mission)	High Family, High Economic Status (St. Francis Wood)
More than once a week	44.2	50.3	55.3	45.8
About once a week	18.0	13.1	16.5	28.0
A few times a month	18.6	22.5	17.0	17.2
About once a month	8.1	3.1	3.5	2.4
A few times a year	6.4	6.3	6.5	4.8
About once a year	1.8	4.2	0.6	1.2
Never	2.9	0.5	0.6	0.6
Total	100.0	100.0	100.0	100.0
No. of cases	(172)	(191)	(170)	(168)

Conversely, in every neighborhood *except* Mission, the rooming-house neighborhood, the proportion of men who have no informal associations is less than 1 per cent, and even in Mission only 2.9 percent of the men have no informal contacts. Thus, whether a man lives in a cheap rooming-house area, an expensive apartment-house area, an area characterized by small detached houses and modest means, or one in which the dwellings are detached, large, and relatively expensive, he is very unlikely to be completely isolated. Axelrod [8] and Greer [9] report corroborating findings for Detroit and Los Angeles, respectively.

The neighborhoods of low family status contain somewhat larger percentages of men who get together informally about once a month or less.[10] Mission contains 19.2 per cent who have few informal contacts compared to Outer Mission's 11.2 per cent, and Pacific Heights contains 14.1 per cent compared to St. Francis Wood's 9.0 per cent. Differences between neighborhoods by economic status at each level of family status are not statistically significant.

Table 2 shows the frequency of participation by type of informal

TABLE 2

PERCENTAGE DISTRIBUTION OF ADULT MALES, BY FREQUENCY OF PARTICIPATION
IN SPECIFIED INFORMAL GROUPS

Frequency of Participation by Group	Low Family, Low Economic Status (Mission)	Low Family, High Economic Status (Pacific Heights)	High Family, Low Economic Status (Outer Mission)	High Family, High Economc Status (St. Francis Wood)
Neighbors:				
About once a week or more	24.4	26.7	31.2	16.7
A few times a month	4.6	7.3	14.1	10.1
About once a month	9.3	5.8	8.8	16.7
A few times a year	3.5	8.9	4.7	23.2
About once a year	1.2	1.6	0.6	1.8
Never	57.0	49.7	40.6	31.5
Total	100.0	100.0	100.0	100.0
No. of cases	(172)	(191)	(170)	(168)
Co-workers: *				
About once a week or more	20.8	21.7	20.1	17.3
A few times a month	5.6	13.3	10.1	11.6
About once a month	11.1	8.4	14.7	16.0
A few times a year	13.9	21.1	16.8	25.0
About once a year	2.1	5.4	5.4	6.4
Never	46.5	30.1	32.9	23.7
Total	100.0	100.0	100.0	100.0
No. of cases	(145)	(166)	(149)	(156)
Relatives: †				
About once a week or more	33.1	29.8	45.3	42.3
A few times a month	10.5	14.7	13.0	13.1
About once a month	12.8	13.1	14.1	11.3
A few times a year	10.5	16.2	13.5	19.0
About once a year	7.5	11.5	4.1	6.0
Never	25.6	14.7	10.0	8.3
Total	100.0	100.0	100.0	100.0
No. of cases	(172)	(191)	(170)	(168)
Friends: ‡				
About once a week or more	36.1	49.7	27.1	39.9
A few times a month	14.5	14.1	14.1	21.4
About once a month	15.7	12.6	21.2	11.9
A few times a year	11.0	13.6	18.2	14.3
About once a year	2.3	1.1	1.8	1.8
Never	20.4	8.9	17.6	10.7
Total	100.0	100.0	100.0	100.0
No. of cases	(172)	(191)	(170)	(168)

* Unemployed men omitted. Also excludes informal contacts at place of work.
† Relatives other than those living with the respondent.
‡ Other than friends who are neighbors, co-workers, or relatives.

group. Those men who report getting together informally with members of a given group "about once a year" or "never" will be considered socially isolated from it. A comparison of the neighborhoods of low family status with those of high family status at each level of economic status shows that social isolation from neighbors and also from relatives varies inversely with family status.[11] The differences are in the same direction in the case of those isolated from co-workers but are not statistically significant. Thus the amount of family life in an urban neighborhood appears to affect the degree to which men are socially isolated from their neighbors and from their relatives, men living in neighborhoods characterized by relatively few children, many women in the labor force, and many multiple dwellings being more isolated from these groups than men living in areas characterized by relatively many children, few women in the labor force, and many single-family detached dwellings.

Comparing Mission to Pacific Heights and Outer Mission to St. Francis Wood will reveal any differences in social isolation from particular informal groups by economic status at each level of family status. No statistically significant differences appear when the economic status of the neighborhood and isolation from neighbors and relatives are considered. However, there is an inverse relationship between isolation from co-workers and neighborhood economic status.[12] Also, men living in neighborhoods of low economic status are more likely to be isolated from friends than are men living in neighborhoods of high economic status.[13] These findings are consistent with those given by Axelrod, who reports similar relationships when relating individual measures of socioeconomic status to frequency of participation in informal groups.[14]

In Table 2 social isolation by type of informal group within each neighborhood can be seen. In Mission and Pacific Heights, the two neighborhoods of low family status, the ranking of the groups from least to most isolation is clear and is as follows: (1) friends, (2) relatives, (3) co-workers, and (4) neighbors. In outer Mission and St. Francis Wood, however, the neighborhoods characterized by a relatively large amount of family life, relatives and neighbors each increase in importance as a source of informal contacts, so that isolation from relatives is not significantly different from isolation from friends, and isolation from neighbors is not significantly different from isolation from co-workers. Isolation from neighbors and co-workers is, however, still greater than isolation from relatives and friends.

Although Table 1 shows that very few men have no informal contacts whatever, it can be seen from Table 2 that many are socially isolated from a given informal group. For example, the proportion of men isolated from neighbors is as high as 58.2 per cent in Mission and even in St. Francis Wood reaches 33.3 per cent. Likewise, fairly large percentages of men seldom or never get together outside of work with their co-workers, the percentage reporting social isolation from this group varying from

48.6 in Mission to 30.1 in St. Francis Wood. The percentage isolated from relatives varies from 33.1 in Mission to 14.1 in Outer Mission, and the percentage isolated from friends varies from 22.7 in Mission to 10.0 in Pacific Heights. This undoubtedly reflects the geographical separation of work and residence, the segmentalization of *personal* relationships, and the resulting increase in freedom to choose one's companions in the city. In contrast, of course, many rural communities consist of persons who are neighbors, who are also kin, and who are also co-workers.

Perhaps the most striking aspect of the findings in Table 2, however, is the importance of the kin group as a source of informal relations in each

TABLE 3
PERCENTAGE OF PARTICIPANTS USUALLY ASSOCIATING IN THEIR HOME
BY TYPE OF GROUP

Group with Which Respondent Associates in the Home	Low Family, Low Economic Status (Mission)	Low Family, High Economic Status (Pacific Heights)	High Family, Low Economic Status (Outer Mission)	High Family, High Economic Status (St. Francis Wood)
Neighbors	67.6	72.9	81.2	79.1
	(74) *	(96)	(101)	(115)
Co-workers †	36.4	29.3	30.0	27.7
	(77)	(116)	(100)	(118)
Relatives	84.4	82.2	81.0	88.3
	(128)	(163)	(153)	(154)
Friends	41.6	43.7	50.0	50.0
	(137)	(174)	(140)	(150)

* Numbers on which the percentages are based are given in parentheses.
† Unemployed persons are excluded.

of these neighborhoods, corroborating Axelrod's comment: "The extended family may have lost its function as an economic producing unit in the city, but relatives continue to be an important source of companionship and mutual support." [15]

On the assumption that informal getting-together in the home may be more intimate and close than that which occurs outside it, each respondent was asked whether or not his associations with a particular group usually occurred at home. These responses are shown in Table 3. By this measure the more intimate contacts seem to occur with relatives and neighbors than with friends and co-workers, although one might question this in the case of neighboring, where physical proximity makes association at home relatively effortless.

In addition, each respondent was asked how many close personal friends he had in each type of informal group. As can be seen from Table 4, in each neighborhood well over half the men report that they have a least one close personal friend in each informal group, providing evidence that informal relations with neighbors, co-workers, relatives, or friends can hardly be described as impersonal.

By this measure of intimacy, co-workers provide more personal relationships than neighbors. Thus the comparison shown in Table 3 between neighbors and co-workers may not in reality indicate differences in degree of intimacy; that is, some men apparently do not see their co-workers in their homes, and yet the relationship is personal and intimate.

In considering both measures of intimacy of informal relations—the degree to which the home is the place of informal interaction and the ex-

TABLE 4

PERCENTAGE OF PARTICIPANTS WITH ONE OR MORE FRIENDS IN THE GROUP
BY TYPE OF GROUP

Group Containing One or More of Respondent's Friends	Low Family, Low Economic Status (Mission)	Low Family, High Economic Status (Pacific Heights)	High Family, Low Economic Status (Outer Mission)	High Family, High Economic Status (St. Francis Wood)
Neighbors	74.3	61.1	78.2	62.6
	(74) *	(96)	(101)	(115)
Co-workers †	89.6	72.4	85.0	79.7
	(77)	(116)	(100)	(118)
Relatives	93.0	88.3	90.8	92.8
	(128)	(163)	(153)	(154)
Friends	89.0	90.8	89.3	92.7
	(137)	(174)	(140)	(150)

* Numbers on which the percentages are based are given in parentheses.
† Unemployed persons are excluded.

tent to which close personal friends are members of a particular informal group—it becomes clear that kin are more likely to provide intimate social contacts than neighbors or co-workers in each neighborhood.

Each respondent was asked how many persons from each group he could call on to take care of him if he were sick for even "as long as a month." By this measure the groups can be ranked according to reliance upon them as follows: (1) relatives, (2) friends, (3) co-workers, and (4) neighbors (see Table 5). Again the importance of kin as a source of ties that bind is evident. This order is maintained in every neighborhood except Outer Mission, in which co-workers seem less depended upon than neighbors. Also in Mission and St. Francis Wood the differences between reliance upon co-workers and upon neighbors are not significant. However, there is no question about the fact that the kin are considered to be the most important in providing relationships that can be counted on in an emergency and that friends are more depended upon than neighbors or co-workers.

Consistent with the finding that men living in neighborhoods of high economic status are less isolated from co-workers and friends, it can be seen from Table 5 that the latter are more depended upon by residents of Pacific Heights and St. Francis Wood than by residents of Mission and Outer Mission respectively.

From the above data the important role of kin and friends in providing city men with close, personal, and intimate contacts seems fairly well established. However, the relative importance of neighbors and co-work-

TABLE 5
PERCENTAGE RELYING ON AT LEAST ONE MEMBER OF THE SPECIFIED GROUP

Group on Which Respondent Relies	Low Family, Low Economic Status (Mission)	Low Family, High Economic Status (Pacific Heights)	High Family, Low Economic Status (Outer Mission)	High Family, High Economic Status (St. Francis Wood)
Neighbors	34.3 (172) *	29.3 (191)	44.7 (170)	39.9 (168)
Co-workers †	39.9 (145)	46.4 (166)	23.5 (149)	43.6 (156)
Relatives	70.9 (172)	83.8 (191)	81.2 (170)	85.1 (168)
Friends	59.9 (172)	65.3 (191)	52.7 (170)	73.2 (168)

* Numbers on which the percentages are based are given in parentheses.
† Unemployed persons are excluded.

ers in relation to one another seems less clear. Table 6 reports the percentage of men who report that, apart from the enjoyment they get out of it, their participation with neighbors or co-workers yields them certain material benefit. We interpret these percentages to indicate the tendency to be calculating of self-seeking and to exploit others. For such persons the association may be a means to some other end, not an end in itself. If this is correct, then it can be concluded that a calculating motive is more

TABLE 6
PERCENTAGE OF PARTICIPANTS BENEFITING MATERIALLY FROM
THEIR PARTICIPATION, BY TYPE OF GROUP

Group from Which Respondent Benefits Materially	Low Family, Low Economic Status (Mission)	Low Family, High Economic Status (Pacific Heights)	High Family, Low Economic Status (Outer Mission)	High Family, High Economic Status (St. Francis Wood)
Neighbors *	51.4 (74) †	32.2 (96)	55.4 (101)	33.9 (115)
Co-workers ‡	18.2 (77)	25.0 (116)	21.0 (100)	28.8 (118)

* Includes only those who get together with neighbors.
† Numbers on which percentages are based are given in parentheses.
‡ Includes only those employed who associate with co-workers.

likely to enter into a man's relationships with neighbors than into his relationships with his co-workers. Taking the neighborhoods separately, however, these differences are not significant in the two neighborhoods of high economic status, although they are significant in the two where economic status is low.

Notice also from Table 6 that men living where economic status is low are more likely to be calculating in their relationships with neighbors than men living where economic status is high.

That the tendency to be calculating in relations with neighbors or co-workers generally is not great is indicated by the fact that only a relatively small percentage of men reported that they would discontinue their informal relations with neighbors or co-workers, respectively, if they *did not* receive any material benefits from them. More than 85 per cent of the men in each neighborhood either do not benefit materially from get-

TABLE 7

PERCENTAGE OF ADULT MALES MEETING ONE OR MORE FRIENDS
IN THE SPECIFIED PLACE

Place of Meeting	Low Family, Low Economic Status (Mission)	Low Family, High Economic Status (Pacific Heights)	High Family, Low Economic Status (Outer Mission)	High Family, High Economic Status (St. Francis Wood)
In the neighborhood	30.2 (172) *	21.6 (191)	43.5 (170)	37.5 (168)
At work	58.3 (172)	55.3 (191)	61.1 (170)	57.6 (168)

* Numbers on which percentages are based are given in parentheses.

ting together with neighbors or co-workers or do not maintain such relationships primarily for "what they get out of it in the way of material benefits." We take this as further evidence that, in general, informal relationships with neighbors and co-workers, when they exist, represent primary, intimate, and personal relationships with little suggestion of exploitation.

Table 7 shows the relative importance of the neighborhood as compared to the place of employment as a source of "close personal friends." In each neighborhood a much larger percentage of men report having met one or more of their good friends at their place of work. This further supports the notion that neighbors are somewhat less important than co-workers in providing satisfying personal relations.

Also Table 7 further affirms the fact that a neighborhood is more highly organized and integrated through informal contacts if it is characterized by high family status; men in Outer Mission and St. Francis Wood are more likely to have met one or more of their good friends in the neighborhood than are men in Mission and Pacific Heights.[16]

To argue that the formal association is not an important activity in the city is to fly in the face of the obvious evidence. However, in spite of the great number of formal associations (business and government agencies were not included) and their generally widespread membership, the question arises as to just how impersonal and anonymous are the relationships. From Table 8 it appears that attendance at a formal meeting serves in part to bring men together in relationships of a primary nature. For example, over 51 per cent of the members of formal associations in each of the neighborhoods report that they have nine or more close per-

TABLE 8

PERCENTAGE DISTRIBUTION OF ADULT MALE PARTICIPANTS IN FORMAL GROUPS
BY NUMBER OF FRIENDS

No. of Friends in Same Formal Groups as Respondent	Low Family, Low Economic Status (Mission)	Low Family, High Economic Status (Pacific Heights)	High Family, Low Economic Status (Outer Mission)	High Family, High Economic Status (St. Francis Wood)
Nine or more	51.2	56.0	55.5	61.3
Four to eight	22.1	22.0	16.0	19.3
One to three	9.9	8.0	14.6	7.1
None	16.8	14.0	13.9	12.3
Total	100.0	100.0	100.0	100.0
No. of cases	(132)	(151)	(137)	(156)

sonal friends who also are members. Conversely, less than 17 per cent report that they have no close personal friends in their associations at all. Thus most individuals find the formal association by no means as impersonal as often assumed.

In conclusion, the findings of this study are that the family and economic characteristics of an urban neighborhood may greatly influence the informal social relations of city residents. Other studies will no doubt demonstrate the relevance of other conditions of the neighborhood.

23. VOLUNTARY ASSOCIATIONS
AND URBANIZATION [1]

Robert T. Anderson and Barbara Gallatin Anderson

*The anthropological history of Dragor, an island suburb of Copen-
hagen, over the past half century, conveys an understanding of the effects
of urbanization upon the social structure of a community. Dragor, a relatively isolated maritime society, was substantially altered by its incorpora-
tion into the growing metropolis and by the impact upon it of Danish national government. Neighborhood, family, and church all lost authority,
influence, and functional integrity as the capacity of government to administer services expanded. Dragor's record of successful voluntary associations, however, carried over into the new period. Organizations to provide mutual aid and to deal with shared interests appeared. Older ones
perished, but the newer interest groups that arose coped effectively with
unmet needs. In this process, they supplemented the network of public
agencies in which the community was coming to participate more
completely.*

OUR RECENT FIELD STUDY of culture change in a Danish village incorporated an investigation of voluntary associations. In less than a half-century Dragor, an island community of fifteen hundred inhabitants, had
made the change from an isolated maritime fishing village to an urban
annex of Copenhagen. Its population had doubled, the physical plan of
its community had vastly expanded, and change was no less penetrating
from the point of view of social organization.

Excerpts reprinted from the *American Journal of Sociology,* November 1959 by permission of the authors and the University of Chicago Press. Copyright 1959 by the University of Chicago.

Our interest came to focus specifically upon the roles and the efficacy of the various social institutions in the process of change—family and kin, class, age groups, associations, the neighborhood, the church, and the local government. The investigation of voluntary associations was particularly compelling because data were available for a comparative analysis not only of their institutional "utility" but of their significance over a span of fifty years within the unlike social structures of a harbor village and an urban community. That Dragor provides the locale of both these communities and a single, changing population leads to unprecedented control and integrity.

Dragor is located on the southeast coast of small (25 square miles) Amager Island.[2] Its location has been decisive in its cultural development, for it is at once strategic and isolating. It is very nearly Denmark's most easterly community. Only Saltholm Island lies between it and Swedish soil. In land miles it is close to the major island of Sjaelland; some 8 miles separate it from the capital city. But, until the turn of the century, inadequate transportation, the poor repair of existent roads and bridges, and, above all, Dragor's distinctly maritime orientation confined communication largely to sea lanes. These, however, were important and much used, for Dragor harbor opens to the turbulent Sound which links the Baltic with the Kattegat and ultimately the North Sea. And until the end of the last century, Dragor's economy depended upon the sea.

Merchant shipping was the most significant occupation, employing ninety skippers, ships' officers, and pilots and a hundred and fifty seamen. Another hundred men were full-time fishermen, and they and the merchant mariners comprised eight-tenths of the adult male population. Aside from three landowning farmers, the rest of the population engaged largely in occupations dependent upon the maritime pursuits, especially shopkeeping and the trades.

By the turn of the century, however, Dragor's economy was adversely affected by technology. The merchant fleet failed to convert from sail to steam, and the fishing fleet could not meet new competition from the mainland. The very rapid consequence was a pervasive undermining of the village's marine-oriented economy. A centuries-old union of the community's culture with the sea was ended. Little by little, however, the technical progress that brought economic crisis to the village also provided its resolution: buses, bicycles, private motorized vehicles, and, above all, a railway, completed in 1907, permitted the arrival of Copenhageners in search of homes beyond the burgeoning city and, at the same time, permitted Dragorians to commute. As the old forms of local occupation became unprofitable, the villagers turned from the sea to the city for a means of earning a living. In the course of two decades, Dragor found itself a suburb of Copenhagen, with its economic base in Denmark's capital city. And now forty fishermen, a scattering of seamen and officers, six pilots, and no active skippers constitute a maritime minority in the present population of suburbanites, of which approximately two-thirds are descended from local families.[3]

Categorically, the institutions that ordered society in the harbor village of the nineties and channeled the personal relations of its men, women, and children persist in the urban community of today. Structurally, however, they have altered, some profoundly, and exemplify varying adaptations to urban pressures. One finds a mounting dependency of the community as well as the individual on voluntary associations which appears particularly in records of family and kin, class, age grades, neighborhood, and church. It is a pre-eminence, however, which voluntary associations must share with another institution—the government. The growth of governmental agencies matches that of voluntary agencies in increased complexity and range of influence.

Family and kin groups have declined in Dragor since 1890. For the early village population the nuclear family was generally an indispensable economic as well as a basic social unit. In fishing families all members gave regular assistance to the head of the family in cleaning, repairing, and constructing equipment: the daily preparation of hooks and traps was a family enterprise; a son, as young as eight years, was commonly a sailing assistant to his father; and many wives peddled their husbands' catch.

. . .

In modern Dragor, familial integrity is considerably lessened both as a social and as an economic force. The myriad joint-labor demands of the extinct fishing-maritime economy no longer exist, and for only a few, now, is solvency contingent upon family solidarity and singleness of effort. The strength of the family as a social unit has been weakened by the widespread daily dispersal of its members at work and by the decrease, often related, in parental authority. Whereas formerly it was common for the father to exercise absolute jurisdiction, with the mother second in command, now, typically, children assume increasing freedom with increasing age—culminating, often in adolescence, in behavior regarded by many adults as rebellious and disobedient. While some parents are less disparaging of the relaxation of standards, all are agreed that the internal structure of the family has altered. Divorce, unrecorded for the nineties, is now an intrusive problem.

. . .

Old Dragor had a tight, rigidly defined class structure. The major basis in ranking individuals was a connection with the sea and, further, one's position in the hierarchy on a ship. Women and children automatically assumed class status in the indelible, marine-marked image of the house-hold head.

The ranking of individuals was correlated with a division of the community into three classes. The skippers, pilots, and ships' officers, together with their near-equivalents, formed the upper class of "fine people" (*fine folk*). A middle class of "ordinary people" (*jaevne folk*) was comprised of most fishermen, seamen, and skilled laborers. A low class of "poor people" (*fattige folk*) was made up of unskilled land laborers and those fishermen and seamen who had lost prestige and material possessions because of moral turpitude—usually chronic alcoholism or chronic aversion to work. While this was, in effect, synonymous with ranking in wealth, the latter differentiation was rarely alluded to and in practice was sometimes inapplicable. Class was synonymous with the division of the community into fixed groups, who dressed differently from one another, sought friendships and entertainment independently of one another, were largely endogamous, and formed voluntary associations for the exclusive diversion of a membership rigidly fixed according to class, in affirmation of the existing social order: the *Skipper Society* for the masters, officers, pilots, and their families, the *Unity* for seamen and fishermen and their families, with *no* association for the prestigeless laboring class. The criteria of class membership were thus simply defined and appear to have been unchallenged so long as the economic base to which the system owed its life and pervasiveness remained unchanged.

· · ·

The old system of acknowledged ranking altered when the prestige of maritime occupation was challenged. Prestige instead came to attach to wealth or power as such. The development of numerical and social supremacy of the middle class was also a factor in the negation of class differences. Of greater significance, however, is the fact that the marked evidence of class has all but disappeared. The meetings and celebrations of the class-delimited voluntary associations, the use of separate rooms in the village inn for each class, and a hierarchical division of the male population in afternoon promenades at the harbor—all these disappeared during World War I. Where there is now evidence of distinctly class-linked voluntary associations, it is for the formerly neglected lower class who today have national as well as local political parties and trade unions.

· · ·

The neighborhood, too, served as the basis for social groups, and Dragorians were socially intimate on the basis of being *naboer* and *genboer*. The *naboer* lived on either side of one's house; the *genboer*, across the street. Neighborhood connections by nature overlapped other institutional relationships, best seen at baptisms and the daily early-evening convocations of the women.

The neighborhood has undergone an ever increasing loss of influence in social relations from the beginnings of the early influx of urban summer residents, strangers to one another and to the community, to the present era of tract-home, community-apartment divisions. Neighborliness persists as an ideal in the old sections of Dragor; it is largely disdained as a potential social encumbrance in newer divisions . . .

In old Dragor the church and community were coterminous in membership. The corporate nature of the community church was evidenced in holiday rituals in which the whole village, under the leadership of the priest, united "to attend the offering." In this service the family head carried a money contribution down the aisle of the church and placed it on each of two tables before the altar. Psychologically, the church united all villagers in the shared experience of the rites of baptism, confirmation, marriage, and internment. The *Indremission,* Dragor's sole voluntary religious association, labored to reaffirm and revitalize this bond, which, in practice, lacked evangelic enthusiasm. Regular Sunday Masses were attended by only a small portion of the community, particularly by the old people.

With the twentieth century, Dragor's church, like her local political institutions, underwent a progressive loss of authority. . . . Today, also, the psychological bond of shared religious experience has vanished with the widespread adoption of secular *rites de passage.*

The domains of activity of voluntary associations themselves and governmental bureaus and agencies have vastly increased, and their developmental adjustment in the face of urbanization show provocative parallels.

. . .

In 1910, the ancient form of communal government was abolished and reorganized according to the national law of 1908. The electorate has been broadened to include all adult men and women over twenty-five years of age. The new form of government provides for a mayor (now called *borgmester*) who is chairman of a council of seven councilmen (now called *byraadsmedlemer*) . . . .

The responsibilities of the communal government have increased greatly and now include extensive projects in public welfare, public insurance, education, public health, public works, and so on. But with the augmented role of the communal government in local affairs has also come an increase in the influence of the national government and the concomitant decrease in the autonomy of local politicians, as more and more jurisdiction is assumed by the national ministries. In effect, the national government now requires the local government to offer a vast array of well-defined services, supervising the administration and financing of these extensive duties.

Nineteenth-century Dragorians met some needs by establishing voluntary associations. . . . Six societies were recorded in the 1890's. The oldest was Dragor Handworkers Sickness and Funeral Treasury (*Dragør Haandvaerkernes Syge- og Begravelseskasse*), founded in 1848 to provide insurance for craftsmen against loss of income due to sickness and for the expense of a funeral. The Dragor Ship Owners and Ships Masters Society of the upper class was founded in the 1870's, and the Unity of the middle class about ten years later. In the 1880's, at the instigation of a retired missionary, a local branch of the nation-wide Inner Missions (*Indremission*) was founded to revitalize religious enthusiasm. Its greatest success was in the nineties, when about three hundred and fifty men and women constructed a two-story brick "Mission House." Cork Society (*Propforeningen*) was also a local branch of a national organization. It united about thirty upper-class men of the village for the purpose of helping poor young people meet the expenses of confirmation. Its yearly dues were contributed to the cause, and the society's name derived from the practice of raising additional funds by fining members each time one was caught without a bottle cork in his pocket. Finally, Dragor's Future (*Dragørs Fremme*) was founded in 1887 by the postman, locally famed as a man of letters, to prepare the village for the breakdown of the old economy in the face of technological developments. It sought, first, a railroad to provide better contact with Copenhagen (the promotion campaign of the society, including pressure-group tactics in the capital, played a part in the laying of the railroad in 1907) ; second, tourist trade; and, finally, a tuberculosis sanatorium to provide local employment. No hospital was constructed, but the tourist trade successfully developed. The major economic change, however, was the inclusion of the local population in the labor market of greater Copenhagen, a development hastened by regular train service.

The viability of the six associations varied during the new century. The Unity died along with the other manifestations of class solidarity. The Skipper Society prolonged its demise by virtue of its prestige, extending its membership to become a purely social club for people of higher income. It is now moribund. Dragor's Future grew less and less active as its leaders grew older, its projects were relegated to other groups, and it finally disbanded in 1931. The Cork Society became extinct during the first World War. Dragor's Handworkers Sickness and Funeral Treasury is still operative but offers only supplementary benefits, since security against illness and unemployment is now a function of the national government, under whose administration most private insurance societies in Denmark have been absorbed.

The old associations did not fare well as time progressed. But new ones appeared. Especially in the solution of problems related to economic adjustment, expansion, and leisure, the voluntary association became a social medium more and more resorted to. After World War II, especially, new societies proliferated, utilizing an essentially unchanged pattern of internal organization.

In 1904 the fishermen formed a society (*Dragør Fiskeriforening*) to cooperate in transporting fish to the market, replacing the old system of individual arrangements, and to deal with the village council in persuading it to reserve a special section of the harbor for the exclusive use of Dragorian fishermen and to restrict for their use beach areas where boiling vats and net racks were kept.

Ship salvage had traditionally provided an income to Dragorian mariners, especially during winter. Whereas formerly the men participated simply by virtue of village residence, by 1921 they organized the Salvage Guild (*Bjaergelav*) to allot work equitably among local mariners and exclude outsiders from the coveted windfalls.

Local brotherhoods of trade unions and professional organizations were formed. Where membership was small, craftsmen and artisans were absorbed into existing Copenhagen groups. Even goosekeepers formed a society. . . .

. . .

In the apartment houses built on the south side of the village after 1945, units were individually owned, and the building was managed by a hired manager under a corporate-trust arrangement. Residents, nevertheless, found it expedient to form associations, to elect officers, and to meet regularly to discuss and vote upon such problems as the allotment of time and space in the communal washing facilities and the control of noise. Similarly, homeowners in the "villa" section north of the old village, formed an association to determine and defend their interests. Finally, associations, usually small and ephemeral, were founded for a variety of specific-interest purposes. A mason, a businessman, and the village doctor formed the still-active Dragor Museum Society (*Dragør Museumsforening*) to acquire and preserve local cultural heirlooms. . . . Another group disbanded after achieving its purpose in preventing the addition of an unaesthetic fourth story to a new building in the heart of town.

The voluntary association is extremely pliant. Easily founded, it is free to adjust with ameba-like fluidity to a flood of problems beyond the scope or ken of other institutions or any combination of them. Its job done, it can go out of business without consequences beyond projects at hand. Danish voluntary associations and forms of government share an organizational structure specifically contrived to facilitate and precipitate change by providing effective, policy making leaders responsive to their electorate. In contrast, the Dragorian household after a half-century of economic change cannot revert to the familial work unit and, like the church, does not know on what basis it can now reallocate its declining authority. The rigid class system of the nineties, the tight little neighborhood, even the exacting northside-southside age groups—all succumbed in the face of change . . .

The voluntary association meets the exigencies of change by uniting people for action on the basis of any shared interest, whether the resultant union coincides with other groupings or cuts a swathe through them.[4] The ultimate result is not just a predominance of special interest associations but a pronounced tendency for other institutions, especially of class, neighborhood, and age, to lose all corporate unity other than that expressed in voluntary associations, so that they become, in effect, no more than part of the large number of special-interest groups. Indeed, when the rationale of these older institutions decreases, the remaining basis for their social coherence is as the points of crystallization of voluntary associations.

. . .

The impetus to multiplication and elaboration of voluntary associations was as much socially linked with the patterns of the community's past as with the more recent urbanism. Because they had existed for at least a couple of generations, were established with pride, and successfully maintained and directed social participation, voluntary associations were seized upon as a traditional social device to cope with the extra-institutional problems that arose with the village's twentieth-century economic and cultural revolution. Dotson found, conversely, that in Guadalajara the growth of voluntary associations was a direct result of diffusion rather than indigenous elaboration of an integrated trait, and he noted a great deal of non-participation.[5] . . .

A weakening of the family, the face-to-face community, and other institutions as social units may well be related to the adverse effect of certain exigencies of urban assimilation, but it does not necessarily follow that voluntary associations have proliferated essentially as a result of this development. Voluntary associations appear either to have had pre-urban recognition and a successful history within the particular population or culture [6] before their city's "flowering," or they are hindered in making significant inroads in the general social structure. In the former case, associations mutiply as . . . their recognized advantage in meeting the mounting individual and group needs for self-expression and the compounding satisfaction of aesthetic, economic, and social interest is exploited. In the latter case, their development is more erratic, dependent perhaps . . . on selective acculturation influences that acquaint special classes with their utility. . . .

24. THE SOCIAL STRUCTURE AND POLITICAL PROCESS OF SUBURBIA

Scott A. Greer

The social organization of suburbia may be derived, as Scott Greer attempts to show, from the type of population encountered there, its style of life, and the implication of its demographic aggregation. The result is a social organization that consists of households within a neighborhood, a residential community bound together by functional need, and, overall, the political municipality. These concentric entities embrace a unifying communication system in addition to a regulative order of norms sanctioning or prohibiting various forms of behavior.

Justifying systematic theory, of course, is its usefulness as a basis for inferring the outcome of situations that contain known variables. In the complete version of this selection Greer proceeds to formulate several kinds of action and individual involvement in the suburb, whether as a social or as a political system. Accordingly, we have child-centered activities, community-political participation, and the fraternal-service kind of behavior as well. Each may be locally centered or related to the larger, environing system. Hypotheses developed in terms of such factors may lead to productive research at the level of community organization.

THE BIFURCATION of work and residence is sometimes taken as one of the defining characteristics of the suburban population.[1] But this bifurcation holds for most of the population in a metropolis; any local residential area is segmental in nature. Because a living area is the site for some, but not all, of the basic social activities of its residents, Janowitz calls it the

Excerpts reprinted from the *American Sociological Review*, August 1960 by permission of the author and the American Sociological Association.

"community of limited liability." [2] Such a community, however, encompasses some very crucial structures and therefore has constraining force —which allows the social scientist some predictive and explanatory power.

The definition of social organization used in the present discussion emphasized functional interdependence. As the unit of analysis, we shall emphasize the spatially defined group. The locality group, or community, is thus viewed as a special case of the social form elsewhere defined as "an aggregate in a state of functional interdependence, from which emerges a flow of communication and a consequent ordering of behavior." [3]

Geographical contiguity, however, has no self-evident sociological meaning. It may become the basis for interdependence only when it constitutes a field for social action. We consider below three such fields, concentric in scope: the neighborhood, the local residential community, and the municipality. Using the definition of the group stated above, we ask three questions about each of these levels of organization: What constitutes the functional interdependence of the members? What are the channels of communication and the contents of the communication flow? What kind of ordered behavior results?

The neighborhood   If the residents of a neighborhood consist of households with familistic ways of life (and consequently similar interests) existing in close proximity, there is a high probability of intersecting trajectories of action. Since surrounding households constitute important and inescapable parts of any given household's organizational environment, there emerge problems of social order, maintenance, and aid. Specifically, it is necessary to regulate the play of children, child-adult relations, and adult-adult relations to the degree that these represent possible blocks to the orderly performance of the household's way of life. To the extent that contiguous sites overlap visually, aurally, and (sometimes) physically, it is also necessary to regulate the use of the sites. The unsightly yard, the noises of the night, the dangerously barricaded sidewalk may constitute such blocks. Finally, similarity of life routines indicates a probable similarity of equipment and tasks: thus the interchangeability of parts is possible. This may range from the traditional borrowing of a cup of bourbon to the baby-sitting pool.

To be sure, similar problems arise in the apartment house districts characterized by a highly urban way of life, but the structure of the neighborhood and the nature of the population result in different kinds of order. The lower rate of communication, due to lack of common or overlapping space, and the separation of routines in time, result in a greater dependence upon formal norms (rules of the building, laws of residency) and upon formal authorities. Thus the apartment house manager, or even the police, may be useful for the maintainance of order and the site. (Their utility, from household to *concierge* to police, is evident in the reliance placed upon such organizations by the state in various European countries.) In the suburbs, however, life-style and the relationships among the sites force inter-household communication.

Communication in the neighborhood may take place at many levels, but in viewing the suburban neighborhood as an organizational unit we shall emphasize casual interaction among those whose paths necessarily intersect. In the adjoining backyards, at bus stops, and local commercial facilities, considerable social interaction is well nigh unavoidable. This interaction may become elaborated into relatively permanent cliques— kaffeeklatsch groups, pools, and the like—and frequently results in a network of close friendships. These differ from "neighboring," or participation in the neighborhood organization, just as friendship within any organization differs from the ongoing structure of activity common to the aggregate.

The resulting patterns of behavior, the structured action, probably vary a good deal according to the type of neighborhood; however, the ubiquity of the phrase "the good neighbor" seems to indicate some generalized role system and normative structure.[4] Orderliness, accessibility in time of need, and cleanliness are salient characteristics rooted in the functional interdependence discussed above. Individual members conform to such norms (whether or not they love their neighbors) because the norms facilitate their ongoing household enterprises.

But the neighborhood is a microcosm. Nor is it the only spatially based social structure mediating between the household and the metropolis. The neighborhood then is a precipitate of interacting households; participation in it does not necessarily indicate a role in the larger local area as community or as political unit. The neighborhood produces, at the least, some order among the small enclave of residents, and communication relevant to the nearby scene.

The local residential area   Neighbors in the suburbs tend to have similar interests, for their ways of life have similar prerequisites, while in the local residential area interdependence results when similar interests are transformed into common interests, based upon the common field in which they operate. Spatial aggregates are the distributing units for many goods and services—public schools, commercial services, and various governmental aids and are frequently available to the individual only through his residence in a geographically delimited aggregate. To the degree that this is true of vital resources, the population of a local residential area is functionally interdependent.[5] At the same time space, as the site of common activities (street, sidewalk, park, playground), is a base of interdependence, as in the neighborhood.

The local residential community as here defined includes a number of neighborhoods. It may or may not be coterminous with a political unit. What is its minimal organizational structure? Communication relevant to the area ordinarily takes place through two channels, the community press and voluntary organizations. While each is a communication channel, we shall stress the communications function of the press and the action function of the voluntary organization.

The local community press in the suburbs, widely distributed and widely read, is a medium available to almost all residents of most local areas.[6] Its utility stems directly from the interdependence of activities within the local area; supported by local merchants, it provides support in turn for the various formal organizations which constitute the "community." To be sure, all areas are not now serviced by a community press, but so useful is the medium (and consequently, so lucrative) that it is rapidly "covering" the suburban areas of contemporary cities. As the press develops where there is a market for its services, this should occur most consistently and widely among the familistic populations.

The suburban paper is quite similar to that described by Janowitz— parochial in its interests, reporting almost exclusively upon local happenings, translating metropolitan events into their effects on the local area, seldom reporting national events.[7] Such local personages as merchants, bureaucrats, and organizational leaders constitute the actors on this stage. Insofar as the local area is a social fact, the latter is reflected in the press and at the same time reinforced in the process of reflection, for the press in perpetuating lines of communication stabilizes norms and roles. If it is chiefly a merchandising mechanism in its economic function, it is also a public platform for the area in its social and political functions.

But what of the local area without a separate government? In this case, what kind of structured action is indicated as the third term in the definition of the area as a social structure? Noting again that spatially defined organization in the residential area is loose, unstructured, and does not engage all of the residents, here we emphasize participation in the local formal organizations. Such organizations are segmental in their membership and purposes; they include those residents who are dependent upon them for basic necessities to their way of life. Community-oriented organizations, improvement associations, child-centered organizations, some fraternal and service clubs are examples. They are particular to the area, their membership is largely limited to those living there, and they are instruments of persuasion and control with respect to various community problems, projects, and festivals. Furthermore, if there is no political structure they are the *only* existing structures through which an interdependence specific to the area (issuing in local problems), communicated through the press (as "community issues"), become manifested in social action.

The suburban municipality   The typical political structure of metropolitan suburbia viewed as a whole is a crazy-quilt of many small municipalities having various eccentric shapes and displaying little obvious order in their boundaries. It is likely, however, that many of these municipalities are roughly coterminous with one or more social communities of the kind discussed above. To the degree that this is the case, the seemingly arbitrary lines on the map may come to represent social communities. The congruence of municipal boundaries with a local residential community permits the translation of common interests into a polity. The common field of activity (and the various segmental interests sited in this field) is contained within a formal organizational structure having the power to control, within wide limits, some of the basic goods and services of the residents. Thus streets, parks, schools (and, to a degree, commercial and residential development) are not only sources of interdependence—their control is so structured as to allow effective action by the

TABLE 1

SOCIAL-POLITICAL STRUCTURES OF SUBURBIA

	Source of Interdependence	Channels of Communication	Structured Action
Neighborhood:	Overlapping field Similar interests	Informal interaction Casual visiting	Regulated interaction Maintenance of the site Mutual aid
Local Area:	Common field	Community press	Segmental interests protection
	Common interests	Local organizations Informal interaction	Diffuse community action (outside political structure)
Municipality:	Common field Common interests Common organizational structure coterminous with both	Local governmental functions Local political organizations Local non-political organizations Community press Informal interaction	Law-abiding (local), tax-paying Voting, holding office Attending meetings Use of bureaucratic structure for complaints and appeals Organization of electoral campaigns

interdependent population. Furthermore, taxation, police power, and other governmental attributes are assigned to the local municipality.

Where such is the case, an additional level is added to the structured action which results from interdependence and the flow of communication within the residential community: political action, within a political community.[8] Communication now incorporates well defined political norms and roles, the latter including the governmental official, political leader, voter, local taxpayer, and so on. But this type of organizational structure does not displace the kinds of voluntary community organizations indicated earlier. Certain modes of action tend to become allocated to the governmental organization; others remain the functions of private and semi-private groups (including the neighborhoods).

The organizational structure of suburbia may be summarized as follows: (1) The overlapping activities of households result in the neighborhoods, which exist as a kind of network spreading throughout the familistic population (for neighborhoods overlap as do households, and the neighborhood structure of a metropolis frequently resembles St. Augustine's definition of God, an infinite circle whose center is everywhere and whose periphery is nowhere). (2) Larger residential areas with a degree of functional interdependence constitute "communities of limited liability." They exhibit communication through informal relations and the community press, and action through voluntary private and semi-private organizations. (3) In many cases, political units are roughly coterminous with, or include, one or more social communities. Neighborhoods are probably nearly omnipresent, though a network need not include all households; so are communities, but they vary widely in degree of organization; political communities may or may not exist. In the summary presented in Table 1, each analytical category is sketched in for each organizational level.

25. THE HYPOTHESIS OF METROPOLITAN DOMINATION

Donald J. Bogue

Much attention has been devoted to the internal organization of the city. Little, however, has gone to the structure of the metropolitan region, that is, the system made up of the leading city in a territory and its surrounding hinterland. Yet the latter is no less tangible a social phenomenon.

Two independent lines of inquiry are seen to converge here upon a common conclusion. Researchers in one line have studied the great city in terms of economic history, technological development, and material progress. Researchers in the other line, urban sociology of the ecological school, have viewed the metropolis as analogous to the processes of growth and adaptation among natural organisms. Bogue shows that both areas of research interpret the metropolitan community as the dominant force within a considerable expanse of territory. This is because of the ability of the metropolitan community to limit the conditions of life for the population of the rural countryside as well as that of the smaller, subordinate cities. It is the superior economic power and civic organization of the great city that gives it the capacity to control the communities in its vicinity. Such macrocosmic social structure is, in fact, characteristic of the present metropolitan stage of urbanization.

OUT OF THE ATTEMPTS to understand cities and their place in the modern world has grown a generalization which may be called the "dominant

Excerpts from *Structure of the Metropolitan Community* by Donald Bogue (1949) published by Horace H. Rackham School of Graduate Studies, University of Michigan. Reprinted by permission of the author.

city" hypothesis or the "hypothesis of metropolitan dominance." . . . It classifies cities on the basis of the functions which they perform and their relative ability to "dominate" other cities and the surrounding country-side. The classification made in formulating this hypothesis is a dichotomous one: cities are divided into "metropolitan centers" and "hinterland cities." The metropolis is usually the largest and most complex (the farthest removed from the "average" city) of all of the cities in the territory. Because it is able to assemble cheaply a varied array of raw materials and products from all parts of the world; because a large number of specialized components and skills are required in the production of the goods required to sustain human beings at their present level of living; because up to a certain point machine production increases in efficiency with an increased scale of operations; and because certain mutual benefits appear to accrue to business enterprises from their location in proximity to each other, the large city is able to produce and distribute more varied goods and services than is a smaller city. The more specialized the goods, and the more the goods are amenable to mass production, the greater these industrial and commercial advantages of large cities seem to become. From these facts it has been concluded that the metropolis, or modern large and complex city, exercises an organizing and integrative influence on the social and economic life of a broad expanse of territory far beyond the civil boundaries, and thereby dominates all other communities within this area. The hypothesis of metropolitan dominance assumes that there is a system of interdependency among cities, and that there are considerable differences between the activities of individual cities. It maintains that the organizing agent, and one of the forces making for intercity differentiation, is the metropolis.

Sufficient evidence has been accumulated to make of this view a very plausible hypothesis. Smaller cities and villages lying in the region about great cities appear to have been drawn into a division of labor with the larger urban center. They exchange for the specialized goods and services of the metropolis such other products as can most effectively be produced from the resources in their immediate locality. Farm operators also appear to have become more dependent upon metropolitan markets, and consequently have regulated their activities to produce, if possible, those products which will yield them the greatest return in the metropolitan market. With these exchanges of material goods has also gone the exchange of ideas and human values. The metropolis appears to have become the focal point not only of our material activities, but of much of our moral and intellectual life as well. Repeatedly it has been pointed out that not only in activities such as non-agricultural production, distribution, and finance, but also in matters of government, progress in the arts and sciences, news dissemination and the formation of public opinion, changed philosophies of religion, and the emergence of new human values, the great metropolis is now the dominating center. To one who accepts such a view, progress toward understanding many economic and social problems of this century can come only from a thorough analysis of the metropolis and its relation to other communities.

Although this hypothesis frequently has been expressed in the form stated here, it has never been submitted to a fair test of verification. However, the research which has been accomplished in the field of metropolitan dominance, although highly selective, is of such high quality that to accomplish the goal of this study it has been necessary to do little more than to assemble the various conclusions drawn by others from partial data, to organize these conclusions systematically as parts of the central hypothesis of metropolitan dominance, and then to devise a procedure for determining their validity.

. . .

Two formulations of the metropolitan hypothesis are outstanding for their completeness of detail and the care with which evidence has been collected for their expression. They are N. S. B. Gras' *An Introduction to Economic History* and R. D. McKenzie's *The Metropolitan Community*. Gras and McKenzie were among the first in their respective fields to attempt to link the present urbanized way of life to pre-industrial organization via the route of community analysis. The research of both men is based upon the premise that the community is the elemental form of social organization. Aside from this common point of view, their techniques, their data, and their modes of analysis differ; yet they reach surprisingly similar conclusions. Gras arrived at the metropolitan hypothesis by an informal case study and natural history approach, using historical and anthropological information covering the entire period of man's recorded history. McKenzie's statement of the metropolitan hypothesis is derived from a more formal statistical study of urbanism in the United States since 1790.

. . . The basic thesis of Gras' *Introduction to Economic History* is that at each stage of technological development man has simultaneously developed a community organization which is suitable to the new techniques of wresting a livelihood from the resources of nature. By using existing information about the technological progress of man through the period of his recorded history, and comparable information about his economic and social organization Gras informally correlates the two. He divides the continuum of technological and communal development of Western Civilization into five major phases or periods: (a) the collectional economy, (b) the cultural nomadic economy, (c) the settled village economy, (d) the town economy, and finally (e) *the metropolitan economy*. Each phase is named for the type of social development dominant in that period. Throughout his history technological change has progressively released man from the necessity of sustaining himself from his immediate

environment. Yet the lessening of this dependence upon the local area
has been achieved only at the expense of a corresponding dependence
upon a more complex system of production and exchange extending over
a wider area. Such a system has invariably involved greater specialization
and division of labor. In order to achieve the potential gains of each new
major technological development, new and larger combinations of population and resources have been required. Consequently, new types of social organization have emerged which have been composed of units better
adapted to operate under the new economy. Each major phase of technological development has been accompanied by a major change in the size,
form, and organization of the community. Thus, according to Gras' interpretation, each of the five types of community enumerated above has
risen to operate a different type of economy, which in turn has been the
result of the attainment of a new level of technological advance.

· · ·

The one situational factor which Gras holds to be absolutely essential
for the development of a city aspirant to metropolitan status is the possession of a *hinterland,* "a tributary adjacent territory, rich in natural resources, accompanied by a productive population and accessible by
means of transportation." We are warned by Gras not to overemphasize
either the metropolis or the hinterland in considering the metropolitan
organization.

· · ·

The striking element about the metropolitan hypothesis as formulated
by Gras is not that great cities exist, nor even that they dominate a broad
expanse of territory, but that *the metropolitan economy is the characteristic and dominant type of modern social and economic organization.*
Thus Gras expresses the metropolitan hypothesis that ours is a "metro-
politanized" culture. The metropolis and the hinterland are held to be
parts of one organic whole. Our present day society operates in terms of,
and is conditioned by, these metropolitan units. According to Gras, the
metropolitan economy is a modern form of social organization by which
man makes effective use of his advanced technology.

· · ·

Human ecology, pursuing its study of human aggregates as an adaption
to the environment, has also arrived at the metropolitan hypothesis. One
of the series of monographs published under the direction of the President's Research Committee on Social Trends was McKenzie's *The Metro-*

politan Community, a work devoted entirely to a development of this hypothesis.

By reducing the scale of local distance, the motor vehicle extended the horizon of the community and introduced a territorial division of labor among local institutions and neighboring centers which is unique in the history of settlement. The large center has been able to extend the radius of its influence; its population and many of its institutions, freed from the dominance of rail transportation, have become widely dispersed throughout surrounding territory. Moreover, formerly independent towns and villages and also rural territory have become part of this enlarged city complex. This new *type of super community organized around a dominant focal point and comprising a multitude of differentiated centers of activity* differs from the metropolitanism established by rail transportation in the complexity of its institutional division of labor and the mobility of its population. Its territorial scope is defined in terms of motor transportation and competition with other regions. Nor is this new type of metropolitan community confined to the great cities. *It has become the communal unit of local relations throughout the entire nation.*[1]

McKenzie accumulated a detailed mass of evidence which demonstrated that the metropolitan center is a true dominant among community types. After reviewing the existing population data and data for many diverse economic activities he concludes:

The super community therefore absorbs varying numbers of separate local communities into its economic and cultural organizations. In this pattern a dominant city—that is, dominant relative to surrounding settlement, functions as the integrating unit . . . In other words, there is developing within the United States, and in fact throughout the modern world, a pattern of settlement which may be designated as city regionalism. This new city regionalism differs from the regionalism of former times in that it is a product of contact and division of labor rather than of mere geographic isolation.[2]

. . .

Gras and McKenzie therefore reached identical conclusions: not cities in general, but metropolitan cities in particular, dominate our society today. This dominance has come about as an orderly change in human organization, through the use of new techniques for supplying the necessities of life from the environment. Such an orientation of activities toward the metropolis is regarded as an epoch of community organization.

. . .

. . . The term "dominance" has been used repeatedly in the foregoing discussion to characterize the relationship between the metropolis and the hinterland. McKenzie's statement of the metropolitan hypothesis from the ecological point of view seems to depend almost entirely upon the use of this term. Gras likewise stated that "commercial dominance" over a wide area is the chief characteristic of metropolitan centers. . . .

. . .

. . . a dominant in nature exercises its control not by ordering and for-bidding, not by virtue of any authority or right to command, *but by controlling the conditions of life.* The right to this control is earned only after a demonstration of the ability to adjust to the wide variety of conditions in the environment. The dominant species may be thought of also as a product of the struggle of all life to adapt. It is a life form which has proved conspicuously successful in surviving, first by adapting to the conditions surrounding it and, second, by reacting upon and altering the environment to benefit its own needs.

When one reflects upon the relationship between the great city and the territory surrounding it, he is impressed by the similarity of this relationship to that found by the bio-ecologist in plant and animal communities. Metropolitan centers have no legal authority to order their smaller neighbors to produce or not to produce a given type of commodity, to inhabit or not to inhabit the land with a given number of persons per square mile, or to think specific thoughts and hold specified beliefs about political, moral, or economic events. If the metropolis does dominate its environment, it does so without coercion and edict.

. . . At the time the territory which is now the United States was first settled, human communities were forced to deal directly with the physical environment. The villages and small cities which were established were in much the position of the lone tree in the field: they drew their nurture from the immediate vicinity, and local catastrophe threatened their existence at all times. They specialized primarily in extracting the most easily obtained resources of the environment, such as fur, lumber, fish, game, and the simpler agricultural products. A considerable amount of the materials extracted or produced were removed from the area by external forces, as were the leaves from the lone tree, for the original colonies were raw material exporters. Just as the single tree derives benefit from the production of leaves, but is able to derive the secondary benefit of the complete consumption of the product only by interacting with others of its kind, so the individual colonies could realize the full benefit of their productive efforts only when they were able to establish intercommunity trade and exert some control over the external forces. . . .

Gradually the interdependences of the colonial cities increased, and as they grew in number and size they achieved a greater degree of control over the environment. The cities had not only adapted to the particular conditions of their environment, but had entered the phase of dominance by modifying and differentiating that environment through new types of activity. Canals, railways, and highways were cut from city to city and from cities into the wilderness. Budding manufacturing activities and new trade opportunities encouraged deforestation and the use of the land to produce raw materials and food for fabrication and exchange through urban centers. As the cities grew they became market centers for each others products and for their respective hinterlands. The value which was placed upon the products and activities of outlying areas came to be less a matter of custom and more a matter of a price established by metropolitan markets. Cities consciously strove to annex new territory to their trade areas to gain for themselves a hinterland. As the frontier advanced westward, "gateway" cities sprang up to provide the functions which earlier colonial towns had performed. Gradually the frontier areas, too, have become "forested" with metropolitan centers. As the number of these centers has multiplied and the system of interchange among them has grown more complex, control over the physical environment has been progressively extended. Presumably this process has not yet attained a climax stage in which a point of equilibrium is attained between the dominating species and the supporting environment. In the meantime, individual communities have thrived when they have adjusted themselves to the conditions imposed by metropolitan centers. When their activities have not been so adapted they have tended to become ghost towns.

Such is the interpretation which can be placed upon the dominance of the great city. Not control through ordering and forbidding, but control through the more subtle means of heightened interdependence, alteration of the physical habitat, and a modification of the conditions under which smaller communities may thrive, are the elements by which the great city may dominate its neighbors. . . .

CHAPTER SIX

DISTRESS, DISSENSUS, AND DISCORD

More than one urban scholar has voiced the fear that cities today, in their failure to adapt human settlements to change, pose for the world its gravest risk short of war. The manifestations of failure are indeed there to be seen. Inadequate housing, widespread poverty, rising crime rates, racial antagonism—these and other conditions compromise the obvious success that modern urban societies have achieved in sanitation, public health, transportation, distribution, entertainment and recreational facilities, and communication.

What Marion J. Levy, Jr., has generalized as states of affairs that are inimical to whole societies, is also applicable to cities.[1] A city is threatened if its population is biologically undermined; if it is rendered so apathetic that it no longer evinces common, cooperative, and collective efforts; or if it is caught up in widespread internal conflict. Stable societies and urban communities avert such terminating situations by doing several things. These include the definition of social roles for individuals to perform; the allocation of rewards, whether material or psychic; the maintenance of effective communication; the preservation of a wide range of agreed-upon goals as well as the means of reaching them; the inhibition of extreme forms of emotion; serviceable socialization; and suppression of tendencies to make drastic use of force and fraud. Organized societies effect these functional provisions skillfully. So too do successful cities.

Even a beginning acquaintance with urban problems, however, suggests that many serious ills are present in the contemporary city. One highly respected school of thought holds, in fact, that urban disorganization is inescapable owing to the continuous social change that cities are instrumental in bringing about. Consider, for instance, the sequence of disturbing changes that overtook Harlan County, Kentucky, as a result of incipient industrialization and urbanization. Paul F. Cressey has ably documented this historical chapter in the American past.[2]

When the railroad was built and coal mining began in 1910 in Harlan County, significant consequences were instantly apparent. Since a person's livelihood now depended on his uncertain, discontinuous employment rather than subsistence farming, the new money economy created a great instability. In addition, a social gap opened between the mine operators and owners on the one hand and their employed workers on the other. This inequality of power and subordination was resented in the mining communities that had sprung up. They were peopled by sizeable numbers of in-migrants, and the established family and neighborhood codes that had been long observed in the rural countryside could no longer regulate behavior. Within the family itself the traditional roles of parents and children were upset, now that the family could not continue as a unified work group. Personal distress showed up in heavy drinking, brawling, gambling, prostitution, and even murder. Finally, too, at the level of government, crassness, cunning, and corruption replaced the earlier system of intense but essentially honest and peaceful rivalries.

Although the foregoing appears clearcut, social problems in general and urban social problems in particular are often as difficult to define as they are to solve. Consider divorce. Is it a problem? Yes, insofar as it signifies a marriage that has failed. No, inasmuch as it represents the solution to a preexisting problem. Again, does unaesthetic architecture constitute a social problem? Yes, says the sophisticated observer who knows about the ennervating effects of uninspiring public buildings. No, answers the average layman in his concern for public economy and in his unawareness of the long-term consequences of flaccid architectural styles. Let us now appraise a third instance. Authorities and experts advocated urban renewal as an answer to urban community tensions, but this has not proved to be true. On the other hand, erotic books and movies were thought even by reputable figures to be pernicious. Few reason so now. Are the supposed solutions to problems themselves problems? And are even the declared problems indeed problems?

In view of these warnings it is understandable that writers differ in their identification of urban social problems. Perhaps most writers feel that a social problem is, first, a general condition that affects a large number of people in a way that threatens or frustrates a social value and, second, a state of affairs that can be remedied by deliberate effort. Death would then not constitute a social problem but some specific cause of early death would.

Not all writers, however, agree with this. Marshall Clinard sees deviance from established norms as being the only true social problems.[3] On the other hand, some writers define problems in humanitarian terms, such as discrimination and pressures toward rigid conformity. These offend cultural standards, to be sure, but they are confined to the welfare of individuals. On the other hand, problems may be defined functionally, like crime, and therefore viewed as detrimental to the continued welfare or stability of the community. Earl Raab and Gertrude J. Selznick lean toward both of these views.[4] That the existence of any social problem depends on definition is certainly truistic. Obviously, it depends on recognition in terms of some value system. Let us take a clear example. Poverty may actually be thought desirable, and given the perniciousness of rising expectations, affluence be deemed intolerably frustrating. Similarly, mental hygiene may not appear to be as much of a social problem as, say, the auto accident rate.

Recognizing these complexities, Richard C. Fuller and Richard R. Myers have formulated a three-part typology of social problems.[5] First we have physical problems, exemplified by droughts and floods, which do not involve moral questions so far as their origins at least are concerned. Second, there are ameliorative problems, that is, criminal behavior and poverty, about which disagreement centers on how best to overcome them. And, third, there are the definitely moral problems—divorce, gambling, and segregation, for example, —on which there is no broad consensus. Confusion, or at least disagreement, exists then, on the definition, the origins, and also the solution of social problems. Consequently, any basic understanding of social problems includes certain derivative principles—among these, multiple causation, the recognition of much ignorance of cause, and the acknowledgement of unfavorable proposed solutions and their side effects.

There are other considerations too. Social problems are interdependent. Take two cases in point. Is unemployment alien to emotional illness, and poverty alien to poor education? Some social problems are hidden from public view, and although they affect many individuals, they do not come to public attention effectively or forcefully except when the problem is brought to attention by exceptional circumstances, such as the publicized death of a woman due to a criminal abortion.

Social values are involved in nearly all conceptions of social problems in the city and elsewhere and they are involved in a variety of ways. Social values cause problems, such as standards of sexual morality. Social values may be in conflict, as in the case of democratic principles that suffer when the pursuit of economic interests leads to racial discrimination. And, too, social values may prevent particular solutions from being adopted. One concrete example of this would be the avoidance of artificial birth control methods. Another, moral opposition to a guaranteed annual income.

However much values are implicated in urban social problems, one exceptionally strong viewpoint, as has already been said, is that such strains are an inseparable part of the currents of social change. Leo F. Schnore has sharply observed that social problems are "correlates, concomitants, or consequences of urban-industrialism." [6] The city violates traditional norms and upsets time-honored institutional safeguards. It destroys established economic security and it engenders short-term or even chronic deprivation, for instance, by ruining the handicrafts market or by disemploying the aged. As a result, urban-industrial society is identified with a wide range of difficulties—including poverty, family disturbances, deviance, and the isolation of the individual.

Major social changes of a distressing kind are being registered currently in even our most advanced metropolitan areas. Greater wealth and leisure are bringing about problems of further economic adjustment. Mass migration from farm to city is exacerbating the problems of acculturation. The expansion of the population occasioned by urban sanitation, medicine, and the like is underscoring the problem of having the unskilled participate in our high-input and high-output industrial establishment. The influx of these at the lowest socioeconomic levels into the metropolitan core and the out-migration of the more affluent to the suburbs is intensifying the imbalance of need and resources in the city.

Very troublesome domestic problems are indeed traceable to urban growth and change. Some are housekeeping difficulties, like sanitation, traffic control, and utility services. Others relate to refractory values, which show up in civic apathy and racial tensions. That the two orders—formal administration, on the one hand, and socio-cultural beliefs and interaction, on the other—are not wholly separate and distinct is an important fact. It can be seen in many cases. One example is the impaired communication among the many segments of the population of a given urban community that prevents funds from being committed to official maintenance activities. Again, poor police control may reflect rifts in the community regarding the means as well as the ends of law enforcement.

As a general change process, urbanization-industrialization affects not only the geographic location and socioeconomic status of age, sex, occupation, and ethnic groups but perhaps even more significantly the images they have of themselves. Thus when other groups refuse to acknowledge such new perspectives and to permit wider social participation, the result is intensified friction. What is more evident than this in the current intergroup discord between blacks and whites?

If social change is vital to the emergence of urban problems, the rate at which it takes place is perhaps equally significant. Crime and delinquency, as one case in point, rise during periods of rapid urban expansion. Likewise the housing problem, which is worsened when a city receives a sudden infusion of back-country migrants. The displacement of men by machines also accompanies swift urbanization, because this augurs a strong market justifying added capital investment. Furthermore, as industrialization proceeds, the tertiary stage of economic development ensues when an advanced use is made of human resources and the resulting élite pull away economically and culturally from the rest of the urban mass and yet still continue to serve as a distant (and hence disturbing) model for the others to aspire to. This is the familiar gold coast and slum complex of anomie.

Once the factor of change is introduced into the theory of urban social problems, then a curious paradox arises. If urban difficulties are not intrinsic to urbanism, however much change may be associated with urban society per se, then *inconsistency* in the rate at which dissensus, distress, and discord appear and the rate at which productive, ameliorative, and controlling social inventions are made is the real, underlying factor that is finally responsible. Consider migration into the city and, again, the traffic dislocation that takes place when a new factory has been built and, on the other hand, the availability of political mechanisms for dealing with them. The view that rate inconsistency is basic assumes the possibility of meeting needs much perhaps as the neo-Malthusians assume the exponential equation of population. Certainly an examination of the history of the city strongly suggests that such remarkable innovations in public health, mass schooling, and transportation have already been made that present issues simply await similar solution.

Two opposing interpretations of society and the social process may, however, be applied to the observation that urban problems are brought about by change. One originated with Durkheim and was given great reinforcement in American sociology by Florian Znaniecki and W. I. Thomas.[7] It holds that at times the cultural consensus breaks down and people become unable to understand, communicate with, and act meaningfully toward one another. The other theory is that people experience social problems because they pursue antagonistic and conflicting interests over the allocation of scarce resources. Karl Marx, Georg Simmel, Albion Small, and more recently Herbert Blumer and Lewis Coser have been notable conflict theorists.[8] Its basic premise is that individuals and groups compete for wealth, power, and prestige, and the differential possession that results constitutes the social problem. Robert Merton's theory of anomie as adherence to goals while one lacks the necessary means of attaining them, takes on great force in the city where social mobility is an imperative even possibly for those of the lowest status.[9] As a theory it underscores the fact that the social-organization and conflict viewpoints are principles that have limited validity. Moreover, even though in the final analysis they relate to antithetical conceptions of the social order, in specific applications such as this one they actually complement each other.

Exponents of the social-organization hypothesis also conceive of personal disorganization. That is to say, war, prolonged economic depression, and large-scale migration give rise to the breakdown of consensus and to the appearance of estrangement, to the confusion of values, and to interpersonal hostility. This is of course an oversimplification, since the conventional indices of personal maladaptation —divorce, crime, and suicide—actually decline during periods of initial social disorganization. Very prolonged periods, however, are accompanied by rising rates. At these times social values come to be frustrated very severely and, as a result, the cohesion that originally created a spirit of élan ebbs away. After prolonged deprivation adherence to social disciplines weakens, probably owing finally to the deterioration of primary groups, and then personal disorganization sets in. This may contribute to large-scale collective phenomena, like organized intergroup aggression, rather than distributive actions alone. Hence it may be closer to the truth to see social and personal disorganization not as unilateral cause and effect but as reinforcing states that are reciprocals of each other.

Thomas and Znaniecki contributed substantially to the theory of social and personal disorganization. They conceived of the former as a condition in which the normative system has little influence, and the latter as the decreasing ability of the individual to arrange things so that he can realize his personal interests. The theory of social disorganization is consistent with a number of carefully established hypotheses. It agrees with the differential association theory of crime advanced by Sutherland, the ecological theory of schizophrenia formulated by Faris and Dunham, and Robert Angell's hypothesis on family instability.[10] In each case weakened adherence to institutionalized standards is crucially apparent.

Considerations of culture, social organization, demography, and ecology have all figured in the analysis of urban strains. For instance, the multiplicity of roles in city life is no doubt a serious factor. Not only is role switching a problem, but there are also incompatible role expectations. The domestic-occupational role of the woman, the business entrepreneur and community leader that the executive is supposed to be, and the otherworldly aspirant and practical administrator which are held up as the beau ideal of the churchman in the urban setting, are examples of prevalent ethical inconsistencies. The demographic interpretation of urban social disorganization has long been pursued with impressive, if not wholly convincing, results. "Natural areas" of deviance have been identified independently by Ernest R. Mowrer, Clifford R. Shaw and Henry D. McKay, and by Robert E. L. Faris and H. Warren Dunham.[11] These are neighborhoods where crime, illness, and social deficit rates are consistently high and as such are related to the peculiar life pattern there and the strains that it consequently entails.

The demographic approach to urban social disorganization shows that urban areas evidence a generally higher level of deviance than rural areas, and that typically the larger the city the greater the extent of violative behavior. If, moreover, the size of the city is related to the frequency of antisocial behavior, so also is the central area of the core city. It is true that occasionally a peripheral or peculiarly located suburban spot will be associated with crime. However, by and large, the incidence of crime is heaviest toward the center of the metropolitan community. Again, though poor physical conditions are present in the inner city, they are in themselves far from being the controlling factor. International studies, in fact, reveal that characteristically the natural areas of deviance are marked by weak social forms that both handicap the inhabitants in competing successfully with those of the surrounding territory and also positively sanction or, at least, condone illicit behavior.

The writings that make up this section on distress, dissensus, and discord in urban society relate to poverty, crime, alienation, racial antipathy, and mass disturbances. They include a presentation of the problem of poverty in urban America and also the concept of the culture of poverty, viewed by Harrington as a constellation of functional responses to deprivation. Clinard's survey of deviant behavior in the city is valuable not only nationally but also internationally. Mizruchi amplifies Durkheim's insight into modern urban secular society, that affluence denotes a relativistic standard with definite tendencies to demoralization. Though focused on the possible reconstruction of Christianity Ross W. Sanderson's essay examines urban social and physical blight through the eyes of the churchman.

Patricia Cayo Sexton enables the reader to turn to the fateful weaknesses of our metropolitan school systems, which are now being called upon to cope with the acculturation of the large, newly-arrived nonwhite populations. The 1968 New York City teachers strike, in its manifestation of the interests of various groups and organizations, as Dr. Sexton reveals, only confirms the relationship of other issues to the general problem.

Judson T. Shaplin, Director of Washington University's Graduate Institute of Education, has declared that our urban public schools, particularly those in the inner city, are in "deep trouble." He attributes this condition to the heavy in-migration of educationally unprepared nonwhites into our big cities, the financial plight of the cities in seeking to finance their schools, and the isolation of the Catholic parochial schools from the major urban public financial and personnel difficulties.

No doubt we are indebted to James B. Conant's *Slums and Suburbs* for first highlighting the urban school crisis. Conant assumed that the poor ghetto whites and blacks are genetically capable of satisfactory academic achievement, that, in short, they have the necessary scholastic aptitude. He was concerned, even alarmed, however, over the growing concentrations of unemployed and frustrated non-white youth in our urban slums. The conditions in the schools, Conant concluded, were inimical to educational progress: high pupil turn-over, the absence of fathers or male heads of households, the low level of educational attainment of the parent generation, extensive crime and delinquency, and socio-cultural alienation and hostility to the gentler values. "The amazing feature of the whole situation," observed Conant, "is that pupils make any progress in schools in some areas of the city." The pervasive influence of the community over the school is also supported by the "Coleman report" and, as Thomas F. Pettigrew has recollected, by three earlier studies employing different measures and samples—those of the Harvard mobility project conducted by the late Samuel A. Stouffer, the study of J. A. Michael, and the survey of residential segregation carried out by A. B. Wilson.

Cities are beset by onerous problems of providing social-welfare services on a very large scale. In 1967, for example, there were 2,073,000 recipients of old-age assistance and 5,309,000 recipients of aid to dependent children. The average monthly payment was only $70 and $40 per person respectively, but old-age assistance payments totaled $1,859,000,000 in 1967 and aid to dependent children, $2,280,000,000. This is a system that has developed willy-nilly over the years and involves all levels of government, principally the federal government as the source though not distributor of funds.

Public provision for ill health is largely of the curative, last-resort variety, with questionable accessibility of services and facilities and with little recognition of the feasibility of thorough precautionary and preventive care. A broad conception of social welfare embraces the adequate supplemental provision of self-development resources in the form of museums, libraries, and parks and recreation areas. Generally the prevailing policy in this respect is one of local initiative, with increasing disparities arising between cities and between municipalities within the same metropolitan area. Income needs are dealt with by complicated assistance and specialized insurance programs, all of them the product of piecemeal legislation. The former are conceived of as charity devices rather than methods of enlarging human resources. Rehabilitative treatment for the handicapped—the blind, amputees, alcoholics, and the mentally ill—varies in quality and scope from one jurisdiction to the next. In general, however, it tends to be meager, even nominal.

The final two readings in this section relate to perhaps the most severe stresses in the contemporary American city—those arising out of intergroup discord. The pernicious consequences of racial separation in the city are systematically presented by Grodzins. As background it illuminates the causes of the 1965 riot in the Los Angeles' Watts area and is reported by the President's Commission on Law Enforcement and Administration of Justice.

26. POVERTY IN AFFLUENCE

Michael Harrington

Michael Harrington subordinates the statistical picture of America's urban poverty to its socioeconomic significance. He does so by presenting the "culture of poverty" that characterizes the poor. Many writers have contributed to the development of this idea, among them Walter Miller, S. M. Miller, Herbert Gans, Frank Riessman, and Oscar Lewis. Harrington takes the position that the culture of poverty is not a normative order, or system of values, to be maintained as an end in itself but is, instead, first a cluster of conditioned responses that are barriers to mobility, such as resignation, and, second, the workings of a set of institutions that perpetuate disadvantage, including government and industry.

In Harrington's work reproduced here, he also reviews some recent economic theory on poverty. Harrington writes with a sense of strong commitment. He is often credited with having more forcefully than anyone else called attention to the plight of the poor, who are ironically so numerous in our large cities and yet at the same time screened from view. Perhaps equally valuable has been Harrington's analysis of the immunity of the poor to the benefits produced by modern society.

THE UNITED STATES in the sixties contains an affluent society within its borders. Millions and tens of millions enjoy the highest standard of life the world has ever known. This blessing is mixed. It is built upon a peculiarly distorted economy, one that often proliferates pseudo-needs

Excerpts reprinted with permission of The Macmillan Company and Penguin Books Ltd. from *The Other America: Poverty in the United States* by Michael Harrington. Copyright © by Michael Harrington 1962.

rather than satisfying human needs. For some, it has resulted in a sense of spiritual emptiness, of alienation. Yet a man would be a fool to prefer hunger to satiety, and the material gains at least open up the possibility of a rich and full existence.

At the same time, the United States contains an underdeveloped nation, a culture of poverty. Its inhabitants do not suffer the extreme privation of the peasants of Asia or the tribesmen of Africa, yet the mechanism of the misery is similar. They are beyond history, beyond progress, sunk in a paralyzing, maiming routine.

.   .   .

I

Perhaps the most important analytic point to have emerged in this description of the other America is the fact that poverty in America forms a culture, a way of life and feeling, that it makes a whole. It is crucial to generalize this idea, for it profoundly affects how one moves to destroy poverty.

The most obvious aspect of this interrelatedness is in the way in which the various subcultures of the other America feed into one another. This is clearest with the aged. There the poverty of the declining years is, for some millions of human beings, a function of the poverty of the earlier years. If there were adequate medical care for everyone in the United States, there would be less misery for old people. It is as simple as that. Or there is the relation between the poor farmers and the unskilled workers. When a man is driven off the land because of the impoverishment worked by technological progress, he leaves one part of the culture of poverty and joins another. If something were done about the low-income farmer, that would immediately tell in the statistics of urban unemployment and the economic underworld. The same is true of the Negroes. Any gain for America's minorities will immediately be translated into an advance for all the unskilled workers. One cannot raise the bottom of a society without benefiting everyone above.

Indeed, there is a curious advantage in the wholeness of poverty. Since the other America forms a distinct system within the United States, effective action at any one decisive point will have a "multiplier" effect; it will ramify through the entire culture of misery and ultimately through the entire society.

Then, poverty is a culture in the sense that the mechanism of impoverishment is fundamentally the same in every part of the system. The vicious circle is a basic pattern. It takes different forms for the unskilled workers, for the aged, for the Negroes, for the agricultural workers, but in each case the principle is the same. There are people in the affluent so-

ciety who are poor because they are poor; and who stay poor because they
are poor.

To realize this is to see that there are some tens of millions of Americans who are beyond the welfare state. Some of them are simply not covered by social legislation: they are omitted from Social Security and from
minimum wage. Others are covered, but since they are so poor they do
not know how to take advantage of the opportunities, or else their coverage is so inadequate as not to make a difference.

The welfare state was designed during the great burst of social creativity that took place in the 1930's. As previously noted its structure corresponds to the needs of those who played the most important role in building it: the middle third, the organized workers, the forces of urban
liberalism, and so on. At the worst, there is "socialism for the rich and
free enterprise for the poor," as when the huge corporation farms are the
main beneficiaries of the farm program while the poor farmers get practically nothing; or when public funds are directed to aid in the construction of luxury housing while the slums are left to themselves (or become
more dense as space is created for the well-off).

So there is the fundamental paradox of the welfare state: that it is not
built for the desperate, but for those who are already capable of helping
themselves. As long as the illusion persists that the poor are merrily free-
loading on the public dole, so long will the other America continue un-
threatened. The truth, it must be understood, is the exact opposite. The
poor get less out of the welfare state than any group in America.

This is, of course, related to the most distinguishing mark of the other
America: its common sense of hopelessness. For even when there are programs designed to help the other Americans, the poor are held back by
their own pessimism.

On one level this fact has been described in this book as a matter of
"aspiration." Like the Asian peasant, the impoverished American tends
to see life as a fate, an endless cycle from which there is no deliverance.
Lacking hope (and he is realistic to feel this way in many cases), that famous solution to all problems—let us educate the poor—becomes less
meaningful. A person has to feel that education will do something for
him if he is to gain from it. Placing a magnificent school with a fine fac-
ulty in the middle of a slum is, I suppose, better than having a run-down
building staffed by incompetents. But it will not really make a difference
so long as the environment of the tenement, the family, and the street
counsels the children to leave as soon as they can and to disregard schooling.

On another level, the emotions of the other America are even more
profoundly disturbed. Here it is not lack of aspiration and of hope; it is a
matter of personal chaos. The drunkenness, the unstable marriages, the
violence of the other America are not simply facts about individuals.
They are the description of an entire group in the society who react this
way because of the conditions under which they live.

In short, being poor is not one aspect of a person's life in this country; it is his life. Taken as a whole, poverty is a culture. Taken on the family level, it has the same quality. These are people who lack education and skill, who have bad health, poor housing, low levels of aspiration and high levels of mental distress. They are, in the language of sociology, "multiproblem" families. Each disability is the more intense because it exists within a web of disabilities. And if one problem is solved, and the others are left constant, there is little gain.

One might translate these facts into the moralistic language so dear to those who would condemn the poor for their faults. The other Americans are those who live at a level of life beneath moral choice, who are so submerged in their poverty that one cannot begin to talk about free choice. The point is not to make them wards of the state. Rather, society must help them before they can help themselves.

II

There is another view about the culture of poverty in America: that by the end of the seventies it will have been halved.

It is important to deal in some detail with this theory. To begin with, it is not offered by reactionaries. The real die-hards in the United States do not even know the poor exist. As soon as someone begins to talk on the subject, that stamps him as a humanitarian. And this is indeed the case with those who look to a relatively automatic improvement in the lot of the other America during the next twenty years or so.

The second reason why this view deserves careful consideration is that it rests, to a considerable extent upon the projection of inevitable and automatic change. Its proponents are for social legislation and for speeding up and deepening this process. But their very argument could be used to justify a comfortable, complacent inaction.

So, does poverty have a future in the United States?

One of the most reasonable and sincere statements of the theme that poverty is coming to an end in America is made by Robert Lampman in the Joint Committee Study Paper "The Low-Income Population and Economic Growth." Lampman estimates that around 20 percent of the nation, some 32,000,000 people, are poor. . . . And he writes, "By 1977–87 we would expect about 10 percent of the population to have low income status as compared to about 20 percent now."

The main point in Lampman's relatively optimistic argument is that poverty will decline naturally with a continuing rate of economic growth. As the sixties begin, however, this assumption is not a simple one. In the postwar period, growth increased until about the mid-fifties. Then a falling off occurred. In each of the postwar recessions, the recovery left a larger reservoir of "normal" prosperity unemployment. Also, long-term unemployment became more and more of a factor among the jobless.

There were more people out of work, and they stayed out of work longer.

In the first period of the Kennedy Administration, various economists presented figures as to what kind of Government action was necessary so as really to attack the problem of depressed areas and low-income occupations. There were differences, of course, but the significant fact is that the legislation finally proposed was usually only a percentage of the need as described by the Administration itself. There is no point now in becoming an economic prophet. Suffice it to say that serious and responsible economists feel that the response of the society has been inadequate.

This has led to a paradoxical situation, one that became quite obvious when economic recovery from the recession began in the spring of 1961. The business indicators were all pointing upward: production and productivity were on the increase. Yet the human indexes of recession showed a tenacity despite the industrial gain. Unemployment remained at high levels. An extreme form of the "class unemployment" described earlier seemed to be built into the economy.

At any rate, one can say that if this problem is not solved the other America will not only persist; it will grow. Thus, the first point of the optimistic thesis strikes me as somewhat ambiguous, for it too quickly assumes that the society will make the needed response.

But even if one makes the assumption that there will be steady economic growth, that will not necessarily lead to the automatic elimination of poverty in the United States. J. K. Galbraith, it will be remembered, has argued that the "new" poverty demonstrates a certain immunity to progress. In making his projection of the abolition of half of the culture of poverty within the next generation, Lampman deals with this point, and it is important to follow his argument.

Lampman rejects the idea that insular (or depressed-areas) poverty will really drag the poor down in the long run. As an example of this point, he cites the fact that the number of rural farm families with incomes of under $2,000 fell during the 1947–1957 period from 3.3 million to 2.4 million because of a movement off the farm.

This point illustrates the problem of dealing with simple statistics. A movement from the farm to the city, that is, from rural poverty to urban poverty, will show an upward movement in money income. This is true, among other reasons, because the money income of the urban poor is higher than that of the country poor. But this same change does not necessarily mean that a human being has actually improved his status, that he has escaped from the culture of poverty. . . . the agricultural poor, these people who are literally driven off the land are utterly unprepared for city life. They come to the metropolis in a time of rising skill requirements and relatively high levels of unemployment. They will often enter the economic underworld. Statistically, they can be recorded as a gain, because they have more money. Socially, they have simply transferred from one part of the culture of poverty to another.

At the same time, it should be noted that although there has been this tremendous exodus of the rural poor, the proportion of impoverished farms in America's agriculture has remained roughly the same.

Then Lampman deals with Galbraith's theory of "case poverty," of those who have certain disabilities that keep them down in the culture of poverty. Here it should be noted again that Galbraith himself is somewhat optimistic about case poverty. He tends to regard the bad health of the poor, physical as well as mental, as being facts about them that are individual and personal. If this book is right, particularly in the discussion of the twisted spirit within the culture of poverty, that is not the case. The personal ills of the poor are a social consequence, not a bit of biography about them. They will continue as long as the environment of poverty persists.

But Lampman's optimism goes beyond that of Galbraith. He believes that disabilities of case poverty ("mental deficiency, bad health, inability to adapt to the discipline of modern economic life, excessive procreation, alcohol, insufficient education") are "moderated over time." And he takes as his main case in point education. "For example, average educational attainment levels will rise in future years simply because younger people presently have better education than older people. Hence, as the current generation of old people pass from the scene, the percent of persons with low educational attainment will fall."

This is true, yet it is misleading if it is not placed in the context of the changes in the society as a whole. It is much more possible today to be poor with a couple of years of high school than it was a generation ago. . . . the skill level of the economy has been changing, and educational deficiency, if anything, becomes an even greater burden as a result. In this case, saying that people will have more education is not saying that they will escape the culture of poverty. It could have a much more ironic meaning: that America will have the most literate poor the world has ever known.

Lampman himself concedes that the aged are "immune" to economic growth. If this is the case, and in the absence of ranging and comprehensive social programs, the increase in the number and percentage of the poor within the next generation will actually increase the size of the other America. Lampman also concedes that families with female heads are immune to a general prosperity, and this is another point of resistance for the culture of poverty.

Finally, Lampman is much more optimistic about "nonwhite" progress than the discussion in this book would justify. . . . Let me simply state the point baldly: the present rate of economic progress among the minorities is agonizingly slow, and one cannot look for dramatic gains from this direction.

Thus, I would agree with Galbraith that poverty in the sixties has qualities that give it a hardiness in the face of affluence heretofore unknown. . . . there are many special factors keeping the unskilled workers, the minorities, the agricultural poor, and the aged in the culture of poverty. If there is to be a way out, it will come from human action, from political change, not from automatic processes.

But finally, let us suppose that Lampman is correct on every point. In that case a generation of economic growth coupled with some social legislation would find America in 1987 with "only" 10 per cent of the nation impoverished. If, on the other hand, a vast and comprehensive program attacking the culture of poverty could speed up this whole development, and perhaps even abolish poverty within a generation, what is the reason for holding back? This suffering is such an abomination in a society where it is needless that anything that can be done should be done.

In all this, I do not want to depict Robert Lampman as an enemy of the poor. In all seriousness, the very fact that he writes about the subject does him credit: he has social eyes, which is more than one can say for quite a few people in the society. And second, Lampman puts forward "A Program to Hasten the Reduction of Poverty" because of his genuine concern for the poor. My argument with him is not over motive or dedication. It is only that I believe that his theory makes the reduction of poverty too easy a thing, that he has not properly appreciated how deeply and strongly entrenched the other America is.

27. CRIME AND THE CITY

Marshall B. Clinard

The incidence and prevalence of certain of the major forms of social deviance—namely, delinquency and crime, mental illness, alcoholism, and suicide—are examined here in relation to urban life. The association of deviance with city size is also measured. In both instances, the findings are generally disquieting in view of the world's continuing urbanization and the persistent growth of metropolitan areas. The specific causes of the different types of social disorganization may be approached, as Clinard recognizes elsewhere, by carefully observing their ecological distribution within the city. In this way, the contributing factors of urbanism, such as differential association, role conflicts, and rapid change, can be assessed. Regional differences are also significant, since variations in deviance rates occur among cities of comparable size, indicating the existence of broad cultural forces apart from the mere facts of urbanism. Cross-cultural studies tend to show disparities in social deviance between urban and rural populations, but they also show striking variations between the cities of different countries.

FOR CENTURIES writers have been concerned about the debauchery and moral conditions of the cities and have generally praised rural life. Hesiod, for example, wrote about the corrupt justice of the cities.[1] The Greeks and Romans compared the city with agricultural areas, noting the greater evils and sources of criminality in the cities. One of the first systematic comparisons of rural and urban peoples was made by Ibn Khaldun in the fourteenth century. This famed Arab historian compared life in the city with that among the nomadic tribes. He found that the nomads had good behavior, whereas evil and corruption were abundant in the city; that honesty and courage were characteristic of the nomads, whereas lying and cowardice were prevalent in the city; and that the city caused decay, stultified initiative, and made men depraved and wicked. In general, rural life has been, and still largely is, a world of close personal relationships which Burgess has thus described:

> But in the main characteristics of small-town life stand out in clear perspective: close acquaintanceship of everyone with everyone else, the dominance of personal relations, and the subjection of the individual to continuous observation and control by the community. . . . This fund of concrete knowledge which everyone has of everyone else in the small town naturally emphasizes and accentuates the role of the personal in all relationships and activities of community life. Approval and disapproval of conduct, likes and dislikes of persons, play correspondingly a tremendous part in social life, in business, in politics, and in the administration of justice.[2]

DELINQUENCY AND CRIME

The types, incidence, and reactions to rural crime, as with urban crime, are a function of the type of life and the various norms and values of the communities. Delinquency and crime rates today are generally much lower in rural areas than in urban. In general, the differences between rural and urban property crimes are greater than the differences in crimes against the person.

Some delinquent and criminal acts committed in rural areas are dealt with informally and not officially reported, and there are undoubtedly more opportunities to commit offenses in urban as compared with rural areas. The differences between rural and urban rates, however, are so great that differential reporting or opportunity could, at most, account for only a small part. Also, there is little evidence to support the theory held by some that the city attracts deviants from rural areas.[3]

As Table 1 shows, burglary rates in the United States, as a whole, are generally almost three times as great in urban areas as in rural, larceny is over three times as great, and robbery over six times.[4] The rates for burglaries known to the police per 100,000 population in 1960 were, for example, 568.9 in urban areas and 210.9 in rural areas. Crimes such as murder, which are relatively infrequent as compared with property crimes, are about the same, with a somewhat higher rate in rural areas where the rate is 6.4 as compared with 4.9 in urban. Rape rates are much higher in urban areas, 10.3 in urban as contrasted with 6.8 in rural.

TABLE 1

RATES PER 100,000 POPULATION FOR CRIMES KNOWN TO THE
POLICE IN RURAL AND URBAN AREAS, UNITED STATES, 1960

| | Rate | |
Offense	Urban	Rural
Murder and nonnegligent manslaughter	4.9	6.4
Forcible rape	10.3	6.8
Robbery	70.7	11.9
Aggravated assault	88.7	42.2
Burglary—breaking or entering	568.9	210.9
Larceny—theft ($50 and over)	340.8	102.8
Automobile theft	243.7	42.1

SOURCE: Derived from Federal Bureau of Investigation, *Uniform Crime Reports* (Annual Bulletin, 1960; Washington, D.C.: Government Printing Office, 1960), p. 33. The population figures used were based on the 1960 census. Rates for the above are based on 1960 census data. "Urban areas" include Standard Metropolitan Statistical Areas.

Specific studies, rather than statistical comparisons, also seem to support the thesis that the urbanization of rural areas and an increase in crime go hand in hand. A study of the southern mountain villages showed that as the hill country was opened to outside contacts criminal activities increased.[5] The most important factor associated with this increase was the growing lack of community identification on the part of individuals as the villages became more urbanized. A study of the rural inmates in an Iowa reformatory revealed that characteristics associated with an urban way of life played a significant role in their criminal behavior.[6]

MENTAL DISORDERS

Most contemporary data on mental disorders, but not all, show that the rates are generally higher in urban than in rural areas. As with crime, many writers feel that the expansion of urbanism is significant in the production of mental illness in our society.[7] One writer has stated that "the data also show that insanity is much more prevalent in urban than in rural areas, a fact of no little significance for the student of rural sociology. . . . there seems to be no doubt of the association between urbanity and insanity." [8] After a study of the prevalence of mental disorder among the urban and rural populations of New York State, Malzberg concluded that the rural regions of the state had less mental disorder than the urban.[9]

In another study, Texas rates for all persons who became psychotic for the first time were found to be two and a half times greater in urban areas than in rural, a difference which was statistically significant.[10] The same differential held for the sexes with an average annual rate per 100,000 for males in urban areas of 76 in contrast with 44 in rural areas;

for females an even greater difference—99 as compared with 36. Even the age-specific psychoses rates were consistently higher in urban areas than for the same rural age group. The disparity between rates for rural and urban areas increased with advancing age. Jaco has summarized the results of the Texas study as follows: "In examining the overall results concerning the incidence rates of mental disorders in the rural and urban areas, no significant evidence was found to support the notion that the large rate differentials between urban and rural areas were due to differences in accessibility to psychiatric treatment facilities or to the type of psychiatric facilities available in the two areas." [11]

Not all the evidence supports the conclusion that the incidence of mental illness is much less in rural areas. The differences may actually be smaller than they now appear to be because of the likelihood that rural families may keep mentally disturbed members at home rather than hospitalize them. A study made in Tennessee concluded that mental health in rural areas is not necessarily as good as the smaller number of commitments to mental institutions might indicate, for almost half the psychotic individuals in rural areas were found to be cared for by their families.[12] For this reason it is possible that mental deviants in urban society may be somewhat more socially visible, and that both unofficial and official tolerance of the deviation will be less.

ALCOHOLISM

The chances that rural persons will become chronic alcoholics are less than half as great as those for urban dwellers, according to estimates made by Yale University's Section on Alcohol Studies. In 1940 the rate per 100,000 adult population in areas of less than 2500 population was 474 as compared with 972 in cities of 100,000 population or over. There were 821 male alcoholics for every 100,000 rural males, as compared with 1894 in large cities; the difference between rural and urban women, computed on a standardized population, is somewhat less. The rates of reported deaths from alcoholism per 100,000 adults in 1940 was nearly twice as great in cities of over 100,000 as in rural areas.[13] Urban commitments for alcoholic psychoses are reported to be three and a half times the rate for rural areas.[14]

The principal reasons for this lower rate of alcoholism in rural areas are the social norms and the amount of social control at the personal level over drinking or excessive drinking. Farm people in the United States are much less likely to drink alcoholic beverages than are city dwellers. One half of the rural people are abstainers, but this proportion decreases as the size of the city increases, until in cities with a population of over 500,000 only one fourth do not drink. Both farm rearing and farm residence are associated with lower proportions of heavy drinkers. A recent Iowa study showed that 58 percent of drinkers in the city were either moderate or heavy drinkers as compared with 43 percent of the farm drinkers.[15] Moreover, the extent of drinking increased among the farm-reared who had migrated to the city but this increase was in moderate rather than heavy drinking.

SUICIDE

On the whole, persons living on farms and villages either in Europe or in America are much less likely to take their lives than persons living in cities. In London the standardized rate, expressed as a percentage of that for the whole of England and Wales, is 115, for the county boroughs 106, for other urban districts 97, and for rural districts 88.[16] In Sweden, Denmark, and Finland wide differences exist between farm and city in the suicide rates, in Finland the urban rate being over twice as high.[17] A detailed study of suicide in France showed that the chances that farm people and persons living in places of less than 2000 population would take their lives were considerably less than for city people.[18] Only in the Irish Free State and the Netherlands have suicides been reported to be greater in rural than in urban areas.[19] This has been partially explained as being due to the large number of old persons in rural areas who, feeling useless from an economic point of view, commit suicide.

The suicide rate in cities of the United States of a population of over 10,000 has generally been almost twice as great as that in smaller cities and rural areas. A student from a small western Kansas town has written of suicides in his community over the past twenty years.

> I know of only four suicides in the last twenty years in the town and its agricultural hinterland. Two of these are dramatic memories of my childhood and occurred in 1932. Both suicides were men (one the president of the Citizens State Bank and the other the county treasurer) who had become involved in dishonest financial affairs. The other two suicides were individuals past middle age and without kinship or community ties. One, a man, whose wife had died several years previously and who was without children, had spent his savings in an attempted rejuvenation. The other suicide, a woman, was separated from her husband and son and was shunned by the women of the community because she talked incessantly. One of the local ministers created a sensation in connection with this woman's funeral sermon—he accused the women of the town of murdering the woman who had committed suicide by refusing to associate with her. To my knowledge, no farmers have committed suicide in this area in the last twenty years.[20]

The differential in rural and urban suicide rates appears to be declining because of the tendency for an urban way of life to characterize rural areas. An analysis of 3081 cases of suicide in Michigan between 1945 and 1949 revealed that rural males exhibited higher suicide rates than urban males.[21] Although "farmers and farm managers" had a high suicide rate in Michigan, the majority of "rural" males who committed suicide were engaged in urban occupations and resided in urbanized fringe areas. It is possible that the high rural rate in this sample was due to two factors: as urban values become more widely disseminated in rural areas they create an intense personal conflict because of the disparity between urban and rural values as they affect behavioral alternatives; and the occupations of rural males who committed suicide are characteristic occupations of urban groups, thus suggesting exposure to conflicting values and norms. Although they lived in the country, these people were oriented to an urban way of life.

SOCIAL DEVIATION AND CITY SIZE

The higher incidence of certain forms of deviant behavior in urban communities has been, in general, demonstrated by a comparison of urban with rural rates, but several questions remain to be answered: (1) If urban rates for certain forms of deviation are, in turn, analyzed by the size of the community, is there a proportional increase as one proceeds from the small city to the great metropolis? (2) Do deviation rates vary according to the distance from a large community? (3) Within any city are there variations in the rates of deviation according to the degree of urbanism of the area?

CRIME RATES BY CITY SIZE

Comparisons in the United States of crime rates by city size show some startling differences and, in most crimes even a continuous progression in rates as the size of the city increases.[22] (See Table 2.) In 1960 the rate per 100,000 population for burglaries reported to the police, for example, which is probably the best comparable index of crime, rose steadily from cities of less than 10,000 with a rate of 288.9, to cities over 250,000 population, with a rate of 742.1, or over twice as great.[23] Robbery rates were nine times as great in the larger cities as compared with the smaller ones.

It is interesting to note that rates by city size are often affected, however, by the cultural factors in the area in which the cities are located.[24] In fact, the regional location of a city seems often to be more related to the crime rate than is the extent of urbanization in the state. Some states, such as California, with a large proportion of urban population, also have high crime rates, whereas Massachusetts, which is also heavily urbanized, has a comparatively low rate. It is likely that the urban "way of life" in a more recently developed area like California is characterized by norm conflicts, rapid change, and other unsettling conditions, whereas in

TABLE 2
RATES PER 100,000 FOR CRIMES KNOWN TO THE POLICE
BY CITY SIZE, UNITED STATES, 1960

	Population	Murder—Nonnegligent manslaughter	Manslaughter by negligence	Forcible rape	Robbery
I	Over 250,000	6.8	4.4	15.2	117.6
II	100,000–250,000	5.6	4.1	7.6	57.5
III	50,000–100,000	3.3	2.9	5.5	36.6
IV	25,000– 50,000	2.9	2.3	4.7	22.6
V	10,000– 25,000	2.4	1.5	4.0	15.7
VI	Under 10,000	2.7	1.3	3.3	12.8

	Population	Aggravated assault	Burglary—Breaking or entering	Larceny $50 and over	Larceny Under $50	Auto theft
I	Over 250,000	154.1	742.1	477.5	1,070.8	368.8
II	100,000–250,000	83.3	668.3	371.2	1,322.6	288.2
III	50,000–100,000	58.9	512.8	343.1	1,107.9	199.0
IV	25,000– 50,000	39.9	433.0	282.9	1,057.7	154.1
V	10,000– 25,000	35.2	347.9	200.1	923.3	112.8
VI	Under 10,000	28.9	288.9	140.8	650.0	82.1

SOURCE: Federal Bureau of Investigation, *Uniform Crime Reports* (Annual Bulletin, 1960; Washington, D.C.: Government Printing Office, 1961), pp. 81–82. Included in this report were 49 cities over 250,-000 population; 80 cities from 100,000 to 250,000; 189 cities from 50,000 to 100,000; 379 cities from 25,000 to 50,000; 880 cities from 10,000 to 25,000; and 1789 cities under 10,000. Population figures on which these rates are based are those included in the 1960 census reports.

older areas, such as New England, these aspects of urbanism may be somewhat attenuated.

ALCOHOLISM

Although cities with a population over 100,000 have estimated rates for chronic alcoholism which are considerably higher than the rates for cities up to 10,000 population, as shown in Table 3, the progression by city

TABLE 3
ESTIMATED RATES OF CHRONIC ALCOHOLISM IN THE ADULT POPULATION
BY SEX AND POPULATION SIZE GROUPS, UNITED STATES, 1940

Population size group	Males per 100,000 adult males	Females per 100,000 adult females	Both sexes per 100,000 adult population
Places of 100,000 and over	1,894	294	972
Places of 10,000 to 100,000	1,422	190	727
Places of 2,500 to 10,000	1,428	217	743
Rural (less than 2,500)	821	154	474

SOURCE: E. M. Jellinek, "Recent Trends in Alcoholism and Alcohol Consumption," *Quarterly Journal of Studies on Alcohol*, 8:23 (June, 1947). Reprinted by permission of the Journal.

size is not continuous. A suggested explanation is that cities ot from 10,000 to 100,000 contain many suburban areas where the rate of alcoholism may be high. This irregular progression in rates for alcoholism is in contrast to the continuous increase in the percentage of drinkers as the size of the city increases.[25]

SUICIDE

Suicide rates appear to increase with the size of the community, until cities of 500,000 and over are reached. The suicide rate per 100,000 population during 1927–1933 ranged from 15.9 in cities of 10,000 to 25,000 population to 19.9 in the 250,000 to 500,000 group, with the rates in cities of over half a million population declining slightly.[26] It has been noted that fast-growing cities tend to have a higher suicide rate.[27]

28. ALIENATION, ANOMIE AND THE AMERICAN DREAM

Ephraim H. Mizruchi

While poverty is usually recognized as a problem of the city, afflu-ence is usually not. Few thinkers hold the position that the inescapable consequence of urban-industrial culture must be dissatisfaction with life. It is true that the original sociological conception of urban society, as for-mulated by Tönnies, Simmel, and Durkheim, contained an implicit anti-urban bias; nonetheless, that view was largely prospective and anticipatory rather than empirically conclusive. No doubt a number of contemporary scholars were guided by these earlier philosophically inclined sociolo-gists, when they pursued the hypothesis that the quality of modern, and predominantly urban, society is inevitably bound to be poor and that the experience of urban-industrial man must similarly be one of de-moralization.

The concomitants of prosperity, it is thus held, are extravagant expec-tations, which are ultimately impossible to gratify, and an aimlessness of purpose that results from the very fact of abundance. Work is deempha-sized in both duration and human significance as the productive process becomes more rational. Paradoxically, then, the debasement of society and its culture occurs pari passu *with the achievement of wealth.*

Mizruchi's essay takes its point of departure, first, from Karl Marx's

Excerpts from *The Substance of Sociology, Codes, Conduct and Consequences* by Ephraim H. Mizruchi, copyright © 1967 by the Meredith Publishing Company. Re-printed by permission of Appleton-Century-Crofts. Also by permission of the Oxford University Press for the author's paper on the same subject published in *The New Sociology: Essays in Honor of C. Wright Mills*, edited by Irving Louis Horowitz (1964). Based on *Success and Opportunity: A Study of Anomie* by Ephraim Mizruchi—permis-sion of the Publisher. Copyright © 1964 by The Free Press, a Division of The Mac-millan Company.

*definition of alienation as estrangement from one's work, from the prod-
uct of that work, from the others with whom one works, and even finally
from oneself as well; and, second, Durkheim's idea of anomie as the state
of affairs in which one strives for unreachable goals. Needless to say, the
latter are generated by the fundamental condition of urban society—a
large volume and high density of population.*

THE ANALYSIS which we have presented here suggests that contemporary
American society is suffering from the combined effects of both alienation
and anomie. Let us look at these processes in several contexts.

WORK AND VALUES

The concern with *rewards* for performance rather than *worthy accomplishment* on the job, or *success* as contrasted with *achievement,* on the
part of our numerically largest segment of the population makes it clear
that work is not seen as an end in itself, a condition predicted by Marx.
The emphasis on *rewards* as contrasted with achievement strongly suggests alienation from work in the relatively lower classes.

Marx, it will be recalled, held that work in industrial societies tended
to give rise to two types of alienation in the occupational sphere. Alienation from the process of work itself represents one type. The second was
alienation from the products of one's work. There is mounting evidence
derived from a great deal of sociological research which supports Marx's
speculative hypotheses. One excellent example of alienation from the
process of work itself is reflected in an interesting study by industrial sociologist Donald F. Roy.

While observing in a factory Roy held a piece-work job on the assembly line. Roy's observations suggest that mental self-manipulation appears to be characteristic of the assembly-line work process . . . "making
out on piece-work could be a stimulating game only as long as the job represented a real challenge to the operator, only as long as the element of
uncertainty was present in the activity's outcome." In short, work typically involved no challenge.

The many studies of work-group control of rate of output on the assembly line including, for example, the Roethlisberger and Dickson
study, suggest that much of the activity which characterizes factory work
is inherently alienative since work satisfaction seemingly is not an inherent outcome of the work process in these contexts.

In addition to the *process* of work itself there is little opportunity for
today's factory worker to enjoy personal attachment to those objects

which he has created, if only in part. The assembly-line method has homogenized the products of the worker's efforts to conform to the needs of a standardized industrial system. Parts made in Toledo, Ohio, must meet precise measures in order to fit other units which are assembled in a Detroit automobile plant.

One of our informants in the community in which the foregoing study was done took the researcher on a tour of the factory in which he has worked for almost two decades. Currently a parts inspector, this man has worked on the line from the beginning of his career. In describing the work and in showing the writer the parts which were made in the plant he seemed to be taking personal pride in the items produced and in the way things were done. But the very handling of the parts, the throwing and dropping and casualness with which they were treated, suggested that there is little opportunity for identification with the material results of one's efforts in this type of work.

In an essay, "The Myth of the Happy Worker," Harvey Swados also addresses himself to the attitudes which workers have toward their work and its products.

> The worker's attitude toward his work is generally compounded of hatred, shame and resignation. . . . They know that there is a difference between working with your back and working with your behind. (I do not make the distinction between hand-work and brain-work, since we are all learning that white-collar work is becoming less and less brain-work.) They know that they work harder than the middle-class for less money. . . . Nor is it simply . . . status-hunger that makes a man hate work that is mindless, endless, stupefying, sweaty, filthy, noisy, exhausting, insecure in its prospects, and practically without hope of advancement.
>
> The plain truth is that factory work is degrading. It is degrading to any man who ever dreams of doing something worthwhile with his life; and it is about time we faced the fact.
>
> *The more a man is exposed to middle-class values, the more sophisticated he becomes and the more production-line work is degrading to him.* [Eds.—Italics Mizruchi's.]

Swados' observations, made during his periodic employment as a factory worker, provide us with more than a description of alienation from the process of work. In the italicized statement it appears that both alienation and anomie are intertwined as factors in the relationship between aspirations associated with the larger society—presumably middle-class consumption values—and the work situation. This is consistent with our position that the two processes are bound up with each other. Furthermore there is the suggestion that one's self-esteem is bound up with work which alludes to alienation from self and others.

Swados also offers some instructive comments with respect to alienation from the product, in this case, the automobile.

On the one hand it is admired and desired as a symbol of freedom, almost a substitute for freedom, not because the worker participated in making it, but because our whole culture is dedicated to the proposition that the automobile is both necessary and beautiful. On the other hand it is hated and despised—so much that if your new car smells bad it may be due to a banana peel crammed down its gullet and sealed up thereafter, so much so that if your dealer can't locate the rattle in your new car you might ask him to open the welds on one of those tail fins and vacuum out the nuts and bolts thrown in by workers sabotaging their own product.

We could well ask, given these circumstances in the working-class occupational sphere, would we expect to find an interest in excellence on the job or achievment values? We could hardly expect this kind of orientation to work. As we noted earlier emphasis on *rewards* is more characteristic of the working class respondents in our sample. *Achievement goals* must be attained in other types of occupations, primarily those associated with the relatively higher classes.

Similarly, emphasis on excellence is more likely to be associated with occupations reflecting emphasis on worthy accomplishments than those which stress rewards. Excellence, as a mode of performing, tends to be integrally bound up with occupations which reflect achievement rather than success values.

But what of the middle-class white collar employee? Is his work challenging and gratifying? While we have suggested earlier that there is a greater tendency to view getting ahead in achievement terms in the relatively higher classes this does not necessarily imply that the vast majority of workers in these classes are actually engaged in more meaningful work than those in the lower classes.

Swados has mentioned that "white collar work is becoming less and less brain-work." Standardization and automation are making robots of the middle-class worker as well. Even in teaching, educational television threatens to make more of an automation of our teachers than the bureaucratic organization of formal education has already accomplished. In the white collar spheres as in industry personal gratification as a result of work as an end in itself and also as a result of the products of one's efforts is a feeling enjoyed by the few rather than the many.

This process was already in evidence during the Lynds' second study of Middletown during the middle 1930's.

It is important to note the strains which current cultural demands for dominance and aggression create in the individual personality. The pursuit of 'success,' particularly in the business world where the males of the culture struggle, involves the acceptance of a heavy burden of disciplines and constraints. Most people, as a result, spend most of their time doing things in which they are not particularly interested, at a tempo which is not their own but dictated by the system. As Lawrence K. Frank has pointed out, to be 'businesslike' means in our present culture to be 'impersonal.' This is but one of the false faces that the culture forces man to wear. Everywhere one is confronted by the demand that one be 'on time,' act 'like a man,' hide one's emotions, talk and appear 'successful,' be 'energetic,' 'sure of oneself,' and so on indefinitely through the stereotypes of being 'regular.' Along with this channeling of individual bent and temperament that the 'success pattern' imposes upon many businessmen must be noted in the case of the workingman the major constraints of inactivity due to recurrent unemployment and to being 'bottom dog' in a culture which habitually stresses and glorifies the traits and possessions of its 'top dogs.'

Galbraith too, has suggested that even achievement may no longer be a worthy goal among higher level employees in this quotation from *The Affluent Society*.

The rise of the public relations industry, which draws its clientele overwhelmingly from among business executives, shows that business achievement is no longer of itself a source of acclaim. At a minimum the achievement must be advertised. But the first task of the public relations man, on taking over a business client, is to 're-engineer' his image to include something besides the production of goods. His subject must be a statesman, a patron of education, or a civic force. Increasingly some artistic or intellectual facet must be found. A businessman who reads *Business Week* is lost to fame. One who reads Proust is marked for greatness.

What we are suggesting here is that: first, the conception of success values may be a reflection of the nature of the work process: second, the material level of living which a group aspires to or has attained and: third, changes are occurring in all spheres of work.

As work becomes more instrumentalized, and current tendencies seem to be in this direction, gratification as a result of the work process will diminish. Indications are that the Protestant Ethic with its emphasis upon work as an end in itself is on the decline as a normative system. If this is indeed occurring then one of the most important sources for meaningful activity and direction in American society is threatened with extinction.

The problem must next be confronted in functional terms. Since one of the important requirements in a social system is a system of *motivation* which will encourage group participants to perform those jobs necessary for the maintenance of organized group life, American society itself may be threatened by the process of increasing instrumentalization.

The problem of motivation leads us to a speculative hypothesis. We suggested above that the middle classes are provided with an already existing avenue for attaining alternate achievement goals. The alternative to which we are referring is formal social participation which affords recognition for the active member of the organized group. It is in the nature of social processes that norms, for example, may emerge as a result of activities which are associated with processes having little to do with the objectives of these acts. We would hypothesize that while in the lower classes criminal norms have, in the least, been reinforced as a result of as-pirational strains, in the middle classes a set of counter norms has emerged which has a tendency to limit the emphasis upon achievement goals in the occupational sphere. As William H. Whyte, Jr., has shown there is a growing tendency for the suburban middle classes to place greater emphasis upon security than on hard work, a major pattern in the quest to attain occupational goals, and an almost intense pattern of par-ticipation in formal associations. If there has been a diminishing empha-sis upon individualism, as both Whyte and David Riesman have held, then this, in part at least, may be viewed against the background of both general affluence and the emergence of a set of norms which have resulted from reactions to the strains associated with circumscribed opportunities and intense competition in the occupational sphere. Whyte has suggested that aspirations have indeed changed although his explanation for the change is at variance with our own. In his words,

> The young men speak of 'the plateau.' If they were to find this haven they would prove that the Social Ethic is personally fulfilling. For the goal of the plateau is in complete consonance with it; one's ambition is not a personal thing that craves achievement for achievement's sake or an ego that demands self-expression. It is an ambition directed outward to the satisfaction of making others happy. Competitive struggle loses its mean-ing; in the harmonious organization one has most of the material rewards necessary for the good life, and none of the gnawing pains of the old kind of striving.

In short, there is a more limited effort to forge ahead in the occupa-tional sphere since achievement goals can be attained with much less haz-ard in other spheres of American life and the minimum material rewards are accumulated, at least for this segment of the population, without a great deal of competitive effort.

Although this hypothesis is highly speculative it is consistent with our explanation for lower class anomie as compared with middle class anomie above.

We held earlier that certain processes, e.g., education, must be pursued as ends in themselves in order to provide optimum performance on the part of the individual. More important, however, we noted that institu-tional processes are characterized by end-valuation rather than means-valuation. Society cannot afford to have certain processes come about as a result of chance factors alone. Thus certain patterns come to be perceived as worthy of one's efforts. Of these patterns some become mandatory and are incorporated into the institutional system.

If work comes to mean little more than a means to a livelihood then it might well be that the functional prerequisites may not be fulfilled in a manner which will, in the very least, maintain the American social sys-tem. In short, if the will to work is threatened the social system is likewise threatened.

PROSPERITY, POVERTY AND ANOMIE

And what of man the person? What will be the sources of personal gratification for him?

The constant proliferation of new hobbies and do-it-yourself programs suggests that these could become the primary source of gratification for man in this society. Many of us are already deluged with the problem of excessive leisure time and the mass culture lamentors have been quick to point out that the leisurely are being misled. Emphasis appears to be directed to the novel and superficial rather than to *haute couture*.

Indeed, Durkheim was not unaware of similar processes accompanying anomie during periods of excessive prosperity. As he pointed out in *Suicide*, "A thirst arises for novelties, unfamiliar pleasures, nameless sensations, all of which lose their savor once known."

Leisure time activities *as they are currently constituted,* it would seem, are not likely to emerge as meaningful alternatives to work.

Although it is hazardous to generalize too broadly there seem to be few situations in American life in which unrealistic expectations do not constitute a problem. Daniel Boorstin has suggested this in somewhat dramatic terms in a recent book, *The Image.* Characterizing Americans in terms similar to Kluckhohn's in *Mirror for Man,* Boorstin describes us as engaged in efforts to "fill our void."

> We [Americans] expect too much of the world. Our expectations are extravagant in the precise dictionary sense of the word—'going beyond the limits of reason or moderation.' They are excessive.
>
> When we pick up our newspaper at breakfast, we expect—we even demand—that it bring us momentous events since the night before. We turn on the car radio as we drive to work and expect 'news' to have occurred since the morning newspaper went to press. Returning in the evening, we expect our house not only to shelter us, to keep us warm in winter and cool in summer, but to relax us, to dignify us, to encompass us with soft music and interesting hobbies, to be a playground, a theatre and a bar. We expect our two week vacation to be romantic, exotic, cheap and effortless. We expect everything to be relaxing, sanitary, and Americanized if we go to a faraway place. We expect new heroes every season, a literary masterpiece every month, a dramatic spectacular every week, a rare sensation every night. We expect everybody to feel free to disagree, yet we expect everybody to be loyal, not to rock the boat or take the Fifth Amendment. We expect everybody to believe deeply in his religion, yet not to think less of others for not believing. We expect our nation to be strong and great and vast and varied and prepared for every challenge; yet we expect our 'national purpose' to be clear and simple, something that gives direction to the lives of nearly two hundred million people and yet can be bought in a paperback at the corner drugstore for a dollar. . . .
>
> We expect anything and everything. We expect the contradicting and the impossible. We expect compact cars which are spacious; luxurious cars which are economical. We expect to be rich and charitable, powerful and

merciful, active and reflective, kind and competitive. We expect to be
inspired by mediocre appeals for 'excellence,' to be made literate by illiterate appeals for literacy. We expect to eat and stay thin, to be constantly
on the move and ever more neighborly, to go to a 'church of our choice'
and yet feel its guiding power over us, to revere God and to be God. . . .

Never have people been more the masters of their environment. Yet
never has a people felt more deceived and disappointed. For never has a
people expected so much more than the world could offer.

The problems associated with the marked tendency towards instrumentalization of work seem to be symptoms of more fundamental conditions
in which the very social fabric, i.e., the normative system is threatened
with annihilation. Indeed, this is the import of the pleas being made by
Erich Fromm, Hannah Arendt and Erich Kahler, to name only a few.

But some writers do not see this in what is simply a foreboding aspect.
William Kornhauser in his *The Politics of Mass Society*, concludes his interesting study with the suggestion that the process of mass society carries
with itself not only the possibility of social alienation but "enhanced opportunities for the creation of new forms of association . . . Modern industry destroys the conditions for a new society of small enterprises, but it
also provides the condition of abundance which frees people to seek new
ways of life."

"Abundance" is, however, a major source of difficulty for contemporary
American society. If there is any one factor which Durkheim stressed
which can be isolated as a major source of malintegration it is abundance.

It is doubtful whether Durkheim could have envisaged a society in
which middle class families could reasonably expect to own two automobiles, as many television sets and untold numbers of radios. Nor is it
likely that he could have imagined how extravagant expectations could
become.

Boorstin's comments could apply only to a society of abundance and
prosperity and this is, indeed, the *type* of condition with which Durkheim was most concerned.

Thus our more general observations, following Durkheim's lead, suggest that contemporary American society is in a paradoxical situation.
Having achieved a very high—but by no means complete—level of *material* prosperity it is in danger of attaining also a condition of social and
cultural *poverty*.

In a suggestive study entitled, *Troublemakers: Youth in an Affluent
Society*, T. R. Fyvel makes some observations which are interesting when
juxtaposed to Kornhauser's statement.

. . . the rise of delinquency has to be seen as one among many similar
symptoms of the growing social unbalance in the affluent society. Looking
at the development in Britain of the last ten years, one can distinguish
something which seems like a built-in conflict in this society—a conflict
between, on one side, a growing sense of widening opportunities, of

expansion, and opposed to it, an alarming drive towards purposelessness.
. . . the affluent society holds out tremendous possibilities of a freer life
for the ordinary man. [But there is also] undeniable evidence that a fairly
large section of British youth felt frustrated, angry, bored and adrift
without firm moral guidance.

Fyvel points out that this condition characterized not only the youth in
British society but adults as well and, similarly, not only the British but
American, Russian and other European societies suffered from the same
condition.

A very recent report by the Council of Europe has provided similar
data. Twelve member countries were requested to report on juvenile delinquency and all noted increases in non-utilitarian acts of theft and violence. Most note-worthy is that these phenomena appear much less often
in the underdeveloped areas.

Fyvel's conclusions and the observations cited in the above report are
compatible with our own. *Increased* opportunities can, if not recognized
and anticipated, have undesirable consequences. And it is to the study of
these factors that sociological research must now turn. Too many of the
problems of deviant behavior and social pathology have been cast in the
mold of poverty conditions. The time is ripe for studies of the concomitants of prosperity.

We Americans have always assumed that unfettered social mobility is
necessarily a desirable condition for all. During times of prosperity mobility not only becomes more attainable but also forces itself upon the
multitude. Few see the high cost which is paid in the form of striving toward unrealizable goals and the consequences in personal demoralization
and despair. Increased opportunity for success has its counterpart in increased opportunity for failure. If a social system is to maintain itself it
must provide a balance between societal needs, personal aspirations and
the possibility of attainment. American society has not solved this problem and, indeed, it has not even seemed willing to entertain the possibility that such a problem does exist.

The fundamental question then becomes one of assessing the American
Dream. Should it be tempered with cautionary folk wisdom or should we
ignore the heavy toll which its pursuit extracts? What would be the consequences for American society of a system of motivation directed by the
oftheard injunction attributed to Confucius, "He who makes his bed
close to the ground does not have far to fall"?

On the other hand there is little chance that the ideology can persist in
the face of the realities of life. Ultimately some economic setback will
occur, some limitations will be felt. What will be the consequences? Will
America wait and watch and speculate or will a new set of goals emerge?

29. THE CHURCH SERVES THE CHANGING CITY

Ross W. Sanderson

Social Christianity, the gospel of redemption through service to society, is spelled out in eight specific points in the following selection. What has motivated the proposed program is the alarming social disorganization found in the great city today. "The urban world is surely upside down," declares Sanderson as he surveys the dreadfully blighted slum of the inner city, racial segregation and discrimination, heterogeneous neighborhoods that are internally estranged, emotional disorder, and inhumane poverty in the presence of dissipated wealth.

There is much attention given here to the administration of the church —not to liturgy or the clarification of doctrine—but the management of professional staff, the church budget, and its material. The Protestant ministry is seen as properly engaged in specialized functions, including social services, in order to provide the city dweller with spiritual opportunity as well as a more benign environment. Equally insistent is the interest expressed in reconstructing a Gemeinschaft *type of neighborhood in which mutuality, instead of indifference and even antagonism toward one another, would flourish.*

1. CHURCH WORK, especially in the changing city, *must be organized in terms of neighborhood need.*

"Every community must make its own program, and the making of the program is itself one of the most important phases of community organization," said Robert A. Woods at Andover-Newton in 1912.[1] When homes lacked baths, Morgan Chapel put them in. When recreation is not organized, alert churches provide it or get it organized in the community. Where social services are absent, churches supply them, at least on an emergency basis. Just what the permanent social work functions of the Church are, whether institutional or in terms of staff, is a question on which there are wide differences of opinion.

There seems to be little question that the supreme function of the Church is to meet continuing basic religious needs. As a consequence there is an observable re-emergence of theology and an increased emphasis on churchmanship. This means a new appreciation of the church edifice, both instrumentally and as a place for spiritual experience. Education in the faith, sometimes called indoctrination, regains its place.

If the need is great, the response must correspond. If equalization of educational opportunity is a sound urban principle, equalization of spiritual opportunity deserves more serious attention.

2. *Inclusiveness is an unavoidable goal.* This applies to social and economic status, to vocation, to all ethnic backgrounds. Congeniality is a normal principle of association, but inadequate in itself. Interest groups have their proper place; but all interests must be served, and all must be constructively related. The best church is one which serves all sorts and conditions of men.

Bilingualism must be regarded as temporary and on the way out. The formation or continuation of nationality churches in America is no longer justified as permanent policy. Continuing external subsidy for any organizational process which deliberately delays assimilation is doubtless unwise. Yet the needs of certain vestigial or emergency groups must be recognized. Just now the Chinese in America constitute a special opportunity. While Italian or Armenian may be decreasingly necessary as a language requirement, it is perfectly natural for birds of a nationalistic or linguistic feather to want to flock together. Only they must learn not to be closed societies; and they need no longer be medicant. There will be later newcomers.

Now that the Supreme Court has spoken about segregation in education, urban Protestantism will have to begin more seriously to mend its ways.

The geographical parish is a continuing responsibility. If no church can serve everybody, all of the churches working together must see that everybody is somehow served. "Whosoever will may come" is a counsel of evangelism, not merely a sentiment in a gospel song. Whatever the social distance that separates Christians, they are members one of another in Christ.

3. *The Group Ministry idea marks a definite advance and meets an urgent vocational need.* Comradeship, the aggregation of specialized func-

tional abilities, and mutual support are invaluable. Recruitment, train-ing, and administration of multiple staffs are still in their experimental infancy. Few senior pastors know how to serve effectively as chief-of-staff. On the other hand, to have no head seems wasteful of time and energy, and as yet dubious or of unproved value.

Not every group will succeed. Group living has failed in the past, it doubtless will in the future. The essentials of success in Group Ministry are now being forged on the anvils of experience.

Perhaps the size of a staff must vary directly with the degree of under-privilege. In any case, the number of members per ordained staff member varies greatly among the cases studied. By and large, churches (like public education) have too high a ratio of persons served to persons serv-ing. Private education does far better but costs far more.

4. *Connections with educational institutions, especially theological seminaries, are valuable where possible.* Unfortunately there are many cities where schools of theology do not exist. Almost everywhere, how-ever, there are institutions of higher learning—municipal universities, teachers' colleges, technical schools, and the like. Whole institutions have grown out of service ministries to inner-city neighborhoods—e.g., the School of Social Service and the Department of Religious Education at Boston University, not to mention the general area of development of the social sciences. The student body can still be reached in terms of *noblesse oblige*. The best trained have something to share with the most needy.

On the other hand, the absence of theological seminaries in some cities may alter some too professional parish patterns for the better, through the larger use of lay volunteers.

5. *Adequate support is imperative.* Effective church work in the chang-ing city costs money, a lot of money. The total costs of the cases studied would be a staggering sum. Subsidy per member is a rather terrifying figure when the question of reproducibility is broached. But it must be remembered that all urban costs are high, including church expenses in the most fortunate parishes.

Endowment is one way of building up reserves against times of special need. In such a situation as that confronting the Church of All Nations in Boston, capital funds might be multiplied ten times without risk of discouraging the regular giving of members.

Wherever possible, cash *subsidy* is to be avoided. The provision of spe-cialized, functional services that could not otherwise be afforded seems less objectionable. When a parish is legitimately receiving outside finan-cial assistance, as often seems necessary, "paternalism must be guarded against, by close association of clergy, staff, and people in their way of life; dependency must be guarded against by developing a sense of finan-cial responsibility in the parish itself" (from a statement of Urban Mis-sion Priests for discussion with laymen). Particularly are members of city parishes to be urged to contribute or otherwise secure all maintenance costs, and to manage the matters of local expense; and no people should be regarded as too impoverished to be missionary.

Public contribution (through community chests, for example) is legitimately sought for social services rendered on a nonsectarian basis, but not at the price of unfair policy control. A recent word of Walter Lippmann's with regard to education is equally pertinent here: "There is an enormous margin of luxury in this country against which we can draw for our total needs." [2] The better churching of the city, and its better service, are a proper claim on personal and corporate generosity. Moreover, there is increasing evidence that the appeal of the changing city to the suburban church pocketbook is being made with increasing effectiveness.

Fees, and member support, need to be adjusted according to changing dollar values, and "good interpretation and active promotion" are as essential in church work as in such agencies as the Y.M.C.A. Yet there is also an obvious danger of over-publicizing, which has been felt by more than one worthy enterprise.

Indigenous financing, or member giving, is to be pushed without apology, whatever the economic status of the constituency of the city church, or the rural church. A study made by Meryl Ruoss, then of the Pathfinding Service of the New York City Mission Society, already cited, "shows that the great growth of work among the Puerto Ricans in New York is generally where its financing and leadership is indigenous."

Alleged fright of local people, when budgets involving thousands of dollars are concerned can be seriously discounted. Whatever the polity of the communion involved, democratic financial controls are of demonstrated value.

Not only is the contribution of money important, but *intelligent understanding and support of program activities is imperative.* Participation needs to be on as broad a membership base as possible. Wide geographical and vocational inclusiveness are desirable, perhaps essential. The discovery and training of *indigenous leadership* is everywhere imperative.

6. *Continuity and duration of effort are essential.* Short pastorates get nowhere in the inner city. Institutional development and functional differentiation are often the slow evolution of decade after decade. New ministries to the underprivileged need not start from scratch, but they must not be impatient of results. In 1892, Robert A. Woods was sure the settlement "must not hurry." In church work too, in the changing city, "haste makes waste."

Yet, if one is to quote proverbs, one must also remember that "the King's business [often] requires haste." That is to say, the time element must not be permitted to serve as an alibi for too little and too late. Bishop Newbigin has recently called attention to the observations made by Roland Allen in *Missionary Methods, St. Paul's or Ours?* [3] Says Allen: "St. Paul leaves behind him in Ephesus, after only two years of missionary work, a fully established Church provided with its own ministry, able to stand entirely on its own feet. Two centuries would be regarded as a more reasonable period by a missionary of the modern era, and, during most of that period the young Church would be treated as a charge on the personal and financial resources of the home base precluding further advance into new regions. The contrast is startling and becomes more so the more it is examined in detail. Our present methods show little sign of being able to achieve the enormous new advances which are necessary if the vast unevangelized regions are to be reached."

What goes for unevangelized peoples goes for the pagan inner city also. Does it not need some Kraemer to tell even the Babes in Christ, "YOU ARE the Church, and you must shoulder its responsibilities"?

7. *Religion should function co-operatively rather than competitively* —"the changing city," Bishop Brent might say, "is too much for a divided Church." Churches should integrate the community rather than divide it. All too often, Woods said, the local church remains "a divisive and disintegrating influence, instead of a center for the promotion of catholic human fellowship and cooperation in its neighborhood, in the local community, for whose democratic progress it stands in the most solemn of all conceivable responsibilities." [4]

Where it is desirable for churches of different denominations to federate or otherwise associate their efforts, the need of new and more inclusive interdenominational "overhead" may be indicated. Successive *ad hoc* arrangements may become wasteful of time and destructive of adequate strategy. Ecumenicity may need to come to grips with the better churching of the changing city and the ecclesiastical administration involved. Neighborhoods were not made for denominations, but denominations to serve people in their natural groupings. If we need new ecclesiastical mechanisms to meet community needs, why not create them? Some of the talk about not developing a "superchurch" seems to betray a fear of greatness. It might be that in the exigencies of the changing city situation we might discover the seeds of greater Christian unity.

SOME PERSONAL CONCLUSIONS

To dwell in thought, as well as physically, month after month, in the changing cities of America does something quite unexpected to one's mind and heart. At the conclusion of his writing this writer found himself automatically erupting in the following perhaps entirely too cryptic paragraph, the expansion of which into a reasoned argument would require more pages.

As one sets the changing city over against the problem of the planet, one is forced to the conclusion that *poverty is too expensive,* that we simply can't afford a world that is partly rich (and a small part at that) and partly desperately poor. Doubtless the hardheaded realist will be appalled at such radicalism. Very well, then. Let unredeemed human nature take its course. That way the problem of the inner city will soon be shelved, for all our cities will be deprived of their insides, and most of their outsides. We walk by faith, or we don't walk.

Suppose we step this down to two less extreme statements.

The city as a whole needs reconstruction and redemption.

To Abbé Michonneau, Paris seemed a "de-Christianized community." Are some American cities any better? How can they be changed?

Robert A. Woods, in the seminary address already cited, declared: "The true point of attack for the Church is the local neighborhood. This is also where the structural upbuilding of society has to begin. This is the distinctive unit and organ of social reconstruction. The neighborhood is the very pith and core and kernel and marrow of organic democracy. Democracy is a cooperative society made up of *people just as they come;* and so far as there is democracy, people must be taken precisely that way, just as they come. Likewise, in its fundamental meaning, the parish is simply a downright practical contrivance for seeing to it that the gospel is imparted to every creature, taking them all as they come, seeing that none is overlooked, and that none get away from the range of the spiritual power of the gospel." [5]

The neighborhood is hard to maintain in the city. It if be lost there, and the Church lose faith in the neighborhood, while more than half of the people live in cities, can democracy survive?

Churches that mean business about the needs of their neighborhoods will understand why St. Margaret's Episcopal Church (940 East 156th Street, New York) devoted its February, 1954, issue of "The Militant" (ten mimeographed pages and cover) to "Christian Concern for Housing," at the same time that it featured a Gospel Preaching Mission during Lent. Neighborhood improvement is a natural clinic in general social reconstruction. The Church will inevitably be concerned with *redevelopment,* if it is interested in people in slum areas.

The truth is, blighted areas were long ago proved to be *too expensive.* The 1952–1953 Annual Report of the National Federation of Settlements and Neighborhood Houses succinctly described how downtown residential areas deteriorate:

"As the growth of the city creates a demand for additional commercial, light manufacturing, warehouse, governmental, and cultural institutions, adjacent residential areas are absorbed. The demand on the part of the city and suburbs for convenient and quick transportation to the central areas brings about the construction of new transportation lines and highways. These throughways disrupt the pattern of old residential areas and render even the most desirable of such neighborhoods noisy, dirty, and dangerous.

"During the past two decades it has become clear that the economic cost of these neighborhoods is beyond the capacity of the city to bear."

But it is not merely the physical city that needs rebuilding at its heart. As Robert Woods put it, "The apparently reckless pouring of its energy out into the open life of the community on the part of any particular local church, with careful avoidance of any appearance of seeking to glorify itself—the stirring of other churches in the vicinity to like action—would mean a new moral and spiritual life in any local community." [6]

And he went on to cite "the great principle upon which the foreign missionary service of the Church has won its amazing triumphs—that *an outlet of service is the essential precursor of an inlet of grace.*"

Accordingly, "we must be fully satisfied with the fact that the leaven is permeating and doing its work. We must avail ourselves of all existing groups, and be prepared to let all the honor and glory be theirs provided the Kingdom of God be advanced. The Church which seeks to label its service or attach to itself the results of its work, or do anything other than freely cast its bread upon the waters, will by just so much fail of its true reward." [7] That is hard doctrine. Is it untrue?

The church in the changing city must be interested in the redemption of persons, of families, of neighborhoods, of the inner city, of the outer city, and of all urban society. Reconstruction is its reason for existence. For this redemption was it founded.

8. Finally, *we must abandon the idea of the impossible.* It is no accident that a former Marine should be found at work as rector of an inner-city church in a situation of extreme difficulty. He asked for it. Does not the Marine Corps "specialize in the impossible"?

There has been some ground for saying that there can be no such thing as an urban neighborhood. Great housing builders, where they can start new, are now deliberately building for small neighborhood contacts, self-contained, unhampered by traffic hazards. Under favorable conditions the neighborhood may stage a comeback.

Can it do so under the most unfavorable?

The settlement movement was a wager that it could. Neighborhood houses sought to re-create the neighborhood, under difficult circumstances. It takes more than good houses to make a neighborhood; it takes a better spirit. Where the housing is bad, so much the harder is it to stir up the better spirit. That is just what East Harlem affords the chance of doing.

As college and university men went into slums to build home-like institutions, so the workers enumerated in these case studies have gone into slum after slum, to live there, to make them *their* neighborhoods, and to help transform them. This is a primary function of the Church. To *live* where one's parishioners live adds to one's testimony, whether of life or of pulpit.

Any ecclesiastical administrator could list for the protection of any-body's pocketbook all the reasons why the city is hopeless. Chief among them is the fact that the administrators' budgetary commitments must be protected, and any wild ideas of mythical sums to be raised by nonexistent "friendly citizens" must not be allowed to run rampant. Fortunately inventive youth has always been willing to tackle the impossible, to smash the stereotypes, to upset the applecarts carefully inscribed "It can't be done."

In an ecclesiastical order whose very burgeoning ecumenicity could easily be satisfied with sanctifying the ecclesiastical *status quo,* there is no need greater than that of *inventiveness.* Nowhere is inventiveness more needed than in the local parish, in the changing city. Paul G. Hoffman, chairman of the Board of the Studebaker Corporation, quotes his father, a successful inventor, as saying, "Many of our greatest inventions came from the minds of men who had not learned too well what can *not* be done." What we are beginning to witness now, in parish, in board offices, and in councils of churches, is a new, heart-searchingly profound refusal to believe that the church job in the changing city cannot be done.

The urban world is surely upside down, and the desire to help set it right side up is more than youthful bravado; it partakes of the New Testament apostolate, based on the heritage of Old Testament prophecy, and strengthened now by centuries of cumulative Christian experience which need not accept the *status quo* as unredeemable.

Impossible? In their various ways, these cases rise up, smiling, to say, "Sorry, brother, but we are *doing* it."

30. CITY SCHOOLS

Patricia Cayo Sexton

 The problem of acculturating and integrating the large non-white minorities into the metropolitan community falls, to a considerable extent, upon the city's public schools. The basic issues affecting urban education may be interpreted in class-struggle terms, as is done in Patricia Sexton's analysis. However, when approached from this perspective, the city's racial question is seen to involve not only local but state and national authorities as well. Broad and narrow interest groups, political parties, and governmental bureaucracies all participate in the complex decision-making processes by which educational services are controlled in the urban community. As a result there is a wide variation in both the range and quality of the services that the schools provide the different social classes. This is perhaps most apparent in regard to racial minorities. The inferior vocational training of nonwhites, for example, may express more a disbelief in their innate ability than the desire to make real opportunities available to them.
 Dr. Sexton devotes most of her attention here to New York City's schools. With respect to the problem of educating the new nonwhite urban minority they may not be atypical.

To TALK ABOUT urban education is to talk about an old phrase fallen in such disrepute during two postwar decades that it has hidden out from scholarly journals like a furtive sex criminal. The phrase "class struggle" now appears in black tie and softened aliases as "slum and suburb," "ine-

Excerpts from *The Annals of the American Academy of Political and Social Science,* March 1964. Reprinted by permission of the author and the publisher.

qualities," problems of the "disadvantaged," of the "culturally deprived," of "integration." However Americanized or blurred the new image may appear, the basic fact seems simple enough: a remarkable "class struggle" now rattles our nation's schools and the scene of sharpest conflict is the city. Southern cities—and New York—were the scenes of first eruptions, but now almost every northern city, and many suburbs, are feeling the new tremors.

A high-ranking official in New Rochelle, New York put it in these words: "It's not just race in our schools . . . it's class warfare!" Class conflict, of course, is not the only issue in city schools. There is ethnic conflict and the special status of Negroes—and of Puerto Ricans and other identifiable groups—at the bottom end of the ladder and the special Rickover pressure-cooked conformism and prestige-college frenzy at the upper end. Nor are the sides in the conflict always clearly formed. But, usually, when the chaff and wheat are separated, what is left is the "haves" in one pile and "have-nots" in another, with some impurities in each—middle-class white "liberals," for example, who support some Negro demands and white have-nots who oppose them. . . .

Other major urban school issues exist—finances, bureaucracy, and the unionization of teachers, among others—and may seem, on the surface, unrelated to class conflict. At second glance, the shortage of school funds can be seen as a product of the antitax ideology of haves. The behemoth bureaucracies may be seen everywhere as more accessible to and influenced by haves, and the decentralization of administration—to which New York's Superintendent Gross and others have devoted themselves— may be seen as a partial response to the growing arousal of have-not groups. The unionization of city teachers may be seen as a response to the hitherto rather rigid conservative control of school systems and the new thrust of liberalism in the cities and the schools, released by have-nots votes and agitation, as well as a defense against the difficult conditions in have-not schools.

LEVELS OF CONFLICT

The class struggle in the schools and the struggle for power which is part of it are carried on at many levels. In some cases, it seems least visible under the spotlight—on the school boards. Through liberal and have-not activity, some city school boards are now composed of middle-class moderates who are more inclined to represent the educational interests of have-nots than were their more conservative predecessors. Some big-city boards, as New York's, seem exemplary public servants, superior in purpose and competence to higher political bodies. Their efforts in behalf of have-nots are limited by several personal as well as external characteristics: they are haves, a quality that usually though not invariably limits

zeal and identity with have-nots; they are moderates in contrast to those
leading the more militant have-not groups. Among the limits set by
school systems are: (1) the traditional conservative reluctance of boards
to interfere in the operations of the bureaucracy; (2) the inertia and resistance of the bureaucracy to pressure from the board; (3) the usual
tendency to become defensive of "their system" and to take criticisms of
the system as personal affronts; (4) influences from middle-class interests
which are usually more insistent and weighty than have-not pressure; (5)
interference from outside groups—such as the unprecedented threat of
the Northcentral Association to withdraw accreditation from the Chicago
schools if the school board insisted on a step which forced Superintendent
Willis into further desegregation. The external limits on the situation,
however, seem more determining: (1) the difficulty of the job to be done,
(2) the lack of sufficient money to do the job.

Services to have-nots within the city system, therefore, are limited by
these conservative factors: (1) the moderate position of most liberal
board members and the insufficiency of zeal or identification to drive
home the grievances of have-nots; (2) conservatism and resistance within
the bureaucracy; (3) conservative influence which acts to shut off funds
to the schools.

In the movement of the class struggle from one end of the continuum,
where a small elite holds total power, to the other extreme, where have-
nots share proportionate influence, there are many points of compromise,
and public officials tend to pursue ever more liberal ends and means. The
white liberals who sit on some city boards may begin to push for more
rapid change or may be replaced soon by representatives who will.

The claim that the city and its school system are so constrained by outside conservatism, especially at the state level, that they can do little
seems largely true, though partially exaggerated. Too often outside interference is made an excuse for inertia. City schools have not given adequate service to have-nots largely because the have-nots were underrepresented in decision-making positions. As cities go, New York's school
board seems unusually enlightened, appointed as it is by a relatively responsive mayor and served by two unusually alert citizen groups—the
Public Education Association and the United Parents Association. Yet a
nine-member board includes only one Negro and no Puerto Rican, although these groups together compose 40 per cent of the city's public
school enrollment. . . . Of some 777 top officials in the system—board
members, superintendents, and principals—it appears that only six are
Negroes, 0.8 per cent of the total.[1]

Although it is sometimes asserted that the interest-group identity of
board members does not affect their decision-making, what may be more
nearly the case, given present knowledge of group dynamics, is that the
group interests of the lone have-not representative may be submerged in
a board's moderate consensus.

Perhaps the "equality lag" within city systems may be more directly attributable to deficiencies in have-not organization than to lack of good faith among liberals and board members. . . . A major weakness of have-nots is their limited understanding of power, who has it and how to get it; they also lack the time, money, and organization often needed to purchase it.[2]

BEYOND THE CITY LIMITS

Local class conflict seems only a dim reflection of a larger conflict. The main drama of class conflict and thrust of conservatism are seen in full dimension in a larger arena—at the federal and state levels. The national scene cannot be ignored in any consideration of the city school situation. Only at this level does there appear a possibility of releasing the funds needed to support high-quality education and the high-level job opportunity that goes with it. The claim that federal aid to education is the *only* school issue and that other concerns are simply distractions is given substantial support by any cursory study of city school budgets and revenue limitations.

Nationally, the conflict seems shaped by at least two major factors:

(1) The congressional system is biased against have-nots and their representatives. The bias results from at least two forms of conservative manipulation: (a) manipulation of rural and small-town interests, North and South, and, through them, congressional apportionment and votes; (b) the additional manipulation of southern rural conservatism—which is given unusual congressional power by the committee seniority system —through the exchange of votes on the race issue.

. . .

(2) Seriously deprived have-nots have failed to enter their full power into the political arena.

THE STATE

If direct federal aid seems distant and the aid formula unlikely to provide much assistance to the cities, fiscal aid from the state may be closer at hand, depending upon how quickly reapportionment will be enforced in the states. New York City received $197 in school aid for each student in its public schools in 1961–1962, while the average in the rest of the state was $314. Miami, Florida paid $47 million in state taxes in one recent year and got back only $1.5 million in grants-in-aid. With sympathetic legislatures, cities may be able to call on other revenues, including an income tax on suburbanites working in the city such as has been adopted in Philadelphia and Detroit.

INEQUALITIES

The consequences of local, state, and national class conflict are seen in the school inequalities and class-biased training given to children even within the most liberal city systems. Only in the past few years has the concern of some unionists, academicians, liberals, and many Negroes brought the full range of inequities to public attention. The "spoils" of the city school, limited as they are by outside controls, are usually divided according to the crude formula "them as has gets." Only now in some cities is there any insistence on the more radical "compensatory" formula —"to each according to need."

Documentary evidence about class inequalities, past and present, is now weighty. My own study of one large city school system, *Education and Income,* describes the various forms of class inequities within one system.[3]. . . In 1955, following Dr. Kenneth Clark's demand for attention to Negro schools, an "outside" study found that Negro and Puerto Rican schools in New York City were generally inferior to "Other" schools.[4]. . . Though the New York Board of Education now claims that Negro and Puerto Rican schools are equal or superior to "Other" schools, Dr. Kenneth Clark still says Harlem schools reflect "a consistent pattern of criminal neglect."

. . .

Inequalities and the compensatory formula now being advocated—reverse inequality—produce only one kind of conflict, one which may be more easily resolved than other disputes because it involves simply the redistribution of money. The "concept" of equality itself seems far less susceptible to change—the notion that, with proper attention, the abilities of have-not children may prove roughly equal to those of haves and that, therefore, they should not be separated, sent off at an early age on different tracks, or given disproportionate access to higher education.

In New York City, fiscal inequality, segregation, and the "concept" of inequality resulted in the following racial distribution of recent graduating classes in New York's special high schools for "gifted children" drawn from the whole city:

	Negroes	Puerto Ricans	Others
Bronx High School of Science	14	2	863
Stuyvesant High School	23	2	629
High School of Music and Art	45	12	638
Brooklyn Technical School	22	6	907

In one recent year, Negroes and Puerto Ricans were about 14 per cent of the graduating class in the city's academic high schools and about 50 per cent in the city's vocational high schools. In the vocational schools, Negroes and Puerto Ricans tend to be heavily concentrated in inferior manual trade schools and seriously underrepresented in the technical schools. . . .

HIGHER EDUCATION

A developing conflict centers on higher education. Though ethnic records are not kept, one expert estimate is that about 2 per cent of students at the University of the City of New York (formerly the city's free colleges) are Negro. One branch of the University is located at the edge of Harlem and is more integrated and accessible to Negroes than other branches, yet less than 5 per cent Negro enrollment is reported there.

In New York, Negroes tend to fall between the free city colleges and the dominant and expensive private universities (New York University, Columbia, and their like). They can neither qualify for the former nor afford the latter. Needs tests are not applied to city-college admissions, and free tuition is extended to the affluent with an 85 high school average and denied the impoverished with an 84 average; enrollments are reported to be now predominantly middle class.[5]

Some critics now say that the only equitable system of tuition charges, in all types of institutions, is a sliding scale based on ability to pay. New York does not have a single state university; what is called the University of the State of New York is simply a scattered collection, mainly in non-urban areas, of teachers colleges, agricultural schools, a few technical schools. Recently, the state gave a 40 per cent subsidy to New York's city colleges, converted by some graduate offerings into the University of the City of New York. The importance of federal funds to education is seen in federal research and development investments in California and the pervading effect such funds have had in underwriting and stimulating growth of educational institutions there.

New York City's effort through the years to provide free college education and to compensate for the void at the state level has been extraordinary. No other city appears to have made any comparable effort. Still the city seems not to have deployed its college resources equitably, and the gathering debate over the city colleges suggests a conflict of view—or interest—between the city's have-nots and its numerous liberal middle class.[6]

. . .

CLASS AND ETHNIC ROLES

Within the city itself, at least these elements seem to have some separate, though often overlapping, identity: (1) Negroes; (2) labor unions; (3)

white have-nots; (4) white liberals; (5) the Jewish community; (6) the Catholic community; (7) business organizations and their allies in city silk-stocking areas.

The roles and activities of these groups in relation to the schools have never been adequately defined, but impressionistic observation seems to indicate the following outlines: The main white support for civil rights in the past several decades has unquestionably come from the leadership within the labor and Jewish communities—with some major assists from middle-class liberal and church groups, particularly in the last several years. The rank-and-file within the labor-union and Jewish communities, more personally threatened by Negroes, have tended to lag some distance behind on civil rights.[7]

In the schools, the class and ethnic lines are distinct, even though less clearly drawn than in the larger community. Some political allies of Negroes have been largely outside the school conflict: unions and large numbers of white have-nots, notably the Poles, Italians, and Irish who have tended to use parochial schools. Some feel it is fortunate that these have-not groups have tended to be outside the public school controversy; others feel that the parochial-public school separation has worked hardships on the public schools and delayed a crisis that would, in the long run, be beneficial to the public schools. Union leaders have been less involved in the schools than in other political affairs because of what seems to be a rather basic alienation from the schools and frequently because of their own parochial background. They have, however, supported school expansion, improvement, financing, and their organized political power, as in New York, has given important direct assistance to the schools and to the claims of Negroes on the schools.

The organized business community has traditionally opposed tax increases for public education, the leadership in these groups usually residing in the suburbs where they have provided ample funds for good schools. Powerful real-estate groups have opposed property taxes as well as school and housing integration. The "swing" group has been the Jewish community and, to some extent, the white liberal. The Jewish community, even middle and upper income, has consistently given solid support to the public schools,[8] but its own heavy stress on education and the fact that it is one of the largest remaining white middle-class groups within many cities have produced some ambivalence in its role and some conflict in unexpected places. The confrontation of these two allies in the city public schools is a source of growing distress to both groups. Because the Jewish community has tended to remain in the city and to use the public schools, it is generally contiguous, geographically and emphatically, with the Negro community and located in the middle of the integration cross fire. Negroes point to Jewish predominance in the "better" high schools, the top "ability" groups, the free city colleges, and in public school administration. In many of the "integrating" areas of the city, the two groups have joined in open conflict, though in other areas they have integrated without friction. Thus, the Jewish community, because it has not fled like others from the city, often finds itself in the same situation as the labor movement with regard to Negroes: competition within a family of mutual interest for a scarcity of opportunities—in the schools in one case and in the job market in the other. . . .

ACCULTURATION AND INTEGRATION

The urban schools now confront the most difficult task they have attempted. Never before has a major *racial* minority been integrated into a nation's school or society. In fact, such integration within a dominantly non-Latin European population is unprecedented in history, the Soviets having settled their racial affairs by geographic separation.

The urban school, whose heavy job has always been the acculturation of immigrant and foreign-speaking ethnic groups, is now taking its first large bite of racial acculturation, as a giant reptile tries to swallow a whole animal. The city is accustomed to educating the immigrant: In New York City in 1960, 48.6 per cent of the population was either foreign-born or had at least one foreign-born parent; in Chicago, the figure was 35.9; in Detroit 32.2; in San Francisco, 43.5. But the Negro group is unique in these respects: (1) it is the largest "immigrant" group of low-income, public-school-using Protestants (many other recent immigrations having skirted the public schools) ; (2) it is the first large racial minority to come to the city schools and the first large group with non-Western origins; (3) it has had a unique history of educational and social deprivation.

The active demand of Negro parents for integration perhaps cannot be fully appeased. Negro—and Puerto Rican—students are approaching a majority in many city public schools and any demand for total, one-for-one integration—which few would make—may be impossible in view of the increasing shortage of white public school students. Rather large-scale integration seems possible, however, as New York City is now beginning to demonstrate. Perhaps the issue will finally be settled by integrated urban renewal, or by setting up superschools and superservices in Negro areas—such as the Amidon school in Washington, D. C.—that will attract white students into Negro areas. Mainly, the urban school integration movement has served the latent function of calling attention to Negro education and arousing concern over the quality of Negro schools. The hope is held by many that, if Negro schools are improved, Negroes will not be so eager to integrate.

Among the newer racial demands in urban schools are: (1) compensatory treatment to balance past inequities; (2) "reverse" integration of schools and the busing of whites into Negro schools in order to "equalize" sacrifice (in New York, the demand has been for compulsory busing of both groups; on this most controversial point, Dr. Kenneth Clark has objected that Harlem schools are not fit either for Negroes or for whites and that busing should be "out" only) ; (3) heterogeneous grouping to scatter Negroes throughout the school population in any given school, rather than segregating them into slow-moving, homogeneous "ability" groups. In New York City and elsewhere, homogeneous grouping has proceeded so far that children in some places are "ability grouped" in kindergarten, based on whether or not they have been to nursery school; these groups, starting almost in the cradle, tend to perpetuate themselves throughout the child's school life.

31. THE METROPOLITAN AREA
AS A RACIAL PROBLEM

Morton Grodzins

New York, Los Angeles, Chicago, Philadelphia, Detroit, San Francisco, Boston, Pittsburgh, St. Louis, Washington, Cleveland, Baltimore, Newark, Minneapolis, and Buffalo—these cities, our fifteen largest metropolitan areas defined as having more than 1,250,000 population in 1960, have attracted the greatest numbers of black in-migrants since 1940. This new urban group consists principally of persons displaced from Southern agriculture. They are a lower-income group and have, initially at least, a high rate of natural increase. They inhabit the central city. For example, in the decade 1940–1950, while the white population of these fifteen great cities increased only 3.7 percent, their Negro population rose 67.8 percent. Still further increase in the numbers of inner-city Negroes is expected in the years ahead.

Some suburbanization of blacks is going on although oftentimes it is merely to adjacent industrial satellites, not true suburbs. As low-income Negroes succeed whites in the generally older sections of the city, and as poverty and discrimination, practiced by individuals and local governments through zoning and arbitrary building codes, hem the Negro in, the ghetto becomes a stark reality. Morton Grodzins discusses its social, economic, and political implications for the metropolitan community.

SOME OF THE CONSEQUENCES of the urban-suburban racial and class schism are already apparent, and others can be reasonably predicted.

Excerpts from *American Race Relations Today*, edited by Earl Raab, published by Anchor Books, Doubleday and Company, Inc. (1962). Reprinted by permission of the University of Pittsburgh Press.

SOCIAL CONSEQUENCES

Within the cities the first result is a spreading of slums. There is no free market for Negro housing. The Negro population always increases faster than the living space available to it. New areas that open up to Negro residence become grossly overcrowded by conversion of one-family houses to multiple dwellings and by squeezing two or more Negro families into apartments previously occupied by a single white one. Though complete statistical evidence is lacking, it is likely that Negroes pay substantially more rent for such accommodations than do whites, and the higher rent itself produces higher densities. Housing occupied by Negroes is more crowded, more dilapidated, and more lacking in amenities such as private baths than housing occupied by whites with equivalent incomes.

Income factors account in part for the condition of life of the Negro community. Negroes are heavily over-represented in low income jobs: in the menial services, in unskilled and semi-skilled factory labor, and in "dirty work" generally. In this respect they are not unlike some earlier immigrants to the city; the Irish and the Poles, for example, also settled mainly in the slums.

Like previous newcomers to the city tasting the freedom of urban life for the first time, a significant portion of the Negro group does not possess the stable patterns of thought and action that characterize the "better" older inhabitants. And, as with all immigrant groups, old community patterns of control do not operate well in the new environment. Family disorganization among urban Negroes is high as measured by such indices as broken marriages, families headed by females, and unrelated individuals living in the same household. The development of social stabilization pivoted on family and community ties take place against great odds. How does a mother keep her teen-age son off the streets if an entire family must eat, sleep, and live in a single room? What utility can be found in sobriety among a society of drinkers and in a block of taverns? What opportunity for quiet amidst the din of a tightly packed, restless neighborhood?

The conditions of urban life, rather than socializing new Negro residents to "desirable" life patterns, frequently have the opposite effect. They encourage rowdiness, casual and competitive sexuality, and a readiness for combat. The result is that the neighborhoods acquired by Negro residents eventually spiral downward. Disease and crime rates are high. Family stability is further prejudiced. Filth accumulates. The slum spreads outward.

These very conditions of life in the predominantly Negro neighborhoods lead the larger population to resist the expansion of Negro residential areas. The racial attribute—skin color—is added to the social attributes of lower class behavior. And while Negroes, like other urban immigrants, can readily lose undesirable social attributes, they cannot lose their color. They therefore do not have the mobility of other immigrant groups. They are racially blocked, whatever their social *bona fides*.

The Negro "black belts" of the great American cities as a consequence are by no means homogeneous. The very concentration of population within them plus the visible badge of color give them a spurious air of likeness. They contain, in fact, wide ranges of every social attribute: from illiteracy to high learning, from filth to hospital-like hygienic standards, from poverty to riches, from political backwardness to sophistication. Though the casual observer of the "black belt" neighborhoods sees only slums, the fact is that in every such area there are sub-areas, frequently on the periphery of the high-density mass, that are anything but slums. These are usually neighborhoods of newest acquisition, inhabited by the well-to-do of the Negro community. Density is low, lawns and gardens are well-tended, church attendance is high, neatness and cleanliness are apparent, parental standards of propriety for children higher than for comparable white groups.

Negro neighborhoods in the shadows of white luxury apartments are not unknown; but the more usual pattern is for low-income non-Negroes to occupy a buffer zone between all-Negro and the better white neighborhoods. Some of these are themselves new migrants to the city: rural white Southerners and Japanese-Americans in Chicago, Puerto Ricans in New York, for example. Others are old residents on the lower ends of the income scale, people who, like the Negroes themselves, do not find success in life, or life itself, easy.

With the exodus of middle and upper classes to the suburbs, lower-income groups constitute a larger and larger fraction of the population of the central cities. Members of these groups generally exhibit a greater degree of intolerance and racial prejudice than do other whites. And the increasing juxtaposing of the Negro and the low-income non-Negro populations produces increased interracial tensions. Shirley Star of the National Opinion Research Center has shown that the greatest white animosity towards Negroes is found on the edge of the expanding Negro residential areas where whites fear their block or neighborhood will soon be "invaded." In these lower class and lower-middle class transitional areas, violence is incipient. Individual differences within the minority group are ignored. A young white resident of such an area in Chicago recently beat a Negro to death with a hammer. "I just wanted to get one of them," he explained, "which one didn't matter."

The total situation produces Negro communities in which people live their whole lives without, or with minimum, contact with the other race. With a Negro population numbering in the hundreds of thousands, and with this population densely concentrated, one can live, eat, shop, work, play, and die in a completely Negro community. The social isolation of the northern urban Negro is, for very large numbers, more complete than it ever was for the Negro rural resident in the South.

Even in education, the urban residential segregation of the non-southern cities has produced consequences that are not dissimilar to what the South is trying to maintain by the use of violence and unconstitutional law. If segregation is defined not in legal terms but in the numbers of students who attend all-Negro schools, then it is undoubtedly true that more Negro students are segregated in the schools of New York and Chicago than in any other cities or some states.

This general picture of segregation needs some qualification. A small number of church groups have succeeded in building interracial congregations. Qualified Negro workers are finding employment in places previously barred to them, not only in manufacturing, but also in the professions and in retail establishments. On a few blocks in urban America, Negroes and whites have demonstrated that they can live together as neighbors. Labor unions, though traditionally anti-Negro, have in some places accepted Negroes as full partners in leadership as well as membership.

These are evidences of advances toward social integration. Other advances have been made within the Negro community itself. As this community in a given city grows larger, satisfactory career lines, economic security, and the home and community life that accompany such developments become possible. Here, however, Negroes and whites meet each other across separate societies rather than within a single group. The Negro shares with whites the better things of life, but he does so in isolation with other Negroes. The disadvantaged segregated community even produces advantages for some individuals within it, providing protected markets for Negro professionals and businessmen and protected constituencies for Negro political and church leaders. Yet even those who profit from segregation suffer from it. They feel the pin-pricks as well as the sledges of discrimination, and they must suppress their dissatisfaction in accordance with standards of conduct expected of all "better" people, whatever their race.

The larger evidence is neither that of social integration nor of intra-community social gains. Rather it is evidence pointing to the expansion of Negro slums within the largest cities and the separation of whites and Negroes by intracity neighborhoods and especially on central city-suburban lines.

ECONOMIC CONSEQUENCES

Population shifts bring with them major economic consequences. Of first importance is the further decline of a large segment of business activity and associated property values, in the central cities. For reasons only remotely related—or unrelated—to the Negro-white population distribution, the economic feasibility of decentralized retail shopping has already been demonstrated. Suburban shopping centers have captured a large segment of the market in clothing, furniture, and other consumption goods; almost everywhere the "downtown" shops of the central cities have lost ground, absolutely and proportionally, to the peripheral developments. Retail sales in the central business district of Chicago decreased by 5 per cent between 1948 and 1954, while sales in the metropolitan area outside the city increased by 53 percent. The relative sales loss of downtown areas has been even greater in other central cities.

Further developments can be foreseen. The downtown stores, with non-white and low-income customers more and more predominant in their clientele, will tend to concentrate on cheaper merchandise. " 'Borax' for downtown, Herman Miller for the suburb," is already a slogan of the furniture business. The decline of the central-city department store will be accompanied by a general deterioration of the downtown area. There are some striking exceptions, most notably in mid-town Manhattan. But in most cities—Chicago, Boston, Los Angeles are good examples—the main streets are becoming infested with sucker joints for tourists: all night jewelry auctions, bargain linens and cheap neckties, hamburger stands and jazz dives. The slums, in other words, are spreading to the central business districts.

A further, though more problematic, development is that the offices of the larger corporations will join the flight from the city, taking along with them their servicing businesses: banks, law offices, advertising agencies, and others. The rapid development of closed circuit television, facsimile reproduction, and other technical aids relieves these businesses of the necessity of clustering at a central point. Their exodus from the city is already underway. New highways will make it easier in many places to get from one suburb to another than from suburb to downtown; and the losses of giving up central headquarters can be amortized over a number of years, frequently at considerable tax savings. Even the downtown hotel is likely to give way to the suburban motel except for convention purposes, an incidental further boost to the honkey-tonk development within the downtown business areas.

The rule seems to be a simple one: retail trade, the white collar shops, and the service industries will follow population. (Once their exodus is well underway, they also lead population.) The same general rule at least partially applies for manufacturing: the greatest suburbanization of manufacturing has taken place in those metropolitan areas where there has also been the most marked suburbanization of population, and some evidence indicates that manufacturing precedes population, rather than vice versa. Though the central cities have lost some manufacturing to both suburban and non-metropolitan areas, they have nevertheless maintained the preponderant share of the nation's total manufacturing enterprise. As

Kitagawa and Bogue have shown, "the over-all spatial distribution [of manufacturing] in the United States has changed comparatively little in the past 50 years." [1] The relative immobility of heavy industry has the result of fixing the laboring and semi-skilled groups, including large numbers of Negroes, within the central cities.

Even a conservative view must anticipate the exodus of a large segment of retail and other non-manufacturing businesses from downtown centers. Abandonment of these centers will lead to a host of municipal problems, not least of which is the loss of a substantial tax base. These economic developments are at once a step towards, and a consequence of, the city-suburban bifurcation of races that promises to transform many central cities into lower class ethnic islands. Successful attempts by central cities to encourage the establishment of new manufacturing plants as a means of rebuilding their tax base will of course hasten this process.

POLITICAL CONSEQUENCES

Whatever the melancholy resemblance between older segregation patterns of the rural South and newer ones of the urban North, one important fact is different: the Negroes of the North possess the suffrage. How will they use it if they become the majority group—or at least the largest single group—in some of the great cities of the nation?

The most likely political development is the organization of Negroes for ends conceived narrowly to the advantage of the Negro community. Such a political effort might aim to destroy zoning and building restrictions for the immediate purpose of enlarging opportunities for desperately needed Negro housing against stubborn social pressures. If successful, the outcome might merely extend the Negro ghetto and cause a further departure of white populations to the suburbs. Yet the short-run political appeal of this action cannot be denied.

What the Negroes seek for themselves in Chicago in 1975 or 1985 might not be any more selfishly conceived than what Irish-dominated city councils in Boston and New York have sought in the past. In one essential field, Negro leadership may be more advantageous to the whole population: lacking devotion to the parochial schools, it would not be mean in the support of public schools. The rub lies in the very visibility of Negro domination. Even on the assumption of Negro leaders and followers demonstrating wisdom and forbearance, what would be the consequence in one or more major cities of the city councils becoming predominantly Negro? What will be the situation in a state legislature when the largest group of big-city representatives are Negroes?

At the very least, cities politically dominated by Negroes will find it more difficult to bring about the urban-suburban cooperation so badly needed in so many fields. They will find greatly exacerbated what is already keenly felt in a majority of states: the conflict between the great urban center and the rural "downstate" or "upstate" areas. Similar unfortunate effects will follow in the national Congress, once a number of large cities are largely represented by Negro congressmen. The pitting of whites against Negroes, and of white policies against Negro policies, does not await actual Negro urban domination. The cry has already been raised in state legislatures. The conflict can only grow more acute as race and class become increasingly coterminous with local government boundaries.

In the long run, it is highly unlikely that the white population will allow Negroes to become dominant in the cities without resistance. The cultural and economic stakes are too high. One countermeasure will surely present itself to the suburbanites: to annex the suburbs with their predominantly white populations, to the cities. This will be a historic reversal of the traditional suburban antipathy to annexation. But in the perception of suburbanites it will be justified: they will be annexing the city to the suburbs.

The use of annexation to curb Negro political powers is already underway. It was an explicit argument used by political leaders favoring an annexation to Nashville in 1952. And other recent annexations, largely confined to the South, have taken place at least partially to deny Negroes political powers they would otherwise achieve.

Other actions to the same end can be expected, especially the gerrymandering of Negro populations so as to deny them equitable representation in legislative bodies of city, state, and nation. Tuskegee, Alabama, was gerrymandered in 1957 to exclude all but a handful of Negro voters from city elections, and steps are currently under way to divide Macon County among five neighboring counties. Negroes have long lived within the city, and the county has for many years been preponderantly Negro, but only recently have the Negroes exercised their franchise in any numbers. In the border city of Cincinnati, fear of growing Negro political power was an important reason for the 1957 action that repealed proportional representation and subsequently defeated the reform City Charter Committee. During the campaign over proportional representation, whispering campaigns urged defeat of the system in order to prevent Theodore M. Berry, Negro vice-mayor, from becoming mayor, as well as to prevent Negroes from moving into white neighborhoods. The total political picture of continued racial bifurcation forecasts a new round of political repression aimed at Negroes. For this one, they will be better armed— effective numbers, economic strength, political sophistication, and allies in the white population.

32. RIOTS

President's Commission on Law Enforcement and the Administration of Justice

Ghetto disorders in twenty American cities during the three summers of *1964, 1965,* and *1966* preceded the so-called Watts riot in Los Angeles. They were all marked by intense hostility toward the police and by much arson, looting, and destruction of property in the black ghetto. New York, Rochester, Jersey City, Paterson, Elizabeth, Chicago, and Philadelphia were each the scene of Negro insurgency before Watts. Later there were notable outbreaks of violence in Detroit, Cleveland, and Newark. In fact, perhaps as many as a hundred of the nation's cities witnessed ghetto riots in the aftermath of Martin Luther King's assassination in April *1968.*

Urban riots had, of course, taken place earlier in Ameican history. New York, in *1863,* East St. Louis, in *1913,* Chicago, in *1919,* and Detroit, in *1943,* had all been the sites of racial disturbances. These riots, however, had been primarily white attacks upon Negroes, not the pattern of blacks rampaging through the streets of their own neighborhoods, leveling buildings, and firing upon the police. It is true that in Harlem, first in *1935* and then again in *1943,* the Watts pattern had been observed, but Watts was the more significant prototype of violence as the outright expression of hostility and as social protest against the conditions of ghetto life. This was probably due to the massive cityward migration that had occurred and the rise in the anticipation that the denial of opportunity to nonwhites would soon come to an end.

Excerpts from *President's Commission on Law Enforcement and the Administration of Justice, the Task Force Report, Crime and Its Impact. An Assessment* (1967): Chapter 9.

THE 5-DAY RIOT that began on Wednesday, August 11, 1965, in the South Central Los Angeles ghetto (the area of which the Watts neighborhood is a small part) has probably been more carefully examined than any riot that has ever occurred. The McCone Commission, appointed by the Governor of California to make a general report on the riot, held 60 formal hearings during which it received sworn testimony from 80 witnesses; it interviewed 90 of those arrested during the riot; and it opened an office in the riot area so that members of its staff could interview local residents.[1] The Bureau of Criminal Statistics of the California Department of Justice made a detailed statistical study of the 3,927 people arrested during the riot.[2] The California National Guard prepared a systematic account of its activities during the riot.[3] Two members of the staff of the riot, wrote the book, *"Burn, Baby, Burn,"* describing the neighborhood, about 7 P.M. on August 11, a day on which the temperature reached 94°, the events of the riot, and a number of the participants in it.[4] Under a grant from the Office of Economic Opportunity, the Institute of Government and Public Affairs of the University of California, Los Angeles, has surveyed the extent of Negro participation in the riot, and Negro and white opinion of the riot and of its causes. Though the Institute's report has not yet been completed, the Commission's staff has had the opportunity to read those chapters that have been drafted.[5]

The Watts riot was, of course, different from the other riots of the last three summers in several ways; no two riots are exactly alike. The most striking difference was its extreme violence and destructiveness. Thirty-four people were killed and 1,032 injured. Two hundred buildings were burned to the ground and 720 more looted or damaged; the total property loss was estimated at $40 million.[6] The resources of the Los Angeles Police Department, the Los Angeles Fire Department, the Los Angeles County Sheriff's Department, and the California Highway Patrol were so overtaxed that 13,400 troops of the California National Guard were finally committed to controlling the riot.

However, there is no evidence that Watts lasted so long and caused so much damage because the Los Angeles ghetto is unique. What was unique in Los Angeles was a conjunction of topographical, organizational, jurisdictional, and operational circumstances that made controlling the riot exceptionally difficult. The area in which rioting occurred is big (46.3 square miles) and flat, and so preventing the riot from spreading required a large number of men. The Los Angeles Police Department had only about 5,000 officers to police a city that is the country's largest in area and second largest in population. Three-quarters of the riot area is in the city of Los Angeles and the rest is in Los Angeles County, which is under the jurisdiction of the county sheriff, and the two departments had done an insufficient amount of joint planning to meet a major emergency. In addition both city and State authorities hesitated for about 2 days to seek the help of the National Guard; when the Guard was deployed, some 52 hours after the first rioting began, the situation rapidly improved, although another 2 days were needed to restore order completely. In short, an examination of how and why the Watts riot became a disaster and other riots did not is of great significance from the point of view of law enforcement and riot control, and of possibly less significance from the point of view of understanding the causes of riots and of preventing them. For the latter purpose, considering the similarities between Watts and other riots, rather than the differences, is more to the point.

South Central Los Angeles does not look any more like Harlem than the Sunset Strip looks like Times Square, but in that the conditions of life there compare unfavorably in all essential respects with those in the rest of the city, it is a typical ghetto.[7] The density of population is greater. The unemployment is higher. The average income is lower. The housing is in worse repair. The average educational achievement is less. The crime rate is higher. The hostility toward the police is greater. And, perhaps the crux of the matter, those residents who have the means and the desire to move to better neighborhoods have only limited opportunities to do so, a fact of which they must be acutely aware; in 1964 the voters of California overwhelmingly repealed by referendum a State fair housing law. It is not too fanciful to compare a district like South Central Los Angeles to a heap of inflammable material that has been carelessly left, out of sight and mind, in an obscure corner of a cellar or an attic; the feeblest, most random spark can ignite it, and sometimes does.

Certainly the spark that ignited Watts was feeble and random.[8] At about 7 P.M. on August 11, a day on which the temperature reached 94°, a Negro driving a pickup truck in a portion of South Central Los Angeles that is outside the city limits called the attention of a white California highway patrolman to the reckless way in which an old gray Buick was being driven north (toward the city limits) on Avalon Boulevard. The patrolman followed the Buick on his motorcycle and determined that it was going 50 miles an hour in a 35-mile-an-hour zone. He turned on his red light and siren, pulled alongside the car and ordered the driver to the curb. The driver, a 21-year-old Negro named Marquette Frye, obeyed at once and without demur. He was evidently drunk and he did not have a driver's license. The patrolman told him he was under arrest and radioed for his backup officer and a transport car to come and help him place Frye in custody. Both arrived promptly. Meanwhile 20 or 30 passersby and residents of nearby buildings had gathered to watch the scene, apparently purely for entertainment. There was no sign of trouble. The patrolman was friendly and polite. Frye was good humored, even jocular.

Suddenly the situation changed. Vociferously and belligerently Frye refused to get into the transport car. The officers attempted to handcuff him. He resisted. The spectators became sullen and hostile. The officers radioed for more help. Frye's stepbrother, who had been riding in the car, and his mother, who owned the car and who had hastened to the scene when a neighbor told her what was happening, came to Frye's assistance. More highway patrolmen and members of the Los Angeles Police Department arrived. The size of the crowd increased. Frye was forcibly subdued, and put in the car. The spectators who by then numbered several hundred, hurled abuse at the police, who by then numbered about 50. Finally the police, with the three Fryes as prisoners, managed to disengage themselves from the crowd and leave the scene, under a shower of rocks and bricks and bottles. In the course of doing so they made another arrest, of a young woman who, according to the police, was spitting and cursing at them and, according to herself, was doing nothing more than talking and giggling. She was a barber and was wearing her professional smock, which gave rise to an impression that the police had manhandled a pregnant woman; a report of this instance of "police brutality" spread through the ghetto area, and as it spread it became a rumor that the police had beaten and kicked Frye's pregnant mother. The crowd did not disperse after the police left. On the contrary, it stayed on Avalon Boulevard, which is a main thoroughfare through South Central Los Angeles, and bombarded passing motorists with whatever missiles were available. Meanwhile angry groups began assembling in other parts of the ghetto. The riot was on.

What is most suggestive—and alarming—about the events that began the Watts riot is the chain of accident and chance. The highway patrolman, responding to a complaint by a Negro citizen, had more than sufficient cause to arrest Frye, and he went about his business with efficiency and propriety. The act for which Frye was arrested, driving drunkenly and recklessly on a main city thoroughfare, could not possibly be interpreted as either a harmless lapse or as a gesture of protest, conscious or unconscious, against white oppression. Frye was not an agitator or a militant; there is not even reason to believe that he was an especially aggrieved young man. The people who first gathered to watch the scene were not looking for trouble, but for amusement. The particular police force against which there was the most antagonism in South Central Los Angeles was not the California Highway Patrol but the Los Angeles Police Department. If the highway patrolmen doing what they did could precipitate a catastrophe like Watts, it is surely safe to say that almost anything might have precipitated it. South Central Los Angeles was ready and willing—and perhaps even eager—to run amok.

WHO RIOTED?

That the Watts riot was a general outbreak in which all kinds of people took part—not just agitators or adolescents or criminals or new arrivals in town or the unemployed or "riff-raff"—is indicated by all the available information about the participants. The California Department of Justice's statistical analysis of those arrested in connection with the riot makes this case strongly.[9] Of the 3,927 people arrested by the Los Angeles Police Department, the Los Angeles Sheriff's Office, the Compton and Long Beach Police Departments, and the California Highway Patrol the large majority, of course, were Negro men and boys; 3,609 were Negroes and 3,409 were males. But beyond these unsurprising figures there are some surprises. The rioters, to the extent that those arrested were a cross section of those who rioted, were not mostly adolescents or young adults. Only 556 were legally juveniles (under 18), while 2,111 were over 25; 602 were over 40. They were not predominantly people with serious criminal histories; 1,113 had no arrest records at all, and of the adults, 965 of those who had been arrested previously had not been convicted. At the other end of the spectrum, 363 adults had served prison terms on criminal convictions, and 52 juveniles had a record of institutional commitment. Considering the fact that a Negro male who grows up in a slum has something like a 75-percent chance of being arrested during his life-time,[10] these figures strongly suggest that the Watts rioters were drawn from all parts of the community.

This suggestion is reinforced by the socioeconomic information that the California Department of Justice was able to extract from the presentence reports that were made on 1,057 adults who were convicted of various offenses in connection with the riot. Of these, 987 were convicted in superior court, which means that they were charged with (though not necessarily convicted of) felonies. Of these 1,057, 410 were married and living with their spouses; 110 owned their own homes; 720 had completed at least the 10th grade; 656 were employed; 389 had incomes of $300 a month or more; 790 had lived in Los Angeles County for 5 years or more. To be sure, this does not present a picture of affluence or education or stability. If it did it would present a most inaccurate picture of South Central Los Angeles. However, these data go far toward refuting the notion that the rioters were predominantly "riff-raff."

The results of the UCLA survey point in the same direction.[11] They indicate that roughly 20 percent of the Negroes in the area actually did participate more or less actively in the riot, and that the general impression in the area was that many more people than that took part; more than 50 percent, by consensus. A more detailed breakdown of the circumstances of those who reported to interviewers that they were active fail to show significant differences between them and those who were inactive, in respect to place of origin, length of residence in Los Angeles, degree of education, importance of religion in childhood, or self-classified social class. For example, 28.6 percent of those who said they were lower class were active; 20.4 percent of those who said they were working class; 23.5 percent of those who said they were middle class, and 15.7 percent of those who said they were upper class. Findings of this sort are not conclusive, of course. For one thing they are based on information volunteered after the riot and not on direct observation at the time of the riot; for another, precise questions about kinds of riot activity could not be asked because the interviewers could not guarantee the interviewees immunity from prosecution. They do not *prove* that the rioters were a fairly representative cross section of the males in the community, but they do suggest it.

A final indication that the riot was not the work of a tiny extremist or criminal minority is the reaction to the riot that the UCLA interviewers found among the Negroes in the area.[12] More than half, 57.9 percent, said that its long-run effects would be favorable; 83.9 percent said that whites were now more aware of Negro problems; 64.4 percent said the victims of the riot deserved being attacked; 61.9 percent said the riot was a Negro protest; 9.9 percent even said that "everyone" in the area supported the riot. In sum, the riot was looked upon favorably by many people from every section of the community, an attitude that again suggests that participation in it was probably representative.

THE "LOGIC" BEHIND WATTS

It appears that the riot was associated with a general sense of grievance among the residents of South Central Los Angeles.[13] What is difficult to establish is to what extent—if at all—it was associated with any specific grievance or grievances. In this connection both the events of the riot itself and the information accumulated by the UCLA survey are ambiguous. Take the relationship between the riot and police-community relations. The police were a principal target of the rioters. They were, from beginning to end, cursed, stoned, and sniped at. A sheriff's deputy was killed and 90 policemen were injured. The UCLA survey shows that there is an almost universal belief in the area that the police misbehave toward Negroes. . . . For example, in response to a question about whether the police use insulting language, some 90 percent answered that it happens in the area; more than half said that it had happened to people they knew; slightly less than half said they had seen it happen, and almost 30 percent said that it had happened to them. On the question of whether the police beat up people in custody, more than 90 percent, again, said it happens in the area; almost half said it had happened to people they knew; some 30 percent said they had seen it happen, and about 5 percent said that it had happened to them. This would imply widespread grievances against the police.[14] Furthermore, the survey showed that those who answered affirmatively questions about police misbehavior were more likely to have been active in the riot than those who answered negatively. On the basis of this data it appears that police brutality—or anyway a popular impression that the police are brutal—was a principal cause of the riot.

However, there are other data that make this conclusion considerably less convincing. For one thing, although the UCLA surveyors found almost no one who believed that firemen performed their duties in a manner that discriminated against Negroes, firemen who tried to put out fires set by the rioters were also subjected to fierce stoning and sniping.[15] Transparently innocent and harmless motorists—teenage couples and mothers with children—on their way through the riot area before effective roadblocks had been set up, were savagely assaulted. When the UCLA surveyors asked open-ended questions along the lines of "What is your biggest complaint about this neighborhood?", mistreatment by the police was seldom mentioned compared with poor physical conditions in the neighborhoods, economic discrimination, inadequate schools, parks and transportation facilities, and a number of other matters. However, other questions such as "What caused the riot?" elicited a sizable (21 percent) citation of police mistreatment.

Similarly, the fact that the great majority of the buildings looted and damaged or destroyed by the rioters were white-owned stores demonstrates pretty clearly that white storeowners are not popular in South Central Los Angeles, but it does not necessarily demonstrate that they are more unpopular than, say, white landlords or for that matter white schoolteachers.[16] Given the choice among burning down or looting the house he lives in, the school his child attends, or the appliance or liquor store he does business with, even the most furiously aggrieved man will probably choose the store. The best evidence seems to be that the targets of the riot were "selected" in the sense that they were the kind of white-owned property that were the most lucrative or least inconvenient to attack.

In summary, the Watts riot appears to have been caused by no one set of people or conditions or grievances. It was a manifestation of a general sense of deep outrage, outrage at every aspect of the lives Negroes are forced to live, outrage at every element of the white community for forcing (or permitting) Negroes to live such lives. According to 56.1 percent of the Negroes interviewed in the course of the UCLA survey, the riot had a "purpose." This purpose, according to more than half of those who said there was one, was to express (in the survey's words) "hostility, resentment, revenge." As has already been noted almost two-thirds of the Negroes interviewed said the victims had deserved the attacks upon them. If the quality of life for so many Americans in Los Angeles, and undoubtedly in other cities as well, is such that they are filled with hostility, resentment, and a desire for revenge, there may be more cause for surprise over how few riots there have been than over how many. And in any case it is surely intolerable for hundreds of thousands, or millions, of Americans to have cause to feel that way, whether or not they riot.

Perhaps the most revealing finding of the UCLA survey was that another 41 percent of the Negroes who said the Watts riot had a purpose described that purpose as being (in the words of the survey again) to "gain attention, let them know, rather than simply to express hostility." In other words, the riot was not only an expression of hostility, but a cry for help. The implication is evident that many Negroes believe that if only the white community realized what the ghetto was like and how its residents felt, the ghetto would not be permitted to exist. . . .

CHAPTER SEVEN

URBAN GOVERNMENT AND THE PHYSICAL ENVIRONMENT

In a public message on the cities late in the 1960s, President Johnson reminded his countrymen that Aristotle had written, "Men come together in cities in order to live. They remain together in order to live the good life." Well might he have referred to the irony in these sentences when they are recalled amidst the many shortcomings that our urban communities manifest, in, as we noted earlier, the tensions being experienced by their vast populations and in their inability to deliver the protective and regulatory services that are the very sine qua non of urban society.

It may be the assumption of unlimited betterment underlying urbanism that is responsible for the perennial critique of the city. Surely unachieved values are evidenced in the claims made early and late that our cities do not provide adequate services. Nonetheless, the insistence with which these charges continue to be leveled would dispute the notion of sheer utopianism. The report to the National Resources Committee which is included in this section of the present volume scored the problems of environmental health in the urban setting, of unsatisfactory provision for beauty and leisure, and of the inefficient placement of industry and the means of transportation in the city a whole generation ago. If anything, the 1968 budget messages of the state governors, though comparable, were less aspiring as they expressed similar concern with urban weaknesses. Singled out for attention in addition to crime and riots were the pollution of air and water, transportation difficulties, and metropolitan consolidation under home rule. That these are nearer solution today than they were then is open to serious doubt.

The National Resources Committee attributed the urban deficiencies it identified three decades ago to an enterprise system unresponsive either to the public interest or to the need for overall technical coordination, and this in spite of a rapidly evolving technology that was continuously upsetting established modes of organization. It also underlined the political fragmentation of our major urban centers. The 1937 report of the NRC Urbanism Committee makes up this section's first reading. In a similar vein but only yesterday political scientist Robert H. Salisbury succinctly catalogued the generic service and structural problems of the modern major American city. The metropolitan area, he declared, is "riotously fragmented"; its fiscal policies and procedures "virtually medieval"; its physical plant "deteriorating"; and its commercial centers being strangled by traffic.[1]

However consensual and even well taken these jeremiads, they should not be allowed to obscure either the basic functional efficiency of the city or the organic, deeply rooted character of the weaknesses ascribed to it. The city is, of course, a huge concentration of people that as a whole achieves definite economies. One is the effect of the division of labor. Another is the "massing of reserves" on a scale that makes possible the eradication of disturbing chance factors. These economies apply to the individual plant, the localized industry, and the entire economy of the city. The demands of economical operation are seen reflected in the phenomenon of centering on the innermost zone, in the clustering of related businesses, in the location of business firms with reference to transportation going in and out of the city, the establishment of companies relative to the labor supply, and the scattering of businesses to be near their customers. It is an obscure pattern to be sure but a definite though unplanned order nonetheless.

And the configuration continues to change in accordance with its implicit dynamics. For example, in 1925 in the entire 22-county New York metropolitan region, 99 percent of the built-up residential area was within a mile of a railroad station. Since then the automobile has indeed given that "tentacled" arrangement a sprawling, weblike appearance in the New York area as well as in more than one other metropolitan community. In fact, as the urban region emerges with greater clarity, and creative federalism develops to coordinate urban affairs, the given city is slowly being absorbed into a more comprehensive order, leading Don Martindale to speculate that "The age of the city seems to be at an end."

Taken as an operational system with an output of regulatory and service functions, the big American city of today is understood more clearly if visualized against the background of the historical changes that have produced it. Economically, the city has witnessed the unfolding of the enterprise system through the stages of mercantile, industrial, finance, and governmental dominance. Technologically, it spans the transition from iron to steel and from water, coal, and oil as fuel to electricity and even nuclear energy. These suggest the complex structures interwoven into the urban fabric, which give the city both its handicaps and its opportunities.

The roots of American urban management lie deeply buried in our social system and its culture. For example, the machinery of checks and balances was carried over from the federal government into that of our cities, with the result that a mosaic of separate municipalities was further rent by a ponderous division of powers. Again, the relation of the citizen to government has been peculiarly American, in that government has been expected to be very responsive to the public and particularly that middle-class segment that has wanted impartiality, efficiency, personal honesty, and devotion to the "common good," even if substantive justice has suffered under the frequently used rule-of-thumb prohibiting municipal discretion, namely, "If there is no state law which says you can do it, you can't."

The history of municipal government in the United States reveals that there was a great deal of diversity in the colonial period when the inherited medieval-like arrangements were being slowly adapted to the circumstances of the New World. With the consolidation of state government following the War for Independence, the acceptance of the charter concept of city government, and the enfranchisement of new segments of the public, the older, controlling Federalist gentry quickly passed from the scene early in the nineteenth century. Soon under the influence of the new corporate elites city government was to become so debased that James Bryce was to deem it "the one conspicuous failure" of American democracy. This was attributable mainly to an unrestrained laissez-faire economy that did not hesitate to compromise the public welfare, and to a disinclination on the part of the public to see more than merely housekeeping services as properly constituting city government, while vital education, religious, and cultural activities were to be organized privately.

Ennervating anti-urban attitudes have been very pronounced in American culture and have further impeded urban progress. The physiocratic philosophy of the Jeffersonians, the patrician planters of the antebellum South, the New England transcendentalists, and the Western populists shared a strong antipathy for the city, its derivative people, and its mercenary practices. Urban America played no strong part in the early development of democracy and consequently earned no public esteem. It had been Boston and New York merchants rather than the townspeople themselves who had agitated for independence from Great Britain. Then the migration of masses of non-Protestant Europeans into our cities late in the nineteenth century tended to offset even the attractiveness that the new urban amenities had for the economically embattled countrymen of the post-Civil War agrarian distress. This only confirmed the already deeply lodged antipathy. However, it should not be ignored that the recognition that cities were essential to economic progress and national strength was born early and never really extinguished, even though the anti-urban bias might have the upper hand during most of our history. Its political Balkanization thus exists only as one among many significant handicaps under which the American city is forced to labor. Edward Banfield has observed another source of confusion in that in our system of municipal government the idea has been that either no one ought to govern or that everyone ought to govern together.[2] In Britain, on the other hand, deferential democracy has held that the voting public gives or withholds its consent from the authorities, but otherwise they exercise their prerogatives freely. The American interpretation of the democratic process has also given sanction to the expression of arbitrary, non-rational interests in politics. In a most suggestive article, "The Local Community as an Ecology of Games," Norton E. Long has made the point that the great "game" of local politics involves a variety of publics each of which has a real or imagined stake in the outcome of the process, except that for many the greatest concern lies in engaging in calculable strategies simply for their own sake.[3] Hence virtually everyone becomes a political participant and even though this gives the system some coordination it also infuses it with a large measure of the adventitious, for people play the game merely for the fun of it. As a result vital problems remain unresolved and even unidentified, for that matter. And rarely are comprehensive plans carried into effect, owing to the absence of enough governmental concentration to do so.

The generic social psychology of the urbanite has also been shown to be unwholesomely related to the composition and style of city politics. Lawrence J. R. Herson for one has written that alienation, disorientation, and group-dependence "are especially useful for their explanation of such vital aspects of urban politics as apathy toward the routine of government, the manipulative powers of the political machine, the urban dweller's unwillingness to experiment freely with the forms of his government, and his affinity for the colorful political leader." In fact, Herson concludes that urban politics is simply the product of the disorientation of urban man.[4]

In another inclusion in this section, Reinhold Wolff surveys the serious difficulties which led to the campaign to replace fragmentation with countywide government in the Miami area. That the process is still in its infancy and perhaps even abortive is suggested by the President's National Commission on Urban Problems. Appointed by Lyndon B. Johnson on January 12, 1967, and chaired by former Senator Paul H. Douglas of Illinois, the Commission was created to inquire into the effects of governmental disunity at the local level, particularly in its bearing on zoning authority and the enforcement of building codes and how, in turn, these thwart efforts to curb poverty and achieve greater social integration. The $1,500,000 study culminating in a 325,000 word report found that in 1967 America's urban areas consisted of 20,745 local governments, or an average of 48 per metropolitan county. The majority, added the report, ring the inner city and by virtue of their resistance to the poverty and minority problem only exacerbate the urban crisis.

If our cities are burdened by a political malaise, they are also less than prepossessing to the senses. Most observers agree no doubt with Norman Rice that cities constitute spectacles of "the smells, the offensive litter, the squalor, the inconsiderate small acts, the tangle of impatient traffic . . . the near view of so many badly conceived structures, the disorder of lights confusing warnings with merchandising, the out-of-control advertising, the grimy little corners and the great slums, which seem to be a part of the heritage of cities and which never quite are coped with in effective and permanent ways." Matthew Arnold's definition of culture as "acquaintance with the best that has been known and said in the world" is a standard unfortunately that beggars the city. True, isolated examples of urban splendor exist: the Acropolis, Paris' great boulevards, the bridges of Venice, the baroque magnificence of Dresden, Chicago's lake front, the Spanish steps in Rome banked with flowers, the stalls along the banks of the Seine, and the out-door art exhibits on the Boston Common. But how few and how remote from the average city where instead of proportion there is only size, instead of movement, confusion, and instead of mass, only irregularity. It is scarcely surprising that Frank Lloyd Wright despised the typical city, although no less an urban critic than Lewis Mumford refused to give up hope.[5] For him two things, language and the city, were "man's greatest work of art" and might yet come to fruition.

On two urban service problems there is great agreement—vehicular congestion and air and water pollution. These are described below by Francis Bello and Mitchell Gordon. They are universally acknowledged as undesirable and for the most part as remediable although, to be sure, the proposed remedies are in dispute, and whatever the programs envisioned the costs of implementing them appear to be huge.

The concentration of people into more densely inhabited areas continues. In 1950, 21.2 percent of the nation lived on the 1.8 percent of our continental land area that made up the Megalopolis of the northeast. Ten years later the same area had only 20.5 percent of the country's population. However, this number was now 37,000,000 persons instead of the previous 32,000,000. And the density per square mile had risen from 596 to 688. In fact, at the three corners of the country—the Washington-Boston corridor, the Florida Gold Coast, and the Los Angeles-San Diego conglomerate—32 percent of the American people were living in 1960 on less than 5 percent of the total land area of the United States. The congestion of traffic that these figures suggest is intense.

The distance from the center to the rim of our solar system measures 4 billion miles. Its circumference stretches some 22 billion miles. Robert Heilbronner has used these statistics as baselines for advancing the magnitude of our traffic problem, for even as long as ten years ago Americans were driving their cars and trucks 700 billion miles annually—not a little of it incidentally, looking for a place to park. Two million Americans were already, in fact, actually living on wheels, in trailers. By 1975, it is estimated, there will be more than 110,000,000 motor vehicles and their use will have risen more than their numbers. These data throw into relief the magnitude of the problems of providing roadways and parking space and of coping with the needs of servicing and junking so large a fleet and of dealing with the exhaust fumes they generate.

Though deplorable, the question of vehicular congestion in our cities is subject to some interpretation. It may, in fact, be less remediable than one might wish. Since 1945, when wartime tire and gas rationing prevented private transportation from being used fully, total mass transit use has declined 65 percent. This includes motor buses, surface railroad, subway and elevated railroad, and trolley cars. Economists at the Rand Corporation, however, have reached the conclusion that in our large cities the private automobile is competitive with other modes of transportation. And as for engineering a reduction in congestion via mass transit, the Minority Report of the House Committee on Banking and Currency, submitted July 3, 1962, points out that approximately 55 percent of the traffic of a transit system is carried in only 20 percent of the 24 hours of the day, that is, in the morning and late afternoon rush hours, a condition susceptible to alterations in scheduling working hours but not simply traffic engineering.

The contribution of the automobile to urban air pollution is significant although industry, of course, is another responsible factor. An indication of the extent to which our air is being poisoned may be obtained from figures compiled by the U. S. Public Health Service. In 1966 the average number of micrograms of smoke, dust, fumes, and droplets of viscuous liquid in the air was 22 for desert

country, 33 for forest, and 27 for mountainous elevations. By contrast it was typically 60–99 over cities of less than 50,000 population
and 100–139 for cities of 1,000,000 or more. In fact, America produces 1,500 pounds of air pollutants per person every year, or a
total rate of 142,000,000 tons a year. Similarly our assaults on the
ground and on our bodies of water continue, with our refuse, garbage, and other solid waste matter now exceeding 800,000,000
pounds every day. Apropos of this Tom Alexander observed, in
1968, "Despite spending some $3 billion annually on municipal ref-
use disposal, most U. S. cities have fallen behind, and most face genuine solid-waste crises within two to 15 years." The problems of
urban government and the management of its physical environment
cannot of course be utterly divorced from its other difficulties arising out of poverty, crime, inadequate education, strained intergroup relations, and the like. Nor do most thinkers attempt to separate them, whatever their own intellectual position may be.
Surveying the problems of metropolitan America, Frank P. Zeidler,
former mayor of Milwaukee, has taken a dim view of the future.
The growing strength of the suburban electorate will, he argues, be
expressed in the increasing concern of state government for suburban areas in opposition to the central cities. The concentration of
poor non-whites in the inner cities will continue, and there will be
increasing tension between the concepts of public ownership and social welfare, on the one hand, and private enterprise on the other.
The creation of more express highways through the big cities will
only favor suburban sprawl. Then as the tax base shrinks and the
school-age population expands, there will be renewed resistance in
the central cities to taxation for educational purposes. Although
tendencies to greater recognition of the legal rights of persons will
continue, the establishment of a polarized, segregated, bi-racial society will become increasingly more apparent.

In a rejoinder to Mayor Zeidler's forebodings, however, Wallace
S. Sayre emphasizes some constructive probabilities. First, that the
alliance of big-city electorates and the federal government can produce new resources and creative structures. Second, that the suburbs
may themselves face dire questions of taxation, zoning, congestion,
and blight, and consequently may find cooperation with the central
cities advantageous. And, third, that the cities may mobilize public
and private enterprise swiftly enough to arrest further deterioration. "I believe," Sayre has concluded, "the cities are on the move,
and . . . suburbia will, however reluctantly at first, follow in their
wake—for the suburbs, too, belong to urban America and must
soon see that nostalgia is less satisfying than common sense." [6]

33. THE PROBLEMS OF URBAN AMERICA

The Urbanism Committee of the National Resources Committee

Perhaps in the customary vein of American utopianism, although this survey was done during the Depression when conditions in the city, as elsewhere, were critical, the report on urbanism made to the National Resources Committee pointed out a broad range of maladjustments in our urban structures, particularly in their relationships to the national economy. The resulting catalogue of weaknesses or failures in the city's protective and regulatory processes remains instructive even today. Among the problems recognized thirty years ago that are still current, if not more aggravated yet, are those of environmental health—pollution, noise, and congestion; inadequate attention to recreation, beauty, renovation, and public improvements; and the improper location and use of both industry and transportation.

Despite the fact that the committee's report is principally an enumeration of deficiencies rather than a study in depth, the forces responsible for them tend to emerge clearly. These are unchecked private enterprise indifferent to the public interest, the multiplicity of governments so inimical to prompt action and cooperation, and rapid technological change coupled with a lag in the legal system making it difficult to plan effectively, avert undesirable consequences, and achieve optimal coordination.

IN THE WAKE OF THE PROCESS of urbanization, a series of maladjustments have bobbed up which militate against the attainment of a satisfactory urban life. The difficulties now confronting the urban community not only prevent the city from making the maximum contribution to our na-

Reprinted from *Our Cities, Their Role in the National Economy* (1937), United States Government Printing Office.

tional economy, but in some instances they actually menace urban existence. . . .

. . . the city is a delicate mechanism which can be thrown out of gear and demoralized at a number of vulnerable points.

How hazardous a place the city can be is indicated by events in time of epidemic, storm, accident, conflagration, war, internal strife, sabotage, strike, or flood. . . . Even in normal times, the breakdown of an electric power station or a transmission line may paralyze the city. A subway accident leaves hundreds of thousands stranded. The bursting of an important water main leaves a whole section of the city without water and exposes it to the hazards of conflagration. The fact that these and other difficulties do not arise more often is a tribute to the smooth functioning of our technology, but when they do happen the effects are swift and serious. . . .

. . . .

DANGERS TO PUBLIC HEALTH

The provision of adequate public-health services is a significant problem of urban life. While urban morbidity and mortality rates in such fields as infants' diseases and tuberculosis compare favorably with the rural rates, in blighted areas and among low-income groups in the city the rates are higher than they would be with adequate, modern, public-health services.

The difficulties of urban public-health regulation are not merely financial, but they involve such irrational and incongruous factors as group selfishness and prudishness. Only under a fearless program recently launched with Federal aid have we deigned to admit the vast prevalence of syphilis and to attack it on a national scale with direct cooperation between the Public Health Service and the cities. It should be possible to restrict within much narrower bounds the common cold so easily transmitted in an urban environment, and its associated diseases of influenza and pneumonia.

DIRT, SMOKE, AND WASTE

Inimical also to the public health are the polluting effects of industrial waste and urban waste in general. In spite of valiant efforts to enforce smoke abatement ordinances, the belching chimneys of factories, office buildings, and apartment houses fill the air with smoke injurious to the respiratory organs, and are inducing neo-modern man to take refuge in air-conditioned buildings. Soot and grime settle on buildings, dirt blackens the streets, and dust seeps into the homes. Garbage, considering the size of the task, is generally well disposed of, but it sometimes piles up in alleys and in outlying dumps, with extremely noxious if not unhealthful consequences. One or a few misplaced industries emitting obnoxious odors at times pollute the air of large sections of the city. Worse still, communities and industries often dump their wastes untreated into the source of the water supply where regulation and legal powers are not adequate to prevent this, or where conflicting State, county, and city boundaries encourage it, with the result that drinking water must be so highly treated with purifying agents as to be nearly unpalatable. The usefulness of many bodies of water is destroyed for much needed recreational purposes as a result of pollution.

NOISE AND STRAIN

The large city and especially its central business district is so characteristically a place of noise that a sudden wave of silence frequently proves to be oppressive to the urbanite for he is accustomed to distracting sounds of all kinds. Screeching brakes, screaming trolley cars, rumbling trucks, rasping auto horns, barking street vendors, shouting newsboys, scolding traffic whistles, rumbling elevated trains, rapping pneumatic hammers, open cut-outs, and now advertising sound trucks and aircraft with radio amplifiers, when added together, constitute a general din for which it would be difficult to find a precedent in the history of cities.

. . .

INADEQUATE RECREATIONAL FACILITIES

The most obvious problem in urban recreation arises out of a lack of sufficient space for play and recreation in some cities and, still more, out of the poor distribution and the consequent ineffectiveness of existing recreational areas in many more cities. This difficulty is due mainly to the failure of municipal authorities to realize the need for recreational facilities until after the cities were built up. As a result, the establishment of adequate parks and playgrounds in the congested sections of cities is made prohibitive by the high cost of land in such districts.

Another emerging problem is that of providing the type of cultural services suitable to a city population which is growing "older" and which is coming to have more leisure time at its disposal. Music, art, light opera, movies, and the theater have not played a large part in the public recreation programs of the past, but with some notable precedents going back to the pre-war period and with the stimulus of the Federal arts, music and theater projects, these forms of recreation may become more widely incorporated into the recreational programs of American cities.

. . .

CONGESTION

The problem of urban congestion arises from the fact that as the city spreads out at its periphery it almost invariably also rises at the center. The skyscraper is a visible symbol of this congestion. As it fills and empties, the streets and traffic facilities, which were designed for smaller cities and lower buildings, are no longer able to carry the load without friction and delays. The extensive remodeling of these facilities to bring them again in scale with the new and greatly more intensive use of private property is inordinately expensive in most cases. For it is precisely at the center, where the region-wide functions of the city are concentrated, where the daily ebb and flow of the human tides converge and where the acquisition of every foot of additional space involves high land costs and building damages, that this remodeling is most needed and space is at a premium.

While the elimination of congestion would involve enormous costs, the aggregate cost of permitting this congestion in our cities to continue represents an imposing waste. Traffic delays where speed and promptness are at a premium, overcrowding of sites and buildings, dark and badly ventilated dwellings and offices, overtaxing of public facilities and services, deficiency in public open space combined with a surplus of unused private open space, undue concentration of land values, and unfair apportionment of the local tax burden—these and other detriments to urban well-being are present in varying degrees in practically every American city. These conditions generally accompany the type of urban growth which is characterized by uninterrupted accretion at the periphery and increasingly more intensive building development, concentration, and congestion in the center, seldom relieved for long, but rather aided and abetted by subways, traffic lights, one-way streets, and the staggering of office hours.

One of the most serious consequences of traffic congestion at the center of urban areas and of the high-speed radial traffic to their outskirts is the increasing rate of street-traffic accidents and the appalling number of fatalities. These constitute a hazard in present-day city life comparable in some respects with the plagues of old.

DISPERSION

Just as extreme concentration is wasteful, so is extreme dispersion. The suburbanite aims to escape at least some of the disadvantages of living in the densely built city but by coming to the central city to earn his living, he creates new problems of overcentralization. The advantages of residen-

tial dispersion are coupled with the disadvantages of atomized administrative areas which tend to break up urban regions into suburban bailiwicks and dormitories independent of the central city.

The real difficulty with the dispersive tendencies of suburbanization
and other centrifugal movements lies in the lack of planning and the consequent waste in public facilities, services, and the use of urban land and
space. Urban expansion being left largely to the whim of the subdivider,
discontinuous, sporadic, suburban settlements or ribbon developments
along the highways, with large undeveloped interstices between them,
greatly increase the cost and difficulties of providing the essential public
facilities and services. . . .

EXPLOITATION OF URBAN LAND

Gambling in land values has contributed to alternate booms and depressions, raising false hopes, encouraging over-ambitious structures, wiping
out private investors, and, all in all, has been one of the major tragedies
of American urban life. Inflated valuations have contributed to vertical
expansion and over-intensive land utilization, with the result that the
private use of land has far outgrown public facilities and services, including water, sewerage, health, police and fire protection, street and transit
facilities, and has created all sorts of congestion.

The dispersive developments of recent years have left blighted vacu-
ums in the interiors of our cities and have themselves been vitiated by
land prices at a level too high to permit a desirable standard of urban development. Boom subdividing has resulted in paper streets with impossible grades and unintelligent gridiron patterns, as well as unneccessary or
premature and poorly planned subdivisions.

. . .

The basic problem . . . is not private exploitation alone but also our
failure to realize that the tenure and use of urban land are matters of urgent public concern; that a larger measure of protection for socially beneficial private uses and of public ownership of land would be in the public
interest; that orderly and speedy reform is essential to the present well-
being and future progress of our cities; and that few of these reforms can
be worked out on an exclusively local scale but require new principles
and policies in urban land economics, country-wide in effect and expressed through State, local, and, perhaps, even through national
legislation.

. . .

OBSOLESCENCE

In the United States generally and, especially, in our cities, there appears to be more obsolescence and demolition of equipment than would seem to be called for in a relatively new country. In an amazingly brief period, as compared with other Nations, American villages have become towns and the towns cities, other cities and towns have become decaying mill sites or ghost towns. Brick houses succeeded frame, apartment hotels replaced residences, office buildings followed shops and lofts, garages of one story were succeeded by garages of several stories, inns have been turned into grand hotels, and the early "cloud scratchers" of the last generation have been torn down to make room for colossal skyscrapers. Cobble-stone and wood-block roads have been replaced by concrete, single tracks have given way to double tracks, and double tracks have soon been transformed by the advent of motorbuses into silent and useless reminders of the trolley age and the days of the suburban and interurban electric lines.

The explanation for this unprecedented rate of obsolescence lies partly in the rapid growth and spread of population and enterprise which in swift succession overtaxed and outmoded existing facilities; in the existence of over-abundant natural resources which discouraged conservation and put a premium on waste; in the rapid but careless workmanship and, as a result, quickly-depreciating construction; in the lack of community stability characteristic of the frontier; in the lack of planning and zoning control which permitted owners to lay out and use their land as they saw fit; and in the general lack of regard for the interest of the community in favor of personal and material gain.

If this unreasonable waste of our physical plant and equipment could but remain physical in its consequences, this problem of obsolescence in American life might prove less serious. But it has had its effects in the disorganization of production, the wastes of unemployment, the destruction of skills, the discouragements to thrift, and the cumulative disregard of community appearance and community values.

UNATTRACTIVE APPEARANCE

Uninspiring buildings, vacant and neglected land parcels, ugly billboards and lack of architectural consistency are characteristic of many American cities. Architectural style may be difficult to regulate, but that it is possible and practicable to do so is evident from European experience. The beautiful cities of the Old World and the few planned cities of America have not become so by accident. They have been deliberately modeled according to well-conceived patterns not only in matters of construction and safety but also in matters of design.

In America we have not given so much attention to the physical attractiveness of cities. Nor have we done much to stimulate among our people an appreciation of beautiful architectural form and civic design. There is practically no effective regulation nor is there an adequate body of custom which would compel owners to conform to the architectural style of the neighborhood. Likewise owners of vacant land are not made to keep their property sightly, let alone to offer these unused areas for recreational or other public purposes. On the contrary, normally there is an attempt to capitalize the space for advertising and cheaply constructed structures of unattractive appearance. While of late years zoning ordinances and building codes have somewhat mitigated this evil, in most of our cities ugly sights and ungainly structures still remain in all too many places.

DISLOCATION OF INDUSTRY

One of the principal urban problems is the articulation of the industries of the community into a structure which will secure the maximum employment of the available labor supply, the minimizing of seasonal and cyclical fluctuations of the total employed payroll of the community, the optimum use of the advantages of location from the standpoint of raw materials and markets, and a balance between the cost of community services to industry and the income derived by the community from industry.

Lacking an appreciation of the need for a selective program of industrial development, communities have attracted and subsidized enterprises without adequate attention to their effects upon the total industrial structure. Too frequently, the test has been not the qualitative test of the effect upon the various parts of the community's industrial mechanism, but the quantitative test of increasing the total amount of industrial activity at the time the new enterprise is established. A poorly balanced local industrial structure throws the entire industrial front out of joint by causing migration of labor, unemployment, lower wages, curtailed purchasing power, less trading business, lower living standards, high cost of relief, high taxes, tax delinquency, untenanted property, stagnation of building enterprises, obsolescence of community plant and depreciation of industrial equipment.

· · ·

INADEQUATE CONTROL OVER TRANSPORT

In addition to industry, the transportation network and the rate structure of the country contributed to the maladjustments in the national urban pattern and urban life. Located principally on natural waterways, the early American cities were soon subjected to the disrupting effects of competing forms of transportation. During the canal era, cities rose up along the new water routes, leaving more mature but less favored places to decay along the old routes. When the railroads came, these canal cities frequently met, in their turn, a similar fate. Then came more railroads, and the rivalries between cities took the form of subsidies, railroad construction by cities themselves, and cutthroat rate reduction.

The consequences were cumulative. Failure of railroads to obtain business on one line led to frantic construction to tap new areas. The tapping of new areas brought about new urban centers which attracted new lines and sought to attract more lines. But the end of this process has not yet been reached. The motortruck and passenger bus are not only cutting into the business of the railways, but they are beginning to influence both the national urban pattern and the local and regional urban structure.

We can only speculate on what may happen as a result of airway development and long-distance electric-power transmission, but unless a less competitive policy is adopted in all these fields, either through private initiative or public regulation, the history of earlier forms of transport may be repeated. Urban communities will attract new forms and facilities of transportation, power, and communication, and largely in the hands of these newer technological developments will lie the cities' future.

· · ·

TRANSPORTATION TERMINALS

The present multiplicity of terminals in urban areas arises from the same competitive practices between transport agencies which characterizes our entire transportation system. Many of these terminals are located in congested central areas. The number of railroad freight stations alone is, for example, as high as 700 in the Philadelphia district.

The fact that in 1932 almost three-fourths of all railway traffic terminated in urban areas, and that over one-third (37 percent) of the total railroad freight operating expenses in 1932 consisted of terminal costs, indicates the importance of the terminal problem from the standpoint of the national and urban economy. The transportation companies, the shippers, and governmental authorities are cognizant of this aspect of the terminal problem but have not adequately appreciated the broader relations between terminals and urban community structure and development as a whole. The location and operation of terminal facilities have profoundly influenced the development of our urban communities, and any major changes in these facilities and their operations are bound to have a material effect on the future physical development of our cities and metropolitan regions.

· · ·

URBAN TRANSIT

Like transportation and terminal facilities, so urban transit and the policies and practices pursued in matters of rates and services, ownership, public regulation, location, and operation, have played a prominent part in determining the development of urban communities and regions. The growth of the urbanized area, the distribution of population and economic activities, land use, land values and the intensity of building development have all been materially influenced by local transit facilities. There is ample evidence to indicate that in spite of the new mobility which came with the general use of the private motor vehicle, the pattern of development of our urban areas still bears the marked imprint of our past transit policies and practices which gave little or no consideration to the interest of the community as a whole. . . .

URBAN PLANNING AND ZONING

Although city planning and zoning as practiced during the past 20 years has, by and large, been beneficial, it has fallen short of expectations and potentialities. It has been, and still is, handicapped by a combination of obstacles, the removal of which is held to be fundamental to really effective and successful urban planning and zoning.

To begin with, city planning bodies lack sufficient legal powers to guide effectively the physical, social, and economic structure of the community through the instrumentality of a comprehensive plan broadly construed. They are subject to uninformed official and public opinion which does not fully appreciate the great importance of community planning. They often encounter jealousy and even opposition on the part of administrative departments. They suffer from insufficient appropriations and a scarcity of competent technical planning personnel. They are themselves sometimes at fault, because they lack sincere interest and vigor in performing their task of which they often have but a limited understanding or a narrow view.

Even where legal powers and planning practices are most advanced, local planning agencies seldom have even advisory authority over *all* public works projects within the area under their jurisdiction, but are limited to projects of their own local government. Nor do they have such authority over the facilities of transportation, transit, and utility agencies, except when the proposed changes directly affect a public facility or public property. Their powers over the layout of real estate subdivisions are inadequate to be fully effective and they are without authority to regulate the quantity of such subdivision developments. In general, local planning agencies need stronger and wider authority in order to exercise jurisdiction over all matters relating to community development, and, where a county or regional planning agency does not exist, not only within the municipal boundaries, but over the entire area now urbanized or likely to become so and as much of the region beyond as bears relation to the proper development of the urban community itself.

. . .

LAG IN PUBLIC IMPROVEMENTS

Urban communities have shown a widespread need for the stimulation of public works and facilities. The difficulties of urban public improvement programs arise first from the historic practice of cities to dispose of their land holdings for a pittance only to be compelled in many cases to buy them back later for their own use at exorbitant prices. The problem of financing public improvements has been only partially relieved by Federal grants and loans recently made available for worthy or self-liquidating public works. The planning of public works has also been neglected both locally, as part of the city plan, and nationally, as part of a broad program for increasing employment directly and for stimulating industrial activity during slump periods.

An additional difficulty has been the existence of a number of overlapping and coordinate governmental authorities in the urban region. Each of these authorities may have a veto power over essential improvements, such as roads, sewers, and sewage disposal plants, and may be unprepared to proceed when all the others are able and willing to do so. . . . City and county, school board and special district, State and Federal Governments almost invariably pursue their land purchasing, construction, or rental policies irrespective of the needs of the others, regardless of the increased bargaining strength of a joint program and apparently unaware of the symbolic and practical values of a single, planned community center for all governmental buildings.

. . .

LEGAL OBSTRUCTIONS TO PHYSICAL IMPROVEMENT

Attempts at improving the physical environment in the city have been blocked at almost every step by the restrictive provisions of State laws, by inadequate grants of power to local governments and by adverse court decisions. In the case of billboard regulation, for example, after some hesitancy about sustaining regulatory ordinances on the basis of the police power, the courts have for years frowned upon regulations which were defended chiefly on aesthetic grounds until in 1935 the Massachusetts Supreme Court upheld an ordinance based purely upon such considerations.

Similarly, the acquisition of land by municipalities has been hampered by narrow legal interpretations of "public use" and of the power to condemn for public use, complex and over-technical eminent domain and land acquisition statutes and procedures, restrictions on excess condemnation, and the absence of a single real estate office within the city government.

Physical improvement programs have also been handicapped by the weaknesses of general property tax administration, uncalled-for tax differentials and exemptions, overburdening special assessments, tax limitations, and slow and inefficient assessment procedures. Even private land transfers are subject to frequently cumbersome and usually expensive procedures and to complex laws relating to title registration, title insurance, mortgage foreclosure and sales of tax delinquent property.

INADEQUATE GOVERNMENTAL POWERS

In contrast to the rapidly increasing responsibilities and services of urban governments, their legal powers are relatively stationary. Legally, the city is the creature of the State, and in practice the city must contend with all sorts of meddlesome State statutory details or conversely with statutory gaps which prove judicially fatal when the city embarks upon new programs. All ranges of urban activity, from petty questions of administrative procedure to general questions of urban policy, are determined by State law. Between 1896 and 1936 the number of Supreme Court cases, State and Federal, involving the exercise of municipal powers, has increased fourfold, and one-third of these cases have been decided against the city. Even constitutional home rule over municipal affairs, though it has been adopted in 18 States, has become a waning movement, and where it has been adopted, courts have, on the whole, tended to construe the grant of municipal powers more narrowly than was expected.

. . .

GOVERNMENTAL DISORGANIZATION OF
METROPOLITAN REGIONS

As has already been pointed out, the process of urbanization has brought larger aggregates of population and wider areas within the orbit of a central dominant city. In continuing to treat the city as a municipal corporation, however, we have obviously allowed the realities of today to be obscured by the artificial and often arbitrary administrative boundaries which are a heritage of the past. Taking only the largest urban areas, i.e., the 96 metropolitan districts containing 55 millions of people or 45 percent of our total population, it is found that the urban governmental system of these districts consists of a bewildering maze of overlapping authorities and of a growing number of suburban and satellite cities.

The multiplicity of governments in the metropolitan areas is best indicated by the fact that, besides a very large number of overlapping authorities, in 1930 there were 272 separate incorporated places in the New York–Northeastern New Jersey metropolitan district, 135 in the Pittsburgh district, 115 in the Chicago area, 92 in the Philadelphia district, and 56 in the Los Angeles district. Together with their over-layers of counties, townships, school districts, sanitary districts, sewer districts, library districts, health districts, park districts, forest preserve districts, street lighting districts, utility districts, water districts, and even mosquito-abatement districts—each of them a separate body politic and corporate —these communities present an odd picture of independent bailiwicks performing related or even identical governmental functions with some degree of cooperation, but with a great degree of competition for municipal revenues, for administrative prestige and for legal powers. Frequently, these districts are too small in area or have insufficient tax resources to support essential public services. All this governmental duplication, confusion and localism are in sharp contrast to the obvious disregard of the network of urban boundary lines by epidemics which complicate urban health work, by criminals who are not stopped by city limits, and by the city and suburban users of highways and transportation facilities who seldom know or care about the maze of political boundaries in metropolitan districts.

The whole problem is aggravated by the customary legal difficulties in applying the earlier, and now unusual, solutions of annexation, consolidation, and federation of metropolitan authorities and suburbs, and in utilizing the more frequent and current devices of special metropolitan authorities, intermunicipal and extra-territorial contractual and functional relations, and interstate and Federal arrangements.

. . .

In their daily or periodic contacts the inhabitants of the metropolitan region, irrespective of municipal, township, county, State, or even national lines, are bound together into a community through industry, public utilities, social and cultural institutions, an interdependent system of transportation and communication, the newspaper, radio, telephone, and postal service, if not through a sense of social solidarity and common interests arising out of common problems. The greatest obstacle to the full emergence of a metropolitan community is the great number of conflicting and overlapping political and administrative units into which the area is divided.

. . .

LACK OF URBAN INFORMATION

In the course of its study, this Committee was continually faced with serious shortcomings in available urban information in the official Federal statistics concerning cities. These deficiencies were apparent in the narrow scope of subjects covered, in the variations in content interfering with comparability of the data from year to year, in the lack of continuity of publication in the unequal periods reported, in the decreasing number of cities covered, in the small number of topics treated during any one year making correlation difficult, and in the use of the area of the city corporate as a unit for the collection of data, instead of including also the urbanized region, thus failing to tell the complete story for the actual city or metropolitan district.

. . .

DISUNITY OF THE CITY

Fundamentally, the United States is suffering from a lack of balance between the urban economy and the entire national economy, between the city and the country, and between the various aspects of urban life itself.

One of our basic urban problems consists of the widespread neglect of cities as a major segment of national existence, the consequent derision of urban politics and depreciation of urban administration as a career, and the cumulative disregard of the city hall as a principal center of American urban life. Indicative of this neglect is the fact that, although the United States has been a predominantly urban nation for more than two decades, this report of the National Resources Committee is the first inquiry on a national, official, and comprehensive scale into the problems of the American urban community.

34. THE CURSE OF MULTIPLICITY

Reinhold P. Wolff

*As survivors from a less interdependent past, multiple governments
continue to plague metropolitan areas with the problems of unequal taxation, inefficient and ineffective services, costly industrial competition,
and an inability to undertake comprehensive planning. The case against
faulty community structure which Reinhold Wolff presents below is
Miami, Florida. He shows that this metropolitan area has long been
handicapped by inadequate intergovernmental cooperation and insufficient coordination of effort. In 1957 areawide metropolitan government
was finally inaugurated in Miami's Dade County but only after decades
of vital neglect, conflict, and piecemeal attempts to achieve functional
unity.*

*The history of unification in metropolitan Miami embraced many of
the devices that any number of similarly beset cities have employed: uniform legislation, partial unification, voluntary cooperation between business firms and municipalities, transfer of city institutions to the county,
regional compacts, and areawide planning. The county manager type of
government initiated under Metro in south Florida began modestly by
centralizing administration in zoning and building, public works, and
traffic management. Even so a referendum movement to restore local autonomy was only narrowly defeated at the polls.*

ALL TOO OFTEN GENERALIZED COMPLAINTS about too many governments
fail to distinguish between those tensions which spring from a desirable
diversity of interests and functions and those that are the result of a
faulty community structure.[1] Unfortunately, Miami had a good many

Excerpts from *Miami Metro, The Road to Urban Unity* by Reinhold P. Wolff (1960).
Reprinted by permission of the University of Miami and the author.

conflicts of the latter type. While its urban structure was less splintered than that of numerous other large cities,[2] there were still many frictions and areas of dispute among its 26 separate municipal authorities. Often these led to open conflict which greatly hindered the business life of the community and the social life of its citizens. Tax inequalities, inadequate and inefficient services, lack of overall planning, can all be blamed on the jumble of local governmental agencies.

Municipal borderlines were established at a time when the towns were isolated places, many of them small in size. Now they have lost their meaning; new settlements have filled in the area between and around them. As a consequence, the circuits of fire and police patrols, the routes of refuse collection, the sewer systems are often crisscrossed, overlapping and ineffectual.[3] Traffic flow along major thoroughfares is impeded by divided jurisdiction of controls.[4] Suburbs of unequal size and uneven income distribution have upset the balance of taxes and complementary services. Competition arises between individual suburbs for attracting trade and industry without regard to the overall needs of the community, and parasitic developments are encouraged where areas without sufficient facilities exploit services offered by the better equipped places. The diversity of interests has often prevented necessary action on a community wide level, and frequently cities have failed to cooperate in matters where the metropolitan area should offer a common front to preserve its interests in dealing with state and federal agencies. It has been pointed out that these matters were of great annoyance to individual business interests, but they also had fargoing consequences for the whole community structure, and thus forced the hands of public officials.

1. Inequity of Taxation, Inequality of Services

Communal taxation, even under the most ideal circumstances, will not be completely equal and equitable. The scale of most city taxes is based on property values, not on income. Regardless of his individual income the resident of a high-class housing area pays a higher tax than the one residing in an area of popular priced homes. In turn, he expects better municipal service which he hopes will contribute to a higher value of his property. Usually we shall find in such communities opposition to centralization and equalization, since residents are understandably opposed to having services in their areas curtailed, or to having their wealth used to lift standards of service in the poorer municipalities.

Of course, high taxation and a high level of service do not always go hand in hand. The fragmentation of the municipal structure has led to overlapping jurisdictions and confusion of services. The citizen often pays high taxes to several bodies and still does not reap the reward of adequate services from any. Conversely, residents of certain areas are benefited by services for which they pay no or inadequate taxes. Besides the injustice to the individual citizen, these conditions have resulted in harmful municipal quarrels. Thus demands for unification of services and taxes have some important backing even in the wealthier communities.

DUPLICATE TAXATION

A favorable subject of criticism in Miami is the duplicate tax structure. Residents of the incorporated places pay a double property tax, namely a county tax plus a municipal levy. On the other hand, residents of unincorporated areas pay only one tax to the county. This led eventually to double standards of taxation for identical situations. Originally this condition was fair to the taxpayer because the unincorporated places were rural areas in which the common municipal services were not available. However, as larger portions of the unincorporated areas became urbanized, the county was forced to give at least a modicum of service, such as refuse collection, police and fire protection, and street maintenance. Yet the county did not obtain a compensating increase in taxes on anything like the scale collected by the municipalities.

Most likely the inequity of the situation is exaggerated in the public mind. Actually, in the Miami area, the bulk of county tax revenue is expended for schools, welfare services and other countywide benefits. The aid extended to the unincorporated areas in terms of specific local services is comparatively small. The county allots only 9.5 per cent of its total expenditures for public safety, and 9.4 per cent for public works, and not all of this goes to the unincorporated areas. These sums amount to about $10.00 per capita for municipal residents. Be that as it may, the argument has certainly helped to sharpen the conflicts between the municipalities and the county, and has supplied ammunition both to the advocates and to the opponents of metropolitan government.

Along the same line of attack is the argument that the cities which are able to make higher contributions to the county treasury in the form of greater ad valorem taxes do not receive a quid pro quo for their larger payment. The city of Miami Beach, for instance, which in 1957 held 7.2 per cent of the population, contributed 26.2 per cent of all property taxes collected in the county. By contrast, Hialeah, which contained 6.1 per cent of the population, paid only 2.6 per cent of the property tax. In some of the beach communities the per capita ad valorem tax reaches enormous proportions. In Bal Harbour, for instance, $1,467 is contributed per capita to the county treasury (in addition to $409 per capita to the local taxing authority), and in the small Indian Creek Village $1,150 per capita per annum goes to the county (plus $500 per capita to the village).[5]

It has been argued that such differentiation in tax payments goes far beyond a "fair" or "normal" degree of gradation. Usually, the argument breaks out in public debate when capital improvements in specific locations are to be undertaken, or special services for certain areas are demanded. The high taxed communities, conscious of the uneven spread of the tax load, oppose such expenditures unless they benefit their own areas.

.   .   .

SPECIAL FEES

In the Miami area the search for new tax sources often caused high charges against non-residents. Some of the communities have obtained unusually high revenue from specific taxes, service charges and fees outside the property tax. Hialeah Gardens in 1957 obtained $192 per capita from fines and forfeitures, largely speeding violations. This was in excess of the total per capita receipts of Miami Beach! The city of Bal Harbour drew high revenue from franchise taxes and business licenses. El Portal has twice as much revenue from fines and forfeitures as from the property tax. The city of Coral Gables received a high per capita income from waste disposal fees. Many of these fees and fines fall on persons who are non-residents but who do business in the area or travel through the area as motorists. The need for unification of traffic rules, motor car inspection and traffic police became one of the strongest arguments for Metro and one of the first reform attempts.

PARASTIC USE OF SERVICES

The inequality of urban service in the city and its fringe areas has led to many parasitic uses of city services by non-tax paying residents of unincorporated areas. It is alleged that the taxpayers in the cities have to support facilities used by residents of non-contributing municipalities or unincorporated places. While some part of this type of parasitic development is probably unavoidable it was bound to reach major proportions in an area in which better than half of the population lives outside the core city, and one-third outside of any incorporated boundaries. Many of the smaller suburbs of Miami have inadequate police forces, inadequate fire prevention programs, no systems for refuse collection and disposal, and very few cultural facilities such as libraries, art galleries and the like.

Typical is the situation with regard to fire protection. A number of the large cities have comprehensive fire prevention programs and consequently enjoy relatively low insurance rates on fire insurance of private residences, business offices and the like. Other cities have only small departments which do not have the necessary resources to carry out effective fire prevention programs. Many of the worst fire hazards in the country are located either in small towns or in unincorporated areas where they are subject to practically no inspection or control, and therefore constitute a very dangerous situation. Naturally, the better equipped city departments are often called to put out fires in areas where no adequate fire protection exists. In order to assist the smaller cities and unincorporated areas, "mutual aid" agreements have been negotiated among most jurisdictions, but these agreements are not really mutual since practically all of the service is rendered by the larger and better equipped departments. They bear the brunt of the burden for fire protection and deplete their own fire fighting resources in the process.

Similar situations exist with respect to police control, refuse collection and cultural establishments. Their advantages are enjoyed by many non-tax paying residents of the unincorporated areas. Of course, situations of this kind are common in any multi-patterned set-up; but they furnish strong arguments for equalization of taxes and charges, and at the same time cause resistance to centralization on the part of the beneficiaries.

Metro was expected to alleviate the conflicts resulting from this disparity of taxes and services.

2. Divided Jurisdictions

In purely local matters, the small municipality is considered the ideal form of government because it brings the citizen closer to his neighbors. The New England town meeting, we teach our children, was democracy at its best. In our densely settled urban communities, however, there are fewer and fewer "local" matters left, and interdependency of adjacent suburbs supplies an overriding argument for centralization of many functions. The street system is integrated with a system of thoroughfares, main arteries and throughways for the entire urban area. Utilities such as water supply plants and waste disposal systems are economical only if operated on a large scale and coordinated in their local service subsidiaries. Even zoning systems and building codes must tie in with the overall pattern of land use for the whole area in order to establish a meaningful order of residential and commercial development—and so it goes with one local function after another.

The road system of the urbanized area, laid out at a time when the city was hardly the size of a little town, proved entirely inadequate when Miami grew into a full metropolis—this despite the fact that Miami's street pattern was designed in an era during which city builders were already familiar with the needs of a motorized age. Even in downtown Miami, city streets are wider, thoroughfares more numerous than they are in many of the older cities built up in the pre-motor era. Still, divided jurisdictions over roads between the central city, the unincorporated areas, and the many smaller municipalities led to innumerable difficulties. Whenever street widening of thoroughfares became necessary, or new roadways had to be planned, these difficulties arose.

Also smaller municipalities insisted on their right of providing un-impeded access to thoroughfares in the interests of business lying in strips alongside the access roads. Unreasonably low speed limits and close se-quence of traffic lights on thoroughfares passing through a town were in-tended to slow down the traffic on shopping streets. One may suspect that the intention was to entice "buying at home." Parking in front of the stores is allowed in most suburban business centers, and the right of way on both sides of the road narrowed. Most plans for throughways, limited access highways and causeways are stalled by objections on the part of some of the participating suburbs. Typical was the objection of a few small beach communities to the building of a state highway across Bis-cayne Bay along 36th Street, which caused a delay of nearly twenty years in the effectuation of this much needed improvement. It would be wrong to assume that the absence of freeways in the Miami area is entirely due to divided jurisdiction, but it is correct to state that such division played a large part in blocking their arrival.

Water supply problems sprang from the inability of the smaller munic-ipalities to provide their own plants. These communities are dependent on the water supply system of the city of Miami, and great inequalities in cost of city water result to citizens of the dependent areas. In the supervi-sion of water rates, the absence of uniform policy resulted in situations that border on the absurd. Private water systems which supply those areas with water had to justify their rate structure by cost elements within a single small municipality, although their cost structure as a whole ob-viously depended on operations throughout the entire area. On the other hand, there were sections in which companies could charge high rates— often had to charge high rates—because of the small size of operations.

Most of the municipalities in Greater Miami are too small to maintain garbage and sewage disposal plants of their own. Again, the lack of city sewers, resulting in the pollution of Biscayne Bay by waste indiscrimi-nately diverted into bay water, cannot entirely be blamed on divided ju-risdictions. There is no doubt, however, that the lack of a uniform waste disposal policy is in part due to the absence of a municipal control body.

One of the greatest sources of confusion and annoyances to the citizen was the multiplicity of the transit systems, some privately owned and some operated by the municipalities. Streetcar systems, later on replaced by buses, originated at a time when the life of each community was cen-tered on its own downtown business district. As the built up area ex-tended beyond city limits, buses picked up and delivered passengers out-side the city proper, and the system as a whole became rather important as a service to the fringe communities. Since most systems are not coordinated with each other, the bus passenger who travels from one end of the Miami area to the other has frequently to shift between two or even three different buses and to pay as many fares. Often adjacent neighborhoods in the outskirts do not have any bus connections. Naturally, the lack of public conveyance facilities increased the percentage of automobile ownership, and indirectly contributed to the traffic congestion in the built up area. In a vicious circle, it also led to operational deficits of bus companies due to infrequent use of the ineffective bus system.

In probably no other field has the conflict of jurisdiction been felt as sharply as in the field of zoning and planning. The lack of comprehensive planning was a key point for many businessmen, and was equally important for the average citizen. Because of uncoordinated zoning many of the upper-class subdivisions, towns and municipalities, such as the resort communities on the east of Biscayne Bay, failed to provide areas for municipal service such as garbage or sewage disposal, cemeteries, districts for colored residents, and other low income sections. For instance, because of the unwritten law of separate areas for Whites and Negroes, Negro service workers of large hotels are banned from living in the neighborhoods close to their places of employment. They have to commute from the municipalities on the west side of Biscayne Bay at great expense in money and time. Miami Beach has no Negro areas, nor have the other beach communities. There are no adequate waste disposal facilities east of the Bay, and no cemeteries. Certain municipalities even refused to make land available for schools, which they consider a nuisance to residential living.

Naturally, such restrictive policies were resented by neighboring municipalities and by the county which has to provide the services for the towns which were not willing to shoulder their own responsibilities. Even in Coral Gables there is only a minimum area where Negro occupancy is tolerated; a sewage disposal plant had to be installed on the University of Miami campus because there was no other place to put it.

Metro was voted in with the expectation that a coordination of planning by the new government would lead to a more meaningful arrangement of service facilities, eliminating duplication in some areas and providing needed additions in others.

3. Cut-Throat Competition for Industry

Thirty years ago when most of the Miami suburbs were still in their infancy, competition started to develop for the lucrative tourist trade. To what extent the shift of the relative center of tourism from Miami to Miami Beach was due to promotional efforts of the city of Miami Beach, and to what extent it was the consequence of a natural development which drove tourism towards the oceanshore, may be a matter of debate.

Indications are that while Miami was in dire financial straits after the bottom dropped out of Florida's land surge, the city of Miami Beach, a high rent area with larger financial resources, was able to initiate a strong city supported campaign for the tourist dollar.

In both cities tax money has been liberally used to support efforts to promote the name of the community as a resort place, to attract conventions and to extend the winter tourist season into the spring and summer. Characteristically, both cities used their chambers of commerce as tourist information centers and subsidized these activities with municipal revenue; both established separate convention bureaus and vied competitively for the meetings of national groups. While the tourist dollar benefited all of Dade County's residents through higher incomes from retailing, wholesaling, and other tourist connected industries, other municipalities were reluctant to contribute to tourist facilities established on Miami Beach. Conversely, the beach communities showed little love for promotional efforts to establish an international trade center, the so-called Interama, because the latter was to be built on the west side of Biscayne Bay. The citizens of Miami and Miami Beach could not even get together on the repair of the main traffic artery which connected the two municipalities—MacArthur Causeway—and which was for many years in a condition of dangerous deterioration. The frequent opening of low causeway bridges impeded the traffic flow between the two cities, but this seemed to be of little concern to either of them. There was no attempt to facilitate other traffic media which served the two cities. Both had separate taxi systems which were not allowed to operate in the confines of the other city, and maintained until 1946 separate streetcar or bus systems.

In the field of industrial development the same pattern of rivalry appeared. The ocean port was located in the city of Miami, but Miami Beach maintained a small harbor of its own. When it became necessary to enlarge the main port, other communities were cool to the plan, and even went to the extent of developing harbor projects of their own. A protracted struggle between the various interests lasted through more than a decade. Finally, a common port project was adopted which would place the main new harbor facilities on Dodge Island, but execution of the plan was delayed for years mainly because of opposition of the city of Miami Beach.

.   .   .

If the hodgepodge of municipal government in Miami created many irritations and hardships for the private citizen as well as for the businessman, it did not create a unique situation. Complaints of unfair assessment of taxes and unequal distribution of tax benefits are heard elsewhere. Multiplicity of government, duplication of efforts in some fields and inadequate, inefficient and uncoordinated efforts in others are common phenomena on the American scene. As in Miami, suburbs fight with each other to boost their own trade or industrial status from Maine to California.

35. BEWARE OF THE AIR

Mitchell Gordon

Nine out of every ten Americans now live in localities that have air-pollution problems. This number includes the entire population of all of our some 230 cities with 50,000 or more people. Industry, the automobile, home heating plants, and incinerators are chiefly responsible for this troublesome and even lethal condition that is common to urban areas all over the globe.

Air pollutants raise laundering, cleaning, and painting costs. They also endanger vegetation, wheat and citrus fruits being two forms that are susceptible to such agents. Human life, too, is placed in jeopardy. Airborne industrial wastes contributed to 63 deaths in the Meuse Valley of Belgium in 1930. Eighteen lives were so lost in 1948 in Donora, Pennsylvania. In 1952, 4,000 deaths were attributed to a pall of smoke and soot that had hung over London for a whole week. That is believed to have been responsible for above normal death rates associated with influenza, bronchitis, pulmonary tuberculosis, and circulatory failure. In view of the growing proportion of the aged in urban society and increased reliance on automobiles and industry, air pollution threatens to remain a serious, if not critical, problem for cities everywhere. Smoke-abatement procedures and internal combustion blow-by devices have not yet substantially reduced this menace.

HUMANS have been fighting polluted air for centuries, and chances are they will still be fighting it centuries from now, if contamination of one

Excerpts reprinted with permission of The Macmillan Company from *Sick Cities* by Mitchell Gordon. © by Mitchell Gordon 1963.

sort or another hasn't cleansed them from the globe by then. King Edward I, son of Henry III, passed the first Smoke Abatement Law back in 1273, shortly after Britons began burning bituminous coal. The problem grew so bad by 1306 that the Parliament formed a special committee to rid the nation of the nuisance. A proclamation forbidding the use of coal in furnaces was issued shortly thereafter, and within the year a violator was executed for failing to heed its dictates. But the prohibition against burning bituminous coal didn't stick.

Five centuries later, air pollution was an even bigger headache in Britain. In 1881, another commission, this time with broader representation from the community, was set up to find a solution to the problem. That same year, on the other side of the Atlantic, the city of Chicago adopted the first ordinance giving a municipality authority to control smoke emission by industry and others. In 1894, commissions to study the problems of air pollution were created in France and Germany as well.

In 1905, Dr. Harold Antoine Des Voeux, a noted British physician who coined the word "smog" to designate the combination of smoke and fog that was becoming increasingly common in Britain's industrial centers, called for an alliance of householders, factory owners, and government officials to study the causes of air polution and develop means for its control. He got nowhere and, in fact, was regarded as something of a crank for his dire warnings on the subject.

Today, from Milan to Mexico City and from Paris to Pretoria, civic bodies are becoming increasingly concerned over what their residents are breathing. And well they might: the normal adult inhales some 15,000 quarts of air daily, about 10 times as much by weight as what he eats and drinks in the same period.

The focus on the control of air pollution is particularly sharp, of course, in the Los Angeles area, largely because of its climate and its vast automotive population. Vehicle registrations in Los Angeles County totaled more than 3 million in 1960—nearly 5 times the figure for the entire state of Florida.

These traveling combustion chambers, like any other combustion devices, spew forth a certain amount of unburned gases—ingredients for the airy stew. Sunshine serves as the cooking element in the photochemical process. The containers, for all intents and purposes, are weak winds which prevent the ingredients from being lost out the sides. And the lid is provided by a phenomenon known as "temperature inversion."

Temperature inversion is produced when a layer of warm air sits atop a layer of cooler air, thus inhibiting the normal processes of vertical ventilation from the rising of warm air.

Los Angeles gets a steady diet of inverted temperature conditions—about three-fourths of the year, in fact—from winds that blow eastward from a predominantly stationary high pressure area about 1,000 miles out to sea and a little to the north. The lower level of that moving air mass is cooled by the sea. Since the cooler air is already low, there is no vertical ventilation from normally rising warm air. Only if the cool air is high enough, 1,500 feet or more, is there enough vertical movement within the cooler surface layer itself to provide the necessary vertical ventilation.

Temperature inversion is not peculiar to Los Angeles. It happens up and down the West Coast from San Francisco to San Diego and even farther south. In fact, practically all coastal areas, except in turbulent polar latitudes, experience it where high pressure areas customarily lie in the direction of their prevailing winds—to the west in northern latitudes and to the east in southern ones.

Thus, if the surface winds are weak, as they frequently are in Los Angeles, if the "lid" of temperature inversion is on (that is, 1,500 feet or lower), the sun isn't hidden behind the clouds, the ingredients are poured into the bowl, and the stew known as "smog" in Los Angeles and by other names elsewhere, isn't long in the serving.

The fact that Los Angeles is ringed in by mountains had long been considered as an aggravator of its smog, turning the basin into a bowl in still another sense, but it may actually help reduce smog: some meteorologists believe mountain slopes act as escalators, heating cool air and sending it gradually upward. Whatever the case may be, Los Angeles would probably have smog with or without its mountains.

Since inversions are common throughout the globe, weak winds not unknown, and sunlight reasonably frequent, only one ingredient is needed to produce the troublesome kind of pollution that plagues Los Angeles: enough unburned gases in the air, especially hydrocarbons and oxides of nitrogen. And these are being provided in more and more places by the growing horde of automobiles.

The poor ventilating characteristics of the Los Angeles basin were observed centuries ago by the Spanish explorer Juan Rodríguez Cabrillo, when in October, 1542, he dropped anchor in what is now known as San Pedro Bay. Cabrillo recorded that while mountain peaks were visible in the distance, their bases could not be seen. Smoke from Indian fires rose into the calm air a few hundred feet and then spread across the valley, known to local Indians as the "Valley of Smokes." Los Angeles is presently getting betwen 39 and 50 days yearly of bad smog, most of it in the hotter months of July, August, September, and October.

Air pollution in Los Angeles, of course, is not the same beast that it is, say, in London. Nor is air pollution in New York the same stew brewed in the air over San Francisco. For one thing, pollutants themselves differ: automotive exhausts may dominate in one city and smoke from burning trash or coal fires in another. The air itself may differ: Los Angeles' air is generally dry, while London's is often wet. Climate, topography, and other factors also exert an influence. The principal targets of air-pollution campaigns thus may vary in different areas.

Too often in the past, problems of air pollution have been regarded as the peculiar product of an unlikely conspiracy of circumstances of the bad habits of a highly unique area. Yet, air pollution has proved time and time again that it may squat almost anywhere for uncomfortably long periods of time. Moreover, the air pollution for so long held peculiar to Los Angeles is proving that it can get around with an automobile as well as any motorist, perhaps better.

A recent study of meteorological and other records revealed that a nine-day siege of air pollution in New York in November, 1953, which is now believed to have taken at least 170 lives, was caused largely by the same phenomenon of "temperature inversion" so often considered peculiar to Los Angeles. In New York's case, the inversion was caused by a combination of weak winds, which might have provided horizontal circulation, and an unusual combination of high- and low-pressure belts.

If Los Angeles' air-pollution experience is a portent of things to come in the air of cities elsewhere, the strategy of combating the problem may similarly be of growing interest—as, indeed, it has been.

The county first took action against air pollution in 1948 by banning burning in open dumps. The city of Whittier nearly seceded from the county because it did not like the idea of incurring added expenses for the disposal of its rubbish by other methods, such as incineration. In all, there were some 54 open-burning rubbish dumps in the county, most of them municipally operated. They were considered a principal contributor of air pollutants at the time.

The banning of open burning, however, proved to be only a preliminary step in the city's arduous war against its ethereal foe. Nine years later, homeowners were prohibited from burning refuse in their backyard incinerators. The edict forced the scrapping of an estimated $48 million worth of the concrete-and-iron backyard furnaces. Detroit, Pittsburgh, Philadelphia, and other cities have since followed Los Angeles' action in banning open burning on dumps and in backyards.

Los Angeles' move against homeowners was followed up within two years by regulations prohibiting the use of smoky fuel oil in the summer months by commercial and industrial establishments and apartment houses. Fuel oil containing over 0.5 percent sulfur was thus banned from burning between the period from April 15th to November 15th throughout the basin. Since fuel oil generally contains more sulfur than that, the regulation, in effect, forced a switch to cleaner but costlier natural and artificial gas during these months along with the installation of equipment necessary to effect the changeover.

The Southern California Edison Company, for one, figured the rule tacked 6 percent, or $3 million, on to its annual fuel bill.

Petroleum refiners came next. In 1960 they were told they would be given a specific period of time—later extended to 1963—to reduce from approximately 18 percent to about 12.5 percent the olefin content of their gasolines, so that autos burning their products would send fewer objectionable gases into the atmosphere. Automakers in the same year were warned by the state that as soon as a specially constituted board certified two or more devices as effective in reducing exhaust gas emissions, they would have to install one of those devices on all new vehicles sold thereafter.

A year later, buyers of used cars were to be compelled to do the same. By the end of the third year, all motorists were to be required to install an approved unit on their vehicles at a cost that was expected to exceed $50 per vehicle.

Approved devices were to eliminate at least 80 percent of the hydrocarbons and at least 60 percent of the carbon monoxide emitted into the air. Nothing was said about nitrogen oxide and other pollutants, which were believed to be less troublesome and anyway threatened to be more difficult to deal with.

Increased number of vehicles, experts agree, will eventually offset the effects of control devices. The devices have to become more and more efficient if they are to prevent the rising number of vehicles from increasing the total volume of pollutants. Ultimately, the solution might lie only in the development of new engines whose waste gases, if any, at least will be less dangerous to the species that must live among them.

It doesn't take much in the way of foreign particles and gases to pollute air. There are about 30,000 tons of air over a square mile at the height of a single-story building. As little as 0.03 tons of pollution in that area—or just one part per million—is enough to make the air unpleasant to breathe. It is not uncommon for a ton of coal to be burned per minute over one square mile of urban dwellings or industry in areas using that fuel in homes or factories. On the average, that volume of coal will produce 0.05 tons of sulfur dioxide and other gases and particles, not counting carbon dioxide.

In automobiles, the waste product emitted in greatest volume is carbon monoxide: autos spew 5 to 6 times the volume of carbon monoxide as they do hydrocarbons and oxides of nitrogen, the chemical compounds that make the most trouble in the air. While carbon monoxide is not particularly troublesome at the moment, experts fear its sheer volume may one day create pollution problems.

Automobiles are the principal producers of air pollution in many cities. Los Angeles' Air Pollution Control District figures the 1,630-square mile Los Angeles basin, which includes more than half of Orange County as well as all of Los Angeles County, received 80 percent of its air pollution from that source in 1961. Its seventy smog-patrol cars wrote some 2,500 notices and citations for excessive exhaust smoke from automobiles in that year; fines for such violations range up to $50.

Los Angeles air-pollution authorities maintain they have reduced—temporarily, at least—both the severity of their smog and the number of days in which smog is bad, but they admit they have not succeeded in arresting its geographical spread nor in keeping down the number of days of moderate smog. The vast San Fernando Valley, a rich agricultural smog-free area until recent years, for instance, is now almost as severely plagued with the malady as Los Angeles itself.

Los Angeles' "smog alerts," sounded when the dreaded ozone content exceeds 50 parts per 100,000,000 parts of air to exhort the public against unnecessary travel or combustion, declined from as many as 15 days a year prior to 1956 to no more than 7 days in any 12-month period thereafter to the time of this writing. Nevertheless, the Los Angeles County Air Pollution Control District reported 96 days "with some degree of smog" in 1960, for example, compared with an average of 88 such days a year over the 7 years through 1960; 31 of the 1960 days were classified as days of heavy eye irritation. Quantities of nitrogen oxide, in the meantime, were observed to be reaching new peaks, rising to a record 3.93 parts per million on January 3, 1961, compared with the previous maximum of 2.00 ppm on January 5, 1960.

Air pollution is growing more widespread on a global scale as well. In Durban, South Africa, the City Council not long ago asked the Standard-Vacuum Refining Company temporarily to close its multimillion-dollar refinery after local residents complained of loss of sleep, nausea, and vomiting from fumes that were said to be issuing from the plant; the company averted the shutdown only by installing a battery of costly control devices. In Japan, the city of Kobe, which has come to be known as the "smoky city," is the scene of increasing clamor for action to clean the air. A thickening mixture of chronic fog and industrial smoke has become a matter of concern among residents of the peaceful Po Valley in Italy. And even Paris in the springtime is not as pleasant as it used to be: the French Association for the Prevention of Atmospheric Pollution reports chimneypot emissions, combined with a growing volume of automobile traffic, are blotting out upper portions of such famous landmarks as the Eiffel Tower and the Montmartre Cathedral.

The Communists are wrestling with the problem, too. A visitor to the Hungarian capital of Budapest reports smog is increasingly obscuring the hills of Buda from the plains of Pest.

Indeed, even the idyllic archipelagoes of the warm Pacific may not be spared the airy blight. Air samples analyzed in Hawaii reveal the presence of increasing quantities of contaminants which may have had their origins many miles distant, perhaps in the continental United States.

36. THE CITY AND THE CAR

Francis Bello

*The changing modes of transportation—the streetcar, elevated, sub-
way, bus, and automobile—have changed the configuration of every city
of any size and have also created difficult problems for it to solve. The
private motor car is now the major transportation question troubling the
urban complex. Generally, mass transit has steadily declined in importance while car registrations continue to rise from 26,000,000 in 1945, to
54,000,00 in 1956, perhaps to and upwards of twice that number by
1975. The automobile has drastically changed the density of population
both at the core of the city and around its perimeter. The Federal-Aid
Highway Act is creating a 40,000-mile network of superhighways around
the country, including 5,500 miles of high capacity urban expressways
ringing or penetrating 90 percent of all our cities of 50,000 population or
more.*

*Transportation within the city is persistently vexatious for the metro-
politan government and economy. Coping with automobile congestion
and movement by building and adapting roads, by providing more parking space, and by strengthening mass transit as either a supporting system
or as a viable alternative is of continuing interest to local, state, and national leadership.*

RESIDENTS of New York City, Chicago, and Philadelphia—where downtown travel is overwhelmingly by public transit—may find it hard to appreciate how heavily most other American cities are dominated by the au-

Excerpts from the October 1957 issue of Fortune Magazine. That article has appeared in
a book, *The Exploding Metropolis*, by Doubleday Company, Inc.

tomobile . . . in fifteen of the nation's twenty-five largest cities, 60 per cent or more of all riders entering the downtown business district arrive by automobile. In eight downtown centers, the percentage of automobile riders exceeds even Los Angeles' 66 per cent.[1] And in five of the eight— Houston, Cincinnati, Kansas City, Dallas, and San Antonio—automobiles carry more than 70 per cent of all those riding into the heart of town. In New York City, by contrast, a scant 17 per cent use automobiles; 83 per cent use public transit.

What is most surprising about automobile use in America's biggest cities is not that the ratio of automobile to public-transit riders varies so widely, but that automobile traffic seems to flow at just about the same speed everywhere, regardless of the size of the city, its age, its geographical assets or handicaps, the number of its expressways, or the cleverness of its traffic engineers. This is perhaps the most striking conclusion that can be drawn from a series of nationwide driving experiments, to determine how fast it is possible to get out of town at the peak of the evening rush hour in the twenty-five largest U.S. cities. . . . With remarkable consistency, the outbound traffic averages just about 20 mph. In only three cities, Boston, St. Louis, and New Orleans, was the average speed as low as 16 mph.

And how fast does the transit rider get home? Against the motorist's average speed of 20 mph, riders using the busiest transit routes in the same cities can expect to average only about 13 mph. The three big exceptions are New York, San Francisco, and Newark, where rail commuters travel at about 34 mph. The slowest transit speed, 8 mph, was recorded in Pittsburgh and San Antonio.

THE ENGINEER'S NIGHTMARE

So the automobile still moves pretty fast, even at rush hours. But how long can this continue? Motor-vehicle registrations have more than doubled since 1945, and the forecast is for over two new vehicles on the road for every three additional Americans; by 1975 the U.S. will have over 100 million vehicles for a population of 220 million.

Nearly half of all motor-vehicle mileage is accumulated on the 373,000 miles of streets that are within city limits. . . .

In Los Angeles, to take an extreme example, Lloyd Braff, general manager of the city's Department of Traffic, estimates that the number of vehicles demanding space on the streets in the peak rush hour is rising at an annual rate of 35,000. To accommodate them . . . his department has:

Banned parking on 300 miles of streets during rush hours.

Timed traffic signals to favor the direction of rush-hour traffic flow. (This increased by nearly 30 per cent the number of vehicles carried on Ventura Boulevard.)

Offset the center line, morning and evening, on twenty-two miles of highway to provide an extra lane for rush-hour traffic.

Used paint liberally to separate traffic lanes. This keeps drivers from weaving in and out and substantially increases a street's capacity.

Painted special left-turn slots at crossings so that left-turning drivers approach each other in the same lane instead of tying up the customary two lanes.

One small invention made by Braff's department will undoubtedly find use elsewhere. So many houses—displaced by new freeways—are carted through Los Angeles streets at night that the job of moving overhead traffic lights to let the houses through became irksome. The solution: a traffic-light arm that swings out of the way when a nut is loosened.

As in Los Angeles, traffic engineers in practically every large city have found ways to move more vehicles through their city's streets than they had believed possible in the past. And all agree that much more can still be done. It may be possible to reserve certain streets exclusively for trucks, buses, or even pedestrians, and perhaps the use should vary with the time of day. (On one downtown street Chicago has already given buses an exclusive lane down the center, with safety islands for riders and pedestrians.)

Eventually, the bulk of all downtown truck deliveries may have to be made at night, and cruising of taxicabs in some cities may have to be curtailed. A recent traffic count on one of New York's busiest thoroughfares, Sixth Avenue, showed the following mix of vehicles: taxis, 48 per cent; private automobiles, 26 per cent; trucks, 20 per cent; and buses, 6 per cent. About one-quarter of the taxis were empty, looking for customers.

Then there is the question of parking. No city ever seems to have enough. A number of big cities—among them San Francisco, Chicago, and Pittsburgh—have floated bond issues to finance large parking garages, which are usually privately operated. Many cities have also held stormy public hearings over proposed ordinances that would require builders to provide a prescribed amount of parking space with all new buildings. Los Angeles has had a requirement of this type for a number of years. In 1954 New York City rejected a measure that would have required most new office buildings to provide off-street parking for 100 to 300 cars. New York's reasons for rejecting the proposal: it would attract more automobiles into the city; it would add inordinately to building costs; and the city preferred to see land put to more productive use.

The fact is that it will never be possible to provide parking space in the largest cities for all the motorists who want to come to them. There wouldn't be anything left worth coming to. If all of New York's transit riders drove in by automobile, for example, all of Manhattan below Fiftieth Street would have to be converted to multiple-deck parking garages.

THE PEDESTRIAN PARADISE

There is one radical solution that is beginning to get a good deal of attention. Keep the cars out. Turn the central city into a pedestrian mall.

Probably the boldest scheme built around this principle is one put forward recently by architect Victor Gruen, who is famous for proposing and designing J. L. Hudson's great shopping center, Northland, ten miles north of Detroit. Asked to prepare a redevelopment plan for downtown Fort Worth, Gruen proposed that the city should counterattack by adopting the most popular features of the suburban shopping center. His plan: let people drive up to the edge of the business center on spacious perimeter expressways, give them plenty of parking space, then make them get out and walk. Allow no cars at all in the central area—and endow it with so many eye-filling, imaginative, and compelling features that workers and shoppers would rather head for the heart of Fort Worth than anywhere else in Texas.

The area that would be closed off and redeveloped—preserving all important buildings—would embrace practically all of the present center of Fort Worth, lying between two railroad lines and the Trinity River. The area is roughly fifteen blocks square. . . . All delivery trucks would be banished underground. Aboveground, there would be no exhaust fumes, honking horns, squealing brakes, or traffic lights—just throngs of happy people, making and spending money.

Fort Worth is still dazzled by the daring concept, . . . and a Greater Fort Worth Planning Committee has been formed to look into it and make recommendations.

Many Fort Worth businessmen favor the plan in principle, especially the perimeter expressways and the ample supply of parking space, but some fear that banning cars from the center of town is too visionary. "People like to do business," says one local businessman, "where there are people and traffic, and where there is the sound and appearance of commercial activity. I don't want to do business in a botanical garden."

60,000 PARKING SPACES

If carried out completely, the Gruen plan might take fifteen years and cost $100 million to $150 million, of which perhaps 10 per cent might be borne by private investors and redevelopers. It is the belief of J. B. Thomas, president of Fort Worth's Texas Electric Service Co. and the man who engaged Gruen to make his study, that the balance of the money would come largely from two sources: revenues from garages and other facilities in the plan, and from increased tax receipts arising from the impact of the plan on property values.

The Gruen plan is based on the estimated needs of 1970, when Fort Worth and its tributary suburbs will have a projected population of some 1,200,000, or about as many people as now live in the Minneapolis-St. Paul metropolitan area—the thirteenth largest in the U.S. The plan provides parking room for 60,000 cars, or some 12,000 more spaces than now exist in downtown Los Angeles, the nominal center of the country's third-largest metropolitan area, with a population of nearly 4,500,000. Presumably something like 60,000 parking spaces will be required to make Fort Worth the genuine regional center that downtown Los Angeles has failed to become.

But almost unnoticed in the Gruen report is a small footnote: the 60,000 parking spaces would be "adequate only with highly efficient rapid-transit system." Actually Gruen's exciting economic projections for a "Greater Fort Worth Tomorrow" assume that *half* of all people traveling to the heart of town will choose to travel by express bus. Since only about 17 per cent of all Fort Worth travelers now use public transit, the Gruen plan seems to be predicated on an enormous reversal of the nationwide trend in travel habits.

So the circle closes. The bold plan that was to solve the downtown traffic and parking problems at one swoop turns out to be based on a great revival of mass transit.

WHAT ABOUT MASS TRANSIT?

As the mass-transit advocates so often point out, one rapid-transit track can move up to 40,000 people past a given point in an hour. To move the same number in automobiles (at the usual occupancy of 1.8 riders per car) would require some sixteen lanes of modern expressway.

Since World War II, however, only two North American cities, Cleveland and Toronto, have had both the inclination and the resources to give modern rapid transit a fresh try. Both were special cases. Cleveland was able to obtain at low cost most of its right-of-way from a stretch of land that had been set aside for a rapid-transit system by the old Van Sweringen interests. Thus, for only $33 million, the city's transit commission could build a 13.5-mile rail line from East Cleveland through downtown Cleveland to a point 5.5 miles west. The Cleveland Rapid Transit Board claims that the new line is operating at only a fraction of its potential. It maintains that rapid-transit riders would increase more than 100 per cent with the addition of a 1.5-mile subway distributing loop under the downtown area, which would cost another $35 million.

The new 4.5-mile Toronto subway, on the other hand, serves the heart of downtown and is widely hailed by transit advocates as a model for other cities to copy. Toronto could afford the line, in the first place, because the efficient and thrifty Toronto Transit Commission had been able to accumulate a surplus of $20 million, largely from heavy World War II patronage of its streetcars and buses. To this sum the commission added $40 million from sale of debentures and built the so-called Yonge Street subway between 1949 and 1954. The subway replaced the city's busiest streetcar route, which carried up to 12,000 riders an hour—possibly a record for streetcar service. The subway now carries up to 32,000 passengers in single peak hours. It seems, however, that there has been no significant increase in the total number of morning and evening riders; it is just that they have discovered that more of them can now ride at one time.

On a typical day, the subway carries about 15 per cent more riders than the old streetcar line. Considering the vast improvement in service, the gain is not too startling. And Yonge Street is still about as crowded with automobiles as ever.

. . .

While difficult to document, it appears that the worker population has increased little if any in the downtown business districts of most big cities. Like the major new population growth, the growth in new job opportunities has taken place at the edge of big cities and in the suburbs. The new jobs for the suburbanites are jobs within—and often beyond—the suburbs. The new home-to-work patterns seem to be beyond any solution based on mass transit. The subway was ideal for moving people between high-density housing and high-density work places. The commuter railroad took over to move people to the same work areas from low-density housing. But there seems no way to provide an efficient mass-transit system that can move people from low-density housing to factories—and even offices—spotted all over the countryside.

The automobile has exploded the metropolis open, and no amount of public transit will jam it back together again. The automobile looks like an unbeatable invention for circulating people from low-density communities to low-density activities of all kinds.

HOW COSTLY A MONSTER?

The automobile, moreover, is not such a costly monster as many planners seem to believe. Curiously, the transit industry claims it has no idea of the length of the average transit trip, but estimating it generously at four miles, transit riders in 1956 paid some $1.4 billion to travel roughly 35 million passenger-miles—an average of 4 cents per mile. Out-of-pocket costs (1956) to the American motorist amounted to $27 billion—which includes the cost of new and used cars, fuel, repairs and parts, tolls, and parking fees. There is no generally accepted figure on depreciation, but $18 billion would be about the right order of magnitude. For his $45 billion the motorist buys about 500 billion vehicle-miles, or—at an average occupancy of 1.8 riders per car—900 billion passenger-miles. Thus the total cost of auto transport comes to 5 cents per passenger-mile. New taxes, averaging a maximum $2 billion yearly over the thirteen-year highway program, will raise the motorist's total outlay, but the cost per passenger-mile will still be below 5½ cents.

And the cost of tomorrow's public transit? No one can be sure, but it is suggested that riders on the proposed San Francisco rapid-transit system would have to pay fares of 2½ cents per mile just to meet the system's maintenance and operating costs. If fares were to cover capital costs as well, the system would have to charge almost 6 cents per passenger-mile. Thus, while it *ought* to be substantially cheaper to move people in masses, it doesn't appear to be. No one, it seems, can afford a chauffeur any more—not even the kind that a transit fare used to buy.

HOPE FOR THE CORE

If the automobile is, in fact, the cheapest—as well as the most rational—way to circulate people in and around tomorrow's lower-density metropolis, this need not mean that every city in the U.S. is fated to look like Los Angeles. Los Angeles had no vital central core to begin with. The core never developed, despite a fine electric railway system in the early years, because the automobile arrived too soon and spattered the city over the countryside.

Virtually every other major U.S. city does have a core, and . . . the core can be preserved and improved by vigorous and imaginative redevelopment.

It is conceivable that there are places where big brand-new rapid-transit systems can be justified. Perhaps San Francisco will turn out to be one of them.

But most U.S. cities will be doing well if they can keep existing transit facilities running and make modest investments to modernize them. It is the persuasive argument of one of the country's leading transportation economists, Wilfred Owen of the Brookings Institution, that it would be unwise to subsidize new transit facilities on a large scale when there are so many other urban needs competing for public funds—new schools and hospitals, new recreation facilities and parks, new water and sewage systems, and slum-clearance and redevelopment projects. The great virtue of the new highways and expressways is that they can be paid for by the users.

True, tomorrow's highways may make a botch of metropolis and confirm the worst fears of the transit people. The Federal-Aid Highway Act leaves the program up to state highway engineers, and the route locations that appeal to them are not necessarily those that may be best for either the city or its suburbs. The problem is to place the new highways so that they do not destroy the amenities of either urban or suburban living.

The automobile metropolis cannot look like the streetcar metropolis. But it should be possible to develop an automobile metropolis that still has a heart and can provide fresh opportunities for those who live both within and without.

CHAPTER EIGHT

COPING WITH
THE URBAN CRISIS

Can the modern metropolitan community actually be managed? With all of its vexing dilemmas and pernicious tensions, is it even humanly possible for us to cope with the megalopolis? Or, as William A. Doebele, Jr., has phrased this despairing question, ". . . [can] one mind or any organized group of minds . . . ever really grasp this restless entity as a whole, or being grasped, [can] human efforts control it?"

So dismaying a query about the viability of urban society (which the preceding two sections of this volume have indeed implied) makes one want to cling, say, to Frank Lloyd Wright's vision of Broadacres as a testimonial to the enduring faith that some men can continue to place in the city.[1] Perhaps now naive in its simplistic equation of architecture with the good society, Wright's passion reminds us, however, that if urban affairs are not to sink into chaos, we must first be convinced that there is a practical alternative to the disorders of the present.

The Committee for Economic Development thus makes the first proposal for urban action. Having examined the potential for federal assistance and also state aid for our cities, the CED endorses metropolitan unity or countywide government, among them Miami (Dade County), Florida, and Nashville (Davidson County), Tennessee. On the other hand, skillful and determined efforts have failed so often recently in the United States that most observers regard the ambition of achieving metropolitan government as futile. Since 1950 consolidation referenda have in fact, gone down to defeat in Newport (Warwick County), Virginia; Albuquerque (Bernalillo County), New Mexico; Macon (Bibb County), Georgia; Cleveland (Cuyahoga County), Ohio; Durham (Durham County), North Carolina; Richmond (Henrico County), Virginia; Columbus (Muscogee County), Georgia; Memphis (Shelby County), Tennessee; St. Louis (St. Louis County), Missouri; and Chattanooga (Hamilton County), Tennessee. A disheartening roster!

What have been the sources of this obdurate resistance? Scott Greer has identified several. The age-old assumption that local government means the immediate, small, grass-roots, autonomous community; and also the public's insistence on ultra-democratic constitutional forms, notably the long ballot, separation of powers, and checks and balances.[2] Other reasons may be added. By and large there is an apathy or listlessness toward local government that is prevalent and that manifests itself in the absence of dissatisfaction with the services that the city offers. For instance, in both St. Louis and Dayton, surveys conducted late in the 1950s failed to uncover any serious complaints about municipal services. Again in Cleveland in 1958, as James A. Norton demonstrated, the percentage "not at all satisfied" ranged from 1 percent concerning fire protection to a high of 28 percent with respect to bus and transit services.[3] Besides, of course, the obvious displeasure of entrenched local officeholders, still another source of opposition to urban consolidation is the fact that metropolitan government is a response to problems so complex, pervasive, implicit, intricate, and involved that they simply tend to escape the average citizen. Consider, for example, pollution, the level of cultural services, and welfare and human resources.

Despite dire warnings of impending peril, local government may have faltered at times—particularly when operating levies have been turned down at the polls—but it certainly has not collapsed. Nor have such vital services as water, sanitation, roads, fire protection, and transit failed disastrously. Doubtlessly recent civil disturbances, rising crime rates, and the sharp decline of many central business districts have given new urgency to the claims of an urban crisis. However, full employment, continued suburbanization, and other difficulties, especially the war in Vietnam and student unrest on university campuses, have acted to blur whatever urban focus these challenges have produced.

Additional changes have been taking place in the city amidst the failure of efforts aimed at comprehensive municipal reform. Important alterations can be observed in land use (high-rise apartments, glass and steel office towers, civic centers); styles of life (yachting, winter vacations, television, home appliances, convenience foods); transportation (jets, expressways, helicopters); industry (automation, computers, chemicals, plastics, industrial parks); and education (school libraries, team teaching, advanced placement, graduate and professional education, and programmed instruction). These have fostered a feeling of unplanned but definite progress and have tended to give the lie to urban Cassandras.

Interlocal governmental cooperation is an alternative to the restructuring of municipal government that many authorities regard as eminently practical. This type of cooperation could take various forms and discharge numerous functions. A 1958 Rockefeller Foundation report, in fact, gave strong impetus to such an approach to urban problems. Cooperation has the real advantage of avoiding an attack on existing units of government and also of allowing operational arrangements to be worked out between governments of different levels as well as between purely local ones. Even more dependable than intergovernmental cooperation is the federation plan. Under this form, authority for given functions and services is entrusted to some consolidated agency, like a metropolitan district, an area authority, or a constituent-unit board, and the agency formulates policy and then engages in whatever administration is called for.

Other perspectives on the problem of local government have taken state and federal systems as their point of departure. Some have simply dismissed metropolitan government at the outset as a practical impossibility. Indeed, it may be argued that area-wide government is itself anachronistic, because it is incapable of coping with the urban region, and no mere metropolitan agency can contend with the megalopolis that stretches for 400 miles from Washington to Boston, or 600 miles from Milwaukee to Pittsburgh. Most scholars, however, have chosen to concentrate on the further extension of state and federal government rather than to advocate the very problematical establishment of a new level of political authority. As Bollens and Schmandt put it, "in terms of the entire metropolitan area, the one-government approach is almost certain to be bypassed increasingly in favor of other techniques." [4]

Through constitutional and legislative measures, each state has greatly influenced its cities. Not only the structure of municipal government, but also its functions and fiscal operations are generally subject to state control. Even though reorganization has long been advocated, the states have limited themselves, except for changing school districts, to providing further financial aid to cities and offering additional direct services, as in air and water pollution abatement and social welfare.

The national government, too, and on an even larger scale than that of the states, has furnished funds and special programs to the cities. Some of these, such as manpower training, public housing, slum clearance, river and harbor improvement, and the support of hospitals have had direct impact. Others have been indirect, although perhaps more significant, in their effects. Included here would be federal mortgage insurance, which accelerated suburbanization, and highway construction, which has had a similar consequence.

Numbers of urban planners, economists, sociologists, and other specialists have urged a stronger federalist approach to urban problems. Gunnar Myrdal, for one, has said that added efforts are needed from Washington in order to provide the massive program essential to urban growth and health. ". . . the war against poverty can be effectively pursued," Myrdal wrote recently in "National Planning for Healthy Cities," "only by national policies, whereas . . . policy efforts at the local level are apt to be frustrated by vested interests and insufficient financial resources." [5] Furthermore, only if rapid and sustained economic growth is realized can there be the resources for coping with poverty and its attendant ills. The latter obviously necessitates national action to provide full employment for individual betterment and the fiscal means for collective measures.

A still longer view of federalism has also been taken. Sam Bass Warner, Jr., has proposed a strategy for programmed federalism *vis-à-vis* the city. "To cope with the changing network of cities, the federal government by its regulatory and public works powers would endeavor to create national minimum standards for open space, clean water and air, and a grid of transport and power services such that the firms and citizens of the United States could move about the landscape in any urban configuration they wished." [6] This strategy calls for a regional concept and the avoidance of concentrating on the single municipality, as has been the case, by means of grants-in-aid, particularly, as Warner declares, "servicing real estate and helping unproductive and unwanted citizens." To back up the national approach other supplementary measures to stabilize the economy and reduce tension levels appear called for, including a guaranteed minimum income, interlocal governmental cooperation, and a vastly expanded federal urban administration.

"Major Factors in Urban Planning," by Robert C. Weaver, our first Secretary of Housing and Urban Development, represents the advocacy of federal assistance together with community action as the foundation for urban reconstruction. Weaver abandons the search for metropolitan government as impractical and chooses instead to rely on existing channels of communication and patterns of influence in the local population. People in any given voluntary association have a number of goals and values in common. Moreover, they heed a certain cadre of leaders. They are, therefore, susceptible to the sentiments that are expressed by their organization and also are prone to concert their efforts in a common cause. The fact too that leaders interact with other leaders gives them access to new views which can subsequently be filtered down to their rank-and-file members. Such a process of deliberate though somewhat informal social action has been observed at work recently in opposition to the maintenance of racial segregation in the public schools and also in controlling riots. It has also been apparent in agitation for the neighborhood control of institutions, including the schools and the police.

The Neighborhood Facilities Grant Program of the 1965 Housing and Urban Development Act made funds available, as President Johnson phrased it, to create and preserve "the sense of community with others which gives us significance and security, a sense of belonging and of sharing in the common life." Included were social services, such as those for legal counsel and consumer education; employment and training benefits; educational services, among them basic adult literacy and Head Start for pre-kindergarteners; housing information for relocation, rehabilitation, and code enforcement; assistance to the aged, notably special health services and handicrafts shops; health, cultural enrichment, and recreation; and, finally a civic participation program providing for organized community action in regard to local problems.

In like manner Title I of the 1966 Demonstration Cities and Metropolitan Development Act called for a "total attack" on urban ills, and designated citizen participation as a vital means in the process. Some indication of the spirit of this legislation with respect to community action may be inferred from one of the criteria for developing a model-cities proposal, namely, "Have all the public officials and private agencies and organizations essential to carrying out a comprehensive program and the citizen groups of the selected neighborhoods been working together to analyze the social and physical problems of the area?" Others of a similar nature could also be cited.

Actually, the civic involvement of the average American citizen is minimal, to say the least. He has little community identification although, not uncommonly, he does take pride in the cleanliness, homes, and landmarks of his city. He does not ordinarily acclaim his local government nor does he take an active interest in civic affairs. In municipal elections that do not coincide with national contests, the voting performance of the public seldom exceeds 50 percent of those who are registered, and as Robert E. Lane has shown, perhaps no more than 2 percent of American adults actively belong to political organizations.

All this would signify that the social nominalism of our modern urban society makes guided social change difficult to realize. Community organization does, however, capitalize on those nonpolitical social ties that are in existence at least in latent fashion. The behavior of the urbanite tends to be directed by the expectations of his role in a given situation rather than by his originally socialized personal attitudes and feelings. Therefore, for example, one may be racially tolerant in political affairs but intolerant occupationally and residentially because one's fellow trade unionists and neighbors so define their respective spheres. Such situational patterning, of course, complicates the administration of any comprehensive general policy.

It does however, imply that specific public programs that are carried out in cooperation with the leadership of private agencies and voluntary associations that have the capacity of redefining and legitimizing expectations may be effective. Hadley Cantril has formulated a principle of opinion and attitude change that is instructive with regard to implementing legislation by means of supportive social action. "When an opinion is held by a slight majority, or when an opinion is not solidly structured, an accomplished fact tends to shift opinion in the direction of acceptance." This would uphold the potential value of the community-action approach in securing the positive kind of school integration that the U. S. Civil Rights Commission declares below is imperative to urban progress. In our larger cities, official action has realized all too little solid accomplishment in school integration.

It should be noted that there is a distinct danger in politicizing the community. The peril lies in the fact that the same process of interest-group activation can be undertaken to maintain accustomed social-status differentials regardless of democratic and humanitarian values simply because they are consensually validated as legitimate. Long ago Max Weber, for one, warned against the bureaucratically administered society that is capable of great efficiency in pursuing temporally legitimate goals while at the same time denying substantive justice. Community action may thus also provide a vehicle for redressing injustices without regard for either due process or the rights of others. Recent experience with "confrontation politics" has made this abundantly clear.

The final reading that appears in the present section is part of the report of the National Advisory Commission on Civil Disorders. Coming on the heels of the major Detroit riot of 1967, the report seemingly satisfied no one fully, despite the fact that it recommended a very broad spectrum of possibly ameliorative measures. It sanctioned greater citizen participation in our metropolitan area governments, expanded social-welfare services, and more concentrated community action—all, however, to be coordinated by charismatic local and state leadership.

The four selections that make up this section of our anthology

deal with the American response to the contemporary urban dilemma. As such, they ignore the systematic but thorough kind of
urban planning that Britain, for example, has engaged in. The British model calls for a hierarchical organization extending from the
local councils at the municipal level to the regional offices of the
Ministry of Housing and Local Government and finally to the national ministry. All levels are assisted by special consultants, commissions, and development corporations, so that both local initiative and general coordination are provided for. The British
government has been planning more "New Towns" in areas away
from the London fringe—in Lancashire, in the West Midlands,
and in County Durham. These undertakings not only reflect the
further nationalization of urban planning in the United Kingdom
but also recognize the need to usher in a decidedly different social
and economic future.

Modern city planning seeks to replace spontaneous and uncoordi-
nated urban decision-making with rational, systematic thought.
Most American planning, however, is for modification and improvement not replacement, although theorists like Ebenezer Howard,
Henry Wright, and Clarence Perry have long urged radical measures.[7] The American experience has been largely eclectic. True,
Radburn, New Jersey, and Greenbelt, Maryland, remain our "New
Towns" of an earlier day. But by and large, urban planning in the
United States has been fragmented, sporadic, and situation, even
crisis, oriented. It has, therefore, from one time to the next and in
one place or another embraced institutional reform at the level of
local government; interlocal cooperation; state and federal assistance; zoning and code enforcement to channelize growth; the recognition of short-term as well as long-term objectives; reliance on persuasion as well as authority; the combination of private and public
investment; the balancing of physical and human needs; the articulation of objectives by means of expressive participation from various segments of the public; and great flexibility regarding the ultimate design of our cities, as to whether they are to be dispersed, to
grow at the periphery, to be ribbonized, or to be rehabilitated at the
center. Simultaneously, racial and related class antagonisms have
taxed the urban crisis in America to the extreme and imparted a
possibly tragic character to an already distressing adventure.

37. MODERNIZING LOCAL GOVERNMENT

Committee for Economic Development

Three alternate routes to municipal reform may be considered: more functional federalism, state action, and the reconstruction of local government. Of these the CED opts for the latter on the grounds that local self-government is imperative though its effectiveness, even its viability perhaps, will depend on consolidation, home rule, the short ballot, a professional civil service, and executive authority.

Despite sharp rises in the costs of the 80,000 local governments in the United States—from $20.1 billion in 1952 to $45.1 billion in 1962—great dissatisfaction exists with the quality of services, high crime rates, school deficiencies, public assistance, transportation, and slums. These conditions continue despite vastly increased amounts of federal aid to cities. Grants-in-aid to local governments amounted to $4 million in 1902. For fiscal 1966–67 Washington budgeted more than $14 billion.

Assuming a somewhat conservative stance with respect to municipal problems, in the sense at least of opposing greater federal authority, the CED addresses itself to such factors as the small size of many of our cities, overlapping jurisdictions, ineffective popular control, the lack of sufficient executive powers, and antiquated administrative organization.

WE ARE CONVINCED that all American communities face urgent problems requiring competent governmental action. We expect these problems to grow, both in variety and intensity, in coming decades. The issues are not

From *Modernizing Local Government*, a statement on national policy by the Research and Policy Committee of the Committee for Economic Development, New York, 1966, pages 13–19. Reprinted by permission.

narrowly confined to matters concerning education, transportation, housing, health and safety, water supply, or air pollution—serious as they are. They extend to all the conditions of modern life, and to the social and material satisfactions that act as incentives for a constructive commitment of human resources.

We are also convinced that many local governments are unequal to the challenge. They are ineffective in coping with present problems, and inadequate in facing the escalation that surely lies ahead. But highly complex problems seldom have simple solutions; nor are acceptable solutions, once found, always easy to apply. There is obvious danger in oversimplification, but we visualize three alternative courses of action open to the nation.

First, recent trends toward "functional government" might go on indefinitely, as in highway administration. This would imply an extension of federal standard-setting, decision-making, and administrative controls —with heavier transfusions of federal funds directly or through state channels. In theory, the present system of local governments could then endure without major structural change or modernization. Functional fragmentation under federal auspices discourages local planning and management on any unified, integral basis. In practice, federal efforts to use *existing* local governments as administrative agencies in executing national policy have already disclosed such serious faults that success cannot be expected within the present framework. Sole reliance on this approach would probably lead to (a) an increase in direct federal management of local affairs, (b) assumption by state governments of a larger share in administrative operations, (c) continued neglect of vital local issues, and (d) excessive costs for the services they render.

Second, the 50 states might expand their administrative mechanisms to supersede local authorities, gradually perhaps, in function after function. This might be done through regional or district centers, in order to relate state action more directly to local situations. Such an alternative would not be endorsed, however, by those who have found their state capitals consistently unresponsive to local needs, whether these are universal or vary from locality to locality.

Third, existing patterns of local government can be drastically revised, to encourage local policy decision-making and to permit effective management of local affairs. This will not be easy, for major structural adjustments are required if we are to preserve the fundamental values in local self-government. But competent local units, responsive to the requirements of an enlightened public, can serve two primary purposes. They can identify local problems and opportunities, and then plan and execute programs with optimum effect. They are also needed to serve in an effective partnership with state agencies, and with the federal government in its expanding fields of activity.

We strongly urge support of the third alternative. Granting the merits of professionalism in functional fields, conceding the importance of federal encouragement and support, and recognizing the need for action by the states consistent with their responsibilities, we still stress the fundamental values of local self-government. These values extend far beyond the efficiencies to be gained through consolidations and reorganizations. Citizen participation in community affairs is the central pillar sustaining a democratic society; it is an invaluable training school for service at other levels. Revitalized local governments will command greater public interest and popular support. Initiatives channeled through effective local units will foster creative experimentation in meeting the diversity of needs from region to region, from urban to rural areas, and from place to place within the same state.

We recognize the obstacles, including vested political interests and civic inertia, found in opposition to any modernization of local institutions of government. But reapportionments of state legislatures and of local governing bodies are creating wide new possibilities for reform. We are convinced that suitable local units can be designed to plan governmental operations fostering rapid community development, to adminster programs effectively, and to contribute materially in their financing. The citizens can obtain the services they need at reasonable cost only through strong local governments, since neither federal nor state governments can be expected to deal competently with local situations.

Efforts to "tidy up" a chaotic situation will not cure the chief illness. Overemphasis on waste, inefficiency, and incompetence may obscure the main point: most American communities lack any instrumentality of government with legal powers, geographic jurisdiction, and independent revenue sources necessary to conduct local government in any valid sense. Our fundamental concern is that every community in the nation be capable of effective management of its local affairs. This is the *sine qua non* of a democratic society geared for entrance into the twenty-first century.

Before a local government can be expected to serve the purposes intended, it must meet four minimum qualifications:

Political unity. Each population governed must have enough common interests, problems, and communications to qualify as a political entity able to produce political leadership responsive to active citizen concern.

Size. Each local unit must be sufficiently large—in population, geographic jurisdiction, and financial resources—to make long-range plans to attract professional staff, and to manage modern services.

Powers. Each government must have legal authority adequate to cope with the problems for which it is responsible, and to enforce its decisions.

Rational structure. Each government must have a representative governing body concerned with policy decisions, and a single chief executive to secure unity in administrative operations.

SUMMARY OF RECOMMENDATIONS

This statement on national policy calls for major changes consistent with these criteria: massive county consolidations to conform with logical geographic and economic boundaries; structural modernization and professional staffing for all local units; and severe reduction in the overlapping layers of local government. Changes of this character will require sweeping action by the states through comprehensive constitutional revisions. Only then—and the process may take a decade in some states—will it be possible to create modern systems of local government able to meet the challenge of the times.

Our proposals are nationwide in scope, and they apply to both urban and rural communities. Valid generalizations are usually subject to various exceptions, but the guidelines that follow have almost universal applicability. They define broad objectives rather than forming a simple blueprint for any state or locality to adopt in detail. And they provide no pat solutions for problems unique to each giant metropolitan complex, or to contiguous urbanized areas forming "strip cities." While specific study of each "megalopolis" is required—supported by such assistance as federal, state, or private foundations may provide—prompt creation of the strong local governments here proposed would permit effective collaboration among them in the search for feasible solutions.

1. *The number of local governments in the United States, now about 80,000, should be reduced by at least 80 per cent.*

Reasonable minimum standards of size would disqualify most present units for continued existence, since average population for all local governments is less than 2,500. Failure to correct this situation, especially in those states where it is most acute, will further cloud the future of local self-government. Local units must be large enough to function effectively if power over local affairs is not to be centralized at higher levels.

2. *The number of overlapping layers of local government found in most states should be severely curtailed.*

Townships and most types of special districts are obvious targets for elimination as independent governments. Small municipalities unable to provide professional administration could continue to set levels of service desired by their citizens through contracts with larger units for their performance, or they could become special assessment "benefit districts" under general government management and without separate elective officials.

3. *Popular election should be confined to members of the policy-making body, and to the chief executive in those governments where the "strong mayor" form is preferred to the "council-manager" plan.*

Half-a-million local officials are elected by the people. Only about half of them are paid for their services, and five-sixths serve part time. We believe local government would benefit greatly from severe reduction of this huge number. Public attention should focus more sharply on key elective positions and major issues, and citizen struggles with the "bed-sheet" ballot should be ended.

4. *Each local unit should have a single chief executive, either elected by the people or appointed by the local legislative body, with all administrative agencies and personnel fully responsible to him; election of department heads should be halted.*

Few Americans would deny the necessity for unitary executive authority in any serious group undertaking. Only in government—and especially in local governments—do we tolerate multiple independent uncoordinated executive authority, with its paralyzing effects. Review and control can be obtained through independent post audits of accounts and operations.

5. *Personnel practices based on merit and professional competence should replace the personal or partisan "spoils" systems found in most counties and many other local units.*

Specialized skills are increasingly essential to solution of most governmental problems, whether in highway engineering, public health and sanitation, police and fire protection, education, pollution control, slum clearance, public finance, or in management as such. Skills require training and experience, as well as innate ability. Persons with high skills must be recruited, developed, and utilized effectively. This is unlikely to occur in a climate of petty partisanship, low salaries, and confused authority.

6. *County modernization should be pressed with special vigor, since counties—everywhere except in New England—have high but underdeveloped potential for solving the problems of rural, urban, and most metropolitan communities.*

Counties are less limited in area, population, and tax base than most local units, and consolidations could correct existing deficiencies in these respects. Their present legal powers are less adequate than those of municipalities, however. And county structural organizations and staffing patterns are obsolete. If the nation is seriously concerned about stronger and better local government, as it should be, these weaknesses must be remedied to permit counties to play a major role.

7. *Once modernized, local governments should be entrusted with broad legal powers permitting them to plan, finance, and execute programs suited to the special needs, interests, and desires of their citizens.*

The reluctance of the states to grant adequate discretion to even the largest city governments continues, although less evident than in the nineteenth century. Powers of other forms of local government are generally much more limited. State constitutions often prohibit legislatures from making effective grants of home rule. But broad grants of power should not be given to outmoded units incapable of using them properly.

8. *The 50 state constitutions should be revamped—either by legislative amendment or through constitutional conventions concentrating on local government modernization—to provide for boundary revisions, extensions of legal authority, and elimination of needless overlapping layers.*

The state legislatures must have authority to establish machinery to revise boundaries for all forms of local government. This function is wholly inappropriate to the local units themselves; they lack objectivity. The legislatures should also be entrusted with the extension of legal powers to the local units, subject to broad state policies.

9. *The terms and conditions of federal—and state—grants-in-aid should be revised to encourage the changes recommended in this statement.*

Presently, some aid programs favor small units over large. Prevailing patterns discourage coordination between governments and between departments of the same government performing different but related functions. Heavy financial aids to archaic structures tend to divert attention from the need to adapt to new conditions. They perpetuate obsolescence.

We are well aware of the sweeping scope of these proposals. Taken in combination they amount to a revolutionary readjustment of local forms designed to preserve the basic values in our federal system of government. Prevailing conditions and trends demand measures of such strength. But adoption of these recommendations—in whole or in major part—will, of course, face stern resistance. Concerted, persistent, and determined efforts must be made by dedicated community leadership before modern and efficient local government based upon the needs of today and the decades immediately ahead can be attained.

38. MAJOR FACTORS
IN URBAN PLANNING

Robert C. Weaver

In sharp contrast to the institutional solution to urban problems proposed earlier by the Committee for Economic Development, Robert Weaver, first Secretary of the Department of Housing and Urban Development, takes a frankly pragmatic position on the issue. Allowing for the possibility that metropolitan government may someday evolve from a fusion of complementary interest groups, Weaver advocates an immediate community-action approach to present difficulties. Judicious federal aid to localities may succeed in improving urban housing, employment opportunities, and education, he says, provided it is utililized in conjunction with responsible voluntary organization that enables the community itself to grow socially and culturally. In this manner it may be able to overcome the dangerous cleavages that it harbors and which hamstring and abort purely administrative programs.

In the process of developing his eclectic hypothesis, Weaver raises a number of theoretical questions concerning community leadership and apathy, the role of physical propinquity in regard to the social acceptance of minorities, and the causal relationship of substandard housing to deviance.

"Frontal attacks on discrimination in housing and residence," writes Weaver, "are already under way and can be expected to increase during the next few years." It might be noted that attacks since then have been formalized in the fair-housing title of the Civil Rights Act of 1968, which

Excerpts from *The Urban Condition*, edited by Leonard J. Duhl, M.D., © 1963 by Basic Books Inc., Publishers, New York, abridged version of Chapter 9. Reprinted by permission of the author and publisher.

outlaws discrimination in the sale or rental and financing of housing with few exceptions, and provides for education and enforcement to implement the law. Also, the U. S. Supreme Court, in the case of Jones v. Mayer Co., *decided in June, 1968, construed the Civil Rights Act of 1866 as forbidding racial discrimination in all housing, public or private.*

. . . IT SEEMS TO ME that we need to recognize frankly that the rational appeal of a comprehensive institutional "solution"—i.e., metropolitan government—is limited to professional students of urban problems. What has been called the "strong bias toward simplicity, uniformity and symmetry of structure" [1] which characterizes proposals for metropolitan organization arises from a professional consensus about an approach to metropolitan problem-solving which seems to have no popular counterpart among the citizens of such areas. In our attempts to find institutional means for coping with problems in metropolitan areas, therefore, it may be necessary to explore the possibilities for pragmatic and proximate adjustments rather than comprehensive remedies.

Second, a number of recent studies cast doubt on the likelihood that the first steps toward solving this institutional problem will be the result of any widespread, popular perception of metropolitan problems or any general consensus about ways of dealing with them. Recently, for example, Robert Dahl has reviewed the process of governmental decision-making in New Haven, where dramatic progress has been made in redeveloping the core area of the city. Most decisions concerned with problems such as this, Dahl notes, took place within a context of relatively complete indifference on the part of a majority of the citizens.[2] Participation in all types of activity related to public concerns was extremely limited, and a study of attitudes revealed that most citizens were primarily concerned with "personal matters, health, jobs, children, and the like . . ." [3]

Even if a majority of the residents of metropolitan areas are not regularly interested in the problems of the larger community, however, is it not likely that the functional problems of the environment will compel their attention? Will problems which impinge directly on individuals and their private interests—the problems of children and schools, the frustrations of the journey to work, the need for "shelter"—mobilize interest and action? . . . As Dahl has noted, "in a political culture where individual achievement and non-governmental techniques are assigned a high priority in problem-solving, men may be frustrated in their primary activities without ever turning to politics for solutions." Dahl concludes from this study that the "ancient myth about the concern of citizens with the life of the democratic *polis* is false in the case of New Haven. Whether or not the myth was a reality in Athens will probably never be known." [4]

Third, the structure and operation of metropolitan organizations will need to reflect the considerable differences which appear to exist in levels of popular awareness and participation in public affairs. If we reject traditional assumptions that everyone is interested in public problems and interested to the same degree, it would appear that unitary institutional solutions will probably be unworkable. While the alternatives may not be subject to detailed description, some observers have stressed the desirability of metropolitan organizations which incorporate a high degree of centralized authority with respect to certain functions and a considerable degree of decentralization with respect to others. In their study of Chicago, Meyerson and Banfield . . . have noted:

> Most of the matters that were decided locally were of local interest. Whether a street was to be paved, the zoning law for a block changed, and the traffic cop transferred were questions which had direct and clearly ascertainable consequences mainly for the locality. . . . Some matters were on the border between being of local and of city-wide interest. . . . In these matters there would be friction because of overlapping jurisdictions of the local and central power holders.[5]

In metropolitan areas, there may be even sharper distinctions which can be drawn between matters of general interest—such as the provision of transportation, public utilities, recreation, and open space—and the concerns of most citizens for the problems of suburb and neighborhood.

Fourth, whatever institutional methods we design for dealing with metropolitan problems, it seems likely that considerable leadership will be necessary to create and sustain them. It might be argued that consensus in our metropolitan areas will be achieved *within* the developing framework of various types of metropolitan organizations, rather than before their creation. Perhaps the history of the federal union of the states provides a useful model in this respect.

If this historic example has any validity, it also suggests among other things that resourceful leadership will be necessary to bring such organizations into existence. . . . As Dahl has observed, "Instead of seeking to explain why citizens are not interested, concerned and active, the task is to explain why a few citizens *are*." [6]

Fifth, among the many tasks which an emerging metropolitan leadership must confront, perhaps none is more important than that of developing a more widespread and effective sense of *membership* in the metropolitan community than exists today. On the one hand, the task of this leadership will be concerned with defining values and assisting in the process of establishing the goals and aims of the community. On the other, it must be concerned with minimizing conflict and bridging the cleavages in race and class which increasingly challenge the values and goals of urban life in the United States.

SEGREGATION AND SOCIAL CLEAVAGES

Beneath the patchwork of local governments that spreads across the metropolis, there has developed a more troubling pattern of racial segregation and socio-economic stratification. In many ways, the increasing urbanization of the nation seems to have involved a centrifugal process by which races and classes are being separated out in terms of residence within metropolitan areas. . . . Increasingly, central cities are tending to become ghettos for the racially and economically underprivileged, so that divisions between city and suburb are becoming ones of race and class.

In analyzing these developments, it is useful to note how they differ from earlier patterns of development in urban areas. As has been noted elsewhere, the middle classes in American cities in the nineteenth century also tended to move away from the newer immigrants. But while the densely concentrated cities of that era also evidenced stratification and segregation, an important point is that this pattern tended to be concentrated largely within the boundaries of one municipality. Thus, an escape from residential proximity to the newer immigrants did not involve an avoidance of the social welfare and other costs which resulted from providing municipal services for these minorities.[7]

The flight to the suburbs in recent years has also been motivated in part by similar desires on the part of today's middle classes, many of whom are the children or grandchildren of yesterday's ethnic newcomers. Because of the pattern of local government in metropolitan areas today, however, this flight often results in an escape from the problems—and their costs. Attempts at metropolitan organization which will require sharing these costs and pooling resources, therefore, are likely to encounter resistance which finds some of its origin in racial prejudice and socio-economic exclusiveness.

The operation of racial prejudice in housing and residence also must be distinguished, in its effects on the Negro, from the effects which prejudice had on earlier ethnic minorities. . . . the goals of better housing, improved neighborhood, and better schools seemed within the reach of earlier minorities once they could secure the economic rewards which resulted from conformity to the Calvinist virtues of thrift, ambition, and industry.

The non-white, however, is confronted with a different situation. The economic status of the Negro has risen considerably during the last twenty years, and a significant Negro middle class is emerging. In their aspirations, self-image, and tastes, this group has taken on most of the traditional characteristics of the American middle class. In contrast to earlier ethnic minorities, however, the Negro is "stuck with pigmentation which in our society is the badge of difference and inferiority." [8] Nowhere is this more apparent than in the matter of housing and residence. Racial prejudice continues to bar the Negro from the type of housing and place of residence for which his income, aspirations, and behavior qualify him.

If the existence of racial prejudice frustrates the attempts of Negroes to secure improved housing in better neighborhoods, it also operates to limit the effectiveness of public programs designed to increase the supply of housing and improve the physical environment of the city. Federal housing programs, for example, have originated in a national consensus on the need to insure that there is decent, safe, and sanitary housing for every American family. The contradiction between national purpose and local prejudice, however, has long been evident. In many cities, low-rent public housing programs are restricted to the crowded older areas, and have resulted in the construction of new housing in an environment of blight and segregation. The Federal Urban Renewal Program has provided the means by which local public agencies could eliminate blighted housing and deteriorated areas of the central cities; but the net gains of this program have been seriously affected in many cities because of the existence of racial prejudice and discrimination. Local attempts to relocate families displaced by urban renewal projects into decent housing and better neighborhoods have been unsuccessful in many instances. During the past year we have recognized these problems, and federal programs are increasingly emphasizing more effective relocation at the local level. But the basic problem still harasses us.

Frontal attacks on discrimination in housing and residence are already under way and can be expected to increase during the next few years. As a result of this struggle, there will be an appearance of less and less understanding between the majority and minority groups. As I have said elsewhere, however, such tensions are frequently evidence of progress.

This prospect of the racial integration of neighborhoods in our cities raises some interesting questions about the degree of social communication and sharing of values which we can expect as a result of such integration. Let me explore this question by examining an assumption which seems to me to underlie some of the thinking in this field.

· · ·

As I listen to some planners, they seem to suggest that physical propinquity between people of differing attitudes and social characteristics in some way produces meaningful social interaction and results in mutual identity and a reduction in social tensions. Planners and others have therefore emphasized the need for "balanced" neighborhoods which include people with a diversity of economic and social characteristics; and have laid emphasis on the physical design or layout of neighborhoods as a way of increasing meaningful communication. More recently there has also been a recrudescence of nostalgia for the "diversity" and "heterogeneity" which characterized certain neighborhoods in the central city.

Again, the implication seems to be that population density and diversity and the physical design of the city exercise some unique and desirable influence on attitudes and behavior.

Stated in another way, one wonders whether mere physical "togetherness" alone will bridge the cleavages which separate race and class in the modern city. Urban ecologists need to take a careful look at these assumptions; and research is needed into questions of how the physical form of the neighborhood and the social characteristics of its residents influence behavior and attitudes. It is conceivable—and I strongly suspect it to be true—that such research would indicate that physical propinquity may be an important, and at times indispensable, element in creating understanding and mutual appreciation among certain elements in our society. However, it may well be that such proximity is only a physical setting in which *other* carefully selected activities are required, to yield maximum results.

Perhaps, indeed, had we not created these consciously homogeneous neighborhoods, we should have less cleavage. But are not the two developments part and parcel of the same forces and attitudes? In part, this is true. But also the drive to sell exclusiveness, so characteristic of the development of suburbia, introduced an element of prestige in single-class and single-race developments. The result is that such neighborhoods today are both the symbol and the embodiment of social distance between classes and ethnic groups. Destruction of this symbol is fundamental to changing class and racial attitudes and distance, but it is doubtful if it, of and in itself, will effect the change.[9]

Recent experience in the urban renewal process tends to magnify the importance which should be assigned to the function of voluntary groups in helping to bring the success of programs to change and improve the environment of the city. In too many communities, plans for the clearing of blighted and obsolete areas have been viewed as matters which can be decided by technicians in consultation with the local power elite. Where these plans have ignored the needs and desires of significant groups in the community, and where the programs have been implemented largely by government action without enlisting the support and advice of citizen groups, urban renewal programs have gotten into serious difficulties.

Elsewhere, the process has been so markedly different that two observers have concluded recently that:

> It seems likely that successful urban renewal in large cities—successful in the sense of widely accepted both within and without the neighborhoods under renewal—will come primarily either in neighborhoods that have indigenous successful community organization or in neighborhoods in which some outside agency manages to create one.[10]

Because of such experience, students of urban problems need to give careful attention to the ways in which voluntary groups can provide the means for stimulating a more widespread sense of interdependence and mutual responsibility in the metropolitan community. . . .

We are reminded by Oscar Handlin of the important part which such groups played in solving the new and unfamiliar problems of the large city of the nineteenth century. Handlin has observed that the social system in cities in that time was

> . . . loosely structured through a large number of autonomous and scarcely articulated associations. The disorder of that situation in some ways added to the problems of expansion. But it provided a viable means through which large populations could act together toward immediate goals under unfamiliar conditions.[11]

Students of urban problems need to investigate whether it is possible for some outside agency to "create" such organizations, as suggested in the quotation cited earlier, particularly in situations where social disorganization and anomie have resulted in a paucity of active voluntary groups. While one of the problems confronting us may be the need for creating a metropolitan community in fact as well as in name, our ability to do this may be seriously conditioned by the success with which we are able to encourage voluntary groups to emerge in response to these problems.

Before prescribing community organization as the sovereign remedy for the social ills of the metropolis, therefore, it might be useful to reflect on the cautionary note sounded by Handlin, a note whose implications need to be investigated by social psychologists and students of culture and personality. Handlin writes:

> The growth of the contemporary suburb has . . . been only symptomatic of broader social changes in the life of the city. Lacking firmly fixed personal or social goals—and swayed by the imprecise standards communicated through the mass media, large parts of its population have lost the capacity for acting meaningfully in groups, except when it comes to matters which touch immediately upon their family life. Outside these narrow personal concerns there has been a perceptible decline in the capacity for group action.[12]

URBAN MIGRANTS AND THEIR ENVIRONMENT

As the third and final example of the problems confronting urban planning, I have chosen some of the issues which involve the newest immigrants to our cities. Southern Negroes, Appalachian Whites, Puerto Ricans, and American Indians have been migrating to the city in large numbers in recent decades. As in the past, they inhabit the worst slums and the most deteriorated neighborhoods of the central cities. While all this is in the classic pattern of earlier immigration, these new arrivals present some unique problems which challenge us to re-examine traditional answers to questions about the methods and goals of acculturation and adjustment to the urban environment.

Perhaps the most obvious of these traditional "answers" involves what John P. Dean has called the "myths of housing reform." [13] Dean and other observers have demonstrated that a great many of the arguments for clearing slums and providing improved housing for slum dwellers were premised upon specious evidence about the supposedly causal role of slums in crime, delinquency, and ill-health. Most of this evidence, which consisted of correlations between evidence about the physical condition of housing and rates of social disorder and disease within slum areas, has been characterized by Robert K. Merton as follows:

> In its early phase social and psychological research on housing was virtually confined to social bookkeeping. During this phase, it was conventionally assumed that research comprised periodic audits of the proportion of substandard dwellings, meticulously described in terms of defective plumbing, defective structures, and, consequently, defective residents. It was devoted to gross and uncritical correlations between something called "bad housing"—typically meaning either slum areas with a high frequency of substandard housing or household groups living in substandard housing —and a series of social morbidities. . . . Yet the long and still continuing series of reports showing uniformly that slum areas, with their defective housing, are characterized by these social morbidities have seldom shown the role played by specifiable aspects of substandard housing.[14]

As a result of the assumption that the physical conditions of housing and neighborhoods have a direct and baneful effect upon the personalities and morals of slum dwellers, it is not surprising that rehousing was justified in terms of the beneficial effects it would have upon their attitudes and behavior. As Dean observed:

> The reformers argued . . . that ill health, uncleanliness, and delinquency are not *innate* characteristics, but are the result of life in the slum environment. Their conception of the slum environment emphasized primarily the inadequate *physical* environment of the slums. It understressed the connection between the *social* environment of the slums and the disorders they want to cure. So it was easy to jump to the conclusion that slum clearance would remove the social ills. . . .[15]

While today few would contend that there is such a direct relationship between physical and social behavior, it may be useful to review past experience if only to remind ourselves of the complexity of the problem we confront in trying to discharge the responsibility which our cities have toward the urban immigrants upon whose labors their economies are so dependent. Clearly, new housing and new neighborhoods are not in and of themselves enough to accomplish the acculturation of the urban immigrant and the slum dweller.

A similar observation has been made recently by James B. Conant, who writes:

Among the preoccupations of those concerned with underprivileged
areas, one often encounters a great emphasis on the importance of adequate, decent housing. To be sure, the inhabitants in slums (Negro and
white) may be living in shockingly bad and even dangerous dwellings.
They may also be living in new housing which is the result of a slum clearance project. I am willing to assume that improving the physical environment improves the lives of the inhabitants. To the extent that increased
housing facilities diminish the mobility of the population, they may even
have a direct bearing on the problem of education. But I am sure new
housing works no miracles. I offer the following hypothesis for professional
social workers and sociologists to demolish—namely, that the correlation
between desirable social attitudes (including attitudes of youths) and job
opportunities is far higher than between the former and housing conditions, as measured by plumbing and heating facilities, and space per
family.[16]

Yet in trying to do "more" than improve housing, we confront several
major problems. The first, and more familiar, concerns the continuing vitality of certain traditional popular beliefs about individualism—"Any
man worth his salt will improve himself"—the debilitating effects of
"charity," and the moral requirements for such charity. In criticizing the
housing reformers for their failure to perceive the necessity of combining
rehousing with extensive programs of social welfare measures, we must
remember that their basic claim about the social right of every American
family to a decent house is still disputed by a number of people in our society. If the traditional ethics of individualism have seriously circumscribed even the limited intentions of the public housing program, these
same beliefs continue to impede the development of improved programs
based upon subsequent insights and broader intentions.

Whatever the content and methods of the programs we devise for assisting urban migrants and slum dwellers, our ability to implement those
programs will depend upon the degree to which there is a growing acceptance and acknowledgement of the community's responsibilities to all
people. In assessing these prospects we must not be too quick in our optimism about assured progress in this sphere. The ethnic tensions and class
antagonisms which marked the urban scene of the nineteenth century
may have abated. It remains to be seen, however, whether our urban society has made strides toward developing more widespread social integration.

The second problem concerns the choice of methods which we will
make and the success which we can expect from them. I mention this because it has lately become fashionable to criticize the naivete which some
have seen as a characteristic of reform movements in America. If we are
to be fashionable and hard-headed, it seems to me that we must acknowledge that dramatic progress in motivating the new urban immigrants to
acculturate to the dominant values of our society is not probable until we
can substantially alter the institutional conditions in our society which
result in low wages, high rates of unemployment, and racial discrimination.

We cannot expect impressive results, for example, in inculcating the economic virtues of thrift in unskilled urban laborers with little job security and few prospects for improvement. There will probably not be dramatic mass conversions to middle class values on the part of Negro immigrants from the South as long as they see their middle class brothers confined by racial prejudice to the same residential ghettos inhabited by the newest arrivals to the city.

Given these problems, it seems to me that our search for the means to assist the urban immigrant must be directed toward several goals and must involve a diversity of techniques.

Perhaps our first objective must be to find techniques for assisting the transition to middle class status of those who are obviously upwardly mobile. For non-whites, for example, this will mean intensified efforts to increase opportunities for training and education which will enable them to enter professional, technical, and managerial groups. It will mean a continued struggle against discrimination in employment. And, as I have mentioned earlier, it will require that racial bars in housing and residence be removed.

The second objective involves the more difficult task of finding ways to "accelerate the effective functioning in urban life of those who do not become middle class." [17] Accepting such an objective may be difficult because it will require us to modify some of our traditional optimistic assumptions, about both the availability of middle class rewards in our society and the ability of individuals whose experiences or expectations have been devoid of middle class rewards to respond quickly to them. Those who refuse to acknowledge any responsibility for the problems of the immigrant and slum dweller probably make some such assumptions, at least tacitly.

This will be more difficult for many of us who are concerned with these problems because it may appear to require compromising basic social goals. One of the results of adopting such an objective, however, may be a distinct improvement in our ability to communicate with those whom we seek to assist. . . . As one perceptive foreign observer has noted, "if society is less frustrating than the subculture prefers to believe, it is also less open than it claims." [18]

In seeking to implement this second objective, it will be necessary to develop a number of new techniques. How, for example, are we to communicate more effectively with cultural groups who attach very different worth to the values of ambition, competition, and consumption, than we do? What are the behavioral norms which are required for successful urban living, and how can they be obtained? What types of cultural conditioning will be most successful in broadening the horizons of those "who have given up trying to escape from the ghetto life?" [19] . . .

In my discussion of this problem of urban immigrants, I have attempted to stress some of our own assumptions, attitudes and "answers" which will require modification and change if we are to be successful in formulating the problems and the programs. It has seemed important to do this because I believe that if we are successful in the pursuit of our basic objective—assisting the immigrants to acculturate to urban life—we can make an important contribution to the quality of urban life in the process. . . .

39. SUCCESSFUL SCHOOL DESEGREGATION

U. S. Commission on Civil Rights

In prescribing techniques to reduce the de facto racial imbalance in the public schools of our large cities, the Civil Rights Commission recognizes that improvement in the quality of education is essential to successful school integration. Open enrollment and busing, the alteration of attendance areas, and cooperation between inner-city and suburban school systems are the primary means by which the commingling of the races can be achieved in urban education. Without, however, forceful state and local leadership to promote a positive interracial climate within the schools, these procedures can be of only limited value.

The Commission has also investigated other ways of securing school integration, notably by the establishment of special-purpose schools permitting interracial use. It has also advocated the improvement of public education through staff development, individual instruction, flexible class organization, and programmed instruction. The successful desegration that it indicates has been accomplished in certain smaller Northern and Western cities the Commission attributes to the size of those cities, allowing strategic site selection or redistricting, and the smaller proportion of Negroes necessitating less extensive changes.

THE SUCCESS that some small cities have experienced in desegregating their schools has not been matched in the Nation's larger cities where the obstacles to desegregation are greater. In a large city, depending on the particular pattern of residential segregation, both Negro and white popu-

From *Racial Isolation in the Public Schools,* Volume 1, A Report of the United States Commission on Civil Rights, 1967.

lation areas may be more extensive in territory. For example, San Francisco has relatively small Negro areas spread throughout the city while Cleveland's Negro population is concentrated heavily in a large ghetto on one side of the city. In a city such as Cleveland, then, the bulk of the Negro population lives relatively farther away from the bulk of the white population. In addition, there have been frequent shifts in the racial character of neighborhoods in large cities. For these reasons, it may be more difficult to achieve school desegregation through strategic selection of school sites, adjustments in attendance area boundaries, or devices which involve enlargement of attendance areas.

Beyond this, the rising Negro population in larger cities makes school desegregation more difficult simply because Negroes tend to constitute a greater proportion of the student enrollment than they do in small cities. This is not universally true. In Boston and Milwaukee, for example, Negroes constitute a relatively small proportion of the school enrollment. But in many large cities, such as Chicago, Baltimore, Detroit, and Philadelphia, the Negro elementary school enrollment already is so great that it is impossible even theoretically to eliminate majority-Negro schools without the cooperation of the suburbs.

Efforts to reduce racial imbalance in most big cities fall generally into three categories: (1) those which seek to reduce imbalance without altering existing attendance areas; (2) those which alter or enlarge attendance areas; and, (3) those which involve cooperation between suburban and central city school jurisdictions.

A number of big city school systems have attempted to reduce racial imbalance without altering established attendance areas. Devices used include open enrollment and busing.

Open Enrollment , An open enrollment plan permits a student to attend an underutilized school outside of the attendance zone in which his residence is located. The purpose of such a plan may be to grant pupils a choice of schools, to relieve racial imbalance, or both.

Under some open enrollment plans, transportation costs must be paid by a family wishing to send its child to a school outside the neighborhood. This is the policy in Boston, where, after school authorities refused to provide transportation, a private busing program—Operation Exodus —was organized and supported by Negro parents in the Roxbury area with the help of contributions from various sources. Operation Exodus sponsored transportation for almost 600 Negro students who transferred from predominantly Negro to predominantly white schools during the 1965–66 school year. Nevertheless, the requirement that transportation expenses be paid by the family imposes obvious limitations on achieving significant desegregation. At its Boston hearing, the Commission heard testimony concerning the difficult financial circumstances under which Operation Exodus was operating in the 1966–67 school year.

Open enrollment plans also are subject to limitations imposed by available space. As part of an overall plan to alleviate racial imbalance, the school board in Rochester, N.Y., adopted in 1963 an open enrollment plan under which transportation was furnished by the school system. The Rochester school superintendent told the Commission of his desire to see open enrollment work in his city:

> When the Board of Education on November 16, 1963, passed unanimously a resolution directing me to prepare administrative regulations to institute open enrollment, I was determined that it was going to work, not to fail.
> I analyzed why open enrollment had failed in many other cities and there were two basic reasons: One, the transportation costs became a burden for the family. . . . Second . . . open enrollment programs suggested in this country failed because the burden was placed on the parent to walk to the school and up to the counter of the secretary or principal and to say, "I want open enrollment," to say it verbally, to come and make personal application. And I vowed to eliminate both those hurdles.

The school system sent letters to parents of children in certain schools located in Negro residential areas, offering the opportunity to transfer. Negro families in significant numbers—more than a thousand—applied. But owing to limitations on the capacity of the receiving schools, only 660 applications could be accepted. Thus even where transportation costs are paid by the school system, open enrollment is limited by the space available in the predominantly white schools.

Open enrollment also has other limitations which restrict its effectiveness as a device to reduce racial imbalance. While experience in Boston and Rochester has shown that many Negro families take advantage of open enrollment, others do not. The reasons are varied. Many Negro families, like many white families, prefer to have their children attend a school close to home. . . . moreover, racial isolation tends to foster negative attitudes toward desegregation for Negroes as well as white persons. Again, Negro parents who gladly might participate in a desegregation plan affecting the entire community may be reluctant to require their children to assume the role of pioneers in an almost all-white school and they may resent being forced to assume the entire burden of desegregation themselves.

There are other limitations inherent in open enrollment. As an advisory committee to the Massachusetts State Commissioner of Education wrote: "Open enrollment alone cannot achieve school integration. Relying on open enrollment places the responsibility for school integration on the uncoordinated actions of thousands of parents, rather than on the planned actions of the schools themselves."

Another drawback of open enrollment is that it does not improve the racial balance of majority-Negro schools. Indeed, where the plan permits white students as well as Negro students to transfer, the result may be to increase isolation at predominantly Negro schools by permitting white students to transfer out of such schools. Still another problem is that open enrollment may drain from majority-Negro schools the students who have the highest aspirations.

Busing   Some school systems have sought to relieve racial imbalance by transporting Negro children from their normal attendance areas to predominantly white schools in other parts of the city. For example, in Portland, Oreg.—a city with an elementary school enrollment of 54,717 of which 4,482 are Negro—some 400 elementary school children, 90 percent of whom are Negroes, currently are being bused with Federal financial aid to 34 white schools outside their regular attendance areas. A Portland school official has acknowledged, however, that busing has not significantly affected the racial composition of Portland's elementary schools because so few children are involved.

In Philadelphia, more than 9,000 elementary and junior high school children—of a total elementary and junior high school enrollment of more than 200,000—are being bused during the 1966–67 school year, both to relieve overcrowding and to reduce racial imbalance. Almost 7,000 of the bused students are from schools that are more than 90 percent Negro. In Philadelphia, 66 percent of the Negro children attended such schools at both the elementary and junior high level in 1965. Approximately 55 percent of the children from the schools which are more than 90 percent Negro are being bused to predominantly white schools. The remainder are being transported to schools that are more than 50 percent Negro. Practically all students bused from overcrowded majority-white schools are assigned to majority-white schools.

ALTERATIONS IN ATTENDANCE AREAS

Among the measures which large cities have used or have contemplated using to reduce racial imbalance are devices which involve changes in attendance areas. Such devices include strategic selection of school sites (which involves the establishment of new attendance areas and concomitant changes in old attendance areas), boundary changes, and school pairing.

Site Selection   The strategic use of site selection as a device to relieve racial imbalance has been mentioned by some school boards, such as those in San Francisco and Philadelphia, in policy statements. In Rochester, school authorities are planning to locate a new junior high school to assure that it will open racially balanced. Some educators, discussing school desegregation in large cities, have suggested that this approach has limitations. The construction of a small school on the periphery of a Negro ghetto may not guarantee stable desegregation, for it is these very areas which frequently experience rapid racial turnover. At the Commission's Cleveland hearing, Paul Briggs, Cleveland Superintendent of Schools, testified that the changing nature of residential patterns in that city made it virtually impossible to achieve school desegregation by this means, even at the high school level:

> When Kennedy Senior High School was first envisioned, if that high school had opened that day in that location, it would have been 60 percent white and 40 percent Negro. When it opened it was 95 percent Negro.

Boundary Changes As a means of eliminating racial imbalance, the adjustment of attendance area boundaries in large school systems essentially has the same limitations as strategic site selection. Only at the periphery of Negro and white areas would boundary adjustments affect a school's racial composition. The small elementary school attendance areas make it unlikely that redistricting can result in lasting desegregation. In New York City, for example, to promote desegregation about 100 boundary changes were made between 1959 and 1963. The Advisory Committee to the State Commissioner of Education pointed out that, despite these changes, the extent of segregation in the city's schools was greater in 1963 than in 1958.

In Chicago, a study of the schools concluded: "Even if the most extreme procedures of redistricting school attendance areas to increase desegregation were to be used, there would still be all-Negro and all-white schools in the city." A study of school redistricting in Boston, which has a relatively small Negro residential area, estimated that the most comprehensive redistricting in that city would reduce the percentage of nonwhite children in majority-Negro elementary schools from 78 to 65. The study did not consider redistricting to be a permanent solution.

School Pairing School pairing involving schools located close to each other and with contiguous attendance zones has enabled some smaller communities to desegregate entire grade divisions of their school systems. In big cities the potential effectiveness of this device is more limited. Desegregation can be achieved by such pairing only when the schools involved are located at or near the border of Negro and white neighborhoods. Large cities have more schools which are located at or near the centers of white and Negro concentrations.

In New York City, the Board of Education in 1964 proposed 21 pairings involving 42 schools. The proposal, however, would have had little impact. Commissioner Allen's Advisory Committee observed:

> If all 21 of the pairings proposed by the board were to be introduced at once . . . school segregation [would have been reduced] by 1 percent. . . .

METROPOLITAN DESEGREGATION

In a few large cities efforts have been made to place youngsters from majority-Negro central city schools in neighboring suburban school systems.

Programs of this kind are operating in the Rochester, N.Y., Boston, Mass., and Hartford, Conn., metropolitan areas.

Rochester   In March 1965, the school board in West Irondequoit, a Rochester suburb, agreed to accept 25 first graders from racially imbalanced Rochester schools. Apart from the transported students, West Irondequoit had four Negro students in an enrollment of approximately 5,800.

The students selected to participate were from a predominantly Negro school located in a middle-class Negro area. The Rochester school administration felt that these children would have the best chance to succeed. The staff screened 58 incoming first-grade children in order to choose those who were average and above average. Parental consent was obtained. Each year approximately 25 more children from central city Rochester schools will enter the first grade in West Irondequoit, until the number of inner-city children reaches 300. Under the plan, no more than four and no less than two Negro children are assigned to the same classroom. Rochester pays the tuition and provides the transportation for the children participating in the program. Most of the tuition and transportation costs are reimbursed by the State and by Federal funds under Title I of the Elementary and Secondary Education Act.

At the Commission's Rochester hearing, William C. Rock, Administrative Director of Planning and Research for the Rochester school system, reported on an evaluation of the program conducted by the Rochester and West Irondequoit school systems. Among the conclusions reached in the study was that "the program is working well and that children at this time are benefiting from the experience." When the achievement of the transferred students and a matched group of students in the sending school was compared, it was found that children in the group going to West Irondequoit were reading consistently at grade level, while the children in the matched control group at the sending school were not reading consistently up to grade level.

All of the children involved in the first year of the West Irondequoit program returned during the 1966–67 school year. Two parents of Negro children participating in the program testified at the Commission hearing in Rochester that their children had had normal school experiences and had adjusted well to school.

Boston   The population of the Boston Metropolitan Area in 1960 was more than 2.5 million. About 3 percent were Negroes who were concentrated primarily within the city of Boston. In September 1966, an organization known at METCO (Metropolitan Council for Educational Opportunities) —a group of private citizens from Boston and surrounding suburban communities who are concerned with educational problems in the metropolitan area—began a program under which 220 children are bused from the predominantly Negro Roxbury-North Dorchester and South End areas of the city to public schools in seven suburban communities. The students selected came from different social class backgrounds and spanned a range of ability. Student participation in METCO is voluntary and the communities taking part have committed themselves to educate the participating children until their graduation from high school.

The METCO program, funded by a private foundation and the U. S. Office of Education under Title III of the Elementary and Secondary Education Act, also is eligible for State assistance under a recently passed law.

METCO leaders hope to expand the busing program next year to include more students and additional communities. Plans to involve 300 additional Boston children in the 1967–68 school year have been announced. Three additional suburban communities have committed themselves informally to participate in METCO next year and 22 other suburban communities have indicated some interest.

Hartford   Of the more than 500,000 persons who live in the Hartford, Conn., Metropolitan Area, nearly 30,000 are Negroes, 25,000 of whom live in the city of Hartford. Since September 1966, 267 Negro elementary school children have been bused from predominantly Negro schools in Hartford to 33 schools in 5 surrounding suburban communities. The program, "Project Concern," is supported by Federal and private foundation funds, and by money from the State and from the city of Hartford. The children from the inner-city schools were chosen at random and no child was excluded because of his ability or achievement level. Less than 5 percent of the children selected declined to participate. The final bused group was 88 percent Negro, 10 percent Puerto Rican, and 2 percent white. The 267 children were assigned to the suburban schools on a vacant seat basis, but with a limit of three Hartford students to a class.

Each child has been placed in the grade he would have attended in the city schools. A supportive team consisting of a teacher and a nonprofessional teacher's aide has been provided for every 25 city children. These teams work with the regular classroom teachers and are concerned primarily with remedial educational activities, to be carried on in small racially mixed groups, and with home-school liaison.

These metropolitan programs affect very small numbers of Negro children and they do not reduce racial isolation in city schools. In spite of their current limitations, however, they show promise. Plans extending beyond central city limits and involving the wider metropolitan area have potential for affecting greater numbers of students and schools than plans confined to the cities alone. This, obviously, is true of cities which have majority-Negro student enrollments.

Progress in reducing racial isolation in city schools has not been extensive. In a number of smaller communities, efforts to eliminate school segregation have been successful. A variety of techniques has been used, mainly involving the enlargement of school attendance areas to overcome residential segregation.

In the Nation's large urban centers, comparatively little progress has been made. Larger areas of racial concentration and rapid racial turnover in peripheral areas have made it difficult for big city school systems to reduce racial imbalance. Techniques that may produce total desegregation in small communities appear to provide few lasting solutions in large cities. In many large cities, school desegregation cannot be achieved without substantial revision of school assignment policies.

In some cities, Negro students already constitute a majority of the public school enrollment. In these cities, solutions not involving suburban participation no longer are possible. John Fischer, reviewing the progress of school desegregation in big cities, has written:

> Twelve years of effort, some ingeniously *pro forma* and some laboriously genuine, have proved that desegregating schools . . . is much more difficult than it first appeared. Attendance area boundaries have been redrawn; new schools have been built in border areas; parents have been permitted, even encouraged, to choose more desirable schools for their children; pupils from crowded slum schools have been bused to outlying schools; "Negro" and "white" schools have been paired and their student bodies merged; but in few cases have the results been wholly satisfactory. Despite some initial success and a few stable solutions, the consequences, for the most part, have proved disappointing. Steady increases in urban Negro population, continuing shifts in the racial character of neighborhoods . . . produce new problems faster than old ones could be solved.

In a few large cities, metropolitan programs are emerging. Small in number and impact, they nevertheless are promising first steps.

40. THE COMMUNITY RESPONSE

National Advisory Commission on Civil Disorders

Appointed by President Johnson after the 1967 Detroit riot, the Advisory Commission on Civil Disorders was mandated to aid the nation in coming to grips with the menace of ghetto violence. The Commission was headed by Governor Otto Kerner of Illinois, with New York's Mayor John Lindsay as Vice-Chairman. Though made promptly, even months ahead of its deadline, the Commission's Report was coolly received by the President, apparently disappointed that the Administration's accomplishments in the field of civil rights and the War on Poverty had not been given proper recognition. Others, like Amitai Etzioni, scorned the Report as a ritual response to grave danger and injustice.

The Commission took the position of the Lemberg Center on Violence, that ghetto disturbances were produced by unresolved grievances accompanied by the conviction that redress was not to be expected. It also concluded that "white racism" was ultimately responsible for the plight of the black minority. Specifically, the Report blamed poor communication between local government and ghetto residents for contributing to the many riots that had recently occurred in America's cities. In addition, the Commission observed that the structure of our municipal governments was ill suited to respond effectively to the multi-problem population that inhabited the inner-city. Although it made many recommendations—too many to be forcefully acted on, its critics said—to improve the economic status of the urban poor, it also stressed reform on the part of city government. The Commission advocated a two-phase program for closing the breach between local government and the ghetto by means of expanded participation in decision-making.

Excerpts from *Report of the National Advisory Commission on Civil Disorders*, Bantam Book edition. © 1968 by The New York Times Company. Reprinted by permission.

No DEMOCRATIC SOCIETY can long endure the existence within its major urban centers of a substantial number of citizens who feel deeply aggrieved as a group, yet lack confidence in the government to rectify perceived injustice and in their ability to bring about needed change.

We are aware that reforms in existing instruments of local government and their relationship to the ghetto population will mean little unless joined with sincere and comprehensive response to the severe social and economic needs of ghetto residents. . . .

We believe, however, that there are measures which can and should be taken now; that they can be put to work without great cost and without delay; that they can be built upon in the future and that they will effectively reduce the level of grievance and tension as well as improve the responsiveness of local government to the needs of ghetto residents.

BASIC STRATEGY AND GOALS

To meet the needs identified above, we recommend pursuit of a comprehensive strategy, which would accomplish the following goals:

- Effective communication between ghetto residents and local government.
- Improved ability of local government to respond to the needs and problems of ghetto residents.
- Expanded opportunities for indigenous leadership to participate in shaping decisions and policies which affect their community.
- Increased accountability of public officials.

We recognize that not all of the programs proposed below to implement the foregoing goals can be instituted with the immediacy which the problem requires. Because the need for action at the local level, where government impinges directly upon the ghetto resident, is particularly urgent, we propose that our suggested programs be implemented in two phases. It is vital, however, that the first phase programs not be regarded or perceived as short term anti-riot efforts calculated to cool already inflamed situations. These programs will have little chance of succeeding unless they are part of a long-range commitment to action designed to eliminate the fundamental sources of grievance and tension.

PROGRAMS: FIRST PHASE ACTIONS

Establishment of Neighborhood Action Task Forces

To open channels of communication between government and ghetto residents, improve the capacity of the city administration to respond effectively to community needs and provide opportunity for meaningful citizen participation in decision-making, we recommend establishment of joint government-community Neighborhood Action Task Forces covering each neighborhood within the city which has a high proportion of low-income minority citizens. While the exact form of these groups will depend upon the size and needs of each municipality, the following basic features should be incorporated:

Composition Each Task Force should include a key official in the mayor's office with direct and immediate access to the mayor, ranking city officials from the operating agencies servicing the ghetto community, elected leaders, representatives from the local business, labor, professional and church communities and neighborhood leaders, including representatives of community organizations of all orientations and youth leaders. Each Task Force would be headed by the mayor's representative. In the larger cities, each of these chairmen would sit as a member of a city-wide Urban Action Task Force.

Functions The Neighborhood Action Task Forces should meet on a regular basis at a location accessible to ghetto residents. These meetings will afford an opportunity for ghetto leaders to communicate directly with the municipal administrators for their area to discuss problems and programs which affect the community. In effect, this device furnishes an inter-agency coordinating mechanism on the one hand and a "community cabinet" on the other.

Ghetto residents should be able to rely on the capacity of the Task Force to cut through the maze of red tape and to overcome bureaucratic barriers in order to make things—collection of garbage, removal of abandoned cars, installation of lights in the park, establishment of playstreets —happen. To accomplish this purpose, the participating city officials should be those with operational decision-making authority. Lesser staff or public relations personnel will not be able to provide the confrontation and interaction with the community representatives which is essential to the effective functioning of the Task Force. Moreover, there is grave danger that opening channels of communication without providing opportunities for obtaining relief will further estrange ghetto residents. If this is not to happen, the Task Force should have a meaningful and realistic capacity for securing redress of grievances. For the same reason, it is essential that the Task Force have the full and energetic support of the mayor and the city council.

The potential for responding effectively to community needs is not limited to available public resources. Acting through business, labor and church members and local Urban Coalitions which have already been formed, the Task Force will have a capacity to involve the resources of the private sector in meeting needs within the ghetto. Possibilities range from support of special summer youth programs (weekend trips, recreation events, camping programs) to provision of cultural and employment opportunities on a year-round basis.

The Neighborhood Action Task Force can play a significant role with respect to youth activities. One possibility involves the establishment of Youth Councils which would employ young street leaders (regardless of previous police records) to develop community programs for other alienated youth. These activities might include organizing and operating remedial libraries, neighborhood cleanup campaigns, police-community dialogues and sports competitions in their own neighborhoods.

Finally, the Task Force can make a major contribution to the prevention of civil disorders. If the Task Force has been successful in achieving the objectives stressed above, its members will have gained the confidence of a wide spectrum of ghetto residents. This will enable it to identify potentially explosive conditions and, working with the police, to take action to defuse the situation.

Similarly, the Task Force could have considerable effectiveness in handling threatening incidents identified by the police. To accomplish this objective, an early warning system could be instituted during the critical summer months. Operating on a 24-hour basis, such a system would have the capacity to receive and evaluate police reports of potentially serious incidents and to initiate an appropriate non-police response, utilizing community contacts and Task Force personnel. Any such operation must have the cooperation of the police, who will be in control of the overall disorder response. To avoid confusion and duplication of effort, the Task Force should have responsibility for coordinating the efforts of all agencies, other than police and fire, once a disturbance has occurred. An example will serve to illustrate how such a system might operate.

Following the slaying last summer of a Negro teen-ager by a Negro detective in the Bedford-Stuyvesant section of Brooklyn, New York, a rumor that the youth had been shot by a white policeman and that the police were trying to suppress this information began to circulate through an already tense neighborhood. The situation became threatening. Yet, within an hour, three white members of the mayor's summer task force group were able to convince a group of black militants that the police version was true. Walking the streets that night and the next two evenings, they worked to dispel the rumor and to restore community stability.

In the larger cities, the Urban Action Task Force could have responsibility or coordinating the programs of various municipal agencies, concentrating their impact on poverty areas and planning for the more effective implementation of existing public efforts.

The Commission believes that the Task Force approach can do precisely what other forms of neighborhood organization have not been able to do. It can connect the real needs and priorities of low-income residents with the energies and resources of both city government and the private sector. It can substantially improve the quality and timeliness of city services to these areas. It will fail unless all of the groups involved are prepared to deal fairly and openly with the problems of the community.

But if it succeeds, it will not only produce improved services but help to generate a new sense of community, as well.

Establishment of Effective Grievance-Response Mechanisms

Effective implementation of the Neighborhood Action Task Forces will depend upon the continuing commitment of the city administration to its success. To ensure continuous attention to many of the sources of tension identified above, we recommend that formal mechanisms for the processing of grievances, many of which will relate to the performance of the city government, be established independent of the local administration.

We are convinced, on the record before this Commission, that the frustration reflected in the recent disorders results, in part at least, from the lack of accessible and visible means of establishing the merits of grievances against the agencies of local and state government, including but not limited to the police. Cities and states throughout the country now have under consideration various forms of grievance-response devices. While we are not prepared to specify the form which such a mechanism should take in any particular community, there are certain criteria which should be met. These include:

• *Independence:* This can be achieved by long term appointment of the administrator, subject to City Council removal. The grievance agency should be separate from operating municipal agencies.

• *Adequate staff and funding:* Exact costs will vary depending on the size and needs of the city's population. It is most important that the agency have adequate funds and staff to discharge its responsibilities.

• *Comprehensive coverage of grievances against public agencies and authorities:* General jurisdiction will facilitate access by grievants. Moreover, unlike specialized complaint agencies, such as civilian review boards, all agencies would be brought equally under public scrutiny. This should facilitate its acceptance by public officials.

• *Power to receive complaints, hold hearings, subpoena witnesses, make public recommendations for remedial action to local authorities and, in cases involving violation of law, bring suit.* These powers are the minimum necessary to the effective operation of the grievance mechanism. As we envision it, the agency's principal power derives from its authority to investigate and make public findings and recommendations. It should, of course, have a conciliation process whereby complaints could be resolved without full investigation and processing.

• *Accessibility:* In large cities, access may require setting up neighborhood offices in ghetto areas. In others, local resident aides could be empowered to receive complaints. It should be possible to file a grievance orally or in writing. If forms are used, they should be easily understood and widely available.

• *Participation in grievance process:* Grievants should be given full opportunity to take part in all proceedings and to be represented by counsel. They should receive prompt advice of action taken, and results of investigations should be made public.

Expanded Legal Service to the Poor

Among the most intense grievances underlying the riots of the summer of 1967 were those which derived from conflicts between ghetto residents and private parties, principally the white landlord and merchant. Though the legal obstacles are considerable, resourceful and imaginative use of available legal processes could contribute significantly to the alleviation of tensions resulting from these and other conflicts. Moreover, through the adversary process which is at the heart of our judicial system, litigants are afforded meaningful opportunity to influence events which affect them and their community. However, effective utilization of the courts requires legal assistance, a resource seldom available to the poor.

Litigation is not the only need which ghetto residents have for legal service. Participation in the grievance procedures suggested above may well require legal assistance. More importantly, ghetto residents have need of effective advocacy of their interests and concerns in a variety of other contexts, from representation before welfare agencies and other institutions of government to advocacy before planning boards and commissions concerned with the formulation of development plans. Again, professional representation can provide substantial benefits in terms of overcoming the ghetto resident's alienation from the institutions of government by implicating him in its processes. Although lawyers function in precisely this fashion for the middle-class clients, they are too often not available to the impoverished ghetto resident.

The Legal Services Program administered by the Office of Economic Opportunity has made a good beginning in providing legal assistance to the poor. Its present level of effort should be substantially expanded through increased private and public funding. In addition, the participation of law schools should be increased through development of programs whereby advanced students can provide legal assistance as a regular part of their professional training. In all of these efforts, the local bar bears major responsibility for leadership and support.

Assistance for Mayors and City Councils

. . . the capacity of the Federal Government to affect local problems depends to a great extent on the capacity of city government to respond competently to federal program initiatives.

In the face of the bewildering proliferation of both community demands and local, state and federal programs, mayors and city councils need to create new mechanisms to aid in decision making, program planning and coordination. At this time, however, no assistance is available to develop these new and critically necessary institutional capabilities or to support the required research, consultants, staff or other vital components of administrative or legislative competence.

The Commission recommends, therefore, that both the state and federal governments provide financial assistance to cities for these purposes as a regular part of all urban program funding.

Hearings on Ghetto Problems and Enactment of Appropriate Local Legislation

Many of the grievances identified in our study of the conditions underlying civil disorders can be redressed only through legislative action. Accordingly, we recommend that the legislative body of each city with a substantial minority population hold, as soon as possible, a series of hearings on ghetto problems. In large cities, these hearings could well be held in the ghetto itself to facilitate full citizen participation.

In addition to establishing a foundation for needed legislative measures, these hearings would constitute a visible demonstration of governmental concern for the problems of ghetto residents. They would also provide a most useful means of bridging the communications gap, contributing to an improved understanding in the white community about the conditions of ghetto life.

Expanded Employment by City Government of Ghetto Residents

We strongly recommend that local government undertake a concerted effort to provide substantial employment opportunities for ghetto residents. Local governments now employ 6.4 million people full time, most of whom live in urban areas; they comprise one of the fastest growing segments of the economy. This offers an opportunity of the greatest significance for local government to respond to one of the most critical needs of ghetto residents and, at the same time, to decrease the distance between city hall and the ghetto by deliberate employment, training and upgrading of Negroes.

To accomplish this goal, we recommend that municipal authorities review applicable civil service policies and job standards and take prompt action to remove arbitrary barriers to employment of ghetto residents. Re-evaluation is particularly necessary with respect to requirements relating to employment qualification tests and police records. Leadership by city government in this vital area is of urgent priority, not only because of the important public employment potential, but also to stimulate private employers to take similar action.

SECOND PHASE ACTIONS

Establishment of Neighborhood City Halls

The Neighborhood Action Task Force concept provides a basis on which lasting structures can be erected. The principal change required in order to transform the official component of the Task Force into a permanent instrument of local government involves the establishment of offices in the neighborhoods served. Depending on the size and composition of the neighborhood, the permanent staff should include an assistant mayor, representatives of the municipal agencies, the city councilman's staff and other institutions and groups included in the Task Force. This facility would function, in effect, as a "Neighborhood City Hall."

The Neighborhood City Hall would accomplish several interrelated objectives. It would contribute to the improvement of public services by providing an effective channel for low-income citizens to communicate their needs and problems to the appropriate public officials and by increasing the ability of local government to respond in a coordinated and timely fashion. It would serve as the eyes and ears of the mayor and council and furnish an informal forum for complaints and grievances. It would make information about government programs and services available to ghetto residents, enabling them to make more effective use of such programs and services and making clear the limitation on the availability of all such programs and services. It would expand opportunities for meaningful community access to and involvement in the planning and implementation of policy affecting their neighborhood. Most important, the Neighborhood City Hall, building on the Task Force approach, affords a significant opportunity to accomplish the democratic goal of making government closer and more accountable to the citizen.

Development of Multi-Service Centers

Frequently, services vital to the ghetto resident—job placement and location, health care, legal assistance—are inaccessible because they are located at considerable distance from the ghetto, a distance often made greater by the lack of efficient public transportation. This problem is compounded by the fact that many key service institutions are fragmented, requiring those seeking assistance to pursue it at various locations scattered throughout a large urban area.

To meet this need, the Office of Economic Opportunity has funded over 700 multi-service centers in ghetto areas throughout the country since 1964. Many of these have been small store-front operations housing OEO-funded services. Some, as in Detroit, have had a fairly wide range of services and have served a large number of families.

The principal problem has been that most centers have not been comprehensive enough. They rarely include traditional city and state agency services. Many relevant federal programs are seldom located in the same center. Manpower and education programs from HEW and the Labor Department, for example, have been housed in separate centers without adequate consolidation or coordination either geographically or programmatically.

The resulting proliferation led the President to call upon the Department of Housing and Urban Development to establish comprehensive "one stop service centers." The experience thus far indicates the need for more effective coordination of federal programs at the national and regional levels. Legislation may be required to simplify grant procedures and assure such coordination.

Each center should have enough neighborhood workers to reach out into the homes of needy people who are not able to seek help. To assure that the service centers are relevant to the needs and styles of the neighborhood, ghetto residents should be trained and employed at all levels. This purpose can well be served through establishment and involvement of Community Service Center Councils to establish overall policy.

We recommend increased federal funding for comprehensive centers and implementation of the policy guidelines proposed above.

Improved Political Representation

It is beyond the scope of this Report to consider in detail the many problems presented by the existing distribution of political power within city governments. But it is plain that the Negro ghetto resident feels deeply that he is not represented fairly and adequately under the arrangements which prevail in many cities. This condition strikes at major democratic values.

To meet this problem, city government and the majority community should revitalize the political system to encourage fuller participation by all segments of the community. Whether this requires adoption of any one system of representation, we are not prepared to say. But it is clear that at-large representation, currently the practice in many American cities, does not give members of the minority community a feeling of involvement or stake in city government. Further, this form of representation dilutes the normal political impact of pressures generated by a particular neighborhood or district.

Negro representation and participation in the formal structure of government can also be furthered by a concerted effort to appoint Negroes to significant policy positions in city government.

More Effective Community Participation

One of the most difficult and controversial problems we have encountered relates to ghetto demands for "self-determination" or "community control." To a limited extent, this concept was made a matter of national policy in the Economic Opportunity Act of 1964 which specified that community action programs should be developed, conducted and administered with "maximum feasible participation" of the residents of the areas and members of the groups served.

In the three years since the beginning of the war on poverty, the effort to put "maximum feasible participation" into effect has met with both success and failure. One measure of its success can be seen in the extent to which the demand for participation, even control, over a variety of programs affecting the ghetto has spilled over into the most traditional areas, such as public school administration.

But the demands made often seem intransigent and the time required for negotiation with residents extravagant. The pulling and hauling of different factions competing for control within the ghetto community sometimes makes it difficult to mount any program. Moreover, it is often easier to organize groups to oppose, complain, demonstrate and boycott than to develop and run programs.

Yet, the demand for a community voice represents a marked and desirable gain over the apathy that existed before. Despite its problems, we believe that meaningful community participation and a substantial measure of involvement in program development is an essential strategy for city government. The democratic values which it advances—providing a stake in the social system, improving the accountability of public officials—as well as the pragmatic benefits which it provides far outweigh these costs.

The essential question which city leadership must face is the ultimate goal of community participation. In this sense, community involvement is directly related to the strategy of decentralization, for with the support of the city, neighborhood groups may become an effective force for carrying on a variety of functions—such as physical renewal and redevelopment—which can be highly disruptive when imposed by outside authority.

If these principles are accomplished, then the choice of mechanisms will depend upon the needs of the particular community and the structure of the local government. We have described earlier in this section opportunities for meaningful community participation in the processes of government. Additional and diverse instrumentalities such as community neighborhood school boards, community planning boards, tenants' councils, youth councils, advisory committees and consumer trade organizations offer further ways of providing institutional channels for effective citizen participation in public decision-making. The crucial issue, however, is whether city government is willing to legitimate these organizations by dealing with them on a regular basis with respect to matters within their competence. We believe that such an approach offers substantial promise of improving the relationship between local government and ghetto residents.

The involvement of the ghetto community in the planning and operation of development programs need not be confined to the public arena. There is great potential in private community development corporations which can emerge from a combined public-private sponsorship and perform mixed functions for the community, including sponsorship of locally owned businesses.

A most promising approach is the neighborhood membership corporation, the first of which was established in Columbus, Ohio, in 1965—the East Central Citizens Organization (ECCO), under an OEO grant. Functioning as a town meeting, its members include all of the residents of a defined ghetto neighborhood (8,150 people). Its activities encompass day-care centers, credit unions, legal and medical services, newspapers, restaurants and business enterprises.

Both money and manpower will be needed from government, foundations and private business to create and assist these corporations and other new community institutions. Technical and professional support will be required. The opportunity that they offer to develop stable community leadership structures and constructive involvement should not be allowed to fail for lack of such support.

CONCLUSION

Finally, there remains the issue of leadership. Now, as never before, the American city has need for the personal qualities of strong democratic leadership. Given the difficulties and delays involved in administrative reorganization or institutional change, the best hope for the city in the short run lies in this powerful instrument. In most cities the mayor will have the prime responsibility.

It is in large part his role now to create a sense of commitment and concern for the problems of the ghetto community and to set the tone for the entire relationship between the institutions of city government and all the citizenry.

Part of the task is to interpret the problems of the ghetto community to the citizenry at large and to generate channels of communication between Negro and white leadership outside of government. Only if all the institutions of the community—those outside of government as well as those inside the structure—are implicated in the problems of the ghetto, can the alienation and distrust of disadvantaged citizens be overcome.

This is now the decisive role for the urban mayor. As leader and mediator, he must involve all those groups—employers, news media, unions, financial institutions and others—which only together can bridge the chasm now separating the racial ghetto from the community. His goal, in effect, must be to develop a new working concept of democracy within the city.

In this effort, state government has a vital role to play. It must equip city leadership with the jurisdictional tools to deal with its problems. It must provide a fuller measure of financial and other resources to urban areas. Most importantly, state leadership is in a unique position to focus the interests and growing resources, political as well as financial, of the suburbs on the physical, social, and cultural environment of the central cities. The crisis confronting city government today cannot be met without regional cooperation. This cooperation can take many forms—metropolitan government, regional planning, joint endeavors. It must be a principal goal, perhaps the overriding concern, of leadership at the state level to fashion a lasting and mutually productive relationship between city and suburban areas.

CHAPTER NINE ⌗

URBAN SOCIOLOGY IN TRANSITION

It was at the University of Chicago at the time of the first World War that Robert E. Park and Ernest W. Burgess laid the foundations for American urban sociology. Although their work was preceded by the Hull House social-work studies, Park and Burgess imparted a degree of generality to their own inquiries that gave them true theoretical significance. The Park and Burgess research was essentially ecological with biotic presuppositions concerning the struggle for life in human society. The result was, therefore, that the basic processes which urban studies came to deal with were conflict, on the one hand, and personal and social organization, disorganization, and reorganization on the other. In his nostalgic review of this early formative period Burgess points out the lack of financial support he and his colleagues experienced, the rudimentary way in which their first investigations were carried on, the formulation of theory that accompanied the compilation of data, and the advances made in research methods (including personal documentation and quantitative description and inference), all of which contributed to establishing Chicago as "a sociological laboratory."

The contributions presented here by Burgess, Hauser, Spinrad, Jacobs, and Keller are a sample of the now considerable literature appraising and evaluating the past and present condition, and the future prospects, of urban sociology. Urban studies have achieved an impressive maturity with respect to the accumulation of systematic data, the refinement of methodology, and the derivation of general hypotheses. Such a conclusion is evident from the writings in this volume as well as from searching symposia like *Urban Research*

Methods, The Study of Urbanization, and *Urban Research and Policy Making.* Much criticism has been directed against urban sociology, however, and on a number of fundamental points there is a good deal of consensus. One point of general agreement concerns the limitations of formal theory. Another, the methodological shortcomings that make even some of the best work turn out, unfortunately, to be little more than impressionistic observation. And still another is the culture-binding historicism of a large part of the urban research done in the Western world.

Some particulars may make these broad strictures clearer. For instance, the supposition that the family declines in importance in urban society has lost a lot of ground. One reason for the change in this supposition is E. Franklin Frazier's study of the Negro family in which he stresses the family's great importance for social integration in the city.[1] Indeed, many researchers have agreed upon the hypothesis that primary relations are only slightly, if at all, a lesser source of social control in the city than they are in the rural community. And, therefore, the implication that the Simmel-Wirth ideal-type mode of urban study has unfortunately taken theory into a blind alley. Again, a major insight of urban sociology (even in the period 1920–1940 when the Chicago school was working under the guidance of deductive, or *a priori,* thought) was that the in-migrant's particular ethnic community serves him as a mechanism of defense, operating apart from the community's political structures.

While urban sociology has been committed to formal theory, it has also been very sensitive to the obligation of solving social problems. To some extent this posture can be attributed to the historical milieu in which social science has been pursued. Ernest Manheim says, in fact, that the city's place in our history as a nation has profoundly affected the very image that the city has projected to the sociologist.[2] Earlier, when the city was a system for the acculturation of the immigrant, its bearing on anomia and institutional disorganization was uppermost. Now, however, massive overseas immigration is over and the city has made us a functioning urban society. Therefore, questions of urban dominance, community structure, and the comparative method of studying cities under different conditions, have become prominent. Still, as we have seen here, the sociological study of the city continues to be motivated by such problems as deviance, family instability, environmental health, inadequate schools, mass culture, public apathy, land use, fiscal policy, and transportation.

Some scholars have, of course, deplored this pragmatic emphasis as myopic; others viewed it as naïve. Thus Schnore and Lampard have asserted, "Serious scientific research must continue to be concerned with fundamental questions of understanding the whole urban phenomenon and not just those aspects that currently appear to be problems to the social engineers." [3] Leonard Reissman has taken the position that precisely because urban sociologists have failed to hew to the line of making urban sociology a unified body of valid and reliable knowledge about cities as social systems, they have, ironically, produced few results even as far as the very problem-solving change they are interested in is concerned.[4]

Nevertheless, conceptual and theoretical unity in urban sociology is easier to aspire to than to achieve. It is difficult to study the kind of complex organization found in the urban setting. As Burgess and Bogue declared in 1961, it "is still a lagging branch of urban research," because the city is so large and intricate a system that it cannot readily be limited to manageable parts and subjected to rigorously controlled observation. Anselm L. Strauss has also addressed the concentration of urban sociology on ideologies, pathologies, and public issues. He has done so with telling cogency, particularly in regard to remedial research strategies.[5]

Although no end of material has been written on urban housing and race, congestion, suburban sprawl, and the like, says Strauss in commenting on the relative lack of attention to urban social structure, "Except from personal experience, no sociologist could begin to write a systematic account of relationships which exist among realtors, bank employees, contractors, local politicians, investment brokers (professional and amateur) and other relevant parties to realtors' transactions." [6] In short, the normal system has been neglected. As an antidote Strauss advocates research into "the unstudied"—varieties of cities, urban images, and social networks within cities—and also, the unusual—whatever is trivial and eccentric, and the variegated life of the streets. In addition, he asserts that "ideological entrapment" should be avoided by being sensitive to glittering generalities, such as urban impersonality, and sensitive to unexamined antipathies, like the general scholarly aversion to suburbia and mass culture. And finally, Strauss also advocates using the comparative method; avoiding single cases and systematically making use of comparable samples.

Philip Hauser is most instructive particularly in regard to comparative urban studies. Hauser considers urban research essential for progress in the world's underdeveloped areas. What is needed to guide national policies, he writes, is insight into the expected and atypical processes of urbanization. Hauser points out that definite decisions as to the allocation of capital resources need to be made if the countries that have not begun to develop are to move forward, and are not to be blocked by their inherited preindustrial and colonial configurations of urban location and function. Manpower development, technological improvement, consumption patterns, land use, migration currents, legal codes, and similar considerations must be strategically controlled for sound economic and political organization.

The modernization of traditional societies that is now going on in the world affords us a golden opportunity to come to a higher level of urban understanding. Gideon Sjoberg has catalogued a number of weaknesses in urban sociology, especially those relating to comparative studies. European cities have been covered extensively, but those of eastern and southern Europe have not had adequate attention. Latin America has also been slighted. Anthropologists, however, have dealt rather thoroughly with Africa, at least with Africa south of the Sahara. The Middle East Institute is stimulating urban research in the Levant, just as UNESCO is in India. Apart from this research in India, Southeast Asia has been largely neglected. And although Japan has been studied, much of this work is not available in English. In somewhat different circumstances, although with the same result, data have been gathered on the cities of the communist bloc, but they are not generally available to outsiders. For these reasons, urban research has not only been uneven in application, it has also been handicapped by inadequate diffusion. Sjoberg concludes that "many American sociologists are unaware of the vast body of materials at hand," so that what is needed is more annotated bibliographies, surveys of the world's literature, and collections of carefully edited readings that bring out the theoretical value of the writings that have been produced,[7] as well as greater interest in *Current Sociology, Sociological Abstracts,* and *Population Index.*

Most urban research, Jack P. Gibbs observes, has been substantive.[8] Relatively few writings on research methodology in urban sociology have accumulated. Rather, problems of method have been attacked as they have arisen in the course of the given inquiry. For example, it is still very much an issue in urban sociology as to whether a city is directed by a unitary or pluralistic power structure and, indeed, whether the pluralistic power structure is in a sufficiently defined form to justify its identification at all. William Spinrad reviews some of the recent literature on this controversy, and in the process he examines some of the methodological questions, such as what power is, how it is wielded, and in which way it may best be observed.

The trend toward cross-cultural urban research will continue to confuse research methods as well as to clarify them. Because of this Sjoberg questions the applicability of standard techniques to comparative studies. W. Lloyd Warner's Index of Status Characteristics (I.S.C.), the Shevky-Williams-Bell social-area analysis, and the Queen and Carpenter urbanism index may turn out to be useless owing to socio-cultural differences and other weaknesses, like the absence of census-tract enumeration in some countries. Therefore, the testing of hypotheses will be impeded unless more proficient methods are developed.

There are pronounced trends in contemporary urban research toward quantification, on the one hand, and macrosociology on the other. Cities are conceived of as complex variables that are shaped by industrialization, particular cultural traditions, and the environing societies within which they exist. In general two major perspectives govern urban sociology today. One is a materialistic stance in which the geographic setting and demographic factors are seen as governing the city's life. The other, an idealistic outlook, attaches causal significance to values and sentiments. The latter viewpoint, in the final analysis, attributes urban phenomena, such as land-use patterns and the level of commercial activity, to cultural elements.

Broad studies designed to test the most general theories tend to suffer, unfortunately, from a lack of scientific rigor. Gibbs has criticized urban research of this sort for being impressionistic, vague, indeterminate, and incommensurate. Its terms, he has declared, are imprecise. Consider "socially heterogeneous, complex, extreme congestion, rational economy, uneven distribution of population, city dominance, technologically advanced, anonymity of social relations, marked spatial segregation, etc."

On the other hand those studies that do rigorously and systematically abstract attributes, that use standardized terms, that quantify their variables, and that make use of limited and comparable units of observation, tend to lack theoretical import. Thus, Burgess and Bogue have warned that the current fad for computer-executed or -assisted research may result in superficial and carelessly designed projects lacking insight and inductive originality, however camouflaged they may be by higher mathematics. All of this, they conclude, may degenerate into a "wave of naive raw empiricism such as that which followed the advent of the IBM counting sorter." In the light of this admonition it is informative to recollect that when Scott Greer's *The Emerging City* was belittled for discursiveness, Morris Janowitz defended it with the recognition that "it is paradoxical but true that a humanistic and literary orientation at times can produce more objectivity than a slavish pursuit of the scientific method." [9]

Value-orientation has emerged as an essential perspective in urban sociology. Its influence on many aspects of the urban system has been documented by Walter Firey, Max Weber, and William F. Whyte, Jr. Among the most articulate culturological critics of formal and mechanistic urban planning is Jane Jacobs. She opposes conventional city planning because typically it refuses to take human needs on their own terms and because it succeeds only in subordinating social factors to the physical aspects of the urban community. Her analysis exposes the over-simplification to which urban planning has been prone, and perhaps she paves the way for a more adequate model for urban studies to use as the basis for policy. Jacobs' thinking emphasizes both the functions of particulars and the need for a *verstehende,* or interpretative, approach to urban phenomena. Hence she argues for a shift from physical to human considerations in city design. Within methodology, she speaks for a shift away from mechanistic surveys to relying on meaningful, but unobtrusive humanistic measuring devices to dig out the valid facts on which to base programs for change.

The task of uniting the inorganic and organic orders of urban phenomena with the superorganic remains unsolved. However, some promising leads have been formulated. Sjoberg has advanced a neo-evolutionary hypothesis to bridge the gap between these two general frames of reference. He would guide empirical research by recognizing that "as industrial urbanization proceeds and as the technological environment becomes increasingly complex, the possibility of evaluating one's external environment in a variety of ways is concomitantly lessened." This would focus attention on revealing the structural correlates of the various urban societies, preindustrial, nascent, and industrial, perhaps by applying a mode of analysis like Parsons' pattern-variable schema.

Power may also become a key variable; the role of special interests in affecting the structures and processes of the urban community as a system in itself, and as a sub-system of a larger national society. Greer regards the city as a social order in which its configuration as a political system is of the highest significance, thus the several institutions are most effectively knit together. Greer defines polity as "a summary of the public decisions that can be enforced by legal sanctions." Polity bears on the myriad of organized groups through which the population of the city express their many interests, including those interests relevant to the geographic environment and demographic system. The polity arbitrates between groups, maintains order, and carries out collective enterprises. In turn, the city itself is a component of a larger social order in which its own conduct as a corporate entity and the activities of its own organized interest groups are further coordinated by the national polity.

Suzanne Keller is included in this chapter for the light that she throws on the neighborhood as a microcosmic unit of urban social structure and systematic planning. Her analysis takes into account recent research and practical experience (much of it discouraging). Interestingly, it also harkens back to the earliest urban sociology at the University of Chicago, that identified the natural-area components of the city. These components, Keller observes, remain viable concepts some forty years later. Like Jacobs and Hauser, she emphasizes the need of taking human and social aspects of urban life into sufficient account in all planning—perhaps by means of a more sophisticated conception of the neighborhood that recognizes actual interaction rather than mere spatial proximity and hypothesized association.

As the pace of urbanization quickens, and as the extent to which the world is urban grows, an understanding of urban phenomena becomes more necessary. Consider, for instance, that Kingsley Davis has projected that India's largest city may have more than 65 million persons by the year 2000! [10] Cities will soon undoubtedly exist on a scale hitherto unrealized and even unimagined. True, a great increase in the funding of urban research has occurred in the past few years. In the United States, the Ford Foundation, the National Science Foundation, the Institute of Public Health, the Social Security Administration, the Department of Housing and Urban Development, and the government's poverty, youth, and manpower programs have all been significantly responsible. It remains to be seen whether the substance and methodology of urban sociology will have been appropriately advanced.

Although knowledge is vital to urban progress, fortunately there are indigenous forces that may automatically compel remedial change. Bollens and Schmandt think that growing affluence will enable people to individually work out their residential and life-style needs more successfully. With wealth should also come the broader realization that one has a socioeconomic stake in the community, and that this realization would promote greater involvement and community stabilization. At the same time, rural migration into the cities will decline, and along with massive efforts for rehabilitation, it will make the inner city a better and safer place to live. Whatever the actual role of urban studies in guiding social change in the city, their significance in understanding urban life will not diminish, but enlarge. The metropolitan community is destined to become, in the words of Burgess and Bogue, "the context of the future."

41. RESEARCH IN URBAN SOCIETY:
A LONG VIEW

Ernest W. Burgess

In what was originally presented to a seminar on "New Directions for Urban Research," Ernest W. Burgess reviews the investigations into the sociology of the city that began at the University of Chicago in 1916. Before that time, from 1908 actually, Edith Abbott and Sophonisba Breckenridge had conducted the Hull House studies in the growing tradition of social-service administration. Waves of immigrants converging on the booming Midwestern metropolis offered tangible evidence for field-work on the urbanization process. Burgess, Robert E. Park, W. I. Thomas, and others participated in a long series of controlled observations of the ecological distribution of social phenomena in Chicago. Basically, they reported that competitive processes result in the dis-organization and reorganization of individual personalities along with sociocultural systems.

Burgess' chronological review of the work done by the early Chicago School is a cogent reminder of the social mapping that eventually permitted the recognition of the concentric zones and natural areas into which a city may be divided. The earlier sociologists who contributed to this sig-nificant part of American urban studies included Clifford R. Shaw, Nels Anderson, Harvey Zorbaugh, Ernest R. Mowrer, Robert E. L. Faris, H. Warren Dunham, Philip M. Hauser, and, of course, Louis Wirth. In this article, Burgess uses a retrospective glance as a basis for the development of more meaningful theory in urban research.

Excerpts from *Contributions to Urban Sociology* edited by Ernest Burgess and Donald J. Bogue (1964). Reprinted by permission of Donald J. Bogue and The University of Chicago Press. © 1964 by the University of Chicago.

. . . I WILL . . . concentrate on describing the program of urban research that came to be called "The City as a Sociological Laboratory." This program, as I knew it, may be subdivided into three phases.

PHASE 1: THE PERIOD WITHOUT FUNDS: DISCOVERING THE PHYSICAL PATTERN OF THE CITY

The first period of our study we might call "the period without funds." Certainly, during our first years there was very little financing for urban research. This covers the period from 1916 to 1923. The work of this period was conducted very largely by the students in our classes. In every course I gave I am sure there were one or two students who made maps. I think the maps of juvenile delinquency were the first ones undertaken. They were followed by maps showing the distribution of motion picture houses. Then came maps showing the distribution of the patrons of the public dance halls. The students made maps of any data we could find in the city that could be plotted.

This phase might also be called, "Discovering the Physical Pattern of the City." We were very impressed with the great differences between the various neighborhoods in the city, and one of our earliest goals was to try to find a pattern to this patchwork of differences, and to "make sense of it." Mapping was the method which seemed most appropriate for such a problem.

At this time we made contacts with agencies throughout the city in search of the data they could furnish. We secured the co-operation of the Juvenile Court, the Health Department, the many social settlements, the Council of Social Agencies that was getting under way, the Association of Commerce, and the Urban League. One of our students collaborated with Graham Romeyn Taylor in publishing the book on the race riots in Chicago. He was Charles S. Johnson, who was later to become president of Fisk University, a leading sociologist, and a leading public figure in this country.

The courses that Dr. Park and I gave at this period may be of interest to you. He gave courses on the Social Survey, the Newspaper, the Negro in America, in addition to his famous course on the Crowd and the Public. Besides the Introduction to Sociology course I gave courses in Social Pathology, Crime and Its Social Treatment, the Theory of Personal Disorganization, and the Family. In the winter of 1918, Dr. Park offered his first field study course. The following autumn I joined him in giving the field study course, and we gave it every quarter as long as he was at the university. After he left, Dr. Wirth and I continued to give this course, as long as we were both at the university.

I should mention one study that was made and published in this period without funds, *The Hobo,* by Nels Anderson. Actually, there was a small fund for this study: $300, that Dr. Ben Reitman, the king of the hobos, solicited from Dr. Evans, who wrote the health column in the Chicago *Tribune.* This small amount of money enabled Nels Anderson to exist in the hobo district, and write this book, which the University of Chicago Press accepted for publication as the first volume in the Sociological Series.

PHASE 2: BIRTH OF AN ORGANIZED RESEARCH PROGRAM

The period with funds came suddenly upon us. Beardsley Ruml, who had been an instructor in psychology at the University of Chicago, became director of the Laura Spelman Rockefeller Foundation. He induced the trustees of this foundation to devote funds to social science research. In 1923 the National Social Science Research Council was established under a grant and with the prospect of funds for research from the same foundation. Dr. Ruml and his board of directors also decided to support social science research at a number of universities. The first university to apply and to have its proposal approved for sponsorship was the University of Chicago. The funds did not descend upon us out of the clouds. We had to make application. We had to show some basis for receiving funds. Fortunately, the studies we had under way made quite an impressive exhibit. Thrasher was already beginning to study the gang, and other studies were in progress. The School of Social Service Administration had a number of projects also under way. So they gave us a grant, as I recall, of $25,000 for the first year. That wouldn't seem very large to social scientists of the present. But when you had had only $300 for one study, it seemed like a great amount, and we were promised much larger funds in the future. I think the next year they gave us $50,000 and $25,000 additional, contingent upon raising $25,000 in the community. This program continued for about ten years and I think every year the civic and social welfare agencies of the community joined with us in raising $25,000 so we could get the extra $25,000 from the foundation.

It was understood that in Chicago, because of the beginning we made in the study of the city, the research would be concentrated and limited to the studies of the community. The first Local Community Research Committee was set up with Dean Leon C. Marshall, who was then the head of the Department of Economics (chairman of the committee), Professor Merriam from political science, Dr. Edith Abbott from social service administration, and Professor Jurnigon from history. I was the representative from sociology.

What were the points of view and the methods of research with which we began our studies? We assumed that the city had a characteristic organization and way of life that differentiated it from rural communities. Like rural communities, however, it was composed of natural areas, each having a particular function in the whole economy and life of the city, each area having its distinctive institutions, groups, and personalities. Often there were wide differences between communities which were very sharply demarcated.

We early decided that the natural areas could be significantly studied in two aspects:

First, their *spatial pattern:* the topography of the local community; the physical arrangements not only of the landscape but of the structures which man had constructed, that sheltered the inhabitants and provided places of work and of play.

Second, their *cultural life:* their modes of living, customs, and standards.

Now the first of these aspects, the spatial aspect, gave rise to ecological studies; all that could be mapped; the distribution, physical structures, institutions, groups, and individuals over an area. It was interesting what discoveries came from mapping data. For example, this first map showed that juvenile delinquents were concentrated in certain areas of the city and that they tended to thin out in other areas. That was quite surprising, strange to say, to the personnel of the juvenile court, because they knew they had cases in all parts of the city. This finding was not accepted by visitors from other cities. They said, "that may be what happens in Chicago; but in our city, juvenile delinquents are evenly scattered all over the area."

But some years later, Clifford R. Shaw studied the spatial distribution of juvenile delinquency in other cities, and found the same phenomena. Delinquents were concentrated in what we call the areas of deterioration and transition; they thinned out and almost disappeared in the better residential neighborhoods. There were, of course, juvenile delinquents in almost every area, but their distribution followed the zonal pattern.

These studies of juvenile delinquency distribution convinced us of the need for basic social data. We realized that population data were essential for social studies of the city. We co-operated with the health department, the Association of Commerce, and with many other agencies including the welfare agencies of the city. We obtained data from the United States Census—unpublished and especially tabulated data, by census tracts. The census tracts for Chicago originally had been laid out in 1910. Little use had been made of them. We secured the tract data for 1920 and 1930. When the census was taken in Chicago in 1930, Dr. Philip M. Hauser was a student. He was in charge of enumeration in one of the districts in the city and began his career that later led him to be the acting director of the 1950 census.

PHASE 3: THE ECONOMIC DEPRESSION AND WAR YEARS

In 1934 we took a population census of Chicago. This was the period of the depression, and of WPA projects. The idea came to me of having a city census. The data could be contrasted with those of 1930 and, later, with those of 1940. I got in touch with the Department of Health and the mayor of the city. I wrote the ordinance under which the census could be conducted. We had the promise of the WPA that they would furnish the enumerators. I attended the meeting of the council because I was afraid if any questions were to be asked of the mayor by the aldermen, he would not be able to answer them. This fear showed my naïveté, because Mayor Kelly made a short speech in which he spoke of all the persons out of work. He said this census would give 1,000 unemployed men jobs. And I heard the aldermen say, "pass, pass." No formal vote was taken. I went over to a reporter and asked what had happened. He said, "Don't you know? They voted unanimously to have this census taken." Two of our graduate students, Charles Newcomb and Richard Lang, directed this census of Chicago. I think it was as good as any other census taken, but the U. S. Bureau of the Census, when it made the 1940 census, did not rely upon the distribution of population which we found in 1934, but went back to their own census of 1930. As a result, they got into real difficulties. Certain areas which we showed having decreased population, had less population than they anticipated, and other areas had gained in population. But I suppose it is only natural that the federal agency would consider that only under its auspices could an adequate census be taken.

An early project was the preparation of a basic map for social data. This map has on it what we regard as basic data, railroads, streetcar lines, business property, residential property, unoccupied property indicated, property occupied by industry, by parks, and by boulevards.

We made a study in order to find the boundaries of the different natural areas of the city. That was the study in which the city was divided into its constituent local communities. The city council passed a resolution that in the future the census division would tabulate population not by wards but by these local communities. This system was accepted by the health department for recording their data and by the Council of Social Agencies for indicating distribution of agencies in the city. The *Local Community Fact Book of Chicago,* of which the first edition, by Wirth and Furez, appeared for 1930, had been reissued after the 1940, 1950, and 1960 censuses. It has been very valuable not only to students engaged in studies but also to the social agencies of the city. It shows population data by local communities.

At that time it was possible to get many research projects accepted by WPA. At one time we had so many research projects in the department, it was said that every graduate student had a project. That wasn't literally true, but there was enough truth in it to warrant the statement. We were able to make certain studies that would otherwise have been impossible, unless we had had grants far beyond the foundation's interest in local community studies. The Ford Foundation at that time had not yet been established.

The book by Faris and Dunham on *Mental Disorders in Urban Areas* would not have been possible without the data that was accumulated in this way. Dr. Hauser wrote his thesis on differential fertility, mortality, and net reproduction in Chicago. He had a force of students employed under WPA at the health department working machines every night, the only time they were available. That would hardly have been possible without great funds. A map showing the distribution of over a hundred thousand relief cases during the depression was made possible in this way.

Statistical data and map-plotting tell us much, but they don't tell us all. They tell us many very interesting things which require further investigation. For example, Shaw, in his studies of all the different social and health conditions related to the distribution of juvenile delinquency, found the highest correlate with juvenile delinquency was tuberculosis. Now, of course, we know that tuberculosis doesn't cause juvenile delinquency; nor does juvenile delinquency cause tuberculosis. But it meant that the same community conditions that give rise to tuberculosis, give rise to juvenile delinquency—non-white population, immigrant population, bad housing. All the factors of community deterioriation that lead to one lead also to the other.

These statistical data raise questions. Many of these questions, of course, can be further studied by statistical investigation; others, to be understood, require us to get below the surface of observable behavior. Cooley thought that these could be studied by what he called sympathetic introspection. He advocated this method as the ideal one for sociologists to use; but it is quite apparent that sympathetic introspection has many fallacies. If you and I try to imagine how a hobo feels—we have not been a homeless man, we have not ridden the rails—our mental picture is quite likely to be very different from what goes on in the mind of a hobo. So the superior method, as sociologists have discovered, is that of communication, of securing personal documents, and the life history. Psychologists and psychiatrists have introduced other methods, other tests, to get beneath the conscious responses of the person to our underlying motivations.

But by the use of a personal document we are able to get at the subjective aspects of life in the city.

Blumenthal, in his book *Small Town Stuff* (a study of a small mining community), exploded the common sense notion that in a small town everybody is constantly rating and re-rating everyone. But when he had interviews with persons, he didn't say, "I want your life history, I want a personal document." He said, "I want you to tell me the history of the community." The history of the community is something that everyone, at least the old-timers, is interested in narrating; and before they knew it, they were telling their life story. Blumenthal found out that what he got from the life story of the individual's self-conception was quite different from his rating in the community.

Of course, this rating in the community is also important, because it enters into the status of a person, into his conception of himself, but is only part of the story. Self-conception is not readily revealed, except perhaps by egocentric persons who will listen, or by the use of the technique of getting personal documents and life histories.

I recall Nels Anderson telling me he was greatly bored by his landlady, in the roominghouse district where he was studying the homeless man, telling him her life history. I told him, "Why, this is valuable, you must get it down on paper." I still have this document; it is most revealing. Who becomes a roominghouse keeper? What are the problems of a roominghouse keeper? Who is the star boarder? How do you keep a roominghouse orderly against all the tendencies toward disorder in a roominghouse district? Out of this one document you get more insight into how life moves in the roominghouse area, and especially from the standpoint of the roominghouse keeper, than you do from a mountain of statistics that might be gathered. So what we get from the life history, of course, also enables us to pose more questions to the statistician, to get to the other answers.

It is very interesting how studies begun in the department tended to get incorporated into other agencies in the community. While working on the study of juvenile delinquency, Mr. Shaw did get some funds during the period without funds from the Chicago Woman's Club, which was interested in the problems of juvenile delinquency. He also lived at a settlement house that was interested in what a sociologist would say about the problems of the gang.

In 1929 Mr. Shaw was appointed head of the Department of Sociological Research at the Institute of Juvenile Research and after that carried on this series of studies and of publications both ecological and cultural. This is a very good illustration of combining statistical methods, of finding out everything in the community that can be correlated with juvenile delinquency, of establishing the delinquency areas of the city, and of securing intensive life histories. *The Jack-Roller* shows how a person becomes a delinquent—an actual history of a delinquent career. Later Mr. Shaw was engaged in another, even more difficult, task of trying to find out the process by which a delinquent is rehabilitated. It seems to be easier to become a delinquent than to cease to be a delinquent; easier to explain why a boy becomes a delinquent than what factors really are involved in his rehabilitation.

The Church Federation of Chicago and the Chicago Theological Seminary employed Dr. Samuel C. Kincheloe to direct research on churches, especially problem churches and dying churches. On the basis of his studies, he presented to the church alternatives to action. One rather interesting effect was this: that the presentation of these facts to the church members hastened the death of many of these dying churches. Otherwise they would have continued the futile struggle to survive years longer.

The Chicago Council of Social Agencies, as I indicated before, adopted the community areas as did also the Recreation Commission and the health department. At Northwestern University Ernest R. Mowrer continued his studies of the family and in his book, *Disorganization—Personal and Social,* presents an exhaustive amount of data on family disorganization classified by the local community areas of the city.

My reason for reviewing the past has been primarily to raise the question of the conceptual system for current urban studies and what seem to be the most appropriate opportunities at present for further studies of the city. It is my firm conviction after a quarter-century of urban research, that *the conceptual system for urban studies should take in the whole field of sociological theory.* Social organization with its class structure; social change as the result of technological discoveries and inventions; collective behavior; social control, ecological studies, and population studies, all give us clues. But whatever is done in one of these fields should not fail to acknowledge principles established by research in other areas of urban life. Personal and social disorganization are of peculiar interest in the study of the city because of the fact of change, because of the change of tempo of city life. But social disorganization needs to be studied not so much from the standpoint of social pathology (although that also requires certain attention) but as an aspect of an interaction and adjustment process that eventually leads into social reorganization. Many trends in social disorganization lead to personal disorganization, community breakdown; but others are attempts at community reorganization. Some of the reorganizational efforts are successful and these of course need to be most carefully observed and studied as they occur. Merely charting past trends, and extrapolating them into the future can never suffice for an entity so dynamic and adaptable as the urban community!

42. COMPREHENSIVE URBAN STUDIES

Philip M. Hauser

Philip M. Hauser's discussion of research into the economic, physical, social, and governmental aspects of the city is guided primarily by considerations of the utility of knowledge for public policy. Hauser writes from the perspective of the developing nations of Southeast Asia, where industrialization and urbanization are underway and innumerable problems are pressing for solution.

Research is especially needed, Hauser observes, on the various consequences of internal migration, on attitudes toward fertility restriction, on changes in the family during different stages of urbanization, on the desirable location of settlements, on the proper allocation of resources between productive and social values, and on the precipitation of pathological forms of personal behavior under the impact of city life. Research along these lines could be valuable in determining governmental programs and administrative procedures. Hauser writes from a background that includes not only a knowledge of urban theory but close acquaintance with officially sponsored studies, such as the conferences and publications for which UNESCO, the Planning Commission of India, the Canadian National Commission, and similar bodies have been responsible.

MANY OF THE DEVELOPING COUNTRIES are acutely aware of present and impending urban problems in relation to their programmes for economic

Excerpts from *Handbook for Social Research in Urban Areas* by Philip Hauser (1964). Reprinted by permission of the United Nations Educational, Scientific and Cultural Organization.

development. Urbanization imposes a heavy requirement for capital formation—for urban infrastructure including public utilities and housing—an especially difficult burden when urbanization is outpacing economic development and productivity. Some developing countries are seeking to decelerate the rate of urbanization or even to induce swelled urban populations to return to rural areas by efforts to increase agricultural productivity and to make village life more attractive and through efforts to decentralize new industrial development. Because of rapid population growth and inability to provide essential facilities and services, many cities in developing areas have experienced serious dis-economies in production (power and transport shortages, etc.) .

In most of the smaller developing countries, especially in South-East Asia, urban population distribution differs from that in the more developed nations in being characterized by the presence of a 'primate' or great city many times, sometimes five to ten times, the size of the second city. These cities are not so much the result of indigenous economic development as the product of economic development oriented essentially to one or more foreign countries. For many cities this external orientation emerged during the colonial period during which the great city developed as a link between the colony and the mother country. In a number of cases the great city still preserves this external orientation in serving as a link between the local *élite* and the outside world rather than an economic outgrowth of the indigenous national economy. . . .

. . .

The relationship between industrialization and urbanization in developing countries is complicated by the presence of the 'primate' city. The fact that the great cities are already there creates a tendency for further centralization of industrial, commercial and service development. Moreover, the great city may also have a paralytic effect on the development of other urban places. Thus, the city in developing countries unlike its counterpart in the more developed areas of the world may be a barrier to, rather than a product of, economic development; it calls for further national economic development to provide it with a sound economic base rather than being a product of such economic development.

Historically the growth and economic characteristics of urban areas in developing countries can be treated in three well-defined phases or stages —namely the pre-industrial, the commercial and industrial. In the pre-industrial phase, subsistence agriculture predominates and means of transportation are fairly primitive. In consequence, the number and size of urban areas in the interior are limited. A large number of urban places in this phase are primarily administrative, military or religious centres with little economic base beyond the performance of these functions. However, even in this stage of economic development there are probably a few large towns especially at the confluence of rivers which, besides being marketing and distribution centres for the tributary area, contain considerable specialized but traditional handicraft manufacture.

With the development of international trade, cities begin to grow on the sea-coast. Sea-coast cities develop a significant economic base in performing the functions of collection, storage, handling and distribution of exports and imports. In time, processing of raw materials received from the hinterland become an added function. During this same period, the improvement of means of transportation widen commercial potentialities among interior urban places. City development during this period is based primarily on commercial activity and in many of the developing countries this commercial phase of urbanization is related to the colonial period.

It is only in recent years that active industrial development has begun in most developing countries. New industrial and mining towns and other specialized single function towns and cities are slowly making their appearance even while industrial development tends, in the main, to be concentrated in the relatively few great cities. The emphasis placed upon industrialization in most plans for economic development contains potentialities for changing the whole character of urbanization in the coming years. At the present time, by reason of the heterogeneous and unintegrated character of underdeveloped economies, many cities are characterized by the coexistence of all three phases of urbanization—pre-industrial, commercial and industrial.

Among the difficult problems posed by continued and accelerated rates of urbanization in developing countries is that relating to locational patterns. Small commercial towns serving agricultural areas tend to be widely distributed largely in accordance with the location of agricultural activity and the density of agricultural population. Larger-size towns are superimposed on the widespread distributional pattern of the smaller commercial centres usually at transport nodal points—river and road junctions and more recently railway junctions. These centres, as well as the seaports are the 'break of bulk' points and serve essentially the function of trans-shipment and distribution of goods between land and water and within the interior. These centres have increasingly become convenient points of location for processing and light manufacturing industry. In most developing countries the development of towns and cities, in respect of economic function, has gone little beyond this point.

With the adoption of Western technology and industrial enterprise new patterns of location of cities are emerging and strategic policy decisions are required. The new locational factors centre around raw material and power sources, the availability of labour and the location of consumer power sources, the availability of labour and the location of consumer markets; and national price policies with respect to centralization and decentralization of industry, regional development and the relation between industrial development and general national economic development.

Increased industrialization necessarily implies a change in the occupational structure of the working force toward non-agricultural activities and specialization in economic function. This means increased population agglomeration and, therefore, increased rates of urbanization because of the difference in the spatial distribution requirements of agricultural and non-agricultural activities. To achieve the gains from the economies of specialization and localization, developing countries are, in the short run, confronted with the need for providing urban economic and social infrastructure or urban overhead investment.

In the earlier stages of economic development in which most developing nations find themselves, the demand for such infrastructure investment is outrunning the pace of economic development in general, and constitutes a serious burden on scarce capital resources. Developing nations in the early crucial stages of industrialization are confronted, therefore, with serious problems of allocating scarce capital resources among infrastructure projects on the one hand, and more immediately productive projects on the other. The question obviously has a bearing on whether new industrial and economic development projects should be located in existing urban centres or in new localities, and vitally affects policy in respect of centralization or decentralization and regional development. The fact that existing urban centres in developing countries are already short of infrastructure facilities makes the problem all the more acute.

Within this framework developing countries are further confronted with two special problems of major import. One is that relating to the choice to be made in the allocation of scarce resources to 'social' as contrasted with 'productive' investment. This is merely a special aspect of the infrastructure problem but, more specifically, concerns the extent to which resources are utilized for 'social' objectives as better housing, environmental sanitation, health projects and education versus the production of general consumer goods. Such 'social' investments are, of course, also 'productive' investments in the longer run, but compete with more immediate productive enterprises in the short run.

The second problem, is that concerning the creation of employment opportunities without retarding technological progress. Emphasis on labour-intensive techniques is frequently necessary but, if carried too far, may adversely affect the growth of the nation's net aggregate product by retarding labour-saving technological development. In general, policy determination presumably aims at obtaining balance in industrial development as between employment opportunities and technology to assure maximum product per head.

Policy makers in developing nations are faced with quite crucial decisions on the problems indicated. Moreover, it may be noted that risks involved in respect of these decisions are much more centralized than were decisions in Western economically-developed countries where risks were widely dispersed in the play of the market mechanism.

Urbanism produces alterations in consumption patterns. Such fragmentary data as are available show that the proportion of consumer expenditures for food in towns and cities decreases appreciably below the village level. Clothing accounts for approximately the same proportion of expenditures in villages, towns and cities. On the other hand, expenditures on amusements, education, transport, services, footwear, rent and taxes tend to rise as do also expenditures on selected food items such as milk and milk products, meat, eggs and fish, fruits and refreshments.

There is also evidence that consumption in urban centers relies more heavily on imported commodities which, of course, increases the drain on foreign exchange. Urban consumption tends also be more modern than rural including increased use of running water, electricity and some durable consumer goods such as sewing machines and electric irons. Once the modern habits are acquired the population seems to grow dependent upon them. City consumption also increases what are regarded by some as 'wasteful' habits such as increased expenditures for smoking, theatre, cinema, tea drinking, etc.

Although it is difficult in view of low national productivity and poverty to analyse the effect of urbanization on saving propensities, the evidence seems to indicate that the propensity to save is reduced in the city as compared with rural areas in developing nations. Studies in Bombay City, Ceylon, Taiwan and Singapore indicate that urban consumer expenditures tend to outrun income and that the worker's family is often in debt. It should be mentioned, however, in respect of the propensity to save that the shift from the rural to urban economy involves the shift from a subsistence to a monetary economy in which mobilization of savings can be facilitated.

Finally, to conclude consideration of some of the more important economic aspects of urbanization in developing nations, it should be observed that the concentration of purchasing power in cities serves as a stimulant to developing industry. The broadening of consumption patterns and ready markets stimulates production on the one hand; the economies of localization derived, for example, from the availability of public utility services, distributive and organizational channels and labour supply, also greatly benefit industrial and commercial enterprise. Moreover, in the urban environment, cultural and social changes, which will be further discussed below, tend to bring about highly significant changes in economic motivation more conducive to increased productivity than that embedded in the rigid socio-economic structure in village communities.

This discussion of the economic aspects of urbanization in developing areas points to the types of problems which may confront economic planners and, therefore, to the types of studies needed to help them in determining policy and programme. Economic studies require high levels of technical competence and training and, in general, should be undertaken only with the participation, or at least with the advice, of economists.

PHYSICAL

The city may also be studied as a physical construction. This is the way the city is viewed by the physical planner who is concerned primarily with its physical problems. The emergence and growth of the city have greatly transformed the physical aspects of man's life. Land-use patterns have become greatly modified and housing has assumed new dimensions and proportions in the urban setting. Aggregative living has also created the need for new types of amenities including water supply, sewerage and drainage, and transport for both persons and goods; and has created problems of congestion, and air and water pollution. Urban living has been accompanied by great increases in the use of non-human energy—the use of power. Finally, urban living also requires the attention of the physical planner to aesthetic recreational and cultural facilities.

.   .   .

SOCIAL

The city represents not only a changed physical environment and new forms of economic organization but it also profoundly affects culture, the social order and man's conduct and thought. Urbanization produces not only the city as a physical and economic structure but also 'urbanism as a way of life.' The abstract aspects of a city—such a size, density and heterogeneity of population—influence the nature, frequency and intensity of social contact and therefore the process of socialization and human nature itself. . . .

.   .   .

Urbanization, especially when accompanied by heterogeneity—differences in background—tends to break down traditional behaviour and produce many problems of personal disorganization. It has precipitated such problems as juvenile delinquency, crime, prostitution, alcoholism, drug addiction, suicide, mental disease, social unrest and political instability. Many of these problems are especially manifest among in-migrant populations who must make the adjustment from rural to urban patterns of living.

ADJUSTMENT OF IN-MIGRANTS

Insight into the nature of social and personal changes in cities of Asia is afforded by a series of five studies prepared for Unesco on the problems of the in-migrant to cities. These studies in Bangkok, Bombay, Dacca, Delhi and Djakarta reveal a recognizable and common pattern in the adjustment of the newcomer to life in the urban setting. They show how the in-migrant, typically from a relatively small and homogeneous place of origin, is confronted in the city with a bewildering and almost incomprehensible vastness and heterogeneity. The newcomer, where possible, lives for some time with his fellow-villagers or relatives and only gradually becomes accommodated to city life. Among the more important new situations to which he must adapt are new and unfamiliar ways of making a living, a money economy, regular working hours, the absence of warm family living, a large number of impersonal contacts with other human beings, new forms of recreation, and a quite different physical setting often involving new forms of housing, sanitation, traffic congestion and noise. The greatest problem of adjustment seems to centre around the shift from a subsistence to a monetary economy and the necessity to have a job for subsistence.

Although the above describes a discernible general pattern, there is also considerable variation evident in the adjustment of newcomers to cities. For example, there are great differences, as between Delhi and Bangkok, in the extent to which religious practices continue to be observed and religious attitudes are modified. There is variability also, as for example between Delhi and Bangkok, in the extent to which the traditional social controls break down and personal disorganization becomes manifest. The observed differences seem largely to depend on the extent to which the in-migrant joins and becomes a part of a relatively homogeneous grouping of relatives or fellow-villagers who manage to maintain many of the elements of a folk society within the urban environment. The situation in Djakarta, which seems more to resemble an agglomeration of villages than a metropolis in the Western sense, affords quite different opportunity for adjustment to the in-migrant than some of the relatively impersonal, heterogeneous and disorganized areas as, for example in Delhi, described in the Unesco studies. Especially difficult are the adjustment problems of footloose refugee populations and 'floating migrants' who have lost all ties to stable and integrated home bases.

.   .   .

THE FAMILY

The family in developing areas as in the West is also being subjected to changes in the city. The structure and organization of the family has been and continues to be diverse among the various nations in Asia, Latin America and Africa. In China and India the family is an extended or joint one—inclusive of a number of generations and subject to the control of a patriarchal head. In other countries, however—Indonesia and Thailand, for example—the small conjugal family (parents and unmarried children) are prevalent; and in still other countries, as in Japan and the Philippines, intermediate types, including married children and other relatives, may be found.

A major point of origin of change in the nature of family in the urban environment may be traced to the disruption of the family as a producing economic unit. This is generally occasioned by the out-migration of its members—sometimes unmarried males, sometimes the married breadwinner, and sometimes entire conjugal units. It is accelerated also by the increasing need in the city to adapt to a monetary as distinguished from a subsistence economy.

The nature of family problems and the character of changes in the family vary considerably with the patterns of internal migration. The problems created by out-migration of unmarried male villagers, both in the place of his origin and his destination, vary considerably from those posed by the out-migration of the husband or father, or of an entire conjugal unit. In many of the cities in developing areas out-migrant males, especially the married ones, maintain contacts with the family in their villages through a constant stream of movement between the city and their home villages. Such shuttling between city and village poses many problems because of its disruptive influence on family life and, also, of urban employment.

Especially in the family which migrates as a group to the city are changes in the traditional family possible. In the urban environment not only is the economic function of the family often drastically altered but the nature of inter-personal relations among its members and the roles of parents, children and siblings may also be modified. Particularly evident may be the tendency for patriarchal authority to diminish, the rights of women to be stressed, the prestige of elders to wane, and increased individualism to characterize all members.

The disruption of traditional family life often has adverse effects on all members of the family and particularly on children, especially when they become victims of child labour practices. The breakdown of traditional family ties is evidenced by increased separation and divorce in the city, by the breakdown of informal social controls manifest in the problems of personal maladjustment and disorganization, and by the acute nature of problems with which the changing family is often unable to cope in the urban setting such as illness, unemployment, orphanhood, old age and widowhood.

These changes are creating increasing pressures among developing nations for legal and institutional changes to meet the problems of the family as a whole and of its members. Protective legislation as represented by child and female labour laws, social security measures and provisions for medical care, and the development of institutions such as schools, orphanages, homes for the aged and hospitals are in large measure designed to meet problems created by the changed situation in the city and the breakdown of traditional family controls.

Although broad changes in the family in developing areas can be described, the data are, on the whole, inadequate and fragmentary as a basis for sound generalization and conclusion. Further information and research on the family in the city in developing areas are badly needed.

SOCIAL DISORGANIZATION

In developing areas, as in Western cities, social disorganization is often a symptom of cultural and social change in the urban environment. Personal disorganization, including crime and delinquency, is a reflection of social disorganization. The breakdown of informal social controls of the folk society is increasingly evident in cities and is manifest partly in the changes in the traditional family discussed above. Problems of personal disorganization in the city include, in addition to delinquency and crime, alcoholism, neurosis, suicide and prostitution. As a special case, prostitution, a fairly widespread social problem in many cities in developing areas, is a product of the predominantly masculine character of in-migration and the economic difficulties experienced by many women in the transition from a subsistence to a monetary economy.

Increased industrialization and urbanization may increase social and personal disorganization, including crime and delinquency. In many cities in developing areas, large elements of the population have not yet become exposed to the urban way of life, have retained many elements of their folk culture and have remained more or less impervious to the disorganizing factors of urban life. With increased industrialization and urbanization the situation is expected to change. It is possible that developing countries may avoid the levels of social disorganization, including crime and delinquency, which occurred in some Western countries under comparable conditions because of the following characteristics of many developing nations: (a) the great general devotion to religion which is an important binding force and a form of social control; (b) the stabilizing effect of the high degree of nationalism prevalent in many developing countries; and (c) the general orientation of the governments toward the concept of the welfare state, in which government is intimately concerned with the well-being of each individual as well as general social progress and social protection. Moreover, the experience of Western countries is available to help developing countries as urbanization progresses.

LABOUR PROBLEMS

In most developing countries, towns have expanded faster, and the exodus from rural areas to the towns has been greater, than warranted by the growth of economic opportunities. A large proportion of the workers who migrate from rural areas find jobs only in casual employment in cities— that is, in service occupations and trades, such as pedlars, trishaw operators, domestic servants, common labourers, etc. 'Tertiary' employment, i.e., service occupations, in many cities in developing areas are an index not of economic progress but of under-employment.

Workers who do become absorbed in expanding industry are faced with difficult adaptations both technical and psychological. Workers abruptly transplanted from rural to urban areas, especially if the shift involves transition from a subsistence to a monetary economy, lack stability, have no training or experience for industrial work, and in consequence have very low productivity. The problem of the in-migrant worker is further aggravated by the fact that he is often separated from his family for long periods, a factor which contributes to his instability and to his return from time to time to his native village. When he is joined by his family, they contribute to the problem of adjustment in the urban environment and often tend to become themselves sources of additional labour problems in the form of female and child labour, frequently under exploitative conditions.

Developing nations are facing a difficult problem in their efforts to protect the in-migrant worker and his family from abuses, to develop training and needed skills in the labour force and to increase productivity.

ARTS AND CRAFTS

Among the social changes set in motion by the city in the developing areas are changes in the arts and crafts and forms of cultural enjoyment. Traditional art was usually utilitarian rather than art *per se*. In the city the traditional products of handicrafts are coming into competition with modern methods of manufacture and in many fields are unable to survive such competition. Some governments are making efforts to preserve the traditional arts, and, at the same time, to support the use of the articles produced through handicrafts. Such efforts cannot be expected to be successful, however, unless the products can, in fact, successfully compete with machine products, either in utility or artistry or both. It must be anticipated that increasing industrialization and urbanization are likely to contribute to the breakdown of many of the traditional forms of art and handicraft.

The city also creates significant changes in forms of recreation and mass participation in cultural activities. Museums and libraries are becoming available in cities in developing areas, although only on a modest scale far below either present or potential demand. A significant change in recreational habits of city-dwellers is visible in the impact of the cinema. Practically all developing countries report an increase in popularity of the motion picture and many question the content and cultural impact of the film. Reports indicate increases in spectator and commercial, as contrasted with participant, forms of recreation. Among the more popular spectator sports, football (soccer) has received a prominent place. It may be expected that the developing countries will experience increases in commercialized recreation and that many of the urban forms of recreation will be diffused to the rural population of the country.

EDUCATION

Educational facilities in the cities in developing nations, as in fact for the nations as a whole, are inadequate both for children and adults. Mass illiteracy, reflecting low levels of living, tends to augment many types of urban problems. Although developing nations are striving to increase educational facilities in urban areas, the need for food, clothing and shelter —particularly for incoming migrants—often claims a higher priority. Provision of more and better educational facilities in the cities of developing countries remains a major problem.

POPULATION

In addition to the other types of problems, urbanization has produced new forms of population problems, that is, problems relating to fertility, mortality, internal migration and composition of the population. In the early history of cities, in general, and in many cities today, death rates are much higher than in rural areas. In contrast, in the urban setting, birth rates tend to be lower than in rural areas in many parts of the world, although not uniformly so.

Since the death rate may be considered a general measurement of all the conditions of life, social, economic and political, that permit the retention of life itself, it deserves careful study for the urban area as a whole, and for specific sub-groupings of the population. In general, however, since the end of the Second World War, the developing areas have been characterized by rapidly declining death rates. Because of continued high birth rates, unprecedented rates of population increase are occurring throughout the nation in urban as well as in rural areas.

The high rates of population growth tend to obstruct efforts to raise levels of living and, in consequence, a number of countries including India, Pakistan, Mainland China, Korea, Egypt and Tunisia have adopted national policies to dampen rates of population increase. In these and other areas, research is needed to provide a basis for planning and administering programmes of family limitation. Information is needed on knowledge about restriction of, and attitudes towards, family size. It goes without saying that such studies should in every instance be consistent with prevalent religious or other value systems. Whether studies focusing on fertility behaviour should be conducted is a matter, of course, for each community to decide for itself in accordance with prevailing norms and policy.

Studies of internal migration and its consequences are often of special importance in developing areas. Large migratory streams from overpopulated rural to urban areas create many problems of adjustment for the in-migrants and for the communities to which they come. Studies of immigration and problems of adjustment and acculturation are a prerequisite to dealing with the many problems generated by internal migratory flows.

Finally, it may be noted that there is need for study of various aspects of population composition. Especially important in such studies is the study of variation in respect to such characteristics as sex, age, ethnicity and race, education, occupational and industrial skills and the like.

.   .   .

GOVERNMENT AND ADMINISTRATION

As has been indicated above, the urban complex and urban living requires mechanisms for integrating and co-ordinating activity. This is evident in the new problems created for local or city government and in the problems requiring re-definition of relationships between local government and state or provincial and national government.

Complex urban problems require increasing numbers of specialists, as well as persons trained in general administration. The urban setting raises many questions relating to the selection, training and recruiting of governmental officials, and the creation of 'civil service' systems. It involves questions of adequate conditions of public service so as to attract able and honest officials. It involves the devising and installing of effective and efficient administrative procedures.

The emergence of the city has posed new problems in the relation of city government to regional or national governments. These problems include consideration of the centralization or decentralization of various functions; the allocation of resources for tax purposes between the national, regional, or municipal government; and broad problems of intergovernmental powers and relationships.

At the local level, many administrative problems arise from the fact that local government boundaries frequently do not coincide with the economic, demographic or geographic or ecological reality referred to as the 'metropolitan area.' In consequence, local governments are often incapable of dealing with the problems of the entire metropolitan area. Finally, it may be noted that it is not clear what governmental levels should be primarily concerned with 'urban problems.' Such difficulties are to be found throughout the world in the economically-advanced as well as in the developing areas. Problems of government in the urban setting require research and attention.

43. POWER IN LOCAL COMMUNITIES

William Spinrad

Two opposing models of community power structure are present in the empirical literature on the city. One holds that decision-making operates in a monolithic system with a business oligarchy uppermost. The other is pluralistic and asserts that the urban community lacks any centralized or coordinated direction, and that whatever decisions are made result from the interaction of a fluid set of varyingly contentious and cooperative groups. Delbert Miller and Robert Dahl are prominently identified with these opposing perspectives that have guided a great deal of recent study.

The sociology of community power structure harbors several significant methodological issues that impede theoretical progress. The conception of power itself is a difficulty, as is the manner in which its exercise is pursued, that is principally whether the point of view of the actor or that of the observer is to be taken. These problems beset current scholarship just as much as the opposing conclusions divide urban sociologists. The idea that at least in American cities a stable network of business, professional, and government leaders directs the outcome of community events has been advanced as a means of reconciling the two dominant views and accelerating cumulative research.

THE EFFORTS AT COMMUNITY POWER ANALYSIS have been many, the findings plentiful, the interpretations challenging. But, despite several suggestive attempts, thorough systematization is still wanting; the rela-

Excerpts from *Social Problems*, Vol. 12, Number 3, 1965. Reprinted by permission of the author and the Society for the Study of Social Problems.

tion between the "power variable" and the entire community social structure is barely sketched.

A meaningful organization of the field would be a posing of the major contending analyses. This, in essence, is the function of a symposium entitled *Power and Democracy in America*.[1] Despite its rather grandiose title and the variety of subjects considered by the major contributors and the editors, the core of the book is the debate between two students of community power, Delbert Miller and Robert Dahl. Utilizing their own researches and other relevant material, the two scholars generally represent and expound the two opposite sides of the methodological and analytical conflict that has characterized recent community power discussion. Miller favors the "reputational" form of investigation and finds a pyramidal, quasi-monolithic structure dominated by a "business elite" more or less typical. He is thus quite in accord with the findings of Hunter's original study. Dahl, utilizing "event analysis," searches for evidence of specific decision makers on particular issues, and concludes that a relatively pluralistic power structure is more prevalent. Of course, the divergencies are more complex and detailed, but these are the summary statements around which the discussion evolves.

The reputational technique, which has, with many variations, become fairly widespread in use, seeks to get knowledgeable informants to select, from a list of leading figures in community organizations and institutional areas, those whom they considered most powerful in "getting things done." Those chosen were then interviewed to learn about the personal and social relations among them, and which people they would themselves solicit if they wanted something adopted or achieved. Reviewing many studies with this research emphasis, including his own "Pacific City," Miller's conclusions are, essentially, the following: [2]

1. Businessmen are overrepresented among "key influentials" and dominate community policy-making in most communities.[3]

2. Local governments are weak power centers. The elected officials are mostly small businessmen, local lawyers, and professional politicians. Policy on important questions is formulated by organized interests groups under the influence of the economic dominants. City councils merely respond to their pressures.

3. Representatives of labor, education, religious, and "cultural" groups are rarely key influentials, are under-represented in city councils.

4. In vivid contrast, Miller reports his investigations of "English City," like "Pacific City" a seaport community of about 500,000 population. Businessmen constitute only a minority of the "key influentials." Labor is significantly represented. There is also an appreciable number from educational, religious, welfare, and "status" leaderships. Furthermore, the city council is the major arena of community decision making, the party organizations the directing groups.

Noting differences between "Regional City" and "Pacific City," Miller does not insist that the power pattern is identical in all American communities. In fact, he develops a typology of possible structures. But the modal type is clearly sketched, particularly in contrast with the findings of his British study.

Dahl's counter propositions are based primarily on his study of New Haven, summarized in the symposium and more fully elaborated in his book *Who Governs?* [4] The power structure of New Haven is seen as relatively pluralistic or, to use his terminology, one of "dispersed inequalities," a metamorphosis from earlier days of oligarchal dominance by "aristocratic patricians" and "entrepreneurs" successively. This is initially indicated in the change in political leadership with the rise of the "ex plebians" from various ethnic groups, often with proletarian backgrounds. The attention is, however, more to the examination of decision-leadership in three issue areas—political nominations, public education, and urban redevelopment, which Dahl insists are both representative and salient. The method in such "event analysis" is typically one of chronological narration of who did what, when, and what effect it had, in this instance supplemented by a more precise systematic tabulation of the kinds of people who held formal positions in the organizations concerned with the above issues and of those who initiated or vetoed significant decisions.

The refutation of the business dominance thesis is quite explicit. Some two hundred "economic notables" were located. Within the issue-areas studied, a significant number occupied formal positions only in connection with urban redevelopment (about fifty), of which seven were actually considered decision leaders. None were formally involved in public education, a handful in political parties.

Even within the area of urban redevelopment, the decision-making role of businessmen was considered minor. Their contributions came largely through their participation in the "Citizens Action Committee," organized by the Mayor with the objective of legitimizing decisions and providing an arena in which objections to the program could be anticipated and avoided. Neither the Committee, nor individual businessmen or business groups, were responsible for many crucial decisions. Dahl believes that they could, if vigorously in opposition, have blocked proposals, but the political officials, led by the Mayor, prevented such contingencies by a "capacity for judging with considerable precision what the existing beliefs and the commitments of the men on the CAC would compel them to agree to if a proposal were presented in the proper way, time, and place." [5] In general, business groups possess many "resources," but they are also limited by many power "liabilities," so that they simply appeared as "one of the groups out of which individuals sporadically emerge to influence the policies and acts of city officials." [6] "Like other groups in the community, from the Negroes on Dixwell Avenue to teachers in the public school, sometimes the Notables have their way and sometimes they do not." [7]

In the decision areas studied, the "inequalities" are not so widely "dispersed." Only a few people make the key decisions in each issue area, but they achieve their hegemony by accepting the indirect influence of larger groups. Nominations are generally determined by a few party leaders, but with attention to the wishes of their followers within the party organizations, especially sub-leaders and representatives of ethnic groups. Most important redevelopment decisions were made by the Mayor and appropriate staff officials, with full sensitivity to the need for getting support from business and other groups. Major public education policy was directed by the Mayor and his appointees on the Board of Education; superintendents, principals, and teachers organizations played some part, but mostly to mobilize support for public education. A few public and party officials thus constituted the directing leadership, each in his own province, with the office and personality of the dynamic Mayor, Richard Lee, supplying the unifying force. We have advisedly called the leading group a "directing" rather than a "dominating" oligarchy. It apparently got its way less from authority or influence, in the communication sense, than from the ability to please others, particularly potentially opposing groups. In fact, the political leaders favored the existence of organized groups as a means of legitimatizing their decisions and mobilizing support, as well as providing an arena where various sentiments could be expressed and somewhat satisfied. The Citizens Action Committee in the urban redevelopment field was one such example. Similarly, school principals and the Board of Education utilized PTAs "to head off or settle conflicts between parents and the school system." [8]

Dahl does not maintain that the New Haven pattern he describes is the only one possible or existent. Like Miller, he offers a model of power types. But the New Haven analysis provides the basic elements around which most of the varied forms are structured.

The dispute between the two major contending approaches to American community power is thus, more or less, joined. Partly methodological, it is, at least initially, a disagreement between a business-elite dominance thesis and an acceptance of a relative pluralism. It is also a disagreement about the role of local government and political leadership. Dahl believes that mayors and their staff have increasingly become the initiators and organizers of important community decisions. Miller insists that the political leaders are uncertain about themselves and wait for cues of others, while businessmen have a clearly defined image "and thus act with more assertion." [9]

Despite their disagreement about the prevailing power picture, Miller and Dahl offer models of possible power structure which are not too dissimilar.[10] Both allow for completely pluralistic patterns, with either particular spheres of influence for specific groups or open struggles by relatively equal groups on the same issues. To Miller, these are subordinate aspects in most American communities. To Dahl, they exist but are less likely possibilities than a system of comparative pluralism with coordination by the political leadership in different ways in different communities, a variant not specifically indicated by Miller. Finally both accept the possibility of domination by an economic elite, but Dahl generally relegates such situations to the past while Miller insists that this pattern, with all its variations, is most common in the United States today.

Whatever evidence is available tends to support Dahl's emphasis against Miller's. Most American communities reveal a relatively pluralistic power structure. On some community-relevant questions, power may be widely dispersed. On the most salient questions, many groups may have an effect on what is decided, but the directing leadership comes from some combination of particular business groups, local government, and, in recent developments, professionals and experts. Communities differ and communities change in the power relations among these elements. A suggestive hypothesis holds that the tendency has been towards their co-ordination into a uniquely composite decision-making collectivity.

44. THE KIND OF PROBLEM A CITY IS

Jane Jacobs

Jane Jacobs is the foe of conventional city planning, whether it is of the simplistic Garden City school or the mechanistic Radiant City variety. Here she surveys the modes of thinking that are characteristic of city planning theory. She does so in terms of the analysis of the history of scientific thought made by Warren Weaver, namely, successive stages dealing, in turn, with problems of, first, organized simplicity; second, disorganized complexity; and, finally, organized complexity. These may be characterized respectively as considerations of two related variables, the method of statistical mechanics; of multiple variables, the method of probability statistics; and, lastly, of the functional interdependence of parts, the method of the life sciences, that she is convinced is essential both to understanding and coping with the phenomena of the big city.

This organic analogy, which presupposes a network of purposeful interaction as basic to the city, directs attention to the human coefficient in the urban milieu. The city is thus sui generis, *and as a thing in itself must be understood in its own terms. Therefore the foundation of successful city planning is to be found in the concrete examination of particulars as aspects of ongoing processes. Only the recognition of significant dynamic details will permit city planning to be carried on effectively. Otherwise it will continue to repeat the mistakes of the past, erring either by opting for total replacement or by electing the atomization of the metropolis into inert scattered fragments. Jane Jacobs' adherence to creative functionalism implies a strong faith in the innate capacity of big cities to*

Excerpts from *The Death and Life of Great American Cities* by Jane Jacobs (1961), Vintage Edition. Reprinted by permission of Random House, Inc.

solve their own problems: witness the way in which they have succeeded in dealing with the earlier problems of human health.

GARDEN CITY PLANNING THEORY had its beginnings in the late nineteenth century, and Ebenezer Howard attacked the problem of town planning much as if he were a nineteenth-century physical scientist analzing a two-variable problem of simplicity. The two major variables in the Garden City concept of planning were the quantity of housing (or population) and the number of jobs. There two were conceived of as simply and directly related to each other, in the form of relatively closed systems. In turn, the housing had its subsidiary variables, related to it in equally direct, simple, mutually independent form: playgrounds, open space, schools, community center, standardized supplies and services. The town as a whole was conceived of, again, as one of the two variables in a direct, simple, town-greenbelt relationship. As a system of order, that is about all there was to it. And on this simple basis of two-variable relationships was created an entire theory of self-contained towns as a means of redistributing the population of cities and (hopefully) achieving regional planning.

Whatever may be said of this scheme for isolated towns, any such simple systems of two-variable relationships cannot possibly be discerned in great cities—and never could be. Such systems cannot be discerned in a town either, the day after the town becomes encompassed in a metropolitan orbit with its multiplicity of choices and complexities of cross-use. But in spite of this fact, planning theory has persistently applied this two-variable system of thinking and analyzing to big cities; and to this day city planners and housers believe they hold a precious nugget of truth about the kind of problem to be dealt with when they attempt to shape or reshape big-city neighborhoods into versions of two-variable systems, with ratios of one thing (as open space) depending directly and simply upon an immediate ratio of something else (as population) .

To be sure, while planners were assuming that cities were properly problems of simplicity, planning theorists and planners could not avoid seeing that real cities were not so in fact. But they took care of this in the traditional way that the incurious (or the disrespectful) have always regarded problems of organized complexity: as if these puzzles were, in Dr. Weaver's words, "in some dark and foreboding way, irrational."

Beginning in the late 1920's in Europe, and in the 1930's here, city planning theory began to assimilate the newer ideas on probability theory developed by physical science. Planners began to imitate and apply these analyses precisely as if cities were problems in disorganized complexity, understandable purely by statistical analysis, predictable by the application of probability mathematics, manageable by conversion into groups of averages.

This conception of the city as a collection of separate file drawers, in effect, was suited very well by the Radiant City vision of Le Corbusier, that vertical and more centralized version of the two-variable Garden City. Although Le Corbusier himself made no more than a gesture toward statistical analysis, his scheme assumed the statistical reordering of a system of disorganized complexity, solvable mathematically; his towers in the park were a celebration, in art, of the potency of statistics and the triumph of the mathematical average.

The new probability techniques, and the assumptions about the kind of problem that underlay the way they have been used in city planning, did not supplant the base idea of the two-variable reformed city. Rather these new ideas were added. Simple, two-variable systems of order were still the aim. But these could be organized even more "rationally" now, from out of a supposed existing system of disorganized complexity. In short, the new probability and statistical methods gave more "accuracy," more scope, made possible a more Olympian view and treatment of the supposed problem of the city.

With the probability techniques, an old aim—stores "properly" related to immediate housing or to a preordained population—became seemingly feasible; there arose techniques for planning standardized shopping "scientifically"; although it was early realized by such planning theorists as Stein and Bauer that preplanned shopping centers within cities must also be monopolistic or semimonopolistic, or else the statistics would not predict, and the city would go on behaving with dark and foreboding irrationality.

With these techniques, it also became feasible to analyze statistically, by income groups and family sizes, a given quantity of people uprooted by acts of planning, to combine these with probability statistics on normal housing turnover, and to estimate accurately the gap. Thus arose the supposed feasibility of large-scale relocation of citizens. In the form of statistics, these citizens were no longer components of any unit except the family, and could be dealt with intellectually like grains of sand, or electrons or billiard balls. The larger the number of uprooted, the more easily they could be planned for on the basis of mathematical averages. On this basis it was actually intellectually easy and sane to contemplate clearance of all slums and re-sorting of people in ten years and not much harder to contemplate it as a twenty-year job.

By carrying to logical conclusions the thesis that the city, as it exists, is a problem in disorganized complexity, housers and planners reached— apparently with straight faces—the idea that almost any specific malfunctioning could be corrected by opening and filling a new file drawer. Thus we get such political party policy statements as this: "The Housing Act of 1959 . . . should be supplemented to include . . . a program of housing for moderate-income families whose incomes are too high for admission to public housing, but too low to enable them to obtain decent shelter in the private market."

With statistical and probability techniques, it also became possible to create formidable and impressive planning surveys for cities—surveys that come out with fanfare, are read by practically nobody, and then drop quietly into oblivion, as well they might, being nothing more nor less than routine exercises in statistical mechanics for systems of disorganized complexity. It became possible also to map out master plans for the statistical city, and people take these more seriously, for we are all accustomed to believe that maps and reality are necessarily related, or that if they are not, we can make them so by altering reality.

With these techniques, it was possible not only to conceive of people, their incomes, their spending money and their housing as fundamentally problems in disorganized complexity, susceptible to conversion into problems of simplicity once ranges and averages were worked out, but also to conceive of city traffic, industry, parks, and even cultural facilities as components of disorganized complexity, convertible into problems of simplicity.

Furthermore, it was no intellectual disadvantage to contemplate "coordinated" schemes of city planning embracing ever greater territories. The greater the territory, as well as the larger the population, the more rationally and easily could both be dealt with as problems of disorganized complexity viewed from an Olympian vantage point. The wry remark that "A Region is an area safely larger than the last one to whose problems we found no solution" is not a wry remark in these terms. It is a simple statement of a basic fact about disorganized complexity; it is much like saying that a large insurance company is better equipped to average out risks than a small insurance company.

However, while city planning has thus mired itself in deep misunderstandings about the very nature of the problem with which it is dealing, the life sciences, unburdened with this mistake, and moving ahead very rapidly, have been providing some of the concepts that city planning needs: along with providing the basic strategy of recognizing problems of organized complexity, they have provided hints about analyzing and handling this kind of problem. These advances have, of course, filtered from the life sciences into general knowledge; they have become part of the intellectual fund of our times. And so a growing number of people have begun, gradually, to think of cities as problems in organized complexity —organisms that are replete with unexamined, but obviously intricately interconnected, and surely understandable, relationships.

This is a point of view which has little currency yet among planners themselves, among architectural city designers, or among the businessmen and legislators who learn their planning lessons, naturally, from what is established and long accepted by planning "experts." Nor is this a point of view that has much appreciable currency in schools of planning (perhaps there least of all).

City planning, as a field, has stagnated. It bustles but it does not advance. Today's plans show little if any perceptible progress in comparison with plans devised a generation ago. In transportation, either regional or local, nothing is offered which was not already offered and popularized in 1938 in the General Motors diorama at the New York World's Fair, and before that by Le Corbusier. In some respects, there is outright retrogression. None of today's pallid imitations of Rockefeller Center is as good as the original, which was built a quarter of a century ago. Even in conventional planning's own given terms, today's housing projects are no improvement, and usually a retrogression, in comparison with those of the 1930's.

As long as city planners, and the businessmen, lenders, and legislators who have learned from planners, cling to the unexamined assumptions that they are dealing with a problem in the physical sciences, city planning cannot possibly progress. Of course it stagnates. It lacks the first requisite for a body of practical and progressing thought: recognition of the kind of problem at issue. Lacking this, it has found the shortest distance to a dead end.

.   .   .

Because the life sciences and cities happen to pose the same kinds of problems does not mean they are the same problems. The organizations of living protoplasm and the organizations of living people and enterprises cannot go under the same microscopes.

However, the tactics for understanding both are similar in the sense that both depend on the microscopic or detailed view, so to speak, rather than on the less detailed, naked-eye view suitable for viewing problems of simplicity or the remote telescopic view suitable for viewing problems of disorganized complexity.

In the life sciences, organized complexity is handled by identifying a specific factor or quantity—say an enzyme—and then painstakingly learning its intricate relationships and interconnections with other factors or quantities. All this is observed in terms of the behavior (not mere presence) of other specific (not generalized) factors or quantities. To be sure, the techniques of two-variable and disorganized-complexity analysis are used too, but only as subsidiary tactics.

In principle, these are much the same tactics as those that have to be used to understand and to help cities. In the case of understanding cities, I think the most important habits of thought are these:

1. To think about processes;

2. To work inductively, reasoning from particulars to the general, rather than the reverse;

3. To seek for "unaverage" clues involving very small quantities, which reveal the way larger and more "average" quantities are operating.

Why think about processes? Objects in cities—whether they are buildings, streets, parks, districts, landmarks, or anything else—can have radically differing effects, depending upon the circumstances and contexts in which they exist. Thus, for instance, almost nothing useful can be understood or can be done about improving city dwellings if these are considered in the abstract as "housing." City dwellings—either existing or potential—are specific and particularized buildings always involved in differing, specific processes such as unslumming, slumming, generation of diversity, self-destruction of diversity.

For cities, processes are of the essence. Furthermore, once one thinks about city processes, it follows that one must think of catalysts of these processes, and this too is of the essence.

The processes that occur in cities are not arcane, capable of being understood only by experts. They can be understood by almost anybody. Many ordinary people already understand them; they simply have not given these processes names, or considered that by understanding these ordinary arrangements of cause and effect, we can also direct them if we want to.

Why reason inductively? Because to reason, instead, from generalizations ultimately drives us into absurdities—as in the case of the Boston planner who knew (against all the real-life evidence he had) that the North End had to be a slum because the generalizations that make him an expert say it is.

This is an obvious pitfall because the generalizations on which the planner was depending are themselves so nonsensical. However, inductive reasoning is just as important for identifying, understanding and constructively using the forces and processes that actually are relevant to cities, and therefore are not nonsensical. I have generalized about these forces and processes considerably, but let no one be misled into believing that these generalizations can be used routinely to declare what the particulars, in this or that place, ought to mean. City processes in real life are too complex to be routine, too particularized for application as abstractions. They are always made up of interactions among unique combinations of particulars, and there is no substitute for knowing the particulars.

Inductive reasoning of this kind is, again, something that can be engaged in by ordinary, interested citizens, and again they have the advantage over planners. Planners have been trained and disciplined in deductive thinking, like the Boston planner who learned his lessons only too well. Possibly because of this bad training, planners frequently seem to be less well equipped intellectually for respecting and understanding particulars than ordinary people, untrained in expertise, who are attached to a neighborhood, accustomed to using it, and so are not accustomed to thinking of it in generalized or abstract fashion.

Why seek "unaverage" clues, involving small quantities? Comprehensive statistical studies, to be sure, can sometimes be useful abstracted measurements of the sizes, ranges, averages and medians of this and that. Gathered from time to time, statistics can tell too what has been happening to these figures. However, they tell almost nothing about how the quantities are working in systems of organized complexity.

To learn how things are working, we need pinpoint clues. For instance, all the statistical studies possible about the downtown of Brooklyn, N.Y., cannot tell us as much about the problem of that downtown and its cause as is told in five short lines of type in a single newspaper advertisement. This advertisement, which is for Marboro, a chain of bookstores, gives the business hours of the chain's five stores. Three of them (one near Carnegie Hall in Manhattan, one near the Public Library and not far from Times Square, one in Greenwich Village) stay open until midnight. A fourth, close to Fifth Avenue and Fifty-ninth Street, stays open until 10 P.M. The fifth, in downtown Brooklyn, stays open until 8 P.M. Here is a management which keeps its stores open late, if there is business to be had. The advertisement tells us that Brooklyn's downtown is too dead by 8 P.M., as indeed it is. No surveys (and certainly no mindless, mechanical predictions projected forward in time from statistical surveys, a boondoggle that today frequently passes for "planning") can tell us anything so relevant to the composition and to the need of Brooklyn's downtown as this small, but specific and precisely accurate, clue to the workings of that downtown.

It takes large quantities of the "average" to produce the "unaverage" in cities. But the mere presence of large quantities—whether people, uses, structures, jobs, parks, streets or anything else—does not guarantee much generation of city diversity. These quantities can be working as factors in inert, low-energy systems, merely maintaining themselves, if that. Or they can make up interacting, high-energy systems, producing by-products of the "unaverage."

The "unaverage" can be physical, as in the case of eye-catchers which are small elements in much larger, more "average" visual scenes. They can be economic, as in the case of one-of-a-kind stores, or cultural, as in the case of an unusual school or out-of-the-ordinary theater. They can be social, as in the case of public characters, loitering places, or residents or users who are financially, vocationally, racially or culturally unaverage.

Quantities of the "unaverage," which are bound to be relatively small, are indispensable to vital cities. However, in the sense that I am speaking of them here, "unaverage" quantities are also important as analytical means—as clues. They are often the only announcers of the way various large quantities are behaving, or failing to behave, in combination with each other. As a rough analogy, we may think of quantitatively minute vitamins in protoplasmic systems, or trace elements in pasture plants. These things are necessary for proper functioning of the systems of which they are a part; however, their usefulness does not end there, because they can and do also serve as vital clues to what is happening in the systems of which they are a part.

This awareness of "unaverage" clues—or awareness of their lack—is, again, something any citizen can practice. City dwellers, indeed, are commonly great informal experts in precisely this subject. Ordinary people in cities have an awareness of "unaverage" quantities which is quite consonant with the importance of these relatively small quantities. And again, planners are the ones at the disadvantage. They have inevitably come to regard "unaverage" quantities as relatively inconsequential, because these are statistically inconsequential. They have been trained to discount what is most vital.

. . .

Now we must dig a little deeper into the bog of intellectual misconceptions about cities in which orthodox reformers and planners have mired themselves (and the rest of us) . Underlying the city planners' deep disrespect for their subject matter, underlying the jejune belief in the "dark and foreboding" irrationality or chaos of cities, lies a long-established misconception about the relationship of cities—and indeed of men—with the rest of nature.

Human beings are, of course, a part of nature, as much so as grizzly bears or bees or whales or sorghum cane. The cities of human beings are as natural, being a product of one form of nature, as are the colonies of prairie dogs or the beds of oysters. The botanist Edgar Anderson has written wittily and sensitively in *Landscape* magazine from time to time about cities as a form of nature. "Over much of the world," he comments, "man has been accepted as a city-loving creature." Nature watching, he points out, "is quite as easy in the city as in the country; all one has to do is accept Man as a part of Nature. Remember that as a specimen of Homo sapiens you are far and away most likely to find that species an effective guide to deeper understanding of natural history."

A curious but understandable thing happened in the eighteenth century. By then, the cities of Europeans had done well enough by them, mediating between them and many harsh aspects of nature, so that something became popularly possible which previously had been a rarity—sentimentalization of nature, or at any rate, sentimentalization of a rustic or a barbarian relationship with nature. Marie Antoinette playing milkmaid was an expression of this sentimentality on one plane. The romantic idea of the "noble savage" was an even sillier one, on another plane. So, in this country, was Jefferson's intellectual rejection of cities of free artisans and mechanics, and his dream of an ideal republic of self-reliant rural yeomen—a pathetic dream for a good and great man whose land was tilled by slaves.

In real life, barbarians (and peasants) are the least free of men—

bound by tradition, ridden by caste, fettered by superstitions, riddled by suspicion and foreboding of whatever is strange. "City air makes free," was the medieval saying, when city air literally did make free the runaway serf. City air still makes free the runaways from company towns, from plantations, from factory-farms, from subsistence farms, from migrant picker routes, from mining villages, from one-class suburbs.

45. THE NEIGHBORHOOD UNIT RECONSIDERED

Suzanne Keller

In his foreword to Suzanne Keller's The Urban Neighborhood, *from which the following selection is taken. C. A. Doxiadis of the Athens Center of Ekistics observes that anyone dealing with human communities must understand how communities operate, why they operate as they do, and finally how they might operate best. It is this fusion of objective inquiry and practical concern that motivates the reexamination of the neighborhood idea concept in Dr. Keller's recent writings.*

Basically, the idea of the neighborhood unit combines the physical and social aspects of urban planning, so that both social intimacy and efficient, economical services are conceived as the goals of community construction and reconstruction. In the material below the neighborhood unit idea is evaluated in the light of social-research findings and also the results of organized efforts in Europe, the United States, and Asia to build new towns altogether and new neighborhoods in already existing communities. Moreover, it considers the merits of alternatives that have been proposed to the neighborhood unit, including the neighborhood circle, the social network, and the roving neighborhood.

As such, this chapter from Dr. Keller's book emphasizes the need for critical thought in urban sociology as well as city planning. In its recollection of the continued validity of earlier research at the University of Chicago it is also a reminder that properly interpreted the older sociological literature is of value even today after much striving has only proved the limited role of physical planning where adequate provision for social unity in the city has not been made.

From *The Urban Neighborhood* by Suzanne Keller (1968). Reprinted by permission of Random House, Inc.

THE NEIGHBORHOOD UNIT IDEA was first applied in the United States and from there went on to conquer and then partly to lose favor with the planning world. Since Perry's original formulation, in which the role of physical design was much more developed than that of the social aspects, the conception has been modified to take into account varied local conditions as well as the accelerated growth rates of modern cities.

Once the conception gained hold, debate centered mainly on the physical size, the population, the types of facilities and services to be provided, and the relation between the neighborhood unit and the larger community of which it was a part. Even on these points, however, agreement has overshadowed disagreement as planners, rather than have to struggle afresh with each new assignment, sought to convert these tentative general assumptions into practical procedural principles.

The two elements on which planners found themselves most in accord were the small size and relative self-sufficiency of such a unit, modified only by its dependence on a larger urban network. Perry, somewhat reluctantly, had proposed as an optimum unit 5,000 people centered on a primary school of 600 pupils serviced by local shops and a local assembly area within walking distance. Ring roads for vehicular traffic providing both the physical boundary as well as the link to the wider world were to encircle the entire area. Several of these neighborhood units were to comprise a community. Thus, size was to be estimated on the basis of the number of families needed to provide the target number of local primary school pupils; distances were to be determined by the criterion of pedestrian access to all essential facilities; and the number of facilities was to be based on existing standards of residents' needs and desires for shops, churches, movies, parks, and clinics near their homes.

Attempts to test the practical validity of this concept have been hampered by its inconsistent applications; each potential test in a "real life" situation represented a somewhat different version of the concept as originally planned. In the British New Towns, for example, the neighborhood unit had to be accommodated to the smaller-size British primary schools, which meant that no single primary school could become the neighborhood core. Also, the number of shops actually servicing the New Town populations fell far short of the plan, whether for financial reasons or special population characteristics is not yet clear.[1] Cinemas, having been displaced by television, can no longer be regarded as essential for each neighborhood unit, and other amenities such as branch libraries and youth and community centers either failed to be established or were too sparsely distributed. In Korangi, Pakistan, to take another example, the absence of certain higher order facilities such as schools and markets likewise altered the plan, thereby precluding a genuine assessment of its actual operation.[2] These practical deviations from the original plan make a full test of the concept difficult; however, they do permit a piecemeal testing of some of its elements.[3]

According to Nicholson, no aspect of life in the British New Towns is more difficult to assess than the neighborhood unit, nor are its presumed advantages everywhere automatically apparent. Subunits for daily shopping and primary schooling may be clearly indicated, and some buffer between individuals and central authorities is also useful. However, the problems of economic duplication of services and thus of competition between neighborhood and town centers and of a division of loyalties between the neighborhood and the town have not as yet been resolved. If people concentrate spiritually, socially, and economically on a neighborhood area, the town as a whole will be deprived of their participation and patronage; whereas if they ignore the neighborhood and concentrate on the town, then the neighborhood unit is clearly superfluous.

In addition to these important practical observations, certain of the concept's fundamental assumptions about human behavior have been challenged in recent years. Increasingly, for example, planners have become less dogmatic about the ideal size of such local units. The pace of population growth as well as revolutionary developments in transportation and communication facilities have forced them to think in terms of larger, more complex sectors. Perry's original target size of 5,000 is considered by some to be too large for genuine neighboring. They assert that it is both insufficiently intimate and insufficiently urban. Experience has shown that if a neighborhood center is to provide a range of standard urban services it needs from three to four times as many consumers as originally stipulated. This would call for two types of local units, a smaller and a larger one, each performing different functions. The larger one would provide basic amenities for somewhere around 20,000 people; the smaller one, whose size remains problematical, would encourage social intimacy.

Planners also hesitate to make the nucleus of neighborhood life a single institution such as a primary school. Just as it is unwise to plan a national economy around a single product so it is unwise to make a single activity the hub of local life. Experience from Sweden and the Soviet Union has indicated that in a changing society a change in the educational system entails a reorganization of all local units whose physical configuration depends on it.

Another basic criticism concerns the undesirable consequences of social segregation stemming from the focus of the neighborhood unit on young families with young children. To make the primary school a nucleus of local life for adults without children or for unmarried individuals is patently absurd. However, in Perry's and his followers' schemes one looks in vain for a consideration of the needs of these groups. Not only do we find an overemphasis on young families with small children, but also within this category the neighborhood unit favors those families valuing the things such units can provide—namely, intimacy, quiet, green spaces, playgrounds for the children, and pedestrian access to primary services.

In addition, their economic similarities further promote a leveling of means and taste in the services desired. In most new towns there is, in fact, an extremely high degree of segregation by income as well as by family composition. Most of the new town residents inhabit standard rent housing; any nonstandard houses tend to be concentrated in one or two neighborhood units so that no balance of social classes is created within these units. Those who consider the mixing of diverse social groups as either undesirable or unfeasible are neither surprised nor dismayed by these findings, but those who see the neighborhood as a miniature of the larger world, as a cornerstone for a more complex, urban existence are disturbed by the failure of neighborhood units to achieve some sort of social balance.

This leads to a final, highly controversial point of criticism concerning the significance of the local area in an urbanized, megalopolitan world. Designing self-contained, or at least self-absorbed, neighborhood units, it is argued, deprives people of some notable advantages of urban life. Some individuals and groups may indeed welcome the intimate small town atmosphere and face-to-face contacts such units intend to foster, but others, truer to the urban ethos, prefer to use the whole city and to travel to their social contacts or work. As we have seen, neighboring, the use of local facilities, and attachment to local areas are highly variable in modern cities, depending on group and class traditions, on general levels of life, and on personal inclination. If this is the case, then how can one expect the neighborhood unit to succeed in all settings? Its utility for certain groups such as the more isolated or immobile may be undeniable, but even here no overall formula is needed.

This is where the incompatibility of the several goals of the neighborhood unit referred to earlier emerges in full force. From its inception the neighborhood unit carried a double burden, which may help account for its erratic performance in practice. On the one hand, it was to provide convenience and comfort and direct, face-to-face contacts in order to restore some sense of community that had been disturbed or destroyed by the specialization and segmentalization of urban life. On the other hand, however, it was also to constitute a special subpart of a larger, more complex totality. In the first case it was to be a somewhat self-contained, personal, "little community." In the second sense it was to be but a specialized fragment of a wider domain, which could not constitute a world for its members, but merely act as one of the means, an instrumentality, for the attainment of larger goals and purposes. Residents are thus under dual, somewhat incompatible pressures, and they may, not surprisingly, develop confused and inconsistent beliefs and conceptions about the significance of their neighborhoods vis-à-vis the city as a whole. As a result of the misgivings and doubts raised by these criticisms, a number of planners and other specialists have proposed alternatives to the neighborhood unit that modify the original concept in significant ways.

ALTERNATIVE PROPOSALS

Not everyone agrees that the principle of the neighborhood unit should be completely abandoned. Some feel that it has never been given a proper chance either because of inadequacies in its design or its application. They urge a proper, full-scale test before the concept is rejected as unworkable, a test that would permit us to specify the reasons for its failure or success under given conditions. In reply one might argue that the reasons for the inconsistent and partial application of the concept may themselves be indirect proof of its conceptual inadequacies. The very need for flexibility to accommodate the variety of needs and demands of a heterogeneous population implies that no single formula may be workable. This rather than a lack of funds or unimaginative design may be at the root of the problem.

A number of planners and social scientists have come to favor alternatives which would not reject the concept in toto but modify it by incorporating research findings on patterns of neighboring and the use of local facilities and services by an urban-industrial population. Among these are the neighborhood circle, the social network, and the roving neighborhood.

PERSONAL AND IMPERSONAL UNITS

The absence of formal constraints on neighboring relationships in urban areas permits individual predispositions and desires to come to the fore. As a result, the boundaries of an individual's choices follow no set or predictable pattern. Some urban residents have extensive ties with other residents, others have few, some go far afield, while others confine their contacts near home. Accordingly, some planners have incorporated these social research findings into their planning schemes by proposing a division of the neighborhood unit into a smaller, personal neighboring circle or network and a larger, impersonal service area. The neighboring circle may include all relatives and acquaintances within a given area, all known by sight, greeted, or chatted with, or only those with whom more intimate contacts are maintained. Studies have found the number of such contacts to vary considerably. In Hamburg, for example, such a circle included up to forty families from houses adjacent to or opposite one's own. Beyond a certain point on that street people were no longer certain whether to greet each other or not. In a well-to-do area of private villas, such uncertainty began with the third house on either side.[4] Bott likewise considers the "social network" to be the significant "immediate social environment of urban families," which, depending on the social similarities among the residents, may be confined to or transcend local area boundaries.[5] Naturally, the shapes of the boundaries established in this subjective fashion will vary as the propensity to neighboring among the inhabitants varies.

Jacqueline Tyrrwhitt, an early advocate of the twofold local unit, suggests the terms "social unit," to consist of about 500 households, or 2,000 persons, within which social contacts between like-minded individuals could unfold, and "urban unit," to designate a much larger area containing from 30,000 to 70,000 people and providing a wide variety of modern urban facilities and services.[6] These suggestions have been taken one step further by Kuper, who links them to his distinction between "reserved" and "sociable" neighbors, suggesting that the service unit is better suited to the reserved type resident and the neighborly unit to the sociable type.[7]

Kuper, along with others, sees an inherent incompatibility between these two types of units. If planners construct a neighborhood unit on the principle of personal, face to face relations, he argues, they are bound to weaken the service unit.

> The very circumstances that favour the service unit are believed to defeat the objective of promoting communities. . . . The smaller the group, the more difficult it is to provide for relative self-sufficiency and the greater the pull to other areas. The larger the group, the more readily may activities of residents be contained within the area, but at the same time, the smaller the likelihood of social relationships ramifying through the neighborhood.[8]

Here we are again reminded of the inverse relationship between the need for and reliance on neighbors and the availability of public services and facilities.

Some would ignore the personal neighboring unit altogether and concentrate entirely on the planning of larger, impersonal areas for shopping, health, culture, and recreation. In fact, Mann observes that since neither the establishment of a community center as a focal point of neighborhood life nor the social mixing of various groups for the sake of social balance has been realized by means of neighborhood units as originally formulated, what remains of the original conception is essentially the idea of "the neighborhood as an amenity area with shops, schools, institutions, open spaces, and road patterns laid down in accordance with a thought-out plan." [9] Many feel that it is only or primarily in this sense that the neighborhood unit "has fully justified itself." Glikson goes so far as to suggest that without some such concept the proper allocation of public amenities and services is virtually impossible.[10]

Planning for amenity areas rather than for neighborhood units in the traditional sense means that planners will continue to search for ways to subdivide a territory into small, more manageable subunits, but they will not expect these to promote primary social relationships. It also means that the use of facilities and services offered in such units need not be confined to residents living in the immediate vicinity. Amenity areas might, therefore, be designed on a numerical and geographical basis with only minimum attention being paid to the social and cultural characteristics of local inhabitants. The services of these areas would draw on users from a variety of points in the urban complex.

In this connection, however, the unavoidable social reality of class and ethnic subdivisions with their impact on tastes and financial resources cannot be ignored. If such realities are not taken into account, the division of an urban area into numerically equal subunits with identical facilities and services may be wasteful and ineffectual. One way to cope with this problem is for planners to concentrate on minimum facilities, such as shops, clinics, and transportation stops, which are not deeply influenced by the social and cultural characteristics of a population. Of course, even here it matters whether the residents are wealthy enough to afford cars and vacations or are tied to mass transport or to recreation near at hand. If it is true that people of "different sexes, ages, and different social classes have different types of interests and different physical areas within which interests are pursued," then any mechanical subdivision according to distance, numbers, or densities is bound to be inappropriate.[11]

Whatever the final resolution of these questions, it is apparent that the neighborhood unit—in its original, inclusive sense—is not in these changing times a useful one. For this reason, perhaps, such units that "formed an essential part of many town development plans have tended to fall into disrepute or be relegated to the status of convenient administrative and service machinery." [12] In some of the more recent British New Towns the concept has been dispensed with altogether. For example, Hook, the town that was never built, had plans to preserve only some of the technical features of the unit concept. The plans provided for the segregation of pedestrian from vehicular traffic and the distribution of primary schools. Similarly, Cumbernauld strove to create a more compact and urban town by doubling densities, by carefully planning vehicular and pedestrian traffic networks, and by making the single town center easily accessible. Its success in achieving its aims must await the completion of the town center along with the attainment of the target population. Some would argue that the retention of such principles or features as the allocation of primary schools on a residential basis and of pedestrian accessibility has only modified but not displaced the neighborhood unit concept. This argument ignores the main innovation of these plans, which was to do away with the idea of identical subunits bearing a uniform residential stamp by explicitly recognizing that "a more mobile community in the motor age makes it fruitless to search for a universal formula." [13]

THE "ROVING NEIGHBORHOOD"

In addition to a personal neighborhood circle, Riemer proposes the "roving neighborhood."[14] He notes that in between large areas that follow the rapid transit lines and divide a city into west, east, north, and south (and are usually devoid of any precise social meaning) and the smaller more intimate area of residential contacts, there develops a sense of identification with some sort of "roving" neighborhood that may be centered around points of interest other than individual residences, such as the local high school or the shopping district. A given individual may belong to several such roving neighborhoods at the same time, with each service focus having its own radius of users. These service radii, sometimes delineated by natural or man-made barriers, may be separate or overlapping. Only if "the service radius happens to coincide for several such facilities, will it be advantageous to integrate them into a unified plan." But to insist in advance that "such integration will have to be related to the walking distance neighborhood" strikes Riemer as an unwarranted assumption.[15] The size of such a service radius will then not be some magic number of 5,000 or 10,000 but will depend on the nature of the shared activities and on their tendency toward clustering or toward dispersion.

Noting that the heterogeneity of cities works against the pedestrian scale in local areas (for example, when church membership must transcend local spatial boundaries to achieve a certain size), Riemer would add five types of "walking distance areas" to supplement these service radii. These areas, based on the most frequent activity around which other contact points are clustered, include the residential, occupational, educational, commercial, and associational walking distance area. The residential walking distance area is thus considered to be only one among several types suited to special groups, such as the very young and their caretakers, the very old, and recent immigrants without means. The other walking distance areas would be focused on other service radii, for example, a drugstore located close to a college or medical services close to places of employment.[16]

A similar notion is contained in the concept of *regroupement intermediaires*. This favors the planning of activities around transportation stops, restaurants near places of employment, cafes, cinemas, or hairdressers, wherever, that is, the same people regularly encounter one another during certain hours, days, or weeks for activities which are habitual rather than communal.[17]

THE "SERVICE NEIGHBORHOOD"

The idea of roving neighborhoods is interesting but difficult to translate into planning practice. Certainly it cannot be put into effect without some concept of a hierarchy of services similar to that proposed by Doxiadis, or earlier, by the MARS group.[18] In these proposals, a large urban area is subdivided into a series of interlocking service areas going from the most inclusive and complex unit, where activities are highly concentrated, to less complex and also smaller ones containing more frequently used or more basic facilities. These units, organized into layers or levels, range from the lowest level comprising a few families on a single street to the highest level servicing more than a half a million people and embracing the entire metropolitan area. In addition to varying by size, population, and principal mode of transport employed, each hierarchical level varies also according to the nature, size, and scope of its center. The advantages of a service hierarchy are its flexibility and the avoidance of monotony by distributing activities, functions, and services in a series of overlapping circles more truly reflective of the urban pattern. Each resident, moreover, does not belong more fully to one subunit—such as the residential one—than to others. His participation is geared to some principle of needs and priorities on which the whole hierarchy is based.

The problem with current versions of service hierarchies concerns the cutting points between levels. Most of these are too empirical. They are based, for example, on how many people are needed to support a wholesale market, flower shops, or an opera house; or they may be based on how many frequent health clinics, universities, or specialty markets, which is bound to vary from place to place according to economic resources and customs. The cut-off points between levels are also arbitrary divisions reflecting personal assumptions about the ways in which people should be using various facilities, how often, and at what distances. As a preliminary tool, such a hierarchy is useful provided it is continually revised as more information on human needs and patterns of movement within cities is made available.

THE NEIGHBORHOOD OF "COLLECTIVE RESPONSIBILITY"

A final alternative is based on insights gained from community organization and action programs. Realizing that the mobility and heterogeneity of urban life have undermined the more traditional forces of social cohesion required for a pooling of collective resources in the solution of common problems, some architects would recommend designs that give local units a collective framework by encouraging local leadership. If local areas were to assume such collective responsibilities as fire and police protection, property maintenance, and recreation, as they did in preindustrial cities, local loyalties and commitments may once again be revived. In the absence of such common undertakings, informal social bonds, even where present, are neither sufficiently stable nor enduring enough to promote local community life. In fact, it has been said that to make personal, variable needs and sentiments bear the burden of creating rather than of merely giving expression to internal moral and emotional cohesion is to take the ephemeral for the substance, to "bind together without a kingpin." [19] Formal organization and local leadership are thus seen as antidotes to urban drift and rootlessness.

This view corresponds on the local scene to major trends in the larger society where formal organizations are likewise designed to promote the continuity and coherence not provided by shifting populations of temporary neighbors, strangers, isolates, and reserved urbanites. The introduction of formally organized, locally based leaders forming the nucleus for sustained local activities and projects encourages and sustains a neighborhood spirit and identity despite rapid rates of residential turnover and the absence of strong bonds of sentiment or tradition among residents.

These neighborhood programs are largely an outgrowth of the urban research carried on at the University of Chicago in the early decades of this century, culminating in what has come to be known as the "Chicago School." This work showed that a number of social phenomena were associated with so-called "natural areas," areas having both an ecological and cultural relation to the rest of the city. The highest rates of delinquency, for example, were concentrated in certain poor, transitional, immigrant zones succumbing to the pressures of a rapidly growing city. The interesting fact about these points of concentration, however, was that the delinquency patterns did not characterize the residents apart from the area. As the older ethnic immigrant groups moved away in their pursuit of the American Dream, the percentage of juvenile delinquents stayed constant in the areas that they abandoned to new and different groups. In the areas to which these groups moved there was a decrease in the delinquency rates. The high rates of delinquency were thus area-bound. This led the original researchers to conclude that the persistence of high delinquency rates in particular areas of the city was due to social disorganization—in particular, to the absence of organized collective efforts to ameliorate local conditions. Their solution was to propose a "program of physical rehabilitation of slum areas and the development of community organization" consisting of a "group of leading citizens of a neighborhood who take the responsibility of a program for delinquency treatment and prevention." [20] Accordingly, they encouraged the establishment of neighborhood discussion and action groups, patterned on the New England Town Meetings, for the purposes of neighborhood improvements. These organizations, patterned along ethnic lines, were at best only moderately successful and died out as their members became absorbed in the mainstream of American political and cultural life.

Similar attempts have been tried since the thirties with equally mixed results. A particularly successful experiment is the "Back of the Yards" rehabilitation effort, organized along the ideas of Saul Alinsky, in a notorious Chicago slum. In this four-square-mile area of more than 100,000 second- and third-generation inhabitants of European Catholic immigrant stock, a physical and economic rebirth followed its organizing along these lines. Preceded by a fifteen-year program of short-range improvement efforts, the large-scale rehabilitation effort succeeded in part because, according to Alinsky, a well-staffed, well-financed community organization gradually took root. It developed into a major power structure and an articulate spokesman for the area in the city government. But while the program increased the self-confidence of the residents by making them more articulate and aware of legal, educational, and health needs and resources, it did not, apparently, decrease crime and delinquency rates. Whatever else its problems, moreover, the area may have derived some advantage from its high proportion of home owners and low rate of residential turnover.[21] One wonders whether such a program would be equally successful under the more typical urban conditions of high residential turnover and the propensity among urban dwellers to rent rather than to own their homes. Such factors, which may be a spur to the initiative and cooperation demanded by such self-help programs, may be crucial variables affecting their outcome. Predictably, traditional neighborhoods with a well-established cultural and social identity would seem to have an advantage under these conditions.

Jane Jacobs also considers self-management necessary for a successful city neighborhood. It should operate at two levels—the street and the district. The street neighborhoods are essentially those where the routine of daily life goes on—meetings, shopping, and just strolling. The vitality, concerns, needs, and interests of residents are expressed there. On the district level the more impersonal, organizational forces of the city become decisive. Jacobs sees these districts, represented by effective leaders or spokesmen, as intermediaries between the powerful city and the powerless street. She correctly observes that self-management means different things at different levels. At the street level it involves resident participation, active concern for common local problems, and a network of interdependent human relationships that give color and meaning to local life. At the district level the ability to formulate broad policies, to relate to the city as a whole, and to deal with city hall directly to obtain necessary public improvements and services becomes crucial. Street and district thus have distinctive, yet equally essential, organizational objectives—one stresses the unique personal character of the local habitat, the other forms a common link to a wider external world on which the local unit depends.[22]

THE ROLE OF THE PHYSICAL PLANNER

What, then, can we say about the role of physical planning in helping to create a sense of community? As a number of studies of newly planned towns and neighborhoods have shown, social solidarity and cooperation are less responsive to physical layout and design than planners would wish. There is considerable reason to doubt that these can, by themselves, either promote or inhibit neighborhood loyalty and sociability. Existing evidence suggests that where residents share certain basic attitudes and ambitions (and these vary by culture and social class), physical features may facilitate social encounters (though not necessarily more intimate personal relationships), but only under rare and unusual circumstances will they also promote an active, purposive community life. In fact, one is tempted to conclude that only where the preconditions are favorable for such a community, can physical design and siting play its intended role at all. Social class and status differences can disrupt the most compact physical arrangements, and the boundaries of gossip chains and other informal social networks do not necessarily, or even usually, conform to the planners' designated boundaries. In conjunction with other factors, most of these yet to be established by careful research, physical and spatial design may contribute to but not determine social interaction. The role of such design is auxiliary rather than autonomous. As we have seen, without acceptable and accepted leaders, common projects, or perceived bonds of interest, utility, or affection, the physically contiguous cannot, apparently, also become socially united.

Notes

Introduction to Chapter One

1. Kingsley Davis, "The Urbanization of the Human Population," in *Cities, A Scientific American Book* (New York: Alfred A. Knopf, 1966), p. 3; also see his "Origin and Growth of Urbanization," *American Journal of Sociology* (March, 1955), 430–437.
2. *Social Organization* (New York: Charles Scribner's Sons, 1909).
3. *Pre-Industrial City* (New York: Free Press of Glencoe, 1960).
4. Cf. *The World's Metropolitan Areas*, 1959, published by the Center.

2. The Greco-Roman Urban Culture

1. The best short survey of Roman culture is Frank G. Moore, *The Roman's World* (1936). Albert Grenier, *The Roman Spirit in Religion, Thought, and Art* (1926), is a statement of the Roman outlook as expressed intellectually and artistically. Interesting commentaries on Roman culture are two works by Grant Showerman, *Eternal Rome: The city and its peoples from the earliest times* (2 vols., 1924) and *Rome and the Romans: A survey and interpretation* (1921). Cyril Bailey, editor, *The Legacy of Rome* (1924), is a discussion of Rome's contributions to Western culture; Cyril Bailey, editor, *The Mind of Rome* (1926), is a useful compilation of selections from Roman writers. W. G. Greene, *The Achievement of Rome* (1934), evaluates various elements of Roman culture. For a detailed topical treatment of Roman culture see Georg Grupp, *Kulturgeschichte der romischen Kaiserzeit* (2 vols., 1904).

The standard reference work for the history of classical culture is Pauly's *Real-Encyclopadie der classischen Altertums-Wissenschaft* (1894–1938, 19 vols. and several supplements).

2. A. H. M. Jones, *The Greek City from Alexander to Justinian* (1940), p. 299. Oxford University Press.

3. On the monuments of Rome see A. W. Van Buren, *Ancient Rome as Revealed by Recent Discoveries* (1936); Leon Homo, *La Rome antique: Histoire-guide des monuments* (ca. 1921); Guiseppe Lugli, *The Classical Monuments of Rome* (ca. 1929); S. B. Platner, *A Topographical Dictionary of Rome* (1929); I. A. Richmond, *The City Wall of Imperial Rome* (1930).

On other Roman cities see R. C. Carrington, *Pompeii* (1936); C. G. Ellaby, *Pompeii and Herculaneum* (1930); Mattes della Corte, *Pompeii, the New*

Excavations (1927); E. G. Barker, *Buried Herculaneum* (1908); Louis Barre, *Herculaneum at Pompeii: Recueil general des peintures, bronzes, mosaques, etc.* (8 vols., 1870–1872).

4. M. I. Rostovtzeff, "The Prehistoric Cities and the Cities of the Ancient Orient," in Richard T. Ely, editor, *Urban Land Economies* (1922), p. 19.

5. See *The Cambridge Ancient History*, Vol. 9, *The Roman Republic* 133–44 B.C. (1932), Chap. XXI, "The Development of the Law under the Republic"; Vol. II, *The Imperial Peace* A.D. 70–192 (1936), Chap. XXI, "Classical Roman Law." See also H. F. Jolosicz, *Historical Introduction to the Study of Roman Law* (1932); C. P. Sherman, *Roman Law in the Modern World* (3 vols., 2nd ed., 1924); W. W. Buckland, *A Textbook of the Roman Law from Augustus to Justinian* (2nd ed., 1932).

3. The Ninth Century

1. Certain authors have believed that demesnial products were destined for sale. See, for example F. Keutgen, *Amter und Zunfte,* Jena, 1903, p. 58. It is a fact that in certain exceptional cases and, for example, in times of famine, selling took place. But as a general rule there was certainly no selling. The texts alleged to prove the contrary are too few in number and too ambiguous to carry conviction. It is evident that the whole economy of the demesnial system of the early Middle Ages is in flagrant opposition to this idea of profit.

4. The Preindustrial City

1. George M. Foster, "What Is Folk Culture?" *American Anthropologist,* LV (1953), 159–73.

2. Gideon Sjoberg, "Folk and 'Feudal' Societies," *American Journal of Sociology,* LVIII (1952), 231–39.

3. Sociologists have devoted almost no attention to the ecology of preindustrial centers. However, works of other social scientists do provide some valuable preliminary data. See, e.g., Marcel Clerget, *Le Caire: Etude de Geographie urbaine et d'histoire economique* (2 vols.; Cairo: E. & R. Schindler, 1934); Robert E. Dickinson, *The West European City* (London: Routledge & Kegan Paul, 1951); Roger Le Tourneau, *Fes: Avant le protectorat* (Casablanca: Societe Marocaine de Librairie et d'Edition, 1949); Edward W. Lane, *Cairo Fifty Years Ago* (London: John Murray, 1896); J. Sauvaget, *Alep* (Paris: Librairie Orientaliste Paul Geuthner, 1941); J. Weulersse, "Antioche: Essai de geographie urbaine," *Bulletin d'etudes orientales,* IV (1934), 27–79; Jean Kennedy, *Here Is India* (New York: Charles Scribner's Sons, 1945); and relevant articles in American geographical journals.

4. Dickinson, *op. cit.,* p. 27; O. H. K. Spate, *India and Pakistan* (London: Methuen & Co., 1954), p. 183.

5. For a discussion of guilds and other facets of the preindustrial city's economy see, e.g., J. S. Burgess, *The Guilds of Peking* (New York: Columbia University Press, 1928); Edward T. Williams, *China, Yesterday and Today* (5th ed.; New York: Thomas Y. Crowell Co., 1932); T'ai-ch'u Liao, "The Apprentices in Chengtu during and after the War," *Yenching Journal of Social Studies,* IV (1948), 90–106; H. A. R. Gibb and Harold Bowen, *Islamic Society and the West* (London: Oxford University Press, 1950), Vol. I, Part I, chap. vi; Le Tourneau, *op. cit.;* Clerget, *op. cit.;* James W. Thompson and Edgar N. Johnson, *An Introduction to Medieval Europe* (New York: W. W. Norton Co., 1937), chap.

xx; Sylvia L. Thrupp, "Medieval Guilds Reconsidered," Journal of Economic History, II (1942), 164–73.

6. For an extreme example of unstandardized currency cf. Robert Coltman, Jr., *The Chinese* (Philadelphia: F. A. Davis, 1891), p. 52. In some traditional societies (e.g., China) the state has sought to standardize economic action in the city by setting up standard systems of currency and/or weights and measures; these efforts, however, generally proved ineffective. Inconsistent policies in taxation, too, hinder the development of a "rational" economy.

7. The status of the true merchant in the preindustrial city, ideally, has been low; in medieval Europe and China many merchants were considered "outcastes." However, in some preindustrial cities a few wealthy merchants have acquired considerable power even though their role has not been highly valued. Even then most of their prestige has come through participation in religious, governmental, or educational activities, which have been highly valued (see, e.g., Ping-ti Ho, "The Salt Merchants of Yang-Chou: A Study of Commercial Capitalism in Eighteenth-Century China," *Harvard Journal of Asiatic Studies*, XVII, 1954, 130–68).

8. For materials on the kinship system and age and sex differentiation see, e.g., Le Tourneau, *op. cit.;* Edward W. Lane, *The Manners and Customs of the Modern Egyptians* (3d ed.; New York: E. P. Dutton Co., 1923); C. Snouck Hurgronje, *Mekka in the Latter Part of the Nineteenth Century*, trans. J. H. Monahan (London: Luzac, 1931); Horace Miner, *The Primitive City of Timbuctoo* (Princeton: Princeton University Press, 1953); Alice M. Bacon, *Japanese Girls and Women* (rev. ed.; Boston: Houghton Mifflin Co., 1902); J. S. Burgess, "Community Organization in China," *Far Eastern Survey*, XIV (1945), 371–73; Morton H. Fried, *Fabric of Chinese Society* (New York: Frederick A. Praeger, 1953); Francis L. K. Hsu, *Under the Ancestors' Shadow* (New York: Columbia University Press, 1948); Cornelius Osgood, *The Koreans and Their Culture* (New York: Ronald Press, 1951), chap. viii; Jukichi Inouye, *Home Life in Tokyo* (2d ed.; Tokyo: Tokyo Printing Co., 1911).

9. Tsung-Lien Shen and Shen-Chi Liu, *Tibet and the Tibetans* (Stanford: Stanford University Press, 1953), pp. 143–44.

10. Osgood, *op. cit.,* p. 146.

11. For information on various aspects of religious behavior see, e.g., Le Tourneau, *op. cit.;* Miner, *op. cit.;* Lane, *Manners and Customs;* Hurgronje, *op. cit.* André Chouraqui, *Les Juifs d' Afrique du Nord* (Paris: Presses Universitaires de France, 1952); Justus Doolittle, *Social Life of the Chinese* (London: Sampson Low, 1868); John K. Shyrock, *The Temples of Anking and Their Cults* (Paris: Privately printed, 1931); Derk Bodde (ed.), *Annual Customs and Festivals in Peking* (Peiping: Henri Vetch 1936); Edwin Benson, *Life in a Medieval City* (New York: Macmillan Co. 1920); Hsu, *op. cit.*

12. Le Tourneau, *op. cit.,* Part VI; Lane, *Manners and Customs,* chap. ii; Charles Bell, *The People of Tibet* (Oxford: Clarendon Press, 1928), chap. xix; O. Olufsen, *The Emir of Bokhara and His Country* (London: William Heinemann, 1911), chap. ix; Doolittle, *op. cit.*

13. Carleton Coon, *Caravan: The Story of the Middle East* (New York: Henry Holt & Co., 1951), p. 259; George W. Gilmore, *Korea from Its Capital* (Philadelphia: Presbyterian Board of Publication, 1892), pp. 51–52.

14. Osgood, *op. cit.,* chap. viii, Gilmore, *op. cit.,* chap. iv.

15. Henri Pirenne, In *Medieval Cities* (Princeton: Princeton University Press, 1925), and others have noted that European cities grew up in opposition to and were separate from the greater society. But this thesis has been overstated for medieval Europe. Most preindustrial cities are integral parts of broader social structures.

16. Some of these cities made extensive use of water power, which possibly fostered deviations from the type.

17. For a discussion of the institutional prerequisites of industrialization see, e.g., Bert F. Hoselitz, "Social Structure and Economic Growth," *Economia internazionale,* VI (1953), 52–77, and Marion J. Levy, "Some Sources of the Vulnerability of the Structures of Relatively Non-industrialized Societies to Those of Highly Industrialized Societies," in Bert F. Hoselitz (ed.), *The Progress of Underdeveloped Areas* (Chicago: University of Chicago Press, 1952), pp. 114 ff.

18. *Op. cit.*

19. This point seems to have been perceived also by Asael T. Hansen in his review of Horace Miner's *The Primitive City of Timbuctoo,* American Journal of Sociology, LIX (1954), 501–2.

20. Ralph L. Beals, "Urbanism, Urbanization and Acculturation," *American Anthropologist,* LIII (1951), 1–10.

21. See, e.g., D. R. Gadgil, *Poona: A Socioeconomic Survey* (Poona: Gokhale Institute of Politics and Economics, 1952), Part II; N. V. Sovani, *Social Survey of Kolhapur City* (Poona: Gokhale Institute of Politics and Economics, 1951), Vol. II; Noel P. Gist, "Caste Differentials in South India," *American Sociological Review,* XIX (1954), 126–37; John Campbell Pelzel, "Social Stratification in Japanese Urban Economic Life" (unpublished Ph.D. dissertation, Harvard University, Department of Social Relations, 1950).

22. Robert Redfield, *The Folk Culture of Yucatan* (Chicago: University of Chicago Press, 1941).

Introduction to Chapter Two

1. See Ferdinand Tonnies, *Community and Society,* tr. and ed. by Charles A. Loomis (East Lansing: Michigan State University, 1957); Henry Maine, *Ancient Law* (London: Oxford University Press, 1931, first published in 1861); Herbert Spencer, *The Principles of Sociology* (New York: Appleton-Century-Crofts, 1877); Emile Durkheim, *The Division of Labor in Society,* tr. from the first French edition, 1893, by George Simpson (New York: Free Press of Glencoe, 1947); and Max Weber, *The Methodology of the Social Sciences,* tr. and ed. by Edward A. Shils and Henry A. Finch (New York: Free Press of Glencoe, 1949).

2. Louis Wirth, "Urbanism as a Way of Life," *American Journal of Sociology* (July, 1938), 1–24.

3. See *The Sociology of Georg Simmel,* tr. by Kurt H. Wolff (New York: Free Press of Glencoe, 1950), 409–422.

4. Max Weber, *The City,* tr. and ed. by Don Martindale and Gertrud Neuwirth (New York: Free Press of Glencoe, 1958).

5. Their work may be consulted in Ernest W. Burgess and Donald J. Bogue (eds.), *Contributions to Urban Sociology* (Chicago: University of Chicago Press, 1964).

6. See Sjoberg, *The Pre-Industrial City, op. cit.;* and also his "Comparative Urban Sociology," in *Sociology Today,* edited by Robert K. Merton and Leonard Broom (New York: Basic Books, 1959), pp. 334–359.

7. Wirth, "Urbanism as a Way of Life," *op. cit.,* also his "Consensus and Mass Communication," *American Sociological Review* (February, 1948), 1–15.

8. Talcott Parsons, *The Social System* (New York: Free Press of Glencoe, 1951), pp. 182–191.

9. See Robert C. Angell, "The Social Integration of Selected American Cities," *American Journal of Sociology* (January, 1942), 575–592, and also his "The

Moral Integration of American Cities," *American Journal of Sociology* (July, 1951), Special Issue, 1–140.

10. Albert Reiss, Jr., "The Sociology of Urban Life, 1946–56" in Paul K. Hatt and Albert Reiss, Jr. (eds.), *Cities and Society: The Revised Reader in Urban Sociology* (New York: Free Press of Glencoe, 1957) and also Otis D. Duncan and Albert Reiss, Jr., *Social Characteristics of Urban and Rural Communities, 1950* (New York: John Wiley, 1956).

11. See Oscar Lewis, "The Folk-Urban Ideal Types," in Philip M. Hauser and Leo F. Schnore (eds.), *The Study of Urbanization* (New York: John Wiley, 1966) pp. 491–503, and Horace Miner, "The Folk-Urban Continuum," *American Sociological Review* (October, 1952), 529–537.

12. Julian H. Stewart, *Theory of Culture Change* (Urbana: University of Illinois Press, 1955).

13. Lewis, "The Folk-Urban Ideal Types," *op. cit.*

7. The Typological Tradition

1. Emile Durkheim, *The Division of Labor in Society* translated from the first French edition, 1893, by George Simpson (Glencoe: The Free Press).

2. Charles H. Cooley, *Social Organization* (New York: Scribners, 1909), 23–34.

3. Charles H. Cooley, *Social Organization, op. cit.* 5.

4. Charles H. Cooley, Robert C. Angell, and Lowell J. Carr, *Introductory Sociology* (New York: 1933), 55–56.

5. To cite just some of the examples of the use of the continuum see Horace Miner, *St. Denis: A French-Canadian Parish* (Chicago: University of Chicago Press, 1939); Herbert Passin and John W. Bennett, "Changing Agricultural Magic in Southern Illinois: A systematic analysis of Folk-Urban Transitions," *Social Forces* XXII (October, 1943), 98–106; Edward Spicer, *Pasuqa: A Yaqui Village in Arizona* (Chicago: University of Chicago Press, 1940). Some of the more significant criticisms are contained in the following: Neal Gross, "Cultural Variables in Rural Communities," *American Journal of Sociology,* LIII (March, 1948), 344–350; Oscar Lewis, *Tepoztlan Revisited* (Urbana: University of Illinois Press, 1951); Julian Steward, *Area Research: Concepts and Methods* (New York: Social Science Research Council, 1950); Gideon Sjoberg, "The Preindustrial City," *American Journal of Sociology,* LX (March 1955) 438–445; and Howard Becker, "Sacred and Secular Societies: Considered with Reference to Folk-State and Similar Classifications" *Social Forces,* XXVIII (May, 1950), 361–376.

6. Robert Redfield, "The Folk Society," *American Journal of Sociology,* LII (January, 1947), 295.

7. See in particular: Howard Becker, *Through Values to Social Interpretation* (Durham: Duke University Press, 1950), 248–280; "1951 Commentary on Value System Terminology" in Howard S. Becker and Harry E. Barnes, *Social Thought from Lore to Science,* second edition (Washington, D.C.: Harren Press, 1952), i–xxii; and "Current Sacred-Secular Theory and Its Development" in Howard Becker and Alvin Boskoff (eds.), *Modern Sociological Theory in Continuity and Change* (New York: Dryden Press, 1957).

8. Charles P. Loomis and J. Allan Beegle, *Rural Social Systems* (New York: Prentice-Hall, 1950).

9. Pitirim A. Sorokin, *Social and Cultural Dynamics* (New York: American Book Co.) Vol. 3, 40. See also *Society, Culture, and Personality* (New York: Harper, 1947), 93–118.

10. We define as "action" any concrete system maintained by a sequence of what Parsons calls "unit acts." "In a unit act there are identifiable as minimum characteristics the following: (1) an end, (2) a situation, analyzable in turn into (a) means and (b) conditions, and (3) at least one selective standard in terms of which the end is related to the situation." *The Structure of Social Action*, second edition, (Glencoe: The Free Press, 1949) , 77.

11. Max Weber, *The Theory of Social and Economic Organization*, translated by A. M. Henderson and Talcott Parsons (New York: Oxford University Press, 1947) 115.

12. Talcott Parsons, *The Structure of Social Action, op. cit.*, 694.

13. For an extensive development of the pattern-variables and their relation to social structure see Talcott Parsons, *The Social System* (Glencoe: The Free Press, 1951) , esp. Chs. 2 and 3.

14. Parsons has stated that he had been dissatisfied with the concepts *Gemeinschaft* and *Gesellschaft* in handling the professions, especially the doctor-patient relationship. However, four out of his five variables place this on the same side; namely, the *Gesellschaft* side. Only on the collectivity orientation vs self orientation does it fall on the *Gemeinschaft* side. It is interesting to note, however, that the collectivity orientation in this relationship rests on an institutional rather than a motivational base. The collectivity orientation of the physician has become built into a set of institutional expectations, and hence it is to a physician's self-interest to act contrary to his own self-interest in an immediate situation (collectivity orientation) —but *not* in the *"long run."* The long run orientation is self rather than collectivity, and hence in this sense all the variables fall on the *Gesellschaft* side. See Talcott Parsons, *The Social System, op. cit.*, 473.

8. Rural and Urban Worlds

1. See a survey and analysis of various definitions of the city and the country in Maunier, R., *L'origine et la fonction economique des villes*, Part I pp. 34 ff.; Sombart, Werner, *Der Moderne Kapitalismus*, 3rd Edition, Vol. I, Chap 9, pp. 124 ff; . . . Bowley, A. L., "Rural Population in England and Wales, a Study of the Changes of Density, Occupations, and Ages," *Journal of R. Statistical Society*, Vol. LXXVII, pp. 597–645, 1914; Wilcox, W. F., "Redefinition of City," *Proceedings of American Sociological Society*, Vol. XX, pp. 97–102, 1926; Coletti, F., *La popolazione rurale in Italia*, pp. 7–10; Anderson, N. and Lindeman, E. C., *Urban Sociology*, Part I.

2. See about this and the universality of application of the typological method in all sciences in Sorokin, P., *Contemporary Sociological Theories*, pp. 719–724. Further references are given there.

9. Rural-Urban Continuum

1. Paul Hatt and Albert J. Reiss, Jr. (eds.) , *Cities and Society* (Glencoe, Ill.: Free Press, 1957) , p. 21.

2. See the discussion of this controversial subject by Reginald Isaacs, "Are Urban Neighborhoods Possible?" and "The 'Neighborhood Unit' Is an Instrument for Segregation," in *Journal of Housing*, V (July and August, 1948) , 178–80, 215–19; Peter H. Mann, "The Concept of Neighborliness," *American Journal of Sociology*, LX (September, 1954) , 163–68; Richard Dewey, "The Neighborhood, Urban Ecology, and City Planners," *American Sociological Review*, XV (August, 1950) , 502–7.

3. See the articles by these writers in Hatt and Reiss, *op. cit.*, and in M. B. Sussman (ed.), *Community Structure and Analysis* (New York: Thomas Y. Crowell Co., 1959).

Introduction to Chapter Three

1. Ernest W. Burgess (ed.), *The Urban Community* (Chicago: University of Chicago Press, 1926); Robert E. Park, "Human Ecology," *American Journal of Sociology* (July, 1936), 1–15; and also Robert E. Park, Ernest W. Burgess and R. D. Mackenzie, *The City* (Chicago: University of Chicago Press, 1925).

2. Ernest W. Burgess and Donald J. Bogue (eds.), *Contributions to Urban Sociology* (Chicago: University of Chicago Press, 1964).

3. Homer Hoyt, *The Structure and Growth of Residential Neighborhoods in American Cities* (Washington, D.C.: Federal Housing Administration, 1939); C. D. Harris and Edward L. Ullman, "The Nature of Cities" *The Annals of the American Academy of Political and Social Science* (November, 1945), 7–17; and Eshref Shevky and Wendell Bell, *Social Areas Analysis* (Palo Alto: Stanford University Press, 1955).

4. See Charles Merriam, *The Making of Citizens* (Chicago: University of Chicago Press, 1931); Calvin F. Schmid, "Research Techniques in Human Ecology," in Pauline V. Young, *Scientific Social Surveys and Research* (Englewood, N.J.: Prentice-Hall, 1966), pp. 432–471; Roderick D. McKenzie, "The Ecological Approach to the Study of the Human Community," *American Journal of Sociology* (November, 1924), 287–301, and his *The Metropolitan Community* (New York: McGraw-Hill, 1933); Nathan L. Whetten, "Suburbanization as a Field for Sociological Research," *Rural Sociology* (December, 1951), 319–328; U.S. National Resources Committee, *Our Cities: Their Role in the National Economy* (Washington, D.C.: Government Printing Office, 1937); and Walter Firey, *Land Use in Central Boston* (Cambridge: Harvard University Press, 1947).

5. Robert E. Dickinson, *City, Region and Regionalism* (London: Kegan Paul, 1947).

6. Stuart Dodd, "A System of Operationally Defined Concepts for Sociology," *American Sociological Review* (Oct. 1939), 619–634.

7. See Hatt and Reiss (eds.), *Cities and Society*, Free Press, p. 21.

8. George Theodorson (ed.) *Studies in Human Ecology* (New York: Harper & Row, 1961).

9. See Maurice R. Davie, "The Pattern of Urban Growth," in *Studies in the Science of Society*, edited by George Peter Murdock (New Haven: Yale University Press, 1937); Milla A. Alihan, *Social Ecology* (New York: Columbia University Press, 1938); August B. Hollingshead, "Human Ecology" in *Principles of Sociology*, edited by Robert E. Park (New York: Barnes and Noble, 1939), and his "A Re-examination of Ecology Theory," *Sociology and Social Research* (January, 1947), 194–204; Warner E. Gettys, "Human Ecology and Social Theory" *Social Forces* (May, 1940), 469–476; Paul K. Hatt, "The Relation of Ecological Location to Status Position and Housing of Ethnic Minorities," *American Sociological Review* (August, 1945), 481–485; C. E. Gehlke and Katherine Biehl, "Certain Effects of Grouping upon the Size of the Correlation Co-efficient in Census Tract Material," *Journal of the American Statistical Association* (March, 1934), Supplement, 167–170; and Otis Duncan and Beverley Davis, "An Alternative to Ecological Correlation," *American Sociological Review* (December, 1953), 665–666.

10. Radhakamal Mukerjee, *Social Ecology* (London: Longmans Green, 1945)

and his "Communities of India, Part II: Traditional Civic Patterns," *Asia* (July, 1940), 375–378 and "Part III: From Village to City," *ibid.* (August, 1940), 439–444.

11. See Theodore Caplow, "Urban Structure in France," *American Sociological Review* (October, 1952), 544–549.

12. See James A. Quinn, "The Nature of Human Ecology: Re-examination and Re-definition," *Social Forces* (December, 1939), 161–68, and Amos H. Hawley, "Ecology and Human Ecology," *Social Forces* (May, 1944), 398–405.

13. Firey, *Land Use in Central Boston, op. cit.;* Christen T. Jonassen, "Cultural Variables in the Ecology of an Ethnic Group," *American Sociological Review* (February, 1949), 32–41; Jerome K. Meyers, "Assimilation to the Ecological and Social Systems of a Community," *American Sociological Review* (June, 1950), 367–72; and Albert Seeman, "Communities in the Salt Lake Basin," *Economic Geography* (July, 1938), 300–308.

14. See Theodore Anderson and Lee L. Bean, "The Shevky-Bell Social Areas: Confirmation of Results and a Re-interpretation," *Social Forces* (December, 1961), 119–124.

10. The Nature of Cities

1. For references see Edward Ullman, "A Theory of Location for Cities," *American Journal of Sociology,* Vol. 46, No. 6 (May 1941), pp. 853–64.

2. Chauncy D. Harris, "A Functional Classification of Cities in the United States" *The Geographical Review,* Vol. 33, No. 1 (Jan. 1943), pp. 85–99.

3. Ernest W. Burgess, "The Growth of the City," in *The City,* ed. by Robert E. Park, Ernest W. Burgess, and Roderick D. McKenzie (Chicago: University of Chicago Press, 1925), pp. 47–62; and Ernest W. Burgess, "Urban Areas," in *Chicago, an Experiment in Social Science Research,* ed. by T. V. Smith and Leonard D. White (Chicago: University of Chicago Press, 1929), pp. 113–38.

4. Homer Hoyt, "City Growth and Mortgage Risk," *Insured Mortgage Portfolio,* Vol. 1, Nos. 6–10 (Dec. 1936–April 1937), *passim;* and U. S. Federal Housing Administration, *The Structure and Growth of Residential Neighborhoods in American Cities* by Homer Hoyt (Washington: Government Printing Office, 1939), *passim.*

5. Exceptions are service-type establishments such as some grocery stores, dry cleaners, and gasoline stations.

6. Chauncy D. Harris, "Suburbs," *American Journal of Sociology,* Vol. 49, No. 1 (July 1943), p. 6.

13. The Politico-Administrative Concept of the City

1. Karl Rathgen, "Gemeindefinanzen" in *Verein für Sozialpolitik* (Leipsig: Duncker & Humblot, 1908–10) and *Allgemeine Verfassungs und Verwaltungsgeschichte* (Leipsig: Huebner, 1911).

2. Hill commanding the pass between Pentelicus and Poenes, occupied by the Spartans in 413.

3. Georg Below, *Der deutsche Staat des Mittelalters* (Leipsig: Zuelle & Meyer, 1914); *Territorium und Stadt* (Munchen: R. Oldenberg, 1900).

4. Weber, *Ancient Judaism,* (New York: Free Press), p. 14 f.

5. *Ibid.,* p. 385 f.

Introduction to Chapter Four

1. James Quinn, *Urban Sociology* (New York: American Book Company, 1955).
2. See her *The City* (Philadelphia: J. B. Lippincott, 1955).
3. Samuel Strong, "Social Types in the Negro Community in Chicago," Unpublished doctoral dissertation, University of Chicago Libraries, 1940. For the writings of Wirth, Anderson, and Zorbaugh, see Bibliographical Notes.
4. See Paul Lazarsfeld and W. N. McPhee, *Voting: A Study of Opinion Formation in a Presidential Campaign* (Chicago: University of Chicago Press, 1954) and Elihu Katz and Paul Lazarsfeld, *Personal Influence* (New York: Free Press of Glencoe, 1955).
5. C. A. McMahan, *Personality and the Urban Environment* (New York: Dryden Press, 1954).
6. Erving Goffman, *The Presentation of Self in Everyday Life* (New York: Doubleday Anchor Books, 1959) and his "Symbols of Class Status," *British Journal of Sociology* (December, 1951), 294–304.
7. David Riesman *et al.*, *The Lonely Crowd, A Study of Changing American Character* (New Haven: Yale University Press, 1950).
8. Daniel Bell, *The End of Ideology* (New York: Free Press of Glencoe, 1960), Ch. 1.
9. Cf. Leonard Reissman and Thomas Ktsanes, "Suburbia: New Homes for Old Values," *Social Problems*, (Winter, 1959), 187–194.
10. See Walter Firey, "Ecological Considerations in Planning for Urban Fringes," *American Sociological Review* (August, 1946), 411–421; A. C. Spectorsky, *Ex-Urbanites* (Philadelphia: J. B. Lippincott, 1955); Herbert Gans, *Levittowners* (New York: Free Press of Glencoe, 1966); Evelyn M. Kitigawa and Donald J. Bogue, *Suburbanization of Manufacturing Activity Within Standard Metropolitan Areas* (Oxford, Ohio: Scripps Foundation for Research in Population Problems, 1955).
11. Cf. Svend Riemer, *The Modern City* (New York: Prentice-Hall, 1952) and his "Urban Personality Reconsidered" in Marvin Sussman (ed.) *Community Structure and Analysis* (New York: Thomas Y. Crowell, 1959), Chapter 21.

18. The Decline of the Protestant Ethic

1. Henry Clews, *Fifty Years in Wall Street* (New York: Irving Publishing Company, 1908).
2. Helping in this task is what a good part of "motivation research" is all about. Motivation researcher Dr. Ernest Dichter, in a bulletin to business, says, "We are now confronted with the problem of permitting the average American to feel moral even when is is flirting, even when he is spending, even when he is not saving, even when he is taking two vacations a year and buying a second or third car. One of the basic problems of this prosperity, then, is to give people the sanction and justification to enjoy it and to demonstrate that the hedonistic approach to his life is a moral, not an immoral one."

19. The Suburban Dislocation

1. Cf. Peter Drucker's discussion of job enlargement and related measures in *Concept of the Corporation* (New York: Harper & Brothers, 1946). Union leaders who once were in the forefront of the drive to make work less exhausting —often an extrapolative matter of lowering hours, allowing the assembly line,

lessening dirt and noise—have seldom moved into the more difficult area of making it less uncreative. (According to Nelson Foote, they have eliminated the former grim silence that suited a Puritanical management.)

2. Cf., e.g., Ely Chinoy, *Automobile Workers and the American Dream* (Garden City, N.Y.: Doubleday & Company, 1955), and, on older patterns of work morality, Eugene A. Friedmann and Robert J. Havighurst, *The Meaning of Work and Retirement* (Chicago: University of Chicago Press, 1954).

3. Cf. "The Found Generation," *The American Scholar,* Vol. 25 (1956), pp. 421–36; see also Eric Larrabee and David Riesman, "Company Town Pastoral: The Role of Business in 'Executive Suite,'" reprinted in Bernard Rosenberg and David Manning White, *Mass Culture* (Glencoe, Ill.: The Free Press, 1956), pp. 325–37.

4. See Nancy C. Morse and Robert S. Weiss, "The Function and Meaning of Work and the Job," *American Sociological Review,* Vol. 20 (1955), pp. 191–98. It should be noted that many men in the professions (the study included only men) and many in sales express great satisfaction with their work.

5. This is somewhat analogous to fad behavior, for individuals no longer live in suburbs as, so to speak, statistical isolates, but live there with recognition of the suburban style as theirs and their country's. Cf. Rolf Meyersohn and Elihu Katz, "Notes on a Natural History of a Fad," *American Journal of Sociology,* Vol. 62. 6 (1957), pp. 594–601.

6. I am indebted to unpublished work on the performing arts in the suburbs done by Philip Ennis at the Bureau of Applied Social Research of Columbia University.

7. Colleges themselves make the same claim that the suburbs do. I recently had occasion to go through a large number of college catalogues as well as the descriptions colleges give in brief compass in the *College Board Handbook;* all but the huge urban universities did their best to present themselves as near the advantages of a large city, but far enough away for suburban safety and charm. (Correspondingly, some teenagers, raised in safe suburbs, find glamor in going downtown, at least for a time.)

8. Cf. Sylvia Fleis Fava, "Contrasts in Neighboring: New York City and a Suburban County," in William Dobriner, Ed., *Reader on the Suburbs* (New York: G. P. Putnam's Sons).

9. To be sure, driving may offer some commuters a change of pace and a chance to be alone. Cf., for a general discussion of the elements of irrationality hiding under slogans of convenience in driving to work in the metropolis, David Riesman and Eric Larrabee, "Autos in America: History Catches up with Ford," *Encounter,* Vol. 8 (1957), pp. 26–36.

10. A few superhighways have been designed to refresh the traveler and increase his sense of visual possibility as well as to speed him on his way; the Taconic State Parkway in New York is a fine example.

11. See Horton and Wohl, "Mass Communication and Para-Social Interaction: Observations on Intimacy at a Distance," *Psychiatry,* Vol. 19 (1956), pp. 215–29.

12. I doubt if even the most superior schools of Scarsdale or Winnetka are as good in the arts as the High School of Music and Art, or in science as the Bronx High School of Science—or at least this was so when New York City was not yet a slum for the Southern and Caribbean migrants. The suburban schools of course, can hardly cope with the crowding their very advantages have brought about—just as the suburbs, to which people go to escape the city's dirt, suffer from a water shortage and may shortly not be able to wash away their own dirt.

13. It is, however, striking how much of this movement, though largely "private" and unorganized and unideological, is determined by fashion—in this respect, resembling residential location itself. On warm winter days Central Park

and its rowboats are often nearly deserted, as is Jackson Park in Chicago; likewise, the Atlantic beaches such as Coney Island, in their off-season magnificence, are as unpopulated as the Labrador coast. People feel it is arbitrary to be cooped up in the city on a summer weekend because they so largely accept the definitions of "living it up" provided by the media and conversation.

14. Cf. Leo Lowenthal, "Biographies in Popular Magazines," in P. F. Lazarsfeld and Frank Stanton, Eds., *Radio Research,* 1942–43 (New York: Duell, Sloane & Pearce) .

15. For a full report on this study, see Robin Jackson and Rolf Meyersohn, "The Social Patterning of Leisure," address to the Annual Institute of the Society for Social Research, Chicago, May 30, 1957. I also draw in this paper on a study, now in the field under the direction of Professor Donald Horton (with the assistance of Robin Jackson) which is concerned with the conflict in styles of leisure in one of the North Shore suburbs, and with the ways in which the institutions of the suburb, particularly the high school, become the foci of that conflict.

16. Highway engineers resemble guided-missile engineers in an understandable irritation with the tiresome "human factor" which is bound to produce accidents—and every effort has typically been made to reduce the functions of individual drivers or soldiers, thus making them more bored and more accident-prone.

Lewis Mumford has been pointing these things out for so long that he resembles the hero in Wells' story, "The Country of the Blind," who comes close to wishing he could share the visual defects of his fellow-men, for it would be more comfortable that way for everybody.

17. It would seem as if Americans, gaining some of the feelings towards the city and its works and ways that Thoreau had, have succeeded in blending his values with those of Carnegie. However, as indicated earlier, they are far from having Andrew Carnegie's concern for hard work, wealth, and thrift—let alone his self-taught passion for literacy—but they do have his interest in serving an image of efficiency, modified by Dale Carnegie's concern for gregarious friendliness.

18. My colleague, Anselm Strauss, has been engaged in a study of the informal tone or aura of cities, their images of themselves; I have profited from conversations with him about city life.

19. Cf. my discussion in "Some Observations on Changes in Leisure Attitudes," *Antioch Review,* Vol. 12 (1952) , pp. 417–36; reprinted in *Individualism Reconsidered.* See also the thoughtful hopefulness concerning changed forms of inventiveness in Conrad M. Arensberg, "Work and the Changing American Scene," in Arensberg, and others, Eds., *Research in Industrial Human Relations* (New York: Harper & Brothers, 1957) .

20. The essay, which originally appeared in *International Quarterly,* Vol. 10 (1904) , pp. 130–55, is reprinted in *American Journal of Sociology,* Vol. 62, No. 6 (1957) , pp. 541–58.

21. I sometimes consider the drive-in movie the archetypical symbol of decentralization where people go to the theater not in stalls which permit circulation of elites but in cars which keep the family or the dating couple together with no sense of the audience or any shared experience outside the sedan.

Introduction to Chapter Five

1. Charles H. Cooley, Robert C. Angell, and Lowell J. Carr, *Introductory Sociology* (New York: Scribner's, 1933) .

2. R. L. Beals "Social Stratification in Latin America," *American Journal of Sociology* (January, 1953), 327–339.

3. Robert Lynd and Helen M. Lynd, *Middletown* (New York: Harcourt, Brace, 1929).

4. Gerhard E. Lenski, "Social Participation and Status Crystallization," *American Sociological Review* (August, 1956), 458–464.

5. See Richard Centers, *The Psychology of Social Classes* (Princeton: Princeton University Press, 1949); A. B. Hollingshead, *Elmtown's Youth* (New York: John Wiley and Sons, 1949); W. Lloyd Warner and Paul S. Lunt, *The Social Life of a Modern Community* (New Haven: Yale University Press, 1941); and Harold Kaufman, *Prestige Classes in a New York Rural Community* (Ithaca: Cornell University Agricultural Experiment Station, 1944).

6. Alvin Boskoff, *The Sociology of Urban Regions* (New York: Appleton-Century-Crofts, 1962), Chapter 10.

7. Refer to Bibliographical Notes for specific citations, particularly Chapter 6.

20. Cleavages in Urban Society

1. See David R. Derge, "Metropolitan and Outstate Alignments in Illinois and Missouri Legislative Delegations," *American Political Science Review*, December, 1958, pp. 1062–1065.

2. For some discussion of these claims by an economist, see Julius Margolis, "Metropolitan Finance Problems," in National Bureau of Economic Research, *Public Finances: Needs, Sources, and Utilization* (Princeton, N.J.: Princeton University Press, 1961), especially pp. 256–259.

3. Peter H. and Alice S. Rossi, "An Historical Perspective on Local Politics," paper delivered at the 1956 meeting of the American Sociological Association (mimeo).

4. Richard Hofstadter, *The Age of Reform* (New York: Alfred A. Knopf, 1955), p. 9.

5. Robert H. Binstock, *A Report on Politics in Worcester, Mass.* (Cambridge, Mass.: Joint Center for Urban Studies, 1961, mimeo), part V, p. 2.

6. Compare the findings of Edgar Litt: "Jewish Ethno-Religious Involvement and Political Liberalism," *Social Forces*, May 1961, pp. 328–332; "Ethnic Status and Political Perspectives," *Midwest Journal of Political Science*, August 1961, pp. 276–283; and "Status, Ethnicity, and Patterns of Jewish Voting Behavior in Baltimore," *Jewish Social Studies*, July 1960, pp. 159–164. Litt argues that the basis of Jewish identification with the Democratic party varies with socio-economic status: upper-class Jews are Democratic because they see the party as an instrument of "social justice" on national and international issues; lower-class Jews are Democratic because they see it as a source of material benefits and economic welfare. These findings are broadly consistent with our argument about political ethos.

7. *Shelley v. Kraemer,* 334 U.S. 1 (1948)

8. M. I. Ostrogorski, *Democracy and the Organization of Political Parties* (New York, 1902), II, 618.

21. Beyond the Melting Pot

1. See Nathan Glazer, *The Social Basis of American Communism*, New York: Harcourt, Brace & World, 1961, Chap. IV.

2. For the complex interplay of religious, ideological, and socioeconomic factors within the American Jewish community, see *American Judaism* by Nathan Glazer, Chicago: University of Chicago Press, 1957.

3. Quoted in the *New York Herald Tribune*, July 2, 1962.

4. See *A Tale of Ten Cities*, Albert Vorspan and Eugene Lipman, New York: Union of American Hebrew Congregations, 1962, pp. 175 ff.

5. Gerhard Lenski, *The Religious Factor*, New York: Doubleday, 1961, gives a great deal of evidence to the effect that value differences between Catholics and white Protestants and Jews (the latter two often linked, but not always) in Detroit have increased as the groups move from working-class and immigrant generation to middle-class and later generations. Parochial schooling plays some part in these differences. For an interesting evocation of the milieu in which Jewish-Catholic political cooperation flourished, see *Al Smith* by Oscar Handlin, Boston: Little, Brown, 1958.

22. Urban Neighborhoods and Informal Social Relations

1. Revised version of a paper read at the annual meetings of the Midwest Sociological Society, Kansas City, Missouri, April, 1956. The first author wishes to express his appreciation to the Carnegie Corporation of New York and the Stanford University Committee for Research in the Social Sciences, which provided the funds for the study, to Maryanne T. Force and to Surinder K. Mehta.

2. *American Journal of Sociology*, XL (July, 1938), 20–21 and 15.

3. E.g., see Morris Axelrod, "Urban Structure and Social Participation," *American Sociological Review*, XXL (February, 1956), 13–18; Donald L. Foley, "Neighbors or Urbanites?" (Rochester, N.Y.: Department of Sociology, University of Rochester, 1952) (mimeographed); Scott Greer, "Urbanism Reconsidered: A Comparative Study of Local Areas in a Metropolis," *American Sociological Review*, XXI (February, 1956), 19–25; Scott Greer and Ella Kube, "Urban Worlds" (Los Angeles: Laboratory in Urban Culture, Occidental College, 1955) (mimeographed); Morris Janowitz, *The Community Press in an Urban Setting* (Glencoe, Ill.: Free Press, 1952); Albert J. Reiss, Jr., "An Analysis of Urban Phenomena," in Robert Moore Fisher (ed.), *The Metropolis in Modern Life* (Garden City, N.Y.: Doubleday and Co., 1955), chap. iii; Joel Smith, William H. Form, and Gregory P. Stone, "Local Intimacy in a Middle-sized City," *American Journal of Sociology*, LX (November, 1954), 276–83; and Gregory P. Stone, "City Shoppers and Urban Identification: Observations on the Social Psychology of City Life," *American Journal of Sociology*, LX (July, 1954), 36–45.

4. For other aspects of the study see Wendell Bell, "The Utility of the Shevky Typology for the Design of Urban Subarea Field Studies," *Journal of Social Psychology* [Editors' note.] (v. 47, February, 1958, 71–83); Wendell Bell and Maryanne T. Force, "Urban Neighborhood Types and Participation in Formal Association," *American Sociological Review*, XXI (February, 1956), 25–34, and "Social Structure and Participation in Different Types of Formal Associations," *Social Forces*, XXXIV (May, 1956), 345–50.

5. For a discussion of social areas and the indexes of economic, family, and ethnic status on which they are based see Eshref Shevky and Wendell Bell, *Social Area Analysis* (Stanford, Calif.: Stanford University Press, 1955).

6. For further information concerning the selection and description of the sample see Bell, *op. cit.*, and Bell and Force, "Urban Neighborhood Types and Participation in Formal Associations," *op. cit.*

7. The calculation involved the summing of the frequency of participation in four informal groups: neighbors, co-workers (outside of work association), relatives (other than those living with the respondent), and friends (other than those who are neighbors, co-workers, and relatives).

8. Morris Axelrod, "A Study of Formal and Informal Group Participation in a Large Urban Community" (unpublished Ph.D. dissertation, University of Michigan, 1953).

9. Op. cit.

10. The sum of the two chi squares equals 6.60, p < .05. The interaction chi square is not significant.

11. The sum of the chi squares in each case indicates p < .01, and the interaction chi square in each case is not significant.

12. The sum of the chi squares equals 7.66, p < .05, and the interaction chi square is not significant.

13. The sum of the chi squares equals 13.93, p < .01, and the interaction chi square is not significant.

14. "Urban Structure and Social Participation," op. cit., p. 17. Cf. Table 6.

15. "Urban Structure and Social Participation," op. cit., p. 17.

16. The sum of the chi squares equals 17.67, p < .01, and the interaction chi square is not significant.

23. Voluntary Associations and Urbanization

1. The field research for this paper was supported by a Research Training Fellowship of the Social Science Research Council and was prepared for publication during the tenure of Postdoctoral Fellowships of the National Science Foundation. The authors are indebted to Professors André Leroi Gourhan, Jean Stoetzel, and Roger Bastid of the Sorbonne for reading earlier drafts of the work.

2. Gallatin Anderson, "L'Évolution culturelle d'un village danois du XIXème au XXème siècle (Dragør)" (doctoral dissertation, University of Paris, 1958); Robert T. Anderson, "The Danish and Dutch Settlements on Amager Island: Four Hundred Years of Socio-cultural Interaction," American Anthropologist, LX (1958), 683–701.

3. According to communal archives, the 1,945 inhabitants of 1890 dropped to about 1,850 in 1900 but thereafter advanced gradually to reach 2,093 in 1940. Approximately 1,000 people arrived in the late forties with the construction of apartment houses and multiple-dwelling units in the southern part of town, and, by 1955, 3,500 residents lived within the village limits.

4. E. D. Chapple and C. S. Coon, Principles of Anthropology (New York: Henry Holt & Co., 1942), p. 418.

5. Floyd Dotson, "A Note on Participation in Voluntary Associations in a Mexican City," American Sociological Review, XVIII (1953), 380–86.

6. Kenneth Little, "The Role of Voluntary Associations in West African Urbanization," American Anthropologist, LIX (1957), 579–96.

24. The Social Structure and Political Process of Suburbia

1. E.g., Walter T. Martin, "The Structuring of Social Relationships Engendered by Suburban Residence," American Sociological Review, 21 (August, 1956) pp. 446–453.

2. Morris Janowitz, The Community Press in an Urban Setting, Glencoe, Ill.: Free Press, 1952. See esp. Chapter 7, "The Social Dimensions of the Local Community."

3. Scott Greer, Social Organization, New York: Random House, 1955. The spatially defined group and the changing nature of the urban sub-community are discussed in Chapters 4 and 5.

4. The norms may vary of course by social rank and ethnicity; to simplify the

argument the effects of these dimensions are considered irrelevant to the major hypotheses. . . .

5. The reader may question the existence of such "local areas" as social fact. However, scattered evidence indicates that the map of the city breaks down into sub-units for the residential population, whether or not these are congruent with ecologically defined "natural areas." The nature and consequences of economic decentralization are explored by Foley, of social and economic decentralization by Janowitz. See Donald L. Foley, "The Use of Local Facilities in a Metropolis," *American Journal of Sociology,* 56 (November, 1950), pp. 238–246, and *Neighbors or Urbanites? The Study of a Rochester Residential District,* Rochester, N.Y.: University of Rochester, 1952; and Janowitz, *op. cit.* A more recent study reports a strong definition of sub-areas among residents of Boston. See Laurence Ross, *The Local Community in the Metropolis,* unpublished Ph.D. thesis, Harvard University, 1959. Furthermore, 98 per cent of the residents of suburban St. Louis County accept the notion and give a distinctive name to their residential area (unpublished research report, Metropolitan St. Louis Survey).

6. Thus 84 per cent of Janowitz's respondents were readers of their local press (*op. cit.*). Similar findings are reported for a Los Angeles suburban sample: of those who received the paper (85 per cent) over 92 per cent were regular readers; see Scott Greer and Ella Kube, *Urban Worlds: A Comparative Study of Four Los Angeles Areas,* Los Angeles: Laboratory in Urban Culture, 1955 (processed).

7. Janowitz, *op. cit.*

8. This does not imply an automatic evolution which presumes that through time interdependence must result in communication and order. The precise processes by which organizational structures evolve are not spelled out here; they would be desirable but are not essential to the purposes of the present paper.

25. The Hypothesis of Metropolitan Domination

1. R. D. McKenzie, *The Metropolitan Community* (New York: McGraw-Hill, 1933) p. 7. (Italics are author's).

2. *Ibid.,* p. 313.

Introduction to Chapter Six

1. Marion J. Levy, Jr., *The Structure of Society* (Princeton: Princeton University Press, 1952).

2. Paul F. Cressey, "Social Disorganization and Reorganization in Harlan County, Kentucky," *American Sociological Review,* (June, 1949), 389–394.

3. Marshall B. Clinard, *Sociology of Deviant Behavior* (New York: Holt, Rinehart and Winston, 1963).

4. Earl Raab and Gertrude J. Selznick, *Major Social Problems* (New York: Harper and Row, 1964).

5. Richard C. Fuller and Richard R. Myers, "The Natural History of a Social Problem," *American Sociological Review,* (June, 1941), 320–329.

6. Leo F. Schnore, "Social Problems in an Urban-Industrial Context," *Social Problems,* (Winter, 1962), p. 228.

7. Emile Durkheim, *The Division of Labor in Society,* tr. from the first French edition, 1893, by George Simpson (New York: Free Press of Glencoe, 1947); Florian Znaniecki and W. I. Thomas, *The Polish Peasant in Europe and America* (New York: Alfred A. Knopf, 1924).

8. For a general survey see Lewis Coser, *The Functions of Social Conflict* (New York: Free Press of Glencoe, 1956).

9. Robert Merton, *Social Theory and Social Structure* (New York: Free Press of Glencoe, 1957), pp. 121–194.

10. R. E. L. Faris and Warren Dunham, *Mental Disorders in Urban Areas* (Chicago: University of Chicago Press, 1939) and Robert Angell, *The Family Encounters the Depression* (New York: Scribner's, 1936).

11. Clifford R. Shaw and Henry D. McKay, *Juvenile Delinquency and Urban Areas* (Chicago: University of Chicago Press, 1942).

27. Crime and the City

1. See Pitirim Sorokin, Carle Zimmerman, and Charles Galpin, *A Systematic Sourcebook in Rural Sociology* (Minneapolis: University of Minnesota Press, 1930), pp. 27–52, 54–68.

2. Ernest W. Burgess, in Albert Blumenthal, *Small-Town Stuff* (Chicago: The University of Chicago Press, 1932), pp. xii–xiii.

3. See page 95 [Marshall B. Clinard, *Sociology of Deviant Behavior*].

4. In such countries as France, Belgium, Switzerland, Holland, Germany, Sweden, Finland, Denmark, and Italy the incidence of urban offenses, crimes known, and convictions per population have been reported as generally higher than among rural areas. In Finland, for example, during the years 1930–1933 there were approximately seven times as many property crimes known to the police in urban areas as in rural.—Hans H. Burchardt, "Kriminalität in Stadt und Land," *Abhandlungen des Kriminalistischen Instituts an der Universität Berlin* (4. Folge, 4 Bd., 1. Heft [1936]). Louis Wirth and Marshall B. Clinard, "Public Safety," in *Urban Government,* Supplementary Report of the Urbanism Committee to the National Resources Committee (Washington, D.C.: Government Printing Office, 1939), I, 247–303. Also see Sorokin, Zimmerman, and Galpin, *op. cit.,* II, 266–302, 315–329.

5. M. Taylor Mathews, *Experience Worlds of the Mountain Peoples* (New York: Columbia University Press, 1937).

6. Clinard, "Rural Criminal Offenders," *American Journal of Sociology,* 50:38–45 (July 1944).

7. For an over-all picture of the general distribution of mental disorder, see Stuart A. Queen, "The Ecological Study of Mental Disorder," *American Sociological Review,* 5:201–209 (April, 1940); Robert E. L. Faris, "Ecological Factors in Human Behavior," in James McV. Hunt, ed., *Personality and the Behavior Disorders* (New York: The Ronald Press Company, 1944), pp. 736–757; C. W. Schroeder, "Mental Disorders in Cities," *American Journal of Sociology,* 47:40–47 (July, 1942); and Abraham Myerson, "Review of Mental Disorders in Urban Areas," *American Journal of Psychiatry,* 96:995–999 (January, 1940).

8. T. Lynn Smith, *The Sociology of Rural Life* (New York: Harper & Row, Publishers, 1940), p. 125.

9. Benjamin Malzberg, "The Prevalence of Mental Disease among the Urban and Rural Populations of New York State." *Psychiatric Quarterly* 9:55–88 (January, 1935).

10. E. Gartly Jaco, *The Social Epidemiology of Mental Diseases* (New York: Russell Sage Foundation, 1960).

11. Jaco, *op. cit.*

12. William F. Roth, Jr., and Frank H. Lutton, "The Mental Health Program in Tennessee," *American Journal of Psychiatry,* 99:662–676 (January, 1943). A study of the Eastern Health District of Baltimore found that one fourth of the rural psychotics were not hospitalized.

13. E. M. Jellinek, "Recent Trends in Alcoholism and Alcohol Consumption," *Quarterly Journal of Studies on Alcohol,* 8:23 (June, 1947).

14. . . . Paul H. Landis, *Rural Life in Process* (New York: McGraw-Hill Book Company, Inc., 1940), p. 320.

15. Harold A. Mulford and Donald E. Miller, "Drinking in Iowa. II. The Extent of Drinking and Selected Socio-Cultural Categories," *Quarterly Journal of Studies on Alcohol,* 21:34–35 (March, 1960).

16. Figures cited in Peter Sainsbury, *Suicide in London: An Ecological Study* (New York: Basic Books, Inc., 1956).

17. Louis I. Dublin and Bessie Bunzel, *To Be or Not to Be* (New York: Harrison Smith and Robert Haas, 1933), p. 82.

18. Maurice Halbwachs, *Les Causes du Suicide* (Paris: Librairie Félix Alcan, 1930).

19. Dublin and Bunzel, *op. cit.,* pp. 82–83.

20. From an unpublished personal document.

21. W. Widick Schroeder and Allan J. Beegle, "Suicide: An Instance of High Rural Rates," *Rural Sociology,* 18:45–52 (March, 1953).

22. Durkheim in France, some fifty years ago, maintained that crime increases directly with the volume and density of the population. A later study by Burchardt concluded that crime rates in European cities generally increase directly with the size of the city. The only exceptions which he found were in the Netherlands and Austria, where the largest cities have the least crime, a situation which he explained as due to unique factors. A comprehensive study of crime in France and Belgium has shown major differences in rates of urban and rural areas, and in those of cities of different sizes. The study found, however, that such rates are affected by the extent of industry and other social factors. See Denis Szabo, *Crimes et Villes* (Louvain: Catholic University of Louvain, 1960).

23. Federal Bureau of Investigation, *Uniform Crime Reports* (Annual Bulletin, 1960; Washington, D.C.: Government Printing Office, 1961). pp. 81–82. The rates for reported burglaries appear to decline in cities of 500,000 or more population, which may be due to a saturation point in urbanization above which size burglary rates do not materially increase.—"Public Safety," *loc. cit.,* p. 265.

24. Wirth and Clinard, "Public Safety," *loc. cit.,* p. 265. Also see Lyle Shannon, "The Spatial Distribution of Criminal Offenses by States," *Journal of Criminal Law, Criminology and Police Science,* 45:264–274 (September–October, 1954).

25. American Institute of Public Opinion Survey, December, 1947.

26. Wirth and Clinard, "Public Safety," *loc. cit.,* p. 271.

27. Henry Wechsler, "Community Growth, Depressive Disorders, and Suicide," *American Journal of Sociology,* 67:9–17 (July, 1961).

29. The Church Serves the Changing City

1. *The Neighborhood in Nation Building,* Boston, Houghton Mifflin, 1912, Chapter XII, "The Recovery of the Parish," p. 139.

2. In *Atlantic Monthly,* May, 1954.

3. New York, World Dominion, 1953.

4. Woods and Kennedy. *The Settlement Horizon,* New York: Russell Sage, 1922, p. 136.

5. *Ibid.,* p. 135.

6. *Ibid.,* p. 137.

7. *Ibid.,* pp. 144, 145.

30. City Schools

1. Daniel Griffiths and Others, *Teacher Mobility in New York City* (New York, 1963).

2. Edward C. Banfield and James Q. Wilson, *City Politics* (Cambridge, Mass.: Harvard University Press and MIT Press, 1963), p. 282. "Organized labor—even if it includes in its ranks the majority of all the adult citizens in the community —is generally regarded as a 'special interest' which must be 'represented'; businessmen, on the other hand, are often regarded, not as 'representing business' as a 'special interest,' but as serving the community as a whole. Businessmen, in Peter Clark's term, often are viewed as 'symbols of civic legitimacy.' Labor leaders rarely have this symbolic quality, but must contend with whatever stigma attaches to being from a lower-class background and associated with a special-interest group. . . . Labor is handicapped not only by having imputed to it less civic virtue but also by a shortage of money and organizational skills."

3. Patricia Cayo Sexton, *Education and Income* (New York: Viking Press, 1961).

4. *The Status of the Public School Education of Negro and Puerto Rican Children in New York City,* October, 1955.

5. A recent admissions change at the city university from sole reliance on high school averages to inclusion of college boards scores is expected further to lighten the skin of enrollees. The Board of Higher Education, however, is now discussing a change of admissions standards to accommodate more Negroes.

6. None of the New York Board of Education's three community colleges (where admissions standards are such that Negroes can, and often do, qualify) are located in Negro areas. One is now scheduled for Manhattan, but the tentative location is between 23rd and 42nd streets, a white area—one of the few in Manhattan. One high ranking public school official is quoted as saying, "The municipal colleges are not equipped to operate vestibule courses for students who have to be civilized."

7. On general political and economic issues, class lines seem quite clearly drawn: Negroes, unions, white have-nots, and a preponderance of the Jewish community appear on the have-not side, and the organized business, middle-class, and upper-class groups on the have side. Strangely, perhaps, and to some large extent understandably, Negroes chose two groups closest to them politically for their first-line offense: unions and the Jewish community. Both were vulnerable, having made continuing proclamations, accompanied by considerable effort, on behalf of equality and brotherhood, yet having done much less than their best to provide equality for Negroes within their own jurisdictions.

8. In Detroit, a recent school-tax election was won, informed observers report, by majorities rolled up in the Negro and Jewish precincts.

31. The Metropolitan Area as a Racial Problem

1. Evelyn M. Kitagawa and Donald J. Bogue, *Suburbanization of Manufacturing Activity Within Standard Metropolitan Areas* (Published jointly by Scripps Foundation for Research in Population Problems, Miami University, and Population Research and Training Center, University of Chicago), 1955, p. 15.

32. Riots

1. The Governor's Commission on the Los Angeles Riots, "Violence in the City—An End or a Beginning" (Los Angeles: Office of the Governor, 1965).

2. State of California, Department of Justice, Bureau of Criminal Statistics, "Watts Riot Arrests" (Los Angeles: California State Printing Office, 1966).

3. California National Guard, "Military Support of Law Enforcement During Civil Disturbances" (Sacramento, 1966).

4. Jerry Cohen and William F. Murphy, "Burn, Baby, Burn: The Los Angeles Race Riots, August 1965" (New York: E. P. Dutton & Co., Inc., 1966).

5. Institute of Government and Public Affairs, "Los Angeles Riot Study," unpublished report prepared for the Office of Economic Opportunity (Los Angeles: Institute of Government and Public Affairs, University of California, 1966). Hereinafter referred to as the UCLA survey.

6. Joseph Boskin, pp. 10–25.

The description and interpretation of the draft riot is derived from Lawrence Lader, "New York's Bloodiest Week." *American Heritage,* 10:44–49, June 1959. The description and interpretation of the other riots are derived from Joseph Boskin, "A History of Race Riots in Urban Areas, 1917–1964." a report prepared for the McCone Commission, 1966. See also Allen D. Grimshaw, "A Study of Social Violence: Urban Race Riots in the United States" (unpublished Ph.D. thesis, University of Pennsylvania, 1959).

7. Evidence supporting the following comparisons are provided in the reports of the UCLA survey.

8. Jerry Cohen and William F. Murphy, *supra* note 15.

9. In the words of the California Department of Justice report, *supra* note 14, p. 37:

> The persons arrested were obviously only a portion of those who participated in the rioting and looting that occurred. Whether or not the arrested persons represent a typical cross section of the unknown total of persons involved is not certain. There may be some reason to believe that the arrested persons are a fair sample on the grounds that in the turmoil of the moment and the tremendous pressures under which the police were operating, the selectivity normally exercised by the police might have been fairly well randomized and those arrested and booked were actually a valid cross section of the total group.

10. Marvin E. Wolfgang, "Crime and Race Conceptions and Mis-Conceptions" (New York: Institute of Human Relations Pamphlet Series, No. 6, 1964), p. 31.

11. UCLA survey, *supra* note 16. (The figures cited come from the as yet unpublished volumes of this survey.)

12. The fact of widespread participation among residents of the poorly organized Negro ghettos is strong evidence against a "conspiracy" theory. There is evidence (see Fred C. Shapiro and James W. Sullivan, "Race Riot New York, 1964" (New York, 1964), pp. 186–189; Assistant U.S. Attorneys Reports, "Chicago, July 22, 1966" (Washington: Office of the Attorney General, 1966); and Jerry Cohen and William F. Murphy, *supra* note 15, pp. 105–106), that extremist groups tried to inflame the riot, but there is no convincing evidence that these groups initially planned or afterwards directed them. After a thorough study of the 1964 riots the FBI, in its "Report on the 1964 Riots" (Washington: Federal Bureau of Investigation, 1965) reported that "aside from the actions of minor organizations or irresponsible individuals there was no systematic planning or organization of any of the city riots" (p. 9). The lack of such planning in the past does not, of course, preclude future attempts at instigation.

13. UCLA, *supra* note 16.

14. There are indications in the National Guard report, *supra* note 14, and in Jerry Cohen and William F. Murphy, *supra* note 15, that the National Guard were less subject to continual attack than were the police.

15. A total of 136 firemen suffered injuries and 1 was killed, according to the official report of the Los Angeles Police Department.

16. See Jerry Cohen and William F. Murphy, *supra* note 15, for an account of the selectivity in choosing targets and the implications of the actions of Negro storeowners in hastily erecting signs such as "Negro-owned," "blood brother," and "blood."

Introduction to Chapter Seven

1. Robert H. Salisbury, "Urban Politics and Education," in Sam Bass Warner, Jr. (ed.), *Planning for a Nation of Cities* (Cambridge: M.I.T. Press, 1966), p. 273.

2. See Edward Banfield, "The Political Implications of Metropolitan Growth," *Daedalus* (Winter, 1960), 61–78; also his *Urban Government* (New York: Free Press of Glencoe, 1961).

3. Norton Long, "The Local Community as an Ecology of Games," *American Journal of Sociology* (November, 1958), 251–261.

4. Lawrence J. R. Herson, "The Lost World of Municipal Government," *American Political Science Review* (June, 1957), 330–345.

5. Lewis Mumford, "Utopia, The City and the Machine," *Daedalus* (Spring, 1965) 271–292; also his *The Culture of Cities* (New York: Harcourt, 1938) and *The City in History* (New York, Harcourt, 1961).

6. Wallace S. Sayre, "Urbanism and Government, 1957–1977: A Rejoinder," *The Annals of the American Academy of Political and Social Science* (November, 1957), 82–85; also see Frank P. Zeidler "Urbanism and Government, 1957–1977," in the *Annals, ibid.,* 77–81.

34. The Curse of Multiplicity

1. Victor Jones, *Metropolitan Government* (Chicago, 1942), lists the following basic problems springing from the multiple city structure: unequalized services, uneven distribution of tax resources, and lack of citizen control of local government.

2. The 19 metropolitan areas with populations of 500,000–1,000,000 had 2,207 governments—an average of over one hundred apiece— (data from 1958 Municipal Yearbook, p. 39).

3. See Public Administration Service: *The Problems of Government in Metropolitan Miami,* pp. 60, ff.

4. The pre-cited Miami Traffic Survey reported (An extensive leadership questionaire survey was conducted by Professor Ross Beiler, who made the findings available to the author.) Business leaders appear to be more alert to the real needs of the community than the rank and file. In Dr. Beiler's survey of leadership, coordinating of planning and zoning was ranked next to the top [behind easing of traffic] as a major community problem: "There is extremely little, if any coordination, cooperation or uniformity between the various governmental agencies in Dade County in determination, installation and operation of traffic control devices and measures." Typical is the diffusion of authority in matters of traffic control and regulation, p. 37. Only three municipalities and the county administration have personnel that work solely for the betterment of traffic conditions.

5. Analysis of 1957 budgets by Bureau of Business and Economic Research, University of Miami.

36. The City and the Car

1. The Los Angeles figure, being for the central city only, does not reflect the dominance of the car in the whole metropolitan area; about 95 per cent of all travel is by automobile—a figure unequaled in any other large city.

Introduction to Chapter Eight

1. Frank Lloyd Wright, *The Living City* (New York: Horizon Press, 1958) and his earlier work, *When Democracy Builds* (Chicago, University of Chicago Press, 1945).

2. See Scott Greer, *Metro-Politics: A Study of Political Culture* (New York: John Wiley, 1963); also *Governing the Metropolis* (New York: John Wiley, 1962) and *The Emerging City: Myth and Reality* (New York: Free Press of Glencoe, 1962).

3. James A. Norton, "General Planning and Planning for Services and Facilities" in Harvey S. Perloff (ed.), *Planning and the Urban Community* (Pittsburgh: University of Pittsburgh Press, 1961), Ch. 8; and his *The Metro Experience* (Cleveland: The Press of Western Reserve University, 1963).

4. John C. Bollens and Henry J. Schmandt, *The Metropolis: Its People, Politics, and Economic Life* (New York: Harper & Row, 1965), p. 438.

5. Gunnar Myrdal, "National Planning for Healthy Cities: Two Challenges To Affluence" in Sam Bass Warner, Jr. (ed.), *Planning for a Nation of Cities* (Cambridge: M.I.T. Press, 1966), Ch. 1.

6. Sam Bass Warner, Jr., "Urban Constraints and Federal Policy," *ibid.*, Ch. 3.

7. See the recent edition of Ebenezer Howard, *Garden Cities of Tomorrow* (Cambridge: The M.I.T. Press, 1965) and Henry Wright, *Re-housing Urban America* (New York: Columbia University Press, 1935). Lewis Mumford idealized the regional city plans of Wright in his writings which have become classic. Refer also to Clarence A. Perry, *Housing for the Machine Age* (New York: Russell Sage Foundation, 1939).

38. Major Factors in Urban Planning

1. Banfield, E. C., and Grodzins, M. *Government and Housing in Metropolitan Areas,* New York: McGraw-Hill, 1958, p. 155.

2. Dahl, R. A., *Who Governs? Democracy and Power in an American City,* New Haven, Conn.: Yale Univ. Press, 1961, pp. 270 ff.

3. *Ibid.*, p. 279.

4. *Ibid.*, pp. 280, 281.

5. Meyerson, M., and Banfield, E.C., *Politics, Planning and the Public Interest,* Glencoe, Ill.: The Free Press, 1955.

6. Dahl, *op. cit.*, p. 279.

7. Weaver, R. C., *Proc. Acad. Pol. Sci.,* 27:31, 1960.

8. ———, *J. Intergroup Rel.,* 2:13, Winter 1960–1961.

9. ———, *Land Economics,* 36:235, 1960.

10. Rossi, P., and Dentler, R. A., *The Politics of Urban Renewal,* New York: The Free Press of Glencoe, 1961, p. 292.

11. Handlin, O., "The Social System," in *The Future Metropolis,* L. Rodwin, ed., New York: Braziller, 1961, p. 40.

12. *Ibid.*, p. 31.

13. Dean, J. P., "The Myths of Housing Reform," in *Reader in Urban Sociology*, P. K. Hatt and A. J. Reiss, eds., Glencoe, Ill.: The Free Press, 1951, p. 664.

14. Merton, R. K., "The Social Psychology of Housing," in *Current Trends in Social Psychology*.

15. Dean, *op. cit.*, p. 667.

16. Conant, J. B., *Slums and Suburbs*, New York: McGraw-Hill, 1961, p. 32.

17. Weaver, R. C., *Proc. Acad. Pol. Sci.*, 27:36, 1960.

18. Marris, P., "A Report on Urban Renewal in the United States," this volume, p. 128.

19. Weaver, R. C., *op. cit.*

Introduction to Chapter Nine

1. Particularly Frazier's *The Negro Family in Chicago* (Chicago: University of Chicago Press, 1932) and "Negro Harlem: An Ecological Study," *American Journal of Sociology* (July, 1937), 72–88.

2. Ernest Manheim, "Theoretical Perspectives of Urban Sociology in an Urbanized Society," *American Journal of Sociology* (November, 1960), 226–229.

3. Leo F. Schnore, "On the Spatial Structure of Cities in the Two Americas," in Philip M. Hauser and Leo F. Schnore (eds.), *The Study of Urbanization* (New York: John Wiley, 1966), and his *The Urban Scene* (New York: Free Press of Glencoe, 1965); and Eric E. Lampard, "Historical Aspects of Urbanization" in Hauser and Schnore, *ibid.*

4. In *The Urban Process* (New York: Free Press of Glencoe, 1964).

5. Anselm L. Strauss, *Images of the American City* (New York: Free Press of Glencoe, 1961).

6. *Ibid.*

7. Gideon Sjoberg, "Theory and Research in Urban Sociology" in Hauser and Schnore, *op. cit.*

8. See Jack P. Gibbs, (ed.), *Urban Research Methods* (Princeton, N.J.: D. Van Nostrand Company, 1961).

9. Janowitz has written extensively on urban phenomena in *The Community Press in an Urban Setting* (N.Y.: Free Press of Glencoe, 1952) and more recently in *Community Political Systems* (N.Y.: Free Press of Glencoe, 1961).

10. Kingsley Davis in Roy Turner, (ed.) *India's Urban Future* (Berkeley: University of California Press, 1962).

43. Power in Local Communities

1. *Power and Democracy in America*, edited by William V. D'Antonio and Howard J. Ehrlich, Notre Dame, Indiana: University of Notre Dame Press, 1961.

2. Actually, the major bulwarks for his thesis are his own and Hunter's research, plus a series of inquiries by Charles Loomis and his associates in Southwestern United States for which no published citations are given. The other references offered actually reveal much more complex patterns. See *Ibid.*, pp. 38–71.

3. *Ibid.*, p. 61.

4. Robert Dahl, *Who Governs? Democracy and Power in an American City*, New Haven and London: Yale University Press, 1961.

5. *Ibid.*, p. 137.

6. *Ibid.*, p. 72.

7. *Ibid.*, p. 75.

8. *Ibid.*, p. 156.

9. D'Antonio and Ehrlich, *op. cit.*, p. 136.

10. D'Antonio and Ehrlich, *op. cit.*, pp. 62–70; Dahl, *op. cit.*, pp. 184–189.

45. The Neighborhood Unit Reconsidered

1. A. Goss, "Neighborhood Units in British New Towns," *Town Planning Review,* XXXII, 1 (April 1961), 66–82.

2. S. Khan, *Social Needs in Neighborhood Planning,* thesis presented to the Graduate School of Ekistics of the Athens Technological Institute, June 1961, p. 119.

3. See, for example, L. R. Vagale, "Neighborhood Planning and Its Relation to Housing," the summary of a lecture at Banglore, June 19, 1964, for an in-service training course organized by the National Buildings Organization, New Delhi.

4. Rainer Mackensen, J. C. Papalekas, E. Pfeid, W. Schuette, and L. Burckhardt, *Daseinformen der Grossstadt* (Tuebingen: Mohr, 1959), p. 163.

5. Elizabeth Bott, *Family and Social Network* (London: Tavistock, 1957), pp. 99, 103.

6. One of the earliest proponents of a twofold unit was Henry S. Churchill, *The City Is the People* (New York: Reynal and Hitchcock, 1945). See also J. Tyrrwhitt, "Town Planning at the Local Level," *The Municipal Journal* (February 10, 1950).

7. Leo Kuper (ed.), *Living in Towns* (London: Crescent, 1953), p. 131.

8. *Ibid.*, pp. 168–69.

9. Peter H. Mann "The Concept of Neighborliness," *American Journal of Sociology,* September 1954, pp. 168–169.

10. Arthur Glikson, "Urban Design and New Towns and Neighborhoods," *Landscape Architecture* (April 1962), p. 171.

11. Mann, *op. cit.*, p. 154.

12. Hilda Jennings, *Societies in the Making* (London: Routledge & Kegan Paul, 1962), p. 225.

13. J. Tetlow and others, *Homes, Towns and Traffic* (New York: International Publications Service, 1965), p. 124.

14. S. Riemer, "Hidden Dimensions of Neighborhood Planning," *Land Economics,* 26 (May 1950), 197–201.

15. *Ibid.*, p. 197.

16. *Ibid.*

17. Paul Henri Chombart de Lauwe, *Des Hommes et des Villes* (Paris: Payot, 1965), p. 16.

18. For a discussion of the MARS plan, see Arthur Korn, *And History Builds the Town* (New York: British Book Center, 1953), pp. 83–103. For the hierarchy of communities proposed by Doxiadis see his numerous writings as well as reports in *Ekistics.*

19. Jennings, *op. cit.*, p. 225.

20. The pattern for Chicago was duplicated in twenty-two other American cities, leading the authors to conclude that "the distribution of juvenile delinquents in space and time follows the pattern of the physical structure and of the social disorganization of the American city." E. W. Burgess and Donald J. Bogue, "The Delinquency Research of Clifford R. Shaw and Henry D. McKay and Associates," in Burgess and Bogue (eds.), *Contributions to Urban Sociology* (Chicago: University of Chicago Press, 1963), p. 607.

21. *Ibid.*, p. 608.

22. Jane Jacobs, *The Death and Life of Great American Cities* (New York: Random House, 1961), pp. 112–130. For other illustrations of community action programs see M. Millspaugh and G. Breckenfield, *The Human Side of Urban Renewal* (New York: Ives and Washburn, 1960), pp. 227–233, and Severyn T. Bruyn, *Communities in Action* (New Haven: College and University Press, 1963).

Suggestions for Further Reading

CHAPTER ONE Emergence and Growth of Cities

The literature on the history of cities is of course voluminous although, as might be expected, some periods have better coverage than others.

Among the major studies which are often cited as source material on the urban centers of the ancient civilizations are those of Robert Redfield, *The Primitive World and Its Transformation* (Ithaca: Cornell University Press, 1953); Shepard Clough, *The Rise and Fall of Civilization* (New York: Columbia University Press, 1961); Rushton Coulborn, *The Origin of Civilized Societies* (Princeton: Princeton University Press, 1959); V. Gordon Childe, *What Happened in History* (New York: Penguin Books, 1946) and *Man Makes Himself* (New York: New American Library, 1951); Tom Jones, *Ancient Civilization* (Chicago: Rand McNally, 1960); S. Piggott (ed.), *The Dawn of Civilization* (London: Thames-Hudson, 1961); Karl Polanji, *The Great Transformation* (New York: Holt, Rinehart and Winston, 1944); and S. Washburn (ed.), *The Social Life of Early Man* (Chicago: Aldine, 1961).

Of all the ancient cities, those of Mesopotamia have been the most completely studied. They are the subject of Robert Braidwood, *The Near East and the Foundations of Civilization* (Eugene, Oregon: Oregon State System of Higher Education, 1952); L. Delaporte, *Mesopotamia, the Babylonian and Assyrian Civilization* (London: Kegan Paul, Trench, Trubner, 1925); Henry Frankfort, *The Birth of Civilization in the Near East* (Bloomington: Indiana University Press, 1951); and Samuel Kramer, *From the Tablets of Sumner* (Indian Hills, Colorado: Falcon's Wing Press, 1956). Very little systematic work has been done on the cities of ancient India. The following, however, provide valuable insight: V. Gordon Childe, *New Light on the Most Ancient East* (London: Routledge and Kegan Paul, 1952); R. C. Majumdar (ed.), *The History and Culture of the Indian People* (Bombay: Bharatiya Vidya Bhawan, 1953), Volume I; S. Piggott, *Pre-historic India* (New York: Penguin Books, 1950); and also Mortimer Wheeler, *The Indus Civilization* (Cambridge: Cambridge University Press, 1953) as well as his *Some Ancient Cities of India* (London: Oxford University Press, 1945).

We do not have adequate material on the cities of early China, the existing writings being of a somewhat general nature. These include Li Chi, *The Beginnings of Chinese Civilization* (Seattle: University of Washington Press, 1957); H. G. Creel, *The Birth of China* (New York: Praeger, 1954); Wolfram

Eberhard, *A History of China* (London: Routledge and Kegan Paul, 1950) ; and K. Latourette, *The Chinese; Their History and Culture* (New York: Macmillan, 1947). Some publications on the more recent trends in the urbanization of China have appeared, notably Wolfram Eberhard, "Data on the Structure of the Chinese City in the Pre-Industrial Period," *Economic Development and Cultural Change* (April, 1956), 253–268; F. Keyes, "Urbanism and Population Distribution in China," *American Journal of Sociology* (May, 1951), 519–527; and Morris Ullman, "Cities of Mainland China: 1953 and 1958," *International Population Reports* (Washington, D.C.: Bureau of the Census, 1961).

For the study of pre-industrial cities in Africa one may consult Basil Davidson, *The Lost Cities of Africa* (Boston: Little, Brown, 1959) ; Horace Miner, *The Primitive City of Timbuctoo* (Princeton: Princeton University Press, 1953) ; W. M. Hailey, *Native Administration in the British African Territories* (London: His Majesty's Stationery Office, 1950–51) ; Philip Hitti, *History of the Arabs* (London: Macmillan, 1946) ; and I. Schapera (ed.), *Western Civilization and the Natives of South Africa* (London: George Routledge and Sons, 1934).

The Central American Mayas had few though impressive cities about which a considerable amount has been written, particularly George Brainerd, *The Maya Civilization* (Los Angeles: University of California Press, 1956) ; Sylvanus Morley, *The Ancient Maya* (Stanford: Stanford University Press, 1956), revised by George Brainerd; J. Thompson, *The Rise and Fall of Maya Civilization* (Norman: University of Oklahoma Press, 1956) ; George Vaillant, *The Aztecs of Mexico* (New York: Penguin Books, 1956) ; and Gordon Willey (ed.), *Prehistoric Settlement Patterns in the New World* (New York: Werner-Gren Foundation, 1956).

There are a number of specific studies treating classical Greek and Roman cities, which include Kathleen Freeman, *Greek City States* (London: Macdonald, 1950) ; G. Glotz, *The Greek City and Its Institutions* (New York: Alfred A. Knopf, 1930) ; A. H. M. Jones, *The Greek City from Alexander to Justinian* (Oxford: Clarendon Press, 1940) and his *The Cities of the Eastern Roman Provinces* (Oxford: Clarendon Press, 1937) ; and R. E. Wycherley, *How the Greeks Built Cities* (New York: Macmillan, 1944). Some general works about the Greco-Roman world afford insight into its urban life, among them Cyril Bailey (ed.), *The Legacy of Rome* (Oxford: Clarendon Press, 1923) ; Jerome Carcopina, *Daily Life in Ancient Rome* (New Haven: Yale University Press, 1940) ; and M. P. Charlesworth, *The Roman Empire* (London: Oxford University Press, 1951).

The economic and social conditions of medieval Europe are dealt with in any number of books, the cities of that period receiving particular emphasis in Edwin Benson, *Life in a Medieval City* (New York: Macmillan, 1920) ; T. A. W. Buckley, *The Great Cities of the Middle Ages* (London: Routledge and Kegan Paul, 1871) ; and Henri Pirenne, *Economic and Social History of Medieval Europe* (New York: Harcourt, Brace, 1936). The waning of the Middle Ages and the beginnings of modern urbanism are treated in Ernest Barker *et al.*, *The Golden Ages of the Great Cities* (London: Thames and Hudson, 1952) ; J. W. Thompson, *Economic and Social History of Europe in the Later Middle Ages* (New York: Century, 1931) ; Robert Dickinson, *The West European City* (London: Routledge and Kegan Paul, 1951) ; T. S. Ashton, *The Industrial Revolution* (London: Oxford University Press, 1948) ; J. L. Hammond and Barbara Hammond, *The Rise of Modern Industry* (New York: Harcourt, Brace, 1926) ; and Paul Mantoux, *The Industrial Revolution in the Eighteenth Century* (New York: Harcourt, Brace, 1927).

For pre-industrial cities readers may profitably refer to Rose Hum Lee, *The City* (Philadelphia: Lippincott, 1955) ; Gideon Sjoberg, *The Pre-Industrial City*,

Past and Present (New York: Free Press, 1960); Svend Riemer, *The Modern City* (Englewood Cliffs: Prentice-Hall, 1952); and selected chapters in John Sirjamaki, *The Sociology of Cities* (New York: Random House, 1964).

Among the outstanding studies of the history of the American city are Carl Bridenbaugh, *Cities in the Wilderness* (New York: Alfred A. Knopf, 1938) and *Cities in Revolt: Urban Life in America* (New York: Alfred A. Knopf, 1955); Constance McLaughlin Green, *American Cities in the Growth of the Nation* (New York: Harper & Row, 1965); Charles Glaab and A. Theodore Brown, *A History of Urban America* (New York: Macmillan, 1967); Amos Hawley, *The Changing Shape of Metropolitan America* (New York: Free Press, 1956) as well as *The American City* (Homewood, Illinois: Dorsey Press, 1963); Blake McKelvey, *The Urbanization of America: 1860–1915* (New Brunswick, New Jersey: Rutgers University Press, 1963) and *The Emergence of Metropolitan America: 1915–1966* (New Brunswick, New Jersey: Rutgers University Press, 1967); R. D. McKenzie, *The Metropolitan Community* (New York: McGraw-Hill, 1933); Arthur Schlesinger, *The Rise of the City: 1878–1898* (New York: Macmillan, 1933); Warren Thompson, *The Growth of Metropolitan Districts in the United States, 1900–1940* (Washington, D.C.: Government Printing Office, 1947); and Jean Gottman, *Megalopolis* (New York: Twentieth Century Fund, 1961).

CHAPTER TWO The Urban Genus

Notable attempts to define and delimit the urban phenomenon may be found in Noel P. Gist, "The Urban Community," in Joseph B. Gittler (ed.), *Review of Sociology: Analysis of a Decade* (New York: Wiley, 1957) and Lewis Mumford, *The Culture of Cities* (New York: Harcourt, Brace, 1938), and subsequently revised. An early textbook, Noel P. Gist and L. A. Halbert, *Urban Society* (New York: Thomas Crowell, 1933), with Sylvia F. Fava having replaced the late Dr. Halbert in more recent editions, continues to be an influence over conceptualization. Other texts too stress the rigorous identification of the distinctive basis of urban life, particularly Stuart A. Queen and David B. Carpenter, *The American City* (New York: McGraw-Hill, 1953); T. Lynn Smith and C. A. McMahan (eds.), *The Sociology of Urban Life* (New York: Dryden Press, 1951); Egon Bergel, *Urban Sociology* (New York: McGraw-Hill, 1955); James Quinn, *Urban Sociology* (New York: American Book Company, 1955); Nels Anderson, *The Urban Community* (New York: Holt, Rinehart and Winston, 1959); Edmund deS. Brunner and W. C. Hallenbeck, *American Society: Urban and Rural Patterns* (New York: Harper, 1955); Alvin Boskoff, *The Sociology of Urban Regions* (New York: Appleton-Century-Crofts, 1962); and John Sirjamaki, *The Sociology of Cities* (New York: Random House, 1964).

A reader of superior quality containing an excellent collection of essays and research reports on the essential character of the urban community remains Paul K. Hatt and Albert J. Reiss (ed.), *Cities and Society* (Glencoe, Illinois: 1951), subsequently re-edited in 1957. Leonard Reissman, *The Urban Process: Cities in Industrial Society* (New York: Free Press, 1964) and Leo Schnore (ed.), *The Urban Scene: Human Ecology and Demography* (New York: Free Press, 1965) provide two additional examples of systematic and comprehensive coverage.

Several articles on the urban concept deserve special mention, namely, Horace Miner, "The Folk-Urban Continuum," *American Sociological Review* (October, 1952), 529–537, which deals with the hypotheses of Robert Redfield and Oscar Lewis; Howard W. Beers, "Rural-Urban Differences: Some Evidence from Public Opinion Polls," *Rural Sociology* (March, 1953), 1–11; Albert Reiss, "An Analysis of Urban Phenomena," in Robert M. Fisher (ed.), *The Metropolis in*

Modern Life (Garden City: Doubleday, 1955) ; and Oscar Lewis and Philip M. Hauser, "The Folk-Urban Ideal Types," in Philip M. Hauser and Leo F. Schnore (eds.), *The Study of Urbanization* (New York: Wiley, 1965) .

CHAPTER THREE Approaches to Urban Sociology

The breadth of thought devoted to the ecological interpretation of urban centers can be suggested though not adequately conveyed by observing that it has taken three major forms—the classical, neo-classical, and socio-cultural. In addition, it has also tended to merge with the literature on demography. Fortunately there are a number of secondary studies which offer valuable guidance to the entire school. Milla Alihan, for example, in *Social Ecology* (New York: Columbia University Press, 1938) reviews the fundamentals of ecological theory, including natural areas and ecological processes. George Clarke, *Elements of Ecology* (New York: Wiley, 1950) and James Quinn, *Human Ecology* (Englewood Cliffs, New Jersey: Prentice-Hall, 1950) are two other standard works.

More original though still general thought may be found in other publications, such as M. R. Davie, "The Pattern of Urban Growth," in George P. Murdock (ed.) , *Studies in the Science of Society* (New Haven: Yale University Press, 1937) ; Robert E. L. Faris, "Ecological Factors in Human Behavior," in James McV. Hunt (ed.), *Personality and the Behavior Disorders* (New York: Ronald Press, 1944) , Volume I; Lee Dice, *Man's Nature and Nature's Man: The Ecology of Human Communities* (Ann Arbor: University of Michigan Press, 1955) ; Warner Gettys, "Human Ecology and Social Theory," *Social Forces* (June, 1939) , 469–476; Walter Firey, *Land Use in Central Boston* (Cambridge: Harvard University Press, 1947) ; and Amos Hawley, *Human Ecology: A Theory of Community Structure* (New York: Ronald Press, 1950) .

Robert Park, "Human Ecology," *American Journal of Sociology* (July, 1936) , 1–15; R. D. McKenzie, "The Scope of Human Ecology," in Ernest W. Burgess, *The Urban Community* (Chicago: University of Chicago Press, 1926) , 161–168; George Theodorson (ed.) , *Studies in Human Ecology* (New York: Harper and Row, 1961) ; and Sidney Wilhelm, *Urban Zoning and Land-Use Theory* (New York: Free Press, 1962) are important contributions that may profitably be compared with one another.

Its close relationship to ecology makes demography a valuable interpretation of urban phenomena in addition to its significance in general. Philip M. Hauser, "Demography and Ecology," supplement to the *Annals of the American Academy of Political and Social Science* (November, 1965) reviews the connections of the two. Kingsley Davis' work in this field is outstanding and may be approached through his *Human Society* (New York: Macmillan, 1949) and more particularly "The Origin and Growth of Urbanization in the World," *American Journal of Sociology* (March, 1955) , 429–437. See also his summary paper "The Sociology of Demographic Behavior" in Robert Merton, Leonard Broom, and Leonard Cottrell (eds.) , *Sociology Today* (New York: Basic Books, 1959) . More extensive treatment is available in Dennis Wrong, *Population and Society* (New York: Random House, 1961) and David Heer, *Society and Population* (Englewood Cliffs, New Jersey: Prentice-Hall, 1968) .

The following demographic studies are also relevant to urban sociology: Otis Duncan and Albert Reiss, Jr., *Social Characteristics of Urban and Rural Communities* (New York: Wiley, 1956) ; Amos Hawley, *The Changing Shape of Metropolitan America: Decentralization since 1920* (New York: Free Press, 1956) ; Joseph Spengler and Otis Duncan (eds.) , *Demographic Analysis* (New

York: Free Press, 1956) ; Philip M. Hauser and Otis Duncan (eds.), *The Study of Population: An Inventory and Appraisal* (Chicago: University of Chicago Press, 1959) ; Leo Schnore, *The Urban Scene: Human Ecology and Demography* (New York: Free Press, 1965) ; Warren Thompson and David Lewis, *Population Problems* (New York: McGraw-Hill, 1965) ; and Donald Bogue, *Principles of Demography* (New York: Wiley, 1969) .

A number of publications that approach the urban community primarily from a cultural standpoint deserve to be cited. These are Robert Redfield and Milton B. Singer, "The Cultural Role of Cities," *Economic Development and Cultural Change* (1954–1955), 53–73; William L. Kolb, "The Social Structure and Functions of Cities," *Economic Development and Cultural Change* (1954–1955), 30–46; Carl H. Kraeling and R. M. Adams (eds.), *City Invincible: Urbanization and Cultural Development in the Ancient Near East* (Chicago: University of Chicago Press, 1960) ; Everett Hughes, "The Cultural Aspect of Urban Research," in L. D. White (ed.), *The State of the Social Sciences* (Chicago: University of Chicago Press, 1956) ; and T. G. McGee, "The Cultural Role of Cities: A Case Study of Kuala Lumpur," *Ekistics* (July, 1964), 19–22 .

CHAPTER FOUR Urban Man

In addition to the sources from which the readings in this volume on the social psychology of the urbanite were drawn, the reader is directed to the following major works: Fustel de Coulanges, *La cite antique* (Paris: Hachette, 1912) ; Louis Wirth, *Community Life and Social Policy* (Chicago: University of Chicago Press, 1956), which is a compilation of his writings; William F. Ogburn, *Social Characteristics of Cities* (Chicago: International City Managers Association of urban personality configurations. Svend Riemer and John McNamara, Josiah Strong, *The Twentieth Century City* (New York: Baker and Taylor, 1898) ; and C. A. McMahan, "Personality in the Urban Environment," in T. Lynn Smith and C. A. McMahan (eds.), *The Sociology of Urban Life* (New York: Dryden Press, 1951) .

Melvin Seeman, "An Evaluation of Current Approaches to Personality Differences in Folk and Urban Society," *Social Forces* (December, 1946), 160–165, summarizes various studies on the influence of the milieu on thought and behavior. Robert C. Angell, "The Social Integration of Selected American Cities," *American Journal of Sociology* (January, 1942), 575–592, and "The Moral Integration of American Cities," *American Journal of Sociology* (July, 1951), special monographic supplement, both provide an institutional consideration of urban personality configurations. Svend Riemer and John McNamara, "Contact Patterns in the City," *Social Forces* (December, 1957), 137–141, reviews the ways in which urban residents participate in organizational activities.

Very influential recent work includes David Riesman, Nathan Glazer, and Reuel Denney, *The Lonely Crowd* (New Haven: Yale University Press, 1950) ; Robert Merton, "Patterns of Influence: Local and Cosmopolitan Influentials," in his *Social Theory and Social Structure* (New York: Free Press, 1957) ; Rupert B. Vance and Nicholas J. Demerath (eds.), *The Urban South* (Chapel Hill: University of North Carolina Press, 1945) ; Clark Kerr et al., *Industrialism and Industrial Man* (Cambridge: Harvard University Press, 1960) ; and William H. Whyte, Jr., *Man and the Modern City* (Pittsburgh: University of Pittsburgh Press, 1963). Vance Packard's books have been very popular: *The Hidden Persuaders* (New York: Pocket Books, 1958) ; *The Status Seekers* (New York: Pocket Books, 1961) ; and *The Waste Makers* (New York: Pocket Books, 1963) .

Suburban life and mentality is dealt with in William M. Dobriner (ed.), *The*

Suburban Community (New York: Putnam, 1948); Sylvia F. Fava, "Suburbanism as a Way of Life," *American Sociological Review* (February, 1956), 34–37; Nathan L. Whetten, "Suburbanization as a Field for Sociological Research," *Rural Sociology* (October, 1951), 319–330; Byron E. Munson, "Attitudes toward Urban and Suburban Residence in Indianapolis," *Social Forces* (October, 1956), 76–80; John R. Seeley *et al., Crestwood Heights: A Study of the Culture of Suburban Life* (New York: Basic Books, 1956); Joseph Bensmen and Bernard Rosenberg, "The Culture of the New Suburbia," *Dissent* (September, 1962), 267–273; and Herbert Gans, *The Levittowners: How People Live and Politic in Suburbia* (New York: Pantheon Books, 1966).

Peter H. Rossi, *Why Families Move: A Study in the Social Psychology of Urban Residential Mobility* (New York: Free Press, 1955) and Herbert Gans, *The Urban Villagers* (New York: Free Press, 1962) have much to offer regarding modes of thought and sentiment characteristic of city populations.

CHAPTER FIVE Urban Social Structure

A great deal has been written on local government and politics in American society, with the following sociologically oriented studies being perhaps among the best: James Coleman, *Community Conflict* (New York: Free Press, 1957); Nelson Polsby, *Community Power and Political Theory* (New Haven: Yale University Press, 1963); Morris Janowitz (ed.), *Community Political Systems* (New York: Free Press, 1959); William Anderson and E. W. Weidner, *American City Government* (New York: Holt, Rinehart and Winston, 1950); Robert Dahl, *Who Governs? Democracy and Power in an American City* (New Haven: Yale University Press, 1961); Robert Wood (with Vladimir Almendinger), *1400 Governments* (Cambridge: Harvard University Press, 1961); Edward Banfield (ed.), *Urban Government* (New York: Free Press, 1961); Charles Adrian, *Governing Urban America* (New York: McGraw-Hill, 1955); Victor Jones, *Metropolitan Government* (Chicago: University of Chicago Press, 1948); Coleman Woodbury (ed.), *The Future of Cities and Urban Redevelopment* (Chicago: University of Chicago Press, 1953); and Floyd Hunter, *Community Power Structure* (Chapel Hill: University of North Carolina Press, 1953).

Among the more permanent monographs on our contemporary urban stratification system, one might well list Robert Lynd and Helen Lynd, *Middletown in Transition* (New York: Harcourt, Brace, 1937); C. Wright Mills, *White Collar* (New York: Oxford University Press, 1953) and *The Power Elite* (New York: Oxford University Press, 1958); Joseph Kahl, *The American Class Structure* (New York: Rinehart, 1957); August Hollingshead and Frederick Redlich, *Social Class and Mental Illness* (New York: Wiley, 1958); Leonard Reissman, *Class in American Society* (New York: Free Press, 1959); Peter M. Blau and Otis Dudley Duncan, *The American Occupational Structure* (New York: Wiley, 1967); James Beshers, *Urban Social Structure* (New York: Free Press, 1962); and John F. Cuber and William F. Kenkel, *Social Stratification in the United States* (New York: Appleton-Century-Crofts, 1959). Books going beyond merely American society include Ralf Dahrendorf, *Class and Class Conflict in Industrial Society* (Palo Alto: Stanford University Press, 1959); Reinhard Bendix and Seymour Lipset (eds.), *Class, Status and Power* (New York: Free Press, 1966); Suzanne Keller, *Beyond the Ruling Class: Strategic Elites in Modern Society* (New York: Random House, 1963); and Seymour Lipset and Reinhard Bendix, *Social Mobility in Industrial Society* (Berkeley: University of California Press, 1959).

The participation of minorities in urban life is the subject of these recent studies: W. Lloyd Warner and Leo Srole, *The Social Systems of American Ethnic Groups* (New Haven: Yale University Press, 1945) ; David Bowers (ed.) , *Foreign Influences in American Life* (Princeton: Princeton University Press, 1944) ; Milton L. Barron (ed.) , *Minorities in a Changing World* (New York: Alfred A. Knopf, 1967) ; Oscar Handlin, *Race and Nationality in American Life* (Boston: Little, Brown, 1950) and *The Newcomers: Negroes and Puerto Ricans in a Changing Metropolis* (Cambridge: Harvard University Press, 1959) ; E. Digby Baltzell, *The Protestant Establishment: Aristocracy and Caste in America* (New York: Random House, 1964) ; Rose Hum Lee, *The Chinese in the United States of America* (Hong Kong: Hong Kong University Press, 1960) ; Celia S. Heller, *Mexican American Youth: Forgotten Youth at the Crossroads* (New York: Random House, 1966) ; and Herbert J. Gans, *The Urban Villagers: Groups and Class in the Life of Italian-Americans* (New York: Free Press, 1962) .

St. Clair Drake and Horace R. Cayton, *Black Metropolis* (New York: Harcourt, Brace, 1945) ; Robin M. Williams, Jr., *Strangers Next Door: Ethnic Relations in American Communities* (Englewood Cliffs, New Jersey: Prentice-Hall, 1964) ; and Allan H. Spear, *Black Chicago* (Chicago: University of Chicago Press, 1967) are three contributions to the study of non-whites in the city. Jews in the American urban milieu receive attention in Judith Kramer and Seymour Levantman, *Children of the Gilded Ghetto* (New Haven: Yale University Press, 1961) and Stephen Birmingham, *"Our Crowd": The Great Jewish Families of New York* (New York: Harper & Row, 1967) .

Voluntary associations in the urban setting are analyzed in very broad perspective by Harold L. Wilensky and Charles N. Lebeaux in their *Industrial Society and Social Welfare* (New York: Russell Sage Foundation, 1958) . Other monographs are Julia Abrahamson, *A Neighborhood Finds Itself* (New York: Harper & Row, 1959) and Nicholas Babchuk, *The Voluntary Association in the Slum* (Lincoln: University of Nebraska Press, 1962) . Floyd Dotson, "Patterns of Voluntary Association among Working-Class Families," *American Sociological Review* (October, 1951) , 687–693; Charles R. Wright and Herbert Hyman, "Voluntary Association Memberships," *American Sociological Review* (June, 1958) , 284–294; John C. Scott, Jr., "Membership and Participation in Voluntary Associations," *American Sociological Review* (June, 1957) , 315–326; Raymond W. Mack and Dennis C. McElrath, "Urban Social Differentiation and the Allocation of Resources," *Annals of the American Academy of Political and Social Science* (April, 1964) , 26–32; and Mirra Komarovsky, "The Voluntary Associations of Urban Dwellers," *American Sociological Review* (December, 1946) , 686–698, contain generalizations on the demographic characteristics of participants as well as projections concerning future urbanization and its bearing on social class and life styles.

Widest of all the concepts of urban social structure is metropolitan dominance, which comprises the focal point of Otis Dudley Duncan *et al., Metropolis and Region* (Baltimore: Johns Hopkins Press, 1960) ; Hans Blumenfeld, "The Modern Metropolis," in *Scientific American, Cities* (New York: Alfred A. Knopf, 1965) ; International Urban Research, *The World's Metropolitan Areas* (Berkeley: University of California Press, 1959) ; Arthur Vidich and Joseph Bensman, *Small Town in Mass Society* (Princeton: Princeton University Press, 1958) ; Stuart F. Chapin and Shirley Weiss (eds.) , *Urban Growth Dynamics in a Regional Cluster of Cities* (New York: Wiley, 1962) ; Rupert Vance and Sara Smith, "Metropolitan Dominance and Urbanization," in Rupert Vance and Nicholas Demerath (eds.) , *The Urban South* (Chapel Hill: University of North Carolina Press, 1955) ; and Raymond Vernon, *Metropolis 1985* (Cambridge: Harvard University Press, 1960) . Titles given earlier in the first section of this bibliography would also be relevant to metropolitan dominance, particularly those by Hawley, McKelvey, Thompson, McKenzie, and Gottman.

CHAPTER SIX Distress, Dissensus, and Discord

The incidence of urban poverty and the characteristics of the poor, at least in American cities, are given in Leon H. Keyserling, *Poverty and Deprivation in the United States* (Washington, D.C.: Conference on Economic Progress, 1962) ; Hanna H. Meissner (ed.), *Poverty in the Affluent Society* (New York: Harper & Row, 1966) ; Ben B. Seligman (ed.), *Poverty as a Public Issue* (New York: Free Press, 1965) ; Gladys O. White, *Yardstick for Need* (Washington, D.C.: Government Printing Office, 1963) ; David Caplowitz, *The Poor Pay More* (New York: Free Press, 1963) ; R. M. MacIver (ed.), *The Assault on Poverty and Individual Responsibility* (New York: Harper and Row, 1965) ; Margaret S. Gordon (ed.), *Poverty in America* (San Francisco: Chandler, 1965) ; James Bryant Conant, *Slums and Suburbs* (New York: McGraw-Hill, 1961) ; Gunnar Myrdal, *Challenge to Affluence* (New York: Pantheon, 1963) ; Kenneth Clark, *Dark Ghetto* (New York: Harper & Row, 1965) ; Louis Ferman *et al., Poverty in America* (Ann Arbor: University of Michigan Press, 1965) ; and Edgar May, *The Wasted Americans* (New York: Harper & Row, 1964) . Special aspects of poverty, such as public assistance, institutional participation, and in-migration, appear in much recent literature, such as Margaret S. Gordon, *The Economics of Welfare Policies* (New York: Columbia University Press, 1963) ; Henry Clark, *The Christian Case against Poverty* (New York: Association Press, 1965) ; Frank Riessman, *The Culturally Deprived Child* (New York: Harper & Row, 1962) ; Peter H. Rossi and Robert A. Dentler, *The Politics of Urban Renewal* (Glencoe: Free Press, 1961) ; and Orlette Ryan and M. F. Greene, *The School Children: Growing Up in the Slums* (New York: Pantheon, 1966) .

The President's Commission on Law Enforcement and the Administration of Justice has published a very impressive series of informative reports on urban crime. Two very valuable collections of articles on deviance in the city that one might also consult are Norman Johnston, Leonard Savitz, and Marvin E. Wolfgang (eds.), *The Sociology of Crime and Delinquency* (New York: Wiley, 1962) and their *The Sociology of Punishment and Correction* (New York: Wiley, 1962) . Over the past several years a number of excellent contributions on the subject have been added in Howard S. Becker, *The Outsiders: Studies in the Sociology of Deviance* (New York: Free Press, 1963) ; Marshall B. Clinard and Richard Quinney, *Criminal Behavior Systems* (New York: Holt, Rinehart and Winston, 1967) ; Simon Dinitz and Walter C. Reckless, *Critical Issues in the Study of Crime* (Boston: Little, Brown, 1968) ; Frank E. Hartung, *Crime, Law, and Society* (Detroit: Wayne State University Press, 1965) ; Leonard Savitz, *Dilemmas in Criminology* (New York: McGraw-Hill, 1967) ; Sarah L. Boggs, "Urban Crime Patterns," *American Sociological Review* (December, 1965) , 899–908; Walter B. Miller, "Implications of Urban Lower Class Culture for Social Work," *Social Service Review* (September, 1959) , 219–236; Hermann Mannheim, *Comparative Criminology* (Boston: Houghton Mifflin, 1965) ; Calvin Schmid, "Urban Crime Areas," Part I, *American Sociological Review* (August, 1960) , 527–542, and Part II, *American Sociological Review* (October, 1960) , 655–678; and Mark Lefton, James K. Skipper, Jr., and Charles H. McCaghy (eds.), *Approaches to Deviance* (New York: Appleton-Century-Crofts, 1968) .

Eric Josephson and Mary Josephson (eds.), *Man Alone: Alienation in Modern Society* (New York: Dell, 1962) ; Ephraim H. Mizruchi, *Success and Opportunity: A Study of Anomie* (New York: Free Press, 1964) ; Richard A. Cloward and Lloyd E. Ohlin, *Delinquency and Opportunity* (Glencoe: Free Press, 1960) ; and Marshall B. Clinard (ed.) , *Anomie and Deviant Behavior* (New York: Free Press, 1964) all focus on the estrangement of persons in the urban milieu. Related studies are Robert E. L. Faris and H. Warren Dunham, *Mental Disorders in Urban Areas* (Chicago: University of Chicago Press, 1939) and Clarence W. Schroeder, "Mental Disorders in Cities," *American Journal of Sociology* (July, 1942) , 40–48.

Religious sentiments under urban conditions receive serious and objective consideration in Joseph Fichter, *Social Relations in an Urban Parish* (Chicago: University of Chicago Press, 1954) ; Will Herberg, *Protestant-Catholic-Jew* (New York: Doubleday, 1955) ; William W. Brickman and Stanley Lehrer (ed.) , *Religion, Government, and Education* (New York: Society for the Advancement of Education, 1961) ; and Richard D. Lambert (ed.) , "Religion in American Society," *The Annals of the American Academy of Political and Social Science* (November, 1960) , which consists of articles on past and present trends in church membership and religious interest, the role of the laity, and the participation of the churches in urban affairs.

Urban Schools in the United States are the subject of Arthur Bestor, *Educational Wastelands: The Retreat from Learning in Our Public Schools* (Urbana: University of Illinois Press, 1953) ; James Bryant Conant, *The American High School Today* (New York: New American Library, 1964) ; Theodore Brameld, *Education for the Emerging Age: Newer Ends and Stronger Means* (New York: Harper & Row, 1961) ; B. J. Chandler *et al., Education in Urban Society* (New York: Dodd, Mead, 1963) ; Daniel Schreiber (ed.) , *The School Drop Out* (Washington, D.C.: National Education Association, 1964) ; Joan Roberts (ed.) , *School Children in the Urban Slum* (New York: Free Press, 1967) ; and Patricia Cayo Sexton, *The American School: A Sociological Analysis* (Englewood Cliffs, New Jersey: Prentice-Hall, 1967) .

Civil disorders at the present time and during the recent past are the subject of Anthony Lewis and *The New York Times, Portrait of a Decade: The Second American Revolution* (New York: Bantam Books, 1965) ; Raymond J. Murphy and James M. Watson, *The Structure of Discontent* (Los Angeles: University of California Institute of Government and Public Affairs, 1967) ; David J. Bordna (ed.) , *The Police: Six Sociological Essays* (New York: Wiley, 1967) ; Arthur Waskow, *From Race Riot to Sit-In* (Garden City: Doubleday, 1966) ; Robert M. Fogelson, "White on Black: A Critique of the McCone Commission Report on the Los Angeles Riots," *Political Science Quarterly* (September, 1967) , 332–367; Robert Blauner, "Whitewash over Watts," *Trans-Action* (March-April, 1966) , 3–9 and 54; Frank Besag, *The Anatomy of a Riot: Buffalo, 1967* (Buffalo: State University of New York Press, 1967) ; Governor's Commission on the Los Angeles Riots (McCone Commission) , *Violence in the City: An End or a Beginning* (Columbia: Lucas, 1965) ; Louis Masotti (ed.) , *Urban Disorders, Violence and Urban Victimization* (Beverly Hills, California: Sage Publications, 1968) ; and Governor's Select Commission on Civil Disorder, State of New Jersey, *Report for Action* (Trenton: Office of the Governor, 1968) .

CHAPTER SEVEN Urban Government and the Physical Environment

One of the most valuable studies of urban transportation—and there have been many—has come from the U. S. Advisory Commission on Inter-Governmental Relations, *Inter-Governmental Responsibilities for Mass Transportation Facilities and Services in Metropolitan Areas* (Washington, D.C.: Government Printing Office, 1961) . Other recent publications include Britton Harris, *Comprehensive Transportation Planning* (Berkeley: Center for Planning and Development, University of California, 1966) and his *Urban Transportation Planning* (Philadelphia: Institute for Environmental Studies, University of Pennsylvania, 1966) ; Anthony Tomazinis, *An Introduction to Urban Transportation Planning* (Philadelphia: Institute for Environmental Studies, University of Pennsylvania, 1966) ; and National Research Council, *Urban Transportation Planning Techniques and Concepts* (Washington, D.C.: Highway Research Board, National Academy of Sciences, National Research Council, 1965) .

Richard Zettel and Richard Carll, *Summary Review of Major Metropolitan Transportation Studies in the United States* (Berkeley: Institute of Transportation and Traffic Engineering, University of California, 1962) ; Harlan Gilmore, *Transportation and the Growth of Cities* (New York: Free Press, 1953) ; Wilfred Owen, *The Metropolitan Transportation Problem* (Washington, D.C.: Brookings Institute, 1956) ; Lowdon Wingo, Jr., *Transportation and Urban Land* (Washington, D.C.: Resources for the Future, 1961) ; Sam Warner, Jr., *Street Car Suburbs* (Cambridge: Harvard University Press, 1965) are informative. Americans will find the Report of the Ministry of Transport, Great Britain, *Traffic in Towns* (London: Her Majesty's Stationery Office, 1963) of interest.

Other aspects of urban maladministration, such as pollution and zoning and code enforcement, may be reviewed in Stuart Chapin, *Urban Land Use Planning* (New York: Harper, 1957) ; Harvey Perloff (ed.), *Planning and the Urban Community* (Pittsburgh: University of Pittsburgh Press, 1961) ; Charles Haar, *Land-Use Planning* (Boston: Little, Brown, 1959) ; Sidney Wilhelm, *Urban Zoning and Land-Use Theory* (New York: Free Press, 1962) ; Clarence S. Stein, *Toward New Towns for America* (Liverpool: Liverpool University Press, 1951) ; Edward Banfield and Morton Grodzins, *Government and Housing in Metropolitan Areas* (New York: McGraw-Hill, 1958) ; James Q. Wilson, *Urban Renewal: The Record and the Controversy* (Cambridge: Massachusetts Institute of Technology Press, 1960) ; "Air Pollution," special issue, *Power* (December, 1960) ; Arthur Stern, *Air Pollution* (New York: Academic Press, 1962) ; William Faith, *Air Pollution Control* (New York: Wiley, 1959) ; and Alan Smith, *Air Pollution* (New York: Pergamon Press, 1966) .

CHAPTER EIGHT Coping with the Urban Crisis

Reforming local government in America is treated in countless books, articles, and reports. Official statements are represented by the House of Representatives, Committee on Government Operations, 87th Congress, 1st Session, *Governmental Structure, Organization and Planning in Metropolitan Areas, A Report by the Advisory Commission on Inter-governmental Relations* (Washington, D.C.: Government Printing Office, 1961) ; Advisory Commission on Inter-governmental Relations, *Alternative Approaches to Inter-governmental Reorganization in Metropolitan Areas* (Washington, D.C.: Government Printing Office, 1962) ; and Sub-committee on Inter-governmental Relations of the Committee on Government Operations, U. S. Senate, 89th Congress, 2nd Session, *Impact of Federal Urban Development Programs on Local Government Organization and Planning, Report of the Advisory Commission on Inter-governmental Relations* (Washington, D.C.: Government Printing Office, 1964) .

Roscoe C. Martin asserts that the solution to urban problems is simply beyond the combined powers of the cities and the states, even when the latter are willing to share in the burden, and accordingly that the cities are claiming a third alternative as the "third partner" in the federal system. See his *Metropolis in Transition: Local Government's Adaptation to Changing Urban Needs* (Washington, D.C.: Housing and Home Finance Agency, 1963) and *The Cities* and Richard H. Leach, *The Federal Government and Metropolitan Areas and the Federal System* (New York: Atherton Press, 1965). Robert H. Connery (Cambridge: Harvard University Press, 1960) also concerns the federalist solution.

Students of metropolitan government will be interested in Philip E. Jacoli and James V. Toscano (eds.), *The Integration of Political Communities* (Philadelphia: Lippincott, 1963); Frank Smallwood, *Metro Toronto: A Decade Later* (Toronto: Bureau of Municipal Research, 1963); Brett W. Hawkins, *Metro: The Politics of City-County Consolidation* (Nashville: Vanderbilt University Press, 1966), which also raises the general question as to the conditions under which proposals for metropolitan unification will succeed or fail; Philip B. Coulter (ed.), *Politics of Metropolitan Areas* (New York: Thomas Y. Crowell, 1967); Leo S. Greene *et al., The States and the Metropolis* (Tuscaloosa: University of Alabama Press, 1968); John C. Bollens (ed.), *Exploring the Metropolitan Community* (Berkeley and Los Angeles: University of California Press, 1961); and John C. Bollens and Henry J. Schmandt, *The Metropolis: Its People, Politics, and Economic Life* (New York: Harper & Row, 1965).

Urban administration in the context of prevailing social conditions has received searching attention in Alan A. Altschuler, *The City Planning Process* (Ithaca: Cornell University Press, 1965), a highly critical analysis; Marshall Clinard, *Slums and Community Development: Experiments in Self-Help* (New York: Free Press, 1966), which is a cross-cultural study; Bernard J. Frieden, *The Future of Old Neighborhoods: Rebuilding for a Changing Population* (Cambridge: Massachusetts Institute of Technology Press, 1964); Harvey S. Perloff, "Social Planning in the Metropolis," in Leonard J. Duhl (ed.), *The Urban Condition: People and Policy in the Metropolis* (New York: Basic Books, 1963). Preceding these was the American Municipal Association's *Action for Cities* (Chicago: Public Administration Service, 1943). J. Clarence Davies, *Neighborhood Groups and Urban Renewal* (New York: Columbia University Press, 1966) and his *The Resurgent Neighborhood* (South Bend: University of Notre Dame Press, 1965) as well as Scott Greer, *Urban Renewal and American Cities* (Indianapolis: Bobbs-Merrill, 1965) are more specialized.

Among additional readings in community organization the student would probably find the following of interest and value: Charles Adrian, *Social Science in Community Action* (East Lansing: Michigan State University Press, 1960); Ronald Lippitt and Bruce Westley, *The Dynamics of Planned Change* (New York: Harcourt, Brace and World, 1958); Walter B. Miller, "The Impact of a Total Community Delinquency Control Project," *Social Problems* (Fall, 1962), 168–191; Robert Morris and Martin Rein, "Goals, Structures and Strategies for Community Change," in *Social Work Practice* (New York: Columbia University Press, 1962); Peter H. Rossi, "Power and Politics: A Road to Social Reform," *Social Service Review* (December, 1961), 359–369; Roland L. Warren, *The Community in America* (Chicago: Rand McNally, 1963); and Irwin T. Sanders, *The Community: An Introduction to a Social System* (New York: Ronald Press, 1966).

CHAPTER NINE Urban Sociology in Transition

Paul K. Hatt and Albert J. Reiss, Jr. (eds.), *Cities and Society* (Glencoe: Free Press, 1951, and revised in 1957), was a very successful attempt to survey the then contemporary state of urban sociology. Philip M. Hauser and Leo F. Schnore (eds.), *The Study of Urbanization* (New York: Wiley, 1965) appeared a decade later. In it Gideon Sjoberg's "Theory and Research in Urban Sociology" provides an excellent appraisal of the field. More recent work is that of Scott Greer *et al.* (eds.), *New Urbanization* (New York: St. Martin's Press, 1968) and Robert Gutman and David Popenoe (eds.), *Urban Studies: Present Trends and Future Prospects in an Emerging Academic Field,* special number, *American Behavioral Scientist* (February, 1963). The Annual Reviews on urban research introduced by the Sage publications may fill a much felt need. The first volume in this series, Leo F. Schnore and Henry Fagin (eds.), *Urban Research and Policy Planning* (New York: Russell Sage Foundation, 1967) was well received. A British book also deserves mention, Peter H. Mann, *An Approach to Urban Sociology* (London: Routledge & Kegan Paul, 1965).

Several other titles also emphasize methodology as well as urban sociological theory. These are Jack P. Gibbs (ed.), *Urban Research Methods* (New York: Van Nostrand, 1961); Wendell Bell, "Social Areas: Typology of Neighborhoods," in Marvin B. Sussman (ed.), *Community Structure and Analysis* (New York: Thomas Y. Crowell, 1959); Scott Greer, "Urbanism Reconsidered: A Comparative Study of Local Areas in a Metropolis," *American Sociological Review* (February, 1956), 19–25; Jack P. Gibbs and Kingsley Davis, "Conventional versus Metropolitan Data in the International Study of Urbanization," *American Sociological Review* (October, 1958), 504–514; and John Walton, "Substance and Artifact: The Current Status of Research in Community Power Structure," *American Journal of Sociology* (January, 1966), 430–438.

Index

ABOUT THE AUTHORS

ALBERT N. COUSINS, currently Professor of Sociology at The Cleveland State University, received his Ph.D. from Harvard in 1951. He has served on the Ohio Board of Regents' Advisory Council on Community Service and on the Cleveland Metropolitan Services Commission. He has also directed several institutes on urban affairs. His published work has appeared in the *Journal of the American Bar Association, Social Forces,* the *American Sociological Review,* the *Indian Journal of Social Research, Federal Probation, Social Education,* and in Norman Bell and Ezra Vogel (eds.) , *A Modern Introduction to the Family.*

HANS NAGPAUL is Assistant Professor of Sociology at The Cleveland State University. He received his graduate training in economics and political science at Punjab University and in community organization at Columbia University. Between 1961 and 1964 he was an urban sociologist with the Indian National Planning Commission. Professor Nagpaul has contributed to the *International Journal of Community Development* (Rome) , the *American Sociological Review,* the *Indian Journal of Social Research,* and the *Indian Journal of Social Work.*

A NOTE ON THE TYPE

THIS BOOK was set on the Linotype in Baskerville. The punches for this face were cut under the supervision of George W. Jones, the eminent English printer and the designer of Granjon and Estienne. Linotype Baskerville is a facsimile cutting from type cast from the original matrices of a face designed by John Baskerville, a writing master of Birmingham, for his own private press. The original face was the forerunner of the "modern" group of type faces, known today as Scotch, Bodoni, etc. After his death in 1775, Baskerville's punches and matrices were sold in France and were used to produce the sumptuous Kehl edition of Voltaire's works.

This book was composed, printed, and bound by Kingsport Press, Inc., Kingsport, Tenn. Typography and binding design by Kenneth Miyamoto.